GREAT
PRESIDENTIAL
DECISIONS

GREAT PRESIDENTIAL DECISIONS

State Papers that Changed the Course of History from Washington to Reagan

NEW AND UPDATED EDITION

BY
RICHARD B. MORRIS
Gouverneur Morris Professor Emeritus of History
Columbia University

AND
JEFFREY B. MORRIS
Department of Political Science
University of Pennsylvania

Richardson, Steirman & Black, Inc.
NEW YORK, 1988

ISBN: 0-931933-57-9

Library of Congress Catalog Number 87-062146

Printed in the United States of America

New, updated Edition
Revised Edition

10   9   8   7   6   5   4   3   2   1

To the Memory of
ALLAN NEVINS
Friend and Fellow Campaigner

Contents

CONTENTS

CONTENTS

FOREWORD TO THE UPDATED EDITION

When the President decides—whether on subjects ranging from disarmament to world trade—his decisions may in retrospect turn out to be misguided. In updating this book since the first edition in 1960 an unusually high number of "great" decisions included herein may be considered as falling in that category. Although the staff available to Presidents to inform and counsel has greatly increased, this has not necessarily guaranteed that the resulting judgments have been based upon adequate information or appropriate decision-making practices, nor have constitutional restraints upon the Presidency or public opinion always been taken into account. As a result, recent Presidents from Lyndon Johnson to Ronald Reagan have discovered the practical limits upon the exercise of Presidential power—whether imposed by the other branches of the government or by public opinion.

The captain is still at the helm and still determines the course, but the course he steers has become increasingly subject to Congressional scrutiny and judicial review. Some recent Presidents have made bold decisions in the face of critical public opinion (Jimmy Carter's fight for the Panama Canal treaties is a prime example) and managed to carry them off. Other decisions have backfired, however, and proved harmful to the national interest, while the implementation of still others has been vetoed by the Congress or the judiciary. The President is expected to guarantee national security and the general welfare and keep federal spending in balance—areas of authority shared with Congress—but members of that body and the public have become increasingly critical of quasi wars fought under Presidential authority, covert actions, and other initiatives impinging upon privacy and hard-won personal liberties.

In the future Presidents will, hopefully, continue to initiate great decisions, but with the recent record in mind, may be expected to act with more prudence, only after adequate briefing, weighing alternatives, and appropriate deliberation. Above all, the President's decisions should manifest a sensitivity to the Constitutional scheme of balanced powers and made with a reasonable assurance that the decisions can win public endorsement.

RICHARD B. MORRIS
JEFFREY B. MORRIS

WHEN THE PRESIDENT DECIDES

In the mid-twentieth century the President of the United States is the acknowledged leader of the free world. His prestige derives not alone from that central role which America plays today in world affairs but also from the nature of the unique office of the Presidency, the traditions that have gathered about that office, and the way its occupants have wielded their powers. Despite its world significance the Presidency is in essence an American institution shaped by the forces of American history. Not inaccurately has the President been described as a kind of "one-man distillation of the American people." The office has constituted a great challenge to those who have won election to it. The Presidency has seemed to endow even average men with unexpected wisdom and strength, with a willingness to place country above narrow partisan considerations and to exercise effective powers in times of crisis. The Presidency is a standing refutation to those who have criticized democracy on the ground that it cannot decide promptly nor act with vigor. This book documents that refutation.

We have come to expect leadership of our Presidents, but they have not always been world leaders nor have they always seized the initiative. There have been arid stretches when the White House was occupied by passive men overshadowed by Congressional leaders of stature and ambition. Increasingly, though, the American people have come to look to the President rather than to Congress or the Supreme Court to exercise initiative, to expound the new principle, to make the important decision. This is as it should be, for it is the President rather than Congress who tends to view national issues in the light of the national welfare rather than in terms of sectional interests or pressure groups or narrow party politics. Elected by the whole people, the President might well seem to have a mandate to act, to shape opinion rather than to follow it. When the President makes up his own mind, he bears out Andrew Jackson's observation that "one man with courage makes a majority."

Some Presidents have not recognized such a mandate and have yielded the initiative to other branches of the government, either because they were by nature indecisive and unadventurous, or because they considered themselves inhibited by the Constitution from assuming leadership. The Founding Fathers, who had led a revolution against George III and his royal governors, were suspicious of the executive power and doubtless would not have made it so considerable had it not been for the flagrant weaknesses of the government under the Articles of Confederation, which lacked a real executive, and had they not expected George Washington to serve as the first President. To so pre-eminent and virtuous a patriot strong powers could confidently be entrusted. Nevertheless the Constitution set up three distinct branches of government and protected each from encroachments by the other through a system of checks and balances. While the Constitution confers the "executive power" upon the President, it gives the lawmaking power to Congress, including the power to declare war. Yet treaties are made by the President, who must secure the consent of two-thirds of the Senate to their ratification. This division of power has restrained cautious Presidents and explains why for long periods of time Congress rather than the Chief Executive made the great decisions.

This book treats the President as a maker of decisions—not just ordinary day-to-day decisions, but large ones which may fairly be said to have shaped the course of history. Whether from the written Constitution, or from custom, or from crises, the President has the power to act. Experience has shown that there are times when only the President can act, when the nation cannot afford the luxury of having the President wait upon Congress for enabling legislation or upon the Supreme Court for a clarifying decision. There are tides in the affairs of men, as John Jay pointed out in the 64th *Federalist* letter, "when days, nay, even when hours, are precious. The loss of a battle, the death of a prince, the removal of a minister, or other circumstances intervening to change the present posture and aspect of affairs, may turn the most favorable tide into a course opposite to our wishes. As in the field, so in the cabinet, there are moments to be seized as they pass, and they who preside in either should be left in capacity to improve them." Since the Chief Executive of the nation is also the commander-in-chief of the armed services, Jay was depicting circumstances which might well confront the President in either of his capacities. Jay as a prophet proved disturbingly accurate, for the Presidents of the future may have at most minutes or hours, not days, or months, or years, as in earlier crises. Such is the effect of military technology upon the traditional division of powers in our Constitution.

Whether the President is to make the big decision or leave it to Congress is really up to the Chief Executive himself. What he will do in such a situation is conditioned by his personality quite as much as by his interpretation of the Presidential powers under the Constitution. Alexander Hamilton, frustrated in his own quest for the Presidency, pointed out that the unity of the Presidential office was a leading element in that executive energy which he sought to nurture and augment. As he pointed out in the 70th *Federalist,* when the power to act is concentrated in a single man, administrative energy is not dissipated. Hamilton's ideas of energy in the Chief Executive were first exemplified, among recent Presidents, by Theodore Roosevelt. A gifted showman with a rare talent for reaching the masses, T. R. in his *Autobiography* set forth his view that the Chief Executive was "a steward of the people bound actively and affirmatively to do all he could for the people, and not to content himself with the negative merit of keeping his talents undamaged in a napkin. I declined to adopt the view that what was imperatively necessary for the Nation could not be done by the President unless he could find some specific authorization to do it." Roosevelt affirmed it as "not only his right but his duty to do anything that the needs of the Nation demanded unless such action was forbidden by the Constitution or by the laws." Acting upon this broad construction of the Presidential powers, T. R. defended his executive actions. "I did not usurp power, but I did greatly broaden the use of executive power," he observed, and students of history and the Constitution would concur.

Roosevelt's successor, William Howard Taft, was a genial, tolerant, and far less volatile personality. He took a strict lawyer's view of the constitutional powers of the President and felt that ascribing "an undefined residuum of power" to that office was an "unsafe" doctrine which might in emergencies lead to acts of an arbitrary character violative of private rights. Roosevelt and Taft gave us a classic polarization of the Presidential powers. The former divided the Presidents into two classes, the "Lincoln Presidents" and the "Buchanan Presidents," and it goes without saying that he ranged himself in the Lincoln class and assigned his successor, against whom he campaigned in 1912, to the Buchanan category. Taft felt that the impartial historian might well find that the differences between T. R. and Abe Lincoln were far greater than the similarities. He was reminded of a story of a friend, who came walking home after a day at the office, to be greeted by his daughter Mary. "Papa," she exclaimed, "I am the best scholar in the class." The father pridefully said, "Why, Mary, you surprise me. When did the teacher tell you? This afternoon?" "Oh, no," Mary replied, "the teacher didn't tell me—I just noticed it myself."

Discounting Theodore Roosevelt's very considerable measure of self-esteem, it is still true that Taft's comment was uncharitable. Many others then and since have recognized the reassertion of Presidential leadership that came with T. R. Woodrow Wilson augmented still further the role of the President as a legislative leader, and Franklin Delano Roosevelt revitalized it again. Congress has become accustomed to receiving proposed drafts of bills from the President, many of them drawn up by White House aides. Through talks with legislative leaders, press conferences, the fireside chat, the patronage power, and the threat of a veto to discourage a crippling amendment, the President has by the mid-twentieth century assumed a much larger role in lawmaking than he customarily exercised in the nineteenth century. Today we expect of the President imaginative leadership and, as Arthur Schlesinger, Jr., has aptly put it, a considerable measure of creative innovation.

Since this book is concerned with Presidential action, it does not consider the times when either Congress or the Supreme Court seized the initiative. In the past Congress has made many important decisions, such as the Missouri Compromise, the mischievous Kansas-Nebraska Act, or the program of radical Reconstruction. Save for the Cleveland administration the whole period from the death of Lincoln to the death of McKinley, both from assassin's bullets, was a time of Congressional decision-making. Viewing the governmental scene in 1885, the young Woodrow Wilson was justified in asserting that "the predominant and controlling force, the center and source of all motive and all regulatory power, is the Congress." In recent years Congress has fought a rearguard action to prevent all important decision-making from being seized by the Chief Executive. The 22nd Amendment limiting the President to two terms is an attempt to forestall the rise of a super-executive power. The late unlamented Bricker Amendment, designed to limit the President's negotiating powers in foreign relations, was another desperate move by men in Congress to reassert a traditional co-partnership in the formulating of foreign policy.

There have been still other occasions when the Supreme Court has handed down the momentous decision. The nationalist opinions of John Marshall's Court are prime examples. Another is the Dred Scott Case, where the Supreme Court held as unconstitutional the long-standing legislative authority of Congress over slavery in the territories, a decision which contributed as much as any single action to the coming of the Civil War. Other examples come readily to mind, drawn chiefly from the post-Civil War period—the Second Legal Tender Case, where the Court, packed by President Grant, reversed an earlier decision and validated the Legal Tender Acts; or the Granger Cases, where the Court upheld state regulation of business "affected with a public interest"; or the Knight Case which crippled the Sherman Antitrust Act. Most recently, the passage of the Civil Rights Act in 1964 constitutes a prime example of Congress following the initiative that had been seized by the Supreme Court.

More and more, though, the big decisions are being made by the President, because neither Congress nor the Supreme Court is structurally able to deal with diplomacy on a global scale. They would need their own ambassadors, their own generals, and their own administrative agencies in order to formulate and execute such global policy. The President alone can command the manifold sources of information upon which he must act in an emergency. The executive arm of the government, under Congress's vigilant eye, is the only practical vehicle for making the big decisions. Napoleon's maxim, "The tools belong to the man who can use them," fits this case. For conducting global diplomacy, for safeguarding the general welfare, for acting in an emergency, the President has the tools, and, if he possesses a measure of courage and wisdom, he is the proper man to use them.

This book is concerned with major decisions, how they were formulated by the Presidents, and the manner in which they were announced. Some of these decisions had an immediate impact. Washington's proclamation against the Whisky Insurrection was followed quickly by a show of force and the capitulation or dispersal of the rebels. Jackson's proclamation to the people of South Carolina forced them to back down on nullification, although a face-saving formula was devised. Truman's announcement that the United States would come to the aid of the Korean Republic signalized the start of a "police action" in which the United States was a major UN participant. Other decisions did not register their full impact at once. Washington's Farewell Address was to be the keystone of our foreign policy for over a hundred years. No one could have anticipated when Jefferson decided to buy Louisiana how quickly that new area would be settled nor what tantalizing problems it would pose for the nation. The Monroe Doctrine caused considerably less stir when it was promulgated than in later years, as the prospective aggressor had already agreed not to intervene in the Western Hemisphere, but the principles Monroe laid down were elaborated by Presidents Polk, Cleveland, and Theodore Roosevelt in directions which might well have startled their initiator. John Quincy Adams' contemporaries could not appreciate the wisdom and boldness of a program which in many particulars foreshadowed the welfare state. The immediate effect of Wilson's decision to insist upon Article X of the League Covenant in its original form was to kill America's entry into the League of Nations. In its longer-range implications that decision may have turned the world from a vision of order to the rule of chaos.

In "The Present Crisis" James Russell Lowell declared that "once to every man and nation comes the moment to decide." But twelve of our Presidents have had two chances and acted on them. Woodrow Wilson made at least three decisions which affected the course of history. Some consideration of the President's role as a decision-maker might well cause us to recast our traditional evaluations of Presidents. Certainly, on the record of action and accomplishment, James K. Polk, despite his lack of personal magnetism, was one of our most effective

Presidents. Millard Fillmore, usually considered a weak and colorless nonentity, deserves credit for two momentous and constructive decisions. His intervention with Congress on behalf of the Compromise of 1850 postponed the sectional crisis for another decade, until the Union was better able to withstand the shock of civil war. And Fillmore's dispatch of Commodore Perry to Japan turned America's eyes to the Pacific and the Orient, with consequences that are still not measurable. The Buffalo lawyer seems in need of upgrading on the Presidential scale. Unfortunate Andrew Johnson was courageous and far-sighted in the decisions he made which conserved the Presidential powers. History should honor him for the enemies he made and not portray him in the words of his vilifiers.

Every decision that is considered in this book was not necessarily the right one at the right time, and every President who acted did not necessarily act from strength. Madison, in weakness, yielded to Congress when he plunged the nation into the War of 1812. James Buchanan is the classic example of the President paralyzed by doubts and indecision. His admission that he lacked the constitutional power to stop secession acted as a catalyst to civil war. Cleveland was pretentious and wrong-minded when he involved the United States in Great Britain's boundary dispute with Venezuela; and William McKinley yielded to Congressional pressures against his best instincts, asking for war with Spain after America's demands had in fact been met. But right or wrong, good or bad, these decisions had momentous consequences, and merit inclusion in this book.

A number of the big decisions reviewed here revolve around the issues of war and peace. Under the Constitution Congress alone has the right to declare war, and yet Congress has never failed to follow a President when he has called for that fateful step. Furthermore, the President as commander-in-chief must take measures to place the country in a posture of defense and to repel attack. Usage and circumstances have in fact transferred the warmaking power from Congress to the President. How far the President can go in leading the nation down the path toward war was a question even the Founding Fathers could not resolve. So ardent an advocate of effective Presidential powers as Alexander Hamilton felt that the President was obliged to put the issue of war to

Congress, and could not declare war on his own. Yet in 1801 he criticized his political opponent President Thomas Jefferson on the ground that the Chief Executive, "for want of the sanction of Congress," had refused to order the capture or detention of the cruisers of Tripoli, although that piratical power had declared war in fact against the United States and had committed overt acts of hostility against our ships and commerce. And Jefferson, who took Louisiana despite his constitutional scruples, observed shortly after his retirement from the Presidency that "to lose our country by a scrupulous adherence to the written law, would be to lose the law itself, with life, liberty, property and all those who are enjoying them with us; thus absurdly sacrificing the end to the means." In short, Jefferson's two terms in the Presidency had converted him to the Hamiltonian principles that in times of national emergency the President must act.

Strong Presidents have always taken this position. Jackson, Lincoln, Theodore Roosevelt, Woodrow Wilson, Franklin Delano Roosevelt, and Harry S. Truman, each as Hamiltonian exponents of energy in the executive, ventured "to act his own opinion with vigor and decision"; each moved first and obtained Congressional sanction afterward. Lincoln, who had denounced Polk's military measures along the Texas border because they were taken without the approval of Congress, made his own fateful decision to supply Fort Sumter. When the Civil War came he met the issue with a series of purely executive measures, for Congress was not convened until July, 1861. Before Congress recognized a state of war, Lincoln had summoned the militia, proclaimed a blockade, expanded the regular army beyond the legal limit, suspended the right of habeas corpus, directed governmental expenditures in advance of Congressional appropriation, and launched an elaborate series of military steps. Similarly, at the time of the Battle of Britain, Franklin Roosevelt, without securing Congressional approval in advance, made the decision to turn over American destroyers in exchange for leases of British bases. President Truman ordered General MacArthur to intervene in Korea before Congress had given him its endorsement. Recognizing that emergencies might leave a mere margin of hours in which to act and that it was necessary to impress Communist China with the fact that the President had the power of decision, Dwight D.

Eisenhower asked Congress in 1958 for a resolution approving in advance such military action as he might order in defense of Formosa.

Once the President decides, he has to formulate his decision and communicate it to Congress and the people. All Presidents have not enjoyed equal literary facility, nor have they all managed to convey that ring of eloquence that came from a Jefferson, a Lincoln, or a Wilson. All of those whose papers have been included in this volume demonstrated their capacity to inform the nation of the seriousness of the issues and to argue persuasively for the course they were recommending. Washington offered his profound counsels to his countrymen as "an old and affectionate friend" in the modest hope that "they may now and then recur to moderate the fury of party spirit, to warn against the mischiefs of foreign intrigue, to guard against the impostures of pretended patriotism." His have been the most cherished counsels ever to emanate from a President.

These historic decisions inspired some grand phrase-making. Take James Madison's war message: "We behold, in fine, on the side of Great Britain a state of war against the United States, and on the side of the United States a state of peace toward Great Britain." Consider the indefatigable optimism of "Old Man Eloquent," John Quincy Adams, when he declared that "the spirit of improvement is abroad upon the earth." Study "Old Hickory's" appeal to the patriotism of South Carolinians, his reminder to them that "There is yet time to show that the descendants of the Pinckneys, the Sumpters, the Rutledges, and of the thousand other names which adorn the pages of your Revolutionary history will not abandon that Union to support which so many of them fought and bled and died. I adjure you, as you honor their memory, as you love the cause of freedom, to which they dedicated their lives, as you prize the peace of your country, the lives of its best citizens, and your own fair fame, to retrace your steps."

The threat of disunion inspired some of the most eloquent appeals. James Buchanan urged the South to pause before it was too late. "It is not every wrong," he pleaded, "nay, it is not every grievous wrong—which can justify a resort to such a fearful alternative. This ought to be the last desperate remedy of a despairing people, after every other constitutional means of conciliation had been exhausted." In his First Inaugural Address Lincoln took a more affirmative position, declaring "that in view of the Constitution and the laws the Union is unbroken, and to the extent of my ability I shall take care, as the Constitution itself expressly enjoins upon me, that the laws of the Union be faithfully executed in all the States." Asserting that "the central idea of secession is the essence of anarchy," Lincoln eloquently reminded the South that "physically speaking we cannot separate. We cannot remove our respective sections from each other nor build an impassable wall between them." Then came the noblest peroration of any Presidential message:

> I am loath to close. We are not enemies, but friends. We must not be enemies. Though passion may have strained it must not break our bonds of affection. The mystic chords of memory, stretching from every battlefield and patriot grave to every living heart and hearthstone all over this broad land, will yet swell the chorus of the Union, when again touched, as surely they will be, by the better angels of our nature.

Perhaps that unattainable level was again reached by Woodrow Wilson, when in his war message he asserted: "But the right is more precious than peace, and we shall fight for the things we have always carried nearest our hearts," and when he closed with this affirmation of America's honorable motives: "God helping her, she can do no other."

The Presidents have to make up their own minds, but their messages often reflect the counsels of those around them. Washington borrowed from Hamilton, and to a lesser degree from Madison and Jay in drafting his Farewell Address. Monroe took at least one notable idea for his Monroe Doctrine from John Quincy Adams. Jackson's inspired Proclamation of Nullification was largely the work of Secretary of State Edward Livingston. Lincoln took the closing paragraph of his Emancipation Proclamation from Salmon P. Chase. President Johnson drew upon Jeremiah Sullivan Black for major assistance in the drafting of his veto of the First Reconstruction Act, and Grover Cleveland toned down Secretary of State Richard Olney's belligerent draft of the Venezuela message, though it still bristled clear through. In preparing his epochal Lend-Lease message F. D. R. drew upon the talents of Robert E. Sherwood and others. This is as it must be. The amount of information that a modern President must sift and digest in order to make a decision is prodigious. He needs the help of experts, but only the President himself can decide how much the country can be told, when, and how. Despite a good deal of collaboration and an increasing amount of ghost-writing, most Presidential papers bear the stamp of their nominal author's own personality and reflect his views.

Unless otherwise indicated the Presidential papers in this volume are based upon the authoritative multivolume compilation of J. D. Richardson.

These notable state papers recapture times of greatness. They bring us face to face with men, superior or average, who put patriotism ahead of party and made the momentous decisions that changed the course of our history. A substantial number of them fit the category of Theodore Roosevelt's doer of deeds—the President who "strives valiantly," and "who at the best knows in the end the triumph of high achievement; and who at worst, if he fails, at least fails while daring greatly; so that his place shall never be with those cold and timid souls who know neither victory nor defeat."

Who can read these state papers without capturing an imperishable moment? Abraham Lincoln, following weeks of tortured indecision, affixing his bold, clear, though "slightly tremulous" signature to the Emancipation Proclamation, after having shaken thousands of hands in a New Year's Day reception at the White House. Wilson, returning from the Capitol following his inspired war message, breaking down and sobbing like a child. F. D. R. cruising aboard the *Tuscaloosa* in the sunlit Caribbean, reading and rereading a message from Winston Churchill disclosing the terrible losses by enemy action suffered by British, Allied, and neutral merchant tonnage, and then within two short days arriving at the momentous decision of Lend-Lease. Each one had enunciated "a new principle for a new age." Each in turn had made the great decision.

RICHARD B. MORRIS

1

THE DECISION
TO UPHOLD THE SUPREMACY
OF THE LAW

Washington Puts Down the Whisky Insurrection

It has been said that the operation of confronting the Whisky rebels in western Pennsylvania would today be entrusted to a few young lawyers in the Internal Revenue Bureau. But the very fact that this would now be no more than a minor-league operation bespeaks the effectiveness with which the first organized refusal to pay taxes was crushed by the Federal government. That we are a nation of taxpayers rather than tax dodgers is the result of good habits begun early, habits instilled at the birth of the nation by two men, George Washington and Alexander Hamilton. When Washington made the crucial decision to use armed force to suppress an insurrection the first President established at one stroke two principles for which the Confederation had been unable to secure recognition—the idea of the supremacy of the law and the power of the Federal government to levy and collect taxes.

The insurrection of a handful of westerners was as much a demonstration against Alexander Hamilton and the things for which he was believed to stand as it was against the Federal government. That brilliant and energetic Secretary of the Treasury was the architect of the entire financial structure of the new government—funding and assumption of the debt, a national bank, and an effective tax program. The excise tax imposed upon distillers by Congress in 1791 was an integral part of that program, and it was supported at that time by Jeffersonian Republicans as well as Federalists. Hamilton was unwilling to use the tariff as the sole source of revenue. He was reluctant to take a step which might slow down foreign trade. At the same time he wanted to forestall the states by seizing upon the excise as a source of revenue for the Federal government.

The West regarded this tax as a manifestation of Hamilton's alleged sectional bias, his alleged favoritism to merchants, manufacturers, and creditors. And westerners were not without grounds for their complaints. A tax of 25 per cent on the net price of a gallon of whisky seemed oppressive in those days when people were unaccustomed to the heavy hand of the tax collector. (Nine dollars per proof gallon is hardly light today either.) Moreover, in the interior parts of the country whisky was accepted as a medium of exchange in the absence of hard money. So long as the Mississippi remained closed to Americans (and the rebels did not realize that it was shortly to be opened to them) the only feasible way of moving grain to market from the interior was over the Alleghenies, as distilled spirits.

Hamilton regarded this tax as a test of the authority of the government, but he also shared the view of a good many that too much hard liquor was being consumed. Doctors on the staff of the College of Physicians of Philadelphia drew up a statement on the evils of intemperance, but in Congress General James Jackson, the fiery Georgia Republican, defiantly asserted the right of his constituents to get drunk. "They have been long in the habit of getting drunk," he insisted. "They will get drunk in defiance of a dozen colleges or all the excise duties which Congress might be weak or wicked enough to impose." In fairness to Hamilton it should be pointed out that excises were also imposed on snuff and loaf sugar, and no rebellion resulted. The manufacturers found they could pass the tax on to the consumer.

As early as 1792 rumblings of discontent were heard in the West. Hamilton, in a letter to John Jay in September of that year, forecast the steps that ultimately would be taken. Inquire, he urged, whether a proclamation from the President would be advisable, warning that the laws would be strictly enforced, and "if the plot should thicken and the application of force should appear to be unavoidable, will it be expedient for the President to repair in person to the scene of the commotion?" These were precisely the steps that Washington took when the little volcano erupted in western Pennsylvania two years later. Federal tax collectors were mauled and terrorized, the Federal courts brought to a halt, and a small body of troops guarding the home of General John Neville, Excise Inspector for Western Pennsylvania, were compelled to surrender. The crowd that gathered at Braddock's Field on August 12, 1794, were in an ugly mood. The insurgents threatened to attack Pittsburgh, which promptly joined the insurrectionary forces.

Hamilton wished for a quick test of the authority of the Federal government within the states, and he was actually spoiling for a fight. On August 2 the apostle of energy in government urged that the government act, and quickly. Washington responded with his proclamation calling upon the insurgents to disperse, and subsequently requesting the huge force of 12,900 men from the states to suppress civil disorder. Writing to the press under the pseudonym of "Tully," Hamilton boldly stated the issue:

> Let us see what is this question. It is plainly this—Shall the majority govern or be governed? Shall the nation rule or be ruled? Shall the general will prevail, or the will of a faction? Shall there be government or no government? . . . Let it be deeply imprinted in your minds, and handed down to your latest posterity, that there is no road to *despotism* more sure or more to be dreaded than that which begins at anarchy.

The military operation against the "Whisky Boys" is signalized by the fact that it was the only occasion in American history when a President, who under the Constitution is commander-in-chief of the armed forces, actually took the field with his troops. Washington accompanied the army as far as Bedford, Pennsylvania, before returning to Philadelphia. But neither he nor any of his men saw any fighting. Nor did Hamilton, who, capitalizing on Secretary of War Knox's absence from the seat of office, was made Acting Secretary of War, and went in person to the field. But those "Whisky Boys" who did not vanish in the face of the army's advance were content to confront the armed forces of the government with liberty poles. Not a single rebel in arms came forth to do battle. The leaders of the overt resistance fled across the Ohio, and the bag of prisoners was meager indeed. Only two of the prisoners were found guilty of high treason. Washington pardoned both, one on the ground that he was a "simpleton," the other as "insane."

In short, as Jefferson acidly observed, "an insurrection was announced and proclaimed and armed against, but could never be found." True, the supremacy of the government had been upheld in a most dramatic demonstration. On sober second thought some persons felt that the government had magnified the affair far beyond its danger to the republic. Not so Hamilton. "Beware," he later wrote Secretary of War McHenry, "of magnifying a riot into an insurrection by employing in the first instance an inadequate force. 'Tis better far to err on the other side. Whenever the government appears in arms, it ought to appear like a *Hercules,* and inspire respect by the display of strength. The consideration of expense is of no moment compared with the advantages of energy."

The voters did not see it that way at all. The suppression of the Whisky Rebellion marks the beginning of the decline in popularity of the Federalist Party. A strong Federalist himself, the eloquent Fisher Ames was led to observe that "a regular government, by overcoming an unsuccessful insurrection, becomes stronger; but elective rulers can scarcely ever employ the physical force of a democracy without turning the moral force, or the power of public opinion, against the government."

A modern postscript: The easiest tax to pass on to the consumer is the tax on hard liquor, yet although a quarter of a century has elapsed since the repeal of the Eighteenth Amendment, the government is still wrestling with the problem of ending the manufacturing and distribution of bootlegged liquor which still manages to evade the excise.

By the President of the United States of America
A PROCLAMATION [1]

Whereas combinations to defeat the execution of the laws laying duties upon spirits distilled within the United States and upon stills have from the time of the commencement of those laws existed in some of the western parts of Pennsylvania; and

Whereas the said combinations, proceeding in a manner subversive equally of the just authority of government and of the rights of individuals, have hitherto effected their dangerous and criminal purpose by the influence of certain irregular meetings whose proceedings have tended to encourage and uphold the spirit of opposition by misrepresentations

[1]Footnote numbers refer to a list of sources, to be found at p. 432.

of the laws calculated to render them odious; by endeavors to deter those who might be so disposed from accepting offices under them through fear of public resentment and of injury to person and property, and to compel those who had accepted such offices by actual violence to surrender or forbear the execution of them; by circulating vindictive menaces against all those who should otherwise, directly or indirectly, aid in the execution of the said laws, or who, yielding to the dictates of conscience and to a sense of obligation, should themselves comply therewith; by actually injuring and destroying the property of persons who were understood to have so complied; by inflicting cruel and humiliating punishments upon private citizens for no other cause than that of appearing to be the friends of the laws; by intercepting the public officers on the highways, abusing, assaulting, and otherwise ill treating them; by going to their houses in the night, gaining admittance by force, taking away their papers, and committing other outrages, employing for these unwarrantable purposes the agency of armed banditti disguised in such manner as for the most part to escape discovery; and

Whereas the endeavors of the Legislature to obviate objections to the said laws by lowering the duties and by other alterations conducive to the convenience of those whom they immediately affect (though they have given satisfaction in other quarters), and the endeavors of the executive officers to conciliate a compliance with the laws by explanations, by forbearance, and even by particular accommodations founded on the suggestion of local considerations, have been disappointed of their effect by the machinations of persons whose industry to excite resistance has increased with every appearance of a disposition among the people to relax in their opposition and to acquiesce in the laws, insomuch that many persons in the said western parts of Pennsylvania have at length been hardy enough to perpetrate acts which I am advised amount to treason, being overt acts of levying war against the United States, the said persons having on the 16th and 17th July last past proceeded in arms (on the second day amounting to several hundreds) to the house of John Neville, inspector of the revenue for the fourth survey of the district of Pennsylvania; having repeatdly attacked the said house with the persons therein, wounding some of them; having seized David Lenox, marshal of the district of Pennsylvania, who previous thereto had been fired upon while in the execution of his duty by a party of armed men, detaining him for some time prisoner, till for the preservation of his life and the obtaining of his liberty he found it necessary to enter into stipulations to forbear the execution of certain official duties touching processes issuing out of a court of the United States; and having finally obliged the said inspector of the said revenue and the said marshal from considerations of personal safety to fly from that part of the country, in order, by a circuitous route, to proceed to the seat of Government, avowing as the motives of these outrageous proceedings an intention to prevent by force of arms the execution of the said laws, to oblige the said inspector of the revenue to renounce his said office, to withstand by open violence the lawful authority of the Government of the United States, and to compel thereby an alteration in the measures of the Legislature and a repeal of the laws aforesaid; and

Whereas by a law of the United States entitled "An act to provide for calling forth the militia to execute the laws of the Union, suppress insurrections, and repel invasions," it is enacted "that whenever the laws of the United States shall be opposed or the execution thereof obstructed in any State by combinations too powerful to be suppressed by the ordinary course of judicial proceedings or by the powers vested in the marshals by that act, the same being notified by an associate justice or the district judge, it shall be lawful for the President of the United States to call forth the militia of such State to suppress such combinations and to cause the laws to be duly executed. And if the militia of a State where such combinations may happen shall refuse or be insufficient to suppress the same, it shall be lawful for the President, if the Legislature of the United States shall not be in session, to call forth and employ such numbers of the militia of any other State or States most convenient thereto as may be necessary; and the use of the militia so to be called forth may be continued, if necessary, until the expiration of thirty days after the commencement of the ensuing session: *Provided always,* That whenever it may be necessary in the judgment of the President to use the military force hereby directed to be called forth, the President shall forthwith, and previous thereto, by proclamation, command such insurgents to disperse and retire peaceably to their respective abodes within a limited time;" and

Whereas James Wilson, an associate justice, on the 4th instant, by writing under his hand, did from evidence which had been laid before him notify to me that "in the counties of Washington and Allegany, in Pennsylvania, laws of the United States are opposed and the execution thereof obstructed by combinations too powerful to be suppressed by the ordinary course of judicial proceedings or by the powers vested in the marshal of that district;" and

Whereas it is in my judgment necessary under the circumstances of the case to take measures for calling forth the militia in order to suppress the combinations aforesaid, and to cause the laws to be duly executed; and I have accordingly determined so to do, feeling the deepest regret for the occasion, but withal the most solemn conviction that the essential interests of the Union demand it, that the very existence of Government and the fundamental principles of social order are materially involved in the issue, and that the patriotism and firmness of all good citizens are seriously called upon, as occasions may require, to aid in the effectual suppression of so fatal a spirit:

Wherefore, and in pursuance of the proviso above recited, I, George Washington, President of the United States, do hereby command all persons being insurgents as aforesaid, and all others whom it may concern, on or before the 1st day of September next to disperse and retire peaceably to their respective abodes. And I do moreover warn all persons whomsoever against aiding, abetting, or comforting the perpetrators of the aforesaid treasonable acts, and do require all officers and other citizens, according to their respective duties and the laws of the land, to exert their utmost endeavors to prevent and suppress such dangerous proceedings.

In testimony whereof I have caused the seal of the United States of America to be affixed to these presents, and signed the same with my hand.

[SEAL] Done at the city of Philadelphia, the 7th day of August, 1794, and of the Independence of the United States of America the nineteenth.

By the President: G^o^ WASHINGTON

EDM: RANDOLPH

2

THE DECISION
TO AVOID ENTANGLEMENTS

Washington's Farewell Address

The decision to stand aloof from European power politics, to avoid entanglements, has been the capstone of American foreign policy from virtually the start of our national life down to very recent times. This rule was embodied in a great state paper, Washington's Farewell Address, but it was in reality the culmination of a series of decisions that started in 1782, when the American peace commissioners in Paris decided to make a separate peace with Great Britain, and to act contrary to explicit instructions from Congress.

Even before the adoption of the Declaration of Independence the isolationist role that America was destined to play could have been forecast. In September, 1775, John Adams, considering the probability of aid from France in an American war for independence, recorded in his *Autobiography* the caution that "we ought not to enter into any alliance with her which should entangle us in any future wars in Europe; that we ought to lay it down as a first principle and a maxim never to be forgotten, to maintain an entire neutrality in all future European wars."

When John Jay joined Franklin in Paris to conduct the preliminary peace negotiations that ended the American Revolution he quickly perceived how the war aims of Spain, France's ally, clashed with those of the United States, notably with respect to America's territorial aspirations to the Mississippi. To preserve national dignity he violated the instructions of Congress not to negotiate without full consultation with France. "I think we have no rational dependence except on God and ourselves," he asserted. Jay's was perhaps the first move toward isolation.

For America the year 1789 was marked by two notable events—the beginning of Washington's Presidency and the start of the French Revolution. Swift-moving events in France—the abolition of the monarchy, the execution of Louis XVI, the Reign of Terror, and the transformation of the French Revolution into a general European war—caused Washington deep concern. Technically, the French alliance of 1778 was still in force. Upon the outbreak early in 1793 of war with Great Britain France hoped to secure aid from the United States, if not direct intervention, at least the conversion of America into a transatlantic base of operations against enemy colonies and commerce. Following the advice of his Secretary of the Treasury, Alexander Hamilton, and ignoring the objections of Thomas Jefferson, his Secretary of State, Washington issued his momentous Proclamation of Neutrality in 1793. This document declared the intention of the United States to "pursue a course friendly and impartial to both belligerent powers" and enjoined upon all citizens its observance under penalty of prosecution. The word "neutrality" was studiously avoided, but the intent was clear, and French sympathizers in America raised shrill voices in protest. Writing under the pseudonym "Pacificus," Hamilton defended both the proclamation and Washington's constitutional right to proclaim it, asserting that the executive power under the Constitution is vested in the President. Later, Jefferson went a step further, and asserted that "the transaction of business with foreign powers is executive altogether."

The Neutrality Proclamation was the first part of a multiple package of foreign policy decisions which is in essence embodied in the Farewell Address. Washington was concerned lest the United States, a young nation and a poorly defended one, be involved in a war on behalf of France to defend her government or in a war against England to maintain American rights. "Foreign influence is truly the Grecian horse to a republic," Hamilton reminded him. On the pretext that the American states had violated the peace treaty of 1783 by confiscating the property of Tories and by raising legal obstacles to the recovery of pre-Revolutionary debts owed to British merchants, the British refused to evacuate the Northwest military posts, which they had been obliged to do under the treaty. Britain thus kept the profitable fur trade in her own hands and the western Indians were heartened in their hostility to the United States. Friction between the two countries was intensified when the British issued Orders in Council in 1793 interfering with neutral shipping. American vessels were seized and American seamen impressed and imprisoned. Indignation swept the country. The followers of Jefferson proposed to boycott all goods shipped to this country by England, but Hamilton convinced Washington that such a step would choke off the chief source of American revenue, the tariff, and the main prop of his fiscal system. To upset commercial relations would, in his judgment, cut our credit to the roots.

Persuaded by Hamilton to seek conciliation, Washington dispatched the Chief Justice, John Jay, to England. Jay managed to wring some concessions from Lord Grenville, England's Foreign Minister. Under the terms of Jay's Treaty the British agreed to withdraw from the Northwest posts and to open the East Indian trade to America on fairly liberal terms. Debts, boundary disputes, and compensation for maritime seizures were referred to joint commissions. The United States was placed on a most-favored-nation basis in trade with the British Isles. But there were glaring omissions—no provision for the issues of impressment, for the removal by the British of slaves during the American Revolution, or for Loyalist claims. A storm of outraged protest greeted the publication of the text of the treaty in March, 1795. Backed by the immense prestige of Washington and fortified by arguments marshaled in its behalf by Hamilton, the treaty won ratification in the Senate by a narrow margin. War with England had been avoided, but at the expense of gravely deteriorating relations with France. That nation took umbrage at the terms of the treaty. The French Directory interfered in American domestic politics even to the extent of recommending that Washington be overthrown by "the right kind of revolution."

It was against this background of Washington's unswerving attachment to peace in the face of outrageous denunciation from the supporters of Jefferson and increasing pressures from the French government that the President's Farewell Address was drafted. That great state paper was long in formulation. Promulgated at the end of Washington's second term, it embodied his fateful decision not to stand for a third term, a decision which for long was accepted as an unwritten law of the Constitution.

Back in February, 1792, when Washington contemplated retiring at the end of his first term, he had asked James Madison to prepare a draft of an address about retirement. Madison sent him a "Form for an Address." When Washington definitely decided to retire at the end of his second term he made a draft of his own, embodying some material from Madison's earlier suggested draft. Then he sent the paper on to Hamilton, who prepared two drafts, faithfully following Washington's scheme of organization and the President's main ideas but rephrasing them in a masterly way. Washington preferred Hamilton's first, or original, draft, but also incorporated some suggestions from John Jay.

Nevertheless the final state paper was very much Washington's own. His rephrasing was felicitous and often less wordy than Hamilton's. For example, Hamilton's "Original Draft" states:

> The great rule of conduct for us in regard to foreign nations ought to be to have as little *political* connection with them as possible.

Washington changed that to read:

> The great rule of conduct for us in regard to foreign nations is, in extending our commercial relations, to have with them as little political connection as possible.

Again Hamilton:

> Why should we forgo the advantages of so felicitous a situation? Why quit our own ground to stand upon foreign ground?

Washington:

> Why forgo the advantages of so peculiar a situation? Why quit our own to stand upon foreign ground?

Hamilton:

> Permanent alliances, intimate connection with any part of the foreign world is to be avoided; so far, (I mean) as we are now at liberty to do it.

Washington:

> It is our true policy to steer clear of permanent alliances with any por-

tion of the foreign world, so far, I mean, as we are now at liberty to do it.

Hamilton:

Taking care always to keep ourselves by suitable establishments in a respectably defensive position, we may safely trust to occasional alliances for extraordinary war emergencies.

Washington:

Taking care always to keep ourselves by suitable establishments on a respectable defensive posture, we may safely trust to temporary alliances for extraordinary emergencies.

In the last illustration there is a subtle but important change of concept, as between "occasional" and "temporary" alliances. It was not Washington but the Jeffersonian Republicans who proclaimed the doctrine of isolationism. "We may lament the fate of Poland and Venice," said Albert Gallatin, "and I never can myself see, without regret, independent nations blotted from the map of the world. But their destiny does not affect us in the least. We have no interest whatever in that balance, and by us it should be altogether forgotten." Nowhere did Washington use the phrase "entangling alliances," later found in Jefferson's First Inaugural.

Early in May, 1796, in a letter to John Jay, Washington disclosed his intention definitely to retire, but he yielded to Hamilton's urging to hold off his public announcement. Hamilton counseled that the timing of the announcement be set for two months before the meeting of the Presidential electors, but Washington did not wait quite that long. Three months before the electors convened he submitted his Farewell Address to the Cabinet, and, four days later, on September 19, 1796, gave it to the people in the columns of the Philadelphia *Daily American Advertiser*. It was never delivered orally.

Washington's political testament to the American people, the Farewell Address, aside from its weighty counsel to his countrymen to avoid sectionalism and the dangers of parties and to cherish the public credit, gave literary articulation to the great decisions which had already been made to avoid war, decisions embodied in the Proclamation of Neutrality and Jay's Treaty, decisions which gave the young nation a necessary breathing spell. To the opposition party the Farewell Address dealt a body blow to the French alliance, soon to be terminated. Considered the "Great Rule" in our foreign policy for many generations, Washington's advice on nonentanglement was dictated by conditions prevailing during his administration and was not meant to be irrevocable. Nevertheless, the "Great Rule" has been the most cherished principle of American diplomacy and stood virtually unaltered until the perils of the twentieth-century world dictated a refashioned and vastly enlarged role for America in world affairs.

FAREWELL ADDRESS [2]

UNITED STATES, *September 17, 1796*

Friends and Fellow-Citizens:

The period for a new election of a citizen to administer the Executive Government of the United States being not far distant, and the time actually arrived when your thoughts must be employed in designating the person who is to be clothed with that important trust, it appears to me proper, especially as it may conduce to a more distinct expression of the public voice, that I should now apprise you of the resolution I have formed to decline being considered among the number of those out of whom a choice is to be made.

I beg you at the same time to do me the justice to be assured that this resolution has not been taken without a strict regard to all the considerations appertaining to the relation which binds a dutiful citizen to his country; and that in withdrawing the tender of service, which silence in my situation might imply, I am influenced by no diminution of zeal for your future interest, no deficiency of grateful respect for your past kindness, but am supported by a full conviction that the step is compatible with both.

The acceptance of and continuance hitherto in the office to which your suffrages have twice called me have been a uniform sacrifice of inclination to the opinion of duty and to a deference for what appeared to be your desire. I constantly hoped that it would have been much earlier in my power, consistently with motives which I was not at liberty to disregard, to return to that retirement from which I had been reluctantly drawn. The strength of my inclination to do this previous to the last election had even led to the preparation of an address to declare it to you; but mature reflection on the then perplexed and critical posture of our affairs with foreign nations and the unanimous advice of persons entitled to my confidence impelled me to abandon the idea. I rejoice that the state of your concerns, external as well as internal, no longer renders the pursuit of inclination incompatible with the sentiment of duty or propriety, and am persuaded, whatever partiality may be retained for my services, that in the present circumstances of our country you will not disapprove my determination to retire.

The impressions with which I first undertook the arduous trust were explained on the proper occasion. In the discharge of this trust I will only say that I have, with good intentions, contributed toward the organization and administration of the Government the best exertions of which a very fallible judgment was capable. Not unconscious in the outset of the inferiority of my qualifications, experience in my own eyes, perhaps still more in the eyes of others, has strengthened the motives to diffidence of myself; and every day the increasing weight of years admonishes me more and more that the shade of retirement is as necessary to me as it will be welcome. Satisfied that if any circumstances have given peculiar value to my services they were temporary, I have the consolation to believe that, while choice and prudence invite me to quit the political scene, patriotism does not forbid it.

In looking forward to the moment which is intended to terminate the career of my political life my feelings do not permit me to suspend the deep acknowledgment of that debt of gratitude which I owe to my beloved country for the many honors it has conferred upon me; still more for the steadfast confidence with which it has supported me, and for the opportunities I have thence enjoyed of manifesting my inviolable attachment by services faithful and persevering, though in usefulness unequal to my zeal. If benefits have resulted to our country from these services, let it always be remembered to your praise and as an instructive example in our annals that under circumstances in which the passions, agitated in every direction, were liable to mislead; amidst appearances sometimes dubious; vicissitudes of fortune often discouraging; in situations in which not unfrequently want of success has countenanced the spirit of criticism, the constancy of your support was the essential prop of the efforts and a guaranty of the plans by which they were effected. Profoundly penetrated with this idea, I shall carry it with me to my grave as a strong incitement to unceasing vows that Heaven may continue to you the choicest tokens of its beneficence; that your union and brotherly affection may be perpetual; that the free Constitution which is the work of your hands may be sacredly maintained;

that its administration in every department may be stamped with wisdom and virtue; that, in fine, the happiness of the people of these States, under the auspices of liberty, may be made complete by so careful a preservation and so prudent a use of this blessing as will acquire to them the glory of recommending it to the applause, the affection, and adoption of every nation which is yet a stranger to it.

Here, perhaps, I ought to stop. But a solicitude for your welfare which can not end but with my life, and the apprehension of danger natural to that solicitude, urge me on an occasion like the present to offer to your solemn contemplation and to recommend to your frequent review some sentiments which are the result of much reflection, of no inconsiderable observation, and which appear to me all important to the permanency of your felicity as a people. These will be offered to you with the more freedom as you can only see in them the disinterested warnings of a parting friend, who can possibly have no personal motive to bias his counsel. Nor can I forget as an encouragement to it your indulgent reception of my sentiments on a former and not dissimilar occasion.

Interwoven as is the love of liberty with every ligament of your hearts, no recommendation of mine is necessary to fortify or confirm the attachment.

The unity of government which constitutes you one people is also now dear to you. It is justly so, for it is a main pillar in the edifice of your real independence, the support of your tranquillity at home, your peace abroad, of your safety, of your prosperity, of that very liberty which you so highly prize. But as it is easy to foresee that from different causes and from different quarters much pains will be taken, many artifices employed, to weaken in your minds the conviction of this truth, as this is the point in your political fortress against which the batteries of internal and external enemies will be most constantly and actively (though often covertly and insidiously) directed, it is of definite moment that you should properly estimate the immense value of your national union to your collective and individual happiness; that you should cherish a cordial, habitual, and immovable attachment to it; accustoming yourselves to think and speak of it as of the palladium of your political safety and prosperity; watching for its preservation with jealous anxiety; discountenancing whatever may suggest even a suspicion that it can in any event be abandoned, and indignantly frowning upon the first dawning of every attempt to alienate any portion of our country from the rest or to enfeeble the sacred ties which now link together the various parts.

For this you have every inducement of sympathy and interest. Citizens by birth or choice of a common country, that country has a right to concentrate your affections. The name of American, which belongs to you in your national capacity, must always exalt the just pride of patriotism more than any appellation derived from local discriminations. With slight shades of difference, you have the same religion, manners, habits, and political principles. You have in a common cause fought and triumphed together. The independence and liberty you possess are the work of joint councils and joint efforts, of common dangers, sufferings, and successes.

But these considerations, however powerfully they address themselves to your sensibility, are greatly outweighed by those which apply more immediately to your interest. Here every portion of our country finds the most commanding motives for carefully guarding and preserving the union of the whole.

The *North,* in an unrestrained intercourse with the *South,* protected by the equal laws of a common government, finds in the productions of the latter great additional resources of maritime and commercial enterprise and precious materials of manufacturing industry. The *South,* in the same intercourse, benefiting by the same agency of the *North,* sees its agriculture grow and its commerce expand. Turning partly into its own channels the seamen of the *North,* it finds its particular navigation invigorated; and while it contributes in different ways to nourish and increase the general mass of the national navigation, it looks forward to the protection of a maritime strength to which itself is unequally adapted. The *East,* in a like intercourse with the *West,* already finds, and in the progressive improvement of interior communications by land and water will more and more find, a valuable vent for the commodities which it brings from abroad or manufactures at home. The *West* derives from the *East* supplies requisite to its growth and comfort, and what is perhaps of still greater consequence, it must of necessity owe the *secure* enjoyment of indispensable *outlets* for its own productions to the weight, influence, and the future maritime strength of the Atlantic side of the Union, directed by an indissoluble community of interest as *one nation.* Any other tenure by which the *West* can hold this essential advantage, whether derived from its own separate strength or from an apostate and unnatural connection with any foreign power, must be intrinsically precarious.

While, then, every part of our country thus feels an immediate and particular interest in union, all the parts combined can not fail to find in the united mass of means and efforts greater strength, greater resource, proportionably greater security from external danger, a less frequent, interruption of their peace by foreign nations, and what is of inestimable value, they must derive from union an exemption from those broils and wars between themselves which so frequently afflict neighboring countries not tied together by the same governments, which their own rivalships alone would be sufficient to produce, but which opposite foreign alliances, attachments, and intrigues would stimulate and imbitter. Hence, likewise, they will avoid the necessity of those overgrown military establishments which, under any form of government, are inauspicious to liberty, and which are to be regarded as particularly hostile to republican liberty. In this sense it is that your union ought to be considered as a main prop of your liberty, and that the love of the one ought to endear to you the preservation of the other.

These considerations speak a persuasive language to every reflecting and virtuous mind, and exhibit the continuance of the union as a primary object of patriotic desire. Is there a doubt whether a common government can embrace so large a sphere? Let experience solve it. To listen to mere speculation in such a case were criminal. We are authorized to hope that a proper organization of the whole, with the auxiliary agency of governments for the respective subdivisions, will afford a happy issue to the experiment. It is well worth a fair and full experiment. With such powerful and obvious motives to union affecting all parts of our country, while experience shall not have demonstrated its impracticability, there will always be reason to distrust the patriotism of those who in any quarter may endeavor to weaken its bands.

In contemplating the causes which may disturb our union it occurs as matter of serious concern that any ground should have been furnished for characterizing parties by *geographical* discriminations—*Northern* and *Southern, Atlantic* and *Western*—whence designing men may endeavor to excite a belief that there is a real difference of local interests and views. One of the expedients of party to acquire influence within particular districts is to misrepresent the opinions and aims of other districts. You can not shield yourselves too much against the jealousies and heartburnings which spring from these misrepresentations; they tend to render alien to each other those who ought to be bound together by fraternal affection. The inhabitants of our Western country have lately had a useful lesson on this head. They have seen in the negotiation by the Executive and in the unanimous ratification by the Senate of the treaty with Spain, and in the universal satisfaction at that event throughout the United States, a decisive proof how unfounded were the suspicions propagated among them of a policy in the General Government and in the Atlantic States unfriendly to their interests in regard to the Mississippi. They have been witnesses to the formation of two treaties—that with Great Britain and that with Spain —which secure to them everything they could desire in respect to our foreign relations toward confirming their prosperity. Will it not be their wisdom to rely for the preservation of these advantages on the union by which they were procured? Will they not henceforth be deaf to those advisers, if such there are, who would sever them from their brethren and connect them with aliens?

To the efficacy and permanency of your union a government for the whole is indispensable. No alliances, however strict, between the parts can be an adequate substitute. They must inevitably experience the infractions and interruptions which all alliances in all times have experienced. Sensible of this momentous truth, you have improved upon your first essay by the adoption of a Constitution of Government better calculated than your former for an intimate union and for the efficacious management of your common concerns. This Government, the offspring of your own choice, uninfluenced and unawed, adopted upon full investigation and mature deliberation, completely free in its principles, in the distribution of its powers, uniting security with energy, and containing within itself a provision for its own amendment, has a just claim to your confidence and your support. Respect for its authority, compliance with its laws, acquiescence in its measures, are duties enjoined by the fundamental maxims of true liberty. The basis of our political systems is the right of the people to make and to alter their constitutions of government. But the constitution which at any time exists till changed by an explicit and authentic act of the whole people is sacredly obligatory upon all. The very idea of the power and the right of the people to establish government presupposes the duty of every individual to obey the established government.

All obstructions to the execution of the laws, all combinations and associations, under whatever plausible character, with the real design to direct, control, counteract, or awe the regular deliberation and action of the constituted authorities, are destructive of this fundamental principle and of fatal tendency. They serve to organize faction; to give it an artificial and extraordinary force; to put in the place of the delegated will of the nation the will of a party, often a small but artful and enterprising minority of the community, and, according to the alternate triumphs of different parties, to make the public administration the mirror of the ill-concerted and incongruous projects of faction rather than the organ of consistent and wholesome plans, digested by common counsels and modified by mutual interests.

However combinations or associations of the above description may now and then answer popular ends, they are likely in the course of time and things to become potent engines by which cunning, ambitious, and unprincipled men will be enabled to subvert the power of the people, and to usurp for themselves the reins of government, destroying afterwards the very engines which have lifted them to unjust dominion.

Toward the preservation of your Government and the permanency of your present happy state, it is requisite not only that you steadily discountenance irregular oppositions to its acknowledged authority, but also that you resist with care the spirit of innovation upon its principles, however specious the pretexts. One method of assault may be to effect in the forms of the Constitution alterations which will impair the energy of the system, and thus to undermine what can not be directly overthrown. In all the changes to which you may be invited remember that time and habit are at least as necessary to fix the true character of governments as of other human institutions; that experience is the surest standard by which to test the real tendency of the existing constitution of a country; that facility in changes upon the credit of mere hypothesis and opinion exposes to perpetual change, from the endless variety of hypothesis and opinion; and remember especially that for the efficient management of your common interests in a country so extensive as ours a government of as much vigor as is consistent with the perfect security of liberty is indispensable. Liberty itself will find in such a government, with powers properly distributed and adjusted, its surest guardian. It is, indeed, little else than a name where the government is too feeble to withstand the enterprises of faction, to confine each member of the society within the limits prescribed by the laws, and to maintain all in the secure and tranquil enjoyment of the rights of person and property.

I have already intimated to you the danger of parties in the State, with particular reference to the founding of them on geographical discriminations. Let me now take a more comprehensive view, and warn you in the most solemn manner against the baneful effects of the spirit of party generally.

This spirit, unfortunately, is inseparable from our nature, having its root in the strongest passions of the human mind. It exists under different shapes in all governments, more or less stifled, controlled, or repressed; but in those of the popular form it is seen in its greatest rankness and is truly their worst enemy.

The alternate domination of one faction over another, sharpened by the spirit of revenge natural to party dissension, which in different ages and countries has perpetrated the most horrid enormities, is itself a frightful despotism. But this leads at length to a more formal and permanent despotism. The disorders and miseries which result gradually incline the minds of men to seek security and repose in the absolute power of an individual, and sooner or later the chief of some prevailing faction, more able or more fortunate than his competitors, turns this disposition to the purposes of his own elevation on the ruins of public liberty.

Without looking forward to an extremity of this kind (which nevertheless ought not to be entirely out of sight), the common and continual mischiefs of the spirit of party are sufficient to make it the interest and duty of a wise people to discourage and restrain it.

It serves always to distract the public councils and enfeeble the public administration. It agitates the community with ill-founded jealousies and false alarms; kindles the animosity of one part against another; foments occasionally riot and insurrection. It opens the door to foreign influence and corruption, which find a facilitated access to the government itself through the channels of party passion. Thus the policy and the will of one country are subjected to the policy and will of another.

There is an opinion that parties in free countries are useful checks upon the administration of the government, and serve to keep alive the spirit of liberty. This within certain limits is probably true; and in governments of a monarchical cast patriotism may look with indulgence, if not with favor, upon the spirit of party. But in those of the popular character, in governments purely elective, it is a spirit not to be encouraged. From their natural tendency it is certain there will always be enough of that spirit for every salutary purpose; and there being constant danger of excess, the effort ought to be by force of public opinion to mitigate and assuage it. A fire not to be quenched, it demands a uniform vigilance to prevent its bursting into a flame, lest, instead of warming, it should consume.

It is important, likewise, that the habits of thinking in a free country should inspire caution in those intrusted with its administration to confine themselves within their respective constitutional spheres, avoiding in the exercise of the powers of one department to encroach upon another. The spirit of encroachment tends to consolidate the powers of all the departments in one, and thus to create, whatever the form of government, a real despotism. A just estimate of that love of power and proneness to abuse it which predominates in the human heart is sufficient to satisfy us of the truth of this position. The necessity of reciprocal checks in the exercise of political power, by dividing and distributing it into different depositories, and constituting each the guardian of the public weal against invasions by the others, has been evinced by experiments ancient and modern, some of them in our country and under our own eyes. To preserve them must be as necessary as to institute them. If in the opinion of the people the distribution or modification of the constitutional powers be in any particular wrong, let it be corrected by an amendment in the way which the Constitution designates. But let there be no change by usurpation; for though this in one instance may be the instrument of good, it is the customary weapon by which free governments are destroyed. The precedent must always greatly overbalance in permanent evil any partial or transient benefit which the use can at any time yield.

Of all the dispositions and habits which lead to political prosperity, religion and morality are indispensable supports. In vain would that man claim the tribute of patriotism who should labor to subvert these great pillars of human happiness—these firmest props of the duties of men and citizens. The mere politician, equally with the pious man, ought to respect and to cherish them. A volume could not trace all their connections with private and public felicity. Let it simply be asked, Where is the security for property, for reputation, for life, if the sense of religious obligation *desert* the oaths which are the instruments of investigation in courts of justice? And let us with caution indulge the supposition that morality can be maintained without religion. Whatever may be conceded to the influence of refined education on minds of peculiar structure, reason and experience both forbid us to expect that national morality can prevail in exclusion of religious principle.

It is substantially true that virtue or morality is a necessary spring of popular government. The rule indeed extends with more or less force to every species of free government. Who that is a sincere friend to it can look with indifference upon attempts to shake the foundation of the fabric? Promote, then, as an object of primary importance, institutions for the general diffusion of knowledge. In proportion as the structure of a government gives force to public opinion, it is essential that public opinion should be enlightened.

As a very important source of strength and security, cherish public credit. One method of preserving it is to use it as sparingly as possible, avoiding occasions of expense by cultivating peace, but remembering also that timely disbursements to prepare for danger frequently prevent much greater disbursements to repel it; avoiding likewise the accumulation of debt, not only by shunning occasions of expense, but by vigorous exertions in time of peace to discharge the debts which unavoidable wars have occasioned, not ungenerously throwing upon posterity the burthen which we ourselves ought to bear. The execution of these maxims belongs to your representatives; but it is necessary that public opinion should cooperate. To facilitate to them the performance of their duty it is essential that you should practically bear in mind that toward the payment of debts there must be revenue; that to have revenue there must be taxes; that no taxes can be devised which are not more or less inconvenient and unpleasant; that the intrinsic embarrassment inseparable from the selection of the proper objects (which is always a choice of difficulties), ought to be a decisive motive for a candid construction of the conduct of the Government in making it, and for a spirit of acquiescence in the measures for obtaining revenue which the public exigencies may at any time dictate.

Observe good faith and justice toward all nations. Cultivate peace and harmony with all. Religion and morality enjoin this conduct. And can it be that good policy does not equally enjoin it? It will be worthy of a free, enlightened, and at no distant period a great nation to give to mankind the magnanimous and too novel example of a people always guided by an exalted justice and benevolence. Who can doubt that in the course of time and things the fruits of such a plan would richly repay any temporary advantages which might be lost by a steady adherence to it? Can it be that Providence has not connected the permanent felicity of a nation with its virtue? The experiment, at least, is recommended by every sentiment which ennobles human nature. Alas! is it rendered impossible by its vices?

In the execution of such a plan nothing is more essential than that permanent, inveterate antipathies against particular nations and passionate attachments for others should be excluded, and that in place of them just and amicable feelings toward all should be cultivated. The nation which indulges toward another an habitual hatred or an habitual fondness is in some degree a slave. It is a slave to its animosity or to its affection, either of which is sufficient to lead it astray from its duty and its interest. Antipathy in one nation against another disposes each more readily to offer insult and injury, to lay hold of slight causes of umbrage, and to be haughty and intractable when accidental or trifling occasions of dispute occur.

Hence frequent collisions, obstinate, envenomed, and bloody contests. The nation prompted by ill will and resentment sometimes impels to war the government contrary to the best calculations of policy. The government sometimes participates in the national propensity, and adopts through passion what reason would reject. At other times it makes the animosity of the nation subservient to projects of hostility, instigated by pride, ambition, and other sinister and pernicious motives. The peace often, sometimes perhaps the liberty, of nations has been the victim.

So, likewise, a passionate attachment of one nation for another produces a variety of evils. Sympathy for the favorite nation, facilitating

43

the illusion of an imaginary common interest in cases where no real common interest exists, and infusing into one the enmities of the other, betrays the former into a participation in the quarrels and wars of the latter without adequate inducement or justification. It leads also to concessions to the favorite nation of privileges denied to others, which is apt doubly to injure the nation making the concessions by unnecessarily parting with what ought to have been retained, and by exciting jealousy, ill-will, and a disposition to retaliate in the parties from whom equal privileges are withheld; and it gives to ambitious, corrupted, or deluded citizens (who devote themselves to the favorite nation) facility to betray or sacrifice the interests of their own country without odium, sometimes even with popularity, gilding with the appearances of a virtuous sense of obligation, a commendable deference for public opinion, or a laudable zeal for public good the base or foolish compliances of ambition, corruption, or infatuation.

As avenues to foreign influence in innumerable ways, such attachments are particularly alarming to the truly enlightened and independent patriot. How many opportunities do they afford to tamper with domestic factions, to practice the arts of seduction, to mislead public opinion, to influence or awe the public councils! Such an attachment of a small or weak toward a great and powerful nation dooms the former to be the satellite of the latter. Against the insidious wiles of foreign influence (I conjure you to believe me, fellow-citizens) the jealousy of a free people ought to be *constantly* awake, since history and experience prove that foreign influence is one of the most baneful foes of republican government. But that jealousy, to be useful, must be impartial, else it becomes the instrument of the very influence to be avoided, instead of a defense against it. Excessive partiality for one foreign nation and excessive dislike of another cause those whom they actuate to see danger only on one side, and serve to veil and even second the arts of influence on the other. Real patriots who may resist the intrigues of the favorite are liable to become suspected and odious, while its tools and dupes usurp the applause and confidence of the people to surrender their interests.

The great rule of conduct for us in regard to foreign nations is, in extending our commercial relations to have with them as little *political* connection as possible. So far as we have already formed engagements let them be fulfilled with perfect good faith. Here let us stop.

Europe has a set of primary interests which to us have none or a very remote relation. Hence she must be engaged in frequent controversies, the causes of which are essentially foreign to our concerns. Hence, therefore, it must be unwise in us to implicate ourselves by artificial ties in the ordinary vicissitudes of her politics or the ordinary combinations and collisions of her friendships or enmities.

Our detached and distant situation invites and enables us to pursue a different course. If we remain one people, under an efficient government, the period is not far off when we may defy material injury from external annoyance; when we may take such an attitude as will cause the neutrality we may at any time resolve upon to be scrupulously respected; when belligerent nations, under the impossibility of making acquisitions upon us, will not lightly hazard the giving us provocation; when we may choose peace or war, as our interest, guided by justice, shall counsel.

Why forego the advantages of so peculiar a situation? Why quit our own to stand upon foreign ground? Why, by interweaving our destiny with that of any part of Europe, entangle our peace and prosperity in the toils of European ambition, rivalship, interest, humor, or caprice?

It is our true policy to steer clear of permanent alliances with any portion of the foreign world, so far, I mean, as we are now at liberty to do it; for let me not be understood as capable of patronizing infidelity to existing engagements. I hold the maxim no less applicable to public than to private affairs that honesty is always the best policy. I repeat, therefore, let those engagements be observed in their genuine sense. But in my opinion it is unnecessary and would be unwise to extend them.

Taking care always to keep ourselves by suitable establishments on a respectable defensive posture, we may safely trust to temporary alliances for extraordinary emergencies.

Harmony, liberal intercourse with all nations are recommended by policy, humanity, and interest. But even our commercial policy should hold an equal and impartial hand, neither seeking nor granting exclusive favors or preferences; consulting the natural course of things; diffusing and diversifying by gentle means the streams of commerce, but forcing nothing; establishing with powers so disposed, in order to give trade a stable course, to define the rights of our merchants, and to enable the Government to support them, conventional rules of intercourse, the best that present circumstances and mutual opinion will permit, but temporary and liable to be from time to time abandoned or varied as experience and circumstances shall dictate; constantly keeping in view that it is folly in one nation to look for disinterested favors from another; that it must pay with a portion of its independence for whatever it may accept under that character; that by such acceptance it may place itself in the condition of having given equivalents for nominal favors, and yet of being reproached with ingratitude for not giving more.

There can be no greater error than to expect or calculate upon real favors from nation to nation. It is an illusion which experience must cure, which a just pride ought to discard.

In offering to you, my countrymen, these counsels of an old and affectionate friend I dare not hope they will make the strong and lasting impression I could wish—that they will control the usual current of the passions or prevent our nation from running the course which has hitherto marked the destiny of nations. But if I may even flatter myself that they may be productive of some partial benefit, some occasional good—that they may now and then recur to moderate the fury of party spirit, to warn against the mischiefs of foreign intrigue, to guard against the impostures of pretended patriotism—this hope will be a full recompense for the solicitude for your welfare by which they have been dictated.

How far in the discharge of my official duties I have been guided by the principles which have been delineated the public records and other evidences of my conduct must witness to you and to the world. To myself, the assurance of my own conscience is that I have at least believed myself to be guided by them.

In relation to the still subsisting war in Europe my proclamation of the 22d of April, 1793, is the index to my plan. Sanctioned by your approving voice and by that of your representatives in both Houses of Congress, the spirit of that measure has continually governed me, uninfluenced by any attempts to deter or divert me from it.

After deliberate examination, with the aid of the best lights I could obtain, I was well satisfied that our country, under all the circumstances of the case, had a right to take, and was bound in duty and interest to take, a neutral position. Having taken it, I determined as far as should depend upon me to maintain it with moderation, perseverance, and firmness.

The considerations which respect the right to hold this conduct it is not necessary on this occasion to detail. I will only observe that, according to my understanding of the matter, that right, so far from being denied by any of the belligerent powers, has been virtually admitted by all.

The duty of holding a neutral conduct may be inferred, without anything more, from the obligation which justice and humanity impose on every nation, in cases in which it is free to act, to maintain inviolate the relations of peace and amity toward other nations.

The inducements of interest for observing that conduct will best be referred to your own reflections and experience. With me a predominant motive has been to endeavor to gain time to our country to settle and mature its yet recent institutions, and to progress without interruption to that degree of strength and consistency which is necessary to give it, humanly speaking, the command of its own fortunes.

Though in reviewing the incidents of my Administration I am unconscious of intentional error, I am nevertheless too sensible of my defects not to think it probable that I may have committed many errors. Whatever they may be, I fervently beseech the Almighty to avert or mitigate the evils to which they may tend. I shall also carry with me the hope that my country will never cease to view them with indulgence, and that, after forty-five years of my life dedicated to its service with an upright zeal, the faults of incompetent abilities will be consigned to oblivion, as myself must soon be to the mansions of rest.

Relying on its kindness in this as in other things, and actuated by that fervent love toward it which is so natural to a man who views in it the native soil of himself and his progenitors for several generations, I anticipate with pleasing expectation that retreat in which I promise myself to realize without alloy the sweet enjoyment of partaking in the midst of my fellow-citizens the benign influence of good laws under a free government—the ever-favorite object of my heart, and the happy reward, as I trust, of our mutual cares, labors, and dangers.

G? Washington

3

THE DECISION
TO AVOID WAR WITH FRANCE

John Adams Flouts the Warmongers in His Own Cabinet

Washington had been concerned lest the European war which broke out in the wake of the French Revolution drag America into the general conflagration. His Proclamation of Neutrality and his dispatch of Jay to London prevented war with England. Washington's successor was confronted with the problem of how to keep America from going to war with France. That nation had made no secret of its disappointment with American neutrality. Under the alliance of 1778, still technically in force, France had counted on using American ports to bring in prizes and to outfit privateers. To the French Jay's Treaty was a provocative act. In retaliation the French Directory broke off diplomatic relations with America, and forced Charles C. Pinckney, whom Washington had sent to France on a diplomatic mission, to flee to Amsterdam. Shortly after his inauguration John Adams called Congress into special session to take such action as "shall convince France and the whole world that we are not a degraded people humiliated under a colonial spirit of fear and sense of inferiority, fitted to be the miserable instruments of foreign influence."

France had, through a succession of ineptly chosen emissaries to America, attempted to drive a wedge between the people and their government. This effort was a failure, but French propaganda had contributed to creating and deepening the rift between the pro-French Jeffersonian Republicans and the Federalists, whom their political opponents labeled Anglophiles. Adams was essentially a man of peace. He sought to conciliate both the Republican opposition and the French government by dispatching a mission to France to negotiate outstanding issues. John Marshall and Elbridge Gerry joined Pinckney in Paris as envoys extraordinary. There they met with three secret agents of the Directory, designated by the ciphers "X" (Hottinguer), "Y" (Bellamy), and "Z" (Hauteval). As a precondition to being officially received by the French government the Americans were advised to pay a bribe to the Directory, make a loan to France, and formally disavow President Adams' recent strictures about the French government. Legend has it that the American commissioners rose in their wrath and declared: "Millions for defense; not one cent for tribute!" These words were the substance of a toast proposed in Marshall's honor on his return to America. The nearest to the legend was the less fiery rebuke attributed to Pinckney: "It is no, no; not a sixpence!" The commissioners were not even united in their indignation. Gerry, who had far less backbone than his colleagues, seemed on the verge of yielding to calculated blackmail and bullying; but then William Vans Murray, the American minister to the Hague, regarded Gerry as an "innocent" who mistook "the lamps of Paris for an illumination on his arrival, and the salutations of fisherwomen for a procession of chaste matrons hailing the great Pacificator." The French agents frightened the wits out of Gerry by warning of war and devastation should their offer be declined. Marshall and Pinckney quit Paris. Gerry stayed on until he, too, realized that the mission was a failure.

The inside story of the "XYZ" affair burst like a bombshell on the American political scene. "The man who, after this mass of evidence, shall be the apologist of France, and the calumniator of his own government, is not an American. The choice for him lies between being deemed a fool, a madman, or a traitor," warned Hamilton. Overnight the Republicans were discredited and every French flag pulled down from the coffee houses. The pro-war faction among the Federalists, headed in the Cabinet by the Secretary of State, Timothy Pickering, wanted an immediate declaration of war against France. Could John Adams resist the tide? He did not evade the issue. While seeing that the country was placed in a warlike posture, he was determined not to give France a *casus belli*. A number of defense measures were enacted. Washington was named commanding general of the army, and Hamilton inspector general and second in command. In July, 1798, Congress repealed the treaties with France, and thus terminated the alliance. On the seas an undeclared naval war began, in which a number of French ships were captured.

If Adams remained cool, Hamilton, the real leader of the Federalists, though outside the Cabinet, became increasingly bellicose and allowed his ambition and his romanticism to convert him into an unrestrained expansionist. Emulating the rising Corsican corporal, he spoke of heading an army that would capture New Orleans in co-operation with the British navy, march into Mexico City, and, with the support of the Venezuelan revolutionary, Francisco Miranda, liberate the Spanish provinces. His exhortations against France became ever more shrill. Fortunately for the country John Adams kept his head. At long last it dawned upon him that Hamilton, not the President, had been directing the Cabinet. Receiving assurances indirectly from Talleyrand that a minister plenipotentiary from America would be received "with the respect due to the representative of a free, independent, and powerful nation," he submitted to the Senate the name of William Vans Murray. The High Federalists were infuriated. A delegation of Senators called upon the President and informed him that they would never confirm the nomination. Thereupon Adams threatened to resign and turn the government over to their arch-enemy, Thomas Jefferson. To the Federalists this was an even worse evil and one to be avoided at all cost. The issue was now compromised by inducing Adams to add two other Federalists to the French Mission, Chief Justice Oliver Ellsworth and Governor William R. Davie of North Carolina, the latter replacing Patrick Henry when the Virginian declined on the grounds of age.

No more courageous decision was ever taken by a President and few more momentous ones. Although the peace move made Adams momentarily popular with the man in the street, it caused an ugly and permanent rift between the President's supporters and the Hamiltonian wing of the party. That rift deepened when Adams, now convinced that he was the victim of a Cabinet conspiracy, ousted Pickering from the State Department and McHenry from the War office. In revenge Hamilton and the High Federalists worked tooth and nail to prevent Adams' re-election. In the late summer of 1800 Hamilton, whom Adams referred to as "the Creole bastard," committed an unpardonable indiscretion. He published a lengthy attack on the President, under his own name but meant for private circulation to top party leaders. Aaron Burr managed to get hold of a copy and had it widely distributed. Hamilton had called Adams an ordinary man who dreams himself to be a Frederick. "To this," Adams wrote, "I shall make but a short answer. When a Miss of the street shall print a pamphlet in London, and call the Queen of England an ordinary woman who dreams herself a Catherine of Russia, no Englishman will have the less esteem for his queen for that impudent libel."

True, Adams had shown himself to be an inept politician and lost the Presidential election of 1800 to Thomas Jefferson, but he had demonstrated that he possessed the qualities of true statesmanship, courage, vision, decisiveness—qualities that kept the country from engaging in a senseless war with an old friend and ally. The negotiations of Adams' commissioners bore fruit. Now that Napoleon, flushed with enormous victories, was First Consul, it was impossible to expect that all the American demands would be met, but a convention was entered into by the two nations under which the quasi-war was brought to a close and the troublesome alliance with France terminated. Historians would indeed support John Adams' own estimate of his decision to send the mission to France as "the most disinterested, the most determined and the most successful of my whole life."

February 18, 1799

Gentlemen of the Senate:

I transmit to you a document which seems to be intended to be a compliance with a condition mentioned at the conclusion of my message to Congress of the 21st of June last.

Always disposed and ready to embrace every plausible appearance of probability of preserving or restoring tranquillity, I nominate William Vans Murray, our minister resident at The Hague, to be minister plenipotentiary of the United States to the French Republic.

If the Senate shall advise and consent to his appointment, effectual care shall be taken in his instructions that he shall not go to France without direct and unequivocal assurances from the French Government, signified by their minister of foreign relations, that he shall be received in character, shall enjoy the privileges attached to his character by the laws of nations, and that a minister of equal rank, title, and powers shall be appointed to treat with him, to discuss and conclude all controversies between the two Republics by a new treaty.

JOHN ADAMS

[Translation]

PARIS, *the 7th Vendémiaire of the 7th Year of the French Republic, One and Indivisible*

The Minister of Exterior Relations to Citizen Pichon, Secretary of Legation of the French Republic near the Batavian Republic:

I have received successively, Citizen, your letters of the 22d and 27th Fructidor [8th and 13th September]. They afford me more and more reason to be pleased with the measure you have adopted, to detail to me your conversations with Mr. Murray. These conversations, at first merely friendly, have acquired consistency by the sanction I have given to them by my letter of the 11th Fructidor. I do not regret that you have trusted to Mr. Murray's honor a copy of my letter. It was intended for you only, and contains nothing but what is conformable to the intentions of Government. I am thoroughly convinced that should explanations take place with confidence between the two Cabinets, irritation would cease, a crowd of misunderstandings would disappear, and the ties of friendship would be more strongly united as each party would discover the hand which sought to disunite them. But I will not conceal from you that your letters of the 2d and 3d Vendémiaire, just received, surprised me much. What Mr. Murray is still dubious of has been very explicitly declared, even before the President's message to Congress of the 3d Messidor [21st June] last was known in France. I had written it to Mr. Gerry, namely, on the 24th Messidor and 4th Thermidor; I did repeat it to him before he sat out. A whole paragraph of my letter to you of the 11th Fructidor, of which Mr. Murray has a copy, is devoted to develop still more the fixed determination of the French Government. According to these bases, you were right to assert that whatever plenipotentiary the Government of the United States might send to France to put an end to the existing differences between the two countries would be undoubtedly received with the respect due to the representative of a free, independent, and powerful nation.

I can not persuade myself, Citizen, that the American Government need any further declarations from us to induce them, in order to renew the negations, to adopt such measures as would be suggested to them by their desire to bring the differences to a peaceable end. If misunderstandings on both sides have prevented former explanations from reaching that end, it is presumable that, those misunderstandings being done away, nothing henceforth will bring obstacles to the reciprocal dispositions. The President's instructions to his envoys at Paris, which I have only known by the copy given you by Mr. Murray, and received by me the 21st Messidor [9th July], announce, if they contain the whole of the American Government's intentions, dispositions which could only have added to those which the Directory has always entertained; and, notwithstanding the posterior acts of that Government, notwithstanding the irritating and almost hostile measures they have adopted, the Directory has manifested its perseverance in the sentiments which are deposited both in my correspondence with Mr. Gerry and in my letter to you of the 11th Fructidor, and which I have hereinbefore repeated in the most explicit manner. Carry, therefore, Citizen, to Mr. Murray those positive expressions in order to convince him of our sincerity, and prevail upon him to transmit them to his Government.

I presume, Citizen, that this letter will find you at The Hague; if not, I ask it may be sent back to you at Paris.

Salute and fraternity,   CH: MAU: TALLEYRAND

February 25, 1799

Gentlemen of the Senate:

The proposition of a fresh negotiation with France in consequence of advances made by the French Government has excited so general an attention and so much conversation as to have given occasion to many manifestations of the public opinion, from which it appears to me that a new modification of the embassy will give more general satisfaction to the Legislature and to the nation, and perhaps better answer the purposes we have in view.

It is upon this supposition and with this expectation that I now nominate Oliver Ellsworth, esq., Chief Justice of the United States; Patrick Henry, esq., late governor of Virginia, and William Vans Murray, esq., our minister resident at The Hague, to be envoys extraordinary and ministers plenipotentiary to the French Republic, with full powers to discuss and settle by a treaty all controversies between the United States and France.

It is not intended that the two former of these gentlemen shall embark for Europe until they shall have received from the Executive Directory assurances, signified by their secretary of foreign relations, that they shall be received in character, that they shall enjoy all the prerogatives attached to that character by the law of nations, and that a minister or ministers of equal powers shall be appointed and commissioned to treat with them.

JOHN ADAMS

4

THE DECISION
TO PURCHASE LOUISIANA

Jefferson Acts on Hamiltonian Principles

To act at the right time and to act decisively is a test of greatness. Such an action was Jefferson's purchase of the vast territory of Louisiana, an acquisition which the President advocated despite his profound belief that the powers of the Federal government must be strictly construed and his sincere doubts that the Constitution conferred upon the Federal government the right to acquire new territories.

In actual fact the acquisition of Louisiana was an accident. What Jefferson really wanted was the undisputed control of the Mississippi River, for the right to navigate the Mississippi freely "to the sea" was long a central focus of American foreign policy. At the peace negotiations in Paris in 1782-83 Spain was unable to prevent America from acquiring territory west to the Mississippi River, but she was determined to keep control of that river herself just as long as she could. During the Confederation period the Spanish government sought fruitlessly to secure an agreement from the United States to "forbear" the navigation of the Mississippi to the sea, but it was clear that ratification by the nine states required by the Articles of Confederation for such a treaty would never be obtained. John Jay, Secretary of Foreign Affairs, proposed that the issue be referred to the new Federal government under the Constitution. In 1795 Thomas Pinckney secured from the Spanish by the Treaty of San Lorenzo both Spain's recognition of the territorial claims of the United States under the Treaty of 1783 and the right of deposit of American goods at New Orleans for three years, and thereafter, if need be, at another point to be designated.

Just when it seemed as though the issue of Mississippi navigation was settled, the situation was dramatically altered. By the secret Treaty of San Ildefonso (October 1, 1800), Louisiana, which France had ceded to Spain in 1762, was returned to France. The transfer was made at the insistence of Napoleon, who projected the revival of the French colonial empire in North America. President Thomas Jefferson was profoundly concerned over the threat posed to American security by a neighboring imperial and aggressive power and alarmed lest the French acquisition of New Orleans result in closing the Mississippi to our western commerce and undoing the good effects of Pinckney's Treaty. His alarm had solid foundation. On October 16, 1802, the Spanish intendant at New Orleans interdicted the right of deposit, an action which caused consternation throughout the West.

Jefferson acted swiftly. He had already anticipated the Spanish move, made at the behest of France, by writing a letter to Robert R. Livingston, our minister to France. "The day that France takes New Orleans," the President declared, "we must marry ourselves to the British fleet and nation"—strong medicine from the doctor who in the '90's had been ready if not eager tó go to war against England and had vigorously opposed Jay's Treaty. Strong medicine indeed from the doctor who, in his First Inaugural Address, had asserted his dedication to the principle of "entangling alliances with none."

It must be kept in mind that what Jefferson wanted was the free navigation of the Mississippi, not a huge expanse of territory west of that river. Accordingly, he instructed Livingston to negotiate for a tract of land on the lower Mississippi for use as a port, or failing this, to obtain an irrevocable guarantee of free navigation and the right of deposit. On January 12, 1803, James Monroe was named minister plenipotentiary to France for the purpose of participating in the negotiations. He was instructed to purchase New Orleans and West Florida with the two million dollars provided by a Congressional appropriation; if need be, he was to go up to ten million dollars.

The immense success which Livingston, with a very slight assist from Monroe, achieved was less a tribute to his skill as a bargainer than to Napoleon's mercurial temperament. Why did Napoleon suffer this *volte-face* so soon after he had acquired Louisiana from Spain? Why give away what had been acquired so effortlessly? The truth is that Bonaparte's dreams of re-establishing a great French empire in America, perhaps of conquering the entire New World, were rudely halted by the native uprising on San Domingo. The Haitian rebels had decimated the pride of the French army. If Napoleon could not suppress a handful of natives, what chance would he have against a vengeful British nation supported by the sharpshooting backwoodsmen of America? Fearful that at any moment England would renew the great war against him, Napoleon was anxious to convert the liability of Louisiana into an asset—cold cash to carry on against Britain. Hence, Barbé Marbois, the negotiator for France, offered Livingston and Monroe much more than they had anticipated or had been authorized to acquire—not only New Orleans, but the whole of Louisiana. The amount to be paid was approximately fifteen million dollars, five million more than had been authorized for a diminutive portion of the territory finally sold. There have been bigger real-estate deals in American history in dollars involved, but this was far and away the best bargain. After affixing his name to the treaty of cession, Livingston rose and shook hands with Monroe and Marbois. "We have lived long," he declared, "but this is the noblest work of our lives."

Under the French Constitution Napoleon had no right to sell this territory without the approval of his legislature. A nice legal question existed also as to whether, in terms of the cession from Spain, Napoleon had any right to offer the land to a third party (Bonaparte had bound himself formally never to alienate Louisiana), but the dictator was contemptuous of agreements and impatient of restraints. Lucien Bonaparte, a younger brother of Napoleon, recounted in his *Mémoires* how irate the First Consul became when members of his immediate family sought to stop him. Informed that the Chambers would not give their consent to the sale, Napoleon called out from his bath, "I shall get along without the consent of anyone at all. Is that clear?" Bonaparte took all the credit, and insisted that the plan had been "conceived by me and negotiated by me, and will be ratified and put through by me alone." With that he splashed water over the remonstrating Joseph and sank back into his bathtub. To the man who declared, "Conquest has made me what I am and conquest alone can maintain me," Louisiana was a step backward, but Napoleon preserved his self-esteem by prophesying: "I have just given England a maritime rival that sooner or later will lay low her pride."

A leading critic of the broad interpretation of the Constitution during the preceding administrations, Jefferson was acutely embarrassed at the idea of acquiring territory which would double the area of the United States without an express provision in the Constitution explicitly authorizing the acquisition of territory. But this was hardly the time for consistency. Jefferson advised the Senate to ratify before Bonaparte changed his mind. He had considered proposing an amendment to the Constitution to legalize the acquisition and government of Louisiana, but decided to allow the Senate to decide the question. In so doing Jefferson and his Republican Party followed Alexander Hamilton's doctrine of implied powers, and were ultimately supported in this by the Supreme Court.

Despite the sniping of a few Federalists, the Louisiana Purchase was overwhelmingly popular, the greatest single achievement of Jefferson's administration and one of the most decisive actions of any American President. Jefferson justified his action by insisting that "the larger our association, the less will it be shaken by local passions." "Is it not better," he asked, "that the opposite bank of the Mississippi should be settled by our own brethren and children than by strangers of another family?" American settlers quickly answered with a rousing affirmation.

The cluster of state papers that follow document Jefferson's momentous decision: his initial letter to Livingston revealing his intentions, his nomination of Livingston and Monroe, his proclamation summoning the Senate into special session, and his submission of the treaty of acquisition to the Senate.

To the U. S. Minister to France (Robert R. Livingston) [3]

WASHINGTON, *Apr. 18, 1802*

Dear Sir—A favorable and a confidential opportunity offering by Mr. Dupont de Nemours, who is revisiting his native country gives me an opportunity of sending you a cipher to be used between us, which will give you some trouble to understand, but, once understood, is the easiest to use, the most indecipherable, and varied by a new key with the greatest facility of any one I have ever known. I am in hopes the explanation

57

inclosed will be sufficient. Let our key of letters be [*some figures which are illegible*] and the key of lines be [*figures illegible*] and lest we should happen to lose our key or be absent from it, it is so formed as to be kept in the memory and put upon paper at pleasure; being produced by writing our names and residences at full length, each of which containing 27 letters is divided into two parts of 9. letters each; and each of the 9. letters is then numbered according to the place it would hold if the 9. were arranged alphabetically, thus [*so blotted as to be illegible*]. The numbers over the letters being then arranged as the letters to which they belong stand in our names, we can always construct our key. But why a cipher between us, when official things go naturally to the Secretary of State, and things not political need no cipher. 1. matters of a public nature, and proper to go on our records, should go to the secretary of state. 2. matters of a public nature not proper to be placed on our records may still go to the secretary of state, headed by the word 'private.' But 3. there may be matters merely personal to ourselves, and which require the cover of a cipher more than those of any other character. This last purpose and others which we cannot foresee may render it convenient and advantageous to have at hand a mask for whatever may need it. But writing by Mr. Dupont I need no cipher. I require from him to put this into your own hand and no other hand, let the delay occasioned by that be what it will.

The cession of Louisiana and the Floridas by Spain to France works most sorely on the U. S. On this subject the Secretary of State has written to you fully. Yet I cannot forbear recurring to it personally, so deep is the impression it makes in my mind. It compleatly reverses all the political relations of the U. S. and will form a new epoch in our political course. Of all nations of any consideration France is the one which hitherto has offered the fewest points on which we could have any conflict of right, and the most points of a communion of interests. From these causes we have ever looked to her as our *natural friend,* as one with which we never could have an occasion of difference. Her growth therefore we viewed as our own, her misfortunes ours. There is on the globe one single spot, the possessor of which is our natural and habitual enemy. It is New Orleans, through which the produce of three-eights of our territory must pass to market, and from its fertility it will ere long yield more than half of our whole produce and contain more than half our inhabitants. France placing herself in that door assumes to us the attitude of defiance. Spain might have retained it quietly for years. Her pacific dispositions, her feeble state, would induce her to increase our facilities there, so that her possession of the place would be hardly felt by us, and it would not perhaps be very long before some circumstance might arise which might make the cession of it to us the price of something of more worth to her. Not so can it ever be in the hands of France. The impetuosity of her temper, the energy and restlessness of her character, placed in a point of eternal friction with us, and our character, which though quiet, and loving peace and the pursuit of wealth, is high-minded, despising wealth in competition with insult or injury, enterprising and energetic as any nation on earth, these circumstances render it impossible that France and the U. S. can continue long friends when they meet in so irritable a position. They as well as we must be blind if they do not see this; and we must be very improvident if we do not begin to make arrangements on that hypothesis. The day that France takes possession of N. Orleans fixes the sentence which is to restrain her forever within her low water mark. It seals the union of two nations who in conjunction can maintain exclusive possession of the ocean. From that moment we must marry ourselves to the British fleet and nation. We must turn all our attentions to a maritime force, for which our resources place us on very high grounds: and having formed and cemented together a power which may render reinforcement of her settlements here impossible to France, make the first cannon, which shall be fired in Europe the signal for tearing up any settlement she may have made, and for holding the two continents of America in sequestration for the common purposes of the united British and American nations. This is not a state of things we seek or desire. It is one which this measure, if adopted by France, forces on us, as necessarily as any other cause, by the laws of nature, brings on its necessary effect. It is not from a fear of France that we deprecate this measure proposed by her. For however greater her force is than ours compared in the abstract, it is nothing in comparison of ours when to be exerted on our soil. But it is from a sincere love of peace, and a firm persuasion that bound to France by the interests and the strong sympathies still existing in the minds of our citizens, and holding relative positions which ensure their continuance we are secure of a long course of peace. Whereas the change of friends, which will be rendered necessary if France changes that position, embarks us necessarily as a belligerent power in the first war of Europe. In that case France will have held possession of New Orleans during the interval of a peace, long or short, at the end of which it will be wrested from her. Will this short-lived possession have been an equivalent to her for the transfer of such a weight into the scale of her enemy? Will not the amalgamation of a young, thriving, nation continue to that enemy the health and force which are at present so evidently on the decline? And will a few years possession of N. Orleans add equally to the strength of France? She may say she needs Louisiana for the supply of her West Indies. She does not need it in time of peace. And in war she could not depend on them because they would be so easily intercepted. I should suppose that all these considerations might in some proper form be brought into view of the government of France. Tho' stated by us, it ought not to give offence; because we do not bring them forward as a menace, but as consequences not controulable by us, but inevitable from the course of things. We mention them not as things which we desire by any means, but as things we deprecate; and we beseech a friend to look forward and to prevent them for our common interests.

If France considers Louisiana however as indispensable for her views she might perhaps be willing to look about for arrangements which might reconcile it to our interests. If anything could do this it would be the ceding to us the island of New Orleans and the Floridas. This would certainly in a great degree remove the causes of jarring and irritation between us, and perhaps for such a length of time as might produce other means of making the measure permanently conciliatory to our interests and friendships. It would at any rate relieve us from the necessity of taking immediate measures for countervailing such an operation by arrangements in another quarter. Still we should consider N. Orleans and the Floridas as equivalent for the risk of a quarrel with France produced by her vicinage. I have no doubt you have urged these considerations on every proper occasion with the government where you are. They are such as must have effect if you can find the means of producing thorough reflection on them by that government. The idea here is that the troops sent to St. Domingo, were to proceed to Louisiana after finishing their work in that island. If this were the arrangement, it will give you time to return again and again to the charge, for the conquest of St. Domingo will not be a short work. It will take considerable time to wear down a great number of souldiers. Every eye in the U. S. is now fixed on this affair of Louisiana. Perhaps nothing since the revolutionary war has produced more uneasy sensations through the body of the nation. Notwithstanding temporary bickerings have taken place with France, she has still a strong hold on the affections of our citizens generally. I have thought it not amiss, by way of supplement to the letters of the Secretary of State to write you this private one to impress you with the importance we affix to this transaction. I pray you to cherish Dupont. He has the best dispositions for the continuance of friendship between the two nations, and perhaps you may be able to make a good use of him. Accept assurances of my affectionate esteem and high consideration.

January 11, 1803

Gentlemen of the Senate:

The cession of the Spanish Province of Louisiana to France, and perhaps of the Floridas, and the late suspension of our right of deposit at New Orleans are events of primary interest to the United States. On both occasions such measures were promptly taken as were thought most likely amicably to remove the present and to prevent future causes of inquietude. The objects of these measures were to obtain the territory on the left bank of the Mississippi and eastward of that, if practicable, on conditions to which the proper authorities of our country would agree, or at least to prevent any changes which might lessen the secure exercise of our rights. While my confidence in our minister plenipotentiary at Paris is entire and undiminished, I still think that these objects might be promoted by joining with him a person sent from hence directly, carrying with him the feelings and sentiments of the nation excited on the late occurrence, impressed by full communications of all the views we entertain on this interesting subject, and thus prepared to meet and to improve to an useful result the counter propositions of the other contracting party, whatsoever form their interests may give to them, and to secure to us the ultimate accomplishment of our object.

I therefore nominate Robert R. Livingston to be minister plenipotentiary and James Monroe to be minister extraordinary and plenipotentiary, with full powers to both jointly, or to either on the death of the other, to enter into a treaty or convention with the First Consul of France for the purpose of enlarging and more effectually securing our rights and interests in the river Mississippi and in the Territories eastward thereof.

But as the possession of these provinces is still in Spain, and the course of events may retard or prevent the cession to France being carried into effect, to secure our object it will be expedient to address equal powers to the Government of Spain also, to be used only in the event of its being necessary.

I therefore nominate Charles Pinckney to be minister plenipotentiary, and James Monroe, of Virginia, to be minister extraordinary and plenipotentiary, with full powers to both jointly, or to either on the death of the other, to enter into a treaty or convention with His Catholic Majesty for the purpose of enlarging and more effectually securing our rights and interests in the river Mississippi and in the Territories eastward thereof.

TH: JEFFERSON

[From the *National Intelligencer,* July 18, 1803]

BY THE PRESIDENT OF THE UNITED STATES OF AMERICA

A PROCLAMATION

Whereas great and weighty matters claiming the consideration of the Congress of the United States form an extraordinary occasion for convening them, I do by these presents appoint Monday, the 17th day of October next, for their meeting at the city of Washington, hereby requiring their respective Senators and Representatives then and there to assemble in Congress, in order to receive such communications as may then be made to them and to consult and determine on such measures as in their wisdom may be deemed meet for the welfare of the United States.

In testimony whereof I have caused the seal of the United States to be hereunto affixed, and signed the same with my hand.

[SEAL]   Done at the city of Washington, the 16th day of July, A. D. 1803, and in the twenty-eighth year of the Independence of the United States

TH: JEFFERSON

By the President:
JAMES MADISON,
Secretary

THIRD ANNUAL MESSAGE

October 17, 1803

To the Senate and House of Representatives of the United States:

In calling you together, fellow-citizens, at an earlier day than was contemplated by the act of the last session of Congress, I have not been insensible to the personal inconveniences necessarily resulting from an unexpected change in your arrangements. But matters of great public concernment have rendered this call necessary, and the interests you feel in these will supersede in your minds all private considerations.

Congress witnessed at their late session the extraordinary agitation produced in the public mind by the suspension of our right of deposit at the port of New Orleans, no assignment of another place having been made according to treaty. They were sensible that the continuance of that privation would be more injurious to our nation than any consequences which could flow from any mode of redress, but reposing just confidence in the good faith of the Government whose officer had committed the wrong, friendly and reasonable representations were resorted to, and the right of deposit was restored.

Previous, however, to this period we had not been unaware of the danger to which our peace would be perpetually exposed whilst so important a key to the commerce of the Western country remained under foreign power. Difficulties, too, were presenting themselves as to the navigation of other streams which, arising within our territories, pass through those adjacent. Propositions had therefore been authorized for obtaining on fair conditions the sovereignty of New Orleans and of other possessions in that quarter interesting to our quiet to such extent as was deemed practicable, and the provisional appropriation of $2,000,-000 to be applied and accounted for by the President of the United States, intended as part of the price, was considered as conveying the sanction of Congress to the acquisition proposed. The enlightened Government of France saw with just discernment the importance to both nations of such liberal arrangements as might best and permanently promote the peace, friendship, and interests of both, and the property and sovereignty of all Louisiana which had been restored to them have on certain conditions been transferred to the United States by instruments bearing date the 30th of April last. When these shall have received the constitutional sanction of the Senate, they will without delay be communicated to the Representatives also for the exercise of their functions as to those conditions which are within the powers vested by the Constitution in Congress.

Whilst the property and sovereignty of the Mississippi and its waters secure an independent outlet for the produce of the Western States and an uncontrolled navigation through their whole course, free from collision with other powers and the dangers to our peace from that source, the fertility of the country, its climate and extent, promise in due season important aids to our Treasury, an ample provision for our posterity, and a wide spread for the blessings of freedom and equal laws.

With the wisdom of Congress it will rest to take those ulterior measures which may be necessary for the immediate occupation and temporary government of the country; for its incorporation into our Union; for rendering the change of government a blessing to our newly adopted brethren; for securing to them the rights of conscience and of property; for confirming to the Indian inhabitants their occupancy and self-government, establishing friendly and commercial relations with them, and for ascertaining the geography of the country acquired. Such materials, for your information, relative to its affairs in general as the short space of time has permitted me to collect will be laid before you when the subject shall be in a state for your consideration.

Another important acquisition of territory has also been made since the last session of Congress. The friendly tribe of Kaskaskia Indians, with which we have never had a difference, reduced by the wars and wants of savage life to a few individuals unable to defend themselves against the neighboring tribes, has transfered its country to the United States, reserving only for its members what is sufficient to maintain them in an agricultural way. The considerations stipulated are that we shall extend to them our patronage and protection and give them certain annual aids in money, in implements of agriculture, and other articles of their choice. This country, among the most fertile within our limits, extending along the Mississippi from the mouth of the Illinois to and up the Ohio, though not so necessary as a barrier since the acquisition of the other bank, may yet be well worthy of being laid open to immediate settlement, as its inhabitants may descend with rapidity in support of the lower country should future circumstances expose that to foreign enterprise. As the stipulations in this treaty also involve matters within the competence of both Houses only, it will be laid before Congress as soon as the Senate shall have advised its ratification.

With many of the other Indian tribes improvements in agriculture and household manufacture are advancing, and with all our peace and friendship are established on grounds much firmer than heretofore. The measure adopted of establishing trading houses among them and of furnishing them necessaries in exchange for their commodities at such moderate prices as leave no gain, but cover us from loss, has the most conciliatory and useful effect on them, and is that which will best secure their peace and good will.

The small vessels authorized by Congress with a view to the Mediterranean service have been sent into that sea, and will be able more effectually to confine the Tripoline cruisers within their harbors and supersede the necessity of convoy to our commerce in that quarter. They will sensibly lessen the expenses of that service the ensuing year.

A further knowledge of the ground in the northeastern and northwestern angles of the United States has evinced that the boundaries established by the treaty of Paris between the British territories and ours in those parts were too imperfectly described to be susceptible of execution. It has therefore been thought worthy of attention for preserving and cherishing the harmony and useful intercourse subsisting between the two nations to remove by timely arrangements what unfavorable incidents might otherwise render a ground of future misunderstanding. A convention has therefore been entered into which provides for a practicable demarcation of those limits to the satisfaction of both parties.

An account of the receipts and expenditures of the year ending the 30th of September last, with the estimates for the service of the ensuing year, will be laid before you by the Secretary of the Treasury so soon as the receipts of the last quarter shall be returned from the more distant States. It is already ascertained that the amount paid into the Treasury for that year has been between $11,000,000 and $12,000,000, and that the revenue accrued during the same term exceeds the sum counted on as sufficient for our current expenses and to extinguish the public debt within the period heretofore proposed.

The amount of debt paid for the same year is about $3,100,000, exclusive of interest, and making, with the payment of the preceding year, a discharge of more than $8,500,000 of the principal of that debt, besides the accruing interest; and there remain in the Treasury nearly $6,000,000. Of these, $880,000 have been reserved for payment of the first installment due under the British convention of January 8, 1802, and two millions are what have been before mentioned as placed by Congress under the power and accountability of the President toward the price of New Orleans and other territories acquired, which, remaining untouched, are still applicable to that object and go in diminution of the sum to be funded for it.

Should the acquisition of Louisiana be constitutionally confirmed and carried into effect, a sum of nearly $13,000,000 will then be added to our public debt, most of which is payable after fifteen years, before which term the present existing debts will all be discharged by the established operation of the sinking fund. When we contemplate the ordinary annual augmentation of impost from increasing population and wealth, the augmentation of the same revenue by its extension to the new acquisition, and the economies which may still be introduced into our public expenditures, I can not but hope that Congress in reviewing their resources will find means to meet the intermediate interest of this additional debt without recurring to new taxes, and applying to this object only the ordinary progression of our revenue. Its extraordinary increase in times of foreign war will be the proper and sufficient fund for any measures of safety or precaution which that state of things may render necessary in our neutral position.

5

THE DECISION
TO FIGHT ENGLAND AGAIN

Madison Plunges the Nation into the War of 1812

James Madison, the man who, according to one Congressional critic, "could not be kicked into a fight," decided after considerable provocation and under great pressure from Congress to go to war against Great Britain in 1812. His predecessor and mentor, Thomas Jefferson, had avoided taking that step. "No two countries upon earth have so many points in common," wrote Jefferson of Great Britain and the United States during the course of extended negotiations, "and their rulers must be great bunglers, indeed, if with such dispositions they break asunder." Yet, break asunder they did, and the blame must be laid to bungling on this side of the ocean as much as to inflexibility on the part of British diplomats.

Truly the War of 1812 was an unnecessary war and an unwanted war. On both sides imaginative statesmanship was lacking. The issues were not new. They went back to the resumption in 1803 of the Napoleonic Wars. In order to deprive each other of the means of war Great Britain and France tightened the restrictions they sought to impose on the neutral carrying trade. Since Britain enjoyed overwhelming naval superiority over France, American commerce suffered more severely from the invasion of her neutral rights by the British than by the French. Again, controversies which had been agitated in the 1790's came to the fore—quarrels over neutral trade, impressment, and blockade. The British no longer permitted American vessels to evade their blockade of the French West Indies by landing a cargo at an American port and securing fresh clearance for a belligerent port. Beginning in 1806, Congress passed the first of the Non-Importation Acts, prohibiting the importation from England of a long list of items. Britain and France each laid down a paper blockade of the other's coastline. Meanwhile the issue of impressment reached a fever pitch when the British frigate *Leopard* attacked the U. S. frigate *Chesapeake* outside the three-mile limit off Norfolk and removed a number of alleged deserters. Jefferson then had Congress pass an embargo on all land and seaborne commerce with foreign nations. This action aroused intense opposition in New England and New York, mercantile areas enjoying a prosperous carrying trade. Then, in March, 1809, Jefferson signed the Non-Intercourse Act, repealing the embargo and reopening trade with all nations except France or Great Britain, and authorizing the President to proclaim resumption of trade with those powers if either or both should cease violating neutral rights.

This was the situation which James Madison inherited on coming into office. The pro-American British minister to the United States, David M. Erskine, gave us assurances that the restrictive orders of the British government as applied to this country would be revoked. Acting on these assurances, Madison legalized trade with Great Britain. The stubborn and myopic British Foreign Secretary, George Canning, repudiated Erskine's agreement. For President Madison there was no alternative but to revive the Non-Intercourse Act against Great Britain. Finally, in 1810 Congress passed a measure known as Macon's Bill No. 2, from its sponsor Nathaniel Macon of North Carolina. This act authorized the President to reopen commerce with Great Britain and France, adding that in the event either one of these powers should before March 3, 1811, modify or revoke her edicts so as to cease violations of American shipping, the President was authorized to prohibit trade with the other. If at the end of three months the other power failed to withdraw her edicts, the President was empowered to revive non-intercourse against her.

Macon's Bill No. 2 turned out to be a trap, and the United States stepped right into it. In a characteristic bit of deception Napoleon informed the United States that he would revoke his controversial decrees on condition that the United States declare non-intercourse against the British unless the Orders in Council were withdrawn. Meantime he issued orders sequestering American vessels that had called at French ports. With astonishing naïveté, Madison accepted the French communication at face value. The British did not revoke their Orders until it was too late. On April 1 Madison recommended to Congress a general embargo, which the moderate Republicans amended to extend from the sixty-day period Madison requested to one of ninety days. The British insisted that Napoleon in fact had not revoked his decrees, and they were entirely correct, but Madison chose to interpret this as final notice of Britain's unyielding position. Toward the close of May he drafted the message given here, calling for an immediate declaration of war, which was communicated to a joint session of Congress on June 1. It has been said that Madison was a prisoner of Congress and the war party, and that having accepted nomination for a second term by a Congressional caucus, he was obliged to go to war. This has not been established, but Madison's action in resisting war and finally yielding to the belligerent summons of Congress may well be compared with McKinley's in a parallel situation.

Wracked by economic distress at home, the British government began to give way, albeit reluctantly. On June 16 Great Britain announced the suspension of the Orders in Council, but two days later, Congress, unaware of the British concession, declared war by a divided vote. In the Senate the vote was 19-13, the closest division on record in any declaration of war in American history. While it is true that expansionist sentiment, fanned by "war hawks" like Henry Clay, John C. Calhoun, William Lowndes, Felix Grundy, and Peter B. Porter lay behind the push toward war on the part of the South and West, the actual grounds for war were maritime seizures and impressment. The Northwesterners desired the conquest of Canada to assure security for an expanding frontier; the Southerners wanted to wrest Florida from Spain, Britain's ally. Madison may have been aware of the expansionist impulse, but in his message to Congress he stressed maritime issues, which in his own mind were more immediate and decisive. To these he added a further grievance, border warfare carried on by the Indians with the connivance, Madison implied, of British traders and garrisons.

Madison's decision, then, gave America a war which would not have broken out had cable or wireless communications been available. "Mr. Madison's War" was presumably fought on behalf of a section of the country, the maritime Northeast, that was implacably opposed to war. Extremists among the New England Federalists actually flirted with the idea of secession. War, when it came, found America totally unprepared due to the failure of the party of Jefferson and Madison to build up the military and naval arms. The management of the war was bungled, and the ultimate stalemate that made a settlement possible was due as much to British preoccupation with European involvements as it was to the achievements of heroic figures like Captain Oliver Hazard Perry, William Henry Harrison, Jacob Brown, Captain Thomas Macdonough, and Andrew Jackson. The latter fought the last major engagement of the war, inflicting a disastrous defeat upon the British at New Orleans, two weeks after the signing of the peace at Ghent.

As for Madison, his diminishing prestige as a war leader reached its nadir when he was forced into ignominious flight from Washington as the British, without meeting serious resistance, entered and burned the capital.

MESSAGE

WASHINGTON, *June 1, 1812*

To the Senate and House of Representatives of the United States:

I communicate to Congress certain documents, being a continuation of those heretofore laid before them on the subject of our affairs with Great Britain.

Without going back beyond the renewal in 1803 of the war in which Great Britain is engaged, and omitting unrepaired wrongs of inferior magnitude, the conduct of her Government presents a series of acts hostile to the United States as an independent and neutral nation.

British cruisers have been in the continued practice of violating the American flag on the great highway of nations, and of seizing and carrying off persons sailing under it, not in the exercise of a belligerent right founded on the law of nations against an enemy, but of a municipal prerogative over British subjects. British jurisdiction is thus extended to neutral vessels in a situation where no laws can operate but the law of nations and the laws of the country to which the vessels belong, and a self-redress is assumed which, if British subjects were wrongfully detained and alone concerned, is that substitution of force for a resort to the responsible sovereign which falls within the definition of war. Could the seizure of British subjects in such cases be regarded as within the exercise of a belligerent right, the acknowledged laws of war, which forbid an article of captured property to be adjudged without a regular investigation before a competent tribunal, would imperiously demand the fairest trial where the sacred rights of persons were at issue. In place of such a trial these rights are subjected to the will of every petty commander.

The practice, hence, is so far from affecting British subjects alone that, under the pretext of searching for these, thousands of American citizens, under the safeguard of public law and of their national flag, have been torn from their country and from everything dear to them; have been dragged on board ships of war of a foreign nation and exposed, under the severities of their discipline, to be exiled to the most distant and deadly climes, to risk their lives in the battles of their oppressors, and to be the melancholy instruments of taking away those of their own brethren.

Against this crying enormity, which Great Britain would be so prompt to avenge if committed against herself, the United States have in vain exhausted remonstrances and expostulations, and that no proof might be wanting of their conciliatory dispositions, and no pretext left for a continuance of the practice, the British Government was formally assured of the readiness of the United States to enter into arrangements such as could not be rejected if the recovery of British subjects were the real and the sole object. The communication passed without effect.

British cruisers have been in the practice also of violating the rights and the peace of our coasts. They hover over and harass our entering and departing commerce. To the most insulting pretensions they have added the most lawless proceedings in our very harbors, and have wantonly spilt American blood within the sanctuary of our territorial jurisdiction. The principles and rules enforced by that nation, when a neutral nation, against armed vessels of belligerents hovering near her coasts and disturbing her commerce are well known. When called on, nevertheless, by the United States to punish the greater offenses committed by her own vessels, her Government has bestowed on their commanders additional marks of honor and confidence.

Under pretended blockades, without the presence of an adequate force and sometimes without the practicability of applying one, our commerce has been plundered in every sea, the great staples of our country have been cut off from their legitimate markets, and a destructive blow aimed at our agricultural and maritime interests. In aggravation of these predatory measures they have been considered as in force from the dates of their notification, a retrospective effect being thus added, as has been done in other important cases, to the unlawfulness of the course pursued. And to render the outrage the more signal these mock blockades have been reiterated and enforced in the face of official communications from the British Government declaring as the true definition of a legal blockade "that particular ports must be actually invested and previous warning given to vessels bound to them not to enter."

Not content with these occasional expedients for laying waste our neutral trade, the cabinet of Britain resorted at length to the sweeping system of blockades, under the name of orders in council, which has been molded and managed as might best suit its political views, its commercial jealousies, or the avidity of British cruisers.

To our remonstrances against the complicated and transcendent injustice of this innovation the first reply was that the orders were reluctantly adopted by Great Britain as a necessary retaliation on decrees of her enemy proclaiming a general blockade of the British Isles at a time when the naval force of that enemy dared not issue from his own ports. She was reminded without effect that her own prior blockades, unsupported by an adequate naval force actually applied and continued, were a bar to this plea; that executed edicts against millions of our property could not be retaliation on edicts confessedly impossible to be executed; that retaliation, to be just, should fall on the party setting the guilty example, not on an innocent party which was not even chargeable with an acquiescence in it.

When deprived of this flimsy veil for a prohibition of our trade with her enemy by the repeal of his prohibition of our trade with Great Britain, her cabinet, instead of a corresponding repeal or a practical discontinuance of its orders, formally avowed a determination to persist in them against the United States until the markets of her enemy should be laid open to British products, thus asserting an obligation on a neutral power to require one belligerent to encourage by its internal regulations the trade of another belligerent, contradicting her own practice toward all nations, in peace as well as in war, and betraying the insincerity of those professions which inculcated a belief that, having resorted to her orders with regret, she was anxious to find an occasion for putting an end to them.

Abandoning still more all respect for the neutral rights of the United States and for its own consistency, the British Government now demands as prerequisites to a repeal of its orders as they relate to the United States that a formality should be observed in the repeal of the French decrees nowise necessary to their termination nor exemplified by British usage, and that the French repeal, besides including that portion of the decrees which operates within a territorial jurisdiction, as well as that which operates on the high seas, against the commerce of the United States should not be a single and special repeal in relation to the United States, but should be extended to whatever other neutral nations unconnected with them may be affected by those decrees. And as an additional insult, they are called on for a formal disavowal of conditions and pretensions advanced by the French Government for which the United States are so far from having made themselves responsible that, in official explanations which have been published to the world, and in a correspondence of the American minister at London with the British minister for foreign affairs such a responsibility was explicitly and emphatically disclaimed.

It has become, indeed, sufficiently certain that the commerce of the United States is to be sacrificed, not as interfering with the belligerent rights of Great Britain; not as supplying the wants of her enemies, which she herself supplies; but as interfering with the monopoly which she covets for her own commerce and navigation. She carries on a war against the lawful commerce of a friend that she may the better carry on a commerce with an enemy—a commerce polluted by the forgeries and perjuries which are for the most part the only passports by which it can succeed.

Anxious to make every experiment short of the last resort of injured nations, the United States have withheld from Great Britain, under successive modifications, the benefits of a free intercourse with their market, the loss of which could not but outweigh the profits accruing from her restrictions of our commerce with other nations. And to entitle these experiments to the more favorable consideration they were so framed as to enable her to place her adversary under the exclusive operation of them. To these appeals her Government has been equally inflexible, as if willing to make sacrifices of every sort rather than yield to the claims of justice or renounce the errors of a false pride. Nay, so far were the attempts carried to overcome the attachment of the British cabinet to its unjust edicts that it received every encouragement within the competency of the executive branch of our Government to expect that a repeal of them would be followed by a war between the United States and France, unless the French edicts should also be repealed. Even this communication, although silencing forever the plea of a disposition in the United States to acquiesce in those edicts originally the sole plea for them, received no attention.

If no other proof existed of a predetermination of the British Government against a repeal of its orders, it might be found in the correspondence of the minister plenipotentiary of the United States at London and the British secretary for foreign affairs in 1810, on the question whether the blockade of May, 1806, was considered as in force or as not in force. It had been ascertained that the French Government, which urged this blockade as the ground of its Berlin decree, was willing in the event of its removal to repeal that decree, which, being followed by alternate repeals of the other offensive edicts, might abolish the whole system on both sides. This inviting opportunity for accomplishing an object so important to the United States, and professed so often to be the desire of both the belligerents, was made known to the British Government. As that Government admits that an actual application of an adequate force is necessary to the existence of a legal blockade, and it was notorious that if such a force had ever been applied its long discontinuance had annulled the blockade in question, there could be no sufficient objection on the part of Great Britain to a formal revocation of it, and no imaginable objection to a declaration of the fact that the blockade did not exist. The declaration would have been consistent with her avowed principles of blockade, and would have enabled the United States to demand from France the pledged repeal of her decrees, either with success, in which case the way would have been opened for a general repeal of the belligerent edicts, or without success, in which case the United States would have been justified in turning their measures exclusively against France. The British Government would, however, neither rescind the blockade nor declare its nonexistence, nor permit its nonexistence to be inferred and affirmed by the American plenipotentiary. On the contrary, by representing the blockade to be comprehended in the orders in council, the United States were compelled so to regard it in their subsequent proceedings.

There was a period when a favorable change in the policy of the British cabinet was justly considered as established. The minister plenipotentiary of His Britannic Majesty here proposed an adjustment of the differences more immediately endangering the harmony of the two countries. The proposition was accepted with the promptitude and cordiality corresponding with the invariable professions of this Government. A foundation appeared to be laid for a sincere and lasting reconciliation. The prospect, however, quickly vanished. The whole proceeding was disavowed by the British Government without any explanations which could at that time repress the belief that the disavowal proceeded from a spirit of hostility to the commercial rights and prosperity of the United States; and it has since come into proof that at the very moment when the public minister was holding the language of friendship and inspiring confidence in the sincerity of the negotiation with which he was charged a secret agent of his Government was employed in intrigues having for their object a subversion of our Government and a dismemberment of our happy union.

In reviewing the conduct of Great Britain toward the United States our attention is necessarily drawn to the warfare just renewed by the savages on one of our extensive frontiers—a warfare which is known to spare neither age nor sex and to be distinguished by features peculiarly shocking to humanity. It is difficult to account for the activity and combinations which have for some time been developing themselves among tribes in constant intercourse with British traders and garrisons without connecting their hostility with that influence and without recollecting the authenticated examples of such interpositions heretofore furnished by the officers and agents of that Government.

Such is the spectacle of injuries and indignities which have been heaped on our country, and such the crisis which its unexampled forbearance and conciliatory efforts have not been able to avert. It might at least have been expected that an enlightened nation, if less urged by moral obligations or invited by friendly dispositions on the part of the United States, would have found in its true interest alone a sufficient motive to respect their rights and their tranquillity on the high seas; that an enlarged policy would have favored that free and general circulation of commerce in which the British nation is at all times interested, and which in times of war is the best alleviation of its calamities to herself as well as to other belligerents; and more especially that the British cabinet would not, for the sake of a precarious and surreptitious intercourse with hostile markets, have persevered in a course of measures which necessarily put at hazard the invaluable market of a great and growing country, disposed to cultivate the mutual advantages of an active commerce.

Other counsels have prevailed. Our moderation and conciliation have had no other effect than to encourage perseverance and to enlarge pretensions. We behold our seafaring citizens still the daily victims of lawless violence, committed on the great common and highway of nations, even within sight of the country which owes them protection. We behold our vessels, freighted with the products of our soil and industry, or returning with the honest proceeds of them, wrested from their lawful destinations, confiscated by prize courts no longer the organs of public law but the instruments of arbitrary edicts, and their unfortunate crews dispersed and lost, or forced or inveigled in British ports into British fleets, whilst arguments are employed in support of these aggressions which have no foundation but in a principle equally supporting a claim to regulate our external commerce in all cases whatsoever.

We behold, in fine, on the side of Great Britain a state of war against the United States, and on the side of the United States a state of peace toward Great Britain.

Whether the United States shall continue passive under these progressive usurpations and these accumulating wrongs, or, opposing force to force in defense of their national rights, shall commit a just cause into the hands of the Almighty Disposer of Events, avoiding all connections which might entangle it in the contest or views of other powers, and preserving a constant readiness to concur in an honorable reestablishment of peace and friendship, is a solemn question which the Constitution wisely confides to the legislative department of the Government. In recommending it to their early deliberations I am happy in the assurance that the decision will be worthy the enlightened and patriotic councils of a virtuous, a free, and a powerful nation.

Having presented this view of the relations of the United States with Great Britain and of the solemn alternative growing out of them, I proceed to remark that the communications last made to Congress on the subject of our relations with France will have shewn that since the revocation of her decrees, as they violated the neutral rights of the United States, her Government has authorized illegal captures by its privateers and public ships, and that other outrages have been practiced on our vessels and our citizens. It will have been seen also that no indemnity had been provided or satisfactorily pledged for the extensive spoliations committed under the violent and retrospective orders of the French Government against the property of our citizens seized within the jurisdiction of France. I abstain at this time from recommending to the consideration of Congress definitive measures with respect to that nation, in the expectation that the result of unclosed discussions between our minister plenipotentiary at Paris and the French Government will speedily enable Congress to decide with greater advantage on the course due to the rights, the interests, and the honor of our country.

6

THE DECISION
TO CURB THE USE OF IMPLIED POWERS

Madison in Farewell Vetoes Calhoun's "Bonus Bill"

Although Jefferson and Madison when out of power had made capital out of the broad construction put upon the Constitution by their chief opponent, Alexander Hamilton, both men when in the Presidency pursued Hamiltonian programs. On what other constitutional ground could one have justified the Louisiana Purchase, or the Embargo, or the seizure of West Florida, or Madison's own signature on a bill creating a new Bank of the United States, whose constitutionality he had at one time denied? Again, Madison signed the tariff act of 1816, a truly Hamiltonian measure to protect American "infant industries" from British competition, and he approved measures strengthening the permanent military and naval establishments—a turnabout from Jefferson's initial policies in the Presidency. Thus, at the very time when the Federalist Party, tarred with the brush of sedition in the War of 1812, was dying, the Jeffersonians were acting like good old-fashioned Federalists themselves.

The great peacetime problem after the end of the second war with Britain was that of internal improvements and how they could best be advanced. Madison recognized the problem, and in his last annual message called the attention of Congress "to the expediency of exercising their sole existing powers, and, where necessary, of resorting to the prescribed mode of enlarging them, in order to effectuate a comprehensive system of roads and canals, such as will have the effect of drawing more closely together every part of our country, by promoting intercourse and improvements and by increasing the share of every part in the common stock of national prosperity."

The rapid expansion of the West spurred demands for connecting links between the Atlantic and the interior, for turnpikes and canals that had already shown themselves practicable and profitable in England. Some states, notably New York, Pennsylvania, and Virginia, were pushing ahead vigorously with plans for such canals, river improvements, and turnpikes, but none of these projects was interstate in character. The West now urged the Federal government to construct those interstate roads and canals which were essential to that section's prosperity and which the states, smitten with jealous rivalry, could not undertake. In Congress men like John C. Calhoun and Henry Clay looked upon the Hamiltonian doctrine of implied powers as justifying public improvements to promote the transportation of the mails and military supplies, to build canals, and to improve the navigation of rivers. The Calhoun of 1817 was quite a different person from the Calhoun of 1831; the young nationalist sounded a different note entirely from the nullificationist of the later period. In that last year of Madison's administration he held it the duty of Congress to "bind the republic together with a perfect system of roads and canals." "Let us conquer space," he exhorted. No one supported Calhoun's program more vigorously than did Henry Clay, because the South Carolinian's notions of that time meshed perfectly with the Kentuckian's principles that the national government should possess broad powers and should vigorously exercise them, especially for the promotion of the interests of the West.

As chairman of the committee to consider the expediency of creating a permanent fund for internal improvements, Calhoun reported on December 23, 1816, a bill providing for the general use by Congress, in the construction of roads and canals, of the bonus of $1,500,000 to be paid by the Bank of the United States, together with the future dividends on the stock of the bank which the United States held. He found his constitutional authority in the "common defense and general welfare" clause and in the power to establish post offices and post roads. "If we are restricted in the use of our money to the enumerated powers," Calhoun asked, "on what principle can the purchase of Louisiana be justified?" Warning that the very extent of the republic exposed the nation to "the greatest of all calamities—next to the loss of liberty—and even to that in its consequences—disunion," he insisted that every tendency to disunion should be counteracted.

The bill, with an amendment proposed by Timothy Pickering which justified the role of the Federal government in internal improvements on the grounds of regulating commerce and national defense and made the consent of the states a requirement to the launching of any project, passed both houses by slender majorities, with the New England states largely opposed for local and sectional reasons. Everyone thought that the constitutional issue had been disposed of, but a shock was in store for the nation. In what was truly his farewell address, Madison returned the bill to the House with a veto message of March 3, 1817. Madison had previously implied that he had some constitutional doubts, and now his scruples prevented him from signing the measure. Teetering on the brink, he feared to take the plunge. Reviewing the acts of his own administration, he had belated misgivings that the application of the doctrine of implied powers was being stretched too far, and that a halt should be called. What gives his message special significance is that Madison had come to look upon the Constitution, of which he was one of the principal authors, as a closed document, not to be enlarged by precedent and usage. He was now turning the clock back to 1787, ignoring the interpretation of the Constitution under both the Federalist and the Jeffersonian administrations.

What made the caution of the administration the more strange was that the Supreme Court under John Marshall was now embarked on a broad nationalist and centralizing interpretation of the Constitution, culminating in 1819 in the famous case of *McCulloch v. Maryland,* in which Marshall invoked the "implied powers" clause of the Constitution to uphold the right of Congress to establish the Bank of the United States and to deny the right of the separate states to tax the Bank. While Madison was in effect turning transportation back to the states, Marshall, in *Gibbons v. Ogden* (1824), freed transportation from the threat of local monopoly and fixed the power of Congress to regulate commerce between the states. Thus, transportation, in effect shackled by the executive, was soon to be liberated by the judiciary.

If the broad constructionists found Madison's veto an unpleasant surprise, they were equally chagrined by President Monroe's first annual message, in which Madison's successor stated it as his settled conviction that Congress did not have the right to pass such legislation.

Congress had all the powers it needed, a special committee reported, citing those that Calhoun and Pickering had earlier marshaled, but a two-thirds vote necessary to override a certain veto of an appropriation bill could not be obtained. The Federal government, at a time of feverish expansion and great sectional and local rivalry to promote transportation facilities with the interior, had withdrawn from the theater of action. Momentarily it seemed that Madison's veto would have hit New York the hardest, for that state was pushing its plans for the Erie Canal. However, the New York legislature, determined to forge ahead regardless, began the enterprise without Federal assistance, and the Pennsylvania legislature appropriated huge sums for canals and turnpikes within that state. Hardest hit by Madison's veto were the Southern states, which evidenced less energy in pressing plans for connecting the headwaters of their chief rivers of the Atlantic slope with those flowing into the Mississippi. Thus, while the North was able to expand and tighten its ties with the West, the South was becoming a sectional enclave, lacking competitive transportation facilities to reach the interior of the country. This was a portent of worse to come.

VETO MESSAGE

March 3, 1817

To the House of Representatives of the United States:
Having considered the bill this day presented to me entitled "An act to set apart and pledge certain funds for internal improvements," and which sets apart and pledges funds "for constructing roads and canals, and improving the navigation of water courses, in order to facilitate, promote, and give security to internal commerce among the several States, and to render more easy and less expensive the means and provisions for the common defense," I am constrained by the insuperable difficulty I feel in reconciling the bill with the Constitution of the United States to return it with that objection to the House of Representatives, in which it originated.

The legislative powers vested in Congress are specified and enumerated in the eighth section of the first article of the Constitution, and it does not appear that the power proposed to be exercised by the bill is among the enumerated powers, or that it falls by any just interpretation within the power to make laws necessary and proper for carrying into execution those or other powers vested by the Constitution in the Government of the United States.

"The power to regulate commerce among the several States" can not include a power to construct roads and canals, and to improve the navigation of water courses in order to facilitate, promote, and secure such a commerce without a latitude of construction departing from the ordinary import of the terms strengthened by the known inconveniences which doubtless led to the grant of this remedial power to Congress.

To refer the power in question to the clause "to provide for the common defense and general welfare" would be contrary to the established and consistent rules of interpretation, as rendering the special and careful enumeration of powers which follow the clause nugatory and improper. Such a view of the Constitution would have the effect of giving to Congress a general power of legislation instead of the defined and limited one hitherto understood to belong to them, the terms "common defense and general welfare" embracing every object and act within the purview of a legislative trust. It would have the effect of subjecting both the Constitution and laws of the several States in all cases not specifically exempted to be superseded by laws of Congress, it being expressly declared "that the Constitution of the United States and laws made in pursuance thereof shall be the supreme law of the land, and the judges of every State shall be bound thereby, anything in the constitution or laws of any State to the contrary notwithstanding." Such a view of the Constitution, finally, would have the effect of excluding the judicial authority of the United States from its participation in guarding the boundary between the legislative powers of the General and the State Governments, inasmuch as questions relating to the general welfare, being questions of policy and expediency, are unsusceptible of judicial cognizance and decision.

A restriction of the power "to provide for the common defense and general welfare" to cases which are to be provided for by the expenditure of money would still leave within the legislative power of Congress all the great and most important measures of Government, money being the ordinary and necessary means of carrying them into execution.

If a general power to construct roads and canals, and to improve the navigation of water courses, with the train of powers incident thereto, be not possessed by Congress, the assent of the States in the mode provided in the bill can not confer the power. The only cases in which the consent and cession of particular States can extend the power of Congress are those specified and provided for in the Constitution.

I am not unaware of the great importance of roads and canals and the improved navigation of water courses, and that a power in the National Legislature to provide for them might be exercised with signal advantage to the general prosperity. But seeing that such a power is not expressly given by the Constitution, and believing that it can not be deduced from any part of it without an inadmissible latitude of construction and a reliance on insufficient precedents; believing also that the permanent success of the Constitution depends on a definite partition of powers between the General and the State Governments, and that no adequate landmarks would be left by the constructive extension of the powers of Congress as proposed in the bill, I have no option but to withhold my signature from it, and to cherishing the hope that its beneficial objects may be attained by a resort for the necessary powers to the same wisdom and virtue in the nation which established the Constitution in its actual form and providently marked out in the instrument itself a safe and practicable mode of improving it as experience might suggest.

7

THE DECISION
TO KEEP EUROPE OUT OF AMERICA

Monroe Enunciates a Famous Message

For the greater part of American history our foreign policy has rested upon three postulates, all found in the Monroe Doctrine, but actually all fashioned from the concept of two separate political systems—an "American System" as opposed to a "European System." This concept is implicit in Washington's Farewell Address and was more explicitly enunciated that very same year by a rising young diplomat named John Quincy Adams, who was destined to play a major role in the formulation of the Monroe Doctrine. The three postulates were: first, that America would not involve herself in Europe's internal affairs; second, that Europe was to keep her hands off the New World; and, third, that she was to cease all further efforts at colonization in the Western Hemisphere.

The great revolutionary movements which swept Latin America after the collapse of Napoleon coincided with a period of fervent nationalism and expansion in the United States. Americans, mindful of their own revolutionary traditions, were sympathetic to the cause of independence for other peoples and concerned lest Europe make some move in the Western Hemisphere that would block American expansion. Recognizing these expansionist trends as inevitable, Spain had renounced all claims to West Florida, which Andrew Jackson had seized, and, in addition, ceded to the United States East Florida. In effect, also, Spain surrendered to the United States her claims to the Pacific Northwest. Meanwhile Czarist Russia was pressing her claims along the Pacific coast to territory as far south as the Oregon country. Russia's claims were challenged by Secretary of State John Quincy Adams in the summer of 1823 in a declaration in which he asserted "that we should contest the right of Russia to *any* territorial establishment on this continent, and that we should assume distinctly the principle that the American continents are no longer subjects for *any* new European colonial establishments." Here was the origin of the principle of noncolonization embodied in the Monroe Doctrine.

The major continental powers of Europe, dedicated to the reactionary principle of "legitimacy" enunciated at the Congress of Vienna, were determined to curb revolutions, whether in Europe or Latin America, and to re-establish the authority of Spain in the New World. The United States had already, at the instigation of President Monroe, recognized the new revolutionary governments of Latin America, and Tory Great Britain, while not sympathetic to the cause of revolution, was anxious to prevent the revival or extension of Spanish and French power in the New World, primarily in order to keep open to British commerce the rich markets of Latin America.

The issue was brought to a head late in 1822, when at the Congress of Verona the Holy Alliance, comprising France, Austria, Russia, and Prussia, agreed to take steps to restore the authority of King Ferdinand VII of Spain, who in 1820 had been forced to accept a constitutional monarchy. The French were authorized to invade Spain, but no action was taken on France's request to intervene in South America. Over this issue of French intervention George Canning, the British Foreign Secretary, broke with the Holy Alliance, and sought to come to an understanding with the United States. It so happened that both countries were suspicious of the other's intentions toward Cuba. John Quincy Adams expressed to Spain "the repugnance of the United States to the transfer of the island of Cuba by Spain to any other power." But England and America satisfied each other that they had no dishonorable intentions toward Spain's turbulent Caribbean island. This no-transfer policy, ancillary to the Monroe Doctrine, was in the course of time to be regarded as part and parcel of it.

Canning now entered into a series of conferences with Richard Rush, the American minister to London, in which he explored the possibility of joint Anglo-American action against intervention in the New World on the part of the Holy Alliance. Rush referred the proposal to Monroe, who turned to his unofficial advisers, former Presidents Jefferson and Madison. Both urged close co-operation with the British. Said Jefferson: "Great Britain is the nation which can do us the most harm of any one, or all on earth; and with her on our side we need not fear the whole world."

Since the United States pressed Britain to recognize the Latin American republics as a preliminary to joint action, and the Tory foreign secretary was disinclined to take precipitate action toward recognizing revolutionary regimes, Canning decided to move on his own. He held a series of conferences with Jules de Polignac, the French ambassador, and secured his objective in the so-called Polignac Agreement, entered into almost two months before Monroe issued his famous message. By that agreement France renounced all intentions to conquer or annex the Spanish-American colonies.

Thus, the immediate threat was over but American officials were unaware of the Anglo-French agreement. John Quincy Adams urged President Monroe to assert America's strength and independence by acting alone. Differing with the two venerable Republican ex-Presidents, he asserted that "it would be more candid, as well as more dignified to avow our principles explicitly to Russia and France, than to come in as a cock-boat in the wake of the British man-of-war." Monroe agreed with Adams that the best course was to go it alone. Although Madison had urged the President to censure France for her interference in Spain and to come out strongly for Greek independence, Monroe acceded to Adams' advice that the formulation of views concerning European affairs should be toned down and the declaration of policy be based wholly on American interest.

Monroe made one important decision on his own. He rejected Adams' recommendation that the declaration should be embodied in diplomatic communications to the various governments. With the support of his Secretary of War, John C. Calhoun, he decided to make the announcement in his annual message to Congress (December 2, 1823). For the actual phraseology of the Monroe Doctrine, except for the lines on the non-colonization principle contributed by Adams, the President must take the credit. On the advice of his Attorney-General, William Wirt, he omitted from his message any unequivocal threat of war, although Congressional leaders like Henry Clay were prepared to go to war against all Europe, even England, should Europe intervene against the Latin American republics.

Between Great Britain and the United States there was never any treaty or agreement, written or unwritten, to uphold the Monroe Doctrine, nor was there ever any understanding that the British navy would support the Monroe Doctrine if it were challenged. This is an historical myth that has no substance in fact. Monroe and Adams refused to be used by Britain to keep the balance of power in Europe. Instead, they were determined that European power politics, including British, should be kept out of the New World. As a result of the Monroe Doctrine Britain was forced to recognize the new Latin American republics, but salvaged some prestige by helping perpetuate for a time the Portuguese monarchy in Brazil. Canning, outmaneuvered by Monroe, defended his Latin American policies in the Commons with the declaration: "I called the New World into existence to redress the balance of the Old." He might have been a little more generous in the attribution of credits.

While on its face a declaration of withdrawal from European affairs, the Monroe Doctrine was really a commitment to leadership in world politics, a bold and far-reaching commitment, modified in the course of time and extended to meet changing circumstances. Constituting the classic definition of the role of the United States in international affairs, it has been with considerable justice called the "most significant of all American state papers."

SEVENTH ANNUAL MESSAGE

WASHINGTON, *December 2, 1823*

Fellow-Citizens of the Senate and House of Representatives:

Many important subjects will claim your attention during the present session, of which I shall endeavor to give, in aid of your deliberations, a just idea in this communication. I undertake this duty with diffidence, from the vast extent of the interests on which I have to treat and of their great importance to every portion of our Union. I enter on it with zeal from a thorough conviction that there never was a period since the establishment of our Revolution when, regarding the condition of the civilized world and its bearing on us, there was greater necessity for devotion in the public servants to their respective duties, or for virtue, patriotism, and union in our constituents.

Meeting in you a new Congress, I deem it proper to present this view of public affairs in greater detail than might otherwise be necessary. I do it, however, with peculiar satisfaction, from a knowledge that in this respect I shall comply more fully with the sound principles of our Government. The people being with us exclusively the sovereign, it is indispensable that full information be laid before them on all important subjects, to enable them to exercise that high power with complete effect. If kept in the dark, they must be incompetent to it. We are all liable to error, and those who are engaged in the management of public affairs are more subject to excitement and to be led astray by their particular interests and passions than the great body of our constituents, who, living at home in the pursuit of their ordinary avocations, are calm but deeply interested spectators of events and of the conduct of those who are parties to them. To the people every department of the Government and every individual in each are responsible, and the more full their information the better they can judge of the wisdom of the policy pursued and of the conduct of each in regard to it. From their dispassionate judgment much aid may always be obtained, while their approbation will form the greatest incentive and most gratifying reward for virtuous actions, and the dread of their censure the best security against the abuse of their confidence. Their interests in all vital questions are the same, and the bond, by sentiment as well as by interest, will be proportionably strengthened as they are better informed of the real state of public affairs, especially in difficult conjunctures. It is by such knowledge that local prejudices and jealousies are surmounted, and that a national policy, extending its fostering care and protection to all the great interests of our Union, is formed and steadily adhered to.

A precise knowledge of our relations with foreign powers as respects our negotiations and transactions with each is thought to be particularly necessary. Equally necessary is it that we should form a just estimate of our resources, revenue, and progress in every kind of improvement connected with the national prosperity and public defense. It is by rendering justice to other nations that we may expect it from them. It is by our ability to resent injuries and redress wrongs that we may avoid them.

The commissioners under the fifth article of the treaty of Ghent, having disagreed in their opinions respecting that portion of the boundary between the Territories of the United States and of Great Britain the establishment of which had been submitted to them, have made their respective reports in compliance with that article, that the same might be referred to the decision of a friendly power. It being manifest, however, that it would be difficult, if not impossible, for any power to perform that office without great delay and much inconvenience to itself, a proposal has been made by this Government, and acceded to by that of Great Britain, to endeavor to establish that boundary by amicable negotiation. It appearing from long experience that no satisfactory arrangement could be formed of the commercial intercourse between the United States and the British colonies in this hemisphere by legislative acts while each party pursued its own course without agreement or concert with the other, a proposal has been made to the British Government to regulate this commerce by treaty, as it has been to arrange in like manner the just claim of the citizens of the United States inhabiting the States and Territories bordering on the lakes and rivers which empty into the St. Lawrence to the navigation of that river to the ocean. For these and other objects of high importance to the interests of both parties a negotiation has been opened with the British Government which it is hoped will have a satisfactory result.

The commissioners under the sixth and seventh articles of the treaty of Ghent having successfully closed their labors in relation to the sixth, have proceeded to the discharge of those relating to the seventh. Their progress in the extensive survey required for the performance of their duties justifies the presumption that it will be completed in the ensuing year.

The negotiation which had been long depending with the French Government on several important subjects, and particularly for a just indemnity for losses sustained in the late wars by the citizens of the United States under unjustifiable seizures and confiscations of their property, has not as yet had the desired effect. As this claim rests on the same principle with others which have been admitted by the French Government, it is not perceived on what just ground it can be rejected. A minister will be immediately appointed to proceed to France and resume the negotiation on this and other subjects which may arise between the two nations.

At the proposal of the Russian Imperial Government, made through the minister of the Emperor residing here, a full power and instructions have been transmitted to the minister of the United States at St. Petersburg to arrange by amicable negotiation the respective rights and interests of the two nations on the northwest coast of this continent. A similar proposal had been made by His Imperial Majesty to the Government of Great Britain, which has likewise been acceded to. The

Government of the United States has been desirous by this friendly proceeding of manifesting the great value which they have invariably attached to the friendship of the Emperor and their solicitude to cultivate the best understanding with his Government. In the discussions to which this interest has given rise and in the arrangements by which they may terminate the occasion has been judged proper for asserting, as a principle in which the rights and interests of the United States are involved, that the American continents, by the free and independent condition which they have assumed and maintain, are henceforth not to be considered as subjects for future colonization by any European powers.

Since the close of the last session of Congress the commissioners and arbitrators for ascertaining and determining the amount of indemnification which may be due to citizens of the United States under the decision of His Imperial Majesty the Emperor of Russia, in conformity to the convention concluded at St. Petersburg on the 12th of July, 1822, have assembled in this city, and organized themselves as a board for the performance of the duties assigned to them by that treaty. The commission constituted under the eleventh article of the treaty of the 22d of February, 1819, between the United States and Spain is also in session here, and as the term of three years limited by the treaty for the execution of the trust will expire before the period of the next regular meeting of Congress, the attention of the Legislature will be drawn to the measures which may be necessary to accomplish the objects for which the commission was instituted.

In compliance with a resolution of the House of Representatives adopted at their last session, instructions have been given to all the ministers of the United States accredited to the powers of Europe and America to propose the proscription of the African slave trade by classing it under the denomination, and inflicting on its perpetrators the punishment, of piracy. Should this proposal be acceded to, it is not doubted that this odious and criminal practice will be promptly and entirely suppressed. It is earnestly hoped that it will be acceded to, from the firm belief that it is the most effectual expedient that can be adopted for the purpose.

At the commencement of the recent war between France and Spain it was declared by the French Government that it would grant no commissions to privateers, and that neither the commerce of Spain herself nor of neutral nations should be molested by the naval force of France, except in the breach of a lawful blockade. This declaration, which appears to have been faithfully carried into effect, concurring with principles proclaimed and cherished by the United States from the first establishment of their independence, suggested the hope that the time had arrived when the proposal for adopting it as a permanent and invariable rule in all future maritime wars might meet the favorable consideration of the great European powers. Instructions have accordingly been given to our ministers with France, Russia, and Great Britain to make those proposals to their respective Governments, and when the friends of humanity reflect on the essential amelioration to the condition of the human race which would result from the abolition of private war on the sea and on the great facility by which it might be accomplished, requiring only the consent of a few sovereigns, an earnest hope is indulged that these overtures will meet with an attention animated by the spirit in which they were made, and that they will ultimately be successful.

The ministers who were appointed to the Republics of Colombia and Buenos Ayres during the last session of Congress proceeded shortly afterwards to their destinations. Of their arrival there official intelligence has not yet been received. The minister appointed to the Republic of Chile will sail in a few days. An early appointment will also be made to Mexico. A minister has been received from Colombia, and the other Governments have been informed that ministers, or diplomatic agents of inferior grade, would be received from each, accordingly as they might prefer the one or the other.

The minister appointed to Spain proceeded soon after his appointment for Cadiz, the residence of the Sovereign to whom he was accredited. In approaching that port the frigate which conveyed him was warned off by the commander of the French squadron by which it was blockaded and not permitted to enter, although apprised by the captain of the frigate of the public character of the person whom he had on board, the landing of whom was the sole object of his proposed entry. This act, being considered an infringement of the rights of ambassadors and of nations, will form a just cause of complaint to the Government of France against the officer by whom it was committed.

The actual condition of the public finances more than realizes the favorable anticipations that were entertained of it at the opening of the last session of Congress. On the 1st of January there was a balance in the Treasury of $4,237,427.55. From that time to the 30th September the receipts amounted to upward of $16,100,000, and the expenditures to $11,400,000. During the fourth quarter of the year it is estimated that the receipts will at least equal the expenditures, and that there will remain in the Treasury on the 1st day of January next a surplus of nearly $9,000,000.

On the 1st of January, 1825, a large amount of the war debt and a part of the Revolutionary debt become redeemable. Additional portions of the former will continue to become redeemable annually until the year 1835. It is believed, however, that if the United States remain at peace the whole of that debt may be redeemed by the ordinary revenue of those years during that period under the provision of the act of March 3, 1817, creating the sinking fund, and in that case the only part of the debt that will remain after the year 1835 will be the $7,000,000 of 5 per cent stock subscribed to the Bank of the United States, and the 3 per cent Revolutionary debt, amounting to $13,296,099.06, both of which are redeemable at the pleasure of the Government.

The state of the Army in its organization and discipline has been gradually improving for several years, and has now attained a high degree of perfection. The military disbursements have been regularly made and the accounts regularly and promptly rendered for settlement. The supplies of various descriptions have been of good quality, and regularly issued at all of the posts. A system of economy and accountability has been introduced into every branch of the service which admits of little additional improvement. This desirable state has been attained by the act reorganizing the staff of the Army, passed on the 14th of April, 1818.

The moneys appropriated for fortifications have been regularly and economically applied, and all the works advanced as rapidly as the amount appropriated would admit. Three important works will be completed in the course of this year—that is, Fort Washington, Fort Delaware, and the fort at the Rigolets, in Louisiana.

The Board of Engineers and the Topographical Corps have been in constant and active service in surveying the coast and projecting the works necessary for its defense.

The Military Academy has attained a degree of perfection in its discipline and instruction equal, as is believed, to any institution of its kind in any country.

The money appropriated for the use of the Ordnance Department has been regularly and economically applied. The fabrication of arms at the national armories and by contract with the Department has been gradually improving in quality and cheapness. It is believed that their quality is now such as to admit of but little improvement.

The completion of the fortifications renders it necessary that there should be a suitable appropriation for the purpose of fabricating the cannon and carriages necessary for those works.

Under the appropriation of $5,000 for exploring the Western waters for the location of a site for a Western armory, a commission was constituted, consisting of Colonel McRee, Colonel Lee, and Captain Talcott, who have been engaged in exploring the country. They have not yet reported the result of their labors, but it is believed that they will be prepared to do it at an early part of the session of Congress.

During the month of June last General Ashley and his party, who were trading under a license from the Government, were attacked by the Ricarees while peaceably trading with the Indians at their request. Several of the party were killed and wounded and their property taken or destroyed.

Colonel Leavenworth, who commanded Fort Atkinson, at the Council Bluffs, the most western post, apprehending that the hostile spirit of the Ricarees would extend to other tribes in that quarter, and that thereby the lives of the traders on the Missouri and the peace of the frontier would be endangered, took immediate measures to check the evil.

With a detachment of the regiment stationed at the Bluffs he successfully attacked the Ricaree village, and it is hoped that such an impression has been made on them as well as on the other tribes on the Missouri as will prevent a recurrence of future hostility.

The report of the Secretary of War, which is herewith transmitted, will exhibit in greater detail the condition of the Department in its various branches, and the progress which has been made in its administration during the three first quarters of the year.

I transmit a return of the militia of the several States according to the last reports which have been made by the proper officers in each to the Department of War. By reference to this return it will be seen that it is not complete, although great exertions have been made to make it so.

As the defense and even the liberties of the country must depend in times of imminent danger on the militia, it is of the highest importance that it be well organized, armed, and disciplined throughout the Union. The report of the Secretary of War shews the progress made during the three first quarters of the present year by the application of the fund appropriated for arming the militia. Much difficulty is found in distributing the arms according to the act of Congress providing for it from the failure of the proper departments in many of the States to make regular returns. The act of May 12, 1820, provides that the system of tactics and regulations of the various corps of the Regular Army shall be extended to the militia. This act has been very imperfectly executed from the want of uniformity in the organization of the militia, proceeding from the defects of the system itself, and especially in its application to that main arm of the public defense. It is thought that this important subject in all its branches merits the attention of Congress.

The report of the Secretary of the Navy, which is now communicated, furnishes an account of the administration of that Department for the three first quarters of the present year, with the progress made in augmenting the Navy, and the manner in which the vessels in commission have been employed.

The usual force has been maintained in the Mediterranean Sea, the Pacific Ocean, and along the Atlantic coast, and has afforded the necessary protection to our commerce in those seas.

In the West Indies and the Gulf of Mexico our naval force has been augmented by the addition of several small vessels provided for by the "act authorizing an additional naval force for the suppression of piracy," passed by Congress at their last session. That armament has been eminently successful in the accomplishment of its object. The piracies by which our commerce in the neighborhood of the island of Cuba had been afflicted have been repressed and the confidence of our merchants in a great measure restored.

The patriotic zeal and enterprise of Commodore Porter, to whom the command of the expedition was confided, has been fully seconded by the officers and men under his command. And in reflecting with high satisfaction on the honorable manner in which they have sustained the reputation of their country and its Navy, the sentiment is alloyed only by a concern that in the fulfillment of that arduous service the diseases incident to the season and to the climate in which it was discharged have deprived the nation of many useful lives, and among them of several officers of great promise.

In the month of August a very malignant fever made its appearance at Thompsons Island, which threatened the destruction of our station there. Many perished, and the commanding officer was severely attacked. Uncertain as to his fate and knowing that most of the medical officers had been rendered incapable of discharging their duties, it was thought expedient to send to that post an officer of rank and experience, with several skillful surgeons, to ascertain the origin of the fever and the probability of its recurrence there in future seasons; to furnish every assistance to those who were suffering, and, if practicable, to avoid the necessity of abandoning so important a station. Commodore Rodgers, with a promptitude which did him honor, cheerfully accepted that trust, and has discharged it in the manner anticipated from his skill and patriotism. Before his arrival Commodore Porter, with the greater part of the squadron, had removed from the island and returned to the United States in consequence of the prevailing sickness. Much useful information has, however, been obtained as to the state of the island and great relief afforded to those who had been necessarily left there.

Although our expedition, cooperating with an invigorated administration of the government of the island of Cuba, and with the corresponding active exertions of a British naval force in the same seas, have almost entirely destroyed the unlicensed piracies from that island, the success of our exertions has not been equally effectual to suppress the same crime, under other pretenses and colors, in the neighboring island of Porto Rico. They have been committed there under the abusive issue of Spanish commissions. At an early period of the present year remonstrances were made to the governor of that island, by an agent who was sent for the purpose, against those outrages on the peaceful commerce of the United States, of which many had occurred. That officer, professing his own want of authority to make satisfaction for our just complaints, answered only by a reference to them to the Government of Spain. The minister of the United States to that court was specially instructed to urge the necessity of the immediate and effectual interposition of that Government, directing restitution and indemnity for wrongs already committed and interdicting the repetition of them. The minister, as has been seen, was debarred access to the Spanish Government, and in the meantime several new cases of flagrant outrage have occurred, and citizens of the United States in the island of Porto Rico have suffered, and others been threatened with assassination for asserting their unquestionable rights even before the lawful tribunals of the country.

The usual orders have been given to all our public ships to seize American vessels engaged in the slave trade and bring them in for adjudication, and I have the gratification to state that not one so employed has been discovered, and there is good reason to believe that our flag is now seldom, if at all, disgraced by that traffic.

It is a source of great satisfaction that we are always enabled to recur to the conduct of our Navy with pride and commendation. As a means of national defense it enjoys the public confidence, and is steadily assuming additional importance. It is submitted whether a more efficient and equally economical organization of it might not in several respects be effected. It is supposed that higher grades than now exist by law would be useful. They would afford well-merited rewards to those who have long and faithfully served their country, present the best incentives to good conduct, and the best means of insuring a proper discipline; destroy the inequality in that respect between military and naval services, and relieve our officers from many inconveniences and mortifications which occur when our vessels meet those of other nations, ours being the only service in which such grades do not exist.

A report of the Postmaster-General, which accompanies this communication, will shew the present state of the Post-Office Department and its general operations for some years past.

There is established by law 88,600 miles of post-roads, on which the mail is now transported 85,700 miles, and contracts have been made for its transportation on all the established routes, with one or two exceptions. There are 5,240 post-offices in the Union, and as many postmasters. The gross amount of postage which accrued from the 1st July, 1822, to the 1st July, 1823, was $1,114,345.12. During the same period the expenditures of the Post-Office Department amounted to $1,169,885.51, and consisted of the following items, viz: Compensation to postmasters, $353,995.98; incidental expenses, $30,866.37; transportation of the mail, $784,600.08; payments into the Treasury, $423.08. On the 1st of July last there was due to the Department from postmasters $135,245.28; from *late* postmasters and contractors, $256,749.31; making a total amount of balances due to the Department of $391,994.59. These balances embrace all delinquencies of postmasters and contractors which have taken place since the organization of the Department. There was due by the Department to contractors on the 1st of July last $26,548.64.

The transportation of the mail within five years past has been greatly extended, and the expenditures of the Department proportionably increased. Although the postage which has accrued within the last three years has fallen short of the expenditures $262,821.46, it appears that collections have been made from the outstanding balances to meet the principal part of the current demands.

It is estimated that not more than $250,000 of the above balances can be collected, and that a considerable part of this sum can only be realized by a resort to legal process. Some improvement in the receipts for postage is expected. A prompt attention to the collection of moneys received by postmasters, it is believed, will enable the Department to continue its operations without aid from the Treasury, unless the expenditures shall be increased by the establishment of new mail routes.

A revision of some parts of the post-office law may be necessary; and it is submitted whether it would not be proper to provide for the appointment of postmasters, where the compensation exceeds a certain amount, by nomination to the Senate, as other officers of the General Government are appointed.

Having communicated my views to Congress at the commencement of the last session respecting the encouragement which ought to be given to our manufactures and the principle on which it should be founded, I have only to add that those views remain unchanged, and that the present state of those countries with which we have the most immediate political relations and greatest commercial intercourse tends to confirm them. Under this impression I recommend a review of the tariff for the purpose of affording such additional protection to those articles which we are prepared to manufacture, or which are more immediately connected with the defense and independence of the country.

The actual state of the public accounts furnishes additional evidence of the efficiency of the present system of accountability in relation to the public expenditure. Of the moneys drawn from the Treasury since the 4th March, 1817, the sum remaining unaccounted for on the 30th of September last is more than a million and a half dollars less than on the 30th of September preceding; and during the same period a reduction of nearly a million of dollars has been made in the amount of the unsettled accounts for moneys advanced previously to the 4th of March, 1817. It will be obvious that in proportion as the mass of accounts of the latter description is diminished by settlement the difficulty of settling the residue is increased from the consideration that in many instances it can be obtained only by legal process. For more precise details on this subject I refer to a report from the First Comptroller of the Treasury.

The sum which was appropriated at the last session for the repairs of the Cumberland road has been applied with good effect to that object. A final report has not yet been received from the agent who was appointed to superintend it. As soon as it is received it shall be communicated to Congress.

Many patriotic and enlightened citizens who have made the subject an object of particular investigation have suggested an improvement of still greater importance. They are of opinion that the waters of the Chesapeake and Ohio may be connected together by one continued canal, and at an expense far short of the value and importance of the object to be obtained. If this could be accomplished it is impossible to calculate the beneficial consequences which would result from it. A great portion of the produce of the very fertile country through which it would pass would find a market through that channel. Troops might be moved with great facility in war, with cannon and every kind of munition, and in either direction. Connecting the Atlantic with the Western country in a line passing through the seat of the National Government, it would contribute essentially to strengthen the bond of union itself. Believing as I do that Congress possess the right to appropriate money for such a national object (the jurisdiction remaining to

95

the States through which the canal would pass), I submit it to your consideration whether it may not be advisable to authorize by an adequate appropriation the employment of a suitable number of the officers of the Corps of Engineers to examine the unexplored ground during the next season and to report their opinion thereon. It will likewise be proper to extend their examination to the several routes through which the waters of the Ohio may be connected by canals with those of Lake Erie.

As the Cumberland road will require annual repairs, and Congress have not thought it expedient to recommend to the States an amendment to the Constitution for the purpose of vesting in the United States a power to adopt and execute a system of internal improvement, it is also submitted to your consideration whether it may not be expedient to authorize the Executive to enter into an arrangement with the several States through which the road passes to establish tolls, each within its limits, for the purpose of defraying the expense of future repairs and of providing also by suitable penalties for its protection against future injuries.

The act of Congress of the 7th of May, 1822, appropriated the sum of $22,700 for the purpose of erecting two piers as a shelter for vessels from ice near Cape Henlopen, Delaware Bay. To effect the object of the act the officers of the Board of Engineers, with Commodore Bainbridge, were directed to prepare plans and estimates of piers sufficient to answer the purpose intended by the act. It appears by their report, which accompanies the documents from the War Department, that the appropriation is not adequate to the purpose intended; and as the piers would be of great service both to the navigation of the Delaware Bay and the protection of vessels on the adjacent parts of the coast, I submit for the consideration of Congress whether additional and sufficient appropriation should not be made.

The Board of Engineers were also directed to examine and survey the entrance of the harbor of the port of Presquille, in Pennsylvania, in order to make an estimate of the expense of removing the obstructions to the entrance, with a plan of the best mode of effecting the same, under the appropriation for that purpose by act of Congress passed 3d of March last. The report of the Board accompanies the papers from the War Department, and is submitted for the consideration of Congress.

A strong hope has been long entertained, founded on the heroic struggle of the Greeks, that they would succeed in their contest and resume their equal station among the nations of the earth. It is believed that the whole civilized world take a deep interest in their welfare.

Although no power has declared in their favor, yet none, according to our information, has taken part against them. Their cause and their name have protected them from dangers which might ere this have overwhelmed any other people. The ordinary calculations of interest and of acquisition with a view to aggrandizement, which mingles so much in the transactions of nations, seem to have had no effect in regard to them. From the facts which have come to our knowledge there is good cause to believe that their enemy has lost forever all dominion over them; that Greece will become again an independent nation. That she may obtain that rank is the object of our most ardent wishes.

It was stated at the commencement of the last session that a great effort was then making in Spain and Portugal to improve the condition of the people of those countries, and that it appeared to be conducted with extraordinary moderation. It need scarcely be remarked that the result has been so far very different from what was then anticipated. Of events in that quarter of the globe, with which we have so much intercourse and from which we derive our origin, we have always been anxious and interested spectators. The citizens of the United States cherish sentiments the most friendly in favor of the liberty and happiness of their fellow-men on that side of the Atlantic. In the wars of the European powers in matters relating to themselves we have never taken any part, nor does it comport with our policy so to do. It is only when our rights are invaded or seriously menaced that we resent injuries or make preparation for our defense. With the movements in this hemisphere we are of necessity more immediately connected, and by causes which must be obvious to all enlightened and impartial observers. The political system of the allied powers is essentially different in this respect from that of America. This difference proceeds from that which exists in their respective Governments; and to the defense of our own, which has been achieved by the loss of so much blood and treasure, and matured by the wisdom of their most enlightened citizens, and under which we have enjoyed unexampled felicity, this whole nation is devoted. We owe it, therefore, to candor and to the amicable relations existing between the United States and those powers to declare that we should consider any attempt on their part to extend their system to any portion of this hemisphere as dangerous to our peace and safety. With the existing colonies or dependencies of any European power we have not interfered and shall not interfere. But with the Governments who have declared their independence and maintained it, and whose independence we have, on great consideration and on just principles, acknowledged, we could not view any interposition for the purpose of oppressing them, or controlling in any other manner their destiny, by any European power in any other light than as the manifestation of an unfriendly disposition toward the United States. In the war between those new Governments and Spain we declared our neutrality at the time of their recognition, and to this we have adhered, and shall continue to adhere, provided no change shall occur which, in the judgment of the competent authorities of this Government, shall make a corresponding change on the part of the United States indispensable to their security.

The late events in Spain and Portugal shew that Europe is still unsettled. Of this important fact no stronger proof can be adduced than that the allied powers should have thought it proper, on any principle satisfactory to themselves, to have interposed by force in the internal concerns of Spain. To what extent such interposition may be carried, on the same principle, is a question in which all independent powers whose governments differ from theirs are interested, even those most remote, and surely none more so than the United States. Our policy in regard to Europe, which was adopted at an early stage of the wars which have so long agitated that quarter of the globe, nevertheless remains the same, which is, not to interfere in the internal concerns of any of its powers; to consider the government *de facto* as the legitimate government for us; to cultivate friendly relations with it, and to preserve those relations by a frank, firm, and manly policy, meeting in all instances the just claims of every power, submitting to injuries from none. But in regard to those continents circumstances are eminently and conspicuously different. It is impossible that the allied powers should extend their political system to any portion of either continent without endangering our peace and happiness; nor can anyone believe that our southern brethren, if left to themselves, would adopt it of their own accord. It is equally impossible, therefore, that we should behold such interposition in any form with indifference. If we look to the comparative strength and resources of Spain and those new Governments, and their distance from each other, it must be obvious that she can never subdue them. It is still the true policy of the United States to leave the parties to themselves, in the hope that other powers will pursue the same course.

If we compare the present condition of our Union with its actual state at the close of our Revolution, the history of the world furnishes no example of a progress in improvement in all the important circumstances which constitute the happiness of a nation which bears any resemblance to it. At the first epoch our population did not exceed 3,000,000. By the last census it amounted to about 10,000,000, and, what is more extraordinary, it is almost altogether native, for the immigration from other countries has been inconsiderable. At the first epoch half the territory within our acknowledged limits was uninhabited and a wilderness. Since then new territory has been acquired of vast extent, comprising with it many rivers, particularly the Mississippi, the navigation of which to the ocean was of the highest importance to the original States. Over this territory our population has expanded in every direction, and new States have been established almost equal in number to those which formed the first bond of our Union. This expansion of our population and accession of new States to our Union have had the happiest effect on all its highest interests. That it has eminently augmented our resources and added to our strength and respectability as a power is admitted by all. But it is not in these important circumstances only that this happy effect is felt. It is manifest that by enlarging the basis of our system and increasing the number of States the system itself has been greatly strengthened in both its branches. Consolidation and disunion have thereby been rendered equally impracticable. Each Government, confiding in its own strength, has less to apprehend from the other, and in consequence each, enjoying a greater freedom of action, is rendered more efficient for all the purposes for which it was instituted. It is unnecessary to treat here of the vast improvement made in the system itself by the adoption of this Constitution and of its happy effect in elevating the character and in protecting the rights of the nation as well as of individuals. To what, then, do we owe these blessings? It is known to all that we derive them from the excellence of our institutions. Ought we not, then, to adopt every measure which may be necessary to perpetuate them?

8

THE DECISION
TO LAUNCH THE GOVERNMENT ON A
CAREER OF PUBLIC IMPROVEMENT

John Quincy Adams Makes His "Perilous Experiment"

Internal improvements were vital to the public welfare and to cementing the nation into a unified whole. The capital requirements were too onerous for individuals or even combinations of entrepreneurs. Without some central plan such improvements might well be carried out on behalf of sectional or local interests. But could the Federal government take the initiative? Madison and Monroe had come increasingly to share Jefferson's doubts about permitting the Constitution to be broadly construed, and, in the absence of clarifying amendments to that document, to believe that matters like internal improvements must be left to the states. Monroe's successor, John Quincy Adams, had supported Jeffersonian policies but found this narrow and restrictive view of the Constitution uncongenial to his basic Federalism. Son of the second President, John Quincy was more of a Washingtonian than his father. After leaving the White House he wrote that "the federalism of Washington, Union, and Internal Improvement have been the three hinges, upon which my political life and fortunes, good and bad, have turned." He advocated Federal expenditures to promote public improvements, and was convinced that only by planning and sensible conservation of natural resources could the nation prosper and expand. This was sound Federalist doctrine, most of it had already been said by Washington himself, but John Quincy Adams was the wrong man and chose the wrong time to enunciate these views.

Perhaps no man, not even Andrew Johnson, ever came into the office of the Presidency under less auspicious circumstances than did John Quincy Adams. He was a minority President chosen by the House of Representatives in an election which quickly gave rise to notorious charges of his having entered into a corrupt bargain with Henry Clay, by which the Kentuckian was to become Secretary of State. In the vituperative harangue of the intemperate John Randolph of Roanoke this association of Adams and Clay was stigmatized as "the coalition of Blifil and Black George—the combination unheard of till then of the Puritan and the black-leg." Opposed as much to parties as he was to sectionalism, Adams refused to bolster his prestige or power by building up a party machine to support his administration through the judicious use of patronage, and even put in his Cabinet persons who were in cahoots with his political enemies. A cold fish to the outside world, Adams rallied few friends about him. Ezekiel Webster observed that people supported Adams' cause "from a cold sense of duty," but soon satisfied themselves that they had discharged "our duty to the cause of any man when we do not entertain for him one personal kind feeling, nor cannot unless we disembowel ourselves like a trussed turkey of all that is human nature within us." Thus, the measures of his administration were "just and wise and every honest man should have supported them," but many did not because they simply could not abide their author, and still others because they were frightened by his centralizing philosophy of government.

Instead of removing obstacles to road and canal bills and placing his signature on Congressional appropriations for internal improvements, Adams, incautiously but courageously, showed his hand in his very first annual message to Congress. A nationalist like Washington and Hamilton, he planned to cement the sections indissolubly together by a network of national highways and canals. He would conserve and develop the public domain, provide for the humane removal and civilizing of the Indians to the west of the Mississippi, and he would finance such a program from the proceeds of the sales of public lands. Internal improvements must be moral as well as physical, he declared. They must be sustained by the example of character in public life, by such institutions as a national university, a national astronomical observatory to emulate the "lighthouses of the skies" maintained by European governments for the advancement of science, a national naval academy, the national sponsorship of research and geographical exploration, a national uniform bankruptcy act, a uniform national system of weights and measures, a more effective patent law to encourage inventors, and a new Department of the Interior.

When Adams read his draft to the Cabinet, Clay recommended discarding the national university. "Let us not recommend anything so unpopular as not likely to succeed," he advised. Adams' Secretary of War, James Barbour, probably alluding to the portion dealing with roads and canals, added: "Let us not propose any thing so popular as to be carried without recommendation." When Clay remarked to the President that "we seem to be stripping off your draft alternately," Adams rejoined with an anecdote from Addison's *Spectator*. "It's like the man with two wives. One is plucking out his white hairs, the other the black, till none are left." Stung by criticisms of the impracticality of some of his proposals, Adams asserted that he had long-range ends in view, not immediate action by Congress. "The plant may come later, though the seed be sown early."

Finally, the Cabinet, without enthusiasm, withdrew their objections and Adams decided to take the plunge. "The perilous experiment is to be made," he noted in his diary that night. "Let me make it with full deliberation, and be prepared for the consequences."

Few messages have ever created so great a stir or have had so little effect on the course of legislation as did that of John Quincy Adams. Some bills for roads and canals were enacted, but no sensible comprehensive scheme. Adams' proposals for the support of scientific and intellectual interests were the laughingstock of the opposition press. Jefferson, in this closing year of his life, regarded the message as symptomatic of the fact that the new leaders had "nothing in them of the feelings and principles of '76," and looked to the setting up of a government under a moneyed aristocracy which would ride and rule "the plundered ploughman and beggared yeomanry." To the sage of Monticello "this will be to them a next blessing to the monarchy of their first aim, and perhaps the surest stepping stone to it."

Adams revealed how far he would go if he could. Would he have gone even further? Would he have moved from internal improvements to moral improvements, of which the foremost was liberty for the enslaved? Before that could come, however, there had to be a strong Union, and to these two causes, freedom for the Negro and union, "Old

Man Eloquent" dedicated his distinguished post-Presidential career in Congress. John Quincy Adams' message had only one fault. It was delivered a century too early. Who is there today who would dispute his vision?

FIRST ANNUAL MESSAGE

WASHINGTON, *December 6, 1825*

Upon this first occasion of addressing the Legislature of the Union, with which I have been honored, in presenting to their view the execution so far as it has been effected of the measures sanctioned by them for promoting the internal improvement of our country, I can not close the communication without recommending to their calm and persevering consideration the general principle in a more enlarged extent. The great object of the institution of civil government is the improvement of the condition of those who are parties to the social compact, and no government, in whatever form constituted, can accomplish the lawful ends of its institution but in proportion as it improves the condition of those over whom it is established. Roads and canals, by multiplying and facilitating the communications and intercourse between distant regions and multitudes of men, are among the most important means of improvement. But moral, political, intellectual improvement are duties assigned by the Author of Our Existence to social no less than to individual man. For the fulfillment of those duties governments are invested with power, and to the attainment of the end—the progressive improvement of the condition of the governed—the exercise of delegated powers is a duty as sacred and indispensable as the usurpation of powers not granted is criminal and odious. Among the first, perhaps the very first, instrument for the improvement of the condition of men is knowledge, and to the acquisition of much of the knowledge adapted to the wants, the comforts, and enjoyments of human life public institutions and seminaries of learning are essential. So convinced of this was the first of my predecessors in this office, now first in the memory, as, living, he was first in the hearts, of our countrymen, that once and again in his addresses to the Congresses with whom he cooperated in the public service he earnestly recommended the establishment of seminaries of learning, to prepare for all the emergencies of peace and war—a national university and a military academy. With respect to the latter, had he lived to the present day, in turning his eyes to the institution at West Point he would have enjoyed the gratification of his most earnest wishes; but in surveying the city which has been honored with his name he would have seen the spot of earth which he had destined and bequeathed to the use and benefit of his country as the site for an university still bare and barren.

In assuming her station among the civilized nations of the earth it would seem that our country had contracted the engagement to contribute her share of mind, of labor, and of expense to the improvement of those parts of knowledge which lie beyond the reach of individual acquisition, and particularly to geographical and astronomical science. Looking back to the history only of the half century since the declaration of our independence, and observing the generous emulation with which the Governments of France, Great Britain, and Russia have devoted the genius, the intelligence, the treasures of their respective nations to the common improvement of the species in these branches of science, is it not incumbent upon us to inquire whether we are not bound by obligations of a high and honorable character to contribute our portion of energy and exertion to the common stock? The voyages of discovery prosecuted in the course of that time at the expense of those nations have not only redounded to their glory, but to the improvement of human knowledge. We have been partakers of that improvement and owe for it a sacred debt, not only of gratitude, but of equal or proportional exertion in the same common cause. Of the cost of these undertakings, if the mere expenditures of outfit, equipment, and completion of the expeditions were to be considered the only charges, it would be unworthy of a great and generous nation to take a second thought. One hundred expeditions of circumnavigation like those of Cook and La Pérouse would not burden the exchequer of the nation fitting them out so much as the ways and means of defraying a single campaign in war. But if we take into account the lives of those benefactors of mankind of which their services in the cause of their species were the purchase, how shall the cost of those heroic enterprises be estimated, and what compensation can be made to them or to their countries for them? Is it not by bearing them in affectionate remembrance? Is it not still more by imitating their example—by enabling countrymen of our own to pursue the same career and to hazard their lives in the same cause?

In inviting the attention of Congress to the subject of internal improvements upon a view thus enlarged it is not my design to recommend the equipment of an expedition for circumnavigating the globe for purposes of scientific research and inquiry. We have objects of useful investigation nearer home, and to which our cares may be more beneficially applied. The interior of our own territories has yet been very imperfectly explored. Our coasts along many degrees of latitude upon the shores of the Pacific Ocean, though much frequented by our spirited commercial navigators, have been barely visited by our public ships. The River of the West, first fully discovered and navigated by a countryman of our own, still bears the name of the ship in which he ascended its waters, and claims the protection of our armed national flag at its mouth. With the establishment of a military post there or at some other point of that coast, recommended by my predecessor and already matured in the deliberations of the last Congress, I would suggest the expediency of connecting the equipment of a public ship for the exploration of the whole northwest coast of this continent.

The establishment of an uniform standard of weights and measures was one of the specific objects contemplated in the formation of our Constitution, and to fix that standard was one of the powers delegated by express terms in that instrument to Congress. The Governments of Great Britain and France have scarcely ceased to be occupied with inquiries and speculations on the same subject since the existence of our Constitution, and with them it has expanded into profound, laborious, and expensive researches into the figure of the earth and the comparative length of the pendulum vibrating seconds in various latitudes from the equator to the pole. These researches have resulted in the composition and publication of several works highly interesting to the cause of science. The experiments are yet in the process of performance. Some of them have recently been made on our own shores, within the walls of one of our own colleges, and partly by one of our own fellow-citizens. It would be honorable to our country if the sequel of the same experiments should be countenanced by the patronage of our Government, as they have hitherto been by those of France and Britain.

Connected with the establishment of an university, or separate from it, might be undertaken the erection of an astronomical observatory, with provision for the support of an astronomer, to be in constant attendance of observation upon the phenomena of the heavens, and for the periodical publication of his observations. It is with no feeling of pride as an American that the remark may be made that on the comparatively small territorial surface of Europe there are existing upward of 130 of these light-houses of the skies, while throughout the whole American hemisphere there is not one. If we reflect a moment upon the discoveries which in the last four centuries have been made in the physical constitution of the universe by the means of these buildings and of observers stationed in them, shall we doubt of their usefulness to every nation? And while scarcely a year passes over our heads without bringing some new astronomical discovery to light, which we must fain receive at second hand from Europe, are we not cutting ourselves off from the means of returning light for light while we have neither observatory nor observer upon our half of the globe and the earth revolves in perpetual darkness to our unsearching eyes?

When, on the 25th of October, 1791, the first President of the United States announced to Congress the result of the first enumeration of the inhabitants of this Union, he informed them that the returns gave the pleasing assurance that the population of the United States bordered on 4,000,000 persons. At the distance of thirty years from that time the last enumeration, five years since completed, presented a population bordering upon 10,000,000. Perhaps of all the evidences of a prosperous and happy condition of human society the rapidity of the increase of population is the most unequivocal. But the demonstration of our prosperity rests not alone upon this indication. Our commerce, our wealth, and the extent of our territories have increased in corresponding proportions, and the number of independent communities associated in our Federal Union has since that time nearly doubled. The legislative representation of the States and people in the two Houses of Congress has grown with the growth of their constituent bodies. The House, which then consisted of 65 members, now numbers upward of 200. The Senate, which consisted of 26 members, has now 48. But the executive and, still more, the judiciary departments are yet in a great measure confined to their primitive organization, and are now not adequate to the urgent wants of a still growing community.

The naval armaments, which at an early period forced themselves upon the necessities of the Union, soon led to the establishment of a Department of the Navy. But the Departments of Foreign Affairs and of the Interior, which early after the formation of the Government had been united in one, continue so united to this time, to the unquestionable detriment of the public service. The multiplication of our relations with the nations and Governments of the Old World has kept pace with that of our population and commerce, while within the last ten years a new family of nations in our own hemisphere has arisen among the inhabitants of the earth, with whom our intercourse, commercial and political, would of itself furnish occupation to an active and industrious department. The constitution of the judiciary, experimental and imperfect as it was even in the infancy of our existing Government, is yet more inadequate to the administration of national justice at our present maturity. Nine years have elapsed since a predecessor in this office, now not the last, the citizen who, perhaps, of all others throughout the Union contributed most to the formation and establishment of our Constitution, in his valedictory address to Congress, immediately preceding his retirement from public life, urgely recommended the revision of the judiciary and the establishment of an additional executive department. The exigencies of the public service and its unavoidable deficiencies, as now in exercise, have added yearly cumulative weight to the considerations presented by him as persuasive to the measure, and in recommending it to your deliberations I am happy to have the influence of his high authority in aid of the undoubting convictions of my own experience.

The laws relating to the administration of the Patent Office are deserving of much consideration and perhaps susceptible of some improvement. The grant of power to regulate the action of Congress upon this subject has specified both the end to be obtained and the means by which it is to be effected, "to promote the progress of science and useful arts by securing for limited times to authors and inventors the exclusive right to their respective writings and discoveries." If an honest pride might be indulged in the reflection that on the records of that office are already found inventions the usefulness of which has scarcely been transcended in the annals of human ingenuity, would not its exultation be allayed by the inquiry whether the laws have effectively insured to the inventors the reward destined to them by the Constitution—even a limited term of exclusive right to their discoveries?

On the 24th of December, 1799, it was resolved by Congress that a marble monument should be erected by the United States in the Capitol at the city of Washington; that the family of General Washington should be requested to permit his body to be deposited under it, and that the monument be so designed as to commemorate the great events of his military and political life. In reminding Congress of this resolution and that the monument contemplated by it remains yet without execution, I shall indulge only the remarks that the works at the Capitol are approaching to completion; that the consent of the family, desired by the resolution, was requested and obtained; that a monument has been recently erected in this city over the remains of another distinguished patriot of the Revolution, and that a spot has been reserved within the walls where you are deliberating for the benefit of this and future ages, in which the mortal remains may be deposited of him whose spirit hovers over you and listens with delight to every act of the representatives of his nation which can tend to exalt and adorn his and their country.

The Constitution under which you are assembled is a charter of limited powers. After full and solemn deliberation upon all or any of the objects which, urged by an irresistible sense of my own duty, I have recommended to your attention should you come to the conclusion that, however desirable in themselves, the enactment of laws for effecting them would transcend the powers committed to you by that venerable instrument which we are all bound to support, let no consideration induce you to assume the exercise of powers not granted to you by the people. But if the power to exercise exclusive legislation in all cases whatsoever over the District of Columbia; if the power to lay and collect taxes, duties, imposts, and excises, to pay the debts and provide for the common defense and general welfare of the United States; if the power to regulate commerce with foreign nations and among the several States and with the Indian tribes, to fix the standard of weights and measures, to establish post-offices and post-roads, to declare war, to raise and support armies, to provide and maintain a navy, to dispose of and make all needful rules and regulations respecting the territory or other property belonging to the United States, and to make all laws which shall be necessary and proper for carrying these powers into execution—if these powers and others enumerated in the Constitution may be effectually brought into action by laws promoting the improvement of agriculture, commerce, and manufactures, the cultivation and encouragement of the mechanic and of the elegant arts, the advancement of literature, and the progress of the sciences, ornamental and profound, to refrain from exercising them for the benefit of the people themselves would be to hide in the earth the talent committed to our charge—would be treachery to the most sacred of trusts.

The spirit of improvement is abroad upon the earth. It stimulates the hearts and sharpens the faculties not of our fellow-citizens alone, but of the nations of Europe and of their rulers. While dwelling with pleasing satisfaction upon the superior excellence of our political institutions, let us not be unmindful that liberty is power; that the nation blessed with the largest portion of liberty must in proportion to its numbers be the most powerful nation upon earth, and that the tenure of power by man is, in the moral purposes of his Creator, upon condition that it shall be exercised to ends of beneficence, to improve the condition of himself and his fellow-men. While foreign nations less blessed with that freedom which is power than ourselves are advancing with gigantic strides in the career of public improvement, were we to slumber in indolence or fold up our arms and proclaim to the world that we are palsied by the will of our constituents, would it not be to cast away the bounties of Providence and doom ourselves to perpetual inferiority? In the course of the year now drawing to its close we have beheld, under the auspices and at the expense of one State of this Union, a new university unfolding its portals to the sons of science and holding up the torch of human improvement to eyes that seek the light. We have seen under the persevering and enlightened enterprise of another State the waters of our Western lakes mingle with those of the ocean. If undertakings like these have been accomplished in the compass of a few years by the authority of single members of our Confederation, can we, the representative authorities of the whole Union, fall behind our fellow-servants in the exercise of the trust committed to us for the benefit of our common sovereign by the accomplishment of works important to the whole and to which neither the authority nor the resources of any one State can be adequate?

Finally, fellow-citizens, I shall await with cheering hope and faithful cooperation the result of your deliberations, assured that, without encroaching upon the powers reserved to the authorities of the respective States or to the people, you will, with a due sense of your obligations to your country and of the high responsibilities weighing upon yourselves, give efficacy to the means committed to you for the common good. And may He who searches the hearts of the children of men prosper your exertions to secure the blessings of peace and promote the highest welfare of our country.

9

THE DECISION
TO END CENTRAL BANKING

Andrew Jackson Kills the "Hydra-headed Monster"

John Quincy Adams sought to enlarge national powers and failed. His successor, Andrew Jackson, fought to expand the powers of the President and triumphed. Elected by a resounding majority, the Hero of New Orleans possessed qualities of personality and political leadership that his predecessor, despite his integrity and intellectual gifts, sadly lacked. Jackson courted popularity. He built up a powerful political machine. He was a master of political strategy and tactics, and he controlled effective organs of propaganda. Posing as the people's champion against the special interests, he succeeded in enlarging the Presidential powers to such an extent that his arch-rival, Henry Clay, was moved to declaim: "We are in the midst of a revolution, hitherto bloodless, but rapidly leading towards a total change of the pure republican character of the government and the concentration of all power in the hands of one man."

Allowing for the political distortion of Clay's accusations, the question might well be asked how this great magnification of Presidential powers was achieved. The answer to that question is found in Jackson's acuteness in discovering popular issues which he adroitly exploited. First among them was the issue over whether or not the charter of the second Bank of the United States should be renewed. The head of that bank was an able Philadelphian named Nicholas Biddle, littérateur, scholar, and statesman, who at the behest of President Monroe became one of the five government directors of the second Bank of the United States, and succeeded to the presidency of that institution. When in his Inaugural Address Andrew Jackson asserted that not only the constitutionality and expediency but also the success of the Bank in creating a sound and firm currency were open to question, Biddle chose to take up the gauntlet. Imprudently he decided to apply to Congress for a new charter in 1832, four years before the old one was due to expire. This proved to be a ghastly mistake, as it projected the Bank issue into a Presidential campaign and gave Jackson a mighty stick with which to beat Henry Clay, a staunch advocate of rechartering the Bank. Clay had welcomed the issue, believing that it would provide good campaign ammunition. Instead, it backfired and destroyed whatever chances he had of being elected President.

When in the summer of 1832 a bill for recharter of the Bank passed both Houses by comfortable majorities Jackson took the occasion to deliver his famous veto message, a masterpiece of propaganda, mobilizing every popular prejudice against the Bank. The message was prepared by Amos Kendall, a member of Jackson's inner circle or "Kitchen Cabinet," and Roger Taney, Attorney General, who put it in final form, with the assistance of the President's secretary, Andrew Donelson. Denying the constitutionality of the Bank, Jackson, employing Taney's phraseology, asserted that the Supreme Court "ought not to control the coordinate authorities of this Government. The Congress, the Executive, and the Court must each for itself be guided by its own opinion of the Constitution." This remarkable assertion accords with the legend that Jackson declared of one Supreme Court decision, "Well, John Marshall has made his decision, now let him enforce it!" But this may only be legend, for in later years Taney, as Chief Justice, denied that Jackson had ever expressed doubt as to his obligation to carry out the acts of Congress, "whatever his own opinion might be of the constitutional question."

In his economic arguments against the Bank Jackson sounded like an old-fashioned agrarian, devoted to the laissez-faire philosophy of government. The message ignored the quasi-public character of the Bank and denied its potentialities for the regulation of banking and currency. The Bank had in fact provided sound central banking operations, aided business expansion, and reduced the threat of inflation posed by a disorganized currency. But some of its fiscal regulations were not popular among borrowers, particularly in the South and West. Located in Philadelphia, the Bank aroused jealousy among business interests elsewhere; Philadelphia's financial leadership was disputed, notably in

New York, which envy Martin Van Buren was quick to exploit.

Jackson's logic and his economics may have been faulty but his emotional appeal was irresistible. He had aligned the Bank on the side of the money trust and the rich and placed himself on the side of the poor. Congress failed to override the veto. The President moved Taney into the Secretaryship of the Treasury, where he was amenable to Jackson's order to remove the government's deposits from the Bank of the United States and place them in state banks, popularly known as "pet banks." For this action Jackson and Taney were censured by the Senate, and the resolution of censure was not expunged until January, 1837. By that date Jackson's triumph over the Bank was complete. Jackson's policies fed a speculative orgy, which the President sought to curb by his Specie Circular of 1836, requiring payment in hard money for public lands. The ensuing Panic of 1837 aroused intense dissatisfaction with the use of state banks as depositories for public funds and helped to crystallize sentiment for the Independent Treasury (1840).

As a politician Jackson had added immeasurably to the popularity and power of the Presidential office by acting as a defender of the common man against a rapacious moneyed aristocracy, but as a tamperer with finance and currency he set the banking system of the country back for a whole generation. That was the real significance of Jackson's momentous decision to exercise his veto.

VETO MESSAGE

WASHINGTON, *July 10, 1832*

To the Senate:

The bill "to modify and continue" the act entitled "An act to incorporate the subscribers to the Bank of the United States" was presented to me on the 4th July instant. Having considered it with that solemn regard to the principles of the Constitution which the day was calculated to inspire, and come to the conclusion that it ought not to become a law, I herewith return it to the Senate, in which it originated, with my objections.

A bank of the United States is in many respects convenient for the Government and useful to the people. Entertaining this opinion, and deeply impressed with the belief that some of the powers and privileges possessed by the existing bank are unauthorized by the Constitution, subversive of the rights of the States, and dangerous to the liberties of the people, I felt it my duty at an early period of my Administration to call the attention of Congress to the practicability of organizing an institution combining all its advantages and obviating these objections. I sincerely regret that in the act before me I can perceive none of those modifications of the bank charter which are necessary, in my opinion, to make it compatible with justice, with sound policy, or with the Constitution of our country.

The present corporate body, denominated the president, directors, and company of the Bank of the United States, will have existed at the time this act is intended to take effect twenty years. It enjoys an exclusive privilege of banking under the authority of the General Government, a monopoly of its favor and support, and, as a necessary consequence, almost a monopoly of the foreign and domestic exchange. The powers, privileges, and favors bestowed upon it in the original charter, by increasing the value of the stock far above its par value, operated as a gratuity of many millions to the stockholders.

An apology may be found for the failure to guard against this result in the consideration that the effect of the original act of incorporation could not be certainly foreseen at the time of its passage. The act before me proposes another gratuity to the holders of the same stock, and in many cases to the same men, of at least seven millions more. This donation finds no apology in any uncertainty as to the effect of the act. On all hands it is conceded that its passage will increase at least 20 or 30 per cent more the market price of the stock, subject to the payment of the annuity of $200,000 per year secured by the act, thus adding in a moment one-fourth to its par value. It is not our own citizens only who are to receive the bounty of our Government. More than eight millions of the stock of this bank are held by foreigners. By this act the American Republic proposes virtually to make them a present of some millions of dollars. For these gratuities to foreigners and to some of our own opulent citizens the act secures no equivalent whatever. They are the certain gains of the present stockholders under the operation of this act, after making full allowance for the payment of the bonus.

Every monopoly and all exclusive privileges are granted at the expense of the public, which ought to receive a fair equivalent. The many millions which this act proposes to bestow on the stockholders of the existing bank must come directly or indirectly out of the earnings of the American people. It is due to them, therefore, if their Government sell monopolies and exclusive privileges, that they should at least exact for them as much as they are worth in open market. The value of the monopoly in this case may be correctly ascertained. The twenty-eight millions of stock would probably be at an advance of 50 per cent, and command in market at least $42,000,000, subject to the payment of the present bonus. The present value of the monopoly, therefore, is $17,000,000, and this the act proposes to sell for three millions, payable in fifteen annual installments of $200,000 each.

It is not conceivable how the present stockholders can have any claim to the special favor of the Government. The present corporation has enjoyed its monopoly during the period stipulated in the original contract. If we must have such a corporation, why should not the Government sell out the whole stock and thus secure to the people the full market value of the privileges granted? Why should not Congress create and sell twenty-eight millions of stock, incorporating the purchasers with all the powers and privileges secured in this act and putting the premium upon the sales into the Treasury?

But this act does not permit competition in the purchase of this monopoly. It seems to be predicated on the erroneous idea that the present stockholders have a prescriptive right not only to the favor but to the bounty of Government. It appears that more than a fourth part of the stock is held by foreigners and the residue is held by a few hundred of our own citizens, chiefly of the richest class. For their benefit does this act exclude the whole American people from competition in the purchase of this monopoly and dispose of it for many millions less than it is worth. This seems the less excusable because some of our citizens not now stockholders petitioned that the door of competition might be opened, and offered to take a charter on terms made much more favorable to the Government and country.

But this proposition, although made by men whose aggregate wealth is believed to be equal to all the private stock in the existing bank, has been set aside, and the bounty of our Government is proposed to be again bestowed on the few who have been fortunate enough to secure the stock and at this moment wield the power of the existing institution. I can not perceive the justice or policy of this course. If our Government must sell monopolies, it would seem to be its duty to take nothing less than their full value, and if gratuities must be made once in fifteen or twenty years let them not be bestowed on the subjects of a foreign government nor upon a designated and favored class of men in our country. It is but justice and good policy, as far as the nature of the case will admit, to confine our favors to our own fellow citizens, and let each in his turn enjoy an opportunity to profit by our bounty. In the bearings of the act before me upon these points I find ample reasons why it should not become a law.

It has been urged as an argument in favor of rechartering the present bank that the calling in its loans will produce great embarrassment and distress. The time allowed to close its concerns is ample, and if it has been well managed its pressure will be light, and heavy only in case its management has been bad. If, therefore, it shall produce distress, the fault will be its own, and it would furnish a reason against renewing a power which has been so obviously abused. But will there ever be a time when this reason will be less powerful? To acknowledge its force is to admit that the bank ought to be perpetual, and as a consequence the present stockholders and those inheriting their rights as successors be established a privileged order, clothed both with great political power and enjoying immense pecuniary advantages from their connection with the Government.

The modifications of the existing charter proposed by this act are not such, in my view, as make it consistent with the rights of the States or the liberties of the people. The qualification of the right of the bank to hold real estate, the limitation of its power to establish branches, and the power reserved to Congress to forbid the circulation of small notes are restrictions comparatively of little value or importance. All the objectionable principles of the existing corporation, and most of its odious features, are retained without alleviation.

The fourth section provides "that the notes or bills of the said corporation, although the same be, on the faces thereof, respectively made payable at one place only, shall nevertheless be received by the said corporation at the bank or at any of the offices of discount and deposit thereof if tendered in liquidation or payment of any balance or balances due to said corporation or to such office of discount and deposit from any other incorporated bank." This provision secures to the State banks a legal privilege in the Bank of the United States which is withheld from all private citizens. If a State bank in Philadelphia owe the Bank of the United States and have notes issued by the St. Louis branch, it can pay the debt with those notes, but if a merchant, mechanic, or other private citizen be in like circumstances he can not by law pay his debt with those notes, but must sell them at a discount or send them to St. Louis to be cashed. This boon conceded to the State banks, though not unjust in itself, is most odious because it does not measure out equal justice to the high and the low, the rich and the poor. To the extent of its practical effect it is a bond of union among the banking establishments of the nation, erecting them into an interest separate from that of the people, and its necessary tendency is to unite the Bank of the United States and the State banks in any measure which may be thought conducive to their common interest.

The ninth section of the act recognizes principles of worse tendency than any provision of the present charter.

It enacts that "the cashier of the bank shall annually report to the Secretary of the Treasury the names of all stockholders who are not resident citizens of the United States, and on the application of the treasurer of any State shall make out and transmit to such treasurer a list of stockholders residing in or citizens of such State, with the amount of stock owned by each." Although this provision, taken in connection with a decision of the Supreme Court, surrenders, by its silence, the right of the States to tax the banking institutions created by this corporation under the name of branches throughout the Union, it is evidently intended to be construed as a concession of their right to tax that portion of the stock which may be held by their own citizens and residents. In this light, if the act becomes a law, it will be understood by the States, who will probably proceed to levy a tax equal to that paid upon the stock of banks incorporated by themselves. In some States that tax is now 1 per cent, either on the capital or on the shares, and that may be assumed as the amount which all citizen or resident stockholders would be taxed under the operation of this act. As it is only the stock *held* in the States and not that *employed* within them which would be subject to taxation, and as the names of foreign stockholders are not to be reported to the treasurers of the States, it is obvious that the stock held by them will be exempt from this burden. Their annual profits will therefore be 1 per cent more than the citizen stockholders, and as the annual dividends of the bank may be safely estimated at 7 per cent, the stock will be worth 10 or 15 per cent more to foreigners than to citizens of the United States. To appreciate the effects which this state of things will produce, we must take a brief review of the operations and present condition of the Bank of the United States.

By documents submitted to Congress at the present session it appears that on the 1st of January, 1832, of the twenty-eight millions of private stock in the corporation, $8,405,500 were held by foreigners, mostly of Great Britain. The amount of stock held in the nine Western and Southwestern States is $140,200, and in the four Southern States is $5,623,100, and in the Middle and Eastern States is about $13,522,000. The profits of the bank in 1831, as shown in a statement to Congress, were about $3,455,598; of this there accrued in the nine Western States about $1,640,048; in the four Southern States about $352,507, and in the Middle and Eastern States about $1,463,041. As little stock is held in the West, it is obvious that the debt of the people in that section to the bank is principally a debt to the Eastern and foreign stockholders; that the interest they pay upon it is carried into the Eastern States and into

Europe, and that it is a burden upon their industry and a drain of their currency, which no country can bear without inconvenience and occasional distress. To meet this burden and equalize the exchange operations of the bank, the amount of specie drawn from those States through its branches within the last two years, as shown by its official reports, was about $6,000,000. More than half a million of this amount does not stop in the Eastern States, but passes on to Europe to pay the dividends of the foreign stockholders. In the principle of taxation recognized by this act the Western States find no adequate compensation for this perpetual burden on their industry and drain of their currency. The branch bank at Mobile made last year $95,140, yet under the provisions of this act the State of Alabama can raise no revenue from these profitable operations, because not a share of the stock is held by any of her citizens. Mississippi and Missouri are in the same condition in relation to the branches at Natchez and St. Louis, and such, in a greater or less degree, is the condition of every Western State. The tendency of the plan of taxation which this act proposes will be to place the whole United States in the same relation to foreign countries which the Western States now bear to the Eastern. When by a tax on resident stockholders the stock of this bank is made worth 10 or 15 per cent more to foreigners than to residents, most of it will inevitably leave the country.

Thus will this provision in its practical effect deprive the Eastern as well as the Southern and Western States of the means of raising a revenue from the extension of business and great profits of this institution. It will make the American people debtors to aliens in nearly the whole amount due to this bank, and send across the Atlantic from two to five millions of specie every year to pay the bank dividends.

In another of its bearings this provision is fraught with danger. Of the twenty-five directors of this bank five are chosen by the Government and twenty by the citizen stockholders. From all voice in these elections the foreign stockholders are excluded by the charter. In proportion, therefore, as the stock is transferred to foreign holders the extent of suffrage in the choice of directors is curtailed. Already is almost a third of the stock in foreign hands and not represented in elections. It is constantly passing out of the country, and this act will accelerate its departure. The entire control of the institution would necessarily fall into the hands of a few citizen stockholders, and the ease with which the object would be accomplished would be a temptation to designing men to secure that control in their own hands by monopolizing the remaining stock. There is danger that a president and directors would then be able to elect themselves from year to year, and without responsibility or control manage the whole concerns of the bank during the existence of its charter. It is easy to conceive that great evils to our country and its institutions might flow from such a concentration of power in the hands of a few men irresponsible to the people.

Is there no danger to our liberty and independence in a bank that in its nature has so little to bind it to our country? The president of the bank has told us that most of the State banks exist by its forbearance. Should its influence become concentered, as it may under the operation of such an act as this, in the hands of a self-elected directory whose interests are identified with those of the foreign stockholders, will there not be cause to tremble for the purity of our elections in peace and for the independence of our country in war? Their power would be great whenever they might choose to exert it; but if this monopoly were regularly renewed every fifteen or twenty years on terms proposed by themselves, they might seldom in peace put forth their strength to influence elections or control the affairs of the nation. But if any private citizen or public functionary should interpose to curtail its powers or prevent a renewal of its privileges, it can not be doubted that he would be made to feel its influence.

Should the stock of the bank principally pass into the hands of the subjects of a foreign country, and we should unfortunately become involved in a war with that country, what would be our condition? Of the course which would be pursued by a bank almost wholly owned by the subjects of a foreign power, and managed by those whose interests, if not affections, would run in the same direction there can be no doubt. All its operations within would be in aid of the hostile fleets and armies without. Controlling our currency, receiving our public moneys, and holding thousands of our citizens in dependence, it would be more formidable and dangerous than the naval and military power of the enemy.

If we must have a bank with private stockholders, every consideration of sound policy and every impulse of American feeling admonishes that it should be *purely American*. Its stockholders should be composed exclusively of our own citizens, who at least ought to be friendly to our Government and willing to support it in times of difficulty and danger. So abundant is domestic capital that competition in subscribing for the stock of local banks has recently led almost to riots. To a bank exclusively of American stockholders, possessing the powers and privileges granted by this act, subscriptions for $200,000,000 could be readily obtained. Instead of sending abroad the stock of the bank in which the Government must deposit its funds and on which it must rely to sustain its credit in times of emergency, it would rather seem to be expedient to prohibit its sale to aliens under penalty of absolute forfeiture.

It is maintained by the advocates of the bank that its constitutionality in all its features ought to be considered as settled by precedent and by the decision of the Supreme Court. To this conclusion I can not assent. Mere precedent is a dangerous source of authority, and should not be regarded as deciding questions of constitutional power except where the acquiescence of the people and the States can be considered as well settled. So far from this being the case on this subject, an argument against the bank might be based on precedent. One Congress, in 1791, decided in favor of a bank; another, in 1811, decided against it. One Congress, in 1815, decided against a bank; another, in 1816, decided in its favor. Prior to the present Congress, therefore, the precedents drawn from that source were equal. If we resort to the States, the expressions of legislative, judicial, and executive opinions against the bank have been probably to those in its favor as 4 to 1. There is nothing in precedent, therefore, which, if its authority were admitted, ought to weigh in favor of the act before me.

If the opinion of the Supreme Court covered the whole ground of this act, it ought not to control the coordinate authorities of this Government. The Congress, the Executive, and the Court must each for itself be guided by its own opinion of the Constitution. Each public officer who takes an oath to support the Constitution swears that he will support it as he understands it, and not as it is understood by others. It is as much the duty of the House of Representatives, of the Senate, and of the President to decide upon the constitutionality of any bill or resolution which may be presented to them for passage or approval as it is of the supreme judges when it may be brought before them for judicial decision. The opinion of the judges has no more authority over Congress than the opinion of Congress has over the judges, and on that point the President is independent of both. The authority of the Supreme Court must not, therefore, be permitted to control the Congress or the Executive when acting in their legislative capacities, but to have only such influence as the force of their reasoning may deserve.

But in the case relied upon the Supreme Court have not decided that all the features of this corporation are compatible with the Constitution. It is true that the court have said that the law incorporating the bank is a constitutional exercise of power by Congress; but taking into view the whole opinion of the court and the reasoning by which they have come to that conclusion, I understand them to have decided that inasmuch as a bank is an appropriate means for carrying into effect the enumerated powers of the General Government, therefore the law incorporating it is in accordance with that provision of the Constitution which declares that Congress shall have power "to make all laws which shall be necessary and proper for carrying those powers into execution." Having satisfied themselves that the word *"necessary"* in the Constitution means *"needful," "requisite," "essential," "conducive to,"* and that "a bank" is a convenient, a useful, and essential instrument in the prosecution of the Government's "fiscal operations," they conclude that to "use one must be within the discretion of Congress" and that "the act to incorporate the Bank of the United States is a law made in pursuance of the Constitution;" "but," say they, *where the law is not prohibited and is really calculated to effect any of the objects intrusted to the Government, to undertake here to inquire into the degree of its necessity would be to pass the line which circumscribes the judicial department and to tread on legislative ground."*

The principle here affirmed is that the "degree of its necessity," involving all the details of a banking institution, is a question exclusively for legislative consideration. A bank is constitutional, but it is the province of the Legislature to determine whether this or that particular power, privilege, or exemption is "necessary and proper" to enable the bank to discharge its duties to the Government, and from their decision there is no appeal to the courts of justice. Under the decision of the Supreme Court, therefore, it is the exclusive province of Congress and the President to decide whether the particular features of this act are *necessary* and *proper* in order to enable the bank to perform conveniently and efficiently the public duties assigned to it as a fiscal agent, and therefore constitutional, or *unnecessary* and *improper,* and therefore unconstitutional.

Without commenting on the general principle affirmed by the Supreme Court, let us examine the details of this act in accordance with the rule of legislative action which they have laid down. It will be found that many of the powers and privileges conferred on it can not be supposed necessary for the purpose for which it is proposed to be created, and are not, therefore, means necessary to attain the end in view, and consequently not justified by the Constitution.

The original act of incorporation, section 21, enacts "that no other bank shall be established by any future law of the United States during the continuance of the corporation hereby created, for which the faith of the United States is hereby pledged: *Provided,* Congress may renew existing charters for banks within the District of Columbia not increasing the capital thereof, and may also establish any other bank or banks in said District with capitals not exceeding in the whole $6,000,000 if they shall deem it expedient." This provision is continued in force by the act before me fifteen years from the 3d of March, 1836.

If Congress possessed the power to establish one bank, they had power to establish more than one if in their opinion two or more banks had been "necessary" to facilitate the execution of the powers delegated to them in the Constitution. If they possessed the power to establish a second bank, it was a power derived from the Constitution to be exercised from time to time, and at any time when the interests of the country or the emergencies of the Government might make it expedient. It was possessed by one Congress as well as another, and by all Congresses alike, and alike at every session. But the Congress of 1816 have taken it away from their successors for twenty years, and the Congress of 1832 proposes to abolish it for fifteen years more. It can not be *"necessary"* or *"proper"* for Congress to barter away or divest themselves of any of the powers vested in them by the Constitution to be exercised for the public good. It is not *"necessary"* to the efficiency of the bank, nor is it *"proper"* in relation to themselves and their successors. They may *properly* use the discretion vested in them, but they may not limit the discretion of their successors. This restriction on themselves and grant of a monopoly to the bank is therefore unconstitutional.

In another point of view this provision is a palpable attempt to amend the Constitution by an act of legislation. The Constitution declares that "the Congress shall have power to exercise exclusive legislation in all cases whatsoever" over the District of Columbia. Its constitutional power, therefore, to establish banks in the District of Columbia and increase their capital at will is unlimited and uncontrollable by any other power than that which gave authority to the Constitution. Yet this act declares that Congress shall *not* increase the capital of existing banks, nor create other banks with capitals exceeding in the whole $6,000,000. The Constitution declares that Congress *shall* have power to exercise exclusive legislation over this District *"in all cases whatsoever,"* and this act declares they shall not. Which is the supreme law of the land? This provision can not be *"necessary"* or *"proper"* or *constitutional* unless the absurdity be admitted that whenever it be "necessary and proper" in the opinion of Congress they have a right to barter away one portion of the powers vested in them by the Constitution as a means of executing the rest.

On two subjects only does the Constitution recognize in Congress the power to grant exclusive privileges or monopolies. It declares that "Congress shall have power to promote the progress of science and useful arts by securing for limited times to authors and inventors the exclusive right to their respective writings and discoveries." Out of this express delegation of power have grown our laws of patents and copyrights. As the Constitution expressly delegates to Congress the power to grant exclusive privileges in these cases as the means of executing the substantive power "to promote the progress of science and useful arts," it is consistent with the fair rules of construction to conclude that such a power was not intended to be granted as a means of accomplishing any other end. On every other subject which comes within the scope of Congressional power there is an ever-living discretion in the use of proper means, which can not be restricted or abolished without an amendment of the Constitution. Every act of Congress, therefore, which attempts by grants of monopolies or sale of exclusive privileges for a limited time, or a time without limit, to restrict or extinguish its own discretion in the choice of means to execute its delegated powers is equivalent to a legislative amendment of the Constitution, and palpably unconstitutional.

This act authorizes and encourages transfers of its stock to foreigners and grants them an exemption from all State and national taxation. So far from being *"necessary and proper"* that the bank should possess this power to make it a safe and efficient agent of the Government in its fiscal operations, it is calculated to convert the Bank of the United States into a foreign bank, to impoverish our people in time of peace, to disseminate a foreign influence through every section of the Republic, and in war to endanger our independence.

The several States reserved the power at the formation of the Constitution to regulate and control titles and transfers of real property, and most, if not all, of them have laws disqualifying aliens from acquiring or holding lands within their limits. But this act, in disregard of the undoubted right of the States to prescribe such disqualifications, gives to alien stockholders in this bank an interest and title, as members of the corporation, to all the real property it may acquire within any of the States of this Union. This privilege granted to aliens is not *"necessary"* to enable the bank to perform its public duties, nor in any sense *"proper,"* because it is vitally subversive of the rights of the States.

The Government of the United States have no constitutional power to purchase lands within the States except "for the erection of forts, magazines, arsenals, dockyards, and other needful buildings," and even for these objects only "by the consent of the legislature of the State in which the same shall be." By making themselves stockholders in the bank and granting to the corporation the power to purchase lands for other purposes they assume a power not granted in the Constitution and grant to others what they do not themselves possess. It is not *necessary* to the receiving, safe-keeping, or transmission of the funds of the Government that the bank should possess this power, and it is not *proper* that Congress should thus enlarge the powers delegated to them in the Constitution.

The old Bank of the United States possessed a capital of only $11,000,-000, which was found fully sufficient to enable it with dispatch and safety to perform all the functions required of it by the Government. The capital of the present bank is $35,000,0000—at least twenty-four more than experience has proved to be *necessary* to enable a bank to perform its public functions. The public debt which existed during the period of the old bank and on the establishment of the new has been nearly paid off, and our revenue will soon be reduced. This increase of capital is therefore not for public but for private purposes.

The Government is the only *"proper"* judge where its agents should reside and keep their offices, because it best knows where their presence will be *"necessary."* It can not, therefore, be *"necessary"* or *"proper"* to authorize the bank to locate branches where it pleases to perform the public service, without consulting the Government, and contrary to its will. The principle laid down by the Supreme Court concedes that Congress can not establish a bank for purposes of private speculation and gain, but only as a means of executing the delegated powers of the General Government. By the same principle a branch bank can not constitutionally be established for other than public purposes. The power which this act gives to establish two branches in any State, without the injunction or request of the Government and for other than public purposes, is not *"necessary"* to the due *execution* of the powers delegated to Congress.

The bonus which is exacted from the bank is a confession upon the face of the act that the powers granted by it are greater than are *"necessary"* to its character of a fiscal agent. The Government does not tax its officers and agents for the privilege of serving it. The bonus of a million and a half required by the original charter and that of three millions proposed by this act are not exacted for the privilege of giving "the necessary facilities for transferring the public funds from place to place within the United States or the Territories thereof, and for distributing the same in payment of the public creditors without charging commission or claiming allowance on account of the difference of exchange," as required by the act of incorporation, but for something more beneficial to the stockholders. The original act declares that it (the bonus) is granted "in consideration of the exclusive privileges and benefits conferred by this act upon the said bank," and the act before me declares it to be "in consideration of the exclusive benefits and privileges continued by this act to the said corporation for fifteen years, as aforesaid." It is therefore for "exclusive privileges and benefits" conferred for their own use and emolument, and not for the advantage of the Government, that a bonus is exacted. These surplus powers for which the bank is required to pay can not surely be "*necessary*" to make it the fiscal agent of the Treasury. If they were, the exaction of a bonus for them would not be "*proper*."

It is maintained by some that the bank is a means of executing the constitutional power "to coin money and regulate the value thereof." Congress have established a mint to coin money and passed laws to regulate the value thereof. The money so coined, with its value so regulated, and such foreign coins as Congress may adopt are the only currency known to the Constitution. But if they have other power to regulate the currency, it was conferred to be exercised by themselves, and not to be transferred to a corporation. If the bank be established for that purpose, with a charter unalterable without its consent, Congress have parted with their power for a term of years, during which the Constitution is a dead letter. It is neither necessary nor proper to transfer its legislative power to such a bank, and therefore unconstitutional.

By its silence, considered in connection with the decision of the Supreme Court in the case of McCulloch against the State of Maryland, this act takes from the States the power to tax a portion of the banking business carried on within their limits, in subversion of one of the strongest barriers which secured them against Federal encroachments. Banking, like farming, manufacturing, or any other occupation or profession, is *a business,* the right to follow which is not originally derived from the laws. Every citizen and every company of citizens in all of our States possessed the right until the State legislatures deemed it good policy to prohibit private banking by law. If the prohibitory State laws were now repealed, every citizen would again possess the right. The State banks are a qualified restoration of the right which has been taken away by the laws against banking, guarded by such provisions and limitations as in the opinion of the State legislatures the public interest requires. These corporations, unless there be an exemption in their charter, are, like private bankers and banking companies, subject to State taxation. The manner in which these taxes shall be laid depends wholly on legislative discretion. It may be upon the bank, upon the stock, upon the profits, or in any other mode which the sovereign power shall will.

Upon the formation of the Constitution the States guarded their taxing power with peculiar jealousy. They surrendered it only as it regards imports and exports. In relation to every other object within their jurisdiction, whether persons, property, business, or professions, it was secured in as ample a manner as it was before possessed. All persons, though United States officers, are liable to a poll tax by the States within which they reside. The lands of the United States are liable to the usual land tax, except in the new States, from whom agreements that they will not tax unsold lands are exacted when they are admitted into the Union. Horses, wagons, any beasts or vehicles, tools, or property belonging to private citizens, though employed in the service of the United States, are subject to State taxation. Every private business, whether carried on by an officer of the General Government or not, whether it be mixed with public concerns or not, even if it be carried on by the Government of the United States itself, separately or in partnership, falls within the scope of the taxing power of the State. Nothing comes more fully within it than banks and the business of banking, by whomsoever instituted and carried on. Over this whole subject-matter it is just as absolute, unlimited, and uncontrollable as if the Constitution had never been adopted, because in the formation of that instrument it was reserved without qualification.

The principle is conceded that the States can not rightfully tax the operations of the General Government. They can not tax the money of the Government deposited in the State banks, nor the agency of those banks in remitting it; but will any man maintain that their mere selection to perform this public service for the General Government would exempt the State banks and their ordinary business from State taxation? Had the United States, instead of establishing a bank at Philadelphia, employed a private banker to keep and transmit their funds, would it have deprived Pennsylvania of the right to tax his bank and his usual banking operations? It will not be pretended. Upon what principle, then, are the banking establishments of the Bank of the United States and their usual banking operations to be exempted from taxation? It is not their public agency or the deposits of the Government which the States claim a right to tax, but their banks and their banking powers, instituted and exercised within State jurisdiction for their private emolument—those powers and privileges for which they pay a bonus, and which the States tax in their own banks. The exercise of these powers within a State, no matter by whom or under what authority, whether by private citizens in their original right, by corporate bodies created by the States, by foreigners or the agents of foreign governments located within their limits, forms a legitimate object of State taxation. From this and like sources, from the persons, property, and business that are found residing, located, or carried on under their jurisdiction, must the States, since the surrender of their right to raise a revenue from imports and exports, draw all the money necessary for the support of their governments and the maintenance of their independence. There is no more appropriate subject of taxation than banks, banking, and bank stocks, and none to which the States ought more pertinaciously to cling.

It can not be *necessary* to the character of the bank as a fiscal agent of the Government that its private business should be exempted from that taxation to which all the State banks are liable, nor can I conceive it *"proper"* that the substantive and most essential powers reserved by the States shall be thus attacked and annihilated as a means of executing the powers delegated to the General Government. It may be safely assumed that none of those sages who had an agency in forming or adopting our Constitution ever imagined that any portion of the taxing power of the States not prohibited to them nor delegated to Congress was to be swept away and annihiliated as a means of executing certain powers delegated to Congress.

If our power over means is so absolute that the Supreme Court will not call in question the constitutionality of an act of Congress the subject of which "is not prohibited, and is really calculated to effect any of the objects intrusted to the Government," although, as in the case before me, it takes away powers expressly granted to Congress and rights scrupulously reserved to the States, it becomes us to proceed in our legislation with the utmost caution. Though not directly, our own powers and the rights of the States may be indirectly legislated away in the use of means to execute substantive powers. We may not enact that Congress shall not have the power of exclusive legislation over the District of Columbia, but we may pledge the faith of the United States that as a means of executing other powers it shall not be exercised for twenty years or forever. We may not pass an act prohibiting the States to tax the banking business carried on within their limits, but we may, as a means of executing our powers over other objects, place that business in the hands of our agents and then declare it exempt from State taxation in their hands. Thus may our own powers and the rights of the States, which we can not directly curtail or invade, be frittered away and extinguished in the use of means employed by us to execute other powers. That a bank of the United States, competent to all the duties which may be required by the Government, might be so organized as not to infringe on our own delegated powers or the reserved rights of the States I do not entertain a doubt. Had the Executive been called upon to furnish the project of such an institution, the duty would have been cheerfully performed. In the absence of such a call it was obviously proper that he should confine himself to pointing out those prominent features in the act presented which in his opinion make it incompatible with the Constitution and sound policy. A general discussion will now take place, eliciting new light and settling important principles; and a new Congress, elected in the midst of such discussion, and furnishing an equal representation of the people according to the last census, will bear to the Capitol the verdict of public opinion, and, I doubt not, bring this important question to a satisfactory result.

Under such circumstances the bank comes forward and asks a renewal of its charter for a term of fifteen years upon conditions which not only operate as a gratuity to the stockholders of many millions of dollars, but will sanction any abuses and legalize any encroachments.

Suspicions are entertained and charges are made of gross abuse and violation of its charter. An investigation unwillingly conceded and so restricted in time as necessarily to make it incomplete and unsatisfactory discloses enough to excite suspicion and alarm. In the practices of the principal bank partially unveiled, in the absence of important witnesses, and in numerous charges confidently made and as yet wholly uninvestigated there was enough to induce a majority of the committee of investigation—a committee which was selected from the most able and honorable members of the House of Representatives—to recommend a suspension of further action upon the bill and a prosecution of the inquiry. As the charter had yet four years to run, and as a renewal now was not necessary to the successful prosecution of its business, it was to have been expected that the bank itself, conscious of its purity and proud of its character, would have withdrawn its application for the present, and demanded the severest scrutiny into all its transactions. In their declining to do so there seems to be an additional reason why the functionaries of the Government should proceed with less haste and more caution in the renewal of their monopoly.

The bank is professedly established as an agent of the executive branch of the Government, and its constitutionality is maintained on that ground. Neither upon the propriety of present action nor upon the provisions of this act was the Executive consulted. It has had no opportunity to say that it neither needs nor wants an agent clothed with such powers and favored by such exemptions. There is nothing in its legitimate functions which makes it necessary or proper. Whatever interest or influence, whether public or private, has given birth to this act, it can not be found either in the wishes or necessities of the executive department, by which present action is deemed premature, and the powers conferred upon its agent not only unnecessary, but dangerous to the Government and country.

It is to be regretted that the rich and powerful too often bend the acts of government to their selfish purposes. Distinctions in society will always exist under every just government. Equality of talents, of education, or of wealth can not be produced by human institutions. In the full enjoyment of the gifts of Heaven and the fruits of superior industry, economy, and virtue, every man is equally entitled to protection by law; but when the laws undertake to add to these natural and just advantages artificial distinctions, to grant titles, gratuities, and exclusive privileges, to make the rich richer and the potent more powerful, the humble members of society—the farmers, mechanics, and laborers—who have neither the time nor the means of securing like favors to themselves, have a right to complain of the injustice of their Government. There are no necessary evils in government. Its evils exist only in its abuses. If it would confine itself to equal protection, and, as Heaven does its rains, shower its favors alike on the high and the low, the rich and the poor, it would be an unqualified blessing. In the act before me there seems to be a wide and unnecessary departure from these just principles.

Nor is our Government to be maintained or our Union preserved by invasions of the rights and powers of the several States. In thus attempting to make our General Government strong we make it weak. Its true strength consists in leaving individuals and States as much as possible to themselves—in making itself felt, not in its power, but in its beneficence; not in its control, but in its protection; not in binding the States more closely to the center, but leaving each to move unobstructed in its proper orbit.

Experience should teach us wisdom. Most of the difficulties our Government now encounters and most of the dangers which impend over our Union have sprung from an abandonment of the legitimate objects of Government by our national legislation, and the adoption of such principles as are embodied in this act. Many of our rich men have not been content with equal protection and equal benefits, but have besought us to make them richer by act of Congress. By attempting to gratify their desires we have in the results of our legislation arrayed section against section, interest against interest, and man against man, in a fearful commotion which threatens to shake the foundations of our Union. It is time to pause in our career to review our principles, and if possible revive that devoted patriotism and spirit of compromise which distinguished the sages of the Revolution and the fathers of our Union. If we can not at once, in justice to interests vested under improvident legislation, make our Government what it ought to be, we can at least take a stand against all new grants of monopolies and exclusive privileges, against any prostitution of our Government to the advancement of the few at the expense of the many, and in favor of compromise and gradual reform in our code of laws and system of political economy.

I have now done my duty to my country. If sustained by my fellow-citizens, I shall be grateful and happy; if not, I shall find in the motives which impel me ample grounds for contentment and peace. In the difficulties which surround us and the dangers which threaten our institutions there is cause for neither dismay nor alarm. For relief and deliverance let us firmly rely on that kind Providence which I am sure watches with peculiar care over the destinies of our Republic, and on the intelligence and wisdom of our countrymen. Through *His* abundant goodness and *their* patriotic devotion our liberty and Union will be preserved.

10

THE DECISION
TO CRUSH NULLIFICATION

Jackson Issues His "Proclamation to the People of South Carolina"

The cement of union was still weak when Old Hickory became President. Spasmodically, as national issues affected specific sections adversely, disunifying cries had been heard, coming first from Virginia and Kentucky in the conflict over the Alien and Sedition Acts, from the West at various times and culminating in Aaron Burr's conspiracy, then from New England in reaction to the War of 1812, and in the year 1832 from the lower South. Suffering gravely from the exhaustion of her cotton lands and recovering all too slowly from the effects of the Panic of 1819, South Carolina took strong exception to the "Tariff of Abominations" of 1828, with its excessively high duties, and her legislature adopted a set of resolutions terming the tariff unconstitutional, oppressive, and unjust.

The leader of this new opposition was that erstwhile nationalist, John C. Calhoun, who prepared for the legislature of his state "The South Carolina Exposition and Protest," an unsigned assertion of the right of a single state to nullify a national law. The whole tariff system, Calhoun held, was unconstitutional and oppressive, and made Southerners "the serfs of the system—out of whose labor is raised, not only the money paid into the Treasury, but the funds out of which are drawn the rich rewards of the manufacturer and his associates in interest. Their encouragement is our discouragement." Calhoun claimed authority for interposition by a state against the "unconstitutional" acts of the national government, citing as authority Hamilton (who would have turned over in his grave) and Madison and Jefferson, whose Virginia and Kentucky Resolves were the seedbed for states'-rights ideologies. Through the instrumentality of a state convention, Calhoun argued, a state could declare null and void an act of the national government.

During Jackson's first term the issue of Union versus states' rights provided a springboard for orators and politicians. In his famous second reply to Senator Robert Y. Hayne, Daniel Webster in 1830 attacked disunionist tendencies, closing his oration with an eloquent peroration celebrating "Liberty *and* Union, now and forever, one and inseparable!" A few months later at the Jefferson Day Dinner in Washington President Jackson offered his toast: "Our Union. It must be preserved!" Calhoun responded: "The Union, next to our liberty, most dear. May we always remember that it can only be preserved by distributing equally the benefits and burdens of the Union."

If there was one thing the protective tariff did not do it was to spread benefits equally. Manufacturers gained protection from English competition while farmers had to pay more for the clothes and tools they purchased. As a concession to the lower South the Tariff of 1832 was enacted, with duties somewhat milder than those of 1828, but still retaining the protectionist principle. Its passage in July of 1832 prompted the South Carolina extremists to take a belligerent posture. The state elections in October resulted in a decisive victory for the nullification party and its extremist leaders, Governor James Hamilton, Jr., and Robert Barnwell Rhett. Meanwhile Calhoun had reaffirmed and elaborated the doctrine of nullification in his Fort Hill Address, which contained the principle of the concurrent majority, and in a letter to Governor Hamilton, in which he defended nullification as a constitutional, conservative, and legitimate means of redress for acts deemed injurious to a state. What it all boiled down to was that the South required a government too weak to interfere with her system of labor just as the North needed a government strong enough to levy and collect import duties. Slavery rather than the tariff issue was really becoming the paramount problem.

The Governor of South Carolina promptly summoned an extraordinary session of the legislature, which in turn called for a state convention. Dominated by extremists, with a bare handful of Unionists in attendance, that convention adopted an ordinance nullifying the tariff acts of 1828 and 1832, prohibiting the collection of duties within the state, forbidding an appeal to the United States Supreme Court of any case in law or equity arising under that ordinance, and asserting that the use of force by the Federal government would be cause for secession. The legislature then authorized the raising of a military force and appropriated funds for arms. The hotheads seemed ready for the showdown. "All appear animated," wrote James H. Hammond, editor of the Columbia *Southern Times*, "by the most thorough conviction that we are unconquerable."

Jackson was rightly incensed. He felt that Calhoun was showing signs of dementia and that South Carolina's attitude was worse than rebellion, that the raising of troops was "positive treason." Outwardly, however, he remained collected. He ordered the Secretary of War to alert the forts in Charleston harbor and gave to Major General Winfield Scott command of the army forces in South Carolina. But he sought to balance his show of force with a gesture of conciliation, adopting what has been appropriately termed "a carrot and stick policy." He recommended to Congress a substantial reduction in tariff rates and the elimination of inequities. Taking the initiative away from the Jacksonians, Henry Clay, desperately seeking to salvage some prestige from his disastrous race for the Presidency, worked out, with the strange collaboration of Calhoun, a compromise tariff of 1833 which was mildly revisionist and did not have that injurious effect on the national economy that Northern manufacturing interests predicted. Again the Great Pacificator managed to keep in the center of the stage.

If John Quincy Adams was dismayed at the conciliatory gesture to South Carolina while she remained contumacious, he was heartened by the "Proclamation to the People of South Carolina" which Jackson issued. The draft of this warning was prepared by Secretary of State Edward Livingston, a distinguished jurist. Ranking as Jackson's most important state paper, the Proclamation forthrightly denied the right of nullification and branded disunion by armed force as treason. In the Force Bill Congress gave the old Hero the authority to enforce the revenue laws by the use of the military if necessary. Upon learning that a compromise tariff was in the making, South Carolina suspended the ordinance of nullification, and rescinded it in March, 1833. As a face-saving, if childish, gesture, the convention adopted an ordinance declaring the Force Bill null and void.

Thus ended the controversy, with both sides claiming victory. The issue of disunion was postponed for a whole generation, but the fire-brands who had precipitated it in 1832 learned nothing from Jackson's powerful and persuasive state paper, nor did they take heed to James Madison's parting counsel to his countrymen in 1836. The aged patriot wrote: "The advice nearest to my heart and deepest in my convictions is that the Union of the States be cherished and perpetuated. Let the open enemy to it be regarded as a Pandora with her box opened; and the disguised one, as a serpent creeping with his wiles into Paradise."

PROCLAMATION

To the People of South Carolina
By Andrew Jackson, President of the United States

Whereas a convention assembled in the State of South Carolina have passed an ordinance by which they declare "that the several acts and parts of acts of the Congress of the United States purporting to be laws for the imposing of duties and imposts on the importation of foreign commodities, and now having actual operation and effect within the United States, and more especially" two acts for the same purposes passed on the 29th of May, 1828, and on the 14th of July, 1832, "are un-authorized by the Constitution of the United States, and violate the true meaning and intent thereof, and are null and void and no law," nor binding on the citizens of that State or its officers; and by the said ordi-nance it is further declared to be unlawful for any of the constituted authorities of the State or of the United States to enforce the payment of the duties imposed by the said acts within the same State, and that it is the duty of the legislature to pass such laws as may be necessary to give full effect to the said ordinance; and

Whereas by the said ordinance it is further ordained that in no case of law or equity decided in the courts of said State wherein shall be drawn in question the validity of the said ordinance, or of the acts of the legislature that may be passed to give it effect, or of the said laws of the United States, no appeal shall be allowed to the Supreme Court of the United States, nor shall any copy of the record be permitted or al-lowed for that purpose, and that any person attempting to take such appeal shall be punished as for contempt of court; and, finally, the said ordinance declares that the people of South Carolina will maintain the said ordinance at every hazard, and that they will consider the passage of any act by Congress abolishing or closing the ports of the said State or otherwise obstructing the free ingress or egress of vessels to and from the said ports, or any other act of the Federal Government to coerce the State, shut up her ports, destroy or harass her commerce, or to enforce the said acts otherwise than through the civil tribunals of the country, as inconsistent with the longer continuance of South Carolina in the Union, and that the people of the said State will thenceforth hold themselves absolved from all further obligation to maintain or preserve their political connection with the people of the other States, and will forthwith proceed to organize a separate government and do all other acts and things which sovereign and independent states may of right do; and

Whereas the said ordinance prescribes to the people of South Carolina a course of conduct in direct violation of their duty as citizens of the United States, contrary to the laws of their country, subversive of its Constitution, and having for its object the destruction of the Union— that Union which, coeval with our political existence, led our fathers, without any other ties to unite them than those of patriotism and a common cause, through a sanguinary struggle to a glorious independence; that sacred Union, hitherto inviolate, which, perfected by our happy Constitution, has brought us, by the favor of Heaven, to a state of prosperity at home and high consideration abroad rarely, if ever, equaled in the history of nations:

To preserve this bond of our political existence from destruction, to maintain inviolate this state of national honor and prosperity, and to justify the confidence my fellow-citizens have reposed in me, I, Andrew Jackson, President of the United States, have thought proper to issue this my proclamation, stating my views of the Constitution and laws applicable to the measures adopted by the convention of South Carolina and to the reasons they have put forth to sustain them, declaring the course which duty will require me to pursue, and, appealing to the understanding and patriotism of the people, warn them of the consequences that must inevitably result from an observance of the dictates of the convention.

Strict duty would require of me nothing more than the exercise of those powers with which I am now or may hereafter be invested for preserving the peace of the Union and for the execution of the laws; but the imposing aspect which opposition has assumed in this case, by clothing itself with State authority, and the deep interest which the people of the United States must all feel in preventing a resort to stronger measures while there is a hope that anything will be yielded to reasoning and remonstrance, perhaps demand, and will certainly justify, a full exposition to South Carolina and the nation of the views I entertain of this important question, as well as a distinct enunciation of the course which my sense of duty will require me to pursue.

The ordinance is founded, not on the indefeasible right of resisting acts which are plainly unconstitutional and too oppressive to be endured, but on the strange position that any one State may not only declare an act of Congress void, but prohibit its execution; that they may do this consistently with the Constitution; that the true construction of that instrument permits a State to retain its place in the Union and yet be bound by no other of its laws than those it may choose to consider as constitutional. It is true, they add, that to justify this abrogation of a law it must be palpably contrary to the Constitution; but it is evident that to give the right of resisting laws of that description, coupled with the uncontrolled right to decide what laws deserve that character, is to give the power of resisting all laws; for as by the theory there is no appeal, the reasons alleged by the State, good or bad, must prevail. If it should be said that public opinion is a sufficient check against the abuse of this power, it may be asked why it is not deemed a sufficient guard against the passage of an unconstitutional act by Congress? There is, however, a restraint in this last case which makes the assumed power of a State more indefensible, and which does not exist in the other. There are two appeals from an unconstitutional act passed by Congress—one to the judiciary, the other to the people and the States. There is no appeal from the State decision in theory, and the practical illustration shows that the courts are closed against an application to review it, both judges and jurors being sworn to decide in its favor. But reasoning on this subject is superfluous when our social compact, in express terms, declares that the laws of the United States, its Constitution, and treaties made under it are the supreme law of the land, and, for greater caution, adds "that the judges in every State shall be bound thereby, anything in the constitution or laws of any State to the contrary notwithstanding." And it may be asserted without fear of refutation that no federative government could exist without a similar provision. Look for a moment to the consequence. If South Carolina considers the revenue laws unconstitutional and has a right to prevent their execution in the port of Charleston, there would be a clear constitutional objection to their collection in every other port; and no revenue could be collected anywhere, for all imposts must be equal. It is no answer to repeat that an unconstitutional law is no law so long as the question of its legality is to be decided by the State itself, for every law operating injuriously upon any local interest will be perhaps thought, and certainly represented, as unconstitutional, and, as has been shown, there is no appeal.

If this doctrine had been established at an earlier day, the Union would have been dissolved in its infancy. The excise law in Pennsylvania, the embargo and nonintercourse law in the Eastern States, the carriage tax in Virginia, were all deemed unconstitutional, and were more unequal in their operation than any of the laws now complained of; but, fortunately, none of those States discovered that they had the right now claimed by South Carolina. The war into which we were forced to support the dignity of the nation and the rights of our citizens might have ended in defeat and disgrace, instead of victory and honor, if the States who supposed it a ruinous and unconstitutional measure had thought they possessed the right of nullifying the act by which it was declared and denying supplies for its prosecution. Hardly and unequally as those measures bore upon several members of the Union, to the legislatures of none did this efficient and peaceable remedy, as it is called, suggest itself. The discovery of this important feature in our Constitution was reserved to the present day. To the statesmen of South Carolina belongs the invention, and upon the citizens of that State will unfortunately fall the evils of reducing it to practice.

If the doctrine of a State veto upon the laws of the Union carries with it internal evidence of its impracticable absurdity, our constitutional history will also afford abundant proof that it would have been repudiated with indignation had it been proposed to form a feature in our Government.

In our colonial state, although dependent on another power, we very early considered ourselves as connected by common interest with each other. Leagues were formed for common defense, and before the declaration of independence we were known in our aggregate character as *the United Colonies of America.* That decisive and important step was taken jointly. We declared ourselves a nation by a joint, not by several acts, and when the terms of our Confederation were reduced to form it was in that of a solemn league of several States, by which they agreed that they would collectively form one nation for the purpose of conducting some certain domestic concerns and all foreign relations. In the instrument forming that Union is found an article which declares that "every State shall abide by the determinations of Congress on all questions which by that Confederation should be submitted to them."

Under the Confederation, then, no State could legally annul a decision of the Congress or refuse to submit to its execution; but no provision was made to enforce these decisions. Congress made requisitions, but they were not complied with. The Government could not operate on individuals. They had no judiciary, no means of collecting revenue.

But the defects of the Confederation need not be detailed. Under its operation we could scarcely be called a nation. We had neither prosperity at home nor consideration abroad. This state of things could not be endured, and our present happy Constitution was formed, but formed in vain if this fatal doctrine prevails. It was formed for important objects that are announced in the preamble, made in the name and by the authority of the people of the United States, whose delegates framed and whose conventions approved it. The most important among these objects—that which is placed first in rank, on which all the others rest—is *"to form a more perfect union."* Now, is it possible that even if there were no express provision giving supremacy to the Constitution and laws of the United States over those of the States, can it be conceived that an instrument made for the purpose of *"forming a more perfect union"* than that of the Confederation could be so constructed by the assembled wisdom of our country as to substitute for that Confederation a form of government dependent for its existence on the local interest, the party spirit, of a State, or of a prevailing faction in a State? Every man of plain, unsophisticated understanding who hears the question will give such an answer as will preserve the Union. Metaphysical subtlety, in pursuit of an impracticable theory, could alone have devised one that is calculated to destroy it.

I consider, then, the power to annul a law of the United States, assumed by one State, *incompatible with the existence of the Union, contradicted expressly by the letter of the Constitution, unauthorized by its spirit, inconsistent with every principle on which it was founded, and destructive of the great object for which it was formed.*

After this general view of the leading principle, we must examine the particular application of it which is made in the ordinance.

The preamble rests its justification on these grounds: It assumes as a fact that the obnoxious laws, although they purport to be laws for raising revenue, were in reality intended for the protection of manufacturers, which purpose it asserts to be unconstitutional; that the operation of these laws is unequal; that the amount raised by them is greater than is required by the wants of the Government; and, finally, that the proceeds are to be applied to objects unauthorized by the Constitution. These are the only causes alleged to justify an open opposition to the laws of the country and a threat of seceding from the Union if any attempt should be made to enforce them. The first virtually acknowledges that the law in question was passed under a power expressly given by the Constitution to lay and collect imposts; but its constitutionality is drawn in question from the *motives* of those who passed it. However apparent this purpose may be in the present case, nothing can be more dangerous than to admit the position that an unconstitutional purpose entertained by the members who assent to a law enacted under a constitutional power shall make that law void. For how is that purpose to be ascertained? Who is to make the scrutiny? How often may bad purposes be falsely imputed, in how many cases are they concealed by false professions, in how many is no declaration of motive made? Admit this doctrine, and you give to the States an uncontrolled right to decide, and every law may be annulled under this pretext. If, therefore, the absurd and dangerous doctrine should be admitted that a State may annul an unconstitutional law, or one that it deems such, it will not apply to the present case.

The next objection is that the laws in question operate unequally. This objection may be made with truth to every law that has been or can be passed. The wisdom of man never yet contrived a system of taxation that would operate with perfect equality. If the unequal operation of a law makes it unconstitutional, and if all laws of that description may be abrogated by any State for that cause, then, indeed, is the Federal Constitution unworthy of the slightest effort for its preservation. We have hitherto relied on it as the perpetual bond of our Union; we have received it as the work of the assembled wisdom of the nation; we have trusted to it as to the sheet anchor of our safety in the stormy times of conflict with a foreign or domestic foe; we have looked to it with sacred awe as the palladium of our liberties, and with all the solemnities of religion have pledged to each other our lives and fortunes here and our hopes of happiness hereafter in its defense and support. Were we mistaken, my countrymen, in attaching this importance to the Constitution of our country? Was our devotion paid to the wretched, inefficient, clumsy contrivance which this new doctrine would make it? Did we pledge ourselves to the support of an airy nothing—a bubble that must be blown away by the first breath of disaffection? Was this self-destroying, visionary theory the work of the profound statesmen, the exalted patriots, to whom the task of constitutional reform was intrusted? Did the name of Washington sanction, did the States deliberately ratify, such an anomaly in the history of fundamental legislation? No; we were not mistaken. The letter of this great instrument is free from this radical fault. Its language directly contradicts the imputation; its spirit, its evident intent, contradicts it. No; we did not err. Our constitution does not contain the absurdity of giving power to make laws and another to resist them.

The sages whose memory will always be reverenced have given us a practical and, as they hoped, a permanent constitutional compact. The Father of his Country did not affix his revered name to so palpable an absurdity. Nor did the States, when they severally ratified it, do so under the impression that a veto on the laws of the United States was reserved to them or that they could exercise it by implication. Search the debates in all their conventions, examine the speeches of the most zealous opposers of Federal authority, look at the amendments that were proposed; they are all silent—not a syllable uttered, not a vote given, not a motion made to correct the explicit supremacy given to the laws of the Union over those of the States, or to show that implication, as is now contended, could defeat it. No; we have not erred. The Constitution is still the object of our reverence, the bond of our Union, our defense in danger, the source of our prosperity in peace. It shall descend, as we have received it, uncorrupted by sophistical construction, to our posterity; and the sacrifices of local interest, of State prejudices, of personal animosities, that were made to bring it into existence, will again be patriotically offered for its support.

The two remaining objections made by the ordinance to these laws are that the sums intended to be raised by them are greater than are required and that the proceeds will be unconstitutionally employed.

The Constitution has given, expressly, to Congress the right of raising revenue and of determining the sum the public exigencies will require. The States have no control over the exercise of this right other than that which results from the power of changing the representatives who abuse it, and thus procure redress. Congress may undoubtedly abuse this discretionary power; but the same may be said of others with which they are vested. Yet the discretion must exist somewhere. The Constitution has given it to the representatives of all the people, checked by the representatives of the States and by the Executive power. The South Carolina construction gives it to the legislature or the convention of a single State, where neither the people of the different States, nor the States in their separate capacity, nor the Chief Magistrate elected by the people have any representation. Which is the most discreet disposition of the power? I do not ask you, fellow-citizens, which is the constitutional disposition; that instrument speaks a language not to be misunderstood. But if you were assembled in general convention, which would you think the safest depository of this discretionary power in the last resort? Would you add a clause giving it to each of the States, or would you sanction the wise provisions already made by your Constitution? If this should be the result of your deliberations when providing for the future, are you, can you, be ready to risk all that we hold dear, to establish, for a temporary and a local purpose, that which you must acknowledge to be destructive, and even absurd, as a general provision? Carry out the consequences of this right vested in the different States, and you must perceive that the crisis your conduct presents at this day would recur whenever any law of the United States displeased any of the States, and that we should soon cease to be a nation.

The ordinance, with the same knowledge of the future that characterizes a former objection, tells you that the proceeds of the tax will be unconstitutionally applied. If this could be ascertained with certainty, the objection would with more propriety be reserved for the law so applying the proceeds, but surely can not be urged against the laws levying the duty.

These are the allegations contained in the ordinance. Examine them seriously, my fellow-citizens; judge for yourselves. I appeal to you to determine whether they are so clear, so convincing, as to leave no doubt of their correctness; and even if you should come to this conclusion, how far they justify the reckless, destructive course which you are directed to pursue. Review these objections and the conclusions drawn from them once more. What are they? Every law, then, for raising revenue, according to the South Carolina ordinance, may be rightfully annulled, unless it be so framed as no law ever will or can be framed. Congress have a right to pass laws for raising revenue and each State have a right to oppose their execution—two rights directly opposed to each other; and yet is this absurdity supposed to be contained in an instrument drawn for the express purpose of avoiding collisions between the States and the General Government by an assembly of the most enlightened statesmen and purest patriots ever embodied for a similar purpose.

In vain have these sages declared that Congress shall have power to lay and collect taxes, duties, imposts, and excises; in vain have they provided that they shall have power to pass laws which shall be necessary and proper to carry those powers into execution, that those laws and that Constitution shall be the "supreme law of the land, and that the judges in every State shall be bound thereby, anything in the constitution or laws of any State to the contrary notwithstanding;" in vain have the people of the several States solemnly sanctioned these provisions, made them their paramount law, and individually sworn to support them whenever they were called on to execute any office. Vain provisions! ineffectual restrictions! vile profanation of oaths! miserable mockery of legislation! if a bare majority of the voters in any one State may, on a real or supposed knowledge of the intent with which a law has been passed, declare themselves free from its operation;

say, here it gives too little; there, too much, and operates unequally; here it suffers articles to be free that ought to be taxed; there it taxes those that ought to be free; in this case the proceeds are intended to be applied to purposes which we do not approve; in that, the amount raised is more than is wanted. Congress, it is true, are invested by the Constitution with the right of deciding these questions according to their sound discretion. Congress is composed of the representatives of all the States and of all the people of all the States. But *we*, part of the people of one State, to whom the Constitution has given no power on the subject, from whom it has expressly taken it away; *we*, who have solemnly agreed that this Constitution shall be our law; *we*, most of whom have sworn to support it—*we* now abrogate this law and swear, and force others to swear, that it shall not be obeyed; and we do this not because Congress have no right to pass such laws—this we do not allege—but because they have passed them with improper views. They are unconstitutional from the motives of those who passed them, which we can never with certainty know; from their unequal operation, although it is impossible, from the nature of things, that they should be equal; and from the disposition which we presume may be made of their proceeds, although that disposition has not been declared. This is the plain meaning of the ordinance in relation to laws which it abrogates for alleged unconstitutionality. But it does not stop there. It repeals in express terms an important part of the Constitution itself and of laws passed to give it effect, which have never been alleged to be unconstitutional.

The Constitution declares that the judicial powers of the United States extend to cases arising under the laws of the United States, and that such laws, the Constitution, and treaties shall be paramount to the State constitutions and laws. The judiciary act prescribes the mode by which the case may be brought before a court of the United States by appeal when a State tribunal shall decide against this provision of the Constitution. The ordinance declares there shall be no appeal—makes the State law paramount to the Constitution and laws of the United States, forces judges and jurors to swear that they will disregard their provisions, and even makes it penal in a suitor to attempt relief by appeal. It further declares that it shall not be lawful for the authorities of the United States or of that State to enforce the payment of duties imposed by the revenue laws within its limits.

Here is a law of the United States, not even pretended to be unconstitutional, repealed by the authority of a small majority of the voters of a single State. Here is a provision of the Constitution which is solemnly abrogated by the same authority.

On such expositions and reasonings the ordinance grounds not only an assertion of the right to annul the laws of which it complains, but to enforce it by a threat of seceding from the Union if any attempt is made to execute them.

This right to secede is deduced from the nature of the Constitution, which, they say, is a compact between sovereign States who have preserved their whole sovereignty and therefore are subject to no superior; that because they made the compact they can break it when in their opinion it has been departed from by the other States. Fallacious as this course of reasoning is, it enlists State pride and finds advocates in the honest prejudices of those who have not studied the nature of our Government sufficiently to see the radical error on which it rests.

The people of the United States formed the Constitution, acting through the State legislatures in making the compact, to meet and discuss its provisions, and acting in separate conventions when they ratified those provisions; but the terms used in its construction show it to be a Government in which the people of all the States, collectively, are represented. We are *one people* in the choice of President and Vice-President. Here the States have no other agency than to direct the mode in which the votes shall be given. The candidates having the majority of all the votes are chosen. The electors of a majority of States may have given their votes for one candidate, and yet another may be chosen. The people, then, and not the States, are represented in the executive branch.

In the House of Representatives there is this difference, that the people of one State do not, as in the case of President and Vice-President, all vote for the same officers. The people of all the States do not vote for all the members, each State electing only its own representatives. But this creates no material distinction. When chosen, they are all representatives of the United States, not representatives of the particular State from which they come. They are paid by the United States, not by the State; nor are they accountable to it for any act done in the performance of their legislative functions; and however they may in practice, as it is their duty to do, consult and prefer the interests of their particular constituents when they come in conflict with any other partial or local interest, yet it is their first and highest duty, as representatives of the United States, to promote the general good.

The Constitution of the United States, then, forms a *government,* not a league; and whether it be formed by compact between the States or in any other manner, its character is the same. It is a Government in which all the people are represented, which operates directly on the people individually, not upon the States; they retained all the power they did not grant. But each State, having expressly parted with so many powers as to constitute, jointly with the other States, a single nation, can not, from that period, possess any right to secede, because such secession does not break a league, but destroys the unity of a nation; and any injury to that unity is not only a breach which would result from the contravention of a compact, but it is an offense against the whole Union. To say that any State may at pleasure secede from the Union is to say that the United States are not a nation, because it would be a solecism to contend that any part of a nation might dissolve its connection with the other parts, to their injury or ruin, without committing any offense. Secession, like any other revolutionary act, may be morally justified by the extremity of oppression; but to call it a constitutional right is confounding the meaning of terms, and can only be done through gross error or to deceive those who are willing to assert a right, but would pause before they made a revolution or incur the penalties consequent on a failure.

Because the Union was formed by a compact, it is said the parties to that compact may, when they feel themselves aggrieved, depart from it; but it is precisely because it is a compact that they can not. A compact is an agreement or binding obligation. It may by its terms have a sanction or penalty for its breach, or it may not. If it contains no sanction, it may be broken with no other consequence than moral guilt; if it have a sanction, then the breach incurs the designated or implied penalty. A league between independent nations generally has no sanction other than a moral one; or if it should contain a penalty, as there is no common superior it can not be enforced. A government, on the contrary, always has a sanction, express or implied; and in our case it is both necessarily implied and expressly given. An attempt, by force of arms, to destroy a government is an offense, by whatever means the constitutional compact may have been formed; and such government has the right by the law of self-defense to pass acts for punishing the offender, unless that right is modified, restrained, or resumed by the constitutional act. In our system, although it is modified in the case of treason, yet authority is expressly given to pass all laws necessary to carry its powers into effect, and under this grant provision has been made for punishing acts which obstruct the due administration of the laws.

It would seem superfluous to add anything to show the nature of that union which connects us, but as erroneous opinions on this subject are the foundation of doctrines the most destructive to our peace, I must give some further development to my views on this subject. No one, fellow-citizens, has a higher reverence for the reserved rights of the States than the Magistrate who now addresses you. No one would make greater personal sacrifices or official exertions to defend them from violation; but equal care must be taken to prevent, on their part, an improper interference with or resumption of the rights they have vested in the nation. The line has not been so distinctly drawn as to avoid doubts in some cases of the exercise of power. Men of the best intentions and soundest views may differ in their construction of some parts of the Constitution; but there are others on which dispassionate reflection can leave no doubt. Of this nature appears to be the assumed right of secession. It rests, as we have seen, on the alleged undivided sovereignty of the States and on their having formed in this sovereign capacity a compact which is called the Constitution, from which, because they made it, they have the right to secede. Both of these positions are erroneous, and some of the arguments to prove them so have been anticipated.

The States severally have not retained their entire sovereignty. It has been shown that in becoming parts of a nation, not members of a league, they surrendered many of their essential parts of sovereignty. The right to make treaties, declare war, levy taxes, exercise exclusive judicial and legislative powers, were all of them functions of sovereign power. The States, then, for all these important purposes were no longer sovereign. The allegiance of their citizens was transferred, in the first instance, to the Government of the United States; they became American citizens and owed obedience to the Constitution of the United States and to laws made in conformity with the powers it vested in Congress. This last position has not been and can not be denied. How, then, can that State be said to be sovereign and independent whose citizens owe obedience to laws not made by it and whose magistrates are sworn to disregard those laws when they come in conflict with those passed by another? What shows conclusively that the States can not be said to have reserved and undivided sovereignty is that they expressly ceded the right to punish treason—not treason against their separate power, but treason against the United States. Treason is an offense against *sovereignty,* and sovereignty must reside with the power to punish it. But the reserved rights of the States are not less sacred because they have, for their common interest, made the General Government the depository of these powers. The unity of our political character (as has been shown for another purpose) commenced with its very existence. Under the royal Government we had no separate character; our opposition to its oppressions began as *united colonies.* We were the *United States* under the Confederation, and the name was perpetuated and the Union rendered more perfect by the Federal Constitution. In none of these stages did we consider ourselves in any other light than as forming one nation. Treaties and alliances were made in the name of all. Troops were raised for the joint defense. How, then, with all these proofs that under all changes of our position we had, for designated purposes and with defined powers, created national governments, how is it that the most perfect of those several modes of union should now be considered as a mere league that may be dissolved at pleasure? It is from an abuse of terms. Compact is used as synonymous with league, although the true term is not employed, because it would at once show the fallacy of the reasoning. It would not do to say that our Constitution was only a league, but it is labored to prove it a compact (which in one sense it is) and then to argue that as a league is a compact every compact between nations must of course be a league, and that from such an engagement every sovereign power has a right to recede. But it has been shown that in this sense the States are not sovereign, and that even if they were, and the national Constitution had been formed by compact, there would be no right in any one State to exonerate itself from its obligations.

So obvious are the reasons which forbid this secession that it is necessary only to allude to them. The Union was formed for the benefit of all. It was produced by mutual sacrifices of interests and opinions. Can those sacrifices be recalled? Can the States who magnanimously surrendered their title to the territories of the West recall the grant? Will the inhabitants of the inland States agree to pay the duties that may be imposed without their assent by those on the Atlantic or the Gulf for their own benefit? Shall there be a free port in one State and onerous duties in another? No one believes that any right exists in a single State to involve all the others in these and countless other evils contrary to engagements solemnly made. Everyone must see that the other States, in self-defense, must oppose it at all hazards.

These are the alternatives that are presented by the convention—a repeal of all the acts for raising revenue, leaving the Government without the means of support, or an acquiescence in the dissolution of our Union by the secession of one of its members. When the first was proposed, it was known that it could not be listened to for a moment. It was known, if force was applied to oppose the execution of the laws, that it must be repelled by force; that Congress could not, without involving itself in disgrace and the country in ruin, accede to the proposition; and yet if this is not done in a given day, or if any attempt is made to execute the laws, the State is by the ordinance declared to be out of the Union. The majority of a convention assembled for the purpose have dictated these terms, or rather this rejection of all terms, in the name of the people of South Carolina. It is true that the governor of the State speaks of the submission of their grievances to a convention of all the States, which, he says, they "sincerely and anxiously seek and desire." Yet this obvious and constitutional mode of obtaining the sense of the other States on the construction of the federal compact, and amending it if necessary, has never been attempted by those who have urged the State on to this destructive measure. The State might have proposed the call for a general convention to the other States, and Congress, if a sufficient number of them concurred, must have called it. But the first magistrate of South Carolina, when he expressed a hope that "on a review by Congress and the functionaries of the General Government of the merits of the controversy" such a convention will be accorded to them, must have known that neither Congress nor any functionary of the General Government has authority to call such a convention unless it be demanded by two-thirds of the States. This suggestion, then, is another instance of the reckless inattention to the provisions of the Constitution with which this crisis has been madly hurried on, or of the attempt to persuade the people that a constitutional remedy had been sought and refused. If the legislature of South Carolina "anxiously desire" a general convention to consider their complaints, why have they not made application for it in the way the Constitution points out? The assertion that they "earnestly seek" it is completely negatived by the omission.

This, then, is the position in which we stand: A small majority of the citizens of one State in the Union have elected delegates to a State convention; that convention has ordained that all the revenue laws of the United States must be repealed, or that they are no longer a member of the Union. The governor of that State has recommended to the legislature the raising of an army to carry the secession into effect, and that he may be empowered to give clearances to vessels in the name of the State. No act of violent opposition to the laws has yet been committed, but such a state of things is hourly apprehended. And it is the intent of this instrument to *proclaim,* not only that the duty imposed on me by the Constitution "to take care that the laws be faithfully executed" shall be performed to the extent of the powers already vested in me by law, or of such others as the wisdom of Congress shall devise and intrust to me for that purpose, but to warn the citizens of South Carolina who have been deluded into an opposition to the laws of the danger they will incur by obedience to the illegal and disorganizing ordinance of the convention; to exhort those who have refused to support it to persevere in their determination to uphold the Constitution and laws of their country; and to point out to all the perilous situation into which the good people of that State have been led, and that the course they are urged to pursue is one of ruin and disgrace to the very State whose rights they affect to support.

Fellow-citizens of my native State, let me not only admonish you, as the First Magistrate of our common country, not to incur the penalty of its laws, but use the influence that a father would over his children whom he saw rushing to certain ruin. In that paternal language, with that paternal feeling, let me tell you, my countrymen, that you are deluded by men who are either deceived themselves or wish to deceive you. Mark under what pretenses you have been led on to the brink of insurrection and treason on which you stand. First, a diminution of the value of your staple commodity, lowered by overproduction in other quarters, and the consequent diminution in the value of your lands were the sole effect of the tariff laws. The effect of those laws was confessedly injurious, but the evil was greatly exaggerated by the unfounded theory you were taught to believe—that its burthens were in proportion to your exports, not to your consumption of imported articles. Your pride was roused by the assertion that a submission to those laws was a state of vassalage and that resistance to them was equal in patriotic merit to the opposition our fathers offered to the oppressive laws of Great Britain. You were told that this opposition might be peaceably, might be constitutionally, made; that you might enjoy all the advantages of the Union and bear none of its burthens. Eloquent appeals to your passions, to your State pride, to your native courage, to your sense of real injury, were used to prepare you for the period when the mask which concealed the hideous features of *disunion* should be taken off. It fell, and you were made to look with complacency on objects which not long since you would have regarded with horror. Look back to the arts which have brought you to this state; look forward to the consequences to which it must inevitably lead! Look back to what was first told you as an inducement to enter into this dangerous course. The great political truth was repeated to you that you had the revolutionary right of resisting all laws that were palpably unconstitutional and intolerably oppressive. It was added that the right to nullify a law rested on the same principle, but that it was a peaceable remedy. This character which was given to it made you receive with too much confidence the assertions that were made of the unconstitutionality of the law and its oppressive effects. Mark, my fellow-citizens, that by the admission of your leaders the unconstitutionality must be *palpable,* or it will not justify either resistance or nullification. What is the meaning of the word *palpable* in the sense in which it is here used? That which is apparent to everyone; that which no man of ordinary intellect will fail to perceive. Is the unconstitutionality of these laws of that description? Let those among your leaders who once approved and advocated the principle of protective duties answer the question; and let them choose whether they will be considered as incapable then of perceiving that which must have been apparent to every man of common understanding, or as imposing upon your confidence and endeavoring to mislead you now. In either case they are unsafe guides in the perilous path they urge you to tread. Ponder well on this circumstance, and you will know how to appreciate the exaggerated language they address to you. They are not champions of liberty, emulating the fame of our Revolutionary fathers, nor are you an oppressed people, contending, as they repeat to you, against worse than colonial vassalage. You are free members of a flourishing and happy Union. There is no settled design to oppress you. You have indeed felt the unequal operation of laws which may have been unwisely, not unconstitutionally, passed; but that inequality must necessarily be removed. At the very moment when you were madly urged on to the unfortunate course you have begun a change in public opinion had commenced. The nearly approaching payment of the public debt and the consequent necessity of a diminution of duties had already produced a considerable reduction, and that, too, on some articles of general consumption in your State. The importance of this change was underrated, and you were authoritatively told that no further alleviation of your burthens was to be expected at the very time when the condition of the country imperiously demanded such a modification of the duties as should reduce them to a just and equitable scale. But, as if apprehensive of the effect of this change in allaying your discontents, you were precipitated into the fearful state in which you now find yourselves.

I have urged you to look back to the means that were used to hurry you on to the position you have now assumed and forward to the consequences it will produce. Something more is necessary. Contemplate the condition of that country of which you still form an important part. Consider its Government, uniting in one bond of common interest and general protection so many different States, giving to all their inhabitants the proud title of *American citizen,* protecting their commerce, securing their literature and their arts, facilitating their intercommunication, defending their frontiers, and making their name respected in the remotest parts of the earth. Consider the extent of its territory, its increasing and happy population, its advance in arts which render life agreeable, and the sciences which elevate the mind! See education spreading the lights of religion, morality, and general information into every cottage in this wide extent of our Territories and States. Behold it as the asylum where the wretched and the oppressed find a refuge and support. Look on this picture of happiness and honor and say, *We too are citizens of America.* Carolina is one of these proud States; her arms have defended, her best blood has cemented, this happy Union. And then add, if you can, without horror and remorse, This happy Union we will dissolve; this picture of peace and prosperity we will deface; this free intercourse we will interrupt; these fertile fields we will deluge with blood; the protection of that glorious flag we renounce; the very name of Americans we discard. And for what, mistaken men? For what do you throw away these inestimable blessings? For what would you exchange your share in the advantages and honor of the Union? For the dream of a separate independence—a dream interrupted by bloody conflicts with your neighbors and a vile dependence on a foreign power. If your leaders could succeed in establishing a separation, what would be your situation? Are you united at home? Are you free from the apprehension of civil discord, with all its fearful consequences? Do our neighboring republics, every day suffering some new revolution or contending with some new insurrection, do they excite your envy? But the dictates of a high duty oblige me solemnly to announce that you can not succeed. The laws of the United States must be executed. I have no discretionary power on the subject; my duty is emphatically pronounced in the Constitution. Those who told you that you might peaceably prevent their execution deceived you; they could not have been deceived themselves. They know that a forcible opposition could alone prevent the execution of the laws, and they know that such opposition must be repelled. Their object is disunion. But be not deceived by names. Disunion by armed forces is *treason*. Are you really ready to incur its guilt? If you are, on the heads of the instigators of the act be the dreadful consequences; on their heads be the dishonor, but on yours may fall the punishment. On your unhappy State will inevitably fall all the evils of the conflict you force upon the Government of your country. It can not accede to the mad project of disunion, of which you would be the first victims. Its First Magistrate can not, if he would, avoid the performance of his duty. The consequences must be fearful for you, distressing to your fellow-citizens here and to the friends of good government throughout the world. Its enemies have beheld our prosperity with a vexation they could not conceal; it was a standing refutation of their slavish doctrines, and they will point to our discord with the triumph of malignant joy. It is yet in your power to disappoint them. There is yet time to show that the descendants of the Pinckneys, the Sumpters, the Rutledges, and of the thousand other names which adorn the pages of your Revolutionary history will not abandon that Union to support which so many of them fought and bled and died. I adjure you, as you honor their memory, as you love the cause of freedom, to which they dedicated their lives, as you prize the peace of your country, the lives of its best citizens, and your own fair fame, to retrace your steps. Snatch from the archives of your State the disorganizing edict of its convention; bid its members to reassemble and promulgate the decided expressions of your will to remain in the path which alone can conduct you to safety, prosperity, and honor. Tell them that compared to disunion all other evils are light, because that brings with it an accumulation of all. Declare that you will never take the field unless the star-spangled banner of your country shall float over you; that you will not be stigmatized when dead, and dishonored and scorned while you live, as the authors of the first attack on the Constitution of your country. Its destroyers you can not be. You may disturb its peace, you may interrupt the course of its prosperity, you may cloud its reputation for stability; but its tranquillity will be restored, its prosperity will return, and the stain upon its national character will be transferred and remain an eternal blot on the memory of those who caused the disorder.

Fellow-citizens of the United States, the threat of unhallowed disunion, the names of those once respected by whom it is uttered, the array of military force to support it, denote the approach of a crisis in our affairs on which the continuance of our unexampled prosperity, our political existence, and perhaps that of all free governments may depend. The conjuncture demanded a free, a full, and explicit enunciation, not only of my intentions, but of my principles of action; and as the claim was asserted of a right by a State to annul the laws of the Union, and even to secede from it at pleasure, a frank exposition of my opinions in relation to the origin and form of our Government and the construction I give to the instrument by which it was created seemed to be proper. Having the fullest confidence in the justness of the legal and constitutional opinion of my duties which has been expressed, I rely with equal confidence on your undivided support in my determination to execute the laws, to preserve the Union by all constitutional means, to arrest, if possible, by moderate and firm measures the necessity of a recourse to force; and if it be the will of Heaven that the recurrence of its primeval curse on man for the shedding of a brother's blood should fall upon our land, that it be not called down by any offensive act on the part of the United States.

Fellow-citizens, the momentous case is before you. On your undivided support of your Government depends the decision of the great question it involves—whether your sacred Union will be preserved and the blessing it secures to us as one people shall be perpetuated. No one can doubt that the unanimity with which that decision will be expressed will be such as to inspire new confidence in republican institutions, and that the prudence, the wisdom, and the courage which it will bring to their defense will transmit them unimpaired and invigorated to our children.

May the Great Ruler of Nations grant that the signal blessings with which He has favored ours may not, by the madness of party or personal ambition, be disregarded and lost; and may His wise providence bring those who have produced this crisis to see the folly before they feel the misery of civil strife, and inspire a returning veneration for that Union which, if we may dare to penetrate His designs, He has chosen as the only means of attaining the high destinies to which we may reasonably aspire.

In testimony whereof I have caused the Seal of the United States to be hereunto affixed, having signed the same with my hand.

Done at the city of Washington, this 10th day of December,
[SEAL]   A. D. 1832, and of the Independence of the United States the fifty-seventh.

ANDREW JACKSON

By the President:
EDW. LIVINGSTON,
Secretary of State

11

THE DECISION
TO STAY EUROPE'S HAND
IN NORTH AMERICA

Polk Reasserts the Monroe Doctrine

James K. Polk, the first "dark horse" in American political history, came to the Presidency at a moment when America's continental destiny seemed about to be decided. An ardent expansionist who made the right decisions at the right time, Polk's reputation suffered for decades from the Whig and antislavery interpretation of the Mexican War which colored our historical literature. George Bancroft, who was a member of Polk's cabinet, later assessed Polk's administration as "perhaps the greatest in our national history, certainly one of the greatest" when "viewed from the standpoint of results."

Polk's accomplishments were due in large measure to his readiness to exercise the Presidential power and his insistence on being the No. 1 man in his administration. To few Presidents have been vouchsafed that inflexible purpose to obtain clear-cut objectives which animated James K. Polk. On the day of his inauguration Polk told Bancroft, according to the latter's account of many years later, that he had four definite objectives: the reduction of the tariff, the re-establishment of the independent treasury, the settlement of the Oregon boundary, and the acquisition of California. It is a matter of record that Polk himself, in his Inaugural Address, declared these to be the main ends of his administration, and that the first three were accomplished with the cooperation of Congress before the end of the session, the fourth before the end of his term.

A dedicated President with no political ambitions beyond his term of office, Polk had serious limitations of personality which counterbalanced his integrity, backbone, and devotion to duty. Cold and suspicious by temperament, he seemed unprepared to find necessary relaxation from the strains of office through ordinary diversions and was devoid of the broad cultural interests of a Jefferson or a Wilson. Despite his unflagging patriotism, he lacked that strong moral and ethical impulse which animated Lincoln. A slaveowner himself, Polk recognized the dangers to the Union from the pressing of the slavery issue by extremists on either side, but no breath of criticism of the institution of slavery is found in any of his state papers. Essentially he was a states'-rights man, a strict constructionist of the Constitution in the Jeffersonian tradition. But his ardent expansionism and his belief in the mission of America, best summed up in the phrase "manifest destiny," stamp him as a political and intellectual heir of Andrew Jackson.

Polk's messages are scholarly and reasoned state papers. Points are often belabored at great length, yet the presentation eschews much of the rhetoric so dear to that generation. In his first annual message, one of his longest, Polk treated the Texas and Oregon issues in great detail and recommended both the adoption of the principle of ad valorem duties and the establishment of an independent Treasury. But the outstanding feature of his message was his reassertion of the Monroe Doctrine. Polk expanded the original doctrine, which was aimed at European colonization and armed intervention. He banned any European territorial aggrandizement in America by any method, even diplomatic intervention. This declaration, according to Dexter Perkins, a leading authority on the doctrine, is "second only in importance" to the original Monroe Doctrine. "It was the beginning of that historic process by which a principle of nonintervention has been transferred into a principle of intervention." Under this principle Polk in 1848 recommended the occupation of Yucatán in order to prevent European intervention in this Mexican state.

In his diary Polk recorded the favorable reactions of Congressmen who called upon him that evening. Regarding the parts dealing with Oregon, Mexico, and Texas, Senator Lewis Cass is reported to have told Polk, "You have struck out the true doctrine, you have cut the Gordian knot." David Wilmot, Democratic Congressman from Pennsylvania whose introduction of the "Wilmot Proviso" was to prove such an embarrassment to the administration, declared that "the doctrines on the tariff were the true doctrines" and that he would support them, while a fellow Pennsylvanian, Senator Simon Cameron, had a few reservations. "We Pennsylvanians," Polk quoted him as saying, "may scratch a little about the tariff but we will not quarrel about it," and he added, "we are well pleased with all the rest of the message."

The more significant portions of the first annual message follow:

FIRST ANNUAL MESSAGE

WASHINGTON, *December 2, 1845*

Fellow-Citizens of the Senate and House of Representatives:

In calling the attention of Congress to our relations with foreign powers, I am gratified to be able to state that though with some of them there have existed since your last session serious causes of irritation and misunderstanding, yet no actual hostilities have taken place. Adopting the maxim in the conduct of our foreign affairs "to ask nothing that is not right and submit to nothing that is wrong," it has been my anxious desire to preserve peace with all nations, but at the same time to be prepared to resist aggression and maintain all our just rights.

In pursuance of the joint resolution of Congress "for annexing Texas to the United States," my predecessor, on the 3d day of March, 1845, elected to submit the first and second sections of that resolution to the Republic of Texas as an overture on the part of the United States for her admission as a State into our Union. This election I approved, and accordingly the chargé d'affaires of the United States in Texas, under instructions of the 10th of March, 1845, presented these sections of the resolution for the acceptance of that Republic. The executive government, the Congress, and the people of Texas in convention have successively complied with all the terms and conditions of the joint resolution. A constitution for the government of the State of Texas, formed by a convention of deputies, is herewith laid before Congress. It is well known, also, that the people of Texas at the polls have accepted the terms of annexation and ratified the constitution. I communicate to Congress the correspondence between the Secretary of State and our chargé d'affaires in Texas, and also the correspondence of the latter with the authorities of Texas, together with the official documents transmitted by him to his own Government. The terms of annexation which were offered by the United States having been accepted by Texas, the public faith of both parties is solemnly pledged to the compact of their union. Nothing remains to consummate the event but the passage of an act by Congress to admit the State of Texas into the Union upon an equal footing with the original States. Strong reasons exist why this should be done at an early period of the session. It will be observed that by the constitution of Texas the existing government is only continued temporarily till Congress can act, and that the third Monday of the present month is the day appointed for holding the first general election. On that day a governor, a lieutenant-governor, and both branches of the legislature will be chosen by the people. The President of Texas is required, immediately after the receipt of official information that the new State has been admitted into our Union by Congress, to convene the legislature, and upon its meeting the existing government will be superseded and the State government organized. Questions deeply interesting to Texas, in common with the other States, the extension of our revenue laws and judicial system over her people and territory, as well as measures of a local character, will claim the early attention of Congress, and therefore upon every principle of republican government she ought to be represented in that body without unnecessary delay. I can not too earnestly recommend prompt action on this important subject. As soon as the act to admit Texas as a State shall be passed the union of the two Republics will be consummated by their own voluntary consent.

This accession to our territory has been a bloodless achievement. No arm of force has been raised to produce the result. The sword has had no part in the victory. We have not sought to extend our territorial possessions by conquest, or our republican institutions over a reluctant people. It was the deliberate homage of each people to the great principle of our federative union. If we consider the extent of territory involved in the annexation, its prospective influence on America, the means by which it has been accomplished, springing purely from the choice of the people themselves to share the blessings of our union, the history of the world may be challenged to furnish a parallel. The jurisdiction of the United States, which at the formation of the Federal Constitution was bounded by the St. Marys on the Atlantic, has passed the capes of Florida and been peacefully extended to the Del Norte. In contemplating the grandeur of this event it is not to be forgotten that the result was achieved in despite of the diplomatic interference of European monarchies. Even France, the country which had been our ancient ally, the country which has a common interest with us in maintaining the freedom of the seas, the country which, by the cession of Louisiana, first opened to us access to the Gulf of Mexico, the country with which we have been every year drawing more and more closely the bonds of successful commerce, most unexpectedly, and to our unfeigned regret, took part in an effort to prevent annexation and to impose on Texas, as a condition of the recognition of her independence by Mexico, that she would never join herself to the United States. We may rejoice that the tranquil and pervading influence of the American principle of self-government was sufficient to defeat the purposes of British and French interference, and that the almost unanimous voice of the people of Texas has given to that interference a peaceful and effective rebuke. From this example European Governments may learn how vain diplomatic arts and intrigues must ever prove upon this continent against that system of self-government which seems natural to our soil, and which will ever resist foreign interference.

Toward Texas I do not doubt that a liberal and generous spirit will actuate Congress in all that concerns her interests and prosperity, and that she will never have cause to regret that she has united her "lone star" to our glorious constellation. . . .

Oregon is a part of the North American continent, to which, it is confidently affirmed, the title of the United States is the best now in existence. For the grounds on which that title rests I refer you to the correspondence of the late and present Secretary of State with the British plenipotentiary during the negotiation. The British proposition of compromise, which would make the Columbia the line south of 49°, with a trifling addition of detached territory to the United States north of that river, and would leave on the British side two-thirds of the whole Oregon Territory, including the free navigation of the Columbia and all the valuable harbors on the Pacific, can never for a moment be entertained by the United States without an abandonment of their just and clear territorial rights, their own self-respect, and the national honor. For the information of Congress, I communicate herewith the correspondence which took place between the two Governments during the late negotiation.

The rapid extension of our settlements over our territories heretofore unoccupied, the addition of new States to our Confederacy, the expansion of free principles, and our rising greatness as a nation are attracting the attention of the powers of Europe, and lately the doctrine has been broached in some of them of a "balance of power" on this continent to check our advancement. The United States, sincerely desirous of preserving relations of good understanding with all nations, can not in silence permit any European interference on the North American continent, and should any such interference be attempted will be ready to resist it at any and all hazards.

It is well known to the American people and to all nations that this Government has never interfered with the relations subsisting between other governments. We have never made ourselves parties to their wars or their alliances; we have not sought their territories by conquest; we have not mingled with parties in their domestic struggles; and believing our own form of government to be the best, we have never attempted to propagate it by intrigues, by diplomacy, or by force. We may claim on this continent a like execution from European interference. The nations of America are equally sovereign and independent with those of Europe. They possess the same rights, independent of all foreign interposition, to make war, to conclude peace, and to regulate their internal affairs. The people of the United States can not, therefore, view with indifference attempts of European powers to interfere with the independent action of the nations on this continent. The American system of government is entirely different from that of Europe. Jealousy among the different sovereigns of Europe, lest any one of them might become too powerful for the rest, has caused them anxiously to desire the establishment of what they term the "balance of power." It can not be permitted to have any application on the North American continent, and especially to the United States. We must ever maintain the principle that the people of this continent alone have the right to decide their own destiny. Should any portion of them, constituting an independent state, propose to unite themselves with our Confederacy, this will be a question for them and us to determine without any foreign interposition. We can never consent that European powers shall interfere to prevent such a union because it might disturb the "balance of power" which they may desire to maintain upon this continent. Near a quarter of a century ago the principle was distinctly announced to the world, in the annual message of one of my predecessors, that—"The American continents, by the free and independent condition which they have assumed and maintain, are henceforth not to be considered as subjects for future colonization by any European powers."

This principle will apply with greatly increased force should any European power attempt to establish any new colony in North America. In the existing circumstances of the world the present is deemed a proper occasion to reiterate and reaffirm the principle avowed by Mr. Monroe and to state my cordial concurrence in its wisdom and sound policy. The reassertion of this principle, especially in reference to North America, is at this day but the promulgation of a policy which no European power should cherish the disposition to resist. Existing rights of every European nation should be respected, but it is due alike to our safety and our interests that the efficient protection of our laws should be extended over our whole territorial limits, and that it should be distinctly announced to the world as our settled policy that no future European colony or dominion shall with our consent be planted or established on any part of the North American continent.

12

THE DECISION
TO GO TO WAR WITH MEXICO

*Polk Charges Mexico with Having "Shed American Blood
upon the American Soil"*

The man who led this country into one of the most spectacular wars in
American history was neither passionate nor impetuous. President
Polk, as a contemporary remarked, "never dreamed of any other war
than a war upon the Whigs." Implacable in his determination to secure
California for the Union, he preferred negotiation to force, but was
prepared to go to war if he could not obtain this objective otherwise.
For the mission to Mexico he picked a states'-rights Democrat from
Louisiana named John Slidell (later to be a Confederate commissioner
to England), and authorized him to pay as much as twenty-five million
dollars for Mexico's claims north of the Rio Grande and including California. When Slidell's efforts proved fruitless, Polk ordered General
Zachary Taylor to move his troops south of the Nueces River to the Rio
Grande, on territory disputed by Mexico and Texas. On April 25, 1846,
a force of 1,600 Mexicans crossed the Rio Grande, and killed or captured a detachment of sixty-three American dragoons, who had ridden
into a trap.

Polk recorded in his diary that at a Cabinet meeting on May 9 he
announced that, despite the absence of news of an "open act of aggression by the Mexican army," the United States had ample cause for war,
and that he thought it was his "duty to send a message to Congress very
soon and recommend definite measures." When polled, the entire Cabinet save Bancroft, Secretary of the Navy, favored Polk's sending a war
message to Congress on May 12. Bancroft agreed that "if any act of
hostility should be committed by the Mexican forces" he would then
be "in favour of immediate war." News of the attack on Taylor's
dragoons reached the White House at 6 P.M. that evening. The Cabinet

was promptly reconvened and unanimously favored a war message to be sent to Congress on Monday, May 11.

In the light of this decision, made in advance of the news of Mexican provocation, Polk's famous message announcing that Mexico had commenced hostilities "and shed American blood upon the American soil" won him the opprobrious title of "Polk the Mendacious." Whether the territory between the Nueces and the Rio Grande, where this act of war took place, was actually United States territory is a moot question. Even granting that Taylor's move to the Rio Grande was defensive, there is no question that in cutting the river and preventing supplies from reaching the Mexican forces Taylor had committed a provocative act. However, even to a man of less fixed purpose than Polk negotiations with Mexico would have proved exceedingly exasperating.

Polk's conduct immediately prior to the Mexican War raises a question as to whether the President is under a constitutional obligation not to risk war without first consulting Congress and obtaining its consent to his diplomatic and military policies. Justifying his vote for the Ashmun resolution of censure, which declared that the President had "unconstitutionally" begun war with Mexico, Abraham Lincoln, then a Whig member of Congress, wrote William H. Herndon at the time:

> Let me first state what I understand to be your position. It is that if it shall become necessary to repel invasion, the President may, without violation of the Constitution, cross the line and invade the territory of another country, and that whether such necessity exists in any given case the President is the sole judge. . . . Allow the President to invade a neighboring nation whenever he shall deem it necessary to repel an invasion and you allow him to do so whenever he may choose to say he deems it necessary for such purpose, and you allow him to make war at pleasure.

This was not the last time this issue was to be raised against a war President. Lincoln, Wilson, Franklin D. Roosevelt, and Harry S. Truman were similarly attacked.

True, there was some justice in the harsh criticism of Polk by the anti-expansionists, but there is also a good deal of evidence to support the President's conclusion in his war message that "the cup of forebearance had been exhausted even before the recent information from the frontier of the Del Norte." It had proved impossible to negotiate with the weak and chaotic government below the Rio Grande, and the atmosphere on both sides of the Texas-Mexican border was inflammatory. "We have more than enough strength to make war. Let us make it, then, and victory will perch upon our banners," proclaimed a leading Mexican newspaper.

Conducting a war of such dimensions and so remote from the seat of government would have tested the talents of any Chief Executive, but Polk was equal to the task. As the commander-in-chief he had the exasperating job of keeping a checkrein on two generals, prima donnas in their own right with grand political aspirations. After keeping "Old Fuss and Feathers" Winfield Scott at home until late in 1846, Polk, dissatisfied with "Old Rough and Ready" Zachary Taylor's insufficiently aggressive tactics and alarmed at his burgeoning Presidential aspirations, stripped him of his infantry and dispatched Scott on an expedition to capture Mexico City, a military exploit unrivaled since the days of Hernando Cortez. In California he had a mutinous general on his hands—John C. Frémont, who happened to have as his father-in-law Thomas Hart Benton, a foremost politician. Making the peace proved even harder than winning the war. A pompous clerk in the State Department named Nicholas P. Trist, who was entrusted with the peace negotiations, started his own private war with Winfield Scott. Then, defying an order to return to Washington, Trist went ahead and wrote a peace treaty with Mexico, which everybody accepted but nobody quite liked—as one disgruntled Whig put it, "the treaty negotiated by an unauthorized agent, with an unacknowledged government, submitted by an accidental President to a dissatisfied Senate."

"Mr. Polk's War" made the United States a great continental power, but it brought in its wake a host of evils—the specter of slavery extension, sectional strife, party disruption, and, finally, civil war. "The United States will conquer Mexico," Ralph Waldo Emerson prophesied, "but it will be as the man who swallows the arsenic which brings him down in turn. Mexico will poison us."

SPECIAL MESSAGE

WASHINGTON, *May 11, 1846*

To the Senate and House of Representatives:

The existing state of the relations between the United States and Mexico renders it proper that I should bring the subject to the consideration of Congress. In my message at the commencement of your present session the state of these relations, the causes which led to the suspension of diplomatic intercourse between the two countries in March, 1845, and the long-continued and unredressed wrongs and injuries committed by the Mexican Government on citizens of the United States in their persons and property were briefly set forth.

As the facts and opinions which were then laid before you were carefully considered, I can not better express my present convictions of the condition of affairs up to that time than by referring you to that communication.

The strong desire to establish peace with Mexico on liberal and honorable terms, and the readiness of this Government to regulate and adjust our boundary and other causes of difference with that power on such fair and equitable principles as would lead to permanent relations of the most friendly nature, induced me in September last to seek the reopening of diplomatic relations between the two countries. Every measure adopted on our part had for its object the furtherance of these desired results. In communicating to Congress a succinct statement of the injuries which we had suffered from Mexico, and which have been accumulating during a period of more than twenty years, every expression that could tend to inflame the people of Mexico or defeat or delay a pacific result was carefully avoided. An envoy of the United States repaired to Mexico with full powers to adjust every existing difference. But though present on the Mexican soil by agreement between the two Governments, invested with full powers, and bearing evidence of the most friendly dispositions, his mission has been unavailing. The Mexican Government not only refused to receive him or listen to his propositions, but after a long-continued series of menaces have at last invaded our territory and shed the blood of our fellow-citizens on our own soil.

It now becomes my duty to state more in detail the origin, progress, and failure of that mission. In pursuance of the instructions given in September last, an inquiry was made on the 13th of October, 1845, in the most friendly terms, through our consul in Mexico, of the minister for foreign affairs, whether the Mexican Government "would receive an envoy from the United States intrusted with full powers to adjust all the questions in dispute between the two Governments," with the assurance that "should the answer be in the affirmative such an envoy would be immediately dispatched to Mexico." The Mexican minister on the 15th of October gave an affirmative answer to this inquiry, requesting at the same time that our naval force at Vera Cruz might be withdrawn, lest its continued presence might assume the appearance of menace and coercion pending the negotiations. This force was immediately withdrawn. On the 10th of November, 1845, Mr. John Slidell, of Louisiana, was commissioned by me an envoy extraordinary and minister plenipotentiary of the United States to Mexico, and was intrusted with full powers to adjust both the questions of the Texas boundary and of indemnification to our citizens. The redress of the wrongs of our citizens naturally and inseparably blended itself with the question of boundary. The settlement of the one question in any correct view of the subject involves that of the other. I could not for a moment entertain the idea that the claims of our much-injured and long-suffering citizens, many of which had existed for more than twenty years, should be postponed or separated from the settlement of the boundary question.

Mr. Slidell arrived at Vera Cruz on the 30th of November, and was courteously received by the authorities of that city. But the Government of General Herrera was then tottering to its fall. The revolutionary party had seized upon the Texas question to effect or hasten its overthrow. Its determination to restore friendly relations with the United States, and to receive our minister to negotiate for the settlement of this question, was violently assailed, and was made the great theme of denunciation against it. The Government of General Herrera, there is good reason to believe, was sincerely desirous to receive our minister; but it yielded to the storm raised by its enemies, and on the 21st of December refused to accredit Mr. Slidell upon the most frivolous pretexts. These are so fully and ably exposed in the note of Mr. Slidell of the 24th of December last to the Mexican minister of foreign relations, herewith transmitted, that I deem it unnecessary to enter into further detail on this portion of the subject.

Five days after the date of Mr. Slidell's note General Herrera yielded the Government to General Paredes without a struggle, and on the 30th of December resigned the Presidency. This revolution was accomplished solely by the army, the people having taken little part in the contest; and thus the supreme power in Mexico passed into the hands of a military leader.

Determined to leave no effort untried to effect an amicable adjustment with Mexico, I directed Mr. Slidell to present his credentials to the Government of General Paredes and ask to be officially received by him. There would have been less ground for taking this step had General Paredes come into power by a regular constitutional succession. In that event his administration would have been considered but a mere constitutional continuance of the Government of General Herrera, and the refusal of the latter to receive our minister would have been deemed conclusive unless an intimation had been given by General Paredes of his desire to reverse the decision of his predecessor. But the Government of General Paredes owes its existence to a military revolution, by which the subsisting constitutional authorities had been subverted. The form of government was entirely changed, as well as all the high functionaries by whom it was administered.

Under these circumstances, Mr. Slidell, in obedience to my direction, addressed a note to the Mexican minister of foreign relations, under date of the 1st of March last, asking to be received by that Government in the diplomatic character to which he had been appointed. This minister in his reply, under date of the 12th of March, reiterated the arguments of his predecessor, and in terms that may be considered as giving just grounds of offense to the Government and people of the United States denied the application of Mr. Slidell. Nothing therefore remained for our envoy but to demand his passports and return to his own country.

Thus the Government of Mexico, though solemnly pledged by official acts in October last to receive and accredit an American envoy, violated their plighted faith and refused the offer of a peaceful adjustment of our difficulties. Not only was the offer rejected, but the indignity of its rejection was enhanced by the manifest breach of faith in refusing to admit the envoy who came because they had bound themselves to receive him. Nor can it be said that the offer was fruitless from the want of opportunity of discussing it; our envoy was present on their own soil. Nor can it be ascribed to a want of sufficient powers; our envoy had full powers to adjust every question of difference. Nor was there room for complaint that our propositions for settlement were unreasonable; permission was not even given our envoy to make any proposition whatever. Nor can it be objected that we, on our part, would not listen to any reasonable terms of their suggestion; the Mexican Government refused all negotiation, and have made no proposition of any kind.

In my message at the commencement of the present session I informed you that upon the earnest appeal both of the Congress and convention of Texas I had ordered an efficient military force to take a position "between the Nueces and the Del Norte." This had become necessary to meet a threatened invasion of Texas by the Mexican forces, for which extensive military preparations had been made. The invasion was threatened solely because Texas had determined, in accordance with a solemn resolution of the Congress of the United States, to annex herself to our Union, and under these circumstances it was plainly our duty to extend our protection over her citizens and soil.

This force was concentrated at Corpus Christi, and remained there until after I had received such information from Mexico as rendered it probable, if not certain, that the Mexican Government would refuse to receive our envoy.

Meantime Texas, by the final action of our Congress, had become an integral part of our Union. The Congress of Texas, by its act of December 19, 1836, had declared the Rio del Norte to be the boundary of that Republic. Its jurisdiction had been extended and exercised beyond the Nueces. The country between that river and the Del Norte had been represented in the Congress and in the convention of Texas, had thus taken part in the act of annexation itself, and is now included within one of our Congressional districts. Our own Congress had, moreover, with great unanimity, by the act approved December 31, 1845, recognized the country beyond the Nueces as a part of our territory by including it within our own revenue system, and a revenue officer to reside within that district has been appointed by and with the advice and consent of the Senate. It became, therefore, of urgent necessity to provide for the defense of that portion of our country. Accordingly, on the 13th of January last instructions were issued to the general in command of these troops to occupy the left bank of the Del Norte. This river, which is the southwestern boundary of the State of Texas, is an exposed frontier. From this quarter invasion was threatened; upon it and in its immediate vicinity, in the judgment of high military experience, are the proper stations for the protecting forces of the Government. In addition to this important consideration, several others occurred to induce this movement. Among these are the facilities afforded by the ports at Brazos Santiago and the mouth of the Del Norte for the reception of supplies by sea, the stronger and more healthful military positions, the convenience for obtaining a ready and a more abundant supply of provisions, water, fuel, and forage, and the advantages which are afforded by the Del Norte in forwarding supplies to such posts as may be established in the interior and upon the Indian frontier.

The movement of the troops to the Del Norte was made by the commanding general under positive instructions to abstain from all aggressive acts toward Mexico or Mexican citizens and to regard the relations between that Republic and the United States as peaceful unless she should declare war or commit acts of hostility indicative of a state of war. He was specially directed to protect private property and respect personal rights.

The Army moved from Corpus Christi on the 11th of March, and on the 28th of that month arrived on the left bank of the Del Norte opposite to Matamoras, where it encamped on a commanding position, which has since been strengthened by the erection of fieldworks. A depot has also been established at Point Isabel, near the Brazos Santiago, 30 miles in rear of the encampment. The selection of his position was necessarily confided to the judgment of the general in command.

The Mexican forces at Matamoras assumed a belligerent attitude, and on the 12th of April General Ampudia, then in command, notified General Taylor to break up his camp within twenty-four hours and to retire beyond the Nueces River, and in the event of his failure to comply with these demands announced that arms, and arms alone, must decide the question. But no open act of hostility was committed until the 24th of April. On that day General Arista, who had succeeded to the command of the Mexican forces, communicated to General Taylor that "he considered hostilities commenced and should prosecute them." A party of dragoons of 63 men and officers were on the same day dispatched from the American camp up the Rio del Norte, on its left bank, to ascertain whether the Mexican troops had crossed or were preparing to cross the river, "became engaged with a large body of these troops, and after a short affair, in which some 16 were killed and wounded, appear to have been surrounded and compelled to surrender."

The grievous wrongs perpetrated by Mexico upon our citizens throughout a long period of years remain unredressed, and solemn treaties pledging her public faith for this redress have been disregarded. A government either unable or unwilling to enforce the execution of such treaties fails to perform one of its plainest duties.

Our commerce with Mexico has been almost annihilated. It was formerly highly beneficial to both nations, but our merchants have been deterred from prosecuting it by the system of outrage and extortion which the Mexican authorities have pursued against them, whilst their appeals through their own Government for indemnity have been made in vain. Our forebearance has gone to such an extreme as to be mistaken in its character. Had we acted with vigor in repelling the insults and redressing the injuries inflicted by Mexico at the commencement, we should doubtless have escaped all the difficulties in which we are now involved.

Instead of this, however, we have been exerting our best efforts to propitiate her good will. Upon the pretext that Texas, a nation as independent as herself, thought proper to unite its destinies with our own she has affected to believe that we have severed her rightful territory, and in official proclamations and manifestoes has repeatedly threatened to make war upon us for the purpose of reconquering Texas. In the meantime we have tried every effort at reconciliation. The cup of forbearance had been exhausted even before the recent information from the frontier of the Del Norte. But now, after reiterated menaces, Mexico has passed the boundary of the United States, has invaded our territory and shed American blood upon the American soil. She has proclaimed that hostilities have commenced, and that the two nations are now at war.

As war exists, and, notwithstanding all our efforts to avoid it, exists by the act of Mexico herself, we are called upon by every consideration of duty and patriotism to vindicate with decision the honor, the rights, and the interests of our country.

Anticipating the possibility of a crisis like that which has arrived, instructions were given in August last, "as a precautionary measure" against invasion or threatened invasion, authorizing General Taylor, if the emergency required, to accept volunteers, not from Texas only, but from the States of Louisiana, Alabama, Mississippi, Tennessee, and Kentucky, and corresponding letters were addressed to the respective governors of those States. These instructions were repeated, and in January last, soon after the incorporation of "Texas into our Union of States," General Taylor was further "authorized by the President to make a requisition upon the executive of that State for such of its militia force as may be needed to repel invasion or to secure the country against apprehended invasion." On the 2d day of March he was again reminded, "in the event of the approach of any considerable Mexican force, promptly and efficiently to use the authority with which he was clothed to call to him such auxiliary force as he might need." War actually existing and our territory having been invaded, General Taylor, pursuant to authority vested in him by my direction, has called on the governor of Texas for four regiments of State troops, two to be mounted and two to serve on foot, and on the governor of Louisiana for four regiments of infantry to be sent to him as soon as practicable.

In further vindication of our rights and defense of our territory, I invoke the prompt action of Congress to recognize the existence of the war, and to place at the disposition of the Executive the means of prosecuting the war with vigor, and thus hastening the restoration of peace. To this end I recommend that authority should be given to call into the public service a large body of volunteers to serve for not less than six or twelve months unless sooner discharged. A volunteer force is beyond question more efficient than any other description of citizen soldiers, and it is not to be doubted that a number far beyond that required would readily rush to the field upon the call of their country. I further recommend that a liberal provision be made for sustaining our entire military force and furnishing it with supplies and munitions of war.

The most energetic and prompt measures and the immediate appearance in arms of a large and overpowering force are recommended to Congress as the most certain and efficient means of bringing the existing collision with Mexico to a speedy and successful termination.

In making these recommendations I deem it proper to declare that it is my anxious desire not only to terminate hostilities speedily, but to bring all matters in dispute between this Government and Mexico to an early and amicable adjustment; and in this view I shall be prepared to renew negotiations whenever Mexico shall be ready to receive propositions or to make propositions of her own.

I transmit herewith a copy of the correspondence between our envoy to Mexico and the Mexican minister for foreign affairs, and so much of the correspondence between that envoy and the Secretary of State and between the Secretary of War and the general in command on the Del Norte as is necessary to a full understanding of the subject.

WASHINGTON, *May 12, 1846*

To the Senate and House of Representatives:

I herewith transmit to Congress a copy of a communication * from the officer commanding the Army in Texas, with the papers which accompanied it. They were received by the Southern mail of yesterday, some hours after my message of that date had been transmitted, and are of a prior date to one of the communications from the same officer which accompanied that message.

JAMES K. POLK

---

* Relating to the operations of the Army near Matamoras, Mexico.

13

THE DECISION
TO POSTPONE THE SECTIONAL SHOWDOWN

Fillmore Advocates the Compromise of 1850

In history texts the thirteenth President of the United States usually rates just a few lines. Millard Fillmore, Chief Executive by accident, is generally characterized as a colorless New York Whig, a neutral mediocrity. But Fillmore was not only a man of personal integrity, dignity, suave manners, and conciliatory temper; he possessed a considerable measure of courage, coolness, and balance. Keeping his head at a time of crisis, his decision helped postpone the final showdown between North and South.

The year 1850 was a critical year in American history. The sectional conflict was now at fever heat. Both sides, free and slave, were determined to preserve a political balance between the sections, but that balance was menaced by the acquisition of new territories in the war with Mexico. A compromise had been effected in 1820, and it had worked for thirty years. Now Henry Clay came up with a new bundle of compromises to preserve the sectional balance. The cluster of resolutions which he offered in the Senate provided for (1) the admission of California as a free state; (2) the organization, without restriction on slavery, of New Mexico as a territory, including the adjustment of the Texas-New Mexico boundary, and the payment by the United States to Texas of ten million dollars in return for the abandonment by Texas of all claims to New Mexico territory; (3) the establishment of a territorial government for Utah, without restriction on slavery; (4) the fugitive slave act, providing machinery for the arrest and return to their owners of runaway slaves; and (5) an act abolishing the slave trade in the District of Columbia.

These compromise proposals inspired the Great Debate, most searching and eloquent in American politics, and marked the last meeting of the Senatorial triumvirate of Calhoun, Clay, and Webster. The South Carolinian, enfeebled by his final illness, had his speech opposing the Compromise read by Senator James M. Mason. He warned against continuing the slavery agitation, and advocated a constitutional amendment restoring "to the South, in substance, the power she possessed of protecting herself before the equilibrium between the sections was destroyed by the action of this government." Three days later, on the seventh of March, Webster made the most eloquent plea in support of the Compromise, speaking "not as a Massachusetts man, nor as a Northern man, but as an American," and for the preservation of the Union. " 'Hear me for my cause,' " he pleaded. But the radical Whigs, like the diehard Democrats, opposed the Compromise, though for completely different reasons. Senator Seward of New York attacked it as "radically wrong and essentially vicious," and Seward's arguments carried enormous weight with the old President Zachary Taylor. The general had come to Washington with Southern sympathies, but was now satisfied that the purposes of the South were revolutionary, if not treasonable. He prepared a message to Congress asserting that he would never permit Texas to seize any part of New Mexico's rightful area, and avowing that he would protect New Mexico to the last extremity.

Taylor's message was never sent to Congress. On July 9 he died of cholera morbus and typhoid fever. Fillmore's succession was a crushing blow to his enemies, the radical Whig faction of Seward and Thurlow Weed. How Fillmore would stand on the Compromise should not have been a secret. When he called on Taylor in July, shortly before the President's death, he informed him, according to his own later account, "that from present appearances, I might be called upon to give a casting vote in the Senate on the Compromise Bill and if I should feel it my duty to vote for it, as I might, I wished him to understand that it was not out of any hostility to him or his Administration, but the vote would be given because I deemed it for the best interests of the country." Within forty-eight hours after Taylor's death, Webster was rejoicing over the turn of events. "I believe Mr. Fillmore favors the compromise," he wrote, "and there is no doubt that recent events have increased the probability of the passage of that measure."

By early August the issue hung precariously in the balance. On August 1 the bill for the admission of California had precipitated a stormy debate on slavery and disunion. Clay carried the brunt of the fight for the bill, but, exhausted by his strenuous labors, he left for Newport to recuperate. The leadership of the pro-Compromise forces was assumed by Senator Stephen A. Douglas of Illinois. The administration now threw its whole weight into the settlement of the issues. In a message to Congress on August 6 President Fillmore urged the propriety and expediency of indemnifying Texas for the surrender of her claims upon New Mexico and added a plea for the adjustment of all outstanding controversies.

Fillmore's message was decisive in persuading Congress, notably the Northern Whigs, to take the first step toward the adoption of the Great Compromise, every part of which passed by decisive majorities. Senator Chase estimated that the message won over six New England senators. Horace Mann was bitter at the unexpected turn of affairs. "Here are twenty, perhaps thirty, men from the North in this House, who, before General Taylor's death, would have sworn, like St. Paul, not to eat or drink until they had voted the proviso, who now, in the face of the world, turn about, defy the instructions of their States, take back their own declarations, a thousand times uttered, and vote against it."

"I can now sleep of nights," Daniel Webster wrote to a friend. Webster, Clay, and Douglas, with President Fillmore's decisive help, had avoided the showdown with the slave states for which old Zachary Taylor had seemed assuredly headed. Had it not been for the change in the Chief Executive it is not inconceivable that secession would have come a decade earlier than it did. Had it come in 1850 the North would have lacked the wise and inspirational leadership of Lincoln, a leadership which preserved the Union.

SPECIAL MESSAGE

WASHINGTON, *August 6, 1850*

To the Senate and House of Representatives:

I herewith transmit to the two Houses of Congress a letter from his excellency the governor of Texas, dated on the 14th day of June last, addressed to the late President of the United States, which, not having been answered by him, came to my hands on his death; and I also transmit a copy of the answer which I have felt it to be my duty to cause to be made to that communication.

Congress will perceive that the governor of Texas officially states that by authority of the legislature of that State he dispatched a special commissioner with full power and instructions to extend the civil jurisdiction of the State over the unorganized counties of El Paso, Worth, Presidio, and Santa Fe, situated on its northwestern limits.

He proceeds to say that the commissioner had reported to him in an official form that the military officers employed in the service of the United States stationed at Santa Fe interposed adversely with the inhabitants to the fulfillment of his object in favor of the establishment of a separate State government east of the Rio Grande, and within the rightful limits of the State of Texas. These four counties, which Texas thus proposes to establish and organize as being within her own jurisdiction, extend over the whole of the territory east of the Rio Grande, which has heretofore been regarded as an essential and integral part of the department of New Mexico, and actually governed and possessed by her people until conquered and severed from the Republic of Mexico by the American arms.

The legislature of Texas has been called together by her governor for the purpose, as is understood, of maintaining her claim to the territory east of the Rio Grande and of establishing over it her own jurisdiction and her own laws by force.

These proceedings of Texas may well arrest the attention of all branches of the Government of the United States, and I rejoice that they occur while the Congress is yet in session. It is, I fear, far from being impossible that, in consequence of these proceedings of Texas, a crisis may be brought on which shall summon the two Houses of Congress, and still more emphatically the executive government, to an immediate readiness for the performance of their respective duties.

By the Constitution of the United States the President is constituted Commander in Chief of the Army and Navy, and of the militia of the several States when called into the actual service of the United States. The Constitution declares also that he shall take care that the laws be faithfully executed and that he shall from time to time give to the Congress information of the state of the Union.

Congress has power by the Constitution to provide for calling forth the militia to execute the laws of the Union, and suitable and appropriate acts of Congress have been passed as well for providing for calling forth the militia as for placing other suitable and efficient means in the hands of the President to enable him to discharge the constitutional functions of his office.

The second section of the act of the 28th of February, 1795, declares that whenever the laws of the United States shall be opposed or their execution obstructed in any State by combinations too powerful to be suppressed by the ordinary course of judicial proceedings or the power vested in the marshals, the President may call forth the militia, as far as may be necessary, to suppress such combinations and to cause the laws to be duly executed.

By the act of March 3, 1807, it is provided that in all cases of obstruction to the laws either of the United States or any individual State or Territory, where it is lawful for the President to call forth the militia for the purpose of causing the laws to be duly executed, it shall be lawful for him to employ for the same purposes such part of the land or naval force of the United States as shall be judged necessary.

These several enactments are now in full force, so that if the laws of the United States are opposed or obstructed in any State or Territory by combinations too powerful to be suppressed by the judicial or civil authorities it becomes a case in which it is the duty of the President either to call out the militia or to employ the military and naval force of the United States, or to do both if in his judgment the exigency of the occasion shall so require, for the purpose of suppressing such combinations. The constitutional duty of the President is plain and peremptory and the authority vested in him by law for its performance clear and ample.

Texas is a State, authorized to maintain her own laws so far as they are not repugnant to the Constitution, laws, and treaties of the United States; to suppress insurrections against her authority, and to punish those who may commit treason against the State according to the forms provided by her own constitution and her own laws.

But all this power is local and confined entirely within the limits of Texas herself. She can possibly confer no authority which can be lawfully exercised beyond her own boundaries.

All this is plain, and hardly needs argument or elucidation. If Texas militia, therefore, march into any one of the other States or into any Territory of the United States, there to execute or enforce any law of Texas, they become at that moment trespassers; they are no longer under the protection of any lawful authority, and are to be regarded merely as intruders; and if within such State or Territory they obstruct any law of the United States, either by power of arms or mere power of numbers, constituting such a combination as is too powerful to be suppressed by the civil authority, the President of the United States has no option left to him, but is bound to obey the solemn injunction of the Constitution and exercise the high powers vested in him by that instrument and by the acts of Congress.

Or if any civil posse, armed or unarmed, enter into any Territory of the United States, under the protection of the laws thereof, with intent to seize individuals, to be carried elsewhere for trial for alleged offenses, and this posse be too powerful to be resisted by the local civil authorities, such seizure or attempt to seize is to be prevented or resisted by the authority of the United States.

The grave and important question now arises whether there be in the Territory of New Mexico any existing law of the United States opposition to which or the obstruction of which would constitute a case calling for the interposition of the authority vested in the President.

The Constitution of the United States declares that—

> This Constitution, and the laws of the United States which shall be made in pursuance thereof, and all treaties made, or which shall be made, under the authority of the United States, shall be the supreme law of the land.

If, therefore, New Mexico be a Territory of the United States, and if any treaty stipulation be in force therein, such treaty stipulation is the supreme law of the land, and is to be maintained and upheld accordingly.

In the letter to the governor of Texas my reasons are given for believing that New Mexico is now a Territory of the United States, with the same extent and the same boundaries which belonged to it while in the actual possession of the Republic of Mexico, and before the late war. In the early part of that war both California and New Mexico were conquered by the arms of the United States, and were in the military possession of the United States at the date of the treaty of peace.

By that treaty the title by conquest was confirmed and these territories, provinces, or departments separated from Mexico forever, and by the same treaty certain important rights and securities were solemnly guaranteed to the inhabitants residing therein.

By the fifth article of the treaty it is declared that—

The boundary line between the two Republics shall commence in the Gulf of Mexico 3 leagues from land, opposite the mouth of the Rio Grande, otherwise called Rio Bravo del Norte, or opposite the mouth of its deepest branch if it should have more than one branch emptying directly into the sea; from thence up the middle of that river, following the deepest channel where it has more than one, to the point where it strikes the southern boundary of New Mexico; thence westwardly, along the whole southern boundary of New Mexico (which runs north of the town called Paso) to its western termination; thence northward along the western line of New Mexico until it intersects the first branch of the river Gila (or, if it should not intersect any branch of that river, then to the point on the said line nearest to such branch, and thence in a direct line to the same); thence down the middle of the said branch and of the said river until it empties into the Rio Colorado; thence across the Rio Colorado, following the division line between Upper and Lower California, to the Pacific Ocean.

The eighth article of the treaty is in the following terms:

Mexicans now established in territories previously belonging to Mexico, and which remain for the future within the limits of the United States as defined by the present treaty, shall be free to continue where they now reside or to remove at any time to the Mexican Republic, retaining the property which they possess in the said territories, or disposing thereof and removing the proceeds wherever they please without their being subjected on this account to any contribution, tax, or charge whatever.

Those who shall prefer to remain in the said territories may either retain the title and rights of Mexican citizens or acquire those of citizens of the United States; but they shall be under the obligation to make their election within one year from the date of the exchange of ratifications of this treaty; and those who shall remain in the said territories after the expiration of that year without having declared their intention to retain the character of Mexicans shall be considered to have elected to become citizens of the United States.

In the said territories property of every kind now belonging to Mexicans not established there shall be inviolably respected. The present owners, the heirs of these, and all Mexicans who may hereafter acquire said property by contract shall enjoy with respect to it guaranties equally ample as if the same belonged to citizens of the United States.

The ninth article of the treaty is in these words:

The Mexicans who, in the territories aforesaid, shall not preserve the character of citizens of the Mexican Republic, conformably with what is stipulated in the preceding article, shall be incorporated into the Union of the United States and be admitted at the proper time (to be judged of by the Congress of the United States) to the enjoyment of all the rights of citizens of the United States according to the principles of the Constitution, and in the meantime shall be maintained and protected in the free enjoyment of their liberty and property and secured in the free exercise of their religion without restriction.

It is plain, therefore, on the face of these treaty stipulations that all Mexicans established in territories north or east of the line of demarcation already mentioned come within the protection of the ninth article, and that the treaty, being a part of the supreme law of the land, does extend over all such Mexicans, and assures to them perfect security in the free enjoyment of their liberty and property, as well as in the free exercise of their religion; and this supreme law of the land, being thus in actual force over this territory, is to be maintained until it shall be displaced or superseded by other legal provisions; and if it be obstructed or resisted by combinations too powerful to be suppressed by the civil authority the case is one which comes within the provisions of law and which obliges the President to enforce those provisions. Neither the Constitution nor the laws nor my duty nor my oath of office leave me any alternative or any choice in my mode of action.

The executive government of the United States has no power or authority to determine what was the true line of boundary between Mexico and the United States before the treaty of Guadalupe Hidalgo, nor has it any such power now, since the question has become a question between the State of Texas and the United States. So far as this boundary is doubtful, that doubt can only be removed by some act of Congress, to which the assent of the State of Texas may be necessary, or by some appropriate mode of legal adjudication; but in the meantime, if disturbances or collisions arise or should be threatened, it is absolutely incumbent on the executive government, however painful the duty, to take care that the laws be faithfully maintained; and he can regard only the actual state of things as it existed at the date of the treaty, and is bound to protect all inhabitants who were then established and who now remain north and east of the line of demarcation in the full enjoyment of their liberty and property, according to the provisions of the ninth article of the treaty. In other words, all must be now regarded as New Mexico which was possessed and occupied as New Mexico by citizens of Mexico at the date of the treaty until a definite line of boundary shall be established by competent authority.

This assertion of duty to protect the people of New Mexico from threatened violence, or from seizure to be carried into Texas for trial for alleged offenses against Texan laws, does not at all include any claim of power on the part of the Executive to establish any civil or military government within that Territory. *That power* belongs exclusively to the legislative department, and Congress is the sole judge of the time and manner of creating or authorizing any such government.

The duty of the Executive extends only to the execution of laws and the maintenance of treaties already in force and the protection of all the people of the United States in the enjoyment of the rights which those treaties and laws guarantee.

It is exceedingly desirable that no occasion should arise for the exercise of the powers thus vested in the President by the Constitution and the laws. With whatever mildness those powers might be executed, or however clear the case of necessity, yet consequences might, nevertheless, follow of which no human sagacity can foresee either the evils or the end.

Having thus laid before Congress the communication of his excellency the governor of Texas and the answer thereto, and having made such observations as I have thought the occasion called for respecting constitutional obligations which may arise in the further progress of things and may devolve on me to be performed, I hope I shall not be regarded as stepping aside from the line of my duty, notwithstanding that I am aware that the subject is now before both Houses, if I express my deep and earnest conviction of the importance of an immediate decision or arrangement or settlement of the question of boundary between Texas and the Territory of New Mexico. All considerations of justice, general expediency, and domestic tranquillity call for this. It seems to be in its character and by position the first, or one of the first, of the questions growing out of the acquisition of California and New Mexico, and now requiring decision.

No government can be established for New Mexico, either State or Territorial, until it shall be first ascertained what New Mexico is, and what are her limits and boundaries. These can not be fixed or known till the line of division between her and Texas shall be ascertained and established; and numerous and weighty reasons conspire, in my judgment, to show that this divisional line should be established by Congress with the assent of the government of Texas. In the first place, this seems by far the most prompt mode of proceeding by which the end can be accomplished. If judicial proceedings were resorted to, such proceedings would necessarily be slow, and years would pass by, in all probability, before the controversy could be ended. So great a delay in this case is to be avoided if possible. Such delay would be every way inconvenient, and might be the occasion of disturbances and collisions. For the same reason I would, with the utmost deference to the wisdom of Congress, express a doubt of the expediency of the appointment of commissioners, and of an examination, estimate, and an award of indemnity to be made by them. This would be but a species of arbitration, which might last as long as a suit at law.

So far as I am able to comprehend the case, the general facts are now all known, and Congress is as capable of deciding on it justly and properly now as it probably would be after the report of the commissioners. If the claim of title on the part of Texas appears to Congress to be well founded in whole or in part, it is in the competency of Congress to offer her an indemnity for the surrender of that claim. In a case like this, surrounded, as it is, by many cogent considerations, all calling for amicable adjustment and immediate settlement, the Government of the United States would be justified, in my opinion, in allowing an indemnity to Texas, not unreasonable or extravagant, but fair, liberal, and awarded in a just spirit of accommodation.

I think no event would be hailed with more gratification by the people of the United States than the amicable adjustment of questions of difficulty which have now for a long time agitated the country and occupied, to the exclusion of other subjects, the time and attention of Congress.

Having thus freely communicated the results of my own reflections on the most advisable mode of adjusting the boundary question, I shall nevertheless cheerfully acquiesce in any other mode which the wisdom of Congress may devise. And in conclusion I repeat my conviction that every consideration of the public interest manifests the necessity of a provision by Congress for the settlement of this boundary question before the present session be brought to a close. The settlement of other questions connected with the same subject within the same period is greatly to be desired, but the adjustment of this appears to me to be in the highest degree important. In the train of such an adjustment we may well hope that there will follow a return of harmony and good will, an increased attachment to the Union, and the general satisfaction of the country.

14

THE DECISION
TO RAISE THE BAMBOO CURTAIN

Fillmore Requests the Emperor to Open Japan to America

By the middle of the nineteenth century the march of Manifest Destiny was converting America into a Pacific power. President Fillmore had shown admirable restraint in refusing to be a party to a rather shady proposal to annex Hawaii; yet he recognized the importance to Americans of this mid-Pacific island chain and was determined that it should not come under the control of any other great power. To Congress he predicted that "at no distant day" a "great trade" would be carried on between the American West Coast and eastern Asia.

Trade with China was already burgeoning. Japan, which exercised a marvelous fascination for Americans, lay athwart the direct route between San Francisco and Shanghai. Not only was the United States interested in protecting shipwrecked whalers who found the Japanese coast hitherto inhospitable, but it was considered imperative that the Navy and Merchant Marine have coaling stations along the Japanese archipelago, as ships were shifting from sail to steam. But Japan remained sealed off to the western world save for special concessions which the Dutch enjoyed under humiliating conditions.

From time to time enterprising Yankee sea captains had defied the boycott of the hated foreigners, but nevertheless found it impossible to raise that bamboo curtain which cut the native Japanese off from contact with the West. George Cleveland, who actually landed goods in Japan as early as 1801, reported: "No person in this country (who has not traded with people who have so little intercourse with the world) can have an idea of the trouble we had in delivering the little Invoice." Other contacts were casual. As late as 1846 an American expedition under Commodore Biddle visited Yedo, only to find the port closed. President Fillmore was determined to keep trade routes open to the Far

East and to expand trans-Pacific commerce and communications. Late in 1850 he transferred Commodore Aulick from the South Atlantic command to the East India squadron, and, in the words of Secretary of State Daniel Webster's instructions, it was stated as "the President's opinion, that steps should be taken at once to enable our enterprising merchants to supply the last link in that great chain which unites all nations of the world by the establishment of a line of steamers from California to China." Webster pointed out the desirability of obtaining supplies of coal from the subjects of the Emperor of Japan, a matter which continued to be on Fillmore's mind. The Aulick mission never got under way because the Commodore was involved in an incident which made him unacceptable for diplomatic duty.

Fillmore and Webster now decided to give the mission a more imposing aspect by sending out an independent fleet under the command of Matthew Calbraith Perry, selected to undertake the most important diplomatic mission ever entrusted to an American naval officer—the negotiation of a treaty with Japan. In preparing a message to the Emperor Fillmore was puzzled about the correct protocol to be employed. He had the American minister to the Netherlands secure from the Dutch foreign office the reply of the shogun in 1844 to an address by William II asking that ports be opened to foreign trade. Fillmore discarded the first draft, and on Webster's death his successor, Edward Everett, prepared a second one, which seems to have been the basis for Fillmore's final letter. A Dutch physician named von Siebold, "the self-constituted court chamberlain of Japan," criticized President Fillmore for being "wanting in the courtly proprieties of diplomatic etiquette," but these are minor flaws in a state paper simply but artfully conceived, whose far-reaching impact may still be felt.

The letter was presented in a ceremony on July 14, 1853, on shore at the village of Kurihama. Commodore Perry was preceded by two boys, dressed for the ceremony, bearing in an envelope of scarlet cloth the boxes which contained his credentials and the President's letter, both written on vellum and bound in blue silk velvet. The documents were delivered to the princes Idzu and Iwami, representatives of the Emperor, in an interview which lasted no more than half an hour. His Imperial Highness, correct protocol or not, got the point of Fillmore's letter, responded through his commissioners in a friendly manner, and on March 31, 1854, made a treaty with the United States granting trade rights at the two ports of Hakodate and Shinoda. The bamboo curtain had at long last been lifted.

To the Mikado of Japan [4]

[Washington, *November 13, 1852*]

Great and Good Friend:

I send you this public letter by Commodore Matthew C. Perry, an officer of the highest rank in the navy of the United States, and commander of the squadron now visiting your imperial majesty's dominions.

I have directed Commodore Perry to assure your imperial majesty that I entertain the kindest feelings toward your majesty's person and government, and that I have no other object in sending him to Japan but to propose to your imperial majesty that the United States and Japan should live in friendship and have commercial intercourse with each other.

The Constitution and laws of the United States forbid all interference with the religious or political concerns of other nations. I have particularly charged Commodore Perry to abstain from every act which could possibly disturb the tranquility of your imperial majesty's dominions.

The United States of America reach from ocean to ocean, and our Territory of Oregon and State of California lie directly opposite to the dominions of your imperial majesty. Our steamships can go from California to Japan in eighteen days.

Our great State of California produces about sixty millions of dollars in gold every year, besides silver, quicksilver, precious stones, and many other valuable articles. Japan is also a rich and fertile country, and produces many very valuable articles. Your imperial majesty's subjects are skilled in many of the arts. I am desirous that our two countries should trade with each other, for the benefit both of Japan and the United States.

We know that the ancient laws of your imperial majesty's government do not allow of foreign trade, except with the Chinese and the Dutch; but as the state of the world changes and new governments are formed, it seems to be wise, from time to time, to make new laws.

There was a time when the ancient laws of your imperial majesty's government were first made.

About the same time America, which is sometimes called the New World, was first discovered and settled by the Europeans. For a long time there were but a few people, and they were poor. They have now become quite numerous; their commerce is very extensive; and they think that if your imperial majesty were so far to change the ancient laws as to allow a free trade between the two countries it would be extremely beneficial to both.

If your imperial majesty is not satisfied that it would be safe altogether to abrogate the ancient laws which forbid foreign trade, they might be suspended for five or ten years, so as to try the experiment. If it does not prove as beneficial as was hoped, the ancient laws can be restored. The United States often limit their treaties with foreign States to a few years, and then renew them or not, as they please.

I have directed Commodore Perry to mention another thing to your imperial majesty. Many of our ships pass every year from California to China; and great numbers of our people pursue the whale fishery near the shores of Japan. It sometimes happens, in stormy weather, that one of our ships is wrecked on your imperial majesty's shores. In all such cases we ask, and expect, that our unfortunate people should be treated with kindness, and that their property should be protected, till we can send a vessel and bring them away. We are very much in earnest in this.

Commodore Perry is also directed by me to represent to your imperial majesty that we understand there is a great abundance of coal and provisions in the Empire of Japan. Our steamships, in crossing the great ocean, burn a great deal of coal, and it is not convenient to bring it all the way from America. We wish that our steamships and other vessels should be allowed to stop in Japan and supply themselves with coal, provisions and water. They will pay for them in money, or anything else your imperial majesty's subjects may prefer; and we request your imperial majesty to appoint a convenient port, in the southern part of the Empire, where our vessels may stop for this purpose. We are very desirous of this.

These are the only objects for which I have sent Commodore Perry, with a powerful squadron, to pay a visit to your imperial majesty's renowned city of Yedo: Friendship, commerce, a supply of coal and provisions, and protection for our shipwrecked people.

We have directed Commodore Perry to beg your imperial majesty's acceptance of a few presents. They are of no great value in themselves; but some of them may serve as specimens of the articles manufactured

181

in the United States, and they are intended as tokens of our sincere and respectful friendship.

May the Almighty have your imperial majesty in His great and holy keeping.

In witness whereof, I have caused the great seal of the United States to be hereunto affixed, and have subscribed the same with my name, at the city of Washington, in America, the seat of my [SEAL] government, on the thirteenth day of the month of November, in the year one thousand eight hundred and fifty-two.

Your good friend,

MILLARD FILLMORE

By the President:

EDWARD EVERETT,
Secretary of State

15

THE DECISION
TO ADMIT KANSAS AS A SLAVE STATE

Buchanan Breaks Up the Democratic Party

In the 1850's slavery weighed heavily on the consciences of enlightened men and women. "I tremble for my country when I reflect that God is just," Jefferson once declared in prophetic vein, and John Quincy Adams warned that " 'Rank corruption, mining all within, infects unseen.' " As the differences over the slavery issue became increasingly irreconcilable, statesmen sought to head off a showdown which would split the Union. The Compromise of 1850 marked a culmination of their efforts. Ironically, Stephen A. Douglas, whose adroit leadership of the Compromise forces in the closing days of the battle had secured the passage of the package measure, was the man who upset the apple cart.

Perhaps no more mischievous bill was ever presented in Congress than the Kansas-Nebraska Act which Douglas sponsored. This bill specifically repealed the Missouri Compromise and recognized the principle of "squatter sovereignty," or self-determination. A group of Northern Democrats, headed by Salmon P. Chase of Ohio, immediately split with the party, and within the territory of Kansas was precipitated a struggle for control verging on civil war. Bitten by the Presidential bee, Douglas was engaged in a flagrant courtship of Southern support at the expense of national harmony. Those who defend him must concede this, but assert in his behalf that he was convinced that by geography and nature these territories would remain free soil, and he was anxious to take steps to open to settlement the region west of Iowa in order to press for a transcontinental railroad along a central route, with Chicago as its eastern terminus, as opposed to a southern one advocated by President Pierce.

The "Kansas Question" converted that territory into a cockpit of civil war waged by armed bands of pro- and antislavery settlers. A proslavery legislature was organized and a proslavery territorial delegate elected by fraud and violence. In opposition, a free-state governor and legislature were elected, but President Franklin Pierce, a weak and superficial statesman, promptly condemned the free government at Topeka as an act of rebellion. House and Senate split sharply over the issue. The former passed a bill in 1856 to admit Kansas as a state under the Topeka constitution, but the measure was quashed in the Senate. During the Congressional debates on Kansas Senator Charles Sumner bitterly denounced the "slave oligarchy" and its "rape" of the territory. In retaliation for Sumner's coarse and insulting aspersions on the characters of several Senators, particularly the absent Andrew P. Butler of South Carolina, Representative Preston S. Brooks, Butler's nephew, brutally assaulted Sumner with a cane as the latter sat at his desk in the Senate chamber.

Whenever a territorial governor tried to pursue a nonpartisan course he found that the Pierce administration would not support him. James Buchanan, on succeeding to the Presidency in 1857, was determined to settle the Kansas issue once and for all. As territorial governor, he dispatched to Kansas—the grave of governors—an expansionist from Mississippi, Robert J. Walker. The new appointee dumfounded the administration by seeking to conciliate the free-state party in Kansas, promising to do his utmost to guarantee that the majority would control the government. When, therefore, a convention at Lecompton prepared a constitution which rigged the issue in such a way as to give the proslavery party an advantage and avoid presenting to the voters a clear-cut opportunity to vote on slavery, Walker tried to persuade Buchanan that the constitution was unacceptable. When he saw that Buchanan was adamant, he resigned in December, 1857, and subsequently joined in the agitation against the Lecompton constitution.

Buchanan, a prisoner of the Southern Democrats in his Cabinet, gave the constitution his open endorsement despite the fact that in the election held on December 21 in Kansas free-state men refused to participate, and that in an election called for by the free-state legislature and held early in January, 1858, the Lecompton constitution was overwhelmingly defeated.

President Buchanan's message to Congress of February 2, 1858, submitting the Lecompton constitution to Congress and recommending the admission of Kansas as a slave state, caused an immediate revolt in his own party. Stephen A. Douglas condemned the constitution as a violation of the principle of "popular sovereignty" and a mockery of justice. Through administrative pressure the Senate voted to admit Kansas under the Lecompton constitution, but the house was deadlocked, until a compromise proposal, combining a popular vote on the constitution to be held in Kansas with a grant to Kansas of some four million acres of public land, mustered enough votes for passage there, and finally in the Senate. But when the issue was submitted to the voters in August the Lecompton constitution was decisively rejected, 11,812 to 1,926.

Buchanan, by his myopic obstinacy, had placed the great prestige of the Presidency behind an issue lacking popular support or moral grounds. His was one of the most willful decisions in the history of the Presidency. It divided the Democratic Party irreconcilably. It handed an up-and-coming prairie lawyer a superb issue to use effectively in his classic debates against the "Little Giant" in the summer of '58, an issue which was to sweep Lincoln into the Presidency in a victory over an opposition party shattered into fragments.

SPECIAL MESSAGE

WASHINGTON, *February 2, 1858*

To the Senate and House of Representatives of the United States:
I have received from J. Calhoun, esq., president of the late constitutional convention of Kansas, a copy, duly certified by himself, of the constitution framed by that body, with the expression of a hope that I would submit the same to the consideration of Congress "with the view of the admission of Kansas into the Union as an independent State." In compliance with this request, I herewith transmit to Congress, for their action, the constitution of Kansas, with the ordinance respecting the public lands, as well as the letter of Mr. Calhoun, dated at Lecompton on the 14th ultimo, by which they were accompanied. Having received but a single copy of the constitution and ordinance, I send this to the Senate.

A great delusion seems to pervade the public mind in relation to the condition of parties in Kansas. This arises from the difficulty of inducing the American people to realize the fact that any portion of them should be in a state of rebellion against the government under which they live. When we speak of the affairs of Kansas, we are apt to refer merely to the existence of two violent political parties in that Territory, divided on the question of slavery, just as we speak of such parties in the States. This presents no adequate idea of the true state of the case. The dividing line there is not between two political parties, both acknowledging the lawful existence of the government, but between those who are loyal to this government and those who have endeavored to destroy its existence by force and by usurpation—between those who sustain and those who have done all in their power to overthrow the Territorial government established by Congress. This government they would long since have subverted had it not been protected from their assaults by the troops of the United States. Such has been the condition of affairs since my inauguration. Ever since that period a large portion of the people of Kansas have been in a state of rebellion against the government, with a military leader at their head of a most turbulent and dangerous character. They have never acknowledged, but have constantly renounced and defied, the government to which they owe allegiance, and have been all the time in a state of resistance against its authority. They have all the time been endeavoring to subvert it and to establish a revolutionary government, under the so-called Topeka constitution, in its stead. Even at this very moment the Topeka legislature are in session. Whoever has read the correspondence of Governor Walker with the State Department, recently communicated to the Senate, will be convinced that this picture is not overdrawn. He always protested against the withdrawal of any portion of the military force of the United States from the Territory, deeming its presence absolutely necessary for the preservation of the regular government and the execution of the laws. In his very first dispatch to the Secretary of State, dated June 2, 1857, he says:

> The most alarming movement, however, proceeds from the assembling on the 9th June of the so-called Topeka legislature, with a view to the enactment of an entire code of laws. Of course it will be my endeavor to prevent such a result, as it would lead to inevitable and disastrous collision, and, in fact, renew the civil war in Kansas.

This was with difficulty prevented by the efforts of Governor Walker; but soon thereafter, on the 14th of July, we find him requesting General Harney to furnish him a regiment of dragoons to proceed to the city of Lawrence; and this for the reason that he had received authentic intelligence, verified by his own actual observation, that a dangerous

186

rebellion had occurred, "involving an open defiance of the laws and the establishment of an insurgent government in that city."

In the governor's dispatch of July 15 he informs the Secretary of State that—

This movement at Lawrence was the beginning of a plan, originating in that city, to organize insurrection throughout the Territory, and especially in all towns, cities, or counties where the Republican party have a majority. Lawrence is the hotbed of all the abolition movements in this Territory. It is the town established by the abolition societies of the East, and whilst there are respectable people there, it is filled by a considerable number of mercenaries who are paid by abolition societies to perpetuate and diffuse agitation throughout Kansas and prevent a peaceful settlement of this question. Having failed in inducing their own so-called Topeka State legislature to organize this insurrection, Lawrence has commenced it herself, and if not arrested the rebellion will extend throughout the Territory.

And again:

In order to send this communication immediately by mail, I must close by assuring you that the spirit of rebellion pervades the great mass of the Republican party of this Territory, instigated, as I entertain no doubt they are, by Eastern societies, having in view results most disastrous to the government and to the Union; and that the continued presence of General Harney here is indispensable, as originally stipulated by me, with a large body of dragoons and several batteries.

On the 20th July, 1857, General Lane, under the authority of the Topeka convention, undertook, as Governor Walker informs us—

to organize the whole so-called Free-State party into volunteers and to take the names of all who refuse enrollment. The professed object is to protect the polls, at the election in August, of the new insurgent Topeka State legislature.

*   *   *   *   *

The object of taking the names of all who refuse enrollment is to terrify the Free-State conservatives into submission. This is proved by recent atrocities committed on such men by Topekaites. The speedy location of large bodies of regular troops here, with two batteries, is necessary. The Lawrence insurgents await the development of this new revolutionary military organization. * * *

In the governor's dispatch of July 27 he says that "General Lane and his staff everywhere deny the authority of the Territorial laws and counsel a total disregard of these enactments."

Without making further quotations of a similar character from other dispatches of Governor Walker, it appears by a reference to Mr. Stanton's communication to General Cass of the 9th of December last that the "important step of calling the legislature together was taken after I [he] had become satisfied that the election ordered by the convention on the 21st instant could not be conducted without collision and bloodshed." So intense was the disloyal feeling among the enemies of the government established by Congress that an election which afforded them an opportunity, if in the majority, of making Kansas a free State, according to their own professed desire, could not be conducted without collision and bloodshed.

The truth is that up till the present moment the enemies of the existing government still adhere to their Topeka revolutionary constitution and government. The very first paragraph of the message of Governor Robinson, dated on the 7th of December, to the Topeka legislature now assembled at Lawrence contains an open defiance of the Constitution and laws of the United States. The governor says:

> The convention which framed the constitution at Topeka originated with the people of Kansas Territory. They have adopted and ratified the same twice by a direct vote, and also indirectly through two elections of State officers and members of the State legislature. Yet it has pleased the Administration to regard the whole proceeding revolutionary.

This Topeka government, adhered to with such treasonable pertinacity, is a government in direct opposition to the existing government prescribed and recognized by Congress. It is a usurpation of the same character as it would be for a portion of the people of any State of the Union to undertake to establish a separate government within its limits for the purpose of redressing any grievance, real or imaginary, of which they might complain against the legitimate State government. Such a principle, if carried into execution, would destroy all lawful authority and produce universal anarchy.

From this statement of facts the reason becomes palpable why the enemies of the government authorized by Congress have refused to vote for delegates to the Kansas constitutional convention, and also afterwards on the question of slavery, submitted by it to the people. It is because they have ever refused to sanction or recognize any other constitution than that framed at Topeka.

Had the whole Lecompton constitution been submitted to the people the adherents of this organization would doubtless have voted against it, because if successful they would thus have removed an obstacle out of the way of their own revolutionary constitution. They would have done this, not upon a consideration of the merits of the whole or any part of the Lecompton constitution, but simply because they have ever resisted the authority of the government authorized by Congress, from which it emanated.

Such being the unfortunate condition of affairs in the Territory, what was the right as well as the duty of the law-abiding people? Were they silently and patiently to submit to the Topeka usurpation, or adopt the necessary measures to establish a constitution under the authority of the organic law of Congress?

That this law recognized the right of the people of the Territory, without any enabling act from Congress, to form a State constitution is too clear for argument. For Congress "to leave the people of the Territory perfectly free," in framing their constitution, "to form and regulate their domestic institutions in their own way, subject only to the Constitution of the United States," and then to say that they shall not be permitted to proceed and frame a constitution in their own way without an express authority from Congress, appears to be almost a contradiction in terms. It would be much more plausible to contend that Congress had no power to pass such an enabling act than to argue that the people of a Territory might be kept out of the Union for an indefinite period, and until it might please Congress to permit them to exercise the right of self-government. This would be to adopt not "their own way," but the way which Congress might prescribe.

It is impossible that any people could have proceeded with more regularity in the formation of a constitution than the people of Kansas have done. It was necessary, first, to ascertain whether it was the desire of the people to be relieved from their Territorial dependence and establish a State government. For this purpose the Territorial legislature in 1855 passed a law "for taking the sense of the people of this Territory upon the expediency of calling a convention to form a State constitution," at the general election to be held in October, 1856. The "sense of the people" was accordingly taken and they decided in favor of a convention. It is true that at this election the enemies of the Territorial government did not vote, because they were then engaged at Topeka, without the slightest pretext of lawful authority, in framing a constitution of their own for the purpose of subverting the Territorial government.

In pursuance of this decision of the people in favor of a convention, the Territorial legislature, on the 27th day of February, 1857, passed an act for the election of delegates on the third Monday of June, 1857, to frame a State constitution. This law is as fair in its provisions as any that ever passed a legislative body for a similar purpose. The right of suffrage at this election is clearly and justly defined. "Every *bona fide* inhabitant of the Territory of Kansas," on the third Monday of June, the day of the election, who was a citizen of the United States above the age of 21, and had resided therein for three months previous to that date, was entitled to vote. In order to avoid all interference from neighboring States or Territories with the freedom and fairness of the election, provision was made for the registry of the qualified voters, and in pursuance thereof 9,251 voters were registered. Governor Walker did his whole duty in urging all the qualified citizens of Kansas to vote at this election. In his inaugural address, on the 27th May last, he informed them that—

> Under our practice the preliminary act of framing a State constitution is uniformly performed through the instrumentality of a convention of delegates chosen by the people themselves. That convention is now about to be elected by you under the call of the Territorial legislature, created and still recognized by the authority of Congress and clothed by it, in the comprehensive language of the organic law, with full power to make such an enactment. The Territorial legislature, then, in assembling this convention, were fully sustained by the act of Congress, and the authority of the convention is distinctly recognized in my instructions from the President of the United States.

The governor also clearly and distinctly warns them what would be the consequences if they should not participate in the election.

> The people of Kansas, then [he says], are invited by the highest authority known to the Constitution to participate freely and fairly in the election of delegates to frame a constitution and State government. The law has performed its entire appropriate function when it extends to the people the right of suffrage, but it can not compel the performance of that duty. Throughout our whole Union, however, and wherever free government prevails those who abstain from the exercise of the right of suffrage authorize those who do vote to act for them in that contingency; and the absentees are as much bound under the law and Constitution, where there is no fraud or violence, by the act of the majority of those who do vote as if all had participated in the election. Otherwise, as voting must be voluntary, self-government would be impracticable and monarchy or despotism would remain as the only alternative.

It may also be observed that at this period any hope, if such had existed, that the Topeka constitution would ever be recognized by Congress must have been abandoned. Congress had adjourned on the 3d March previous, having recognized the legal existence of the Territorial legislature in a variety of forms, which I need not enumerate. Indeed, the Delegate elected to the House of Representatives under a Territorial law had been admitted to his seat and had just completed his term of service on the day previous to my inauguration.

This was the propitious moment for settling all difficulties in Kansas. This was the time for abandoning the revolutionary Topeka organization and for the enemies of the existing government to conform to the laws and to unite with its friends in framing a State constitution; but this they refused to do, and the consequences of their refusal to submit to lawful authority and vote at the election of delegates may yet prove to be of a most deplorable character. Would that the respect for the laws of the land which so eminently distinguished the men of the past generation could be revived. It is a disregard and violation of law which have for years kept the Territory of Kansas in a state of almost open rebellion against its government. It is the same spirit which has produced actual rebellion in Utah. Our only safety consists in obedience and conformity to law. Should a general spirit against its enforcement prevail, this will prove fatal to us as a nation. We acknowledge no master but the law, and should we cut loose from its restraints and everyone do what seemeth good in his own eyes our case will indeed be hopeless.

The enemies of the Territorial government determined still to resist the authority of Congress. They refused to vote for delegates to the convention, not because, from circumstances which I need not detail, there was an omission to register the comparatively few voters who were inhabitants of certain counties of Kansas in the early spring of 1857, but because they had predetermined at all hazards to adhere to their revolutionary organization and defeat the establishment of any other constitution than that which they had framed at Topeka. The election was therefore suffered to pass by default. But of this result the qualified electors who refused to vote can never justly complain.

From this review it is manifest that the Lecompton convention, according to every principle of constitutional law, was legally constituted and was invested with power to frame a constitution.

The sacred principle of popular sovereignty has been invoked in favor of the enemies of law and order in Kansas. But in what manner is popular sovereignty to be exercised in this country if not through the instrumentality of established law? In certain small republics of ancient times the people did assemble in primary meetings, passed laws, and directed public affairs. In our country this is manifestly impossible. Popular sovereignty can be exercised here only through the ballot box; and if the people will refuse to exercise it in this manner, as they have done in Kansas at the election of delegates, it is not for them to complain that their rights have been violated.

The Kansas convention, thus lawfully constituted, proceeded to frame a constitution, and, having completed their work, finally adjourned on the 7th day of November last. They did not think proper to submit the whole of this constitution to a popular vote, but they did submit the question whether Kansas should be a free or a slave State to the people. This was the question which had convulsed the Union and shaken it to its very center. This was the question which had lighted up the flames of civil war in Kansas and had produced dangerous sectional parties throughout the Confederacy. It was of a character so paramount in respect to the condition of Kansas as to rivet the anxious attention of the people of the whole country upon it, and it alone. No person thought of any other question. For my own part, when I instructed Governor Walker in general terms in favor of submitting the constitution to the people, I had no object in view except the all-absorbing question of slavery. In what manner the people of Kansas might regulate their other concerns was not a subject which attracted any attention. In fact, the general provisions of our recent State constitutions, after an experience of eight years, are so similar and so excellent that it would be difficult to go far wrong at the present day in framing a new constitution.

I then believed and still believe that under the organic act the Kansas convention were bound to submit this all-important question of slavery to the people. It was never, however, my opinion that, independently of this act, they would have been bound to submit any portion of the constitution to a popular vote in order to give it validity. Had I entertained such an opinion, this would have been in opposition to many precedents in our history, commencing in the very best age of the Republic. It would have been in opposition to the principle which pervades our institutions, and which is every day carried out into practice, that the people have the right to delegate to representatives chosen by themselves their sovereign power to frame constitutions, enact laws, and perform many other important acts without requiring that these should be subjected to their subsequent approbation. It would be a most inconvenient limitation of their own power, imposed by the people upon themselves, to exclude them from exercising their sovereignty in any lawful manner they think proper. It is true that the people of Kansas might, if they had pleased, have required the convention to submit the constitution to a popular vote; but this they have not done. The only remedy, therefore, in this case is that which exists in all other similar cases. If the delegates who framed the Kansas constitution have in any manner violated the will of their constituents, the people always possess the power to change their constitution or their laws according to their own pleasure.

The question of slavery was submitted to an election of the people of Kansas on the 21st December last, in obedience to the mandate of the constitution. Here again a fair opportunity was presented to the adherents of the Topeka constitution, if they were the majority, to decide this exciting question "in their own way" and thus restore peace to the distracted Territory; but they again refused to exercise their right of popular sovereignty, and again suffered the election to pass by default.

I heartily rejoice that a wiser and better spirit prevailed among a large majority of these people on the first Monday of January, and that they did on that day vote under the Lecompton constitution for a governor and other State officers, a Member of Congress, and for members of the legislature. This election was warmly contested by the parties, and a larger vote was polled than at any previous election in the Territory. We may now reasonably hope that the revolutionary Topeka organization will be speedily and finally abandoned, and this will go far toward the final settlement of the unhappy differences in Kansas. If frauds have been committed at this election, either by one or both parties, the legislature and the people of Kansas, under their constitution, will know how to redress themselves and punish these detestable but too common crimes without any outside interference.

The people of Kansas have, then, "in their own way" and in strict accordance with the organic act, framed a constitution and State government, have submitted the all-important question of slavery to the people, and have elected a governor, a Member to represent them in Congress, members of the State legislature, and other State officers. They now ask admission into the Union under this constitution, which is republican in its form. It is for Congress to decide whether they will admit or reject the State which has thus been created. For my own part, I am decidedly in favor of its admission, and thus terminating the Kansas question. This will carry out the great principle of nonintervention recognized and sanctioned by the organic act, which declares in express language in favor of "nonintervention by Congress with slavery in the States or Territories," leaving "the people thereof perfectly free to form and regulate their domestic institutions in their own way, subject only to the Constitution of the United States." In this manner, by localizing the question of slavery and confining it to the people whom it immediately concerned, every patriot anxiously expected that this question would be banished from the halls of Congress, where it has always exerted a baneful influence throughout the whole country.

It is proper that I should briefly refer to the election held under an act of the Territorial legislature on the first Monday of January last on the

Lecompton constitution. This election was held after the Territory had been prepared for admission into the Union as a sovereign State, and when no authority existed in the Territorial legislature which could possibly destroy its existence or change its character. The election, which was peaceably conducted under my instructions, involved a strange inconsistency. A large majority of the persons who voted against the Lecompton constitution were at the very same time and place recognizing its valid existence in the most solemn and authentic manner by voting under its provisions. I have yet received no official information of the result of this election.

As a question of expediency, after the right has been maintained, it may be wise to reflect upon the benefits to Kansas and to the whole country which would result from its immediate admission into the Union, as well as the disasters which may follow its rejection. Domestic peace will be the happy consequence of its admission, and that fine Territory, which has hitherto been torn by dissensions, will rapidly increase in population and wealth and speedily realize the blessings and the comforts which follow in the train of agricultural and mechanical industry. The people will then be sovereign and can regulate their own affairs in their own way. If a majority of them desire to abolish domestic slavery within the State, there is no other possible mode by which this can be effected so speedily as by prompt admission. The will of the majority is supreme and irresistible when expressed in an orderly and lawful manner. They can make and unmake constitutions at pleasure. It would be absurd to say that they can impose fetters upon their own power which they can not afterwards remove. If they could do this, they might tie their own hands for a hundred as well as for ten years. These are fundamental principles of American freedom, and are recognized, I believe, in some form or other by every State constitution; and if Congress, in the act of admission, should think proper to recognize them I can perceive no objection to such a course. This has been done emphatically in the constitution of Kansas. It declares in the bill of rights that "all political power is inherent in the people and all free governments are founded on their authority and instituted for their benefit, and therefore they have at all times an inalienable and indefeasible right to alter, reform, or abolish their form of government in such manner as they may think proper." The great State of New York is at this moment governed under a constitution framed and established in direct opposition to the mode prescribed by the previous constitution. If, therefore, the provision changing the Kansas constitution after the year 1864 could by possibility be construed into a prohibition to make such a change previous to that period, this prohibition would be wholly unavailing. The legislature already elected may at its very first session submit the question to a vote of the people whether they will or will not have a convention to amend their constitution and adopt all necessary means for giving effect to the popular will.

It has been solemnly adjudged by the highest judicial tribunal known to our laws that slavery exists in Kansas by virtue of the Constitution of the United States. Kansas is therefore at this moment as much a slave State as Georgia or South Carolina. Without this the equality of the sovereign States composing the Union would be violated and the use and enjoyment of a territory acquired by the common treasure of all the States would be closed against the people and the property of nearly half the members of the Confederacy. Slavery can therefore never be prohibited in Kansas except by means of a constitutional provision, and in no other manner can this be obtained so promptly, if a majority of the people desire it, as by admitting it into the Union under its present constitution.

On the other hand, should Congress reject the constitution under the idea of affording the disaffected in Kansas a third opportunity of prohibiting slavery in the State, which they might have done twice before if in the majority, no man can foretell the consequences.

If Congress, for the sake of those men who refused to vote for delegates to the convention when they might have excluded slavery from the constitution, and who afterwards refused to vote on the 21st December last, when they might, as they claim, have stricken slavery from the constitution, should now reject the State because slavery remains in the constitution, it is manifest that the agitation upon this dangerous subject will be renewed in a more alarming form than it has ever yet assumed.

Every patriot in the country had indulged the hope that the Kansas and Nebraska act would put a final end to the slavery agitation, at least in Congress, which had for more than twenty years convulsed the country and endangered the Union. This act involved great and fundamental principles, and if fairly carried into effect will settle the question. Should the agitation be again revived, should the people of the sister States be again estranged from each other with more than their former bitterness, this will arise from a cause, so far as the interests of Kansas are concerned, more trifling and insignificant than has ever stirred the elements of a great people into commotion. To the people of Kansas the only practical difference between admission or rejection depends simply upon the fact whether they can themselves more speedily change the present constitution if it does not accord with the will of the majority, or frame a second constitution to be submitted to Congress hereafter. Even if this were a question of mere expediency, and not of right, the small difference of time one way or the other is of not the least importance when contrasted with the evils which must necessarily result to the whole country from a revival of the slavery agitation.

In considering this question it should never be forgotten that in proportion to its insignificance, let the decision be what it may so far as it may affect the few thousand inhabitants of Kansas who have from the beginning resisted the constitution and the laws, for this very reason the rejection of the constitution will be so much the more keenly felt by the people of fourteen of the States of this Union, where slavery is recognized under the Constitution of the United States.

Again, the speedy admission of Kansas into the Union would restore peace and quiet to the whole country. Already the affairs of this Territory have engrossed an undue proportion of public attention. They have sadly affected the friendly relations of the people of the States with each other and alarmed the fears of patriots for the safety of the Union. Kansas once admitted into the Union, the excitement becomes localized and will soon die away for want of outside aliment. Then every difficulty will be settled at the ballot box.

Besides—and this is no trifling consideration—I shall then be enabled to withdraw the troops of the United States from Kansas and employ them on branches of service where they are much needed. They have been kept there, on the earnest importunity of Governor Walker, to maintain the existence of the Territorial government and secure the execution of the laws. He considered that at least 2,000 regular troops, under the command of General Harney, were necessary for this purpose. Acting upon his reliable information, I have been obliged in some degree to interfere with the expedition to Utah in order to keep down rebellion in Kansas. This has involved a very heavy expense to the Government. Kansas once admitted, it is believed there will no longer be any occasion there for troops of the United States.

I have thus performed my duty on this important question, under a deep sense of responsibility to God and my country. My public life will terminate within a brief period, and I have no other object of earthly ambition than to leave my country in a peaceful and prosperous condition and to live in the affections and respect of my countrymen. The dark and ominous clouds which now appear to be impending over the Union I conscientiously believe may be dissipated with honor to every portion of it by the admission of Kansas during the present session of Congress, whereas if she should be rejected I greatly fear these clouds will become darker and more ominous than any which have ever yet threatened the Constitution and the Union.

16

THE DECISION
NOT TO STOP SECESSION

Buchanan Confesses He Lacks the Power to Act

The American Presidency offers no sharper contrasts than Andrew Jackson and James Buchanan. When South Carolina nullified the tariff, Old Hickory promptly proclaimed nullification unconstitutional and strengthened the military posture of the Federal government in that refractory state. South Carolina was morally and legally ostracized. No other Southern states followed her along the path of interposition, and the threatened rebellion fizzled out. Contrariwise, when the states of the Lower South, on news of Lincoln's election, appeared on the verge of taking the irrevocable step of secession, Buchanan did not use force or even the threat of force. Instead, he urged upon Congress an "exploratory" amendment to the Constitution to protect slave property and thereby settle the issues between North and South. The only time the Civil War could have been stopped was before it broke out. But in those crucial days between November 6, 1860 and March 4, 1861, Buchanan lived through an agony of indecision. In one respect, however, his message to Congress of December 3, 1860, was decisive. It resolved all doubts in the minds of the hotheads who were about to secede. They now were assured that the President would make no move to stop them. The results were fateful to the cause of Union.

In order to understand the setting and significance of Buchanan's message, it is necessary to consider the chronology of events. On November 6, election night, the early wires carried the news of Lincoln's victory. The President-elect had but 39 per cent of the vote, but a majority in the Electoral College. The revolt against Lincoln began even before all the returns were in. South Carolina moved first. On the morning after the national election Federal District Judge Magrath addressed the grand jury: "For the last time I have, as a Judge of the

United States, administered the laws of the United States within the limits of the State of South Carolina." So far as he was concerned, he added, "the Temple of Justice . . . is now closed." Other Federal officials in South Carolina quickly followed his example. Still, secession enthusiasm was largely confined to the six or seven states of the Lower South. The border states and Virginia gave no indication of extreme action. All looked to the President for direction, but found no clear path marked out for them.

Buchanan, crowding seventy, nervous and irritable, hoped to postpone the catastrophe until he left office. What he needed most was a Cabinet that would stiffen his backbone, but his own advisers were sharply divided. Secretary of the Treasury Howell Cobb was ready to take the plunge to secession, along with others, notably his careless, if not actually dishonest, Secretary of War John B. Floyd, who at this very time was engaged in shipping arms and heavy guns to the South —embezzlement if not treason. The chief Unionists in his Cabinet were Secretary of State Lewis Cass, who soon resigned in disgust because of Buchanan's failure to order the reinforcement of the Charleston forts, and the temperamental and eccentric Jeremiah Sullivan Black, Attorney General.

The President was undecided whether to issue a proclamation as Andrew Jackson had done in like circumstances or to send a message to Congress. Finding no support in the Cabinet for a proclamation, Buchanan then prepared his message, taking legal advice from his Attorney General. While the President declared the Union to be perpetual and denied the right of secession, he did concede the right of resistance, which he found "embodied in strong and express language in our own Declaration of Independence." He weakened his case further by confessing that the executive had no authority to act in this situation. It was up to Congress to decide whether the present laws could be so amended as to carry out the objects of the Constitution and avoid civil strife. Buchanan spoke eloquently of the Union, but reserved most of his fire for the abolitionists who were staying in the Union, not for the Southern extremists who were already getting out.

Then Buchanan stiffened momentarily. After ordering Major Robert Anderson to withdraw his garrison from Fort Moultrie to the more formidable Fort Sumter, he dispatched to Fort Sumter the *Star of the West,* an unarmed ship with reinforcements and provisions. But the ship was repulsed with fire from South Carolina shore batteries and returned to New York. Fort after fort and arsenal after arsenal belonging to the Federal government were seized by state forces in the Lower South during January and February. Buchanan did nothing. In his message to Congress of December 3, 1860, he had already made his fateful decision not to act, and now it was too late for him to turn back.

During the same period one after another of the states of the Lower South seceded, and the Upper South was perilously poised for the plunge. Buchanan, tense and troubled, could only wait for the freedom that Lincoln's inauguration would bring him. As an old Pennsylvania friend of the President put it, "This, at first, a squabble of politicians, has outgrown their capacity to govern, and now plain men with a stake in the country must stiffen one another in their actions." A plain man with a stake in the country became President on the fourth of March. The hour of decision had finally come.

FOURTH ANNUAL MESSAGE

WASHINGTON CITY, *December 3, 1860*

Fellow-Citizens of the Senate and House of Representatives:
Throughout the year since our last meeting the country has been eminently prosperous in all its material interests. The general health has been excellent, our harvests have been abundant, and plenty smiles throughout the land. Our commerce and manufactures have been prosecuted with energy and industry, and have yielded fair and ample returns. In short, no nation in the tide of time has ever presented a spectacle of greater material prosperity than we have done until within a very recent period.

Why is it, then, that discontent now so extensively prevails, and the Union of the States, which is the source of all these blessings, is threatened with destruction?

The long-continued and intemperate interference of the Northern people with the question of slavery in the Southern States has at length produced its natural effects. The different sections of the Union are now arrayed against each other, and the time has arrived, so much dreaded by the Father of his Country, when hostile geographical parties have been formed.

I have long foreseen and often forewarned my countrymen of the now impending danger. This does not proceed solely from the claim on the part of Congress or the Territorial legislatures to exclude slavery from the Territories, nor from the efforts of different States to defeat the execution of the fugitive-slave law. All or any of these evils might have been endured by the South without danger to the Union (as others have been) in the hope that time and reflection might apply the remedy. The immediate peril arises not so much from these causes as from the fact that the incessant and violent agitation of the slavery question throughout the North for the last quarter of a century has at length produced its malign influence on the slaves and inspired them with vague notions of freedom. Hence a sense of security no longer exists around the family altar. This feeling of peace at home has given place to apprehensions of servile insurrections. Many a matron throughout the South retires at night in dread of what may befall herself and children before the morning. Should this apprehension of domestic danger, whether real or imaginary, extend and intensify itself until it shall pervade the masses of the Southern people, then disunion will become inevitable. Self-preservation is the first law of nature, and has been implanted in the heart of man by his Creator for the wisest purpose; and no political union, however fraught with blessings and benefits in all other respects, can long continue if the necessary consequence be to render the homes and the firesides of nearly half the parties to it habitually and hopelessly insecure. Sooner or later the bonds of such a union must be severed. It is my conviction that this fatal period has not yet arrived, and my prayer to God is that He would preserve the Constitution and the Union throughout all generations.

But let us take warning in time and remove the cause of danger. It can not be denied that for five and twenty years the agitation at the North against slavery has been incessant. In 1835 pictorial handbills and inflammatory appeals were circulated extensively throughout the South of a character to excite the passions of the slaves, and, in the language of General Jackson, "to stimulate them to insurrection and produce all the horrors of a servile war." This agitation has ever since been continued by the public press, by the proceedings of State and county conventions and by abolition sermons and lectures. The time of Congress has been occupied in violent speeches on this never-ending subject, and appeals, in pamphlet and other forms, indorsed by distinguished names, have been sent forth from this central point and spread broadcast over the Union.

How easy would it be for the American people to settle the slavery question forever and to restore peace and harmony to this distracted country! They, and they alone, can do it. All that is necessary to accomplish the object, and all for which the slave States have ever contended, is to be let alone and permitted to manage their domestic institutions in their own way. As sovereign States, they, and they alone, are responsible before God and the world for the slavery existing among them. For this the people of the North are not more responsible and have no more right to interfere than with similar institutions in Russia or in Brazil.

Upon their good sense and patriotic forbearance I confess I still greatly rely. Without their aid it is beyond the power of any President, no matter what may be his own political proclivities, to restore peace and harmony among the States. Wisely limited and restrained as is his power under our Constitution and laws, he alone can accomplish but little for good or for evil on such a momentous question.

And this brings me to observe that the election of any one of our fellow-citizens to the office of President does not of itself afford just cause for dissolving the Union. This is more especially true if his election has been effected by a mere plurality, and not a majority of the people, and has resulted from transient and temporary causes, which may probably never again occur. In order to justify a resort to revolutionary resistance, the Federal Government must be guilty of "a deliberate, palpable, and dangerous exercise" of powers not granted by the Constitution. The late Presidential election, however, has been held in strict conformity with its express provisions. How, then, can the result justify a revolution to destroy this very Constitution? Reason, justice, a regard for the Constitution, all require that we shall wait for some overt and dangerous act on the part of the President elect before resorting to such a remedy. It is said, however, that the antecedents of the President elect have been sufficient to justify the fears of the South that he will attempt to invade their constitutional rights. But are such apprehensions of contingent danger in the future sufficient to justify the immediate destruction of the noblest system of government ever devised by mortals? From the very nature of his office and its high responsibilities he must necessarily be conservative. The stern duty of administering the vast and complicated concerns of this Government affords in itself a guaranty that he will not attempt any violation of a clear constitutional right.

After all, he is no more than the chief executive officer of the Government. His province is not to make but to execute the laws. And it is a remarkable fact in our history that, notwithstanding the repeated efforts of the antislavery party, no single act has ever passed Congress, unless we may possibly except the Missouri compromise, impairing in the slightest degree the rights of the South to their property in slaves; and it may also be observed, judging from present indications, that no probability exists of the passage of such an act by a majority of both Houses, either in the present or the next Congress. Surely under these circumstances we ought to be restrained from present action by the precept of Him who spake as man never spoke, that "sufficient unto the day is the evil thereof." The day of evil may never come unless we shall rashly bring it upon ourselves.

It is alleged as one cause for immediate secession that the Southern States are denied equal rights with the other States in the common Territories. But by what authority are these denied? Not by Congress, which has never passed, and I believe never will pass, any act to exclude slavery from these Territories; and certainly not by the Supreme Court, which has solemnly decided that slaves are property, and, like all other property, their owners have a right to take them into the common Territories and hold them there under the protection of the Constitution.

So far, then, as Congress is concerned, the objection is not to anything they have already done, but to what they may do hereafter. It will surely be admitted that this apprehension of future danger is no good reason for an immediate dissolution of the Union. It is true that the Territorial legislature of Kansas, on the 23d February, 1860, passed in great haste an act over the veto of the governor declaring that slavery "is and shall be forever prohibited in this Territory." Such an act, however, plainly violating the rights of property secured by the Constitution, will surely be declared void by the judiciary whenever it shall be presented in a legal form.

Only three days after my inauguration the Supreme Court of the United States solemnly adjudged that this power did not exist in a Territorial legislature. Yet such has been the factious temper of the times that the correctness of this decision has been extensively impugned before the people, and the question has given rise to angry political conflicts throughout the country. Those who have appealed from this judgment of our highest constitutional tribunal to popular assemblies would, if they could, invest a Territorial legislature with power to annul the sacred rights of property. This power Congress is expressly forbidden by the Federal Constitution to exercise. Every State legislature in the Union is forbidden by its own constitution to exercise it.

It can not be exercised in any State except by the people in their highest sovereign capacity, when framing or amending their State constitution. In like manner it can only be exercised by the people of a Territory represented in a convention of delegates for the purpose of framing a constitution preparatory to admission as a State into the Union. Then, and not until then, are they invested with power to decide the question whether slavery shall or shall not exist within their limits. This is an act of sovereign authority, and not of subordinate Territorial legislation. Were it otherwise, then indeed would the equality of the States in the Territories be destroyed, and the rights of property in slaves would depend not upon the guaranties of the Constitution, but upon the shifting majorities of an irresponsible Territorial legislature. Such a doctrine, from its intrinsic unsoundness, can not long influence any considerable portion of our people, much less can it afford a good reason for a dissolution of the Union.

The most palpable violations of constitutional duty which have yet been committed consist in the acts of different State legislatures to defeat the execution of the fugitive-slave law. It ought to be remembered, however, that for these acts neither Congress nor any President can justly be held responsible. Having been passed in violation of the Federal Constitution, they are therefore null and void. All the courts, both State and national, before whom the question has arisen have from the beginning declared the fugitive-slave law to be constitutional. The single exception is that of a State court in Wisconsin, and this has not only been reversed by the proper appellate tribunal, but has met with such universal reprobation that there can be no danger from it as a precedent. The validity of this law has been established over and over again by the Supreme Court of the United States with perfect unanimity. It is founded upon an express provision of the Constitution, requiring that fugitive slaves who escape from service in one State to another shall be "delivered up" to their masters. Without this provision it is a well-known historical fact that the Constitution itself could never have been adopted by the Convention. In one form or other, under the acts of 1793 and 1850, both being substantially the same, the fugitive-slave law has been the law of the land from the days of Washington until the present moment. Here, then, a clear case is presented in which it will be the duty of the next President, as it has been my own, to act with vigor in executing this supreme law against the conflicting enactments of State legislatures. Should he fail in the performance of this high duty, he will then have manifested a disregard of the Constitution and laws, to the great injury of the people of nearly one-half of the States of the Union But are we to presume in advance that he will thus violate his duty? This would be at war with every principle of justice and of Christian charity. Let us wait for the overt act. The fugitive-slave law has been carried into execution in every contested case since the commencement of the present Administration, though often, it is to be regretted, with great loss and inconvenience to the master and with considerable expense to the Government. Let us trust that the State legislatures will repeal their unconstitutional and obnoxious enactments. Unless this shall be done without unnecessary delay, it is impossible for any human power to save the Union.

The Southern States, standing on the basis of the Constitution, have a right to demand this act of justice from the States of the North. Should it be refused, then the Constitution, to which all the States are parties, will have been willfully violated by one portion of them in a provision essential to the domestic security and happiness of the remainder. In that event the injured States, after having first used all peaceful and constitutional means to obtain redress, would be justified in revolutionary resistance to the Government of the Union.

I have purposely confined my remarks to revolutionary resistance, because it has been claimed within the last few years that any State, whenever this shall be its sovereign will and pleasure, may secede from the Union in accordance with the Constitution and without any violation of the constitutional rights of the other members of the Confederacy; that as each became parties to the Union by the vote of its own people assembled in convention, so any one of them may retire from the Union in a similar manner by the vote of such a convention.

In order to justify secession as a constitutional remedy, it must be on the principle that the Federal Government is a mere voluntary association of States, to be dissolved at pleasure by any one of the contracting parties. If this be so, the Confederacy is a rope of sand, to be penetrated and dissolved by the first adverse wave of public opinion in any of the States. In this manner our thirty-three States may resolve themselves into as many petty, jarring, and hostile republics, each one retiring from the Union without responsibility whenever any sudden excitement might impel them to such a course. By this process a Union might be entirely broken into fragments in a few weeks which cost our forefathers many years of toil, privation, and blood to establish.

Such a principle is wholly inconsistent with the history as well as the character of the Federal Constitution. After it was framed with the greatest deliberation and care it was submitted to conventions of the people of the several States for ratification. Its provisions were discussed at length in these bodies, composed of the first men of the country. Its opponents contended that it conferred powers upon the Federal Government dangerous to the rights of the States, whilst its advocates maintained that under a fair construction of the instrument there was no foundation for such apprehensions. In that mighty struggle between the first intellects of this or any other country it never occurred to any individual, either among its opponents or advocates, to assert or even to intimate that their efforts were all vain labor, because the moment that any State felt herself aggrieved she might secede from the Union. What a crushing argument would this have proved against those who dreaded that the rights of the States would be endangered by the Constitution! The truth is that it was not until many years after the origin of the Federal Government that such a proposition was first advanced. It was then met and refuted by the conclusive arguments of General Jackson, who in his message of the 16th of January, 1833, transmitting the nullifying ordinance of South Carolina to Congress, employs the following language:

> The right of the people of a single State to absolve themselves at will and without the consent of the other States from their most solemn obligations, and hazard the liberties and happiness of the millions composing this Union, can not be acknowledged. Such authority is believed to be utterly repugnant both to the principles upon which the General Government is constituted and to the objects which it is expressly formed to attain.

It is not pretended that any clause in the Constitution gives countenance to such a theory. It is altogether founded upon inference; not from any language contained in the instrument itself, but from the sovereign character of the several States by which it was ratified. But is it beyond the power of a State, like an individual, to yield a portion of its sovereign rights to secure the remainder? In the language of Mr. Madison, who has been called the father of the Constitution—

> It was formed by the States; that is, by the people in each of the States acting in their highest sovereign capacity, and formed, consequently, by the same authority which formed the State constitutions. * * * Nor is the Government of the United States, created by the Constitution, less a government, in the strict sense of the term, within the sphere of its powers than the governments created by the constitutions of the States are within their several spheres. It is, like them, organized into legislative, executive, and judiciary departments. It operates, like them, directly on persons and things, and, like them, it has at command a physical force for executing the powers committed to it.

It was intended to be perpetual, and not to be annulled at the pleasure of any one of the contracting parties. The old Articles of Confederation were entitled "Articles of Confederation and Perpetual Union between the States," and by the thirteenth article it is expressly declared that "the articles of this Confederation shall be inviolably observed by every State, and the Union shall be perpetual." The preamble to the Constitution of the United States, having express reference to the Articles of Confederation, recites that it was established "in order to form a more perfect union." And yet it is contended that this "more perfect union" does not include the essential attribute of perpetuity.

But that the Union was designed to be perpetual appears conclusively from the nature and extent of the powers conferred by the Constitution on the Federal Government. These powers embrace the very highest attributes of national sovereignty. They place both the sword and the purse under its control. Congress has power to make war and to make peace, to raise and support armies and navies, and to conclude treaties with foreign governments. It is invested with the power to coin money and to regulate the value thereof, and to regulate commerce with foreign nations and among the several States. It is not necessary to enumerate the other high powers which have been conferred upon the Federal Government. In order to carry the enumerated powers into effect, Congress possesses the exclusive right to lay and collect duties on imports, and, in common with the States, to lay and collect all other taxes.

But the Constitution has not only conferred these high powers upon Congress, but it has adopted effectual means to restrain the States from interfering with their exercise. For that purpose it has in strong prohibitory language expressly declared that—

No State shall enter into any treaty, alliance, or confederation; grant letters of marque and reprisal; coin money; emit bills of credit; make anything but gold and silver coin a tender in payment of debts; pass any bill of attainder, *ex post facto* law, or law impairing the obligation of contracts.

Moreover—

No State shall without the consent of the Congress lay any imposts or duties on imports or exports, except what may be absolutely necessary for executing its inspection laws.

And if they exceed this amount the excess shall belong to the United States. And—

No State shall without the consent of Congress lay any duty of tonnage, keep troops or ships of war in time of peace, enter into any agreement or compact with another State or with a foreign power, or engage in war, unless actually invaded or in such imminent danger as will not admit of delay.

In order still further to secure the uninterrupted exercise of these high powers against State interposition, it is provided that—

> This Constitution and the laws of the United States which shall be made in pursuance thereof, and all treaties made or which shall be made under the authority of the United States, shall be the supreme law of the land, and the judges in every State shall be bound thereby, anything in the constitution or laws of any State to the contrary notwithstanding.

The solemn sanction of religion has been superadded to the obligations of official duty, and all Senators and Representatives of the United States, all members of State legislatures, and all executive and judicial officers, "both of the United States and of the several States, shall be bound by oath or affirmation to support this Constitution."

In order to carry into effect these powers, the Constitution has established a perfect Government in all its forms—legislative, executive, and judicial; and this Government to the extent of its powers acts directly upon the individual citizens of every State, and executes its own decrees by the agency of its own officers. In this respect it differs entirely from the Government under the old Confederation, which was confined to making requisitions on the States in their sovereign character. This left it in the discretion of each whether to obey or to refuse, and they often declined to comply with such requisitions. It thus became necessary for the purpose of removing this barrier and "in order to form a more perfect union" to establish a Government which could act directly upon the people and execute its own laws without the intermediate agency of the States. This has been accomplished by the Constitution of the United States. In short, the Government created by the Constitution, and deriving its authority from the sovereign people of each of the several States, has precisely the same right to exercise its power over the people of all these States in the enumerated cases that each one of them possesses over subjects not delegated to the United States, but "reserved to the States respectively or to the people."

To the extent of the delegated powers the Constitution of the United States is as much a part of the constitution of each State and is as binding upon its people as though it had been textually inserted therein.

This Government, therefore, is a great and powerful Government, invested with all the attributes of sovereignty over the special subjects to which its authority extends. Its framers never intended to implant in its bosom the seeds of its own destruction, nor were they at its creation guilty of the absurdity of providing for its own dissolution. It was not intended by its framers to be the baseless fabric of a vision, which at the touch of the enchanter would vanish into thin air, but a substantial and mighty fabric, capable of resisting the slow decay of time and of defying the storms of ages. Indeed, well may the jealous patriots of that day have indulged fears that a Government of such high powers might violate the reserved rights of the States, and wisely did they adopt the rule of a strict construction of these powers to prevent the danger. But they did not fear, nor had they any reason to imagine, that the Constitution would ever be so interpreted as to enable any State by her own act, and without the consent of her sister States, to discharge her people from all or any of their federal obligations.

It may be asked, then, Are the people of the States without redress against the tyranny and oppression of the Federal Government? By no means. The right of resistance on the part of the governed against the oppression of their governments can not be denied. It exists independently of all constitutions, and has been exercised at all periods of the world's history. Under it old governments have been destroyed and new ones have taken their place. It is embodied in strong and express language in our own Declaration of Independence. But the distinction must ever be observed that this is revolution against an established government, and not a voluntary secession from it by virtue of an inherent constitutional right. In short, let us look the danger fairly in the face. Secession is neither more nor less than revolution. It may or it may not be a justifiable revolution, but still it is revolution.

What, in the meantime, is the responsibility and true position of the Executive? He is bound by solemn oath, before God and the country, "to take care that the laws be faithfully executed," and from this obligation he can not be absolved by any human power. But what if the performance of this duty, in whole or in part, has been rendered impracticable by events over which he could have exercised no control? Such at the present moment is the case throughout the State of South Carolina so far as the laws of the United States to secure the administration of justice by means of the Federal judiciary are concerned. All the Federal officers within its limits through whose agency alone these laws can be carried into execution have already resigned. We no longer have a district judge, a district attorney, or a marshal in South Carolina. In fact, the whole machinery of the Federal Government necessary for the distribution of remedial justice among the people has been demolished, and it would be difficult, if not impossible, to replace it.

The only acts of Congress on the statute book bearing upon this subject are those of February 28, 1795, and March 3, 1807. These authorize

208

the President, after he shall have ascertained that the marshal, with his *posse comitatus,* is unable to execute civil or criminal process in any particular case, to call forth the militia and employ the Army and Navy to aid him in performing this service, having first by proclamation commanded the insurgents "to disperse and retire peaceably to their respective abodes within a limited time." This duty can not by possibility be performed in a State where no judicial authority exists to issue process, and where there is no marshal to execute it, and where, even if there were such an officer, the entire population would constitute one solid combination to resist him.

The bare enumeration of these provisions proves how inadequate they are without further legislation to overcome a united opposition in a single State, not to speak of other States who may place themselves in a similar attitude. Congress alone has power to decide whether the present laws can or can not be amended so as to carry out more effectually the objects of the Constitution.

The same insuperable obstacles do not lie in the way of executing the laws for the collection of the customs. The revenue still continues to be collected as heretofore at the custom-house in Charleston, and should the collector unfortunately resign a successor may be appointed to perform this duty.

Then, in regard to the property of the United States in South Carolina. This has been purchased for a fair equivalent, "by the consent of the legislature of the State," "for the erection of forts, magazines, arsenals," etc., and over these the authority "to exercise exclusive legislation" has been expressly granted by the Constitution to Congress. It is not believed that any attempt will be made to expel the United States from this property by force; but if in this I should prove to be mistaken, the officer in command of the forts has received orders to act strictly on the defensive. In such a contingency the responsibility for consequences would rightfully rest upon the heads of the assailants.

Apart from the execution of the laws, so far as this may be practicable, the Executive has no authority to decide what shall be the relations between the Federal Government and South Carolina. He has been invested with no such discretion. He possesses no power to change the relations heretofore existing between them, much less to acknowledge the independence of that State. This would be to invest a mere executive officer with the power of recognizing the dissolution of the confederacy among our thirty-three sovereign States. It bears no resemblance to the recognition of a foreign *de facto* government, involving no such responsibility. Any attempt to do this would, on his part, be a naked act of usurpation. It is therefore my duty to submit to Congress the whole question in all its bearings. The course of events is so rapidly hastening forward that the emergency may soon arise when you may be called upon to decide the momentous question whether you possess the power by force of arms to compel a State to remain in the Union. I should feel myself recreant to my duty were I not to express an opinion on this important subject.

The question fairly stated is, Has the Constitution delegated to Congress the power to coerce a State into submission which is attempting to withdraw or has actually withdrawn from the Confederacy? If answered in the affirmative, it must be on the principle that the power has been conferred upon Congress to declare and to make war against a State. After much serious reflection I have arrived at the conclusion that no such power has been delegated to Congress or to any other department of the Federal Government. It is manifest upon an inspection of the Constitution that this is not among the specific and enumerated powers granted to Congress, and it is equally apparent that its exercise is not "necessary and proper for carrying into execution" any one of these powers. So far from this power having been delegated to Congress, it was expressly refused by the Convention which framed the Constitution.

It appears from the proceedings of that body that on the 31st May, 1787, the clause *"authorizing an exertion of the force of the whole against a delinquent State"* came up for consideration. Mr. Madison opposed it in a brief but powerful speech, from which I shall extract but a single sentence. He observed:

> The use of force against a State would look more like a declaration of war than an infliction of punishment, and would probably be considered by the party attacked as a dissolution of all previous compacts by which it might be bound.

Upon his motion the clause was unanimously postponed, and was never, I believe, again presented. Soon afterwards, on the 8th June, 1787, when incidentally adverting to the subject, he said: "Any government for the United States formed on the supposed practicability of using force against the unconstitutional proceedings of the States would prove as visionary and fallacious as the government of Congress," evidently meaning the then existing Congress of the old Confederation.

Without descending to particulars, it may be safely asserted that the power to make war against a State is at variance with the whole spirit and intent of the Constitution. Suppose such a war should result in the conquest of a State; how are we to govern it afterwards? Shall we hold it as a province and govern it by despotic power? In the nature of things, we could not by physical force control the will of the people and compel them to elect Senators and Representatives to Congress and to perform all the other duties depending upon their own volition and required from the free citizens of a free State as a constituent member of the Confederacy.

But if we possessed this power, would it be wise to exercise it under existing circumstances? The object would doubtless be to preserve the Union. War would not only present the most effectual means of destroying it, but would vanish all hope of its peaceable reconstruction. Besides, in the fraternal conflict a vast amount of blood and treasure would be expended, rendering future reconciliation between the States impossible. In the meantime, who can foretell what would be the sufferings and privations of the people during its existence?

The fact is that our Union rests upon public opinion, and can never be cemented by the blood of its citizens shed in civil war. If it can not live in the affections of the people, it must one day perish. Congress possesses many means of preserving it by conciliation, but the sword was not placed in their hand to preserve it by force.

But may I be permitted solemnly to invoke my countrymen to pause and deliberate before they determine to destroy this the grandest temple which has ever been dedicated to human freedom since the world began? It has been consecrated by the blood of our fathers, by the glories of the past, and by the hopes of the future. The Union has already made us the most prosperous, and ere long will, if preserved, render us the most powerful, nation on the face of the earth. In every foreign region of the globe the title of American citizen is held in the highest respect, and when pronounced in a foreign land it causes the hearts of our countrymen to swell with honest pride. Surely when we reach the brink of the yawning abyss we shall recoil with horror from the last fatal plunge.

By such a dread catastrophe the hopes of the friends of freedom throughout the world would be destroyed, and a long night of leaden despotism would enshroud the nations. Our example for more than eighty years would not only be lost, but it would be quoted as a conclusive proof that man is unfit for self-government.

It is not every wrong—nay, it is not every grievous wrong—which can justify a resort to such a fearful alternative. This ought to be the last desperate remedy of a despairing people, after every other constitutional means of conciliation had been exhausted. We should reflect that under this free Government there is an incessant ebb and flow in public opinion. The slavery question, like everything human, will have its day. I firmly believe that it has reached and passed the culminating point. But if in the midst of the existing excitement the Union shall perish, the evil may then become irreparable.

Congress can contribute much to avert it by proposing and recommending to the legislatures of the several States the remedy for existing evils which the Constitution has itself provided for its own preservation. This has been tried at different critical periods of our history, and always with eminent success. It is to be found in the fifth article, providing for its own amendment. Under this article amendments have been proposed by two-thirds of both Houses of Congress, and have been "ratified by the legislatures of three-fourths of the several States," and have consequently become parts of the Constitution. To this process the country is indebted for the clause prohibiting Congress from passing any law respecting an establishment of religion or abridging the freedom of speech or of the press or of the right of petition. To this we are also indebted for the bill of rights which secures the people against any abuse of power by the Federal Government. Such were the apprehensions justly entertained by the friends of State rights at that period as to have rendered it extremely doubtful whether the Constitution could have long survived without those amendments.

Again the Constitution was amended by the same process, after the election of President Jefferson by the House of Representatives, in February, 1803. This amendment was rendered necessary to prevent a recurrence of the dangers which had seriously threatened the existence of the Government during the pendency of that election. The article for its own amendment was intended to secure the amicable adjustment of conflicting constitutional questions like the present which might arise between the governments of the States and that of the United States. This appears from contemporaneous history. In this connection I shall merely call attention to a few sentences in Mr. Madison's justly celebrated report, in 1799, to the legislature of Virginia. In this he ably and conclusively defended the resolutions of the preceding legislature against the strictures of several other State legislatures. These were mainly founded upon the protest of the Virginia legislature against the "alien and sedition acts," as "palpable and alarming infractions of the Constitution." In pointing out the peaceful and constitutional remedies—and he referred to none other—to which the States were authorized to resort on such occasions, he concludes by saying that—

> The legislatures of the States might have made a direct representation to Congress with a view to obtain a rescinding of the two offensive acts, or they might have represented to their respective Senators in Congress their wish that two-thirds thereof would propose an explanatory amendment to the Constitution; or two-thirds of themselves, if

such had been their option, might by an application to Congress have obtained a convention for the same object.

This is the very course which I earnestly recommend in order to obtain an "explanatory amendment" of the Constitution on the subject of slavery. This might originate with Congress or the State legislatures, as may be deemed most advisable to attain the object. The explanatory amendment might be confined to the final settlement of the true construction of the Constitution on three special points:

1. An express recognition of the right of property in slaves in the States where it now exists or may hereafter exist.

2. The duty of protecting this right in all the common Territories throughout their Territorial existence, and until they shall be admitted as States into the Union, with or without slavery, as their constitutions may prescribe.

3. A like recognition of the right of the master to have his slave who has escaped from one State to another restored and "delivered up" to him, and of the validity of the fugitive-slave law enacted for this purpose, together with a declaration that all State laws impairing or defeating this right are violations of the Constitution, and are consequently null and void. It may be objected that this construction of the Constitution has already been settled by the Supreme Court of the United States, and what more ought to be required? The answer is that a very large proportion of the people of the United States still contest the correctness of this decision, and never will cease from agitation and admit its binding force until clearly established by the people of the several States in their sovereign character. Such an explanatory amendment would, it is believed, forever terminate the existing dissensions, and restore peace and harmony among the States.

It ought not to be doubted that such an appeal to the arbitrament established by the Constitution itself would be received with favor by all the States of the Confederacy. In any event, it ought to be tried in a spirit of conciliation before any of these States shall separate themselves from the Union. . . .

17

THE DECISION
TO PRESERVE THE UNION

*Lincoln Warns that the Union "Will Constitutionally
Defend and Maintain Itself"*

When Abraham Lincoln was elected President everybody knew how he stood on the question of slavery. He had made it clear that he was no radical abolitionist, rather a conservative, ready to make reasonable concessions to Southern sensibilities. On December 22, 1860, he wrote to Alexander H. Stephens: "Do the people of the South really entertain fears that a Republican administration would, directly or indirectly, interfere with the slaves, or with them about the slaves?" Lincoln assured Stephens that "there is no cause for such fears," that the South "would be in no more danger in this respect" than it was "in the days of Washington." On the other hand, Lincoln was inflexibly opposed to the extension of slavery in the territories, and advised his supporters in Congress that Senator John J. Crittenden's peace resolution, which would have recognized slavery in territories south of 36° 30', the old Missouri Compromise line, was unacceptable to him. Unable to agree on any compromise proposition which would conciliate the South, Congress, to whom Buchanan had turned over the burden of settling the issue, accomplished no more than did the retiring President.

On the slavery issue Lincoln had shown himself to be moderate. Would he compromise the issue of Union? In his journey to the capital from Springfield, which he left, "not knowing when or whether I ever may return, with a task before me greater than that which rested upon Washington," the President-elect avoided disclosing the specific steps he would take. He was opposed to bloodshed, he told a Philadelphia audience. "The government will not use force, unless force is used against it."

People wondered when they heard Lincoln during these fateful days whether this prairie lawyer had the wisdom and courage to settle an issue which had divided the greatest statesmen of the land for a troubled decade. Henry Villard, a news reporter, recounts how, as the Presidential train traveled east from Springfield, Lincoln disappointed many who saw him for the first time, who noted his shrill, high-pitched voice, his "most unprepossessing features, the gawkiest figure, and the most awkward manners." Very tall, he stooped a little and walked shamblingly. Walt Whitman, who saw him when he came to New York, recognized the nobility of the man, "his dress of complete black, stovepipe hat pushed on the head, dark-brown complexion, seam'd and wrinkled yet canny-looking face, black bushy head of hair, disproportionately long neck." To do justice to the figure of Lincoln would have required, in Whitman's opinion, "the eyes and brains and finger-touch of Plutarch and Aeschylus and Michelangelo, assisted by Rabelais."

People wondered, too, whether Lincoln would ever get the chance to deliver his Inaugural Address. Reports of a widespread conspiracy were in the air. "It is beyond a doubt that the revolutionists have determined to take forcible possession of the Government at Washington before the fourth of March, and perhaps within thirty days," reported Charles Francis Adams. Advised of an assassination plot against him in Baltimore, Lincoln pulled no punches in his talk at Philadelphia. He told his audience that the ideals of the Declaration of Independence were still alive and offered them hope "that in due time the weights would be lifted from the shoulders of all men, and that all should have an equal chance." If the country could not be saved without giving up that principle, he added, "I would rather be assassinated on this spot than surrender it." But those responsible for getting him safely to the capital would take no chances. Foregoing speaking engagements in Baltimore, Lincoln reached that city at 3:30 in the morning, took a carriage from one railroad station to the other unnoticed (according to a colorful but inaccurate story, wearing a "Scotch plaid cap" and a "long military cloak"), and arrived safely in Washington.

As the clock struck noon on a threatening Inauguration Day Lincoln entered President Buchanan's carriage at Willard's Hotel. Buchanan seemed grave and silent, Lincoln was reported "calm and but little affected by the excitement around him." Facing a vast throng, Lincoln read his Inaugural Address on a temporary platform at the east front of the unfinished Capitol. Then he swore to "defend the Constitution," the oath being administered by Chief Justice Taney, whose Court's authority to decide issues of constitutionality Lincoln had only just questioned in his message.

Would the Inaugural Address reveal Lincoln's course of action? Lincoln made it clear again that he had no intention of interfering with slavery in the states where it existed or of endangering the peace and security of any section of the country. Reiterating Buchanan's point that the Union was "perpetual," he did not dodge the issue of how to keep it from being broken up, as Buchanan had. The Union, he pronounced, will "defend and maintain itself." However, he went so far toward pacifying the insurgent section as to state that in regions where opposition was "great and universal" the performance of Federal functions would be suspended, that he deemed it better to "forego" the strict legal right for the time being. In other words, force was not to be the policy. In closing, he appealed to "the mystic chords of memory" stretching from the patriot dead to the living, which, he prophesied, would "yet swell the chorus of the Union when again touched, as surely they will be, by the better angels of our nature."

The nation had not heard such simple eloquence in an Inaugural Address since President Jefferson. "In our youth," Justice Oliver Wendell Holmes once wrote, "our hearts were touched with fire." Some of that fire doubtless came from the eloquent phrasing, the Biblical simplicity, and the grand vision of Abraham Lincoln's speeches and state papers. Each word of this message was significant. It had been worked over in numerous drafts. Lincoln originally had included an endorsement of the Republican Party platform. Now he dropped it out. In his final draft he referred to the Southern ordinance of secession as "revolutionary" instead of "treasonable," and instead of pledging that his power would be "used to reclaim the public property and places" already seized, confined himself to the pledge that he would "hold, occupy, and possess" the government's property.

In his original draft Lincoln closed on a more belligerent note. "With you, and not with me, is the solemn question of 'Shall it be

216

peace, or a sword.'" On the advice of William H. Seward, Lincoln discarded this ending and revised an alternative paragraph which Seward had submitted. Seward's passage read: "The mystic chords which, proceeding from so many battle-fields and so many patriot graves, pass through all the hearts and all the hearths in this broad continent of ours, will yet again harmonize in their ancient music when breathed upon by the guardian angel of the nation." Lincoln's simpler version was more poetic and more moving.

It is a fitting commentary on the temper of the South at that time to point out that, despite the reasoned and conciliatory tone of the Inaugural Address and its eloquent appeal for Union, it was denounced in the South as a call to arms. Historians differ as to whether Lincoln at this time planned to use force to preserve the Union, but the Inaugural Address, considered in relation to the dramatic events that quickly followed, should have dispelled doubts. Historians also differ as to whether or not Lincoln provoked the South into shooting first by sending naval vessels to the relief of Fort Sumter. Lincoln's course has been compared by his critics to Bismarck's alleged conduct in the Ems dispatch incident and Franklin D. Roosevelt's alleged behavior at the time of Pearl Harbor. But in sending food to beleaguered Sumter Lincoln went no farther than Buchanan had, and it is hard to justify Jefferson Davis's view of Lincoln's act as "a declaration of war." It is for this reason that the Inaugural Address cannot be separated in context from the series of proclamations issued after the start of the war. On April 14, 1861, Major Robert Anderson formally surrendered Fort Sumter. The next day Lincoln issued his far-reaching proclamation, calling out the militia of the nonrebellious states "to suppress" these powerful "combinations" and "to cause the laws to be duly executed." Other proclamations quickly followed, announcing a blockade of the rebellious states and calling for volunteers.

Can a few discontented individuals break up their government? Lincoln asked. "Is there, in all republics, this inherent and fatal weakness?" "Must a Government, of necessity, be too *strong* for the liberties of its own people, or too *weak* to maintain its own existence?" Lincoln answered his own rhetorical questions: "So viewing the issue, no choice was left but to call out the war power of the Government; and so to resist force employed for its destruction, by force for its preservation."

FIRST INAUGURAL ADDRESS

Fellow-Citizens of the United States:

In compliance with a custom as old as the Government itself, I appear before you to address you briefly and to take in your presence the oath prescribed by the Constitution of the United States to be taken by the President "before he enters on the execution of his office."

I do not consider it necessary at present for me to discuss those matters of administration about which there is no special anxiety or excitement.

Apprehension seems to exist among the people of the Southern States that by the accession of a Republican Administration their property and their peace and personal security are to be endangered. There has never been any reasonable cause for such apprehension. Indeed, the most ample evidence to the contrary has all the while existed and been open to their inspection. It is found in nearly all the published speeches of him who now addresses you. I do but quote from one of those speeches when I declare that—

> I have no purpose, directly or indirectly, to interfere with the institution of slavery in the States where it exists. I believe I have no lawful right to do so, and I have no inclination to do so.

Those who nominated and elected me did so with full knowledge that I had made this and many similar declarations and had never recanted them; and more than this, they placed in the platform for my acceptance, and as a law to themselves and to me, the clear and emphatic resolution which I now read:

> *Resolved,* That the maintenance inviolate of the rights of the States, and especially the right of each State to order and control its own domestic institutions according to its own judgment exclusively, is essential to that balance of power on which the perfection and endurance of our political fabric depend; and we denounce the lawless invasion by armed force of the soil of any State or Territory, no matter under what pretext, as among the gravest of crimes.

I now reiterate these sentiments, and in doing so I only press upon the public attention the most conclusive evidence of which the case is susceptible that the property, peace, and security of no section are to be in any wise endangered by the now incoming Administration. I add, too, that all the protection which, consistently with the Constitution and the laws, can be given will be cheerfully given to all the States when lawfully demanded, for whatever cause—as cheerfully to one section as to another.

There is much controversy about the delivering up of fugitives from service or labor. The clause I now read is as plainly written in the Constitution as any other of its provisions:

No person held to service or labor in one State, under the laws thereof, escaping into another, shall in consequence of any law or regulation therein be discharged from such service or labor, but shall be delivered up on claim of the party to whom such service or labor may be due.

It is scarcely questioned that this provision was intended by those who made it for the reclaiming of what we call fugitive slaves; and the intention of the lawgiver is the law. All members of Congress swear their support to the whole Constitution—to this provision as much as to any other. To the proposition, then, that slaves whose cases come within the terms of this clause "shall be delivered up" their oaths are unanimous. Now, if they would make the effort in good temper, could they not with nearly equal unanimity frame and pass a law by means of which to keep good that unanimous oath?

There is some difference of opinion whether this clause should be enforced by national or by State authority, but surely that difference is not a very material one. If the slave is to be surrendered, it can be of but little consequence to him or to others by which authority it is done. And should anyone in any case be content that his oath shall go unkept on a merely unsubstantial controversy as to *how* it shall be kept?

Again: In any law upon this subject ought not all the safeguards of liberty known in civilized and humane jurisprudence to be introduced, so that a free man be not in any case surrendered as a slave? And might it not be well at the same time to provide by law for the enforcement of that clause in the Constitution which guarantees that "the citizens of each State shall be entitled to all privileges and immunities of citizens in the several States"?

I take the official oath to-day with no mental reservations and with no purpose to construe the Constitution or laws by any hypercritical rules; and while I do not choose now to specify particular acts of Congress as proper to be enforced, I do suggest that it will be much safer for all, both in official and private stations, to conform to and abide by all those acts which stand unrepealed than to violate any of them trusting to find impunity in having them held to be unconstitutional.

It is seventy-two years since the first inauguration of a President under our National Constitution. During that period fifteen different and greatly distinguished citizens have in succession administered the executive branch of the Government. They have conducted it through many perils, and generally with great success. Yet, with all this scope of precedent, I now enter upon the same task for the brief constitutional term of four years under great and peculiar difficulty. A disruption of the Federal Union, heretofore only menaced, is now formidably attempted.

I hold that in contemplation of universal law and of the Constitution the Union of these States is perpetual. Perpetuity is implied, if not expressed, in the fundamental law of all national governments. It is safe to assert that no government proper ever had a provision in its organic law for its own termination. Continue to execute all the express provisions of our National Constitution, and the Union will endure forever, it being impossible to destroy it except by some action not provided for in the instrument itself.

Again: If the United States be not a government proper, but an association of States in the nature of contract merely, can it, as a contract, be peaceably unmade by less than all the parties who made it? One party to a contract may violate it—break it, so to speak—but does it not require all to lawfully rescind it?

Descending from these general principles, we find the proposition that in legal contemplation the Union is perpetual confirmed by the history of the Union itself. The Union is much older than the Constitution. It was formed, in fact, by the Articles of Association in 1774. It was matured and continued by the Declaration of Independence in 1776. It was further matured, and the faith of all the then thirteen States expressly plighted and engaged that it should be perpetual, by the Articles of Confederation in 1778. And finally, 1778, one of the declared objects for ordaining and establishing the Constitution was *"to form a more perfect Union."*

But if destruction of the Union by one or by a part only of the States be lawfully possible, the Union is *less* perfect than before the Constitution, having lost the vital element of perpetuity.

It follows from these views that no State upon its own mere motion can lawfully get out of the Union; that *resolves* and *ordinances* to that effect are legally void, and that acts of violence within any State or States against the authority of the United States are insurrectionary or revolutionary, according to circumstances.

I therefore consider that in veiw of the Constitution and the laws the Union is unbroken, and to the extent of my ability I shall take care, as the Constitution itself expressly enjoins upon me, that the laws of the Union be faithfully executed in all the States. Doing this I deem to be only a simple duty on my part, and I shall perform it so far as practicable unless my rightful masters, the American people, shall withhold the requisite means or in some authoritative manner direct the contrary. I trust this will not be regarded as a menace, but only as the declared purpose of the Union that it *will* constitutionally defend and maintain itself.

In doing this there needs to be no bloodshed or violence, and there shall be none unless it be forced upon the national authority. The power confided to me will be used to hold, occupy, and possess the property and places belonging to the Government and to collect the duties and imposts; but beyond what may be necessary for these objects, there will be no invasion, no using of force against or among the people anywhere. Where hostility to the United States in any interior locality shall be so great and universal as to prevent competent resident citizens from holding the Federal offices, there will be no attempt to force obnoxious strangers among the people for that object. While the strict legal right may exist in the Government to enforce the exercise of these offices, the attempt to do so would be so irritating and so nearly impracticable withal that I deem it better to forego for the time the uses of such offices.

The mails, unless repelled, will continue to be furnished in all parts of the Union. So far as possible the people everywhere shall have that sense of perfect security which is most favorable to calm thought and reflection. The course here indicated will be followed unless current events and experience shall show a modification or change to be proper, and in every case and exigency my best discretion will be exercised, according to circumstances actually existing and with a view and a hope of a peaceful solution of the national troubles and the restoration of fraternal sympathies and affections.

That there are persons in one section or another who seek to destroy the Union at all events and are glad of any pretext to do it I will neither affirm nor deny; but if there be such, I need address no word to them. To those, however, who really love the Union may I not speak?

Before entering upon so grave a matter as the destruction of our national fabric, with all its benefits, its memories, and its hopes, would it not be wise to ascertain precisely why we do it? Will you hazard so desperate a step while there is any possibility that any portion of the ills you fly from have no real existence? Will you, while the certain ills you fly to are greater than all the real ones you fly from, will you risk the commission of so fearful a mistake?

All profess to be content in the Union if all constitutional rights can be maintained. Is it true, then, that any right plainly written in the Constitution has been denied? I think not. Happily, the human mind is so constituted that no party can reach to the audacity of doing this. Think, if you can, of a single instance in which a plainly written provision of the Constitution has ever been denied. If by the mere force of numbers a majority should deprive a minority of any clearly written constitutional right, it might in a moral point of view justify revolution; certainly would if such right were a vital one. But such is not our case. All the vital rights of minorities and of individuals are so plainly assured to them by affirmations and negations, guaranties and prohibitions, in the Constitution that controversies never arise concerning them. But no organic law can ever be framed with a provision specifically applicable to every question which may occur in practical administration. No foresight can anticipate nor any document of reasonable length contain express provisions for all possible questions. Shall fugitives from labor be surrendered by national or by State authority? The Constitution does not expressly say. *May* Congress prohibit slavery in the Territories? The Constitution does not expressly say. *Must* Congress protect slavery in the Territories? The Constitution does not expressly say.

From questions of this class spring all our constitutional controversies, and we divide upon them into majorities and minorities. If the minority will not acquiese, the majority must, or the Government must cease. There is no other alternative, for continuing the Government is acquiescence on one side or the other. If a minority in such case will secede rather than acquiesce, they make a precedent which in turn will divide and ruin them, for a minority of their own will secede from them whenever a majority refuses to be controlled by such minority. For instance, why may not any portion of a new confederacy a year or two hence arbitrarily secede again, precisely as portions of the present Union now claim to secede from it? All who cherish disunion sentiments are now being educated to the exact temper of doing this.

Is there such perfect identity of interests among the States to compose a new union as to produce harmony only and prevent renewed secession?

Plainly the central idea of secession is the essence of anarchy. A majority held in restraint by constitutional checks and limitations, and always changing easily with deliberate changes of popular opinions and sentiments, is the only true sovereign of a free people. Whoever rejects it does of necessity fly to anarchy or to despotism. Unanimity is impossible. The rule of a minority, as a permanent arrangement, is wholly inadmissible; so that, rejecting the majority principle, anarchy or despotism in some form is all that is left.

I do not forget the position assumed by some that constitutional questions are to be decided by the Supreme Court, nor do I deny that such decisions must be binding in any case upon the parties to a suit as to the object of that suit, while they are also entitled to very high respect and consideration in all parallel cases by all other departments of the Government. And while it is obviously possible that such decision may be erroneous in any given case, still the evil effect following it, being limited to that particular case, with the chance that it may be overruled and never become a precedent for other cases, can better be borne than could the evils of a different practice. At the same time, the candid citizen must confess that if the policy of the Government upon vital questions affecting the whole people is to be irrevocably fixed by decisions of the Supreme Court, the instant they are made in ordinary litigation between parties in personal actions the people will have ceased to be their own rulers, having to that extent practically resigned their Government into the hands of that eminent tribunal. Nor is there in this view any assault upon the court or the judges. It is a duty from which they may not shrink to decide cases properly brought before them, and it is no fault of theirs if others seek to turn their decisions to political purposes.

One section of our country believes slavery is *right* and ought to be extended, while the other believes it is *wrong* and ought not to be extended. This is the only substantial dispute. The fugitive-slave clause of the Constitution and the law for the suppression of the foreign slave trade are each as well enforced, perhaps, as any law can ever be in a community where the moral sense of the people imperfectly supports the law itself. The great body of the people abide by the dry legal obligation in both cases, and a few break over in each. This, I think, can not be perfectly cured, and it would be worse in both cases *after* the separation of the sections than before. The foreign slave trade, now imperfectly suppressed, would be ultimately revived without restriction in one section, while fugitive slaves, now only partially surrendered, would not be surrendered at all by the other.

Physically speaking, we can not separate. We can not remove our respective sections from each other nor build an impassable wall between them. A husband and wife may be divorced and go out of the presence and beyond the reach of each other, but the different parts of our country can not do this. They can not but remain face to face, and intercourse, either amicable or hostile, must continue between them. Is it possible, then, to make that intercourse more advantageous or more satisfactory *after* separation than *before?* Can aliens make treaties easier than friends can make laws? Can treaties be more faithfully enforced between aliens than laws can among friends? Suppose you go to war, you can not fight always; and when, after much loss on both sides and no gain on either, you cease fighting, the identical old questions, as to terms of intercourse, are again upon you.

This country, with its institutions, belongs to the people who inhabit it. Whenever they shall grow weary of the existing Government, they can exercise their *constitutional* right of amending it or their *revolutionary* right to dismember or overthrow it. I can not be ignorant of the fact that many worthy and patriotic citizens are desirous of having the National Constitution amended. While I make no recommendation of amendments, I fully recognize the rightful authority of the people over the whole subject, to be exercised in either of the modes prescribed in the instrument itself; and I should, under existing circumstances, favor rather than oppose a fair opportunity being afforded the people to act upon it. I will venture to add that to me the convention mode seems preferable, in that it allows amendments to originate with the people themselves, instead of only permitting them to take or reject propositions originated by others, not especially chosen for the purpose, and which might not be precisely such as they would wish to either accept or refuse. I understand a proposed amendment to the Constitution— which amendment, however, I have not seen—has passed Congress, to the effect that the Federal Government shall never interfere with the domestic institutions of the States, including that of persons held to service. To avoid misconstruction of what I have said, I depart from my purpose not to speak of particular amendments so far as to say that, holding such a provision to now be implied constitutional law, I have no objection to its being made express and irrevocable.

The Chief Magistrate derives all his authority from the people, and they have conferred none upon him to fix terms for the separation of the States. The people themselves can do this also if they choose, but the Executive as such has nothing to do with it. His duty is to administer the present Government as it came to his hands and to transmit it unimpaired by him to his successor.

Why should there not be a patient confidence in the ultimate justice of the people? Is there any better or equal hope in the world? In our present differences, is either party without faith of being in the right? If the Almighty Ruler of Nations, with His eternal truth and justice, be on your side of the North, or on yours of the South, that truth and that justice will surely prevail by the judgment of this great tribunal of the American people.

By the frame of the Government under which we live this same people have wisely given their public servants but little power for mischief, and have with equal wisdom provided for the return of that little to their own hands at very short intervals. While the people retain their virtue and vigilance no Administration by any extreme of wickedness or folly can very seriously injure the Government in the short space of four years.

My countrymen, one and all, think calmly and *well* upon this whole subject. Nothing valuable can be lost by taking time. If there be an object to *hurry* any of you in hot haste to a step which you would never take *deliberately,* that object will be frustrated by taking time; but no good object can be frustrated by it. Such of you as are now dissatisfied still have the old Constitution unimpaired, and, on the sensitive point, the laws of your own framing under it; while the new Administration will have no immediate power, if it would, to change either. If it were admitted that you who are dissatisfied hold the right side in the dispute, there still is no single good reason for precipitate action. Intelligence, patriotism, Christianity, and a firm reliance on Him who has never yet forsaken this favored land are still competent to adjust in the best way all our present difficulty.

In *your* hands, my dissatisfied fellow-countrymen, and not in *mine,* is the momentous issue of civil war. The Government will not assail *you.* You can have no conflict without being yourselves the aggressors. *You* have no oath registered in heaven to destroy the Government, while *I* shall have the most solemn one to "preserve, protect, and defend it."

I am loath to close. We are not enemies, but friends. We must not be enemies. Though passion may have strained it must not break our bonds of affection. The mystic chords of memory, stretching from every battlefield and patriot grave to every living heart and hearthstone all over this broad land, will yet swell the chorus of the Union, when again touched, as surely they will be, by the better angels of our nature.

March 4, 1861

SPECIAL MESSAGE

WASHINGTON, *March 26, 1861*

To the Senate of the United States:

I have received a copy of a resolution of the Senate passed on the 25th

225

instant, requesting me, if in my opinion not incompatible with the public interest, to communicate to the Senate the dispatches of Major Robert Anderson to the War Department during the time he has been in command of Fort Sumter.

On examining the correspondence thus called for I have, with the highest respect for the Senate, come to the conclusion that at the present moment the publication of it would be inexpedient.

ABRAHAM LINCOLN

BY THE PRESIDENT OF THE UNITED STATES
A PROCLAMATION

Whereas the laws of the United States have been for some time past and now are opposed and the execution thereof obstructed in the States of South Carolina, Georgia, Alabama, Florida, Mississippi, Louisiana, and Texas by combinations too powerful to be suppressed by the ordinary course of judicial proceedings or by the powers vested in the marshals by law:

Now, therefore, I, Abraham Lincoln, President of the United States, in virtue of the power in me vested by the Constitution and the laws, have thought fit to call forth, and hereby do call forth, the militia of the several States of the Union to the aggregate number of 75,000, in order to suppress said combinations and to cause the laws to be duly executed.

The details for this object will be immediately communicated to the State authorities through the War Department.

I appeal to all loyal citizens to favor, facilitate, and aid this effort to maintain the honor, the integrity, and the existence of our National Union and the perpetuity of popular government and to redress wrongs already long enough endured.

I deem it proper to say that the first service assigned to the forces hereby called forth will probably be to repossess the forts, places, and property which have been seized from the Union; and in every event the utmost care will be observed, consistently with the objects aforesaid, to avoid any devastation, any destruction of or interference with property, or any disturbance of peaceful citizens in any part of the country.

And I hereby command the persons composing the combinations aforesaid to disperse and retire peaceably to their respective abodes within twenty days from this date.

Deeming that the present condition of public affairs presents an extraordinary occasion, I do hereby, in virtue of the power in me vested by the Constitution, convene both Houses of Congress. Senators and

Representatives are therefore summoned to assemble at their respective chambers at 12 o'clock noon on Thursday, the 4th day of July next, then and there to consider and determine such measures as, in their wisdom, the public safety and interest may seem to demand.

In witness whereof I have hereunto set my hand and caused the seal of the United States to be affixed.

Done at the city of Washington, this 15th day of April, [SEAL] A. D. 1861, and of the Independence of the United States the eighty-fifth.

ABRAHAM LINCOLN

By the President:

WILLIAM H. SEWARD, *Secretary of State*

BY THE PRESIDENT OF THE UNITED STATES OF AMERICA

A PROCLAMATION

Whereas an insurrection against the Government of the United States has broken out in the States of South Carolina, Georgia, Alabama, Florida, Mississippi, Louisiana, and Texas, and the laws of the United States for the collection of the revenue can not be effectually executed therein conformably to that provision of the Constitution which requires duties to be uniform throughout the United States; and

Whereas a combination of persons engaged in such insurrection have threatened to grant pretended letters of marque to authorize the bearers thereof to commit assaults on the lives, vessels, and property of good citizens of the country lawfully engaged in commerce on the high seas and in waters of the United States; and

Whereas an Executive proclamation has been already issued requiring the persons engaged in these disorderly proceedings to desist therefrom, calling out a militia force for the purpose of repressing the same, and convening Congress in extraordinary session to deliberate and determine thereon:

Now, therefore, I, Abraham Lincoln, President of the United States, with a view to the same purposes before mentioned and to the protection of the public peace and the lives and property of quiet and orderly citizens pursuing their lawful occupations, until Congress shall have assembled and deliberated on the said unlawful proceedings or until the same shall have ceased, have further deemed it advisable to set on foot a blockade of the ports within the States aforesaid, in pursuance of the laws of the United States and of the law of nations in such case

227

provided. For this purpose a competent force will be posted so as to prevent entrance and exit of vessels from the ports aforesaid. If, there-fore, with a view to violate such blockade, a vessel shall approach or shall attempt to leave either of the said ports, she will be duly warned by the commander of one of the blockading vessels, who will indorse on her register the fact and date of such warning, and if the same vessel shall again attempt to enter or leave the blockaded port she will be captured and sent to the nearest convenient port for such proceedings against her and her cargo as prize as may be deemed advisable.

And I hereby proclaim and declare that if any person, under the pre-tended authority of the said States or under any other pretense, shall molest a vessel of the United States or the persons or cargo on board of her, such person will be held amenable to the laws of the United States for the prevention and punishment of piracy.

In witness whereof I have hereunto set my hand and caused the seal of the United States to be affixed.

Done at the city of Washington, this 19th day of April, [SEAL] A. D. 1861, and of the Independence of the United States the eighty-fifth.

ABRAHAM LINCOLN

By the President:
WILLIAM H. SEWARD, *Secretary of State*

By the President of the United States of America

A PROCLAMATION

Whereas, for the reasons assigned in my proclamation of the 19th instant, a blockade of the ports of the States of South Carolina, Georgia, Florida, Alabama, Louisiana, Mississippi, and Texas was ordered to be established; and

Whereas since that date public property of the United States has been seized, the collection of the revenue obstructed, and duly com-missioned officers of the United States, while engaged in executing the orders of their superiors, have been arrested and held in custody as prisoners or have been impeded in the discharge of their official duties, without due legal process, by persons claiming to act under authorities of the States of Virginia and North Carolina, an efficient blockade of the ports of those States will also be established.

In witness whereof I have hereunto set my hand and caused the seal of the United States to be affixed.

Done at the city of Washington, this 27th day of April,

[SEAL] A. D. 1861, and of the Independence of the United States the eighty-fifth.

ABRAHAM LINCOLN

By the President:

WILLIAM H. SEWARD, *Secretary of State*

BY THE PRESIDENT OF THE UNITED STATES

A PROCLAMATION

Whereas existing exigencies demand immediate and adequate measures for the protection of the National Constitution and the preservation of the National Union by the suppression of the insurrectionary combinations now existing in several States for opposing the laws of the Union and obstructing the execution thereof, to which end a military force in addition to that called forth by my proclamation of the 15th day of April in the present year appears to be indispensably necessary:

Now, therefore, I, Abraham Lincoln, President of the United States and Commander in Chief of the Army and Navy thereof and of the militia of the several States when called into actual service, do hereby call into the service of the United States 42,034 volunteers to serve for the period of three years, unless sooner discharged, and to be mustered into service as infantry and cavalry. The proportions of each arm and the details of enrollment and organization will be made known through the Department of War.

And I also direct that the Regular Army of the United States be increased by the addition of eight regiments of infantry, one regiment of cavalry, and one regiment of artillery, making altogether a maximum aggregate increase of 22,714 officers and enlisted men, the details of which increase will also be made known through the Department of War.

And I further direct the enlistment for not less than one or more than three years of 18,000 seamen, in addition to the present force, for the naval service of the United States. The details of the enlistment and organization will be made known through the Department of the Navy.

The call for volunteers hereby made and the direction for the increase of the Regular Army and for the enlistment of seamen hereby given, together with the plan of organization adopted for the volunteer and for the regular forces hereby authorized, will be submitted to Congress as soon as assembled.

In the meantime I earnestly invoke the cooperation of all good citizens in the measures hereby adopted for the effectual suppression of unlawful violence, for the impartial enforcement of constitutional laws, and for the speediest possible restoration of peace and order, and with these of happiness and prosperity, throughout our country.

In testimony whereof I have hereunto set my hand and caused the seal of the United States to be affixed.

Done at the city of Washington, this 3d day of May, A.D. [SEAL] 1861, and of the Independence of the United States the eighty-fifth.

ABRAHAM LINCOLN

By the President:
WILLIAM H. SEWARD, *Secretary of State*

BY THE PRESIDENT OF THE UNITED STATES OF AMERICA

A PROCLAMATION

Whereas an insurrection exists in the State of Florida by which the lives, liberty, and property of loyal citizens of the United States are endangered; and

Whereas it is deemed proper that all needful measures should be taken for the protection of such citizens and all officers of the United States in the discharge of their public duties in the State aforesaid:

Now, therefore, be it known that I, Abraham Lincoln, President of the United States, do hereby direct the commander of the forces of the United States on the Florida coast to permit no person to exercise any office or authority upon the islands of Key West, the Tortugas, and Santa Rosa which may be inconsistent with the laws and Constitution of the United States, authorizing him at the same time, if he shall find it necessary, to suspend there the writ of *habeas corpus* and to remove from the vicinity of the United States fortresses all dangerous or suspected persons.

In witness whereof I have hereunto set my hand and caused the seal of the United States to be affixed.

Done at the city of Washington, this 10th day of May, A. D. [SEAL] 1861, and of the Independence of the United States the eighty-fifth.

ABRAHAM LINCOLN

By the President:
WILLIAM H. SEWARD,
Secretary of State

18

THE DECISION
TO FREE THE SLAVES

Lincoln Turns the Civil War into a Great Crusade

By a stroke of the pen President Lincoln converted a war between the states into a great moral crusade. But his was no hasty or impulsive act. It came as the result of long and tortuous deliberations and its timing was perfect. In his public utterances at the beginning of the conflict Lincoln had indicated that he had no intention of interfering with the institution of slavery within the states, but once war came the issue could not be kept on ice. In one way or the other the question kept arising almost every single day. Generals tried to deal with the question when slaves crowded into Union camps. Courts had to deal with the problem of applying the fugitive slave act to Negroes fleeing from one Union state to another. Congress had taken piecemeal measures. On March 13, 1862, it prohibited the use of the armed forces for the restoration of escaping slaves, and on July 17 of the same year it passed an act declaring that slaves whose owners were hostile to the United States, and who found their way within Union lines were free. Later in the war the fugitive slave acts—the old measure of 1793 and the drastic law of 1850—were repealed. In addition, drafted slaves as well as colored volunteers were declared free, with compensation to loyal owners.

For a long time Lincoln shied away from outright emancipation. He was on the contrary ardent in promoting colonization, a plan once favored in the South but long discredited by radical abolitionists. Addressing a Negro delegation in August of 1862, he told them that "it is better for us both" that we be separated. But such a program was really too little and too late. As one ardent abolitionist put it, "as a tub to the whale, it may do to provide for voluntary colonization. But if Emancipation waits on colonization, that means eternal slavery."

Lincoln was under insistent pressure from the abolitionists to take a more radical course. By midsummer of '62, the President later re-counted, he realized that it was necessary to change tactics "or lose the game." It was then that he determined upon adopting the emancipa-tion policy. He did so very secretively. "Without consultation with, or the knowledge of, the Cabinet, I prepared the original drafts of the proclamation, and, after much anxious thought, called a Cabinet meet-ing upon the subject." When he broached the proclamation to the cabinet on July 22, Seward, while approving the course, suggested post-poning the issue "until you can give it to the country supported by military success." The "wisdom" of this view struck Lincoln "with very great force." He put the proclamation aside, waiting for victory. Meantime Unionist Democrats urged him to come out for a restoration of the Union as it was, while abolitionists shrilly demanded a strong stand on slavery. In an editorial, "Prayer of Twenty Millions," Greeley's *Tribune* declared that an "immense majority of the Loyal Millions" of his countrymen required of Lincoln a frank execution of the laws as the abolitionists interpreted them. The President replied in a celebrated letter to Horace Greeley:

My paramount object in this struggle is to save the Union, and is not either to save or destroy slavery. If I could save the Union without freeing any slave, I would do it; and if I could save it by freeing all the slaves, I would do it; and if I could save it by freeing some and leav-ing others alone, I would also do that. What I do about slavery and the colored race, I do because I believe it helps to save the Union; and what I forbear, I forbear because I do not believe it would help to save the Union. . . .

I have here stated my purpose according to my view of official duty; and I intend no modification of my oft-expressed personal wish that all men everywhere could be free.

When General Lee's attempt to invade the Northern states was re-pulsed at Antietam, Lincoln decided that the opportune movement had arrived. Completing the second draft of the preliminary proclama-tion, he called his Cabinet together. First, he made them listen to a reading from a popular humorist, Artemus Ward. Then, assuming a "graver tone," he told them that his mind was made up "to issue a Proclamation of Emancipation." With becoming humility, he confessed that "many others" might do better than he, but since he knew of no constitutional way of putting any other person in his place, he had to do the best he could and "bear the responsibility of taking the course which I feel I ought to take."

When it came to the text of the proclamation Secretary of State Seward suggested that, after the word "recognize," the words "and maintain" should be added. Although Lincoln rejoined that he was not entirely sure that he could perform that promise, he yielded to the Secretary of State's insistence. Lincoln then issued at once the preliminary Emancipation Proclamation, declaring that if the states then in rebellion did not return to their allegiance by January 1, 1863, the President would issue another proclamation whereby the slaves in those states would become "forever free." Accordingly, since the rebel states chose to ignore the first proclamation, Lincoln, dispelling doubts that he might be wavering, issued the final proclamation as scheduled. His hand was so wearied after three hours of handshaking at the New Year's reception at the White House that, according to Sumner, "he held the pen with difficulty." At the prompting of his Secretary of the Treasury, Salmon P. Chase, Lincoln included the closing justification of the proclamation as "an act of justice, warranted by the Constitution," and, significantly, added his own words "upon military necessity," representing his own judgment as to the legal basis of the action.

The Emancipation Proclamation freed not a single slave. The only regions to which it extended were those in which the Confederacy was still in control. As Earl Russell, Britain's foreign secretary, declared: "It professes to emancipate all slaves in places where the United States' authorities cannot ... now make emancipation a reality," but not where "emancipation, if decreed, might have been carried into effect." Joyfully greeted by liberals in the North, savagely denounced in the South and among Northern Copperhead Democrats, the proclamation had its greatest impact in England. In a remarkable series of mass meetings in leading English cities the lower and middle classes demonstrated their heartfelt endorsement of Lincoln's action and their support to the cause of the Union. President Lincoln, in his famous letter "To the Working-Men of Manchester," "deeply" deplored the sufferings which they, together with workingmen throughout Europe, were forced to endure because of the blockade of the cotton states, but he placed these sufferings at the door "of our disloyal citizens." Lincoln congratulated them on their "decisive utterances." This was only fair and proper, because the Emancipation Proclamation, while it lacked immediate legal impact in the United States, so heartened the antislavery sentiment of British labor that it prevented the British government from recognizing the independence of the Confederacy, as it may have contemplated doing. Though in itself it did not free any slaves—that remained for later legislation and the Thirteenth Amendment—it proved a major stroke in diplomacy and marked finis to the efforts of the Confederacy to secure overt backing from England and France. Lincoln was right. No European nation could now afford to come out in the open in support of a government resting upon "human slavery" and in opposition to a government "built upon human rights."

By the President of the United States of America

A PROCLAMATION

Whereas on the 22d day of September, A. D. 1862, a proclamation was issued by the President of the United States, containing, among other things, the following, to wit:

That on the 1st day of January, A.D. 1863, all persons held as slaves within any State or designated part of a State the people whereof shall then be in rebellion against the United States shall be then, thenceforward, and forever free; and the executive government of the United States, including the military and naval authority thereof, will recognize and maintain the freedom of such persons and will do no act or acts to repress such persons, or any of them, in any efforts they may make for their actual freedom.

That the Executive will on the 1st day of January aforesaid, by proclamation, designate the States and parts of States, if any, in which the people thereof, respectively, shall then be in rebellion against the United States; and the fact that any State or the people thereof shall on that day be in good faith represented in the Congress of the United States by members chosen thereto at elections wherein a majority of the qualified voters of such States shall have participated shall, in the absence of strong countervailing testimony, be deemed conclusive evidence that such State and the people thereof are not then in rebellion against the United States.

Now, therefore, I, Abraham Lincoln, President of the United States, by virtue of the power in me vested as Commander in Chief of the Army and Navy of the United States in time of actual armed rebellion against the authority and Government of the United States, and as a fit and necessary war measure for suppressing said rebellion, do, on this 1st day of January, A. D. 1863, and in accordance with my purpose so to do, publicly proclaimed for the full period of one hundred days from the day first above mentioned, order and designate as the States and parts of States wherein the people thereof, respectively, are this day in rebellion against the United States the following, to wit:

Arkansas, Texas, Louisiana (except the parishes of St. Bernard, Plaquemines, Jefferson, St. John, St. Charles, St. James, Ascension, Assumption, Terrebonne, Lafourche, St. Mary, St. Martin, and Orleans, including the city of New Orleans), Mississippi, Alabama, Florida, Georgia, South Carolina, North Carolina, and Virginia (except the forty-eight counties designated as West Virginia, and also the counties of Berkeley, Accomac, Northampton, Elizabeth City, York, Princess Anne, and Norfolk, including the cities of Norfolk and Portsmouth), and which excepted parts are for the present left precisely as if this proclamation were not issued.

And by virtue of the power and for the purpose aforesaid, I do order and declare that all persons held as slaves within said designated States and parts of States are and henceforward shall be free, and that the executive government of the United States, including the military and naval authorities thereof, will recognize and maintain the freedom of said persons.

And I hereby enjoin upon the people so declared to be free to abstain from all violence, unless in necessary self-defense; and I recommend to them that in all cases when allowed they labor faithfully for reasonable wages.

And I further declare and make known that such persons of suitable condition will be received into the armed service of the United States to garrison forts, positions, stations, and other places and to man vessels of all sorts in said service.

And upon this act, sincerely believed to be an act of justice, warranted by the Constitution upon military necessity, I invoke the considerate judgment of mankind and the gracious favor of Almighty God.

In witness whereof I have hereunto set my hand and caused the seal of the United States to be affixed.

[SEAL]   Done at the city of Washington, this 1st day of January, A. D. 1863, and of the Independence of the United States of America the eighty-seventh.

ABRAHAM LINCOLN

By the President:

WILLIAM H. SEWARD, *Secretary of State*

19

THE DECISION
TO CHECK THE CONGRESSIONAL PROGRAM
OF REVENGE

Johnson Vetoes the First Reconstruction Act

Long before Appomattox the gulf was widening between President Lincoln and the Radical leaders in Congress over the policy to be adopted toward the rebellious states once the war had ended. Ever the moderate, Lincoln was firm but conciliatory. In his Amnesty and Reconstruction plan he had proposed that as soon as 10 per cent of the voters of the year 1860 in any of the seceded states should form a loyal government, that government should be recognized as legal. The incensed Radicals passed a bill nullifying Lincoln's program and insisting that a majority of the voters must declare themselves loyal before their state could be taken back into the fold and that the new state constitutions must prohibit slavery. Lincoln pocket-vetoed the bill, and when Congress adjourned issued a proclamation setting forth his reasons for so doing.

Despite vindictive attacks by the Radicals, it is clear that Lincoln, had he lived, would have continued to oppose their punitive program. In his Second Inaugural Lincoln urged that the war be brought to a conclusion "with malice toward none, with charity for all." At a Cabinet meeting on April 14 the President advised that "if we were wise and discreet we should re-animate the states and get their governments in successful operation." He himself, he revealed, did not share the "feelings of hate and vindictiveness" which possessed certain men in Congress. Lincoln, according to Secretary of the Navy Gideon Welles, expressed the hope that "there would be no persecution, no bloody work, after the war was over." At 10:15 P.M. that evening he was fatally wounded by an assassin's bullet.

No Vice-President in American history, not even Harry Truman, ever faced, upon succeeding to the Presidency, so complex and emotionally packed an issue as did the self-schooled tailor's apprentice, Andrew Johnson. A Unionist Democrat, he had been appointed by President Lincoln military governor of Tennessee, where he had learned at first hand some of the problems of reconstructing the unreconstructable rebels. In January, 1865, Johnson informed Lincoln of the passage by a convention, however irregular in composition, of constitutional amendments that would bring about the abolition of slavery in Tennessee. These were later ratified by popular vote.

Johnson, on assuming the Presidency, pushed ahead with a modified version of Lincoln's plan of reconstruction. His general proclamation of amnesty of May 29, 1865, listed fourteen classes of persons who must make special application for pardon, but excepted from pardon persons whose taxable property exceeded $20,000. He then issued proclamations which had in view the establishment of loyal governments in the Southern states, but he did not demand a necessary proportion of loyal voters (Lincoln's plan had required one-tenth), nor did he insist that certain specific actions first be taken by state conventions or legislatures. Under Johnson's plan new state constitutions were adopted, the ordinances of secession repealed, slavery abolished, and the Thirteenth Amendment ratified by all the Southern states except Mississippi. Johnson's program was vulnerable because the new governments failed to extend the suffrage to a few highly qualified Negroes, as he had suggested, and because the new Black Codes which these legislatures adopted were viewed in the North as perpetuating slavery in fact if not in law.

Alarmed at the insistence of the President on pushing his own plan of reconstruction, so different from that of Congress, the Radicals now subjected him to a barrage of invective. He was accused unfairly of "bootlicking proclivity" toward Southern aristocracy, denounced as "a vile, sneaking traitor" who had "obtained political goods on false pretences." Branded a drunkard merely on the basis of his unfortunate appearance at the inauguration under the influence of liquor, accused of turning the White House into a brothel, and falsely charged with being behind Lincoln's assassination, Johnson, stung to the quick, struck back in a "swing around the circle." However his counter-charges boomeranged and the trip was a failure. The American people do not like to see a President stoop as low as his enemies.

Johnson's enemies had their own plan and quickly set it in motion. Previously, when the Thirty-ninth Congress had met on December 4, 1865, it had refused to seat the new Congressmen and Senators from the Southern states. The vindictive Thaddeus Stevens, insisting that the Southern states must come in as new states or remain conquered provinces, moved for the setting up of the notorious joint committee of fifteen, which was fated to play a leading role during Reconstruction. Determined that Republican rule should be established in the South, the Radicals insisted on extending the franchise to the freedmen, on further Constitutional amendments restricting the power of the states over the civil rights of the Negro, and on severely curtailing the powers of the President. The Radicals considered that their program was vindicated by the smashing victory they won in the fall elections of '66, and pushed ahead by passing the First Reconstruction Act. This measure divided the ten states not yet restored to the Union into five military districts subject to martial law. To achieve restoration these states were required to call new constitutional conventions, elected by universal manhood suffrage, which were to establish state governments guaranteeing Negro suffrage and ratifying the Fourteenth Amendment. Congress reserved to itself the power to review each case, end military rule, and seat representatives. This, in short, was Congressional government of conquered provinces.

Recognizing that this measure took out of his hands completely the policy-making of the peace, President Johnson met the challenge with a stinging veto. Rather than sign a measure depriving citizens of the right of habeas corpus, he declared, "I would sever my right arm from my body." Declaring the measure unconstitutional, he pointed out that it set up a military dictatorship, which he labeled an "absolute despotism." The section of the act authorizing military commissions for the trial and punishment of offenders, was, as Johnson correctly pointed out, in direct and contemptuous disregard of the Supreme Court's opinion in *Ex parte Milligan*, rendered less than three months before, and was based on the untenable theory that a state of war still existed. Johnson closed with a warning that one section of the country was now legislating for all parts of the country, "not only during the life of the present generation, but for ages to come."

Johnson's extemporaneous speeches did his reputation little good, for they were undignified, ill-tempered, sometimes even illiterate, but his prepared addresses and messages are models of clarity and persuasive reasoning, and, what is more, he wrote many of them himself. In this veto message, however, the President had the major assistance of Jeremiah Sullivan Black.

A disdainful Congress repassed the measure over Johnson's veto, and he faithfully enforced the measure, along with supplementary reconstruction acts. But Johnson had really addressed his message to the people and sought to arouse the nation to the fact that a revolutionary step was being initiated by Congress. Much has been written about the Radical Reconstruction program. Actually many good and necessary things were achieved, but the reconstruction of the Southern attitude of mind could not be brought about by legislation or military government. It still has not been brought about. A decade was to pass after the struggle between Johnson and the Radicals, and the nation, sick to death of the punitive program, returned once more to the policy of compromise and conciliation advocated by Lincoln and Johnson.

VETO MESSAGE

WASHINGTON, *March 2, 1867*

To the House of Representatives:

I have examined the bill "to provide for the more efficient government of the rebel States" with the care and anxiety which its transcendent importance is calculated to awaken. I am unable to give it my assent, for reasons so grave that I hope a statement of them may have some influence on the minds of the patriotic and enlightened men with whom the decision must ultimately rest.

The bill places all the people of the ten States therein named under the absolute domination of military rulers; and the preamble undertakes to give the reason upon which the measure is based and the ground upon which it is justified. It declares that there exists in those States no legal governments and no adequate protection for life or property, and asserts the necessity of enforcing peace and good order

239

within their limits. Is this true as matter of fact?

It is not denied that the States in question have each of them an actual government, with all the powers—executive, judicial, and legislative—which properly belong to a free state. They are organized like the other States of the Union, and, like them, they make, administer, and execute the laws which concern their domestic affairs. An existing *de facto* government, exercising such functions as these, is itself the law of the state upon all matters within its jurisdiction. To pronounce the supreme law-making power of an established state illegal is to say that law itself is unlawful.

The provisions which these governments have made for the preservation of order, the suppression of crime, and the redress of private injuries are in substance and principle the same as those which prevail in the Northern States and in other civilized countries. They certainly have not succeeded in preventing the commission of all crime, nor has this been accomplished anywhere in the world. There, as well as elsewhere, offenders sometimes escape for want of vigorous prosecution, and occasionally, perhaps, by the inefficiency of courts or the prejudice of jurors. It is undoubtedly true that these evils have been much increased and aggravated, North and South, by the demoralizing influences of civil war and by the rancorous passions which the contest has engendered. But that these people are maintaining local governments for themselves which habitually defeat the object of all government and render their own lives and property insecure is in itself utterly improbable, and the averment of the bill to that effect is not supported by any evidence which has come to my knowledge. All the information I have on the subject convinces me that the masses of the Southern people and those who control their public acts, while they entertain diverse opinions on questions of Federal policy, are completely united in the effort to reorganize their society on the basis of peace and to restore their mutual prosperity as rapidly and as completely as their circumstances will permit.

The bill, however, would seem to show upon its face that the establishment of peace and good order is not its real object. The fifth section declares that the preceding sections shall cease to operate in any State where certain events shall have happened. These events are, first, the selection of delegates to a State convention by an election at which negroes shall be allowed to vote; second, the formation of a State constitution by the convention so chosen; third, the insertion into the State constitution of a provision which will secure the right of voting at all elections to negroes and to such white men as may not be disfranchised for rebellion or felony; fourth, the submission of the constitution for ratification to negroes and white men not disfranchised, and its actual ratification by their vote; fifth, the submission of the State constitution to Congress for examination and approval, and the actual approval of it by that body; sixth, the adoption of a certain amendment to the Federal Constitution by a vote of the legislature elected under the new constitution; seventh, the adoption of said amendment by a sufficient number of other States to make it a part of the Constitution of the United States. All these conditions must be fulfilled before the people of any of these States can be relieved from the bondage of military domination; but when they are fulfilled, then immediately the pains and penalties of the bill are to cease, no matter whether there be peace and order or not, and without any reference to the security of life or property. The excuse given for the bill in the preamble is admitted by the bill itself not to be real. The military rule which it establishes is plainly to be used, not for any purpose of order or for the prevention of crime, but solely as a means of coercing the people into the adoption of principles and measures to which it is known that they are opposed, and upon which they have an undeniable right to exercise their own judgment.

I submit to Congress whether this measure is not in its whole character, scope, and object without precedent and without authority, in palpable conflict with the plainest provisions of the Constitution, and utterly destructive to those great principles of liberty and humanity for which our ancestors on both sides of the Atlantic have shed so much blood and expended so much treasure.

The ten States named in the bill are divided into five districts. For each district an officer of the Army, not below the rank of a brigadier-general, is to be appointed to rule over the people; and he is to be supported with an efficient military force to enable him to perform his duties and enforce his authority. Those duties and that authority, as defined by the third section of the bill, are "to protect all persons in their rights of person and property, to suppress insurrection, disorder, and violence, and to punish or cause to be punished all disturbers of the public peace or criminals." The power thus given to the commanding officer over all the people of each district is that of an absolute monarch. His mere will is to take the place of all law. The law of the States is now the only rule applicable to the subjects placed under his control, and that is completely displaced by the clause which declares all interference of State authority to be null and void. He alone is permitted to determine what are rights of person or property, and he may protect them in such way as in his discretion may seem proper. It places at his free disposal all the lands and goods in his district, and he may distribute them without let or hindrance to whom he pleases. Being bound by no State law, and there being no other law to regulate the subject, he may make a criminal code of his own; and he can make it as bloody as any recorded in history, or he can reserve the privilege of acting upon the impulse of his private passions in each case that arises. He is bound by no rules of evidence; there is, indeed, no provision by which he is authorized or required to take any evidence at all. Everything is a crime which he chooses to call so, and all persons are condemned whom he pronounces to be guilty. He is not bound to keep any record or make any report of his proceedings. He may arrest his victims wherever he finds them, without warrant, accusation, or proof of probable cause. If he gives them a trial before he inflicts the punishment, he gives it of his grace and mercy, not because he is commanded so to do.

To a casual reader of the bill it might seem that some kind of trial was secured by it to persons accused of crime, but such is not the case. The officer "may allow local civil tribunals to try offenders," but of course this does not require that he shall do so. If any State or Federal court presumes to exercise its legal jurisdiction by the trial of a malefactor without his special permission, he can break it up and punish the judges and jurors as being themselves malefactors. He can save his friends from justice, and despoil his enemies contrary to justice.

It is also provided that "he shall have power to organize military commissions or tribunals;" but this power he is not commanded to exercise. It is merely permissive, and is to be used only "when in his judgment it may be necessary for the trial of offenders." Even if the sentence of a commission were made a prerequisite to the punishment of a party, it would be scarcely the slightest check upon the officer, who has authority to organize it as he pleases, prescribe its mode of proceeding, appoint its members from his own subordinates, and revise all its decisions. Instead of mitigating the harshness of his single rule, such a tribunal would be used much more probably to divide the responsibility of making it more cruel and unjust.

Several provisions dictated by the humanity of Congress have been inserted in the bill, apparently to restrain the power of the commanding officer; but it seems to me that they are of no avail for that purpose. The fourth section provides: First. That trials shall not be unnecessarily delayed; but I think I have shown that the power is given to punish without trial; and if so, this provision is practically inoperative. Second. Cruel or unusual punishment is not to be inflicted; but who is to decide what is cruel and what is unusual? The words have acquired a legal meaning by long use in the courts. Can it be expected that military officers will understand or follow a rule expressed in language so purely technical and not pertaining in the least degree to their profession? If not, then each officer may define cruelty according to his own temper, and if it is not usual he will make it usual. Corporal punishment, imprisonment, the gag, the ball and chain, and all the almost insupportable forms of torture invented for military punishment lie within the range of choice. Third. The sentence of a commission is not to be executed without being approved by the commander, if it affects life or liberty, and a sentence of death must be approved by the President. This applies to cases in which there has been a trial and sentence. I take it to be clear, under this bill, that the military commander may condemn to death without even the form of a trial by a military commission, so that the life of the condemned may depend upon the will of two men instead of one.

It is plain that the authority here given to the military officer amounts to absolute despotism. But to make it still more unendurable, the bill provides that it may be delegated to as many subordinates as he chooses to appoint, for it declares that he shall "punish or cause to be punished." Such a power has not been wielded by any monarch in England for more than five hundred years. In all that time no people who speak the English language have borne such servitude. It reduces the whole population of the ten States—all persons, of every color, sex, and condition, and every stranger within their limits—to the most abject and degrading slavery. No master ever had a control so absolute over the slaves as this bill gives to the military officers over both white and colored persons.

It may be answered to this that the officers of the Army are too magnanimous, just, and humane to oppress and trample upon a subjugated people. I do not doubt that army officers are as well entitled to this kind of confidence as any other class of men. But the history of the world has been written in vain if it does not teach us that unrestrained authority can never be safely trusted in human hands. It is almost sure to be more or less abused under any circumstances, and it has always resulted in gross tyranny where the rulers who exercise it are strangers to their subjects and come among them as the representatives of a distant power and more especially when the power that sends them is unfriendly. Governments closely resembling that here proposed have been fairly tried in Hungary and Poland, and the suffering endured by those people roused the sympathies of the entire world. It was tried in Ireland, and, though tempered at first by principles of English law, it gave birth to cruelties so atrocious that they are never recounted without just indignation. The French Convention armed its deputies with this power and sent them to the southern departments of the Republic. The massacres, murders, and other atrocities which they committed show what the passions of the ablest men in the most civilized society will tempt them to do when wholly unrestrained by law.

The men of our race in every age have struggled to tie up the hands of their governments and keep them within the law, because their own experience of all mankind taught them that rulers could not be relied on to concede those rights which they were not legally bound to respect. The head of a great empire has sometimes governed it with a mild and paternal sway, but the kindness of an irresponsible deputy never yields what the law does not extort from him. Between such a master and the people subjected to his domination there can be nothing but enmity; he punishes them if they resist his authority, and if they submit to it he hates them for their servility.

I come now to a question which is, if possible, still more important. Have we the power to establish and carry into execution a measure like this? I answer, Certainly not, if we derive our authority from the Constitution and if we are bound by the limitations which it imposes.

This proposition is perfectly clear, that no branch of the Federal Government—executive, legislative, or judicial—can have any just powers except those which it derives through and exercises under the organic law of the Union. Outside of the Constitution we have no legal authority more than private citizens, and within it we have only so much as that instrument gives us. This broad principle limits all our functions and applies to all subjects. It protects not only the citizens of States which are within the Union, but it shields every human being who comes or is brought under our jurisdiction. We have no right to do in one place more than in another that which the Constitution says we shall not do at all. If, therefore, the Southern States were in truth out of the Union, we could not treat their people in a way which the fundamental law forbids.

Some persons assume that the success of our arms in crushing the opposition which was made in some of the States to the execution of the Federal laws reduced those States and all their people—the innocent as well as the guilty—to the condition of vassalage and gave us a power over them which the Constitution does not bestow or define or limit. No fallacy can be more transparent than this. Our victories subjected the insurgents to legal obedience, not to the yoke of an arbitrary despotism. When an absolute sovereign reduces his rebellious subjects, he may deal with them according to his pleasure, because he had that power before. But when a limited monarch puts down an insurrection, he must still govern according to law. If an insurrection should take place in one of our States against the authority of the State government and end in the overthrow of those who planned it, would that take away the rights of all the people of the counties where it was favored by a part or a majority of the population? Could they for such a reason be wholly outlawed and deprived of their representation in the legislature? I have always contended that the Government of the United States was sovereign within its constitutional sphere; that it executed its laws, like the States themselves, by applying its coercive power directly to individuals, and that it could put down insurrection with the same effect as a State and no other. The opposite doctrine is the worst heresy of those who advocated secession, and can not be agreed to without admitting that heresy to be right.

Invasion, insurrection, rebellion, and domestic violence were anticipated when the Government was framed, and the means of repelling and suppressing them were wisely provided for in the Constitution; but it was not thought necessary to declare that the States in which they might occur should be expelled from the Union. Rebellions, which were invariably suppressed, occurred prior to that out of which these questions grow; but the States continued to exist and the Union remained unbroken. In Massachusetts, in Pennsylvania, in Rhode Island, and in New York, at different periods in our history, violent and armed opposition to the United States was carried on; but the relations of those States with the Federal Government were not supposed to be interrupted or changed thereby after the rebellious portions of their population were defeated and put down. It is true that in these earlier cases there was no formal expression of a determination to withdraw from the Union, but it is also true that in the Southern States the ordinances of secession were treated by all the friends of the Union as mere nullities and are now acknowledged to be so by the States themselves. If we admit that they had any force or validity or that they did in fact take the States in which they were passed out of the Union, we sweep from under our feet all the grounds upon which we stand in justifying the use of Federal force to maintain the integrity of the Government.

This is a bill passed by Congress in time of peace. There is not in any one of the States brought under its operation either war or insurrection. The laws of the States and of the Federal Government are all in undisturbed and harmonious operation. The courts, State and Federal, are open and in the full exercise of their proper authority. Over every State comprised in these five military districts, life, liberty, and property are secured by State laws and Federal laws, and the National Constitution is everywhere in force and everywhere obeyed. What, then, is the ground on which this bill proceeds? The title of the bill announces that it is intended "for the more efficient government" of these ten States. It is recited by way of preamble that no legal State governments "nor adequate protection for life or property" exist in those States, and that peace and good order should be thus enforced. The first thing which arrests attention upon these recitals, which prepare the way for martial law, is this, that the only foundation upon which martial law can exist under our form of government is not stated or so much as pretended. Actual war, foreign invasion, domestic insurrection —none of these appear; and none of these, in fact, exist. It is not even recited that any sort of war or insurrection is threatened. Let us pause here to consider, upon this question of constitutional law and the power of Congress, a recent decision of the Supreme Court of the United States in *ex parte Milligan*.

I will first quote from the opinion of the majority of the court:

> Martial law can not arise from a threatened invasion. The necessity must be actual and present, the invasion real, such as effectually closes the courts and deposes the civil administration.

We see that martial law comes in only when actual war closes the courts and deposes the civil authority; but this bill, in time of peace, makes martial law operate as though we were in actual war, and becomes the *cause* instead of the *consequence* of the abrogation of civil authority. One more quotation:

> It follows from what has been said on this subject that there are occasions when martial law can be properly applied. If in foreign invasion or civil war the courts are actually closed, and it is impossible to administer criminal justice according to law, *then,* on the theater of active military operations, where war really prevails, there is a necessity to furnish a substitute for the civil authority thus overthrown, to preserve the safety of the army and society; and as no power is left but the military, it is allowed to govern by martial rule until the laws can have their free course.

I now quote from the opinion of the minority of the court, delivered by Chief Justice Chase:

> We by no means assert that Congress can establish and apply the laws of war where no war has been declared or exists. Where peace exists, the laws of peace must prevail.

This is sufficiently explicit. Peace exists in all the territory to which this bill applies. It asserts a power in Congress, in time of peace, to set aside the laws of peace and to substitute the laws of war. The minority, concurring with the majority, declares that Congress does not possess

246

that power. Again, and, if possible, more emphatically, the Chief Justice, with remarkable clearness and condensation, sums up the whole matter as follows:

There are under the Constitution three kinds of military jurisdiction —one to be exercised both in peace and war; another to be exercised in time of foreign war without the boundaries of the United States, or in time of rebellion and civil war within States or districts occupied by rebels treated as belligerents; and a third to be exercised in time of invasion or insurrection within the limits of the United States, or during rebellion within the limits of the States maintaining adhesion to the National Government, when the public danger requires its exercise. The first of these may be called jurisdiction under military law, and is found in acts of Congress prescribing rules and articles of war or otherwise providing for the government of the national forces; the second may be distinguished as military government, superseding as far as may be deemed expedient the local law, and exercised by the military commander under the direction of the President, with the express or implied sanction of Congress; while the third may be denominated martial law proper, and is called into action by Congress, or temporarily, when the action of Congress can not be invited, and in the case of justifying or excusing peril, by the President, in times of insurrection or invasion or of civil or foreign war, within districts or localities where ordinary law no longer adequately secures public safety and private rights.

It will be observed that of the three kinds of military jurisdiction which can be exercised or created under our Constitution there is but one that can prevail in time of peace, and that is the code of laws enacted by Congress for the government of the national forces. That body of military law has no application to the citizen, nor even to the citizen soldier enrolled in the militia in time of peace. But this bill is not a part of that sort of military law, for that applies only to the soldier and not to the citizen, whilst, contrariwise, the military law provided by this bill applies only to the citizen and not to the soldier.

I need not say to the representatives of the American people that their Constitution forbids the exercise of judicial power in any way but one—that is, by the ordained and established courts. It is equally well known that in all criminal cases a trial by jury is made indispensable by the express words of that instrument. I will not enlarge on the inestimable value of the right thus secured to every freeman or speak of the danger to public liberty in all parts of the country which must ensue from a denial of it anywhere or upon any pretense. A very recent decision of the Supreme Court has traced the history, vindicated the dignity, and made known the value of this great privilege so clearly that nothing more is needed. To what extent a violation of it might be excused in time of war or public danger may admit of discussion, but we are providing now for a time of profound peace, when there is not an armed soldier within our borders except those who are in the service of the Government. It is in such a condition of things that an act of Congress is proposed which, if carried out, would deny a trial by the lawful courts and juries to 9,000,000 American citizens and to their posterity for an indefinite period. It seems to be scarcely possible that anyone should seriously believe this consistent with a Constitution which declares in simple, plain, and unambiguous language that all persons shall have that right and that no person shall ever in any case be deprived of it. The Constitution also forbids the arrest of the citizen without judicial warrant, founded on probable cause. This bill authorizes an arrest without warrant, at the pleasure of a military commander. The Constitution declares that "no person shall be held to answer for a capital or otherwise infamous crime unless on presentment by a grand jury." This bill holds every person not a soldier answerable for all crimes and all charges without any presentment. The Constitution declares that "no person shall be deprived of life, liberty, or property without due process of law." This bill sets aside all process of law, and makes the citizen answerable in his person and property to the will of one man, and as to his life to the will of two. Finally, the Constitution declares that "the privilege of the writ of *habeas corpus* shall not be suspended unless when, in case of rebellion or invasion, the public safety may require it;" whereas this bill declares martial law (which of itself suspends this great writ) in time of peace, and authorizes the military to make the arrest, and gives to the prisoner only one privilege, and that is a trial "without unnecessary delay." He has no hope of release from custody, except the hope, such as it is, of release by acquittal before a military commission.

The United States are bound to guarantee to each State a republican form of government. Can it be pretended that this obligation is not palpably broken if we carry out a measure like this, which wipes away every vestige of republican government in ten States and puts the life, property, liberty, and honor of all the people in each of them under the domination of a single person clothed with unlimited authority?

The Parliament of England, exercising the omnipotent power which it claimed, was accustomed to pass bills of attainder; that is to say, it would convict men of treason and other crimes by legislative enactment. The person accused had a hearing, sometimes a patient and fair one, but generally party prejudice prevailed instead of justice. It often became necessary for Parliament to acknowledge its error and reverse its own action. The fathers of our country determined that no such thing should occur here. They withheld the power from Congress, and thus forbade its exercise by that body, and they provided in the Constitution that no State should pass any bill of attainder. It is therefore impossible for any person in this country to be constitutionally convicted or punished for any crime by a legislative proceeding of any sort. Nevertheless, here is a bill of attainder against 9,000,000 people at once. It is based upon an accusation so vague as to be scarcely intelligible and found to be true upon no credible evidence. Not one of the 9,000,000 was heard in his own defense. The representatives of the doomed parties were excluded from all participation in the trial. The conviction is to be followed by the most ignominious punishment ever inflicted on large masses of men. It disfranchises them by hundreds of thousands and degrades them all, even those who are admitted to be guiltless, from the rank of freemen to the condition of slaves.

The purpose and object of the bill—the general intent which pervades it from beginning to end—is to change the entire structure and character of the State governments and to compel them by force to the adoption of organic laws and regulations which they are unwilling to accept if left to themselves. The negroes have not asked for the privilege of voting; the vast majority of them have no idea what it means. This bill not only thrusts it into their hands, but compels them, as well as the whites, to use it in a particular way. If they do not form a constitution with prescribed articles in it and afterwards elect a legislature which will act upon certain measures in a prescribed way, neither blacks nor whites can be relieved from the slavery which the bill imposes upon them. Without pausing here to consider the policy or impolicy of Africanizing the southern part of our territory, I would simply ask the attention of Congress to that manifest, well-known, and universally acknowledged rule of constitutional law which declares that the Federal Government has no jurisdiction, authority, or power to regulate such subjects for any State. To force the right of suffrage out of the hands of the white people and into the hands of the negroes is an arbitrary violation of this principle.

This bill imposes martial law at once, and its operations will begin so soon as the general and his troops can be put in place. The dread alternative between its harsh rule and compliance with the terms of this measure is not suspended, nor are the people afforded any time for free deliberation. The bill says to them, take martial law first, *then* deliberate. And when they have done all that this measure requires them to do other conditions and contingencies over which they have no control yet remain to be fulfilled before they can be relieved from martial law.

Another Congress must first approve the Constitution made in conformity with the will of this Congress and must declare these States entitled to representation in both Houses. The whole question thus remains open and unsettled and must again occupy the attention of Congress; and in the meantime the agitation which now prevails will continue to disturb all portions of the people.

The bill also denies the legality of the governments of ten of the States which participated in the ratification of the amendment to the Federal Constitution abolishing slavery forever within the jurisdiction of the United States and practically excludes them from the Union. If this assumption of the bill be correct, their concurrence can not be considered as having been legally given, and the important fact is made to appear that the consent of three-fourths of the States—the requisite number—has not been constitutionally obtained to the ratification of that amendment, thus leaving the question of slavery where it stood before the amendment was officially declared to have become a part of the Constitution.

That the measure proposed by this bill does violate the Constitution in the particulars mentioned and in many other ways which I forbear to enumerate is too clear to admit of the least doubt. It only remains to consider whether the injunctions of that instrument ought to be obeyed or not. I think they ought to be obeyed, for reasons which I will proceed to give as briefly as possible.

In the first place, it is the only system of free government which we can hope to have as a nation. When it ceases to be the rule of our conduct, we may perhaps take our choice between complete anarchy, a consolidated despotism, and a total dissolution of the Union; but national liberty regulated by law will have passed beyond our reach.

It is the best frame of government the world ever saw. No other is or can be so well adapted to the genius, habits, or wants of the American people. Combining the strength of a great empire with unspeakable blessings of local self-government, having a central power to defend the general interests, and recognizing the authority of the States as the guardians of industrial rights, it is "the sheet anchor of our safety abroad and our peace at home." It was ordained "to form a more perfect union, establish justice, insure domestic tranquillity, promote the general welfare, provide for the common defense, and secure the blessings of liberty to ourselves and to our posterity." These great ends have been attained heretofore, and will be again by faithful obedience to it; but they are certain to be lost if we treat with disregard its sacred obligations.

It was to punish the gross crime of defying the Constitution and to vindicate its supreme authority that we carried on a bloody war of four years' duration. Shall we now acknowledge that we sacrificed a million of lives and expended billions of treasure to enforce a Constitution which is not worthy of respect and preservation?

Those who advocated the right of secession alleged in their own justification that we had no regard for law and that their rights of property, life, and liberty would not be safe under the Constitution as administered by us. If we now verify their assertion, we prove that they were in truth and in fact fighting for their liberty, and instead of branding their leaders with the dishonoring name of traitors against a righteous and legal government we elevate them in history to the rank of self-sacrificing patriots, consecrate them to the admiration of the world, and place them by the side of Washington, Hampden, and Sidney. No; let us leave them to the infamy they deserve, punish them as they should be punished, according to law, and take upon ourselves no share of the odium which they should bear alone.

It is a part of our public history which can never be forgotten that both Houses of Congress, in July, 1861, declared in the form of a solemn resolution that the war was and should be carried on for no purpose of subjugation, but solely to enforce the Constitution and laws, and that when this was yielded by the parties in rebellion the contest should cease, with the constitutional rights of the States and of individuals unimpaired. This resolution was adopted and sent forth to the world unanimously by the Senate and with only two dissenting voices in the House. It was accepted by the friends of the Union in the South as well as in the North as expressing honestly and truly the object of the war. On the faith of it many thousands of persons in both sections gave their lives and their fortunes to the cause. To repudiate it now by refusing to the States and to the individuals within them the rights which the Constitution and laws of the Union would secure to them is a breach of our plighted honor for which I can imagine no excuse and to which I can not voluntarily become a party.

The evils which spring from the unsettled state of our Government will be acknowledged by all. Commercial intercourse is impeded, capital is in constant peril, public securities fluctuate in value, peace itself is not secure, and the sense of moral and political duty is impaired. To avert these calamities from our country it is imperatively required that we should immediately decide upon some course of administration which can be steadfastly adhered to. I am thoroughly convinced that any settlement or compromise or plan of action which is inconsistent with the principles of the Constitution will not only be unavailing, but mischievous; that it will but multiply the present evils, instead of removing them. The Constitution, in its whole integrity and vigor, throughout the length and breadth of the land, is the best of all compromises. Besides, our duty does not, in my judgment, leave us a choice between that and any other. I believe that it contains the remedy that is so much needed, and that if the coordinate branches of the Government would unite upon its provisions they would be found broad enough and strong enough to sustain in time of peace the nation which they bore safely through the ordeal of a protracted civil war. Among the most sacred guaranties of that instrument are those which declare that "each State shall have at least one Representative," and that "no State, without its consent, shall be deprived of its equal suffrage in the Senate." Each House is made the "judge of the elections, returns, and qualifications of its own members," and may, "with the concurrence of two-thirds, expel a member." Thus, as heretofore urged, "in the admission of Senators and Representatives from any and all of the States there can be no just ground of apprehension that persons who are disloyal will be clothed with the powers of legislation, for this could not happen when the Constitution and the laws are enforced by a vigilant and faithful Congress." "When a Senator or Representative presents his certificate of election, he may at once be admitted or rejected; or, should there be any question as to his eligibility, his credentials may be referred for investigation to the appropriate committee. If admitted to a seat, it must be upon evidence satisfactory to the House of which he thus becomes a member that he possesses the requisite constitutional and legal qualifications. If refused admission as a member for want of due allegiance to the Government, and returned to his constituents, they are admonished that none but persons loyal to the United States will be allowed a voice in the legislative councils of the nation, and the political power and moral influence of Congress are thus effectively exerted in the interests of loyalty to the Government and fidelity to the Union." And is it not far better that the work of restoration should be accomplished by simple compliance with the plain requirements of the Constitution than by a recourse to measures which in effect destroy the States and threaten the subversion of the General Government? All that is necessary to settle this simple but important question without further agitation or delay is a willingness on the part of all to sustain the Constitution and carry its provisions into practical operation. If tomorrow either branch of Congress would declare that upon the presentation of their credentials members constitutionally elected and loyal to the General Government would be admitted to seats in Congress, while all others would be excluded and their places remain vacant until the selection by the people of loyal and qualified persons, and if at the same time assurance were given that this policy would be continued until all the States were represented in Congress, it would send a thrill of joy throughout the entire land, as indicating the inauguration of a system which must speedily bring tranquillity to the public mind.

While we are legislating upon subjects which are of great importance to the whole people, and which must affect all parts of the country, not only during the life of the present generation, but for ages to come, we should remember that all men are entitled at least to a hearing in the councils which decide upon the destiny of themselves and their children. At present ten States are denied representation, and when the Fortieth Congress assembles on the 4th day of the present month sixteen States will be without a voice in the House of Representatives. This grave fact, with the important questions before us, should induce us to pause in a course of legislation which, looking solely to the attainment of political ends, fails to consider the rights it transgresses, the law which it violates, or the institutions which it imperils.

20

THE DECISION
TO PRESERVE THE PRESIDENCY

Johnson Vetoes the Tenure-of-Office Act

March 2, 1867, was a fateful day in American history. Congress had to digest two major messages from President Andrew Johnson, one, vetoing the Congressional plan of reconstruction, the other, vigorously dissenting from a bill "to regulate the tenure of civil offices." Andrew Johnson was not only fighting for his political life. He was fighting a battle for all future Presidents, to keep the division of powers of the three great branches of the Federal government free from paralyzing raids by the system of checks and balances. Had he lost, the executive and the judiciary would have been subject to the caprice of the legislative will.

Emboldened by their sweeping victory in the election of 1866, the Radicals in Congress overrode Johnson's vetoes and enacted legislation curbing the power of the Chief Executive, who was prevented from appointing new Supreme Court justices. Congress called itself into special session on January 22, 1867, and passed a bill virtually depriving the President of command of the army. Then, to make sure that Johnson could not remove the hostile members from his own Cabinet, it enacted the Tenure-of-Office Act, prohibiting the President from removing officials appointed by and with the advice of the Senate without Senatorial approval. Cabinet officers were specifically included in the measure, but with the proviso that they should "hold their offices respectively for and during the term of the President by whom they may have been appointed and for one month thereafter, subject to removal" with the consent of the Senate.

Edwin M. Stanton, Secretary of War, played very much the same role in Johnson's Cabinet as Pickering had in John Adams'. He was an informer and adviser of the opposition, thoroughly disloyal to the Chief

Executive. Even though he had explicitly stated that he considered the Tenure-of-Office Act unconstitutional, Stanton had consistently worked behind the scenes against Johnson's program. When the President learned that Stanton had personally drafted the Supplementary Reconstruction Act which Congress had just passed, he addressed the following terse note to his Secretary of War:

Sir:
   Public considerations of a high character constrain me to say that your resignation as Secretary of War will be accepted.

Very respectfully yours,
ANDREW JOHNSON

He held off sending the note for a few days until word came to him that Stanton had deliberately withheld from the President a recommendation for clemency in the case of Mrs. Mary E. Surratt, involved in the Lincoln assassination plot. Convinced that he had been duped into signing a death warrant for the woman, Johnson changed the date of his note to Stanton from August 1 to August 5 and added beneath his signature the title, "The President of the United States." Stanton, "for public considerations of a high character," refused to give up the office. General Grant was commissioned secretary *ad interim,* but when the Senate refused to concur in the dismissal, the general, whose behavior in this incident is not very creditable, turned the office back to Stanton in violation of his understanding with Johnson. Stanton then refused to turn the office over to General Lorenzo Thomas, *ad interim.*

This was the spark that ignited the flame. Thaddeus Stevens and John A. Bingham now appeared at the bar of the Senate and impeached the President of high crimes and misdemeanors in office, in fulfillment of a vote of the House the day before. The great impeachment trial began on Friday, March 13, 1868, with Chief Justice Chase presiding over the Senate proceedings. The only issue, as Johnson's able legal counsel pointed out, involved the constitutionality of the Tenure-of-Office Act, but the managers for the prosecution dragged a variety of red herrings into the trial, turning the impeachment proceedings into what one historian has called "a solemn theatrical fiasco." Every schoolboy knows that the prosecution mustered one less than the number necessary for conviction, and the President stood acquitted. As a distinguished scholar once put it, "The single vote by which Andrew Johnson escaped conviction marks the narrow margin by which the Presidential element in our system escaped destruction."

That was the real significance of Johnson's historic and courageous message vetoing the Tenure-of-Office Act. His arguments, finally vindicated by a later Supreme Court, and his successful defense in the impeachment trial, preserved a Presidential power of removal which had been often used by his predecessors and, what is vastly more important, preserved the Presidency itself.

VETO MESSAGE

WASHINGTON, *March 2, 1867*

To the Senate of the United States:
I have carefully examined the bill "to regulate the tenure of certain civil offices." The material portion of the bill is contained in the first section, and is of the effect following, namely:

> That every person holding any civil office to which he has been appointed, by and with the advice and consent of the Senate, and every person who shall hereafter be appointed to any such office and shall become duly qualified to act therein, is and shall be entitled to hold such office until a successor shall have been appointed by the President, with the advice and consent of the Senate, and duly qualified; and that the Secretaries of State, of the Treasury, of War, of the Navy, and of the Interior, the Postmaster-General, and the Attorney-General shall hold their offices respectively for and during the term of the President by whom they may have been appointed and for one month thereafter, subject to removal by and with the advice and consent of the Senate.

These provisions are qualified by a reservation in the fourth section, "that nothing contained in the bill shall be construed to extend the term of any office the duration of which is limited by law." In effect the bill provides that the President shall not remove from their places any of the civil officers whose terms of service are not limited by law without the advice and consent of the Senate of the United States. The bill in this respect conflicts, in my judgment, with the Constitution of the United States. The question, as Congress is well aware, is by no means a new one. That the power of removal is constitutionally vested in the President of the United States is a principle which has been not more distinctly declared by judicial authority and judicial commentators than it has been uniformly practiced upon by the legislative and executive departments of the Government. The question arose in the House of Representatives so early as the 16th of June, 1789, on the bill for establishing an Executive Department denominated "the Department of Foreign Affairs." The first clause of the bill, after recapitulating the functions of that officer and defining his duties, had these words: "To be removable from office by the President of the United States." It was moved to strike out these words and the motion was sustained with great ability and vigor. It was insisted that the President could not constitutionally exercise the power of removal exclusively of the Senate; that the Federalists so interpreted the Constitution when arguing for its adoption by the several States; that the Constitution had nowhere given the President power of removal, either expressly or by strong implication, but, on the contrary, had distinctly provided for removals from office by impeachment only.

A construction when denied the power of removal by the President was further maintained by arguments drawn from the danger of the abuse of the power; from the supposed tendency of an exposure of public officers to capricious removal to impair the efficiency of the civil service; from the alleged injustice and hardship of displacing incumbents dependent upon their official stations without sufficient consideration; from a supposed want of responsibility on the part of the President, and from an imagined defect of guaranties against a vicious President who might incline to abuse the power. On the other hand, an exclusive power of removal by the President was defended as a true exposition of the text of the Constitution. It was maintained that there are certain causes for which persons ought to be removed from office without being guilty of treason, bribery, or malfeasance, and that the nature of things demands that it should be so. "Suppose," it was said, "a man becomes insane by the visitation of God and is likely to ruin our affairs; are the hands of the Government to be confined from warding off the evil? Suppose a person in office not possessing the talents he was judged to have at the time of the appointment; is the error not to be corrected? Suppose he acquires vicious habits and incurable indolence or total neglect of the duties of his office, which shall work mischief to the public welfare; is there no way to arrest the threatened danger? Suppose he becomes odious and unpopular by reason of the measures he pursues—and this he may do without committing any positive offense against the law; must he preserve his office in despite of the popular will? Suppose him grasping for his own aggrandizement and the elevation of his connections by every means short of the treason defined by the Constitution, hurrying your affairs to the precipice of destruction, endangering your domestic tranquillity, plundering you of the means of defense, alienating the affections of your allies and promoting the spirit of discord; must the tardy, tedious, desultory road by way of impeachment be traveled to overtake the man who, barely confining himself within the letter of the law, is employed in drawing off the vital principle of the Government? The nature of things, the great objects of society, the express objects of the Constitution itself, require that this thing should be otherwise. To unite the Senate with the President in the exercise of the power," it was said, "would involve us in the most serious difficulty. Suppose a discovery of any of those events should take place when the Senate is not in session; how is the remedy to be applied? The evil could be avoided in no other way than by the Senate sitting always." In regard to the danger of the power being abused if exercised by one man it was said "that the danger is as great with respect to the Senate, who are assembled from various parts of the continent, with different impressions and opinions;" "that such a body is more likely to misuse the power of removal than the man whom the united voice of America calls to the Presidential chair. As the nature of government requires the power of removal," it was maintained "that it should be exercised in this way by the hand capable of exerting itself with effect; and the power must be conferred on the President by the Constitution as the executive officer of the Government."

Mr. Madison, whose adverse opinion in the Federalist had been relied upon by those who denied the exclusive power, now participated in the debate. He declared that he had reviewed his former opinions, and he summed up the whole case as follows:

> The Constitution affirms that the executive power is vested in the President. Are there exceptions to this proposition? Yes; there are. The Constitution says that in appointing to office the Senate shall be associated with the President, unless in the case of inferior officers, when the law shall otherwise direct. Have we (that is, Congress) a right to extend this exception? I believe not. If the Constitution has invested all executive power in the President, I venture to assert that the Legislature has no right to diminish or modify his executive authority. The question now resolves itself into this: Is the power of displacing an executive power? I conceive that if any power whatsoever is in the Executive it is the power of appointing, overseeing, and controlling those who execute the laws. If the Constitution had not qualified the power of the President in appointing to office by associating the Senate with him in that business, would it not be clear that he would have the right by virtue of his executive power to make such

appointment? Should we be authorized in defiance of that clause in the Constitution, "The executive power shall be vested in the President," to unite the Senate with the President in the appointment to office? I conceive not. If it is admitted that we should not be authorized to do this, I think it may be disputed whether we have a right to associate them in removing persons from office, the one power being as much of an executive nature as the other; and the first one is authorized by being excepted out of the general rule established by the Constitution in these words: "The executive power shall be vested in the President."

The question, thus ably and exhaustively argued, was decided by the House of Representatives, by a vote of 34 to 20, in favor of the principle that the executive power of removal is vested by the Constitution in the Executive, and in the Senate by the casting vote of the Vice-President.

The question has often been raised in subsequent times of high excitement, and the practice of the Government has, nevertheless, conformed in all cases to the decision thus early made.

The question was revived during the Administration of President Jackson, who made, as is well recollected, a very large number of removals, which were made an occasion of close and rigorous scrutiny and remonstrance. The subject was long and earnestly debated in the Senate, and the early construction of the Constitution was, nevertheless, freely accepted as binding and conclusive upon Congress.

The question came before the Supreme Court of the United States in January, 1839, *ex parte* Hennen. It was declared by the Court on that occasion that the power of removal from office was a subject much disputed, and upon which a great diversity of opinion was entertained in the early history of the Government. This related, however, to the power of the President to remove officers appointed with the concurrence of the Senate, and the great question was whether the removal was to be by the President alone or with the concurrence of the Senate, both constituting the appointing power. No one denied the power of the President and Senate jointly to remove where the tenure of office was not fixed by the Constitution, which was a full recognition of the principle that the power of removal was incident to the power of appointment; but it was very early adopted as a practical construction of the Constitution that this power was vested in the President alone, and such would appear to have been the legislative construction of the Constitution, for in the organization of the three great Departments of State, War, and Treasury, in the year 1789, provision was made for the appointment of a subordinate officer by the head of the Department, who should have charge of the records, books, and papers appertaining to the office when the head of the Department should be removed from office by the President of the United States. When the Navy Department was established, in the year 1798, provision was made for the charge and custody of the books, records, and documents of the Department in case of vacancy in the office of Secretary by removal or otherwise. It is not here said "by removal of the President," as is done with respect to the heads of the other Departments, yet there can be no doubt that he holds his office with the same tenure as the other Secretaries and is removable by the President. The change of phraseology arose, probably, from its having become the settled and well-understood construction of the Constitution that the power of removal was vested in the President alone in such cases, although the appointment of the officer is by the President and Senate. (13 Peters, p. 139.)

Our most distinguished and accepted commentators upon the Constitution concur in the construction thus early given by Congress, and thus sanctioned by the Supreme Court. After a full analysis of the Congressional debate to which I have referred, Mr. Justice Story comes to this conclusion:

> After a most animated discussion, the vote finally taken in the House of Representatives was affirmative of the power of removal in the President, without any cooperation of the Senate, by the vote of 34 members against 20. In the Senate the clause in the bill affirming the power was carried by the casting vote of the Vice-President. That the final decision of this question so made was greatly influenced by the exalted character of the President then in office was asserted at the time and has always been believed; yet the doctrine was opposed as well as supported by the highest talents and patriotism of the country. The public have acquiesced in this decision, and it constitutes, perhaps, the most extraordinary case in the history of the Government of a power conferred by implication on the Executive by the assent of a bare majority of Congress which has not been questioned on many other occasions.

The commentator adds:

> Nor is this general acquiescence and silence without a satisfactory explanation.

Chancellor Kent's remarks on the subject are as follows:

> On the first organization of the Government it was made a question whether the power of removal in case of officers appointed to hold at pleasure resided nowhere but in the body which appointed, and, of course, whether the consent of the Senate was not requisite to remove. This was the construction given to the Constitution, while it was pending for ratification before the State conventions, by the author of the Federalist. But the construction which was given to the Constitution by Congress, after great consideration and discussion, was different.

The words of the act [establishing the Treasury Department] are: "And whenever the same shall be removed from office by the President of the United States, or in any other case of vacancy in the office, the assistant shall act." This amounted to a legislative construction of the Constitution, and it has ever since been acquiesced in and acted upon as a decisive authority in the case. It applies equally to every other officer of the Government appointed by the President, whose term of duration is not specially declared. It is supported by the weighty reason that the subordinate officers in the executive department ought to hold at the pleasure of the head of the department, because he is invested generally with the executive authority, and the participation in that authority by the Senate was an exception to a general principle and ought to be taken strictly. The President is the great responsible officer for the faithful execution of the law, and the power of removal was incidental to that duty, and might often be requisite to fulfill it.

Thus has the important question presented by this bill been settled, in the language of the late Daniel Webster (who, while dissenting from it, admitted that it was settled), by construction, settled by precedent, settled by the practice of the Government, and settled by statute. The events of the last war furnished a practical confirmation of the wisdom of the Constitution as it has hitherto been maintained in many of its parts, including that which is now the subject of consideration. When the war broke out, rebel enemies, traitors, abettors, and sympathizers were found in every Department of the Government, as well in the civil service as in the land and naval military service. They were found in Congress and among the keepers of the Capitol; in foreign missions; in each and all the Executive Departments; in the judicial service; in the post-office, and among the agents for conducting Indian affairs. Upon probable suspicion they were promptly displaced by my predecessor, so far as they held their offices under executive authority, and their duties were confided to new and loyal successors. No complaints against that power or doubts of its wisdom were entertained in any quarter. I sincerely trust and believe that no such civil war is likely to occur again. I can not doubt, however, that in whatever form and on whatever occasion sedition can raise an effort to hinder or embarrass or defeat the legitimate action of this Government, whether by preventing the collection of revenue, or disturbing the public peace, or separating the States, or betraying the country to a foreign enemy, the power of removal from office by the Executive, as it has heretofore existed and been practiced, will be found indispensable.

Under these circumstances, as a depository of the executive authority of the nation, I do not feel at liberty to unite with Congress in reversing it by giving my approval to the bill. At the early day when this question was settled, and, indeed, at the several periods when it has subsequently been agitated, the success of the Constitution of the United States, as a new and peculiar system of free representative government, was held doubtful in other countries, and was even a subject of patriotic apprehension among the American people themselves. A trial of nearly eighty years, through the vicissitudes of foreign conflicts and of civil war, is confidently regarded as having extinguished all such doubts and apprehensions for the future. During that eighty years the people of the United States have enjoyed a measure of security, peace, prosperity, and happiness never surpassed by any nation. It can not be doubted that the triumphant success of the Constitution is due to the wonderful wisdom with which the functions of government were distributed between the three principal departments—the legislative, the executive, and the judicial—and to the fidelity with which each has confined itself or been confined by the general voice of the nation within its peculiar and proper sphere. While a just, proper, and watchful jealousy of executive power constantly prevails, as it ought ever to prevail, yet it is equally true that an efficient Executive, capable, in the language of the oath prescribed to the President, of executing the laws and, within the sphere of executive action, of preserving, protecting, and defending the Constitution of the United States, is an indispensable security for tranquillity at home and peace, honor, and safety abroad. Governments have been erected in many countries upon our model. If one or many of them have thus far failed in fully securing to their people the benefits which we have derived from our system, it may be confidently asserted that their misfortune has resulted from their unfortunate failure to maintain the integrity of each of the three great departments while preserving harmony among them all.

Having at an early period accepted the Constitution in regard to the Executive office in the sense in which it was interpreted with the concurrence of its founders, I have found no sufficient grounds in the arguments now opposed to that construction or in any assumed necessity of the times for changing those opinions. For these reasons I return the bill to the Senate, in which House it originated, for the further consideration of Congress which the Constitution prescribes. Insomuch as the several parts of the bill which I have not considered are matters chiefly of detail and are based altogether upon the theory of the Constitution from which I am obliged to dissent, I have not thought it necessary to examine them with a view to make them an occasion of distinct and special objections.

Experience, I think, has shown that it is the easiest, as it is also the most attractive, of studies to frame constitutions for the self-government of free states and nations. But I think experience has equally shown that it is the most difficult of all political labors to preserve and maintain such free constitutions of self-government when once happily established. I know no other way in which they can be preserved and maintained except by a constant adherence to them through the various vicissitudes of national existence, with such adaptations as may become necessary, always to be effected, however, through the agencies and in the forms prescribed in the original constitutions themselves.

Whenever administration fails or seems to fail in securing any of the great ends for which republican government is established, the proper course seems to be to renew the original spirit and forms of the Constitution itself.

21

THE DECISION
TO RETURN TO A SOUND DOLLAR

Cleveland Vetoes the Sherman Silver Purchase Act

The man who dealt decisively with the money crisis of 1893 was a conscientious, hard-working minister's son, who, through fortuitous political circumstances, rose spectacularly from mayor of Buffalo to President of the United States in the space of four short years. The first Democrat to hold the Presidency since Buchanan, Grover Cleveland has the additional distinction of being the only man ever to return to the White House after he failed once to secure a second term.

Cleveland did not bring to office any advanced notions of government. Honest, courageous, if unimaginative, he opposed paternalism in government and was committed to the notion that economic forces must be allowed free play without state interference. His one major departure from this traditional view of the role of the government was his fight for tariff reform. Cleveland's great message of 1887 advocating tariff reduction still stands as one of the truly heroic state papers, but because it was badly timed it failed of its objective and helped lose the election of 1888 for Cleveland.

Cleveland looked upon government as an umpire and not a partisan in the play of economic forces. He was opposed equally to excessive pensions for veterans and their dependents and to high tariffs to shelter industry. "A fair field and no favor" was his motto. Victorious in the election of '92, he returned to office with a less objective point of view, and might fairly have been labeled pro-business. He sent Federal troops to break the Pullman strike of '94, and he seemed curiously insensitive to the plight of the farmer. As William C. Whitney, Cleveland's multimillionaire campaign manager, wrote the President in 1892, "the impression of you got by the people is that you do not appreciate their suffering and poverty." Whitney dismissed these notions as "the usual twaddle," but Cleveland did little to dispel them. Charles A. Dana called him the "stuffed prophet" of a naked conservatism.

It is perhaps difficult for Americans today to understand the currency issues of the post-Civil War period, since we have been off the gold standard and on a managed currency for almost three decades. For Cleveland's generation, any departure from fiscal orthodoxy aroused violent emotions. In fact, the currency issue had not died down since the government during the Civil War had issued "greenbacks," paper money not backed by specie. The business world insisted that this depreciated currency be redeemed in gold. This was its idea of "sound money." The farmers, contrariwise, were "cheap money" men, who demanded more and more greenbacks to boost farm prices from their depressed levels. In 1875 a Republican Congress yielded to the "sound money" men and passed a bill making paper currency redeemable on demand with metallic money. Rebounding from their temporary defeat, the farmers joined hands in the 1870's with the silver-mining interests and demanded the free and unlimited coinage of all silver mined at the ratio of 16 to 1. Congress compromised, and passed over President Hayes's veto the Bland-Allison Act of 1878, providing that the Treasury, instead of coining all silver presented, as the West wished, purchase from two to four million dollars' worth of bullion a month and coin it into dollars.

In the '80's prices skidded downward. Farmers and other debt-burdened groups were concerned about the deflated currency. Although business and industrial activity had increased many times over in the twenty-year period ending in 1890, money in circulation had barely risen. In short, money was tight, and there was no doubt about it. Meantime, during the years 1889 and 1890 six new Western states with strong silver interests were admitted to the Union, greatly strengthening the silver bloc in the Senate. The Western silver interests cynically agreed to support a protective tariff if the East would back a silver bill. From this pact of mutual detestation there emerged the Sherman Silver Purchase Act of 1890, under which the Treasury was obligated to buy a total of 4,500,000 ounces of silver monthly—about all that was being mined—and pay for it in notes redeemable in either silver or gold. This law roughly doubled the minimum amount of silver that could be acquired under the old Bland-Allison Law. If it did not help anybody else, it proved a great boon to the silver-mining interests.

When Grover Cleveland, running on a sound-money plank, unseated Benjamin Harrison, he was immediately confronted with a business panic compounded by a government deficit. Under the Sherman Silver Purchase Act the Treasury was required to issue legal tender notes for the silver bullion it bought; the bearers of the paper could present it for gold; new notes were issued as more silver was bought and the new note-holders would repeat the process. In this way the Treasury was being drained of its gold reserve, which had dropped below $100,000,-000, popularly regarded as the safe minimum for supporting some $350,000,000 in greenbacks. Action was imperative. Cleveland summoned Congress in an extra session in the summer of 1893. Before he had a chance to deliver his message the President had to undergo in secret an operation for removal of a cancer from the roof of his mouth. Had he died, the "soft money" Vice President, Adlai E. Stevenson (grandfather of the Democratic standard bearer in 1952 and 1956), would have succeeded him. But Cleveland recovered from the operation, and set to work on his message. He had before him a rather belligerent draft drawn up by Attorney General Olney. This draft needlessly offended the silver groups and not only urged upon Congress the repeal of the silver-purchase clauses but also demanded that Congress provide that all outstanding obligations of the government should be payable in gold coin. Cleveland tactfully struck out both sections. The final message was moderate in temper and shrewdly directed toward the interests of the wage-earner rather than the businessman.

Cleveland's notable message evoked a spirited debate. The administration marshaled to its cause such effective orators as Bourke Cochran and Thomas B. Reed, but the most eloquent voice heard in the halls of Congress was that of the silverite William Jennings Bryan, that "circuit-riding evangelist in politics." Despite Bryan's eloquent appeal for the "unnumbered throng," "work-worn and dust-begrimed," who make their "mute appeal," Cleveland won a decisive victory. The Silver Purchase Act was repealed. Cleveland's sound-money policy was endorsed by the people in the election of 1896 when Bryan, capturing the Democratic nomination with his sensational "Cross of Gold" speech, went down to stinging defeat at the hands of "hard money" McKinley. The tide of the "silver heresy" rapidly receded. Cleveland may have been inflexible and insensitive on this issue, but he settled it for his generation.

SPECIAL SESSION MESSAGE

EXECUTIVE MANSION, *August 8, 1893*

To the Congress of the United States:

The existence of an alarming and extraordinary business situation, involving the welfare and prosperity of all our people, has constrained me to call together in extra session the people's representatives in Congress, to the end that through a wise and patriotic exercise of the legislative duty, with which they solely are charged, present evils may be mitigated and dangers threatening the future may be averted.

Our unfortunate financial plight is not the result of untoward events nor of conditions related to our natural resources, nor is it traceable to any of the afflictions which frequently check national growth and prosperity. With plenteous crops, with abundant promise of remunerative production and manufacture, with unusual invitation to safe investment, and with satisfactory assurance to business enterprise, suddenly financial distrust and fear have sprung up on every side. Numerous moneyed institutions have suspended because abundant assets were not immediately available to meet the demands of frightened depositors. Surviving corporations and individuals are content to keep in hand the money they are usually anxious to loan, and those engaged in legitimate business are surprised to find that the securities they offer for loans, though heretofore satisfactory, are no longer accepted. Values supposed to be fixed are fast becoming conjectural, and loss and failure have invaded every branch of business.

I believe these things are principally chargeable to Congressional legislation touching the purchase and coinage of silver by the General Government.

This legislation is embodied in a statute passed on the 14th day of July, 1890, which was the culmination of much agitation on the subject involved, and which may be considered a truce, after a long struggle, between the advocates of free silver coinage and those intending to be more conservative.

Undoubtedly the monthly purchases by the Government of 4,500,000 ounces of silver, enforced under that statute, were regarded by those interested in silver production as a certain guaranty of its increase in price. The result, however, has been entirely different, for immediately following a spasmodic and slight rise the price of silver began to fall after the passage of the act, and has since reached the lowest point ever known. This disappointing result has led to renewed and persistent effort in the direction of free silver coinage.

Meanwhile not only are the evil effects of the operation of the present law constantly accumulating, but the result to which its execution must inevitably lead is becoming palpable to all who give the least heed to financial subjects.

This law provides that in payment for the 4,500,000 ounces of silver bullion which the Secretary of the Treasury is commanded to purchase monthly there shall be issued Treasury notes redeemable on demand in gold or silver coin, at the discretion of the Secretary of the Treasury, and that said notes may be reissued. It is, however, declared in the act to be "the established policy of the United States to maintain the two metals on a parity with each other upon the present legal ratio or such ratio as may be provided by law." This declaration so controls the action of the Secretary of the Treasury as to prevent his exercising the discretion nominally vested in him if by such action the parity between gold and silver may be disturbed. Manifestly a refusal by the Secretary to pay these Treasury notes in gold if demanded would necessarily result in their discredit and depreciation as obligations payable only in silver, and would destroy the parity between the two metals by establishing a discrimination in favor of gold.

Up to the 15th day of July, 1893, these notes had been issued in payment of silver-bullion purchases to the amount of more than $147,000,-000. While all but a very small quantity of this bullion remains uncoined and without usefulness in the Treasury, many of the notes given in its purchase have been paid in gold. This is illustrated by the statement that between the 1st day of May, 1892, and the 15th day of July, 1893, the notes of this kind issued in payment for silver bullion amounted to a little more than $54,000,000, and that during the same period about $49,000,000 were paid by the Treasury in gold for the redemption of such notes.

The policy necessarily adopted of paying these notes in gold has not spared the gold reserve of $100,000,000 long ago set aside by the Government for the redemption of other notes, for this fund has already been subjected to the payment of new obligations amounting to about $150,000,000 on account of silver purchases, and has as a consequence for the first time since its creation been encroached upon.

We have thus made the depletion of our gold easy and have tempted other and more appreciative nations to add it to their stock. That the opportunity we have offered has not been neglected is shown by the large amounts of gold which have been recently drawn from our Treasury and exported to increase the financial strength of foreign nations. The excess of exports of gold over its imports for the year ending June 30, 1893, amounted to more than $87,500,000.

Between the 1st day of July, 1890, and the 15th day of July, 1893, the gold coin and bullion in our Treasury decreased more than $132,000,000, while during the same period the silver coin and bullion in the Treasury increased more than $147,000,000. Unless Government bonds are to be constantly issued and sold to replenish our exhausted gold, only to be again exhausted, it is apparent that the operation of the silver-purchase law now in force leads in the direction of the entire substitution of silver for the gold in the Government Treasury, and that this must be followed by the payment of all Government obligations in depreciated silver.

At this stage gold and silver must part company and the Government must fail in its established policy to maintain the two metals on a parity with each other. Given over to the exclusive use of a currency greatly depreciated according to the standard of the commercial world, we could no longer claim a place among nations of the first class, nor could our Government claim a performance of its obligation, so far as such an obligation has been imposed upon it, to provide for the use of the people the best and safest money.

If, as many of its friends claim, silver ought to occupy a larger place in our currency and the currency of the world through general international cooperation and agreement, it is obvious that the United States will not be in a position to gain a hearing in favor of such an arrangement so long as we are willing to continue our attempt to accomplish the result singlehanded.

The knowledge in business circles among our own people that our Government can not make its fiat equivalent to intrinsic value nor keep inferior money on a parity with superior money by its own independent efforts has resulted in such a lack of confidence at home in the stability of currency values that capital refuses its aid to new enterprises, while millions are actually withdrawn from the channels of trade and commerce to become idle and unproductive in the hands of timid owners. Foreign investors, equally alert, not only decline to purchase American securities, but make haste to sacrifice those which they already have.

It does not meet the situation to say that apprehension in regard to the future of our finances is groundless and that there is no reason for lack of confidence in the purposes or power of the Government in the premises. The very existence of this apprehension and lack of confidence, however caused, is a menace which ought not for a moment to be disregarded. Possibly, if the undertaking we have in hand were the maintenance of a specific known quantity of silver at a parity with gold, our ability to do so might be estimated and gauged, and perhaps, in view of our unparalleled growth and resources, might be favorably passed upon. But when our avowed endeavor is to maintain such parity in regard to an amount of silver increasing at the rate of $50,000,000 yearly, with no fixed termination to such increase, it can hardly be said that a problem is presented whose solution is free from doubt.

The people of the United States are entitled to a sound and stable currency and to money recognized as such on every exchange and in every market of the world. Their Government has no right to injure them by financial experiments opposed to the policy and practice of other civilized states, nor is it justified in permitting an exaggerated and unreasonable reliance on our national strength and ability to jeopardize the soundness of the people's money.

This matter rises above the plane of party politics. It vitally concerns every business and calling and enters every household in the land. There is one important aspect of the subject which especially should never be overlooked. At times like the present, when the evils of unsound finance threaten us, the speculator may anticipate a harvest gathered from the misfortune of others, the capitalist may protect himself by hoarding or may even find profit in the fluctuations of values; but the wage earner—the first to be injured by a depreciated currency and the last to receive the benefit of its correction—is practically defenseless. He relies for work upon the ventures of confident and contented capital. This failing him, his condition is without alleviation, for he can neither prey on the misfortunes of others nor hoard his labor. One of the greatest statesmen our country has known, speaking more than fifty years ago, when a derangement of the currency had caused commercial distress, said:

> The very man of all others who has the deepest interest in a sound currency and who suffers most by mischievous legislation in money matters is the man who earns his daily bread by his daily toil.

These words are as pertinent now as on the day they were uttered, and ought to impressively remind us that a failure in the discharge of our duty at this time must especially injure those of our countrymen who labor, and who because of their number and condition are entitled to the most watchful care of their Government.

270

It is of the utmost importance that such relief as Congress can afford in the existing situation be afforded at once. The maxim "He gives twice who gives quickly" is directly applicable. It may be true that the embarrassments from which the business of the country is suffering arise as much from evils apprehended as from those actually existing. We may hope, too, that calm counsels will prevail, and that neither the capitalists nor the wage earners will give way to unreasoning panic and sacrifice their property or their interests under the influence of exaggerated fears. Nevertheless, every day's delay in removing one of the plain and principal causes of the present state of things enlarges the mischief already done and increases the responsibility of the Government for its existence. Whatever else the people have a right to expect from Congress, they may certainly demand that legislation condemned by the ordeal of three years' disastrous experience shall be removed from the statute books as soon as their representatives can legitimately deal with it.

It was my purpose to summon Congress in special session early in the coming September, that we might enter promptly upon the work of tariff reform, which the true interests of the country clearly demand, which so large a majority of the people, as shown by their suffrages, desire and expect, and to the accomplishment of which every effort of the present Administration is pledged. But while tariff reform has lost nothing of its immediate and permanent importance and must in the near future engage the attention of Congress, it has seemed to me that the financial condition of the country should at once and before all other subjects be considered by your honorable body.

I earnestly recommend the prompt repeal of the provisions of the act passed July 14, 1890, authorizing the purchase of silver bullion, and that other legislative action may put beyond all doubt or mistake the intention and the ability of the Government to fulfill its pecuniary obligations in money universally recognized by all civilized countries.

22

THE DECISION
TO STRETCH THE MONROE DOCTRINE
TO INCLUDE BOUNDARY DISPUTES

Cleveland Tells England: Arbitrate with Venezuela, or Else

On a number of occasions in the course of the nineteenth century the Monroe Doctrine was reasserted and expanded. President Polk made it clear that the United States would not tolerate any expansion by a European power in the Americas. President Grant declared that the United States would not suffer the transfer of American territory from one European state to another. How far dared the United States go in curbing the territorial claims of European nations? The test came in the second administration of Grover Cleveland.

For many years the boundary between British Guiana on the east and Venezuela on the west had been unsettled and a source of contention between the two countries. A tentative boundary was drawn up by Sir Robert Schomburgk in 1840, which the British came to view as final, but the Venezuelans found unacceptable. Prospects of a settlement vanished when gold was discovered in the disputed area. The Venezuelan government appealed to President Cleveland to intervene, and imperialists at home kept pressing him to take a strong stand. Henry Cabot Lodge, in a magazine piece at the time, asserted that "the American people are not ready to abandon the Monroe Doctrine, or give up their rightful supremacy in the Western Hemisphere. On the contrary, they are as ready now to fight to maintain both as they were when they forced the French out of Mexico." Lodge insisted that "the supremacy of the Monroe Doctrine should be established and at once—peaceably if we can, forcibly if we must." Senator William V. Allen went further. He interpreted the Monroe Doctrine to mean that "wherever territory is essential to the safety and security of this country we should not only insist that such powers should not acquire additional territory, but we should also insist that this Government shall have the right to such territory by purchase."

For many years twisting the lion's tail had been a favorite pastime of State Department officials. Considering the depth of anti-British feeling among Americans of Irish origin located in key states, such a bold posture was always politically expedient.

Yielding to jingoist pressures, Richard Olney, Cleveland's new Secretary of State, issued a flamboyant note on July 20, 1895, in the course of which he declared that "the United States is practically sovereign on this continent, and its fiat is law upon the subjects to which it confines its interposition." America, he asserted, would "treat as an injury to itself the forcible assumption by an European power of political control over an American state." He concluded his belligerent missive by demanding from Great Britain a definite decision on whether or not she was prepared to submit the Venezuelan boundary dispute to impartial arbitration. Cleveland later dubbed the note a "twenty-inch gun" blast. The British were not cowed by the unwarranted tone of the blustering Secretary of State. After some delay Lord Salisbury, England's Foreign Minister, peremptorily rejected the arbitration proposal and denied the applicability of the Monroe Doctrine to this situation.

Grover Cleveland was "mad clear through." The result was a bristling Presidential message to Congress. The first draft was written by Olney, but Cleveland sat up all night rewriting it. When he finished at dawn, as he said later, he could not tell what he had written from what was Olney's part. Cleveland asked Congress to appropriate money for a commission to determine the true Venezuelan boundary, and declared that it would be the duty of the United States to maintain this boundary against aggression. The President felt that in forcing a quick settlement he could keep Congress from doing real mischief, but the truculent passages of the message sounded like a call to arms, and so it was regarded by the jingoist elements in the country.

Why did the British yield to Cleveland even though this boundary dispute could not conceivably be considered a further acquisition of territory within the original meaning of the Monroe Doctrine and even though the British case was so much stronger than the Venezuelan?

The answer was provided by Germany. On January 2, 1896, the undiplomatic Kaiser Wilhelm II dispatched a telegram to President Kruger of the Transvaal congratulating the Boers on their capture of an unauthorized British raiding party. Overnight, British anger was deflected toward Germany, now a formidable naval and maritime rival. Lord Salisbury admitted blandly when Parliament met in February, 1896, that "from some points of view the mixture of the United States in this matter conduces to results which will be satisfactory to us more rapidly than if the United States had not interfered."

The boundary dispute was finally referred to an arbitral tribunal of five, and the ultimate decision, handed down in 1899, upheld the principal British contentions. Henceforth, a broad interpretation of the Monroe Doctrine came into more general acceptance, Americans were increasingly disposed to accept overseas responsibilities, and, more important, a long and lasting entente with England was initiated. All this could hardly have been foreseen by Cleveland when he rewrote Olney's truculent draft, but then history has proved kinder to him in this affair than he deserved.

SPECIAL MESSAGE

EXECUTIVE MANSION, *December 17, 1895*

To the Congress:

In my annual message addressed to the Congress on the 3d instant I called attention to the pending boundary controversy between Great Britain and the Republic of Venezuela and recited the substance of a representation made by this Government to Her Britannic Majesty's Government suggesting reasons why such dispute should be submitted to arbitration for settlement and inquiring whether it would be so submitted.

The answer of the British Government, which was then awaited, has since been received, and, together with the dispatch to which it is a reply, is hereto appended.

Such reply is embodied in two communications addressed by the British prime minister to Sir Julian Pauncefote, the British ambassador at this capital. It will be seen that one of these communications is devoted exclusively to observations upon the Monroe doctrine, and claims that in the present instance a new and strange extension and development of this doctrine is insisted on by the United States; that the reasons justifying an appeal to the doctrine enunciated by President Monroe are generally inapplicable "to the state of things in which we live at the present day," and especially inapplicable to a controversy involving the boundary line between Great Britain and Venezuela.

Without attempting extended argument in reply to these positions, it may not be amiss to suggest that the doctrine upon which we stand is strong and sound, because its enforcement is important to our peace and safety as a nation and is essential to the integrity of our free institutions and the tranquil maintenance of our distinctive form of government. It was intended to apply to every stage of our national life and can not become obsolete while our Republic endures. If the balance of power is justly a cause for jealous anxiety among the Governments of the Old World and a subject for our absolute noninterference, none the less is an observance of the Monroe doctrine of vital concern to our people and their Government.

Assuming, therefore, that we may properly insist upon this doctrine without regard to "the state of things in which we live" or any changed conditions here or elsewhere, it is not apparent why its application may not be invoked in the present controversy.

If a European power by an extension of its boundaries takes possession of the territory of one of our neighboring Republics against its will and in derogation of its rights, it is difficult to see why to that extent such European power does not thereby attempt to extend its system of government to that portion of this continent which is thus taken. This is the precise action which President Monroe declared to be "dangerous to our peace and safety," and it can make no difference whether the European system is extended by an advance of frontier or otherwise.

It is also suggested in the British reply that we should not seek to apply the Monroe doctrine to the pending dispute because it does not embody any principle of international law which "is founded on the general consent of nations," and that "no statesman, however eminent, and no nation, however powerful, are competent to insert into the code of international law a novel principle which was never recognized before and which has not since been accepted by the government of any other country."

Practically the principle for which we contend has peculiar, if not exclusive, relation to the United States. It may not have been admitted in so many words to the code of international law, but since in international councils every nation is entitled to the rights belonging to it, if the enforcement of the Monroe doctrine is something we may justly claim it has its place in the code of international law as certainly and as securely as if it were specifically mentioned; and when the United

275

States is a suitor before the high tribunal that administers international law the question to be determined is whether or not we present claims which the justice of that code of law can find to be right and valid.

The Monroe doctrine finds its recognition in those principles of international law which are based upon the theory that every nation shall have its rights protected and its just claims enforced.

Of course this Government is entirely confident that under the sanction of this doctrine we have clear rights and undoubted claims. Nor is this ignored in the British reply. The prime minister, while not admitting that the Monroe doctrine is applicable to present conditions, states:

> In declaring that the United States would resist any such enterprise if it was contemplated, President Monroe adopted a policy which received the entire sympathy of the English Government of that date.

He further declares:

> Though the language of President Monroe is directed to the attainment of objects which most Englishmen would agree to be salutary, it is impossible to admit that they have been inscribed by any adequate authority in the code of international law.

Again he says:

> They [Her Majesty's Government] fully concur with the view which President Monroe apparently entertained, that any disturbance of the existing territorial distribution in that hemisphere by any fresh acquisitions on the part of any European State would be a highly inexpedient change.

In the belief that the doctrine for which we contend was clear and definite, that it was founded upon substantial considerations and involved our safety and welfare, that it was fully applicable to our present conditions and to the state of the world's progress, and that it was directly related to the pending controversy, and without any conviction as to the final merits of the dispute, but anxious to learn in a satisfactory and conclusive manner whether Great Britain sought under a claim of boundary to extend her possessions on this continent without right, or whether she merely sought possession of territory fairly included within her lines of ownership, this Government proposed to the Government of Great Britain a resort to arbitration as the proper means of settling the question, to the end that a vexatious boundary dispute between the two contestants might be determined and our exact standing and relation in respect to the controversy might be made clear.

It will be seen from the correspondence herewith submitted that this proposition has been declined by the British Government upon grounds which in the circumstances seem to me to be far from satisfactory. It is deeply disappointing that such an appeal, actuated by the most friendly feelings toward both nations directly concerned, addressed to the sense of justice and to the magnanimity of one of the great powers of the world, and touching its relations to one comparatively weak and small, should have produced no better results.

The course to be pursued by this Government in view of the present condition does not appear to admit of serious doubt. Having labored faithfully for many years to induce Great Britain to submit this dispute to impartial arbitration, and having been now finally apprised of her refusal to do so, nothing remains but to accept the situation, to recognize its plain requirements, and deal with it accordingly. Great Britain's present proposition has never thus far been regarded as admissible by Venezuela, though any adjustment of the boundary which that country may deem for her advantage and may enter into of her own free will can not of course be objected to by the United States.

Assuming, however, that the attitude of Venezuela will remain unchanged, the dispute has reached such a stage as to make it now incumbent upon the United States to take measures to determine with sufficient certainty for its justification what is the true divisional line between the Republic of Venezuela and British Guiana. The inquiry to that end should of course be conducted carefully and judicially, and due weight should be given to all available evidence, records, and facts in support of the claims of both parties.

In order that such an examination should be prosecuted in a thorough and satisfactory manner, I suggest that the Congress make an adequate appropriation for the expenses of a commission, to be appointed by the Executive, who shall make the necessary investigation and report upon the matter with the least possible delay. When such report is made and accepted it will, in my opinion, be the duty of the United States to resist by every means in its power, as a willful aggression upon its rights and interests, the appropriation by Great Britain of any lands or the exercise of governmental jurisdiction over any territory which after investigation we have determined of right belongs to Venezuela.

In making these recommendations I am fully alive to the responsibility incurred and keenly realize all the consequences that may follow.

I am, nevertheless, firm in my conviction that while it is a grievous thing to contemplate the two great English-speaking peoples of the world as being otherwise than friendly competitors in the onward march of civilization and strenuous and worthy rivals in all the arts of peace, there is no calamity which a great nation can invite which equals that which follows a supine submission to wrong and injustice and the consequent loss of national self-respect and honor, beneath which are shielded and defended a people's safety and greatness.

23

THE DECISION
TO INTERVENE IN CUBA

McKinley Asks for War Against Spain

As wars go, the war with Spain was a little one, but our entry into it marked the assumption by the United States of responsibilities as a world power and stretched the line of American security across the wide Pacific to the Far East. One might well assume that so fateful a step would have been preceded by careful military planning and by a judicious weighing of alternatives and consequences. Instead, the war was an impulsive measure, entered into only *after* our major demands had been met by Spain, and decided upon by a President, well-intentioned and honorable, but deficient in backbone and with intellectual limitations.

The revolution which broke out in Cuba in 1895 was the last of a century of revolts against the waning power of Spain in the New World. This one was precipitated by a combination of Spanish misrule and a depression in the Cuban sugar industry set off by an American tariff against Cuban sugar. Ravaged intermittently by insurgency, Cuba had long seemed a tempting morsel to American expansionists, and only the firm hand of earlier Presidents had shut the door to annexation. The Cuban war was conducted savagely by both sides. The insurgents aimed to disorganize the economic life of the island by terror and pillaging, and set about burning sugar cane fields and driving the natives into the towns. Traditionally sympathetic with the Cuban patriots, the Americans chose to ignore these acts of devastation and to concentrate their fire on the Spanish commander, General Valeriano Weyler, whom the American press denounced as "the butcher," "that human hyena," and "the fiendish despot."

A good case could be made for the charge that our war with Cuba was over synthetic issues and was hatched by rival New York newspapers, William Randolph Hearst's *Journal* and Joseph Pulitzer's *World,* engaged in a fierce circulation war of their own. When Hearst sent Frederic Remington to Cuba to sketch the civil war, the well-known artist wired back: "Everything is quiet. There is no trouble here. There will be no war." Hearst's reply is apocryphal: "You furnish the pictures, and I'll furnish the war."

The newspapers' drive for war was buttressed from within the Republican Party, where a group of younger political figures, including the brash Theodore Roosevelt, Assistant Secretary of War, and the strong-minded Senator from Massachusetts, Henry Cabot Lodge, regarded Cuba as the key to the domination of the Caribbean. Disciples of Alfred Thayer Mahan, whose doctrines of the importance of sea power and strategically located naval bases fed the flames of expansionism, Roosevelt and Lodge were now in positions that afforded them the power to carry out such objectives.

Moderate and conciliatory in temper, President McKinley showed considerable forbearance in avoiding a call for war immediately after the sinking of the battleship *Maine* in Havana harbor on February 15, 1898, under circumstances that remain mysterious. But the pressures mounted. Backed overwhelmingly by the people, the warmakers in Congress were clearly in the driver's seat. "Remember the *Maine!*" became the national slogan, and the liberation of Cuba took on the dimensions of a crusade.

"I pray God," President McKinley told a delegation of insurgent Congressmen, "that we may be able to keep the peace." His critics unfairly accused him of subservience to Wall Street, which was opposed to war.

Meantime, in Madrid, General Stewart L. Woodford, a New York lawyer who was the American minister to Spain, was making genuine progress in the settlement of the outstanding issues between that nation and the United States. Woodford cabled the White House that in all matters except the question of an armistice Spain had bowed to the United States. She had agreed to submit the differences over the *Maine* to arbitration; she was appropriating a large sum for Cuban relief, and would also accept proffered aid from the United States, and she had proclaimed the revocation of the *reconcentrado* order, by which many

Cuban civilians had been herded into frightfully unsanitary concentration camps where they could not give assistance to the armed *insurrectos*. Spain had gone further in making concessions on Cuba than she had ever gone before, but because that proud nation found it "inconvenient to accept at once a suspension of hostilities asked for by the insurgents," McKinley, feeling he had no choice but to yield to an impatient Congress, began the preparation of a message of intervention.

Sleepless, harried, dreading the suffering that war entailed, the President seemed headed for a breakdown. More reassuring news was coming in. General Woodford cabled that peace was imminent, and on Saturday night, April 9, the President was informed that as a result of the efforts of European powers and the Pope the Queen Regent had instructed Spain's new governor-general of Cuba to proclaim the suspension of hostilities. This was the news for which McKinley had devoutly prayed on the night of March 31, but now it came too late. The President felt that there was no way to control the war spirit in Congress. The next morning his message was carried to the Capitol.

In the message McKinley asked Congress for authority to use the military and naval forces to secure peace and a stable government in Cuba. He asked for neutral intervention, without recognition of Cuban independence, because he did not feel that the self-styled republic of the insurgents could legally claim to represent the Cuban people. In drafting this part of the message the President had called on the able assistance of Attorney General John W. Griggs.

McKinley's was indeed a curious war message. Dry and dispassionate in tone, it lacks the ring of Polk's message calling for war with Mexico, the crusading mood of Wilson's great war message, or the denunciatory line of Franklin Delano Roosevelt's message on Pearl Harbor. Its tone revealed, in fact, President McKinley's own mixed feelings and his lack of enthusiasm for the martial venture. Most anomalous are the last two paragraphs, in which the President refers almost casually to the recent announcement by the Spanish government that it would accede to all the principal demands of the United States. In other words, McKinley chose to end his war message with the revelation that there was in fact no *casus belli*.

Congress, it goes without saying, chose to ignore these paragraphs and to concentrate on just four words in McKinley's message: "I AWAIT YOUR ACTION." But the action that Congress took could well be considered a repudiation of the President's moderate course. Not only did Congress declare war against Spain, but it explicitly recognized the insurgent republic, although by the Teller Amendment it disclaimed any intention of the United States to exercise sovereignty over Cuba, except for its pacification.

Any doubts as to whether the Teller Amendment marked the downfall of the annexationists were dispelled when the President made the military decision to send Dewey's fleet to attack the Philippines, and when the American commissioners insisted on the acquisition of the Philippines as a precondition to peace with Spain. McKinley's fateful decision, then, really involved two steps—the first, to go to war, and the second, to annex a far Pacific empire. Both decisions were his own. When a visiting delegation of churchmen visited the White House McKinley told them how he came to the latter decision:

I walked the floor of the White House night after night until midnight; and I am not ashamed to tell you, gentlemen, that I went down on my knees and prayed Almighty God for light and guidance more than one night. And one night late it came to me this way—I don't know how it was, but it came . . . that there was nothing left for us to do but to take them all, and to educate the Filipinos, and uplift them and civilize and Christianize them, and by God's grace do the very best we could by them, as our fellow-men for whom Christ also died. And then I went to bed, and went to sleep, and slept soundly, and the next morning I sent for the chief engineer of the War Department (our map-maker), and I told him to put the Philippines on the map of the United States, and there they are, and there they will stay while I am President!

MESSAGE

EXECUTIVE MANSION, *April 11, 1898*

To the Congress of the United States:
Obedient to that precept of the Constitution which commands the President to give from time to time to the Congress information of the

state of the Union and to recommend to their consideration such measures as he shall judge necessary and expedient, it becomes my duty to now address your body with regard to the grave crisis that has arisen in the relations of the United States to Spain by reason of the warfare that for more than three years has raged in the neighboring island of Cuba.

I do so because of the intimate connection of the Cuban question with the state of our own Union and the grave relation the course which it is now incumbent upon the nation to adopt must needs bear to the traditional policy of our Government if it is to accord with the precepts laid down by the founders of the Republic and religiously observed by succeeding Administrations to the present day.

The present revolution is but the successor of other similar insurrections which have occurred in Cuba against the dominion of Spain, extending over a period of nearly half a century, each of which during its progress has subjected the United States to great effort and expense in enforcing its neutrality laws, caused enormous losses to American trade and commerce, caused irritation, annoyance, and disturbance among our citizens, and, by the exercise of cruel, barbarous, and uncivilized practices of warfare, shocked the sensibilities and offended the humane sympathies of our people.

Since the present revolution began, in February, 1895, this country has seen the fertile domain at our threshold ravaged by fire and sword in the course of a struggle unequaled in the history of the island and rarely paralleled as to the numbers of the combatants and the bitterness of the contest by any revolution of modern times where a dependent people striving to be free have been opposed by the power of the sovereign state.

Our people have beheld a once prosperous community reduced to comparative want, its lucrative commerce virtually paralyzed, its exceptional productiveness diminished, its fields laid waste, its mills in ruins, and its people perishing by tens of thousands from hunger and destitution. We have found ourselves constrained, in the observance of that strict neutrality which our laws enjoin and which the law of nations commands, to police our own waters and watch our own seaports in prevention of any unlawful act in aid of the Cubans.

Our trade has suffered, the capital invested by our citizens in Cuba has been largely lost, and the temper and forbearance of our people have been so sorely tried as to beget a perilous unrest among our own citizens, which has inevitably found its expression from time to time in the National Legislature, so that issues wholly external to our own body politic engross attention and stand in the way of that close devotion to domestic advancement that becomes a self-contained commonwealth whose primal maxim has been the avoidance of all foreign entanglements. All this must needs awaken, and has, indeed, aroused, the utmost concern on the part of this Government, as well during my predecessor's term as in my own.

In April, 1896, the evils from which our country suffered through the Cuban war became so onerous that my predecessor made an effort to bring about a peace through the mediation of this Government in any way that might tend to an honorable adjustment of the contest between Spain and her revolted colony, on the basis of some effective scheme of self-government for Cuba under the flag and sovereignty of Spain. It failed through the refusal of the Spanish government then in power to consider any form of mediation or, indeed, any plan of settlement which did not begin with the actual submission of the insurgents to the mother country, and then only on such terms as Spain herself might see fit to grant. The war continued unabated. The resistance of the insurgents was in no wise diminished.

The efforts of Spain were increased, both by the dispatch of fresh levies to Cuba and by the addition to the horrors of the strife of a new and inhuman phase happily unprecedented in the modern history of civilized Christian peoples. The policy of devastation and concentration, inaugurated by the Captain-General's *bando* of October 21, 1896, in the Province of Pinar del Rio was thence extended to embrace all of the island to which the power of the Spanish arms was able to reach by occupation or by military operations. The peasantry, including all dwelling in the open agricultural interior, were driven into the garrison towns or isolated places held by the troops.

The raising and movement of provisions of all kinds were interdicted. The fields were laid waste, dwellings unroofed and fired, mills destroyed, and, in short, everything that could desolate the land and render it unfit for human habitation or support was commanded by one or the other of the contending parties and executed by all the powers at their disposal.

By the time the present Administration took office, a year ago, reconcentration (so called) had been made effective over the better part of the four central and western provinces—Santa Clara, Matanzas, Havana, and Pinar del Rio.

The agricultural population to the estimated number of 300,000 or more was herded within the towns and their immediate vicinage, deprived of the means of support, rendered destitute of shelter, left poorly clad, and exposed to the most unsanitary conditions. As the scarcity of food increased with the devastation of the depopulated areas of production, destitution and want became misery and starvation. Month by month the death rate increased in an alarming ratio. By March, 1897, according to conservative estimates from official Spanish sources, the mortality among the reconcentrados from starvation and the diseases thereto incident exceeded 50 per cent of their total number.

No practical relief was accorded to the destitute. The overburdened towns, already suffering from the general dearth, could give no aid. So called "zones of cultivation" established within the immediate areas of effective military control about the cities and fortified camps proved illusory as a remedy for the suffering. The unfortunates, being for the most part women and children, with aged and helpless men, enfeebled by disease and hunger, could not have tilled the soil without tools, seed, or shelter for their own support or for the supply of the cities. Reconcentration, adopted avowedly as a war measure in order to cut off the resources of the insurgents, worked its predestined result. As I said in my message of last December, it was not civilized warfare; it was extermination. The only peace it could beget was that of the wilderness and the grave.

Meanwhile the military situation in the island had undergone a noticeable change. The extraordinary activity that characterized the second year of the war, when the insurgents invaded even the thitherto unharmed fields of Pinar del Rio and carried havoc and destruction up to the walls of the city of Havana itself, had relapsed into a dogged struggle in the central and eastern provinces. The Spanish arms regained a measure of control in Pinar del Rio and parts of Havana, but, under the existing conditions of the rural country, without immediate improvement of their productive situation. Even thus partially restricted, the revolutionists held their own, and their conquest and submission, put forward by Spain as the essential and sole basis of peace, seemed as far distant as at the outset.

In this state of affairs my Administration found itself confronted with the grave problem of its duty. My message of last December reviewed the situation and narrated the steps taken with a view to relieving its acuteness and opening the way to some form of honorable settlement. The assassination of the prime minister, Canovas, led to a change of government in Spain. The former administration, pledged to subjugation without concession, gave place to that of a more liberal party, committed long in advance to a policy of reform involving the wider principle of home rule for Cuba and Puerto Rico.

The overtures of this Government made through its new envoy, General Woodford, and looking to an immediate and effective amelioration of the condition of the island, although not accepted to the extent of admitted mediation in any shape, were met by assurances that home rule in an advanced phase would be forthwith offered to Cuba, without waiting for the war to end, and that more humane methods should thenceforth prevail in the conduct of hostilities. Coincidentally with these declarations the new government of Spain continued and completed the policy, already begun by its predecessor, of testifying friendly regard for this nation by releasing American citizens held under one charge or another connected with the insurrection, so that by the end of November not a single person entitled in any way to our national protection remained in a Spanish prison.

While these negotiations were in progress the increasing destitution of the unfortunate reconcentrados and the alarming mortality among them claimed earnest attention. The success which had attended the limited measure of relief extended to the suffering American citizens among them by the judicious expenditure through the consular agencies of the money appropriated expressly for their succor by the joint resolution approved May 24, 1897, prompted the humane extension of a similar scheme of aid to the great body of sufferers. A suggestion to this end was acquiesced in by the Spanish authorities.

On the 24th of December last I caused to be issued an appeal to the American people inviting contributions in money or in kind for the succor of the starving sufferers in Cuba, following this on the 8th of January by a similar public announcement of the formation of a central Cuban relief committee, with headquarters in New York City, composed of three members representing the American National Red Cross and the religious and business elements of the community.

The efforts of that committee have been untiring and have accomplished much. Arrangements for free transportation to Cuba have greatly aided the charitable work. The president of the American Red Cross and representatives of other contributory organizations have generously visited Cuba and cooperated with the consul-general and the local authorities to make effective distribution of the relief collected through the efforts of the central committee. Nearly $200,000 in money and supplies has already reached the sufferers, and more is forthcoming. The supplies are admitted duty free, and transportation to the interior has been arranged, so that the relief, at first necessarily confined to Havana and the larger cities, is now extended through most, if not all, of the towns where suffering exists.

Thousands of lives have already been saved. The necessity for a change in the condition of the reconcentrados is recognized by the Spanish Government. Within a few days past the orders of General Weyler have been revoked. The reconcentrados, it is said, are to be permitted to return to their homes and aided to resume the self-supporting pursuits of peace. Public works have been ordered to give them employment and a sum of $600,000 has been appropriated for their relief.

The war in Cuba is of such a nature that, short of subjugation or extermination, a final military victory for either side seems impracticable. The alternative lies in the physical exhaustion of the one or the other party, or perhaps of both—a condition which in effect ended the ten years' war by the truce of Zanjon. The prospect of such a protraction and conclusion of the present strife is a contingency hardly to be contemplated with equanimity by the civilized world, and least of all by the United States, affected and injured as we are, deeply and intimately, by its very existence.

Realizing this, it appeared to be my duty, in a spirit of true friendliness, no less to Spain than to the Cubans, who have so much to lose by the prolongation of the struggle, to seek to bring about an immediate termination of the war. To this end I submitted on the 27th ultimo, as a result of much representation and correspondence, through the United States minister at Madrid, propositions to the Spanish Government looking to an armistice until October 1 for the negotiation of peace with the good offices of the President.

In addition I asked the immediate revocation of the order of reconcentration, so as to permit the people to return to their farms and the needy to be relieved with provisions and supplies from the United States, cooperating with the Spanish authorities, so as to afford full relief.

The reply of the Spanish cabinet was received on the night of the 31st ultimo. It offered, as the means to bring about peace in Cuba, to confide the preparation thereof to the insular parliament, inasmuch as the concurrence of that body would be necessary to reach a final result, it being, however, understood that the powers reserved by the constitution to the central Government are not lessened or diminished. As the Cuban parliament does not meet until the 4th of May next, the Spanish Government would not object for its part to accept at once a suspension of hostilities if asked for by the insurgents from the general in chief, to whom it would pertain in such case to determine the duration and conditions of the armistice.

The propositions submitted by General Woodford and the reply of the Spanish Government were both in the form of brief memoranda, the texts of which are before me and are substantially in the language above given. The function of the Cuban parliament in the matter of "preparing" peace and the manner of its doing so are not expressed in the Spanish memorandum, but from General Woodford's explanatory reports of preliminary discussions preceding the final conference it is understood that the Spanish Government stands ready to give the insular congress full powers to settle the terms of peace with the insurgents, whether by direct negotiation or indirectly by means of legislation does not appear.

With this last overture in the direction of immediate peace, and its disappointing reception by Spain, the Executive is brought to the end of his effort.

In my annual message of December last I said:

> Of the untried measures there remain only: Recognition of the insurgents as belligerents; recognition of the independence of Cuba; neutral intervention to end the war by imposing a rational compromise between the contestants, and intervention in favor of one or the other party. I speak not of forcible annexation, for that can not be thought of. That, by our code of morality, would be criminal aggression.

Thereupon I reviewed these alternatives in the light of President Grant's measured words, uttered in 1875, when, after seven years of sanguinary, destructive, and cruel hostilities in Cuba, he reached the conclusion that the recognition of the independence of Cuba was impracticable and indefensible and that the recognition of belligerence was not warranted by the facts according to the tests of public law. I commented especially upon the latter aspect of the question, pointing out the inconveniences and positive dangers of a recognition of belligerence, which, while adding to the already onerous burdens of neutrality within our own jurisdiction, could not in any way extend our influence or effective offices in the territory of hostilities.

Nothing has since occurred to change my view in this regard, and I recognize as fully now as then that the issuance of a proclamation of neutrality, by which process the so-called recognition of belligerents is published, could of itself and unattended by other action accomplish nothing toward the one end for which we labor—the instant pacification of Cuba and the cessation of the misery that afflicts the island.

Turning to the question of recognizing at this time the independence of the present insurgent government in Cuba, we find safe precedents in our history from an early day. They are well summed up in President Jackson's message to Congress, December 21, 1836, on the subject of the recognition of the independence of Texas. He said:

> In all the contests that have arisen out of the revolutions of France, out of the disputes relating to the crowns of Portugal and Spain, out of the revolutionary movements of those Kingdoms, out of the separa-

tion of the American possessions of both from the European Governments, and out of the numerous and constantly occurring struggles for dominion in Spanish America, so wisely consistent with our just principles has been the action of our Government that we have under the most critical circumstances avoided all censure and encountered no other evil than that produced by a transient estrangement of good will in those against whom we have been by force of evidence compelled to decide.

It has thus been made known to the world that the uniform policy and practice of the United States is to avoid all interference in disputes which merely relate to the internal government of other nations, and eventually to recognize the authority of the prevailing party, without reference to our particular interests and views or to the merits of the original controversy.

* * * * *

* * * But on this as on every trying occasion safety is to be found in a rigid adherence to principle.

In the contest between Spain and her revolted colonies we stood aloof and waited, not only until the ability of the new States to protect themselves was fully established, but until the danger of their being again subjugated had entirely passed away. Then, and not till then, were they recognized. Such was our course in regard to Mexico herself. * * * It is true that, with regard to Texas, the civil authority of Mexico has been expelled, its invading army defeated, the chief of the Republic himself captured, and all present power to control the newly organized Government of Texas annihilated within its confines. But, on the other hand, there is, in appearance at least, an immense disparity of physical force on the side of Mexico. The Mexican Republic under another Executive is rallying its forces under a new leader and menacing a fresh invasion to recover its lost dominion.

Upon the issue of this threatened invasion the independence of Texas may be considered as suspended, and were there nothing peculiar in the relative situation of the United States and Texas our acknowledgement of its independence at such a crisis could scarcely be regarded as consistent with that prudent reserve with which we have heretofore held ourselves bound to treat all similar questions.

Thereupon Andrew Jackson proceeded to consider the risk that there might be imputed to the United States motives of selfish interest in view of the former claim on our part to the territory of Texas and of the avowed purpose of the Texans in seeking recognition of independence as an incident to the incorporation of Texas in the Union, concluding thus:

Prudence, therefore, seems to dictate that we should still stand aloof and maintain our present attitude, if not until Mexico itself or one of the great foreign powers shall recognize the independence of the new Government, at least until the lapse of time or the course of events shall have proved beyond cavil or dispute the ability of the people of that country to maintain their separate sovereignty and to uphold the Government constituted by them. Neither of the contending parties can justly complain of this course. By pursuing it we are but carrying out the long-established policy of our Government—a policy which has secured to us respect and influence abroad and inspired confidence at home.

These are the words of the resolute and patriotic Jackson. They are evidence that the United States, in addition to the test imposed by public law as the condition of the recognition of independence by a neutral state (to wit, that the revolted state shall "constitute in fact a body politic, having a government in substance as well as in name, possessed of the elements of stability," and forming *de facto,* "if left to itself, a state among the nations, reasonably capable of discharging the duties of a state"), has imposed for its own governance in dealing with cases like these the further condition that recognition of independent statehood is not due to a revolted dependency until the danger of its being again subjugated by the parent state has entirely passed away.

This extreme test was, in fact, applied in the case of Texas. The Congress to whom President Jackson referred the question as one "probably leading to war," and therefore a proper subject for "a previous understanding with that body by whom war can alone be declared and by whom all the provisions for sustaining its perils must be furnished," left the matter of the recognition of Texas to the discretion of the Executive, providing merely for the sending of a diplomatic agent when the President should be satisfied that the Republic of Texas had become "an independent state." It was so recognized by President Van Buren, who commissioned a chargé d'affaires March 7, 1837, after Mexico had abandoned an attempt to reconquer the Texas territory, and when there was at the time no *bona fide* contest going on between the insurgent province and its former sovereign.

I said in my message of December last:

> It is to be seriously considered whether the Cuban insurrection possesses beyond dispute the attributes of statehood, which alone can demand the recognition of belligerency in its favor.

The same requirement must certainly be no less seriously considered when the graver issue of recognizing independence is in question, for no less positive test can be applied to the greater act than to the lesser, while, on the other hand, the influences and consequences of the struggle upon the internal policy of the recognizing state, which form important factors when the recognition of belligerency is concerned, are secondary, if not rightly eliminable, factors when the real question is whether the community claiming recognition is or is not independent beyond peradventure.

Nor from the standpoint of expediency do I think it would be wise or prudent for this Government to recognize at the present time the independence of the so-called Cuban Republic. Such recognition is not necessary in order to enable the United States to intervene and pacify the island. To commit this country now to the recognition of any particular government in Cuba might subject us to embarrassing conditions of international obligation toward the organization so recognized. In case of intervention our conduct would be subject to the approval or disapproval of such government. We would be required to submit to its direction and to assume to it the mere relation of a friendly ally.

When it shall appear hereafter that there is within the island a government capable of performing the duties and discharging the functions of a separate nation, and having as a matter of fact the proper forms and attributes of nationality, such government can be promptly and readily recognized and the relations and interests of the United States with such nation adjusted.

There remain the alternative forms of intervention to end the war, either as an impartial neutral, by imposing a rational compromise between the contestants, or as the active ally of the one party or the other.

As to the first, it is not to be forgotten that during the last few months the relation of the United States has virtually been one of friendly intervention in many ways, each not of itself conclusive, but all tending to the exertion of a potential influence toward an ultimate pacific result, just and honorable to all interests concerned. The spirit of all our acts hitherto has been an earnest, unselfish desire for peace and prosperity in Cuba, untarnished by differences between us and Spain and unstained by the blood of American citizens.

The forcible intervention of the United States as a neutral to stop the war, according to the large dictates of humanity and following many historical precedents where neighboring states have interfered to check the hopeless sacrifices of life by internecine conflicts beyond their borders, is justifiable on rational grounds. It involves, however, a hostile constraint upon both the parties to the contest, as well as to enforce a truce as to guide the eventual settlement.

The grounds for such intervention may be briefly summarized as follows:

First. In the cause of humanity and to put an end to the barbarities, bloodshed, starvation, and horrible miseries now existing there, and which the parties to the conflict are either unable or unwilling to stop or mitigate. It is no answer to say this is all in another country, belonging to another nation, and is therefore none of our business. It is specially our duty, for it is right at our door.

Second. We owe it to our citizens in Cuba to afford them that protection and indemnity for life and property which no government there can or will afford, and to that end to terminate the conditions that deprive them of legal protection.

Third. The right to intervene may be justified by the very serious injury to the commerce, trade, and business of our people and by the wanton destruction of property and devastation of the island.

Fourth, and which is of the utmost importance. The present condition of affairs in Cuba is a constant menace to our peace and entails upon this Government an enormous expense. With such a conflict waged for years in an island so near us and with which our people have such trade and business relations; when the lives and liberty of our citizens are in constant danger and their property destroyed and themselves ruined; where our trading vessels are liable to seizure and are seized at our very door by war ships of a foreign nation; the expeditions of filibustering that we are powerless to prevent altogether, and the irritating questions and entanglements thus arising—all these and others that I need not mention, with the resulting strained relations, are a constant menace to our peace and compel us to keep on a semi war footing with a nation with which we are at peace.

These elements of danger and disorder already pointed out have been strikingly illustrated by a tragic event which has deeply and justly moved the American people. I have already transmitted to Congress the report of the naval court of inquiry on the destruction of the battle ship *Maine* in the harbor of Havana during the night of the 15th of February. The destruction of that noble vessel has filled the national heart with inexpressible horror. Two hundred and fifty-eight brave sailors and marines and two officers of our Navy, reposing in the fancied security of a friendly harbor, have been hurled to death, grief and want brought to their homes and sorrow to the nation.

The naval court of inquiry, which, it is needless to say, commands the unqualified confidence of the Government, was unanimous in its conclusion that the destruction of the *Maine* was caused by an exterior explosion—that of a submarine mine. It did not assume to place the responsibility. That remains to be fixed.

In any event, the destruction of the *Maine*, by whatever exterior cause, is a patent and impressive proof of a state of things in Cuba that is intolerable. That condition is thus shown to be such that the

Spanish Government can not assure safety and security to a vessel of the American Navy in the harbor of Havana on a mission of peace, and rightfully there.

Further referring in this connection to recent diplomatic correspondence, a dispatch from our minister to Spain of the 26th ultimo contained the statement that the Spanish minister for foreign affairs assured him positively that Spain will do all that the highest honor and justice require in the matter of the *Maine*. The reply above referred to, of the 31st ultimo, also contained an expression of the readiness of Spain to submit to an arbitration all the differences which can arise in this matter, which is subsequently explained by the note of the Spanish minister at Washington of the 10th instant, as follows:

> As to the question of fact which springs from the diversity of views between the reports of the American and Spanish boards, Spain proposes that the facts be ascertained by an impartial investigation by experts, whose decision Spain accepts in advance.

To this I have made no reply.

President Grant, in 1875, after discussing the phases of the contest as it then appeared and its hopeless and apparent indefinite prolongation, said:

> In such event I am of opinion that other nations will be compelled to assume the responsibility which devolves upon them, and to seriously consider the only remaining measures possible—mediation and intervention. Owing, perhaps, to the large expanse of water separating the island from the peninsula, * * * the contending parties appear to have within themselves no depository of common confidence to suggest wisdom when passion and excitement have their sway and to assume the part of peacemaker. In this view in the earlier days of the contest the good offices of the United States as a mediator were tendered in good faith, without any selfish purpose, in the interest of humanity, and in sincere friendship for both parties, but were at the time declined by Spain, with the declaration, nevertheless, that at a future time they would be indispensable. No intimation has been received that in the opinion of Spain that time has been reached. And yet the strife continues, with all its dread horrors and all its injuries to the interests of the United States and of other nations. Each party seems quite capable of working great injury and damage to the other, as well as to all the relations and interests dependent on the existence of peace in the island; but they seem incapable of reaching any adjustment, and both have thus far failed of achieving any success whereby one party shall possess and control the island to the exclusion of the other. Under these circumstances the agency of others, either by media-

tion or by intervention, seems to be the only alternative which must, sooner or later, be invoked for the termination of the strife.

In the last annual message of my immediate predecessor, during the pending struggle, it was said:

> When the inability of Spain to deal successfully with the insurrection has become manifest and it is demonstrated that her sovereignty is extinct in Cuba for all purposes of its rightful existence, and when a hopeless struggle for its reestablishment has degenerated into a strife which means nothing more than the useless sacrifice of human life and the utter destruction of the very subject-matter of the conflict, a situation will be presented in which our obligations to the sovereignty of Spain will be superseded by higher obligations, which we can hardly hesitate to recognize and discharge.

In my annual message to Congress December last, speaking to this question, I said:

> The near future will demonstrate whether the indispensable condition of a righteous peace, just alike to the Cubans and to Spain, as well as equitable to all our interests so intimately involved in the welfare of Cuba, is likely to be attained. If not, the exigency of further and other action by the United States will remain to be taken. When that time comes, that action will be determined in the line of indisputable right and duty. It will be faced, without misgiving or hesitancy, in the light of the obligation this Government owes to itself, to the people who have confided to it the protection of their interests and honor, and to humanity.
>
> Sure of the right, keeping free from all offense ourselves, actuated only by upright and patriotic considerations, moved neither by passion nor selfishness, the Government will continue its watchful care over the rights and property of American citizens and will abate none of its efforts to bring about by peaceful agencies a peace which shall be honorable and enduring. If it shall hereafter appear to be a duty imposed by our obligations to ourselves, to civilization, and humanity to intervene with force, it shall be without fault on our part and only because the necessity for such action will be so clear as to command the support and approval of the civilized world.

The long trial has proved that the object for which Spain has waged the war can not be attained. The fire of insurrection may flame or may smolder with varying seasons, but it has not been and it is plain that it can not be extinguished by present methods. The only hope of relief and repose from a condition which can no longer be endured is the enforced pacification of Cuba. In the name of humanity, in the name of civilization, in behalf of endangered American interests which give us the right and the duty to speak and to act, the war in Cuba must stop.

In view of these facts and of these considerations I ask the Congress to authorize and empower the President to take measures to secure a full and final termination of hostilities between the Government of Spain and the people of Cuba, and to secure in the island the establishment of a stable government, capable of maintaining order and observing its international obligations, insuring peace and tranquillity and the security of its citizens as well as our own, and to use the military and naval forces of the United States as may be necessary for these purposes.

And in the interest of humanity and to aid in preserving the lives of the starving people of the island I recommend that the distribution of food and supplies be continued and that an appropriation be made out of the public Treasury to supplement the charity of our citizens.

The issue is now with the Congress. It is a solemn responsibility. I have exhausted every effort to relieve the intolerable condition of affairs which is at our doors. Prepared to execute every obligation imposed upon me by the Constitution and the law, I await your action.

Yesterday, and since the preparation of the foregoing message, official information was received by me that the latest decree of the Queen Regent of Spain directs General Blanco, in order to prepare and facilitate peace, to proclaim a suspension of hostilities, the duration and details of which have not yet been communicated to me.

This fact, with every other pertinent consideration, will, I am sure, have your just and careful attention in the solemn deliberations upon which you are about to enter. If this measure attains a successful result, then our aspirations as a Christian, peace-loving people will be realized. If it fails, it will be only another justification for our contemplated action.

24

THE DECISION
TO WIELD THE "BIG STICK"
ON LAWLESS BUSINESS

Theodore Roosevelt's Message on the Trusts

From the death of Lincoln Congress had been supreme in the nation, and, save for Andrew Johnson and perhaps Cleveland, Presidents had been the creatures of the Congressional machine. The Republican Party which controlled Congress in the time of McKinley was content to let power remain where it was then lodged. Dominated by the great industrial and financial interests, the party considered McKinley the inevitable and safe choice for renomination in 1900, but agreed with some misgivings to the selection as his running mate of the reformist governor of New York, Theodore Roosevelt. In fact, Boss Platt of the Empire State was anxious to get the Rough Rider into a post where he would cause conservative Republicans the least possible anxiety. And what better one was available than the Vice Presidency, graveyard of political ambitions?

When Platt first presented the proposition, Mark Hanna of Ohio, McKinley's manager and the pre-eminent party leader, is reputed to have responded coldly. "Don't any of you realize," Hanna is alleged to have remarked, "that there's only one life between this madman and the White House!" Hanna yielded, the Republicans won in 1900, and in September, 1901, when an assassin mortally wounded McKinley at Buffalo, "that damned cowboy," as Hanna called Roosevelt, was President of the United States.

T. R.'s accession to office marked not only the resurgence of Presidential leadership but the beginning of a more concerted effort by the Federal government to regulate large industrial combinations engaged in monopolistic practices. In addition to state antitrust legislation, the Federal Sherman Antitrust Act of 1890 had prohibited combinations in restraint of trade. Yet, as a result of ineffectual enforcement by the Department of Justice, the law fell into neglect and even contempt.

Determined to investigate and publicize business mergers, and to press for the vigorous prosecution of monopolies, Roosevelt fired his opening gun with his first message to Congress in December, 1901. In its total context, the message was more of a popgun than a Krupp. It was by no means a revolutionary document. T. R. came out against assassins and anarchists, supported the existing tariff schedules, and asked for a subsidized Merchant Marine. Nothing very adventurous in all that. He saved his fire for the trusts, characterizing the growth of great corporations as a "natural" phenomenon, but stating without equivocation that the old laws and customs regulating the accumulation of wealth were now inadequate. Calling for "practical efforts" to correct such "real and grave evils" of large industry as overcapitalization, he specifically proposed the creation of a new Department of Commerce with a Bureau of Corporations, an act to expedite antitrust prosecutions, and a railroad bill barring rebates on freight shipments. Coming from a person of Roosevelt's impulsive and pugnacious temperament, this was indeed a prudent document, but it contained the seeds of much of his future legislative program. Mr. Dooley succinctly summarized it. "Th' trusts, says he, are heejoous monsthers built up be th' enlightened intherprise iv th' men that have done so much to advance progress in our beloved country, he says. On wan hand I wud stamp them undher fut; on th' other hand not so fast."

Mr. Dooley was right. Roosevelt was not opposed to bigness *per se,* but to the misuse of power by large aggregations of capital. He believed in government regulation of giant corporations, not their dissolution. Blocked by a stubborn and conservative Congress, which only gave him part of the legislation he demanded, he used the existing antitrust laws to bring lawless business to book through prosecutions judiciously instituted by the Department of Justice.

T. R.'s initial suit, to dissolve the Northern Securities Company in 1902, was followed by numerous other prosecutions of trusts, among them the Beef Trust, in which competition was not effectively restored until the early 1920's, the Standard Oil Company, and the American Tobacco Company. His dual program of publicity and prosecution was carried forward at an even more intensive pace by President Taft, whose most important victories, against the oil and tobacco trusts, were scored in proceedings that Roosevelt had instituted. T. R. did not bring about the demise of big business, but his message flashed a warning signal that monopolies and oligopolies henceforth would be under constant surveillance and held to account, and that the government regarded the maintenance of competition as essential for the general welfare. The age of lawless business was over.

FIRST ANNUAL MESSAGE

WHITE HOUSE, *December 3, 1901*

To the Senate and House of Representatives:

The Congress assembles this year under the shadow of a great calamity. On the sixth of September, President McKinley was shot by an anarchist while attending the Pan-American Exposition at Buffalo, and died in that city on the fourteenth of that month.

Of the last seven elected Presidents, he is the third who has been murdered, and the bare recital of this fact is sufficient to justify grave alarm among all loyal American citizens. Moreover, the circumstances of this, the third assassination of an American President, have a peculiarly sinister significance. Both President Lincoln and President Garfield were killed by assassins of types unfortunately not uncommon in history; President Lincoln falling a victim to the terrible passions aroused by four years of civil war, and President Garfield to the revengeful vanity of a disappointed office-seeker. President McKinley was killed by an utterly depraved criminal belonging to that body of criminals who object to all governments, good and bad alike, who are against any form of popular liberty if it is guaranteed by even the most just and liberal laws, and who are as hostile to the upright exponent of a free people's sober will as to the tyrannical and irresponsible despot.

It is not too much to say that at the time of President McKinley's death he was the most widely loved man in all the United States; while we have never had any public man of his position who has been so wholly free from the bitter animosities incident to public life. His political opponents were the first to bear the heartiest and most generous tribute to the broad kindliness of nature, the sweetness and gentleness of character which so endeared him to his close associates. To a standard of lofty integrity in public life he united the tender affections and home virtues which are all-important in the make-up of national character. A gallant soldier in the great war for the Union, he also shone as an example to all our people because of his conduct in the most sacred and intimate of home relations. There could be no personal hatred of him, for he never acted with aught but consideration for the welfare of others. No one could fail to respect him who knew him in public or private life. The defenders of those murderous criminals who seek to excuse their criminality by asserting that it is exercised for political ends, inveigh against wealth and irresponsible power. But for this assassination even this base apology cannot be urged.

President McKinley was a man of moderate means, a man whose stock sprang from the sturdy tillers of the soil, who had himself belonged among the wage-workers, who had entered the Army as a private soldier. Wealth was not struck at when the President was assassinated, but the honest toil which is content with moderate gains after a lifetime of unremitting labor, largely in the service of the public. Still less was power struck at in the sense that power is irresponsible or centered in the hands of any one individual. The blow was not aimed at tyranny or wealth. It was aimed at one of the strongest champions the wage-worker has ever had; at one of the most faithful representatives of the system of public rights and representative government who has ever risen to public office. President McKinley filled that political office for which the entire people vote, and no President —not even Lincoln himself—was ever more earnestly anxious to represent the well thought-out wishes of the people, his one anxiety in every crisis was to keep in closest touch with the people—to find out what they thought and to endeavor to give expression to their thought, after having endeavored to guide that thought aright. He had just been re-elected to the Presidency because the majority of our citizens, the majority of our farmers and wage-workers, believed that he had faithfully upheld their interests for four years. They felt that he represented so well and so honorably all their ideals and aspirations that they wished him to continue for another four years to represent them.

And this was the man at whom the assassin struck! That there might be nothing lacking to complete the Judas-like infamy of his act, he took advantage of an occasion when the President was meeting the people generally; and advancing as if to take the hand out-stretched to him in kindly and brotherly fellowship he turned the noble and generous confidence of the victim into an opportunity to strike the fatal blow. There is no baser deed in all the annals of crime.

The shock, the grief of the country are bitter in the minds of all who saw the dark days, while the President yet hovered between life and death. At last the light was stilled in the kindly eyes and the breath went from the lips that even in mortal agony uttered no words save of forgiveness to his murderer, of love for his friends, and of unfaltering trust in the will of the Most High. Such a death, crowning the glory of such a life, leaves us with infinite sorrow, but with such pride in what he had accomplished and in his own personal character, that we feel the blow not as struck at him, but as struck at the Nation. We mourn a good and great President who is dead; but while we mourn we are lifted up by the splendid achievements of his life and the grand heroism with which he met his death.

When we turn from the man to the Nation, the harm done is so great as to excite our gravest apprehensions and to demand our wisest and most resolute action. This criminal was a professed anarchist, inflamed by the teachings of professed anarchists, and probably also by the reckless utterances of those who, on the stump and in the public press, appeal to the dark and evil spirits of malice and greed, envy and sullen hatred. The wind is sowed by the men who preach such doctrines, and they cannot escape their share of responsibility for the whirlwind that is reaped. This applies alike to the deliberate demagogue, to the exploiter of sensationalism, and to the crude and foolish visionary who, for whatever reason, apologizes for crime or excites aimless discontent.

The blow was aimed not at this President, but at all Presidents; at every symbol of government. President McKinley was as emphatically the embodiment of the popular will of the Nation expressed through the forms of law as a New England town meeting is in similar fashion the embodiment of the law-abiding purpose and practice of the people of the town. On no conceivable theory could the murder of the President be accepted as due to protest against "inequalities in the social order," save as the murder of all the freemen engaged in a town meeting could be accepted as a protest against that social inequality which puts a malefactor in jail. Anarchy is no more an expression of "social discontent" than picking pockets or wife-beating.

The anarchist, and especially the anarchist in the United States, is merely one type of criminal, more dangerous than any other because he represents the same depravity in a greater degree. The man who advocates anarchy directly or indirectly, in any shape or fashion, or the man who apologizes for anarchists and their deeds, makes himself morally accessory to murder before the fact. The anarchist is a criminal whose perverted instincts lead him to prefer confusion and chaos to the most beneficent form of social order. His protest of concern for workingmen is outrageous in its impudent falsity; for if the political institutions of this country do not afford opportunity to every honest and intelligent son of toil, then the door of hope is forever closed against him. The anarchist is everywhere not merely the enemy of system and of progress, but the deadly foe of liberty. If ever anarchy is triumphant, its triumph will last for but one red moment, to be succeeded for ages by the gloomy night of despotism.

For the anarchist himself, whether he preaches or practices his doctrines, we need not have one particle more concern than for any ordinary murderer. He is not the victim of social or political injustice. There are no wrongs to remedy in his case. The cause of his criminality is to be found in his own evil passions and in the evil conduct of those who urge him on, not in any failure by others or by the State to do justice to him or his. He is a malefactor and nothing else. He is in no sense, in no shape or way, a "product of social conditions," save as a highwayman is "produced" by the fact that an unarmed man happens to have a purse. It is a travesty upon the great and holy names of liberty and freedom to permit them to be invoked in such a cause. No man or body of men preaching anarchistic doctrines should be allowed at large any more than if preaching the murder of some specified private individual. Anarchistic speeches, writings, and meetings are essentially seditious and treasonable.

I earnestly recommend to the Congress that in the exercise of its wise discretion it should take into consideration the coming to this country of anarchists or persons professing principles hostile to all government and justifying the murder of those placed in authority. Such individuals as those who not long ago gathered in open meeting to glorify the murder of King Humbert of Italy perpetrate a crime, and the law should ensure their rigorous punishment. They and those like them should be kept out of this country; and if found here they should be promptly deported to the country whence they came; and far-reaching provision should be made for the punishment of those who stay. No matter calls more urgently for the wisest thought of the Congress.

The Federal courts should be given jurisdiction over any man who kills or attempts to kill the President or any man who by the Constitution or by law is in line of succession for the Presidency, while the punishment for an unsuccessful attempt should be proportioned to the enormity of the offense against our institutions.

Anarchy is a crime against the whole human race; and all mankind should band against the anarchist. His crime should be made an offense against the law of nations, like piracy and that form of manstealing known as the slave trade; for it is of far blacker infamy than either. It should be so declared by treaties among all civilized powers. Such treaties would give to the Federal Government the power of dealing with the crime.

A grim commentary upon the folly of the anarchist position was afforded by the attitude of the law toward this very criminal who had just taken the life of the President. The people would have torn him limb from limb if it had not been that the law he defied was at once invoked in his behalf. So far from his deed being committed on behalf of the people against the Government, the Government was obliged at once to exert its full police power to save him from instant death at the hands of the people. Moreover, his deed worked not the slightest dislocation in our governmental system, and the danger of a recurrence of such deeds, no matter how great it might grow, would work only in the direction of strengthening and giving harshness to the forces of order. No man will ever be restrained from becoming President by any fear as to his personal safety. If the risk to the President's life became great, it would mean that the office would more and more come to be filled by men of a spirit which would make them resolute and merciless in dealing with every friend of disorder. This great country will not fall into anarchy, and if anarchists should ever become a serious menace to its institutions, they would not merely be stamped out, but would involve in their own ruin every active or passive sympathizer with their doctrines. The American people are slow to wrath, but when their wrath is once kindled it burns like a consuming flame.

During the last five years business confidence has been restored, and the nation is to be congratulated because of its present abounding prosperity. Such prosperity can never be created by law alone, although it is easy enough to destroy it by mischievous laws. If the hand of the Lord is heavy upon any country, if flood or drought comes, human wisdom is powerless to avert the calamity. Moreover, no law can guard us against the consequences of our own folly. The men who are idle or credulous, the men who seek gains not by genuine work with head or hand but by gambling in any form, are always a source of menace not only to themselves but to others. If the business world loses its head, it loses what legislation cannot supply. Fundamentally the welfare of each citizen, and therefore the welfare of the aggregate of citizens which makes the nation, must rest upon individual thrift and energy, resolution, and intelligence. Nothing can take the place of this individual capacity; but wise legislation and honest and intelligent administration can give it the fullest scope, the largest opportunity to work to good effect.

The tremendous and highly complex industrial development which went on with ever accelerated rapidity during the latter half of the nineteenth century brings us face to face, at the beginning of the twentieth, with very serious social problems. The old laws, and the old customs which had almost the binding force of law, were once quite sufficient to regulate the accumulation and distribution of wealth. Since the industrial changes which have so enormously increased the productive power of mankind, they are no longer sufficient.

The growth of cities has gone on beyond comparison faster than the growth of the country, and the upbuilding of the great industrial centers has meant a startling increase, not merely in the aggregate of wealth, but in the number of very large individual, and especially of very large corporate, fortunes. The creation of these great corporate fortunes has not been due to the tariff nor to any other governmental action, but to natural causes in the business world, operating in other countries as they operate in our own.

The process has aroused much antagonism, a great part of which is wholly without warrant. It is not true that as the rich have grown richer the poor have grown poorer. On the contrary, never before has the average man, the wage-worker, the farmer, the small trader, been so well off as in this country and at the present time. There have been abuses connected with the accumulation of wealth; yet it remains true that a fortune accumulated in legitimate business can be accumulated by the person specially benefited only on condition of conferring immense incidental benefits upon others. Successful enterprise, of the type which benefits all mankind, can only exist if the conditions are such as to offer great prizes as the rewards of success.

The captains of industry who have driven the railway systems across this continent, who have built up our commerce, who have developed our manufactures, have on the whole done great good to our people. Without them the material development of which we are so justly proud could never have taken place. Moreover, we should recognize the immense importance of this material development of leaving as unhampered as is compatible with the public good the strong and forceful men upon whom the success of business operations inevitably rests. The slightest study of business conditions will satisfy anyone capable of forming a judgment that the personal equation is the most important factor in a business operation; that the business ability of the man at the head of any business concern, big or little, is usually the factor which fixes the gulf between striking success and hopeless failure.

An additional reason for caution in dealing with corporations is to be found in the international commercial conditions of today. The same business conditions which have produced the great aggregations of corporate and individual wealth have made them very potent factors in international commercial competition. Business concerns which have the largest means at their disposal and are managed by the ablest men are naturally those which take the lead in the strife for commercial supremacy among the nations of the world. America has only just begun to assume that commanding position in the international business world which we believe will more and more be hers. It is of the utmost importance that this position be not jeopardized, especially at a time when the overflowing abundance of our own natural resources and the skill, business energy, and mechanical aptitude of our people make foreign markets essential. Under such conditions it would be most unwise to cramp or to fetter the youthful strength of our Nation.

Moreover, it cannot too often be pointed out that to strike with ignorant violence at the interests of one set of men almost inevitably endangers the interests of all. The fundamental rule in our national life—the rule which underlies all others—is that, on the whole, and in the long run, we shall go up or down together. There are exceptions; and in times of prosperity some will prosper far more, and in times of adversity, some will suffer far more, than others; but speaking generally, a period of good times means that all share more or less in them, and in a period of hard times all feel the stress to a greater or less degree. It surely ought not to be necessary to enter into any proof of this statement; the memory of the lean years which began in 1893 is still vivid, and we can contrast them with the conditions in this very year which is now closing. Disaster to great business enterprises can never have its effects limited to the men at the top. It spreads throughout, and while it is bad for everybody, it is worst for those farthest down. The capitalist may be shorn of his luxuries; but the wage-worker may be deprived of even bare necessities.

The mechanism of modern business is so delicate that extreme care must be taken not to interfere with it in a spirit of rashness or ignorance. Many of those who have made it their vocation to denounce the great industrial combinations which are popularly, although with technical inaccuracy, known as "trusts," appeal especially to hatred and fear. These are precisely the two emotions, particularly when combined with ignorance, which unfit men for the exercise of cool and steady judgment. In facing new industrial conditions, the whole history of the world shows that legislation will generally be both unwise and ineffective unless undertaken after calm inquiry and with sober self-restraint. Much of the legislation directed at the trusts would have been exceedingly mischievous had it not also been entirely ineffective. In accordance with a well-known sociological law, the ignorant or reckless agitator has been the really effective friend of the evils which he has been nominally opposing. In dealing with business interests, for the Government to undertake by crude and ill-considered legislation to do what may turn out to be bad, would be to incur the risk of such far-reaching national disaster that it would be preferable to undertake nothing at all. The men who demand the impossible or the undesirable serve as the allies of the forces with which they are nominally at war, for they hamper those who would endeavor to find out in rational fashion what the wrongs really are and to what extent and in what manner it is practicable to apply remedies.

All this is true; and yet it is also true that there are real and grave evils, one of the chief being over-capitalization because of its many baleful consequences; and a resolute and practical effort must be made to correct these evils.

There is a widespread conviction in the minds of the American people that the great corporations known as trusts are in certain of their features and tendencies hurtful to the general welfare. This springs from no spirit of envy or uncharitableness, nor lack of pride in the great industrial achievements that have placed this country at the head of the nations struggling for commercial supremacy. It does not rest upon a lack of intelligent appreciation of the necessity of meeting changing and changed conditions of trade with new methods, nor upon ignorance of the fact that combination of capital in the effort to accomplish great things is necessary when the world's progress demands that great things be done. It is based upon sincere conviction that combination and concentration should be, not prohibited, but supervised and within reasonable limits controlled; and in my judgment this conviction is right.

It is no limitation upon property rights or freedom of contract to require that when men receive from Government the privilege of doing business under corporate form, which frees them from individual responsibility, and enables them to call into their enterprises the capital of the public, they shall do so upon absolutely truthful representations as to the value of the property in which the capital is to be invested. Corporations engaged in interstate commerce should be regulated if they are found to exercise a license working to the public injury. It should be as much the aim of those who seek for social betterment to rid the business world of crimes of cunning as to rid the entire body politic of crimes of violence. Great corporations exist only because they are created and safeguarded by our institutions; and it is therefore our right and our duty to see that they work in harmony with these institutions.

The first essential in determining how to deal with the great industrial combinations is knowledge of the facts—publicity. In the interest of the public, the Government should have the right to inspect and examine the workings of the great corporations engaged in interstate business. Publicity is the only sure remedy which we can now invoke. What further remedies are needed in the way of governmental regulation, or taxation, can only be determined after publicity has been obtained, by process of law, and in the course of administration. The first requisite is knowledge, full and complete—knowledge which may be made public to the world.

Artificial bodies, such as corporations and joint stock or other associations, depending upon any statutory law for their existence or privileges, should be subject to proper governmental supervision, and full and accurate information as to their operations should be made public regularly at reasonable intervals.

The large corporations, commonly called trusts, though organized in one State, always do business in many States, often doing very little business in the State where they are incorporated. There is utter lack of uniformity in the State laws about them; and as no State has any exclusive interest in or power over their acts, it has in practice proved impossible to get adequate regulation through State action. Therefore, in the interest of the whole people, the Nation should, without interfering with the power of the States in the matter itself, also assume power of supervision and regulation over all corporations doing an interstate business. This is especially true where the corporation derives a portion of its wealth from the existence of some monopolistic element or tendency in its business. There would be no hardship in such supervision; banks are subject to it, and in their case it is now accepted as a simple matter of course. Indeed, it is probable that supervision of corporations by the National Government need not go so far as is now the case with the supervision exercised over them by so conservative a State as Massachusetts, in order to produce excellent results.

When the Constitution was adopted, at the end of the eighteenth century, no human wisdom could foretell the sweeping changes, alike in industrial and political conditions, which were to take place by the beginning of the twentieth century. At that time it was accepted as a matter of course that the several States were the proper authorities to regulate, so far as was then necessary, the comparatively insignificant and strictly localized corporate bodies of the day. The conditions are now wholly different and wholly different action is called for. I believe that a law can be framed which will enable the National Government to exercise control along the lines above indicated; profiting by the experience gained through the passage and administration of the Interstate-Commerce Act. If, however, the judgment of the Congress is that it lacks the constitutional power to pass such an act, then a constitutional amendment should be submitted to confer the power.

There should be created a Cabinet officer, to be known as Secretary of Commerce and Industries, as provided in the bill introduced at the last session of the Congress. It should be his province to deal with commerce in its broadest sense; including among many other things whatever concerns labor and all matters affecting the great business corporations and our merchant marine.

The course proposed is one phase of what should be a comprehensive and far-reaching scheme of constructive statesmanship for the purpose of broadening our markets, securing our business interests on a safe basis, and making firm our new position in the international industrial world; while scrupulously safeguarding the rights of wage-worker and capitalist, of investor and private citizen, so as to secure equity as between man and man in this Republic. . . .

25

THE DECISION
TO ASSUME RESPONSIBILITY FOR PRESERV-
ING ORDER IN THE WESTERN HEMISPHERE

T. R.'s Corollary to the Monroe Doctrine

That Teddy Roosevelt would stretch the meaning of the Monroe Doctrine to its furthest limits seemed a safe bet in view of his past record
as an outspoken and uninhibited expansionist. When Police Commissioner of New York City Roosevelt had praised the manner in
which President Cleveland had handled the Venezuelan boundary dispute. "Speak softly and carry a big stick; you will go far," was his
favorite motto, but in matters of diplomacy he seldom used the *sotto
voce* approach. The man who later boasted with much justice, "I took
the Canal Zone," accepted the Monroe Doctrine as the cornerstone of
American belligerency. Not that T. R. hungered after more territory.
By 1901 the United States seemed to have ample breathing space.
When, owing to the incessant turmoil in Santo Domingo, the question
of our intervention came up, Roosevelt remarked: "As for annexing
the island, I have about the same desire as a gorged boa constrictor
might have to swallow a porcupine wrong-end-to."

Disorders and maladministration in Latin America provoked the
President into declaring his hand. Roosevelt believed that there were
two kinds of nations, civilized and semibarbaric, and the former might
have to use the big stick on the latter occasionally. His ideas came into
focus in 1902, when England and Germany threatened to use force to
collect their debts from Venezuela. Roosevelt's position at the time is
a matter of dispute, but fortunately Venezuela's President finally agreed
to arbitrate the issues. The incident aroused T. R.'s liveliest suspicions
of Germany's intentions in the Western Hemisphere.

Two years later that "unspeakably villainous little monkey," as
Roosevelt characterized Venezuela's Castro, proved rambunctious again.

The President wrote privately that American intervention would have "a very healthy effect." "It will show these Dagos that they will have to behave decently." These strong views found formal expression in his celebrated Corollary to the Monroe Doctrine, delivered as a portion of his annual message to Congress in December, 1904. He declared then that any country in the Western Hemisphere that "keeps order and pays its obligations" need not fear interference from the United States, but in the case of "chronic wrongdoing, or an impotence which results in a general loosening of the ties of civilized society," the adherence of the United States to the Monroe Doctrine might force America, "however reluctantly, in flagrant cases of such wrongdoing or impotence, to the exercise of an international police power."

The Roosevelt Corollary was spelled out in the case of Santo Domingo, where dictatorships and revolution had reduced the island republic to bankruptcy. Fearing that European nations might intervene to collect debts due their nationals and might even seize the territory, Roosevelt now took the position that if there was any policing to be done only the United States could, under the Monroe Doctrine, undertake the disagreeable task. Accordingly, T. R. dispatched American agents to the island to take charge of the customs, pending ratification by the Senate of a special treaty with Santo Domingo. When Roosevelt failed to secure the two-thirds vote of the Senate necessary for ratification, he made an executive agreement on his own to stabilize Santo Domingo's finances and assure the payment of her foreign debts. The Senate, said Mr. Roosevelt, was "such a helpless body when efficient work for good is to be done." Two years later the Senate reluctantly put its seal of approval on a modified Dominican agreement.

The President, in his annual message of December, 1905, justified the course of action he had pursued. He maintained that "it is far better that this country" intervene to collect debts than to "allow any foreign country to undertake it." T. R. rationalized that such prompt action would forestall our clashing with a major power. Intervention now became the path to peace, although it did not work out as smoothly as T. R. had assumed. His Corollary led to protracted and unhappy spells of intervention, not only in Santo Domingo, but also in Haiti, Nicaragua, and Cuba, although in the case of the last-named republic

Roosevelt moved more gingerly. "I am doing my best," he said, "to persuade the Cubans that if only they will be good they will be happy; I am seeking the very minimum of interference necessary to make them good."

Neither Europe nor Latin America was "happy" about the Roosevelt Corollary. European newspapers denounced it as the "grafting of Caesarism upon Republican institutions." Henceforth Uncle Sam became the symbol of force and imperialism in Latin America, and whatever good will we had earned by our aid to Cuba speedily evaporated. New times brought a new and happier policy. Under Presidents Hoover and Franklin Delano Roosevelt the old Roosevelt Corollary was repudiated, the United States renounced any right it had once claimed to intervene in the affairs of sister states, American receiverships were liquidated, and American troops finally withdrawn in the interest of a Good Neighbor policy.

FOURTH ANNUAL MESSAGE

WHITE HOUSE, *December 6, 1904*

To the Senate and House of Representatives:

In treating of our foreign policy and of the attitude that this great Nation should assume in the world at large, it is absolutely necessary to consider the Army and the Navy, and the Congress, through which the thought of the Nation finds its expression, should keep ever vividly in mind the fundamental fact that it is impossible to treat our foreign policy, whether this policy takes shape in the effort to secure justice for others or justice for ourselves, save as conditioned upon the attitude we are willing to take toward our Army, and especially toward our Navy. It is not merely unwise, it is contemptible, for a nation, as for an individual, to use high-sounding language to proclaim its purposes, or to take positions which are ridiculous if unsupported by potential force, and then to refuse to provide this force. If there is no intention of providing and of keeping the force necessary to back up a strong attitude, then it is far better not to assume such an attitude.

The steady aim of this Nation, as of all enlightened nations, should be to strive to bring ever nearer the day when there shall prevail throughout the world the peace of justice. There are kinds of peace which are highly undesirable, which are in the long run as destructive as any war. Tyrants and oppressors have many times made a wilderness and called it peace. Many times peoples who were slothful or timid or shortsighted, who had been enervated by ease or by luxury, or misled by false teachings, have shrunk in unmanly fashion from doing duty that was stern and that needed self-sacrifice, and have sought to hide from their own minds their shortcomings, their ignoble motives, by calling them love of peace. The peace of tyrannous terror, the peace of craven weakness, the peace of injustice, all these should be shunned as we shun unrighteous war. The goal to set before us as a nation, the goal which should be set before all mankind, is the attainment of the peace of justice, of the peace which comes when each nation is not merely safe-guarded in its own rights, but scrupulously recognizes and performs its duty toward others. Generally peace tells for righteousness; but if there is conflict between the two, then our fealty is due first to the cause of righteousness. Unrighteous wars are common, and unrighteous peace is rare; but both should be shunned. The right of freedom and the responsibility for the exercise of that right can not be divorced. One of our great poets has well and finely said that freedom is not a gift that tarries long in the hands of cowards. Neither does it tarry long in the hands of those too slothful, too dishonest, or too unintelligent to exercise it. The eternal vigilance which is the price of liberty must be exercised, sometimes to guard against outside foes; although of course far more often to guard against our own selfish or thoughtless shortcomings.

If these self-evident truths are kept before us, and only if they are so kept before us, we shall have a clear idea of what our foreign policy in its larger aspects should be. It is our duty to remember that a nation has no more right to do injustice to another nation, strong or weak, than an individual has to do injustice to another individual; that the same moral law applies in one case as in the other. But we must also remember that it is as much the duty of the Nation to guard its own rights and its own interests as it is the duty of the individual so to do. Within the Nation the individual has now delegated this right to the State, that is, to the representative of all the individuals, and it is a maxim of the law that for every wrong there is a remedy. But in international law we have not advanced by any means as far as we have advanced in municipal law. There is as yet no judicial way of enforcing a right in international law. When one nation wrongs another or wrongs many others, there is no tribunal before which the wrongdoer can be brought. Either it is necessary supinely to acquiesce or else it is necessary for the aggrieved nation valiantly to stand up for its rights. Until some method is devised by which there shall be a degree of international control over offending nations, it would be a wicked thing for the most civilized powers, for those with most sense of international obligations and with keenest and most generous appreciation of the difference between right and wrong, to disarm. If the great civilized nations of the present day should completely disarm, the result would mean an immediate recrudescence of barbarism in one form or another. Under any circumstances a sufficient armament would have to be kept up to serve the purposes of international police; and until international cohesion and the sense of international duties and rights are far more advanced than at present, a nation desirous both of securing respect for itself and of doing good to others must have a force adequate for the work which it feels is allotted to it as its part of the general world duty. Therefore it follows that a self-respecting, just, and far-seeing nation should on the one hand endeavor by every means to aid in the development of the various movements which tend to provide substitutes for war, which tend to render nations in their actions toward one another, and indeed toward their own peoples, more responsive to the general sentiment of humane and civilized mankind; and on the other hand that it should keep prepared, while scrupulously avoiding wrongdoing itself, to repel any wrong, and in exceptional cases to take action which in a more advanced stage of international relations would come under the head of the exercise of the international police. A great free people owes it to itself and to all mankind not to sink into helplessness before the powers of evil.

We are in every way endeavoring to help on, with cordial good will, every movement which will tend to bring us into more friendly relations with the rest of mankind. In pursuance of this policy I shall shortly lay before the Senate treaties of arbitration with all powers which are willing to enter into these treaties with us. It is not possible at this period of the world's development to agree to arbitrate all matters, but there are many matters of possible difference between us and other nations which can be thus arbitrated. Furthermore, at the request of the Interparliamentary Union, an eminent body composed of practical statesmen from all countries, I have asked the Powers to join with this Government in a second Hague conference, at which it is hoped that the work already so happily begun at The Hague may be carried some steps further toward completion. This carries out the desire expressed by the first Hague conference itself.

It is not true that the United States feels any land hunger or entertains any projects as regards the other nations of the Western Hemisphere save such as are for their welfare. All that this country desires is to see the neighboring countries stable, orderly, and prosperous. Any country whose people conduct themselves well can count upon our hearty friendship. If a nation shows that it knows how to act with reasonable efficiency and decency in social and political matters, if it keeps order and pays its obligations, it need fear no interference from the United States. Chronic wrongdoing, or an impotence which results in a general loosening of the ties of civilized society, may in America, as elsewhere, ultimately require intervention by some civilized nation, and in the Western Hemisphere the adherence of the United States to the Monroe Doctrine may force the United States, however reluctantly, in flagrant cases of such wrongdoing or impotence, to the exercise of an international police power. If every country washed by the Caribbean Sea would show the progress in stable and just civilization which with the aid of the Platt amendment Cuba has shown since our troops left the island, and which so many of the republics in both Americas are constantly and brilliantly showing, all question of interference by this Nation with their affairs would be at an end. Our interests and those of our southern neighbors are in reality identical. They have great natural riches, and if within their borders the reign of law and justice obtains, prosperity is sure to come to them. While they thus obey the primary laws of civilized society they may rest assured that they will be treated by us in a spirit of cordial and helpful sympathy. We would interfere with them only in the last resort, and then only if it became evident that their inability or unwillingness to do justice at home and abroad had violated the rights of the United States or had invited foreign aggression to the detriment of the entire body of American nations. It is a mere truism to say that every nation, whether in America or anywhere else, which desires to maintain its freedom, its independence, must ultimately realize that the right of such independence can not be separated from the responsibility of making good use of it.

In asserting the Monroe Doctrine, in taking such steps as we have taken in regard to Cuba, Venezuela, and Panama, and in endeavoring to circumscribe the theater of war in the Far East, and to secure the open door in China, we have acted in our own interest as well as in the interest of humanity at large. There are, however, cases in which, while our own interests are not greatly involved, strong appeal is made to our sympathies. Ordinarily it is very much wiser and more useful for us to concern ourselves with striving for our own moral and material betterment here at home than to concern ourselves with trying to better the condition of things in other nations. We have plenty of sins of our own to war against, and under ordinary circumstances we can do more for the general uplifting of humanity by striving with heart and soul to put a stop to civic corruption, to brutal lawlessness and violent race prejudices here at home than by passing resolutions about wrongdoing elsewhere. Nevertheless there are occasional crimes committed on so vast a scale and of such peculiar horror as to make us doubt whether it is not our manifest duty to endeavor at least to show our disapproval of the deed and our sympathy with those who have suffered by it. The cases must be extreme in which such a course is justifiable. There must be no effort made to remove the mote from our brother's eye if we refuse to remove the beam from our own. But in extreme cases action may be justifiable and proper. What form the action shall take must depend upon the circumstances of the case; that is, upon the degree of the atrocity and upon our power to remedy it. The cases in which we could interfere by force of arms as we interfered to put a stop to intolerable conditions in Cuba are necessarily very few. Yet it is not to be expected that a people like ours, which in spite of certain very obvious shortcomings, nevertheless as a whole shows by its consistent practice its belief in the principles of civil and religious liberty and of orderly freedom, a people among whom even the worst crime, like the crime of lynching, is never more than sporadic, so that individuals and not classes are molested in their fundamental rights—it is inevitable that such a nation should desire eagerly to give expression to its horror on an occasion like that of the massacre of the Jews in Kishenef, or when it witnesses such systematic and long-extended cruelty and oppression as the cruelty and oppression of which the Armenians have been the victims, and which have won for them the indignant pity of the civilized world.

Even where it is not possible to secure in other nations the observance of the principles which we accept as axiomatic, it is necessary for us firmly to insist upon the rights of our own citizens without regard to their creed or race; without regard to whether they were born here or born abroad. It has proved very difficult to secure from Russia the right for our Jewish fellow-citizens to receive passports and travel through Russian territory. Such conduct is not only unjust and irritating toward us, but it is difficult to see its wisdom from Russia's standpoint. No conceivable good is accomplished by it. If an American Jew or an American Christian misbehaves himself in Russia he can at once be driven out; but the ordinary American Jew, like the ordinary American Christian, would behave just about as he behaves here, that is, behave as any good citizen ought to behave; and where this is the case it is a wrong against which we are entitled to protest to refuse him his passport without regard to his conduct and character, merely on racial and religious grounds. In Turkey our difficulties arise less from the way in which our citizens are sometimes treated than from the indignation inevitably excited in seeing such fearful misrule as has been witnessed both in Armenia and Macedonia.

The strong arm of the Government in enforcing respect for its just rights in international matters is the Navy of the United States. I most earnestly recommend that there be no halt in the work of upbuilding the American Navy. There is no more patriotic duty before us as a people than to keep the Navy adequate to the needs of this country's position. We have undertaken to build the Isthmian Canal. We have undertaken to secure for ourselves our just share in the trade of the Orient. We have undertaken to protect our citizens from improper treatment in foreign lands. We continue steadily to insist on the application of the Monroe Doctrine to the Western Hemisphere. Unless our attitude in these and all similar matters is to be a mere boastful sham we can not afford to abandon our naval programme. Our voice is now potent for peace, and is so potent because we are not afraid of war. But our protestations upon behalf of peace would neither receive nor deserve the slightest attention if we were impotent to make them good.

FIFTH ANNUAL MESSAGE

WHITE HOUSE, *December 5, 1905*

To the Senate and House of Representatives:

The first conference of nations held at The Hague in 1899, being unable to dispose of all the business before it, recommended the consideration and settlement of a number of important questions by another conference to be called subsequently and at an early date. These questions were the following. (1) The rights and duties of neutrals; (2) the limitation of the armed forces on land and sea, and of military budgets; (3) the use of new types and calibres of military and naval guns; (4) the inviolability of private property at sea in times of war; (5) the bombardment of ports, cities, and villages by naval forces. In October, 1904, at the instance of the Interparliamentary Union, which, at a conference held in the United States, and attended by the lawmakers of fifteen different nations, had reiterated the demand for a second conference of nations, I issued invitations to all the powers signatory to The Hague Convention to send delegates to such a conference, and suggested that it be again held at The Hague. In its note of December 16, 1904, the United States Government communicated to the representatives of foreign governments its belief that the confer-

315

ence could be best arranged under the provisions of the present Hague treaty.

From all the powers acceptance was received, coupled in some cases with the condition that we should wait until the end of the war then waging between Russia and Japan. The Emperor of Russia, immediately after the treaty of peace which so happily terminated this war, in a note presented to the President on September 13, through Ambassador Rosen, took the initiative in recommending that the conference be now called. The United States Government in response expressed its cordial acquiescence, and stated that it would, as a matter of course, take part in the new conference and endeavor to further its aims. We assume that all civilized governments will support the movement, and that the conference is now an assured fact. This Government will do everything in its power to secure the success of the conference, to the end that substantial progress may be made in the cause of international peace, justice, and good will.

This renders it proper at this time to say something as to the general attitude of this Government toward peace. More and more war is coming to be looked upon as in itself a lamentable and evil thing. A wanton or useless war, or a war of mere aggression—in short, any war begun or carried on in a conscienceless spirit, is to be condemned as a peculiarly atrocious crime against all humanity. We can, however, do nothing of permanent value for peace unless we keep ever clearly in mind the ethical element which lies at the root of the problem. Our aim is righteousness. Peace is normally the hand-maiden of righteousness; but when peace and righteousness conflict then a great and upright people can never for a moment hesitate to follow the path which leads toward righteousness, even though that path also leads to war. There are persons who advocate peace at any price; there are others who, following a false analogy, think that because it is no longer necessary in civilized countries for individuals to protect their rights with a strong hand, it is therefore unnecessary for nations to be ready to defend their rights. These persons would do irreparable harm to any nation that adopted their principles, and even as it is they seriously hamper the cause which they advocate by tending to render it absurd in the eyes of sensible and patriotic men. There can be no worse foe of mankind in general, and of his own country in particular, than the demagogue of war, the man who in mere folly or to serve his own selfish ends continually rails at and abuses other nations, who seeks to excite his countrymen against foreigners on insufficient pretexts, who excites and inflames a perverse and aggressive national vanity, and who may on occasions wantonly bring on conflict between his nation and some other nation. But there are demagogues of peace just as there are demagogues of war, and in any such movement as this for The Hague conference it is essential not to be misled by one set of extremists any more than by the other. Whenever it is possible for a nation or an individual to work for real peace, assuredly it is failure of duty not so to strive, but if war is necessary and righteous then either the man or the nation shrinking from it forfeits all title to self-respect. We have scant sympathy with the sentimentalist who dreads oppression less than physical suffering, who would prefer a shameful peace to the pain and toil sometimes lamentably necessary in order to secure a righteous peace. As yet there is only a partial and imperfect analogy between international law and internal or municipal law, because there is no sanction of force for executing the former while there is in the case of the latter. The private citizen is protected in his rights by the law, because he can call upon the police, upon the sheriff's posse, upon the militia, or in certain extreme cases upon the army, to defend him. But there is no such sanction of force for international law. At present there could be no greater calamity than for the free peoples, the enlightened, independent, and peace-loving peoples, to disarm while yet leaving it open to any barbarism or despotism to remain armed. So long as the world is as unorganized as now the armies and navies of those peoples who on the whole stand for justice, offer not only the best, but the only possible, security for a just peace. For instance, if the United States alone, or in company only with the other nations that on the whole tend to act justly, disarmed, we might sometimes avoid bloodshed, but we would cease to be of weight in securing the peace of justice—the real peace for which the most law-abiding and high-minded men must at times be willing to fight. As the world is now, only that nation is equipped for peace that knows how to fight, and that will not shrink from fighting if ever the conditions become such that war is demanded in the name of the highest morality.

So much it is emphatically necessary to say in order both that the position of the United States may not be misunderstood, and that a genuine effort to bring nearer the day of the peace of justice among the nations may not be hampered by a folly which, in striving to achieve the impossible, would render it hopeless to attempt the achievement of the practical. But, while recognizing most clearly all above set forth, it remains our clear duty to strive in every practicable way to bring nearer the time when the sword shall not be the arbiter among nations. At present the practical thing to do is to try to minimize the number of cases in which it must be the arbiter, and to offer, at least to all civilized powers, some substitute for war which will be available in at least a considerable number of instances. Very much can be done through another Hague conference in this direction, and I most earnestly urge that this Nation do all in its power to try to further the movement and to make the result of the decisions of The Hague conference effective. I earnestly hope that the conference may be able to devise some way to make arbitration between nations the customary way of settling international disputes in all save a few classes of cases, which should themselves be as sharply defined and rigidly limited as the present governmental and social development of the world will permit. If possible, there should be a general arbitration treaty negotiated among all the nations represented at the conference. Neutral rights and property should be protected at sea as they are protected on land. There should be an international agreement to this purpose and a similar agreement defining contraband of war.

During the last century there has been a distinct diminution in the number of wars between the most civilized nations. International relations have become closer and the development of The Hague tribunal is not only a symptom of this growing closeness of relationship, but is a means by which the growth can be furthered. Our aim should be from time to time to take such steps as may be possible toward creating something like an organization of the civilized nations, because as the world becomes more highly organized the need for navies and armies will diminish. It is not possible to secure anything like an immediate disarmament, because it would first be necessary to settle what peoples are on the whole a menace to the rest of mankind, and to provide against the disarmament of the rest being turned into a movement which would really chiefly benefit these obnoxious peoples; but it may be possible to exercise some check upon the tendency to swell indefinitely the budgets for military expenditure. Of course such an effort could succeed only if it did not attempt to do too much; and if it were undertaken in a spirit of sanity as far removed as possible from a merely hysterical pseudo-philanthropy. It is worth while pointing out that since the end of the insurrection in the Philippines this Nation has shown its practical faith in the policy of disarmament by reducing its little army one-third. But disarmament can never be of prime importance; there is more need to get rid of the causes of war than of the implements of war.

I have dwelt much on the dangers to be avoided by steering clear of any mere foolish sentimentality because my wish for peace is so genuine and earnest; because I have a real and great desire that this second Hague conference may mark a long stride forward in the direction of securing the peace of justice throughout the world. No object is better worthy the attention of enlightened statesmanship than the establishment of a surer method than now exists of securing justice as between nations, both for the protection of the little nations and for the prevention of war between the big nations. To this aim we should endeavor not only to avert bloodshed, but, above all, effectively to strengthen the forces of right. The Golden Rule should be, and as the world grows in morality it will be, the guiding rule of conduct among nations as among individuals; though the Golden Rule must not be construed, in fantastic manner, as forbidding the exercise of the police power. This mighty and free Republic should ever deal with all other States, great or small, on a basis of high honor, respecting their rights as jealously as it safeguards its own.

One of the most effective instruments for peace is the Monroe Doctrine as it has been and is being developed by this Nation and accepted by other nations. No other policy could have been as efficient in promoting peace in the Western Hemisphere and in giving to each nation thereon the chance to develop along its own lines. If we had refused to apply the doctrine to changing conditions it would now be completely outworn, would not meet any of the needs of the present day, and, indeed, would probably by this time have sunk into complete oblivion. It is useful at home, and is meeting with recognition abroad because we have adapted our application of it to meet the growing and changing needs of the hemisphere. When we announce a policy such as the Monroe Doctrine we thereby commit ourselves to the consequences of the policy, and those consequences from time to time alter. It is out of the question to claim a right and yet shirk the responsibility for its exercise. Not only we, but all American republics who are benefited by the existence of the doctrine, must recognize the obligations each nation is under as regards foreign peoples no less than its duty to insist upon its own rights.

That our rights and interests are deeply concerned in the maintenance of the doctrine is so clear as hardly to need argument. This is especially true in view of the construction of the Panama Canal. As a mere matter of self-defense we must exercise a close watch over the approaches to this canal; and this means that we must be thoroughly alive to our interests in the Caribbean Sea.

There are certain essential points which must never be forgotten as regards the Monroe Doctrine. In the first place we must as a Nation make it evident that we do not intend to treat it in any shape or way as an excuse for aggrandizement on our part at the expense of the republics to the south. We must recognize the fact that in some South

American countries there has been much suspicion lest we should interpret the Monroe Doctrine as in some way inimical to their interests, and we must try to convince all the other nations of this continent once and for all that no just and orderly Government has anything to fear from us. There are certain republics to the south of us which have already reached such a point of stability, order, and prosperity that they themselves, though as yet hardly consciously, are among the guarantors of this doctrine. These republics we now meet not only on a basis of entire equality, but in a spirit of frank and respectful friendship, which we hope is mutual. If all of the republics to the south of us will only grow as those to which I allude have already grown, all need for us to be the especial champions of the doctrine will disappear, for no stable and growing American Republic wishes to see some great non-American military power acquire territory in its neighborhood. All that this country desires is that the other republics on this continent shall be happy and prosperous; and they cannot be happy and prosperous unless they maintain order within their boundaries and behave with a just regard for their obligations toward outsiders. It must be understood that under no circumstances will the United States use the Monroe Doctrine as a cloak for territorial aggression. We desire peace with all the world, but perhaps most of all with the other peoples of the American Continent. There are, of course, limits to the wrongs which any self-respecting nation can endure. It is always possible that wrong actions toward this Nation, or toward citizens of this Nation, in some State unable to keep order among its own people, unable to secure justice from outsiders, and unwilling to do justice to those outsiders who treat it well, may result in our having to take action to protect our rights; but such action will not be taken with a view to territorial aggression, and it will be taken at all only with extreme reluctance and when it has become evident that every other resource has been exhausted.

Moreover, we must make it evident that we do not intend to permit the Monroe Doctrine to be used by any nation on this Continent as a shield to protect it from the consequences of its own misdeeds against foreign nations. If a republic to the south of us commits a tort against a foreign nation, such as an outrage against a citizen of that nation, then the Monroe Doctrine does not force us to interfere to prevent punishment of the tort, save to see that the punishment does not assume the form of territorial occupation in any shape. The case is more difficult when it refers to a contractual obligation. Our own Government has always refused to enforce such contractual obligations on behalf of its citizens by an appeal to arms. It is much to be wished that all foreign governments would take the same view. But they do not; and in consequence we are liable at any time to be brought face to face with disagreeable alternatives. On the one hand, this country would certainly decline to go to war to prevent a foreign government from collecting a just debt; on the other hand, it is very inadvisable to permit any foreign power to take possession, even temporarily, of the custom houses of an American Republic in order to enforce the payment of its obligations; for such temporary occupation might turn into a permanent occupation. The only escape from these alternatives may at any time be that we must ourselves undertake to bring about some arrangement by which so much as possible of a just obligation shall be paid. It is far better that this country should put through such an arrangement, rather than allow any foreign country to undertake it. To do so insures the defaulting republic from having to pay a debt of an improper character under duress, while it also insures honest creditors of the republic from being passed by in the interest of dishonest or grasping creditors. Moreover, for the United States to take such a position offers the only possible way of insuring us against a clash with some foreign power. The position is, therefore, in the interest of peace as well as in the interest of justice. It is of benefit to our people; it is of benefit to foreign peoples; and most of all it is really of benefit to the people of the country concerned.

This brings me to what should be one of the fundamental objects of the Monroe Doctrine. We must ourselves in good faith try to help toward peace and order those of our sister republics which need such help. Just as there has been a gradual growth of the ethical element in the relations of one individual to another, so we are, even though slowly, more and more coming to recognize the duty of bearing one another's burdens, not only as among individuals, but also as among nations.

Santo Domingo, in her turn, has now made an appeal to us to help her, and not only every principle of wisdom but every generous instinct within us bids us respond to the appeal. It is not of the slightest consequence whether we grant the aid needed by Santo Domingo as an incident to the wise development of the Monroe Doctrine or because we regard the case of Santo Domingo as standing wholly by itself, and to be treated as such, and not on general principles or with any reference to the Monroe Doctrine. The important point is to give the needed aid, and the case is certainly sufficiently peculiar to deserve to be judged purely on its own merits. The conditions in Santo Domingo have for a number of years grown from bad to worse until a year ago all society was on the verge of dissolution. Fortunately, just at this time a ruler sprang up in Santo Domingo, who, with his colleagues, saw the dangers threatening their country and appealed to the friend- ship of the only great and powerful neighbor who possessed the power, and as they hoped also the will to help them. There was imminent danger of foreign intervention. The previous rulers of Santo Domingo had recklessly incurred debts, and owing to her internal disorders she had ceased to be able to provide means of paying the debts. The pa- tience of her foreign creditors had become exhausted, and at least two foreign nations were on the point of intervention, and were only pre- vented from intervening by the unofficial assurance of this Government that it would itself strive to help Santo Domingo in her hour of need. In the case of one of these nations, only the actual opening of negoti- ations to this end by our Government prevented the seizure of territory in Santo Domingo by a European power. Of the debts incurred some were just, while some were not of a character which really renders it obligatory on or proper for Santo Domingo to pay them in full. But she could not pay any of them unless some stability was assured her Government and people.

Accordingly, the Executive Department of our Government nego- tiated a treaty under which we are to try to help the Dominican people to straighten out their finances. This treaty is pending before the Senate. In the meantime a temporary arrangement has been made which will last until the Senate has had time to take action upon the treaty. Under this arrangement the Dominican Government has ap- pointed Americans to all the important positions in the customs service, and they are seeing to the honest collection of the revenues, turning over 45 per cent. to the Government for running expenses and putting the other 55 per cent. into a safe depository for equitable division in case the treaty shall be ratified, among the various creditors, whether European or American.

The Custom Houses offer well-nigh the only sources of revenue in Santo Domingo, and the different revolutions usually have as their real aim the obtaining of these Custom Houses. The mere fact that the Collectors of Customs are Americans, that they are performing their duties with efficiency and honesty, and that the treaty is pending in the Senate gives a certain moral power to the Government of Santo Domingo which it has not had before. This has completely discouraged all revolutionary movement, while it has already produced such an increase in the revenues that the Government is actually getting more from the 45 per cent. that the American Collectors turn over to it than it got formerly when it took the entire revenue. It is enabling the poor, harassed people of Santo Domingo once more to turn their attention to industry and to be free from the cure of interminable revolutionary disturbance. It offers to all bona-fide creditors, American and European, the only really good chance to obtain that to which they are justly entitled, while it in return gives to Santo Domingo the only opportunity of defense against claims which it ought not to pay, for now if it meets the views of the Senate we shall ourselves thoroughly examine all these claims, whether American or foreign, and see that none that are improper are paid. There is, of course, opposition to the treaty from dishonest creditors, foreign and American, and from the professional revolutionists of the island itself. We have already reason to believe that some of the creditors who do not dare expose their claims to honest scrutiny are endeavoring to stir up sedition in the island and opposition to the treaty. In the meantime, I have exercised the authority vested in me by the joint resolution of the Congress to prevent the introduction of arms into the island for revolutionary purposes.

Under the course taken, stability and order and all the benefits of peace are at last coming to Santo Domingo, danger of foreign intervention has been suspended, and there is at last a prospect that all creditors will get justice, no more and no less. If the arrangement is terminated by the failure of the treaty chaos will follow; and if chaos follows, sooner or later this Government may be involved in serious difficulties with foreign Governments over the island, or else may be forced itself to intervene in the island in some unpleasant fashion. Under the proposed treaty the independence of the island is scrupulously respected, the danger of violation of the Monroe Doctrine by the intervention of foreign powers vanishes, and the interference of our Government is minimized, so that we shall only act in conjunction with the Santo Domingo authorities to secure the proper administration of the customs, and therefore to secure the payment of just debts and to secure the Dominican Government against demands for unjust debts. The proposed method will give the people of Santo Domingo the same chance to move onward and upward which we have already given to the people of Cuba. It will be doubly to our discredit as a Nation if we fail to take advantage of this chance; for it will be of damage to ourselves, and it will be of incalculable damage to Santo Domingo. Every consideration of wise policy, and, above all, every consideration of large generosity, bids us meet the request of Santo Domingo as we are now trying to meet it.

26

THE DECISION
TO SUPPORT A HIGH TARIFF

Taft Defends the Payne-Aldrich Act

For almost a century the tariff had been a major issue in American politics. The Civil War marked the triumph of high tariff protection for American industry. In President McKinley's administration tariff rates reached a new high, and reform elements in both parties felt that in the interest of the consumer and the farmer something had to be done, and soon. In 1908 the Republican Party platform pledged tariff reform, and William Howard Taft, T. R.'s hand-picked successor, was enthusiastically committed to it. The public was led to expect lower prices, and seldom if ever has the consumer been more cruelly deceived.

Taft, who had proved himself an able jurist and administrator, was temperamentally unsuited to engage in the battles that come in the course of the Presidency. The four years he spent in the White House were probably the unhappiest of his whole life. He was unwilling to dominate his party and therefore unable to control it. Not sharing Theodore Roosevelt's conception of the Presidency as a stewardship of the public welfare, he left the legislative initiative in the main to Congress.

The reform wing in the Republican Party at first held high hopes for Taft, but he was disinclined to badger and bully Congress or to use the patronage as a club. The first obstacle in the way of tariff reform was "Uncle Joe" Cannon, Speaker of the House, who was implacably opposed to downward tariff revision and manipulated the rules of procedure to block every move to bring it about. Taft regarded Cannon as "dirty and vulgar," and wrote T. R. that he would "have to go." The President let people know that he was opposed to the re-election of the Speaker, and after he had built up the expectations of the Cannon opposition, he dropped the fight when the going became rough. Finally, and without Taft's help, the insurgents and Democrats, although unable to prevent Cannon's re-election, changed the House rules and deprived the parliamentary czar of his dictatorial power to appoint the crucial Committee on Rules. In this fight the insurgents felt that Taft had let them down.

The real showdown came over the tariff. To the tariff bill proposed by Representative Sereno E. Payne in the House, Nelson W. Aldrich, the Senatorial spokesman of privilege, offered some eight hundred amendments, mostly in an upward direction, and specifically on iron and steel products, textiles and lumber. Upon reading the Aldrich bill, Mr. Dooley felicitated the suffering senators, "steamin' away under the majestic tin dome of the capitol," trying to reduce the tariff "to a weight at which it could stand on the same platform as the President without endangering his life." He predicted that the Aldrich amendments would make life easier for everybody, since the Rhode Island Senator had thoughtfully left curling stones, false teeth, canary-bird seed, hog bristles, silkworm eggs, and other such vital necessaries on the free list. "Th' new Tariff Bill," Mr. Dooley concluded, "put these familyar commodyties within th' reach iv all."

The insurgents took up the gage of battle. They were led by such Midwestern political personages as Robert La Follette of Wisconsin, Albert Cummins of Iowa, and Albert J. Beveridge of Indiana. On May 4, 1909, they launched their oratorical attack upon the tariff bill. Taft, unwilling to blackmail Congress, abdicated leadership in the fight. "I have no disposition," he told Aldrich, "to exert any other influence than that which it is my function under the Constitution to exercise." He suffered the reactionaries to run with the ball, then he joined their team. In justice to the President it should be pointed out that he did succeed in getting a number of rates reduced, in having the bill provide for the establishment of a tariff commission and impose a Federal tax on corporations engaged in interstate commerce. Taft also called upon Congress to adopt a joint resolution for submission to the states of a constitutional amendment permitting the Federal income tax. As a source of revenue, the income tax was soon to dwarf the tariff and revolutionize taxation in the United States.

Despite Taft's efforts the final result was "an eastern-made bill made to protect eastern products," a high tariff levied at the expense of the producers of raw materials in the South and West and, of course, of the consumer. By now thoroughly annoyed by the "yelping and snarling" at Boss Cannon and the Payne-Aldrich Tariff on the part of the Middle Western Republicans, known by 1909 as progressives, Taft virtually read them out of the party and considered them "assistant Democrats." Aware of the rising unrest in the corn and wheat country, the President decided upon a cross-country speaking tour to rally support for the administration. This tour was to be as fateful for his administration as Andrew Johnson's and Woodrow Wilson's proved for their respective programs.

The climax came in September, 1909, at the Winona, Minnesota, Opera House, where, in a speech dictated hurriedly the day before on the train, Taft defended the Payne-Aldrich Tariff as "the best tariff bill" that had ever been passed. In the course of the speech he mentioned one of the most controversial features of that tariff, Schedule K, which dealt with wool. The President had favored a cut in wool, but the insurgent Western woolgrowers opposed it, along with the Eastern woolen manufacturers. Taft conceded that this schedule was "the one important defect" in the tariff bill. But that is all he conceded. After the Winona address Taft was labeled a reactionary by the progressive elements in the Republican Party. That speech set the stage for the great secession from the Republican Party three years later and for the candidacy of Taft's erstwhile friend and sponsor, Teddy Roosevelt, running on the "Bull Moose" ticket.

More than any speeches made during the entire 1912 campaign, the Winona address assured the election of Woodrow Wilson to the Presidency, and left to the Democrats the credit for lowering tariff schedules. "We must abolish everything that bears even the semblance of privilege or of any kind of artificial advantage," Woodrow Wilson stated in his message asking for revision of the Payne-Aldrich Tariff. Henceforth, asserted Princeton's former president, the objective of tariff duties "must be effective competition, the whetting of American wits by contest with the wits of the rest of the world."

ADDRESS ON THE TARIFF LAW OF 1909

By President Taft at Winona, Minn., September 17, 1909

My fellow citizens: As long ago as August 1906, in the congressional campaign in Maine, I ventured to announce that I was a tariff revisionist and thought that the time had come for a readjustment of the schedules. I pointed out that it had been ten years prior to that time that the Dingley bill had been passed; that great changes had taken place in the conditions surrounding the productions of the farm, the factory, and the mine, and that under the theory of protection in that time the rates imposed in the Dingley bill in many instances might have become excessive; that is, might have been greater than the difference between the cost of production abroad and the cost of production at home with a sufficient allowance for a reasonable rate of profit to the American producer. I said that the party was divided on the issue, but that in my judgment the opinion of the party was crystallizing and would probably result in the near future in an effort to make such revision. I pointed out the difficulty that there always was in a revision of the tariff, due to the threatened disturbance of industries to be affected and the suspension of business, in a way which made it unwise to have too many revisions. In the summer of 1907 my position on the tariff was challenged, and I then entered into a somewhat fuller discussion of the matter. It was contended by the so-called "standpatters" that rates beyond the necessary measure of protection were not objectionable, because behind the tariff wall competition always reduced the prices, and thus saved the consumer. But I pointed out in that speech what seems to me as true to-day as it then was, that the danger of excessive rates was in the temptation they created to form monopolies in the protected articles, and thus to take advantage of the excessive rates by increasing the prices, and therefore, and in order to avoid such a danger, it was wise at regular intervals to examine the question of what the effect of the rates had been upon the industries in this country, and whether the conditions with respect to the cost of production here had so changed as to warrant a reduction in the tariff, and to make a lower rate truly protective of the industry.

It will be observed that the object of the revision under such a statement was not to destroy protected industries in this country, but it was to continue to protect them where lower rates offered a sufficient protection to prevent injury by foreign competition. That was the object of the revision as advocated by me, and it was certainly the object of the revision as promised in the Republican platform.

I want to make as clear as I can this proposition, because, in order to determine whether a bill is a compliance with the terms of that platform, it must be understood what the platform means. A free trader is opposed to any protected rate because he thinks that our manufacturers, our farmers, and our miners ought to withstand the competition of foreign manufacturers and miners and farmers, or else go out of business and find something else more profitable to do. Now, certainly the promises of the platform did not contemplate the downward revision of the tariff rates to such a point that any industry theretofore protected should be injured. Hence, those who contend that the promise of the platform was to reduce prices by letting in foreign competition are contending for a free trade, and not for anything that they had the right to infer from the Republican platform.

The Ways and Means Committee of the House, with Mr. Payne at its head, spent a full year in an investigation, assembling evidence in reference to the rates under the tariff, and devoted an immense amount of work in the study of the question where the tariff rates could be reduced and where they ought to be raised with a view to maintaining a reasonably protective rate, under the principles of the platform, for every industry that deserved protection. They found that the determination of the question, what was the actual cost of production and whether an industry in this country could live under a certain rate and withstand threatened competition from abroad, was most difficult. The manufacturers were prone to exaggerate the injury which a reduction in the duty would give and to magnify the amount of duty that was needed; while the importers, on the other hand, who were interested in developing the importation from foreign shores, were quite likely to be equally biased on the other side.

Mr. Payne reported a bill—the Payne Tariff bill—which went to the Senate and was amended in the Senate by increasing the duty on some things and decreasing it on others. The difference between the House bill and the Senate bill was very much less than the newspapers represented. It turns out upon examination that the reductions in the Senate were about equal to those in the House, though they differed in character. Now, there is nothing quite so difficult as the discussion of a tariff bill, for the reason that it covers so many different items, and the meaning of the terms and the percentages are very hard to understand. The passage of a new bill, especially where a change in the method of assessing the duties has been followed, presents an opportunity for various modes and calculations of the percentages of increases and decreases that are most misleading and really throw no light at all upon the changes made.

One way of stating what was done is to say what the facts show—that under the Dingley law there were 2,024 items. This included dutiable items only. The Payne law leaves 1,150 of these items unchanged. There are decreases in 654 of the items and increases in 220 of the items. Now, of course, that does not give a full picture, but it does show the proportion of decreases to have been three times those of the increases. Again, the schedules are divided into letters from A to N. The first schedule is that of chemicals, oils, etc. There are 232 items in the Dingley law; of these, 81 were decreased, 22 were increased, leaving 129 unchanged. Under Schedule B—earths, earthenware and glassware—there were 170 items in the Dingley law; 46 were decreased, 12 were increased, and 112 left unchanged. C is the schedule of metals and manufactures. There were 321 items in the Dingley law; 185 were decreased, 30 were increased, and 106 were left unchanged. D is the schedule of wood and manufactures of wood. There were 35 items in the Dingley law; 18 were decreased, 3 were increased, and 14 were left unchanged. There were 38 items in sugar, and of these 2 were decreased and 36 left unchanged. Schedule F covers tobacco and manufactures of tobacco, of which there were 8 items; they were all left unchanged. In the schedule covering agricultural products and provisions there were 187 items in the Dingley law; 14 of them were decreased, 19 were increased, and 154 left unchanged. Schedule H—that of spirits and wines—contained 33 items in the Dingley law; 4 were decreased, 23 increased, and 6 left unchanged. In cotton manufactures there were 261 items; of these 28 were decreased, 47 increased, and 186 left unchanged. In Schedule J—flax, hemp, and jute—there were 254 items in the Dingley law; 187 were reduced, 4 were increased, and 63 left unchanged. In wool, and manufactures thereof, there were 78 items; 3 were decreased, none were increased, and 75 left unchanged. In silk and silk goods there were 78 items; of these, 21 were decreased, 31 were increased, and 26 were left unchanged. In pulp, papers, and books there were 59 items in the Dingley law, and of these 11 were decreased, 9 were increased, and 39 left unchanged. In sundries there were 270 items, and of these 54 were decreased, 20 were increased, and 196 left unchanged. So that the total showed 2,024 items in the Dingley law, of which 654 were decreased, 220 were increased, making 874 changes, and 1,150 left unchanged.

Changes in Dingley Law by Payne Law

Schedule	Items in Dingley law	Decreases	Increases	Total Changes	Unchanged
A—Chemicals, oils, etc.	232	81	22	103	129
B—Earths, earthen- and glassware	170	46	12	58	112
C—Metals, and manufactures of	321	185	30	215	106
D—Wood, and manufactures of	35	18	3	21	14
E—Sugar, molasses, and manufactures of	38	2	0	2	36
F—Tobacco, and manufactures of	8	0	0	0	8
G—Agricultural products and provisions	187	14	19	33	154
H—Spirits, wines, etc.	33	4	23	27	6
I—Cotton manufactures	261	28	47	75	186
J—Flax, hemp, jute, manufactures of	254	187	4	191	63
K—Wool, and manufactures of	78	3	0	3	75
L—Silk and silk goods	78	21	31	52	26
M—Pulp, papers, and books	59	11	9	20	39
N—Sundries	270	54	20	74	196
Total	2,024	654	220	874	1,150

Attempts have been made to show that the real effect of these changes has been by comparing the imports under the various schedules, and assuming that the changes and their importance were in proportion to the importations. Nothing could be more unjust in a protective tariff which also contains revenue provisions. Some of the tariff is made for the purpose of increasing the revenue by increasing importations which shall pay duty. Other items in the tariff are made for the purpose of reducing competition, that is, by reducing importations, and, therefore, the question of the importance of a change in rate can not in the slightest degree be determined by the amount of imports that take place. In order to determine the importance of the changes, it is much fairer to take the articles on which the rates of duty have been reduced and those on which the rates of duty have been increased, and then determine from statistics how large a part the articles upon which duties have been reduced play in the consumption of the country, and how large a part those upon which the duties have been increased play in the consumption of the country. Such a table has been prepared by

Mr. Payne, than whom there is no one who understands better what the tariff is and who has given more attention to the details of the schedule.

Now, let us take Schedule A—chemicals, oils, and paints. The articles upon which the duty has been decreased are consumed in this country to the extent of $433,000,000. The articles upon which the duty has been increased are consumed in this country to the extent of $11,000,000. Take Schedule B. The articles on which the duty has been decreased entered in the consumption of the country to the amount of $128,000,000, and there has been no increase in duty on such articles. Take Schedule C—metals and their manufactures. The amount to which such articles enter into the consumption of the country is $1,221,000,000, whereas the articles of the same schedule upon which there has been an increase enter into the consumption of the country to the extent of only $37,000,000. Take Schedule D—lumber. The articles in this schedule upon which there has been a decrease enter into the consumption of the country to the extent of $566,000,000, whereas the articles under the same schedule upon which there has been an increase enter into its consumption to the extent of $31,000,000. In tobacco there has been no change. In agricultural products, those in which there has been a reduction of rates enter into the consumption of the country to the extent of $483,000,000; those in which there has been an increase enter into the consumption to the extent of $4,000,000. In the schedule of wines and liquors, the articles upon which there has been an increase, enter into the consumption of the country to the extent of $462,000,000. In cottons there has been a change in the higher-priced cottons and an increase. There has been no increase in the lower-priced cottons, and of the increases the high-priced cottons enter into the consumption of the country to the extent of $41,000,000. Schedule J—flax, hemp, and jute: The articles upon which there has been a decrease enter into the consumption of the country to the extent of $22,000,000, while those upon which there has been an increase enter into the consumption to the extent of $804,000. In Schedule K as to wool, there has been no change. In Schedule L as to silk, the duty has been decreased on articles which enter into the consumption of the country to the extent of $8,000,000, and has been increased on articles that enter into the consumption of the country to the extent of $106,000,000. On paper and pulp the duty has been decreased on articles, including print paper, that enter into the consumption of the country to the extent of $67,000,000 and increased on articles that enter into the consumption of the country to the extent of $81,000,000. In sundries, or Schedule N, the duty has been decreased on articles that enter into the consumption of the country to the extent of $1,719,000,000; and increased on articles that enter into the consumption of the country to the extent of $101,-000,000.

It will be found that in Schedule A the increases covered only luxuries —perfumes, pomades, and like articles; Schedule H—wines and liquors —which are certainly luxuries and are made subject to increase in order to increase the revenues, amounting to $462,000,000; and in Schedule L—silks—which are luxuries, certainly, $106,000,000, making a total of the consumption of those articles upon which there was an increase and which were luxuries of $579,000,000, leaving a balance of increase on articles which were not luxuries of value in consumption of only $272,000,-000, as against $5,000,000,000, representing the amount of articles entering into the consumption of the country, mostly necessities, upon which there has been a reduction of duties, and to which the 650 decreases applied.

STATEMENT

Schedule	Consumption value Duties decreased	Duties increased
A—Chemicals, oils, and paints	$ 433,099,846	$ 11,105,820
B—Earths, earthenware, and glassware	128,423,732	
C—Metals, and manufactures of	1,221,956,620	37,675,804
D—Wood, and manufactures of	566,870,950	31,280,372
E—Sugar, molasses, and manufactures of	300,965,953	
F—Tobacco, and manufactures of (no change of rates)		
G—Agricultural, products and provisions	483,430,637	4,380,043
H—Spirits, wines, and other beverages		462,001,856
I—Cotton manufactures		41,622,024
J—Flax, hemp, jute, and manufactures of	22,127,145	804,445
K—Wool and manufactures of wool. (No production statistics available for articles affected by changes of rates)		
L—Silks, and silk goods	7,947,568	106,742,646
M—Pulp, papers, and books	67,628,055	81,486,466
N—Sundries	1,719,428,069	101,656,598
Total	$4,951,878,575	$878,756,074

Of the above increases the following are luxuries, being articles strictly of voluntary use:

Schedule A. Chemicals, including perfumeries, pomades
and like articles $ 11,105,820
Schedule H. Wines and liquors   462,001,856
Schedule L. Silks   106,742,646
　　Total $579,850,322

This leaves a balance of increases which are not on articles of luxury of $298,905,752, as against decreases on about five billion dollars of consumption.

Now this statement shows as conclusively as possible the fact that there was a substantial downward revision on articles entering into the general consumption of the country which can be termed necessities, for the proportion is $5,000,000,000 representing the consumption of articles to which decreases applied, to less than $300,000,000 of articles of necessity to which the increases applied.

Now, the promise of the Republican platform was not to revise everything downward, and in the speeches which have been taken as interpreting that platform, which I made in the campaign, I did not promise that everything should go downward. What I promised was, that there should be many decreases, and that in some few things increases would be found to be necessary; but that on the whole I conceived that the change of conditions would make the revision necessarily downward—and that, I contend, under the showing which I have made, has been the result of the Payne bill. I did not agree, nor did the Republican party agree, that we would reduce rates to such a point as to reduce prices by the introduction of foreign competition. That is what the free traders desire. That is what the revenue tariff reformers desire; but that is not what the Republican platform promised, and it is not what the Republican party wished to bring about. To repeat the statement with which I opened this speech, the proposition of the Republican party was to reduce rates so as to maintain a difference between the cost of production abroad and the cost of production here, insuring a reasonable profit to the manufacturer on all articles produced in this country; and the proposition to reduce rates and prevent their being excessive was to avoid the opportunity for monopoly and the suppression of competition, so that the excessive rates could be taken advantage of to force prices up.

Now, it is said that there was not a reduction in a number of the schedules where there should have been. It is said that there was no reduction in the cotton schedule. There was not. The House and the

333

Senate took evidence and found from cotton manufacturers and from other sources that the rates upon the lower class of cottons were such as to enable them to make a decent profit—but only a decent profit—and they were contented with it; but that the rates on the high grades of cotton cloth, by reason of court decisions, had been reduced so that they were considerably below those of the cheaper grades of cotton cloth, and that by undervaluations and otherwise the whole cotton schedule had been made unjust and the various items were disproportionate in respect to the varying cloths. Hence, in the Senate a new system was introduced attempting to make the duties more specific rather than ad valorem, in order to prevent by judicial decision or otherwise a disproportionate and unequal operation of the schedule. Under this schedule it was contended that there had been a general rise of all the duties on cotton. This was vigorously denied by the experts of the Treasury Department. At last, the Senate in conference consented to a reduction amounting to about 10 per cent. on all the lower grades of cotton and thus reduced the lower grades substantially to the same rates as before and increased the higher grades to what they ought to be under the Dingley law and what they were intended to be. Now, I am not going into the question of evidence as to whether the cotton duties were too high and whether the difference between the cost of production abroad and at home, allowing only a reasonable profit to the manufacturer here, is less than the duties which are imposed under the Payne bill. It was a question of evidence which Congress passed upon, after they heard the statements of cotton manufacturers and such other evidence as they could avail themselves of. I agree that the method of taking evidence and the determination was made in a general way, and that there ought to be other methods of obtaining evidence and reaching a conclusion more satisfactory.

Criticism has also been made of the crockery schedule and the failure to reduce that. The question whether it ought to have been reduced or not was a question of evidence which both committees of Congress took up, and both concluded that the present rates on crockery were such as were needed to maintain the business in this country. I had been informed that the crockery schedule was not high enough, and mentioned that in one of my campaign speeches as a schedule probably where there ought to be some increases. It turned out that the difficulty was rather in undervaluations than in the character of the schedule itself, and so it was not changed. It is entirely possible to collect evidence to attack almost any of the schedules, but one story is good until another is told, and I have heard no reason for sustaining the contention that the crockery schedule is unduly high. So with respect

to numerous details—items of not great importance—in which, upon what they regarded as sufficient evidence, the committee advanced the rates in order to save a business which was likely to be destroyed.

I have never known a subject that will evoke so much contradictory evidence as the question of tariff rates and the question of cost of production at home and abroad. Take the subject of paper. A committee was appointed by Congress a year before the tariff sittings began, to determine what the difference was between the cost of production in Canada of print paper and the cost of production here, and they reported that they thought that a good bill would be one imposing $2 a ton on paper, rather than $6, the Dingley rate, provided that Canada could be induced to take off the export duties and remove the other obstacles to the importation of spruce wood in this country out of which wood pulp is made. An examination of the evidence satisfied Mr. Payne—I believe it satisfied some of the Republican dissenters—that $2, unless some change was made in the Canadian restrictions upon the exports of wood to this country, was much too low, and that $4 was only a fair measure of the difference between the cost of production here and in Canada. In other words, the $2 found by the special committee in the House was rather an invitation to Canada and the Canadian print-paper people to use their influence with their government to remove the wood restrictions by reducing the duty on print paper against Canadian print-paper mills. It was rather a suggestion of a diplomatic nature than a positive statement of the difference in actual costs of production under existing conditions between Canada and the United States.

There are other subjects which I might take up. The tariff on hides was taken off because it was thought that it was not necessary in view of the high price of cattle thus to protect the man who raised them, and that the duty imposed was likely to throw the control of the sale of hides into the hands of the meat packers in Chicago. In order to balance the reduction on hides, however, there was a great reduction in shoes, from 25 to 10 per cent.; on sole leather, from 20 to 5 per cent.; on harness, from 45 to 20 per cent. So there was a reduction in the duty on coal of 33⅓ per cent. All countervailing duties were removed from oil, naphtha, gasoline, and its refined products. Lumber was reduced from $2 to $1.25; and these all on articles of prime necessity. It is said that there might have been more. But there were many business interests in the South, in Maine, along the border, and especially in the far Northwest, which insisted that it would give great advantage to Canadian lumber if the reduction were made more than 75 cents. Mr. Pinchot, the Chief Forester, thought that it would tend to make

better lumber in this country if a duty were retained on it. The lumber interests thought that $2 was none too much, but the reduction was made and the compromise effected. Personally I was in favor of free lumber, because I did not think that if the tariff was taken off there would be much suffering among the lumber interests. But in the controversy the House and Senate took a middle course, and who can say they were not justified.

With respect to the wool schedule, I agree that it probably represents considerably more than the difference between the cost of production abroad and the cost of production here. The difficulty about the woolen schedule is that there were two contending factions early in the history of Republican tariffs, to wit, woolgrowers and the woolen manufacturers, and that finally, many years ago, they settled on a basis by which wool in the grease should have 11 cents a pound, and by which allowance should be made for the shrinkage of the washed wool in the differential upon woolen manufactures. The percentage of duty was very heavy—quite beyond the difference in the cost of production, which was not then regarded as a necessary or proper limitation upon protective duties.

When it came to the question of reducing the duty at this hearing in the tariff bill on wool, Mr. Payne, in the House, and Mr. Aldrich, in the Senate, although both favored reduction in the schedule, found that in the Republican party the interests of the woolgrowers of the Far West and the interests of the woolen manufacturers in the East and in other States, reflected through their representatives in Congress, was sufficiently strong to defeat any attempt to change the woolen tariff, and that had it been attempted it would have beaten the bill reported from either committee. I am sorry this is so, and I could wish that it had been otherwise. It is the one important defect in the present Payne tariff bill and in the performance of the promise of the platform to reduce rates to a difference in the cost of production, with reasonable profit to the manufacturer. That it will increase the price of woolen cloth or clothes, I very much doubt. There have been increases by the natural product, but this was not due to the tariff, because the tariff was not changed. The increase would, therefore, have taken place whether the tariff would have been changed or not. The cost of woolen cloths behind the tariff wall, through the effect of competition, has been greatly less than the duty, if added to the price, would have made it.

There is a complaint now by the woolen clothiers and by the carded woolen people of this woolen schedule. They have honored me by asking in circulars sent out by them that certain questions be put to

336

me in respect to it, and asking why I did not veto the bill in view of the fact that the woolen schedule was not made in accord with the platform. I ought to say in respect to this point that all of them in previous tariff bills were strictly in favor of maintaining the woolen schedule as it was. The carded woolen people are finding that carded wools are losing their sales because they are going out of style. People prefer worsteds. The clothing people who are doing so much circularizing were contented to let the woolen schedule remain as it was until very late in the tariff discussion, long after the bill had passed the House, and, indeed, they did not grow very urgent until the bill had passed the Senate. This was because they found that the price of woolen cloth was going up, and so they desired to secure reduction in the tariff which would enable them to get cheaper material. They themselves are protected by a large duty, and I can not with deference to them ascribe their intense interest only to a deep sympathy with the ultimate consumers, so-called. But, as I have already said, I am quite willing to admit that allowing the woolen schedule to remain where it is, is not a compliance with the terms of the platform as I interpret it and as it is generally understood.

On the whole, however, I am bound so say that I think the Payne tariff bill is the best tariff bill that the Republican party ever passed; that in it the party has conceded the necessity for following the changed conditions and reducing tariff rates accordingly. This is a substantial achievement in the direction of lower tariffs and downward revision, and it ought to be accepted as such. Critics of the bill utterly ignore the very tremendous cuts that have been made in the iron schedule, which heretofore has been subject to criticism in all tariff bills. From iron ore, which was cut 75 per cent., to all the other items as low as 20 per cent., with an average of something like 40 or 50 per cent., that schedule has been reduced so that the danger of increasing prices through a monopoly of the business is very much lessened, and that was the chief purposes of revising the tariff downward under Republican protective principles. The severe critics of the bill pass this reduction in the metal schedule with a sneer, and say that the cut did not hurt the iron interests of the country. Well, of course it did not hurt them. It was not expected to hurt them. It was expected only to reduce excessive rates, so that business should still be conducted at a profit, and the very character of the criticism is an indication of the general injustice of the attitude of those who make it, in assuming that it was the promise of the Republican party to hurt the industries of the country by the reductions which they were to make in the tariff, whereas it expressly indicated as plainly as possible in the platform that all of the industries were to be protected against injury by foreign competition, and the promise only went to the reduction of excessive rates beyond what was necessary to protect them.

The high cost of living, of which 50 per cent. is consumed in food, 25 per cent. in clothing, and 25 per cent. in rent and fuel, has not been produced by the tariff, because the tariff has remained the same while the increases have gone on. It is due to the change of conditions the world over. Living has increased everywhere in cost—in countries where there is free trade and in countries where there is protection—and that increase has been chiefly seen in the cost of food products. In other words, we have had to pay more for the products of the farmer, for meat, for grain, for everything that enters into food. Now, certainly no one will contend that protection has increased the cost of food in this country, when the fact is that we have been the greatest exporters of food products in the world. It is only that the demand has increased beyond the supply, that farm lands have not been opened as rapidly as the population, and the demand has increased. I am not saying that the tariff does not increase prices in clothing and in building and in other items that enter into the necessities of life, but what I wish to emphasize is that the recent increases in the cost of living in this country have not been due to the tariff. We have a much higher standard of living in this country than they have abroad, and this has been made possible by higher income for the workingman, the farmer, and all classes. Higher wages have been made possible by the encouragement of diversified industries, built up and fostered by the tariff.

Now, the revision downward of the tariff that I have favored will not, I hope, destroy the industries of the country. Certainly it is not intended to. All that it is intended to do, and that is what I wish to repeat, is to put the tariff where it will protect industries here from foreign competition, but will not enable those who will wish to monopolize to raise prices by taking advantage of excessive rates beyond the normal difference in the cost of production.

If the country desires free trade, and the country desires a revenue tariff and wishes the manufacturers all over the country to go out of business, and to have cheaper prices at the expense of the sacrifice of many of our manufacturing interests, then it ought to say so and ought to put the Democratic party in power if it thinks that party can be trusted to carry out any affirmative policy in favor of a revenue tariff. Certainly in the discussions in the Senate there was no great manifestation on the part of our Democratic friends in favor of reducing rates on necessities. They voted to maintain the tariff rates on everything that came from their particular sections. If we are to have free trade,

338

certainly it can not be had through the maintenance of Republican majorities in the Senate and House and a Republican administration.

And now the question arises, what was the duty of a Member of Congress who believed in a downward revision greater than that which has been accomplished, who thought that the wool schedules ought to be reduced, and that perhaps there were other respects in which the bill could be improved? Was it his duty because, in his judgment, it did not fully and completely comply with the promises of the party platform as he interpreted it, and indeed as I had interpreted it, to vote against the bill? I am here to justify those who answer this question in the negative. Mr. Tawney was a downward revisionist like myself. He is a low-tariff man, and has been known to be such in Congress all the time he has been there. He is a prominent Republican, the head of the Appropriations Committee, and when a man votes as I think he ought to vote, and an opportunity such as this presents itself, I am glad to speak in behalf of what he did, not in defense of it, but in support of it.

This is a government by a majority of the people. It is a representative government. People select some 400 members to constitute the lower House and some 92 members to constitute the upper House through their legislatures, and the varying views of a majority of the voters in eighty or ninety millions of people are reduced to one resultant force to take affirmative steps in carrying on a government by a system of parties. Without parties popular government would be absolutely impossible. In a party, those who join it, if they would make it effective, must surrender their personal predilections on matters comparatively of less importance in order to accomplish the good which united action on the most important principles at issue secures.

Now, I am not here to criticise those Republican Members and Senators whose views on the subject of the tariff were so strong and intense that they believed it their duty to vote against their party on the tariff bill. It is a question for each man to settle for himself. The question is whether he shall help maintain the party solidarity for accomplishing its chief purposes, or whether the departure from principle in the bill as he regards it is so extreme that he must in conscience abandon the party. All I have to say is, in respect to Mr. Tawney's action, and in respect to my own in signing the bill, that I believed that the interests of the country, the interests of the party, required me to sacrifice the accomplishment of certain things in the revision of the tariff which I had hoped for, in order to maintain party solidarity, which I believe to be much more important than the reduction of rates in one or two schedules of the tariff. Had Mr. Tawney voted against the bill, and there had been others of the House sufficient in number to have defeated the bill, or if I had vetoed the bill because of the absence of a reduction of rates in the wool schedule, when there was a general downward revision, and a substantial one though not a complete one, we should have left the party in a condition of demoralization that would have prevented the accomplishment of purposes and a fulfillment of other promises which we had made just as solemnly as we had entered into that with respect to the tariff. When I could say without hesitation that this is the best tariff bill that the Republican party has ever passed, and therefore the best tariff bill that has been passed at all, I do not feel that I could have reconciled any other course to my conscience than that of signing the bill, and I think Mr. Tawney feels the same way. Of course, if I had vetoed the bill I would have received the applause of many Republicans who may be called low-tariff Republicans, and who think deeply on that subject, and of all the Democracy. Our friends the Democrats would have applauded, and then laughed in their sleeve at the condition in which the party would have been left; but, more than this, and waiving considerations of party, where would the country have been had the bill been vetoed, or been lost by a vote? It would have left the question of the revision of the tariff open for further discussion during the next session. It would have suspended the settlement of all our business down to a known basis upon which prosperity could proceed and investments be made, and it would have held up the coming of prosperity to this country certainly for a year and probably longer. These are the reasons why I signed it.

But there are additional reasons why the bill ought not to have been beaten. It contained provisions of the utmost importance in the interest of this country in dealing with foreign countries and in the supplying of a deficit which under the Dingley bill seemed inevitable. There has been a disposition in some foreign countries taking advantage of greater elasticity in their systems of imposing tariffs and of making regulations to exclude our products and exercise against us undue discrimination. Against these things we have been helpless, because it required an act of Congress to meet the difficulties. It is now proposed by what is called the maximum and minimum clause, to enable the President to allow to come into operation a maximum or penalizing increase of duties over the normal or minimum duties whenever in his opinion the conduct of the foreign countries has been unduly discriminatory against the United States. It is hoped that very little use may be required of this clause, but its presence in the law and the power conferred upon the Executive, it is thought, will prevent in the future such undue discriminations. Certainly this is most important to our exporters of agricultural products and manufactures.

Second. We have imposed an excise tax upon corporations measured by 1 per cent. upon the net income of all corporations except fraternal and charitable corporations after exempting $5,000. This, it is thought, will raise an income of 26 to 30 millions of dollars, will supply the deficit which otherwise might arise without it, and will bring under federal supervision more or less all the corporations of the country. The inquisitorial provisions of the act are mild but effective, and certainly we may look not only for a revenue but for some most interesting statistics and the means of obtaining supervision over corporate methods that has heretofore not obtained.

Then, we have finally done justice to the Philippines. We have introduced free trade between the Philippines and the United States, and we have limited the amount of sugar and the amount of tobacco and cigars that can be introduced from the Philippines to such a figure as shall greatly profit the Philippines and yet in no way disturb the products of the United States or interfere with those engaged in the tobacco or sugar interests here. These features of the bill were most important, and the question was whether they were to be sacrificed because the bill did not in respect to wool and woolens and in some few other matters meet our expectations. I do not hesitate to repeat that I think it would have been an unwise sacrifice of the business interests of the country, it would have been an unwise sacrifice of the solidarity, efficiency, and promise-performing power of the party, to have projected into the next session another long discussion of the tariff, and to have delayed or probably defeated the legislation needed in the improvement of our interstate commerce regulation, and in making more efficient our antitrust law and the prosecutions under it. Such legislation is needed to clinch the Roosevelt policies, by which corporations and those in control of them shall be limited to a lawful path and shall be prevented from returning to those abuses which a recurrence of prosperity is too apt to bring about unless definite, positive steps of a legislative character are taken to mark the lines of honest and lawful corporate management.

Now, there is another provision in the new tariff bill that I regard as of the utmost importance. It is a provision which appropriates $75,000 for the President to employ persons to assist him in the execution of the maximum and minimum tariff clause and in the administration of the tariff law. Under that authority, I conceive that the President has the right to appoint a board, as I have appointed it, who shall associate with themselves, and have under their control, a number of experts who shall address themselves, first, to the operation of foreign tariffs upon the exports of the United States, and then to the operation of the United States tariff upon imports and exports. There are provisions in the general tariff procedure for the ascertainment of the cost of production of articles abroad and the cost of production of articles here. I intend to direct the board in the course of these duties and in carrying them out, in order to assist me in the administration of the law, to make what might be called a glossary of the tariff, or a small encyclopedia of the tariff, or something to be compared to the United States Pharmacopoeia with reference to information as to drugs and medicines. I conceive that such a board may very properly, in the course of their duties, take up separately all the items of the tariff, both those on the free list and those which are dutiable, describe what they are, where they are manufactured, what their uses are, the methods of manufacture, the cost of production abroad and here, and every other fact with respect to each item which would enable the Executive to understand the operation of the tariff, the value of the article, and the amount of duty imposed, and all those details which the student of every tariff law finds it so difficult to discover. I do not intend, unless compelled or directed by Congress, to publish the result of these investigations, but to treat them merely as incidental facts brought out officially from time to time, and as they may be ascertained and put on record in the department, there to be used when they have all been accumulated and are sufficiently complete to justify executive recommendation based on them. Now, I think it is utterly useless, as I think it would be greatly distressing to business, to talk of another revision of the tariff during the present Congress. I should think that it would certainly take the rest of this administration to accumulate the data upon which a new and proper revision of the tariff might be had. By that time the whole Republican party can express itself again in respect to the matter and bring to bear upon its Representatives in Congress that sort of public opinion which shall result in solid party action. I am glad to see that a number of those who thought it their duty to vote against the bill insist that they are still Republicans and intend to carry on their battle in favor of lower duties and a lower revision within the lines of the party. That is their right and, in their view of things, is their duty.

It is vastly better that they should seek action of the party than that they should break off from it and seek to organize another party, which would probably not result in accomplishing anything more than merely defeating our party and inviting in the opposing party, which does not believe, or says that it does not believe, in protection. I think that we ought to give the present bill a chance. After it has been operating for two or three years, we can tell much more accurately than we can today its effect upon the industries of the country and the necessity for any amendment in its provisions.

I have tried to state as strongly as I can, but not more strongly than I think the facts justify, the importance of not disturbing the business interests of this country by an attempt in this Congress or the next to make a new revision; but meantime I intend, so far as in me lies, to secure official data upon the operation of the tariff, from which, when a new revision is attempted, exact facts can be secured.

I have appointed a tariff board that has no brief for either side in respect to what the rates shall be. I hope they will make their observations and note their data in their record with exactly the same impartiality and freedom from anxiety as to result with which the Weather Bureau records the action of the elements or any scientific bureau of the Government records the results of its impartial investigations. Certainly the experience in this tariff justifies the statement that no revision should hereafter be attempted in which more satisfactory evidence of an impartial character is not secured.

I am sorry that I am not able to go into further detail with respect to the tariff bill, but I have neither the information nor the time in which to do it. I have simply stated the case as it seemed to Mr. Tawney in his vote and as it seemed to me in my signing the bill.

27

THE DECISION
TO GO TO WAR WITH GERMANY

Wilson's Message to Congress

The Lesson is Plain:
If you want WAR, vote for Hughes!
If you Want Peace with Honor
V O T E   F O R   W I L S O N !

The above advertisement appeared in the leading newspapers of the country on the eve of the Presidential election of 1916. This was a variation on the theme of the keynote address of the Democratic Convention at St. Louis, when Governor Martin H. Glynn of New York asserted that the United States was "constrained by the tradition of its past, by the logic of its present and by the promise of its future to hold itself apart from European warfare." From this keynote was coined the Democratic slogan, "He kept us out of war," the greatest single factor in effecting the re-election of Woodrow Wilson in his contest with Charles Evans Hughes, the Republican standard-bearer.

On the record a strong case could have been made out for the slogan. When war broke out in Europe in August, 1914, President Wilson had acted promptly. He issued a proclamation of neutrality and shortly thereafter appealed to Americans to be "impartial in thought as well as in action." This was hard to do, even for a nation of traditional isolationists, for the sympathies of the majority of Americans were with the Allies from the start, and Allied war purchases fed a war boom on this side of the ocean and brought about a closening of financial ties between American bankers and the Allied nations.

Both belligerents violated America's neutral rights, and Wilson was shortly involved in sharp diplomatic exchanges with the Allies as well as with the Central Powers. The British proclaimed a blockade of Germany, reinterpreted the doctrine of continuous voyage to justify

344

the seizure of shipments from the United States to a neutral port where the cargo was ultimately destined for the enemy, steadily enlarged their contraband list, and took liberties with the traditional rules governing the visit and search of neutral merchant vessels. The impact of the State Department's protests was blunted by our own Anglophile Ambassador to Great Britain, Walter Hines Page, who on one occasion told Sir Edward Grey, Britain's Foreign Secretary, "I have now read the dispatch, but I do not agree with it. Let us consider how it should be answered!"

Germany's violations of neutral rights grew out of her resort to the U-boat. The submarine determined the kind of counter-blockade that Germany could actually enforce. In announcing a blockade of the waters around the British Isles Germany declared that all Allied vessels found there by submarines would be destroyed without warning. Such action violated the traditional rules which required that before destroying an enemy merchant vessel a belligerent warship must stop it, ascertain its identity, and provide for the safety of passengers and crew. But if the submarine observed these rules it would have exposed itself to danger and destruction, as its thin hull could be pierced by shells from the decks of armed merchant vessels or rammed by the faster ship. In short, the British policy toward neutrals affected property not lives, while the German threatened both. That difference was dramatically highlighted by the sinking of the *Lusitania* on May 7, 1915, with the loss of many lives, including 128 Americans. A wave of horror and resentment swept the United States. Theodore Roosevelt demanded that the United States intervene, but neither the public nor the President felt that war was warranted. "There is such a thing as a man being too proud to fight," Wilson told a Philadelphia audience on May 10, 1915. "There is such a thing as a nation being so right that it does not need to convince others by force that it is right."

When, on August 19, 1915, the British passenger liner *Arabic* was torpedoed without warning, with the loss of two American lives, Wilson, under threat of breaking off diplomatic relations, secured from the German ambassador a pledge that henceforth U-boats would not sink liners without warning and without providing for the safety of the noncombatants. Again, on March 24, 1916, the Germans torpedoed

345

an unarmed French steamer, the *Sussex,* plying the English Channel. Wilson sent Germany an ultimatum, and again the Germans yielded, promising that their U-boats would no longer sink merchant vessels without warning, either in or out of the war zone.

Wilson was neither insensitive nor aloof. He was profoundly concerned about the Armageddon which was laying Europe waste, and regarded his role as that of a neutral mediator. His confidential aide, Colonel Edward M. House, had prepared on February 22, 1916 a joint memorandum with Sir Edward Grey, the substance of which was that Wilson was ready, on hearing from France and England that the moment was opportune, to propose a conference to end the war. Should the Allies accept and Germany decline, the United States would "probably" enter the war against Germany, which it would also "probably" do if at such a conference terms "not unfavorable to the Allies" could not be obtained. Wilson endorsed the memorandum. The "probably" was his contribution. Here was indeed a moral commitment to the Allied cause. Wilson was moving rapidly from pacifism to preparedness. Would he now move from neutralist isolation to participation?

The Democratic Party campaign slogan of 1916 was a source of embarrassment to Wilson. "I can't keep the country out of war," he said privately. "They talk of me as though I were a god. Any little German lieutenant can put us into the war at any time by some calculated outrage." Earlier he had reminded his audience that "at any moment" the time might come "when I cannot preserve both the honor and the peace of the United States. Do not exact of me an impossible and contradictory thing."

After his re-election Wilson made a final effort to bring about peace, dispatching notes to the warring nations on December 18, 1916. Again, on January 22, 1917, he went before the Senate and defined the conditions of a just and enduring peace, calling for a League of Nations, the equality of nations, the freedom of the seas, government by consent of the governed, and the limitation of armaments. "Only a peace between equals can last," he urged with great moral force.

Then, Germany took the calculated risk which forced Wilson's hand. At a secret conference held on January 9, 1917, the militarists decided to renew the U-boat campaign, gambling that their submarines could choke off the supply lines to Great Britain and knock the Allies out of the war before America could send her troops into action. Notified on January 31, 1917, of the decision to resume unrestricted submarine warfare, Wilson severed diplomatic relations with Berlin. Yet he was disinclined to arm American merchant ships. His hand was forced, however, by a message from the German Foreign Secretary, Arthur Zimmermann, to the German minister in Mexico. Intercepted and decoded by British Naval Intelligence, the document revealed that Germany, in return for an alliance with Mexico, was offering our southern neighbor her "lost territory" of Texas, New Mexico, and Arizona. A dozen noninterventionists in the Senate were able to kill by filibuster the Armed Ship Bill which the House had passed, and which Wilson now strongly supported. "A little group of willful men, representing no opinion but their own," Wilson charged, "have rendered the great Government of the United States helpless and contemptible."

On March 18, 1917, German U-boats sank without warning three unarmed American merchant vessels. Two days later Wilson called Congress into special session for April 2. Anguished and sleepless, the President worked on his war message. "If there is any alternative" to war, Wilson said to Frank I. Cobb, editor of the New York *World,* "for God's sake, let's take it." At half past eight on the evening of April 2 he appeared before a joint session of Congress and read his war message. The President had set a high standard of eloquence in his own First Inaugural Message, which ranks with the classic First Inaugural Addresses of Jefferson and Lincoln. The war message was equally eloquent, and at the same time was touched by fire and ennobled by moral authority.

To Woodrow Wilson came the war he never really wanted. Could he now make the just and lasting peace to which his thoughts would increasingly turn?

WAR MESSAGE

[Delivered to Joint Session of Congress, April 2, 1917]

Gentlemen of the Congress:

I have called the Congress into extraordinary session because there are serious, very serious, choices of policy to be made, and made im-

347

mediately which it was neither right nor constitutionally permissible that I should assume the responsibility of making.

On the third of February last, I officially laid before you the extraordinary announcement of the Imperial German Government that on and after the first day of February it was its purpose to put aside all restraints of law or of humanity and use its submarines to sink every vessel that sought to approach either the ports of Great Britain and Ireland or the western coast of Europe or any of the ports controlled by the enemies of Germany within the Mediterranean. That had seemed to be the object of the German submarine warfare earlier in the war; but since April of last year the Imperial Government had somewhat restrained the commanders of its undersea craft, in conformity with its promise then given to us that passenger boats should not be sunk, and that due warning would be given to all other vessels which its submarines might seek to destroy, when no resistance was offered or escape attempted, and care taken that their crews were given at least a fair chance to save their lives in their open boats. The precautions taken were meager and haphazard enough, as was proved in distressing instance after instance in the progress of the cruel and unmanly business, but a certain degree of restraint was observed.

The new policy has swept every restriction aside. Vessels of every kind, whatever their flag, their character, their cargo, their destination, their errand, have been ruthlessly sent to the bottom without warning and without thought of help or mercy for those on board—the vessels of friendly neutrals along with those of belligerents. Even hospital ships and ships carrying relief to the sorely bereaved and stricken people of Belgium, though the latter were provided with safe conduct through the proscribed areas by the German Government itself, and were distinguished by unmistakable marks of identity, have been sunk with the same reckless lack of compassion or of principle.

I was for a little while unable to believe that such things would in fact be done by any government that had hitherto subscribed to the humane practices of civilized nations. International law had its origin in the attempt to set up some law which would be respected and observed upon the seas, where no nation had right of dominion and where lay the free highways of the world. By painful stage after stage has that law been built up, with meager enough results, indeed, after all was accomplished that could be accomplished, but always with a clear view, at least, of what the heart and conscience of mankind demanded.

This minimum of right the German Government has swept aside under the plea of retaliation and necessity, and because it had no weapons which it could use at sea except these which it is impossible to employ as it is employing them without throwing to the winds all scruples of humanity or of respect for the understandings that were supposed to underlie the intercourse of the world.

I am not now thinking of the loss of property involved, immense and serious as that is, but only of the wanton and wholesale destruction of the lives of non-combatants, men, women, and children, engaged in pursuits which have always, even in the darkest period of modern history, been deemed innocent and legitimate. Property can be paid for; the lives of peaceful and innocent people can not be.

The present German submarine warfare against commerce is a warfare against mankind. It is a war against all nations. American ships have been sunk, American lives taken in ways which it has stirred us very deeply to learn of, but the ships and people of other neutral and friendly nations have been sunk and overwhelmed in the waters in the same way. There has been no discrimination. The challenge is to all mankind. Each nation must decide for itself how it will meet it. The choice we make for ourselves must be made with a moderation of counsel and a temperateness of judgment befitting our character and our motives as a nation.

We must put excited feeling away. Our motive will not be revenge or the victorious assertion of the physical might of the nation, but only the vindication of right, of human right, of which we are only a single champion.

When I addressed the Congress on the 26th of February last, I thought that it would suffice to assert our neutral right with arms; our right to use the sea against unlawful interference; our right to keep our people safe against unlawful violence. But armed neutrality, it now appears, is impracticable. Because submarines are in effect outlaws when used as the German submarines have been used against merchant shipping, it is impossible to defend ships against their attacks as the law of nations has assumed that merchantmen would defend themselves against privateers or cruisers, visible craft giving chase upon the open sea. It is common prudence in such circumstances, grim necessity indeed, to endeavor to destroy them before they have shown their own intention. They must be dealt with upon sight, if dealt with at all.

The German Government denies the right of neutrals to use arms at all within the areas of the sea which it has prescribed, even in the defense of rights which no modern publicist has ever before questioned their right to defend. The intimation is conveyed that the armed guards which we have placed on our merchant ships will be treated as beyond the pale of law and subject to be dealt with as pirates would be. Armed neutrality is ineffectual enough at best; in such circumstances and in the face of such pretensions, it is worse than ineffectual; it is likely only to produce what it was meant to prevent; it is practically certain to draw us into the war without either the rights or the effectiveness of belligerents.

There is one choice we cannot make, we are incapable of making— we will not choose the path of submission and suffer the most sacred rights of our nation and our people to be ignored or violated. The wrongs against which we now array ourselves are no common wrongs; they cut to the very roots of human life.

With a profound sense of the solemn and even tragical character of the step I am taking and of the grave responsibilities which it involves, but in unhesitating obedience to what I deem my constitutional duty, I advise that the Congress declare the recent course of the Imperial German Government to be, in fact, nothing less than war against the Government and people of the United States; that it formally accept the status of belligerent which has thus been thrust upon it; and that it take immediate steps not only to put the country in a more thorough state of defense, but also to exert all its power and employ all its resources to bring the Government of the German Empire to terms and end the war.

What this will involve is clear. It will involve the utmost practicable co-operation in counsel and action with the governments now at war with Germany; and, as incident to that, the extension to those governments of the most liberal financial credits, in order that our resources may, so far as possible, be added to theirs. It will involve the organization and mobilization of all the material resources of the country to supply the materials of war and serve the incidental needs of the nation in the most abundant and yet the most economical and efficient way possible. It will involve the immediate full equipment of the navy in all respects, but particularly in supplying it with the best means of dealing with the enemy's submarines. It will involve the immediate addition to the armed forces of the United States already provided for by law in case of war at least 500,000 men, who should, in my opinion, be chosen upon the principle of universal liability to service, and also the authorization of subsequent additional increments of equal force so soon as they may be needed and can be handled in training.

It will involve also, of course, the granting of adequate credits to the Government, sustained, I hope, so far as they can equitably be sustained, by the present generation, by well-conceived taxation. I say sustained so far as may be equitable by taxation because it seems to me that it would be most unwise to base the credits which will now be necessary entirely on money borrowed. It is our duty, I most respectfully urge, to protect our people so far as we may against the very serious hardships and evils which would be likely to arise out of the inflation which would be produced by vast loans.

In carrying out the measures by which these things are to be accomplished, we should keep constantly in mind the wisdom of interfering as little as possible in our own preparation and in the equipment of our own military forces with the duty—for it will be a very practical duty—of supplying the nations already at war with Germany with the materials which they can obtain only from us or by our assistance. They are in the field, and we should help them in every way to be effective there.

I shall take the liberty of suggesting, through the several executive departments of the Government, for the consideration of your committees, measures for the accomplishment of the several objects I have mentioned. I hope that it will be your pleasure to deal with them as having been framed after very careful thought by the branch of the Government upon which the responsibility of conducting the war and safeguarding the nation will most directly fall.

While we do these things, these deeply momentous things, let us be very clear, and make very clear to all the world what our motives and our objects are. My own thought has not been driven from its habitual and normal course by the unhappy events of the last two months, and I do not believe that the thought of the nation has been altered or clouded by them.

I have exactly the same things in mind now that I had in mind when I addressed the Senate on the 22d of January last; the same that I had in mind when I addressed the Congress on the 3d of February and on the 26th of February. Our object now, as then, is to vindicate the principles of peace and justice in the life of the world as against selfish and autocratic power and to set up among the really free and self-governed peoples of the world such a concert of purpose and of action as will henceforth insure the observance of those principles.

Neutrality is no longer feasible or desirable where the peace of the world is involved and the freedom of its peoples, and the menace to that peace and freedom lies in the existence of autocratic governments backed by organized force which is controlled wholly by their will, not by the will of their people. We have seen the last of neutrality in such circumstances.

We are at the beginning of an age where it will be insisted that the same standards of conduct and of responsibility for wrong done shall be observed among nations and their governments that are observed among the individual citizens of civilized states.

We have no quarrel with the German people. We have no feeling toward them but one of sympathy and friendship. It was not upon their impulse that their Government acted in entering this war. It was not with their previous knowledge or approval.

It was a war determined upon as wars used to be determined upon in the old, unhappy days when peoples were nowhere consulted by their rulers and wars were provoked and waged in the interest of dynasties or of little groups of ambitious men who were accustomed to use their fellow-men as pawns and tools.

Self-governed nations do not fill their neighbor states with spies or set the course of intrigue to bring about some critical posture of affairs which will give them an opportunity to strike and make conquest. Such designs can be successfully worked out only under cover and where no one has the right to ask questions.

Cunningly contrived plans of deception or aggression, carried, it may be, from generation to generation, can be worked out and kept from the light only within the privacy of courts or behind the carefully guarded confidences of a narrow and privileged class. They are happily impossible where public opinion commands and insists upon full information concerning all the nation's affairs.

A steadfast concert for peace can never be maintained except by a partnership of democratic nations. No autocratic government could be trusted to keep faith within it or observe its covenants. It must be a league of honor, a partnership of opinion. Intrigue would eat its vitals away; the plottings of inner circles who could plan what they would and render account to no one would be a corruption seated at its very heart. Only free peoples can hold their purpose and their honor steady to a common end and prefer the interests of mankind to any narrow interest of their own.

Does not every American feel that assurance has been added to our hope for the future peace of the world by the wonderful and heartening things that have been happening within the last few weeks in Russia?

Russia was known by those who knew her best to have been always in fact democratic at heart, in all the vital habits of her thought, in all the intimate relationships of her people that spoke their natural instinct, their habitual attitude toward life.

The autocracy that crowned the summit of her political structure, long as it had stood and terrible as was the reality of its power, was not in fact Russian in origin, character or purpose; and now it has been shaken off and the great generous Russian people have been added in all their native majesty and might to the forces that are fighting for a freedom in the world, for justice and for peace. Here is a fit partner for a league of honor.

One of the things that has served to convince us that the Prussian autocracy was not and could never be our friend is that from the very outset of the present war it has filled our unsuspecting communities and even our offices of government with spies and set criminal intrigues everywhere afoot against our national unity of council, our peace within and without, our industries and our commerce.

Indeed, it is now evident that its spies were here even before the war began; and it unhappily is not a matter of conjecture, but a fact proved in our courts of justice, that the intrigues which have more than once come perilously near to disturbing the peace and dislocating the industries of the country have been carried on at the instigation, with the support, and even under the personal direction of official agents of the Imperial Government accredited to the Government of the United States.

Even in checking these things and trying to extirpate them, we have sought to put the most generous interpretation possible upon them because we knew that their source lay, not in any hostile feeling or purpose of the German people toward us (who were, no doubt, as ignorant of them as we ourselves were), but only in the selfish designs of a government that did what it pleased and told its people nothing. But they have played their part in serving to convince us at last that that government entertains no real friendship for us and means to act against our peace and security at its convenience. That it means to stir up enemies against us at our very doors, the intercepted note to the German Minister at Mexico City is eloquent evidence.

We are accepting this challenge of hostile purpose because we know that in such a government, following such methods, we can never have a friend; and that in the presence of its organized power always lying in wait to accomplish we know not what purpose, there can be no assured security for the democratic governments of the world.

We are now about to accept gage of battle with this natural foe to liberty and shall, if necessary, spend the whole force of the nation to check and nullify its pretensions and end its power. We are glad, now that we see the facts with no veil of false pretense about them, to fight thus for the ultimate peace of the world and for the liberation of its peoples, the German peoples included; for the rights of nations great and small and the privilege of men everywhere to choose their way of life and of obedience. The world must be made safe for democracy. Its peace must be planted upon the tested foundations of political liberty.

We have no selfish ends to serve. We desire no conquest, no dominion. We seek no indemnities for ourselves, no material compensation for the sacrifices we shall freely make. We are but one of the champions of the rights of mankind. We shall be satisfied when those rights have been made as secure as the faith and the freedom of the nations can make them.

Just because we fight without rancor and without selfish object, seeking nothing for ourselves but what we shall wish to share with all free peoples, we shall, I feel confident, conduct our operations as belligerents without passion and ourselves observe with proud punctilio the principles of right and of fair play we profess to be fighting for.

I have said nothing of the Governments allied with the Imperial Government of Germany because they have not made war upon us or challenged us to defend our right and our honor. The Austro-Hungarian Government has, indeed, avowed its unqualified indorsement and acceptance of the reckless and lawless submarine warfare adopted now without disguise by the Imperial German Government, and it has therefore not been possible for this Government to receive Count Tarnowski, the Ambassador recently accredited to this Government by the Imperial and Royal Government of Austria-Hungary; but that Government has not actually engaged in warfare against citizens of the United States on the seas, and I take the liberty, for the present at least, of postponing a discussion of our relations with the authorities at Vienna. We enter this war only where we are clearly forced into it because there are no other means of defending our rights.

It will be all the easier for us to conduct ourselves as belligerents in a high spirit of right and fairness because we act without animus, not in enmity toward a people nor with the desire to bring any injury or disadvantage upon them, but only in armed opposition to an irresponsible Government which has thrown aside all considerations of humanity and of right and is running amuck.

We are, let me say again, the sincere friends of the German people, and shall desire nothing so much as the early re-establishment of intimate relations of mutual advantage between us—however hard it may be for them, for the time being, to believe that this is spoken from our hearts. We have borne with their present Government through all these bitter months because of that friendship—exercising a patience and forbearance which would otherwise have been impossible. We shall, happily, still have an opportunity to prove that friendship in our daily attitude and actions toward the millions of men and women of German birth and native sympathy who live among us and share our life, and we shall be proud to prove it toward all who are in fact loyal to their neighbors and to the Government in the hour of test. They are, most of them, as true and loyal Americans as if they had never known any other fealty or allegiance. They will be prompt to stand with us in rebuking and restraining the few who may be of a different mind and purpose.

If there should be disloyalty, it will be dealt with with a firm hand of stern repression; but if it lifts its head at all, it will lift it only here and there and without countenance, except from a lawless and malignant few.

It is a distressing and oppressive duty, gentlemen of the Congress, which I have performed in thus addressing you. There are, it may be, many months of fiery trial and sacrifice ahead of us. It is a fearful thing to lead this great peaceful people into war, into the most terrible and disastrous of all wars, civilization itself seeming to be in the balance. But the right is more precious than peace, and we shall fight for the things which we have always carried nearest our hearts—for democracy, for the right of those who submit to authority to have a voice in their own governments, for the rights and liberties of small nations, for a universal domination of right by such a concert of free peoples as shall bring peace and safety to all nations and make the world itself at last free. To such a task we can dedicate our lives and our fortunes, everything that we are and everything that we have, with the pride of those who know that the day has come when America is privileged to spend her blood and her might for the principles that gave her birth and happiness and the peace which she has treasured. God helping her, she can do no other.

28

THE DECISION
TO PREPARE A BLUEPRINT FOR
WORLD PEACE

Wilson's Fourteen Points

Woodrow Wilson and America were now engaged in a great crusade, and it was in a crusading spirit that the President, combining in equal proportions qualities of obstinate self-righteousness and messianic zeal, set about drawing a blueprint for world peace.

Wilson's great mistake was made at the beginning. He did not secure in advance of America's entry into the war a commitment by the Allies to accept his peace objectives. The Allies had entered into secret treaties under which they planned to share territories and colonies taken from the Central Powers. By May, 1917, Wilson knew of these treaties, but chose to ignore them, and even found it politic to tell the Senate Committee on Foreign Relations that he had not learned of the treaties until he got to Paris more than a year and a half later. Wilson felt that once the war was over he could mobilize world opinion and force Britain and France to accept a peace settlement on his terms. A cruel disillusionment was in store for him.

Everywhere people yearned for a peace which would put an end to war once and for all, and everywhere they turned to Woodrow Wilson as the one disinterested spokesman with vision and idealism. Following the Russian Revolution the Kerensky regime in May, 1917, called for a peace based on the principles of self-determination, no annexations, no indemnities. In midsummer Pope Benedict XV appealed to the warring powers to consider as a basis for a durable peace such principles as the renunciation of indemnities, disarmament, a guarantee of the independence of Belgium, freedom of the seas, and the examination of territorial claims in a "spirit of equity and justice." Following the November Revolution in Russia, the Bolsheviks published the secret treaties concluded by the Allies and denounced them as evidence of imperialist war aims. The need for a statement of Allied peace objectives became exigent. When the Allies were unable to agree, Colonel House urged Wilson to issue a formulation on his own.

The result was one of the most influential state papers in American history, Wilson's message to Congress of January 8, 1918, setting forth as "the only possible program" his famous Fourteen Points. Acclaimed in the Allied nations as a manifesto of the war for democracy, the message had a powerful effect upon the German people. It proved to be one of the great propaganda documents of modern times. By this speech Wilson brought himself to the forefront among world leaders.

Wilson, in subsequent addresses, expatiated on his war aims. In an address made before Washington's tomb at Mount Vernon on July 4, 1918, the President stressed the mission concept of America's role. The Founding Fathers, he declared, spoke, "not for a class, but for a people," and now it was up to America to speak "not for a single people only, but for all mankind." America's objectives were epitomized in one eloquent sentence: "What we seek is the reign of law, based upon the consent of the governed and sustained by the organized opinion of mankind." In subsequent talks he pledged that the peace settlement would avoid "such covenants of selfishness and compromise as were entered into at the Congress of Vienna," and singled out Point 14 as the paramount peace objective. "The constitution of that League of Nations," Wilson insisted, in the uncompromising tone which was to characterize his later remarks, "and the clear definition of its objects must be a part, in a sense the most essential part of the peace settlement itself."

Wilson's idealism captured the masses but left the realistic leaders of the Allied nations cold and even contemptuous. As Premier Georges Clemenceau of France reportedly commented: "God gave us his Ten Commandments, and we broke them. Wilson gave us his Fourteen Points—we shall see." Realizing the growing resistance of the Allied leaders, Wilson remarked in the summer of 1918 that if necessary he would "reach the people of Europe over the heads of their rulers."

The Germans accepted the Fourteen Points unconditionally, but the Allies would not consider them as a basis for ending the war until Wilson agreed to two reservations. He yielded to the Allies full liberty of action on the subject of the freedom of the seas and made the substantive concession requiring Germany to pay reparations for all war damages to civilians. On this basis the German representatives signed the armistice on November 11, 1918, at Marshal Foch's headquarters in a railroad car in Compiègne Forest.

Woodrow Wilson's Fourteen Points had brought the war to an end. Could a durable peace be erected on the principles he formulated?

ADDRESS TO CONGRESS, JANUARY 8, 1918

[On War Aims and Peace Terms]

Gentlemen of the Congress:

Once more, as repeatedly before, the spokesmen of the Central Empires have indicated their desire to discuss the objects of the war and the possible basis of a general peace. Parleys have been in progress at Brest-Litovsk between Russian representatives and representatives of the Central Powers, to which the attention of all the belligerents has been invited for the purpose of ascertaining whether it may be possible to extend these parleys into a general conference with regard to terms of peace and settlement. The Russian representatives presented not only a perfectly definite statement of the principles upon which they would be willing to conclude peace, but also an equally definite program for the concrete application of those principles. The representatives of the Central Powers, on their part, presented an outline of settlement which, if much less definite, seemed susceptible of liberal interpretation until their specific program of practical terms was added. That program proposed no concessions at all, either to the sovereignty of Russia or to the preferences of the population with whose fortunes it dealt, but meant, in a word, that the Central Empires were to keep every foot of territory their armed forces had occupied—every province, every city, every point of vantage—as a permanent addition to their territories and their power. It is a reasonable conjecture that the general principles of settlement which they at first suggested originated with the more liberal statesmen of Germany and Austria, the men who have begun to feel the force of their own peoples' thought and purpose, while the concrete terms of actual settlement came from the military leaders who have no thought but to keep what they have got. The negotiations have been broken off. The Russian representatives were sincere and in earnest. They cannot entertain such proposals of conquest and domination.

The whole incident is full of significance. It is also full of perplexity. With whom are the Russian representatives dealing? For whom are the representatives of the Central Empires speaking? Are they speaking for the majorities of their respective Parliaments or for the minority parties, that military and imperialistic minority which have so far dominated their whole policy and controlled the affairs of Turkey and of the Balkan States which have felt obliged to become their associates in this war? The Russian representatives have insisted, very justly, very wisely, and in the true spirit of modern democracy, that the conferences they have been holding with the Teutonic and Turkish statesmen should be held with open, not closed, doors, and all the world has been audience, as was desired. To whom have we been listening, then? To those who speak the spirit and intention of the resolutions of the German Reichstag of the ninth of July last, the spirit and intention of the liberal leaders and parties of Germany, or to those who resist and defy that spirit and intention and insist upon conquest and subjugation? Or are we listening, in fact, to both, unreconciled and in open and hopeless contradiction? These are very serious and pregnant questions. Upon the answer to them depends the peace of the world.

But whatever the results of the parleys at Brest-Litovsk, whatever the confusions of counsel and of purpose in the utterances of the spokesmen of the Central Empires, they have again attempted to acquaint the world with their objects in the war and have again challenged their adversaries to say what their objects are and what sort of settlement they would deem just and satisfactory. There is no good reason why that challenge should not be responded to, and responded to with the utmost candor. We did not wait for it. Not once, but again and again, we have laid our whole thought and purpose before the world, not in general terms only, but each time with sufficient definition to make it clear what sort of definite terms of settlement must necessarily spring out of them. Within the last week Mr. Lloyd George has spoken with admirable candor and in admirable spirit for the people and Government of Great Britain. There is no confusion of counsel among the adversaries of the Central Powers, no uncertainty of principle, no vagueness of detail. The only secrecy of counsel, the only lack of fearless frankness, the only failure to make definite statement of the objects of the war, lie with Germany and her allies. The issues of life and death hang upon these definitions. No statesman who has the least conception of his responsibility ought for a moment to permit himself to continue this tragical and appalling outpouring of blood and treasure unless he is sure beyond a peradventure that the objects of the vital sacrifice are part and parcel of the very life and society and that the people for whom he speaks think them right and imperative as he does.

There is, moreover, a voice calling for these definitions of principle and of purpose which is, it seems to me, more thrilling and more compelling than any of the many moving voices with which the troubled air of the world is filled. It is the voice of the Russian people. They are prostrate and all but helpless, it would seem, before the grim power of Germany, which has hitherto known no relenting and no pity. Their power apparently is shattered. And yet their soul is not subservient. They will not yield in principle or in action. Their conception of what is right, of what is humane and honorable for them to accept, has been stated with a frankness, a largeness of view, a generosity of spirit, and a universal human sympathy which must challenge the admiration of every friend of mankind; and they have refused to compound their ideals or desert others that they themselves may be safe. They call to us to say what it is that we desire, in what, if in anything, our purpose and our spirit differ from theirs; and I believe that the people of the United States would wish me to respond with utter simplicity and frankness. Whether their present leaders believe it or not, it is our heartfelt desire and hope that some way may be opened whereby we may be privileged to assist the people of Russia to attain their utmost hope of liberty and ordered peace.

It will be our wish and purpose that the processes of peace, when they are begun, shall be absolutely open, and that they shall involve and permit henceforth no secret understandings of any kind. The day of conquest and aggrandizement is gone by; so is also the day of secret covenants entered into the interest of particular governments and likely at some unlooked-for moment to upset the peace of the world. It is this happy fact, now clear to the view of every public man whose thoughts do not still linger in an age that is dead and gone, which makes it possible for every nation whose purposes are consistent with justice and the peace of the world to avow now or at any other time the objects it has in view.

We entered this war because violations of right had occurred which touched us to the quick and made the life of our own people impossible unless they were corrected and the world secured once for all against their recurrence. What we demand in this war, therefore, is nothing peculiar to ourselves. It is that the world be made fit and safe to live in; and particularly that it be made safe for every peace-loving nation which, like our own, wishes to live its own life, determine its own institutions, be assured of justice and fair dealings by the other peoples of the world, as against force and selfish aggression. All the peoples of the world are in effect partners in this interest, and for our own part we see very clearly that unless justice be done to others it will not be done to us.

The program of the world's peace, therefore, is our program, and that program, the only possible program, as we see it, is this:

I.—Open covenants of peace, openly arrived at, after which there shall be no private international understandings of any kind, but diplomacy shall proceed always frankly and in the public view.

II.—Absolute freedom of navigation upon the seas, outside territorial waters, alike in peace and in war, except as the seas may be closed in whole or in part by international action for the enforcement of international covenants.

III.—The removal, so far as possible, of all economic barriers and the establishment of an equality of trade conditions among all the nations consenting to the peace and associating themselves for its maintenance.

IV.—Adequate guarantees given and taken that national armaments will be reduced to the lowest point consistent with domestic safety.

V.—Free, open-minded, and absolutely impartial adjustment of all colonial claims, based upon a strict observance of the principle that in determining all such questions of sovereignty the interests of the population concerned must have equal weight with the equitable claims of the Government whose title is to be determined.

VI.—The evacuation of all Russian territory and such a settlement of all questions affecting Russia as will secure the best and freest co-operation of the other nations of the world in obtaining for her an unhampered and unembarrassed opportunity for the independent determination of her own political development and national policy, and assure her of a sincere welcome into the society of free nations under institutions of her own choosing; and, more than a welcome, assistance also of every kind that she may need and may herself desire. The treatment accorded Russia by her sister nations in the months to come will be the acid test of their good-will, of their comprehension of her needs as distinguished from their own interests, and of their intelligent and unselfish sympathy.

VII.—Belgium, the whole world will agree, must be evacuated and restored, without any attempt to limit the sovereignty which she enjoys in common with all other free nations. No other single act will serve as this will serve to restore confidence among the nations in the laws which they have themselves set and determined for the government of their relations with one another. Without this healing act the whole structure and validity of international law is forever impaired.

VIII.—All French territory should be freed and the invaded portions restored, and the wrong done to France by Prussia in 1871 in the matter of Alsace-Lorraine, which has unsettled the peace of the world for nearly fifty years, should be righted, in order that peace may once more be made secure in the interest of all.

IX.—A readjustment of the frontiers of Italy should be effected along clearly recognizable lines of nationality.

X.—The peoples of Austria-Hungary, whose place among the nations we wish to see safeguarded and assured, should be accorded the freest opportunity of autonomous development.

XI.—Rumania, Serbia, and Montenegro should be evacuated; occupied territories restored; Serbia accorded free and secure access to the sea; and the relations of the several Balkan States to one another determined by friendly counsel along historically established lines of allegiance and nationality; and international guarantees of the political and economic independence and territorial integrity of the several Balkan States should be entered into.

XII.—The Turkish portions of the present Ottoman Empire should be assured a secure sovereignty, but the other nationalities which are now under Turkish rule should be assured an undoubted security of life and an absolutely unmolested opportunity of autonomous development, and the Dardanelles should be permanently opened as a free passage to the ships and commerce of all nations under international guarantees.

XIII.—An independent Polish State should be erected which should include the territories inhabited by indisputably Polish populations, which should be assured a free and secure access to the sea, and whose political and economic independence and territorial integrity should be guaranteed by international covenant.

XIV.—A general association of nations must be formed under specific covenants for the purpose of affording mutual guarantees of political independence and territorial integrity to great and small states alike.

In regard to these essential rectifications of wrong and assertions of right, we feel ourselves to be intimate partners of all the governments and peoples associated together against the imperialists. We cannot be separated in interest or divided in purpose. We stand together until the end.

For such arrangements and covenants we are willing to fight and to continue to fight until they are achieved; but only because we wish the right to prevail and desire a just and stable peace, such as can be secured only by removing the chief provocations to war, which this program does remove. We have no jealousy of German greatness, and there is nothing in this program that impairs it. We grudge her no achievement or distinction of learning or of pacific enterprise such as have made her record very bright and very enviable. We do not wish to injure her or to block in any way her legitimate influence or power. We do not wish to fight her either with arms or with hostile arrangements of trade, if she is willing to associate herself with us and the other peace-loving nations of the world in covenants of justice and law and fair dealing. We wish her only to accept a place of equality among the peoples of the world—the new world in which we now live—instead of a place of mastery.

Neither do we presume to suggest to her any alteration or modification of her institutions. But it is necessary, we must frankly say, and necessary as a preliminary to any intelligent dealings with her on our part, that we should know whom her spokesmen speak for when they speak to us, whether for the Reichstag majority or for the military party and the men whose creed is imperial domination.

We have spoken, now, surely, in terms too concrete to admit of any further doubt or question. An evident principle runs through the whole program I have outlined. It is the principle of justice to all peoples and nationalities, and their right to live on equal terms of liberty and safety with one another, whether they be strong or weak. Unless this principle be made its foundation, no part of the structure of international justice can stand. The people of the United States could act upon no other principle, and to the vindication of this principle they are ready to devote their lives, their honor, and everything that they possess. The moral climax of this, the culminating and final war for human liberty, has come, and they are ready to put their own strength, their own highest purpose, their own integrity and devotion to the test.

29

THE DECISION
TO INSIST UPON ARTICLE X

Wilson's Exposition of the League of Nations Covenant

"It was an innocent man's war," is the way Laurence Stallings recently characterized America's part in the First World War, and it was led by an innocent man. Woodrow Wilson's armor was not only fortified by innocence but strengthened further by a consuming belief that those who were against his ideas were mortal personal enemies. In his approach to settling differences with other people Wilson as President of the United States had learned nothing from his years as president of Princeton University. At Old Nassau he had refused to compromise on the issues of the eating clubs and the graduate school, had refused to treat with diplomacy and tolerance those who opposed him. His failure in both these controversies can be attributed very largely to certain fatal weaknesses in his make-up. In the great struggle over the peacemaking Wilson demonstrated his unhappy faculty for diverting high causes into personal feuds.

Wilson's conduct of the peace was marked by a series of political blunders. First of all, the President ended the wartime truce in American politics when, in the fall of 1918, he made a direct appeal to the voters to return a Democratic Congress. He foolishly staked his prestige on the outcome of the mid-term elections, and lost, and at the same time he united the opposing factions in the Republican Party.

Wilson's next mistake was to participate personally in the peacemaking. Before his time no President had ever gone abroad when in office. Wilson's announced intention to sail for Europe was denounced as evidence of a messiah complex, or, as former President Taft put it, of a desire "to hog the whole show." He exposed himself to pressures at the peace table that he never would have faced had he stayed in Washington and avoided direct personal involvement in the negotiations. To add to the indignation of the opposition, Wilson named to the peace commission only one Republican out of the five remaining members of the delegation, and that one was at best a minor-league Republican. Wilson was uncomfortable with people who challenged his position, and hence he carefully avoided inviting along with him such pre-eminent Republicans as ex-President Taft, Elihu Root, or Henry Cabot Lodge, chairman of the Senate's Committee on Foreign Relations. He would pay dearly for this mistake.

Around the Paris peace table Wilson pushed for agreement on the Covenant of the League of Nations, which was drafted at incredible speed. When he returned to the United States to take care of pressing bills he was soon confronted with a round robin signed by 39 Senators or Senators-elect, and sponsored by Senator Lodge, objecting to having the peace treaty combined with the League Covenant in a single document. Even though more than enough Senators had now gone on record to indicate that such a treaty would not be ratified, Wilson defied his opponents and warned that the League Covenant would be so tied into the treaty that it could not be cut out without killing the pact.

On his return to Paris Wilson was confronted with Allied demands for a punitive peace which would carry out the provisions of the secret treaties. He showed remarkable tenacity in curbing imperialist appetites and in forcing the Allies to accept a treaty far short of their own goals. But he had to make concessions all along the line, to compromise some of his Fourteen Points in order to secure agreement on the League, upon which he now staked all for establishing a just and durable peace. Commented historian Thomas A. Bailey, "he was like the mother who throws her younger children to the pursuing wolves in order to save her sturdy first-born son."

Wilson had worked at a killing pace in Paris and he returned to Washington a very tired man, with a big fight on his hands. The battle lines were being formed when he presented the Treaty and the Covenant to the Senate on July 10, 1919. At that time probably a heavy majority of the American people and somewhat more than two-thirds of the Senate favored ratifying the Covenant. A small group of Senators led by Borah and Johnson constituted the "Battalion of Death" in implacable opposition. A substantial number of Senators ranked among "the mild reservationists," who favored moderate amendments. If the "mild reservationists" and outright supporters of the Covenant could reach an accord, America's entry into the League was assured.

It was then that Wilson made the fateful decision not to compromise. It was set forth in his statement, given here, at a three-hour conference with the members of the Senate Committee on Foreign Relations, held on August 19, 1919, and in his answers to the innumerable questions about the Covenant and the Treaty that the committee members raised. The big issue revolved around Article X of the Covenant, by which the member nations pledged themselves "to respect and preserve as against external aggression the territorial integrity and existing political independence of all Members of the League." Wilson conceded that the United States would still maintain her freedom of action and that Article X would exert only a moral force on this country, but he refused flatly to incorporate any such interpretation into the Covenant. "Article X seems to me to constitute the very backbone of the whole covenant. Without it the League would be hardly more than an influential debating society." With these words Wilson had flung down the gage of battle. Now the struggle assumed the character and proportions of a Greek tragedy.

Even before this dramatic three-hour confrontation a fierce personal animosity had developed between Wilson and Lodge. "I never expected to hate anyone in politics with the hatred I feel towards Wilson," wrote Lodge back in 1915. But there was something more than a personal feud and party politics behind this division. There was a lurking fear on the part of traditional isolationists of the dangers ahead for America if she allowed herself to be involved in world affairs. Whether Lodge was sincere in wanting to safeguard American interests or was actually determined to defeat the Treaty on one ground or another is difficult to determine. But if Lodge was really bluffing, Wilson never called the bluff.

Instead, embittered by "the little group of willful men" in the Senate, Wilson set out from Washington to carry his case to the people. At first indifferently received in the Middle West, he was getting increasingly enthusiastic receptions in the far West. On September 25 he delivered his fortieth speech at Pueblo, Colorado. That night he collapsed. His face drooped on one side; his left arm and leg were paralyzed for a time. Rushed back to Washington, he carried on the battle for the Treaty and the League from his sickroom in the White House.

On November 6, 1919, Senator Lodge reported the Treaty with fourteen reservations, including one providing that unless Congress made specific provision by joint resolution, the United States would assume no obligations under Article X of the Covenant to respect and preserve against external aggression the territorial integrity or political independence of any country, to intervene in controversies between nations, or to employ its armed forces to uphold the provisions of the treaty. Wilson was pressed by Colonel House and Senator Gilbert M. Hitchcock, acting Democratic leader of the Senate, to accept the reservations. "Let Lodge compromise!" Wilson shot back from his sickbed. Article X was still, for him, "the heart of the Covenant." Even the British announced that they would accept the Lodge reservations. But Wilson instructed the Democrats to vote against the Treaty with reservations, and all but four Democratic Senators combined with the "irreconcilables" to defeat ratification when it came up to a vote on November 19. Wilson by his fateful decision had killed the chances of America's joining the League of Nations, even though it is clear that 77 Senators were then in favor of ratification, with or without reservations, and only 17 were opposed to the Treaty in any form. Wilson lost another chance on March 19, 1920, when he again directed the Democrats to vote down the Treaty with the League reservations, although this time the motion commanded a majority but lacked the necessary two-thirds vote.

It is idle to speculate on what the course of world history might have been had the United States assumed its rightful place in the League of Nations after World War I. The responsibility for the failure must be shared equally by Wilson for his supreme intransigence, by Lodge for exploiting personal and political animosities, and by the American people for their unreadiness to assume world responsibilities. In his last public utterance on Armistice Day, 1923, Woodrow Wilson prophetically declared: "I am not one of those that have the least anxiety about the triumph of the principles I have stood for. That we shall prevail is as sure as that God reigns."

TREATY OF PEACE WITH GERMANY [5]

REPORT OF THE CONFERENCE BETWEEN MEMBERS OF THE SENATE COMMITTEE ON FOREIGN RELATIONS AND THE PRESIDENT OF THE UNITED STATES

August 19, 1919

STATEMENT OF THE PRESIDENT:

The President. Mr. Chairman, I have taken the liberty of writing out a little statement in the hope that it might facilitate discussion by speaking directly on some points that I know have been points of controversy and upon which I thought an expression of opinion would not be unwelcome. I am absolutely glad that the committee should have responded in this way to my intimation that I would like to be of service to it. I welcome the opportunity for a frank and full interchange of views.

I hope, too, that this conference will serve to expedite your consideration of the treaty of peace. I beg that you will pardon and indulge me if I again urge that practically the whole task of bringing the country back to normal conditions of life and industry waits upon the decision of the Senate with regard to the terms of the peace.

I venture thus again to urge my advice that the action of the Senate with regard to the treaty be taken at the earliest practicable moment because the problems with which we are face to face in the readjustment of our national life are of the most pressing and critical character, will require for their proper solution the most intimate and disinterested cooperation of all parties and all interests, and can not be postponed without manifest peril to our people and to all the national advantages we hold most dear. May I mention a few of the matters which can not be handled with intelligence until the country knows the character of the peace it is to have? I do so only by a very few samples.

The copper mines of Montana, Arizona, and Alaska, for example, are being kept open and in operation only at a great cost and loss, in part upon borrowed money; the zinc mines of Missouri, Tennessee, and Wisconsin are being operated at about one-half their capacity; the lead of Idaho, Illinois, and Missouri reaches only a portion of its former market; there is an immediate need for cotton belting, and also for

368

lubricating oil, which can not be met—all because the channels of trade are barred by war when there is no war. The same is true of raw cotton, of which the Central Empires alone formerly purchased nearly 4,000,000 bales. And these are only examples. There is hardly a single raw material, a single important foodstuff, a single class of manufactured goods which is not in the same case. Our full, normal profitable production waits on peace.

Our military plans of course wait upon it. We can not intelligently or wisely decide how large a naval or military force we shall maintain or what our policy with regard to military training is to be until we have peace not only, but also until we know how peace is to be sustained, whether by the arms of single nations or by the concert of all the great peoples. And there is more than that difficulty involved. The vast surplus properties of the Army include not food and clothing merely, whose sale will affect normal production, but great manufacturing establishments also which should be restored to their former uses, great stores of machine tools, and all sorts of merchandise which must lie idle until peace and military policy are definitively determined. By the same token there can be no properly studied national budget until then.

The nations that ratify the treaty, such as Great Britain, Belgium, and France, will be in a position to lay their plans for controlling the markets of central Europe without competition from us if we do not presently act. We have no consular agents, no trade representatives there to look after our interests.

There are large areas of Europe whose future will lie uncertain and questionable until their people know the final settlements of peace and the forces which are to administer and sustain it. Without determinate markets our production can not proceed with intelligence or confidence. There can be no stabilization of wages because there can be no settled conditions of employment. There can be no easy or normal industrial credits because there can be no confident or permanent revival of business.

But I will not weary you with obvious examples. I will only venture to repeat that every element of normal life amongst us depends upon and awaits the ratification of the treaty of peace; and also that we can not afford to lose a single summer's day by not doing all that we can to mitigate the winter's suffering, which, unless we find means to prevent it, may prove disastrous to a large portion of the world, and may, at its worst, bring upon Europe conditions even more terrible than those wrought by the war itself.

Nothing, I am led to believe, stands in the way of the ratification of

369

the treaty except certain doubts with regard to the meaning and implication of certain articles of the covenant of the league of nations; and I must frankly say that I am unable to understand why such doubts should be entertained. You will recall that when I had the pleasure of a conference with your committee and with the Committee of the House of Representatives on Foreign Affairs at the White House in March last the questions now most frequently asked about the league of nations were all canvassed with a view to their immediate clarification. The covenant of the league was then in its first draft and subject to revision. It was pointed out that no express recognition was given to the Monroe doctrine; that it was not expressly provided that the league should have no authority to act or to express a judgment on matters of domestic policy; that the right to withdraw from the league was not expressly recognized; and that the constitutional right of the Congress to determine all questions of peace and war was not sufficiently safeguarded. On my return to Paris all these matters were taken up again by the commission on the league of nations and every suggestion of the United States was accepted.

The views of the United States with regard to the questions I have mentioned had, in fact, already been accepted by the commission and there was supposed to be nothing inconsistent with them in the draft of the covenant first adopted—the draft which was the subject of our discussion in March—but no objection was made to saying explicitly in the text what all had supposed to be implicit in it. There was absolutely no doubt as to the meaning of any one of the resulting provisions of the covenant in the minds of those who participated in drafting them, and I respectfully submit that there is nothing vague or doubtful in their wording.

The Monroe doctrine is expressly mentioned as an understanding which is in no way to be impaired or interfered with by anything contained in the covenant and the expression "regional understandings like the Monroe doctrine" was used, not because anyone of the conferees thought there was any comparable agreement anywhere else in existence or in contemplation, but only because it was thought best to avoid the appearance of dealing in such a document with the policy of a single nation. Absolutely nothing is concealed in the phrase.

With regard to domestic questions article 16 of the covenant expressly provides that, if in case of any dispute arising between members of the league the matter involved is claimed by one of the parties "and is found by the council to arise out of a matter which by international law is solely within the domestic jurisdiction of that party, the council shall so report, and shall make no recommendation as to its settlement."

The United States was by no means the only Government interested in the explicit adoption of this provision, and there is no doubt in the mind of any authoritative student of international law that such matters as immigration, tariffs, and naturalization are incontestably domestic questions with which no international body could deal without express authority to do so. No enumeration of domestic questions was undertaken because to undertake it, even by sample, would have involved the danger of seeming to exclude those not mentioned.

The right of any sovereign State to withdraw had been taken for granted, but no objection was made to making it explicit. Indeed, so soon as the views expressed at the White House conference were laid before the commission it was at once conceded that it was best not to leave the answer to so important a question to inference. No proposal was made to set up any tribunal to pass judgment upon the question whether a withdrawing nation had in fact fulfilled "all its international obligations and all its obligations under the covenant." It was recognized that that question must be left to be resolved by the conscience of the nation proposing to withdraw; and I must say that it did not seem to me worth while to propose that the article be made more explicit, because I knew that the United States would never itself propose to withdraw from the league if its conscience was not entirely clear as to the fulfillment of all its international obligations. It has never failed to fulfill them and never will.

Article 10 is in no respect of doubtful meaning when read in the light of the covenant as a whole. The council of the league can only "advise upon" the means by which the obligations of that great article are to be given effect to. Unless the United States is a party to the policy or action in question, her own affirmative vote in the council is necessary before any advice can be given, for a unanimous vote of the council is required. If she is a party, the trouble is hers anyhow. And the unanimous vote of the council is only advice in any case. Each Government is free to reject it if it pleases. Nothing could have been made more clear to the conference than the right of our Congress under our Constitution to exercise its independent judgment in all matters of peace and war. No attempt was made to question or limit that right. The United States will, indeed, undertake under article 10 to "respect and preserve as against external aggression the territorial integrity and existing political independence of all members of the league," and that engagement constitutes a very grave and solemn moral obligation. But it is a moral, not a legal, obligation, and leaves our Congress absolutely free to put its own interpretation upon it in all cases that call for action. It is binding in conscience only, not in law.

Article 10 seems to me to constitute the very backbone of the whole covenant. Without it the league would be hardly more than an influential debating society.

It has several times been suggested, in public debate and in private conference, that interpretations of the sense in which the United States accepts the engagements of the covenant should be embodied in the instrument of ratification. There can be no reasonable objection to such interpretations accompanying the act of ratification provided they do not form a part of the formal ratification itself. Most of the interpretations which have been suggested to me embody what seems to me the plain meaning of the instrument itself. But if such interpretations should constitute a part of the formal resolution of ratification, long delays would be the inevitable consequence, inasmuch as all the many governments concerned would have to accept, in effect, the language of the Senate as the language of the treaty before ratification would be complete. The assent of the German Assembly at Weimar would have to be obtained, among the rest, and I must frankly say that I could only with the greatest reluctance approach that assembly for permission to read the treaty as we understand it and as those who framed it quite certainly understood it. If the United States were to qualify the document in any way, moreover, I am confident from what I know of the many conferences and debates which accompanied the formulation of the treaty that our example would immediately be followed in many quarters, in some instances with very serious reservations, and that the meaning and operative force of the treaty would presently be clouded from one end of its clauses to the other.

Pardon me, Mr. Chairman, if I have been entirely unreserved and plain-spoken in speaking of the great matters we all have so much at heart. If excuse is needed, I trust that the critical situation of affairs may serve as my justification. The issues that manifestly hang upon the conclusions of the Senate with regard to peace and upon the time of its action are so grave and so clearly insusceptible of being thrust on one side or postponed that I have felt it necessary in the public interest to make this urgent plea, and to make it as simply and as unreservedly as possible.

I thought that the simplest way, Mr. Chairman, to cover the points that I knew to be points of interest?

30

THE DECISION
TO PUT AN END TO FEAR

Franklin D. Roosevelt's First Inaugural Address

In the same year, 1933, just a few months apart, Adolf Hitler became Chancellor of Germany and Franklin Delano Roosevelt became President of the United States. In Germany a depressed people, in a mood of resurgent nationalism, had turned to a new messiah to lead them to destruction. In more sober mood the American people had elected to the Presidency a man who would set their steps on the road out of the great and terrible depression. The economic crisis which gripped the nation had stemmed from a number of conditions, domestic and international, but was touched off by the panic and crash of 1929. When the inflated prosperity of its greatest bull market vanished, America awakened to the sober day-after of its most tragic and persistent depression.

Despite alarming economic indices, the two previous Presidents had been unable or unwilling to take the stern measures that should have been taken to head off the economic crisis. Calvin Coolidge's public utterances had added fuel to the fires of speculation and justified William Allen White's characterization of him as pursuing "that masterly inactivity for which he was so splendidly equipped." His successor, Herbert Hoover, was an abler man by far, with a deeper grasp of economic issues, and a background of remarkable administrative achievements, but he was committed from the start to the principles of "rugged individualism" and *laissez faire*. Though cool to governmental intervention in the economy, he had taken a number of halting and piecemeal steps to check the downward economic spiral. He advocated a policy of decentralized work relief and pinned his hopes for economic recovery on the assumption that government loans to banks and railroads would stop deflation in agriculture and industry and ultimately restore the levels of employment and purchasing power. He signed an exorbitantly high tariff measure, which made it impossible for foreign nations to sell their wares in this country, and then proposed a moratorium for one year on both interallied debts and reparations. This went into effect too late to keep the banks of Germany from closing, which, in turn, forced Great Britain off the gold standard. In short, it was a program of too little and too late.

In his campaign for election in 1932 Franklin D. Roosevelt set forth a program of economic nationalism and social reconstruction shaped by him with the aid of a group of assistants known as the "Brain Trust." Appealing to the "forgotten man at the bottom of the economic pyramid," Roosevelt in his Commonwealth Club address expounded the function of government as that of meeting "the problem of underconsumption, of adjusting production to consumption, of distributing wealth and products more equitably, of adapting existing economic organizations to the service of the people." Nevertheless, he assured his listeners that such economic regulation would be adopted "only as a last resort."

This philosophy of government was roundly condemned by Mr. Hoover, running for a second term. He considered it "a radical departure" from the American way of life. In a prophetic vein he warned that should the New Deal come to power, "the grass will grow in streets of a hundred cities, a thousand towns; the weeds will overrun the fields of millions of farms." Such Cassandra-like forebodings stirred little response from a nation facing the perils of bankruptcy, unemployment, starvation, and possibly even revolution. In the November election Roosevelt carried 42 states, with an overwhelming popular vote.

In the interim between the election and the inauguration of Franklin Delano Roosevelt economic conditions reached gravely critical proportions. Industrial production dropped to an all-time low. Runs on banks became increasingly frequent. The hoarding of currency set in on a large scale. Bank holidays were spreading throughout the country, and by Inauguration Day virtually every bank in the United States had been closed or placed under restrictions by state proclamations.

In his speech accepting the nomination, F. D. R., the imperturbable aristocrat with a heart for the common man and a genius for political maneuver, had pledged "a new deal for the American people." What could this mean? Could it foreshadow the nationalization of banking, dictatorship, fascism, communism? It was to mean none of these things. In its initial stages, the New Deal meant a program of relief and recovery aimed at revitalizing the economy of private capitalism by a series of emergency measures passed in the "Hundred Days" after the inauguration. In its later stages it meant the acceptance of a welfare-state economy. Roosevelt himself was no doctrinaire statesman. He believed in improvisation and experimentation. "It is common sense," he had said in 1932, "to take a method and try it. If it fails, admit it frankly and try another. But above all, try something."

Unlike Hoover, Franklin Roosevelt regarded the Presidency as something more than an efficiency-expert's job. He considered it to be "preeminently a place of moral leadership," and he seized the occasion of his very first speech to the nation as President to assert that leadership. The millions who listened on their radios to F. D. R.'s Inaugural Message were reassured by his tone, voice, and words that "the only thing we have to fear is fear itself" and his recognition that "we must act, and act quickly."

At long last the initiative had returned to the White House, and vigor and experimentation would be in the new order of things. To the nation in crisis it was reassuring to know that the Man in the White House would "try something." Within a week the acute panic was at an end, and confidence had been restored.

The New Deal was launched.

INAUGURAL ADDRESS [6]

March 4, 1933

President Hoover, Mr. Chief Justice, my friends:

I am certain that my fellow Americans expect that on my induction into the Presidency I will address them with a candor and a decision which the present situation of our nation impels.

This is pre-eminently the time to speak the truth, the whole truth, frankly and boldly. Nor need we shrink from honestly facing conditions in our country today. This great nation will endure as it has endured, will revive and will prosper.

So first of all let me assert my firm belief that the only thing we have to fear is fear itself—nameless, unreasoning, unjustified terror which paralyzes needed efforts to convert retreat into advance.

In every dark hour of our national life a leadership of frankness and vigor has met with that understanding and support of the people themselves which is essential to victory. I am convinced that you will again give that support to leadership in these critical days.

In such a spirit on my part and on yours we face our common difficulties. They concern, thank God, only material things. Values have shrunken to fantastic levels; taxes have risen; our ability to pay has fallen, government of all kinds is faced by serious curtailment of income; the means of exchange are frozen in the currents of trade; the withered leaves of industrial enterprise lie on every side; farmers find no markets for their products; the savings of many years in thousands of families are gone.

More important, a host of unemployed citizens face the grim problem of existence, and an equally great number toil with little return. Only a foolish optimist can deny the dark realities of the moment.

Yet our distress comes from no failure of substance. We are stricken by no plague of locusts. Compared with the perils which our forefathers conquered because they believed and were not afraid, we have still much to be thankful for. Nature still offers her bounty and human efforts have multiplied it. Plenty is at our doorstep, but a generous use of it languishes in the very sight of the supply.

Primarily, this is because the rulers of the exchange of mankind's goods have failed through their own stubbornness and their own incompetence, have admitted their failure and abdicated. Practices of the unscrupulous money changers stand indicted in the court of public opinion, rejected by the hearts and minds of men.

True, they have tried, but their efforts have been cast in the pattern of an outworn tradition. Faced by failure of credit, they have proposed only the lending of more money.

Stripped of the lure of profit by which to induce our people to follow their false leadership, they have resorted to exhortations, pleading tearfully for restored confidence. They know only the rules of a generation of self-seekers.

They have no vision, and when there is no vision the people perish.

The money changers have fled from their high seats in the temple of our civilization. We may now restore that temple to the ancient truths.

The measure of the restoration lies in the extent to which we apply social values more noble than mere monetary profit.

Happiness lies not in the mere possession of money; it lies in the joy of achievement, in the thrill of creative effort. The joy and moral stimulation of work no longer must be forgotten in the mad chase of evanescent profits. These dark days will be worth all they cost us if they teach us that our true destiny is not to be ministered unto but to minister to ourselves and to our fellow men.

Recognition of the falsity of material wealth as the standard of success goes hand in hand with the abandonment of the false belief that public office and high political position are to be valued only by the standards of pride of place and personal profit; and there must be an end to a conduct in banking and in business which too often has given to a sacred trust the likeness of callous and selfish wrongdoing.

Small wonder that confidence languishes, for it thrives only on honesty, on honor, on the sacredness of obligations, on faithful protection, on unselfish performance; without them it cannot live.

Restoration calls, however, not for changes in ethics alone. This nation asks for action, and action now.

Our greatest primary task is to put people to work. This is no unsolvable problem if we face it wisely and courageously. It can be accomplished in part by direct recruiting by the Government itself, treating the task as we would treat the emergency of a war, but at the same time, through this employment, accomplishing greatly needed projects to stimulate and reorganize the use of our natural resources.

Hand in hand with this we must frankly recognize the overbalance of population in our industrial centers and, by engaging on a national scale in a redistribution, endeavor to provide a better use of the land for those best fitted for the land.

The task can be helped by definite efforts to raise the values of agricultural products and with this the power to purchase the output of our cities.

It can be helped by preventing realistically the tragedy of the growing loss, through foreclosure, of our small homes and our farms.

It can be helped by insistence that the Federal, State and local governments act forthwith on the demand that their cost be drastically reduced.

It can be helped by the unifying of relief activities which today are often scattered, uneconomical and unequal. It can be helped by national planning for and supervision of all forms of transportation and of communications and other utilities which have a definitely public character.

There are many ways in which it can be helped, but it can never be helped merely by talking about it. We must act, and act quickly.

Finally, in our progress toward a resumption of work we require two safeguards against a return of the evils of the old order; there must be a strict supervision of all banking and credits and investments; there must be an end to speculation with other people's money, and there must be provision for an adequate but sound currency.

These are the lines of attack. I shall presently urge upon a new Congress, in special session, detailed measure for their fulfillment, and I shall seek the immediate assistance of the several States.

Through this program of action we address ourselves to putting our own national house in order and making income balance outgo. Our international trade relations, though vastly important, are in point of time and necessity secondary to the establishment of a sound national economy. I favor as a practical policy the putting of first things first. I shall spare no effort to restore world trade by international economic readjustment, but the emergency at home cannot wait on that accomplishment.

The basic thought that guides these specific means of national recovery is not narrowly nationalistic.

It is the insistence, as a first consideration, upon the interdependence of the various elements in, and parts of, the United States—a recognition of the old and permanently important manifestation of the American spirit of the pioneer.

It is the way to recovery. It is the immediate way. It is the strongest assurance that the recovery will endure.

In the field of world policy I would dedicate this nation to the policy of the good neighbor—the neighbor who resolutely respects himself and, because he does so, respects the rights of others—the neighbor who respects his obligations and respects the sanctity of his agreements in and with a world of neighbors.

If I read the temper of our people correctly, we now realize as we have never realized before our interdependence on each other; that we can not merely take but we must give as well; that if we are to go forward, we must move as a trained and loyal army willing to sacrifice for the good of a common discipline, because without such discipline no progress is made, no leadership becomes effective.

We are, I know, ready and willing to submit our lives and property to such discipline because it makes possible a leadership which aims at a larger good.

This I propose to offer, pledging that the larger purposes will bind upon us all as a sacred obligation with a unity of duty hitherto evoked only in time of armed strife.

With this pledge taken, I assume unhesitatingly the leadership of this great army of our people, dedicated to a disciplined attack upon our common problems.

Action in this image and to this end is feasible under the form of government which we have inherited from our ancestors.

Our Constitution is so simple and practical that it is possible always to meet extraordinary needs by changes in emphasis and arrangement without loss of essential form. That is why our constitutional system has proved itself the most superbly enduring political mechanism the modern world has produced. It has met every stress of vast expansion of territory, of foreign wars, of bitter internal strife, of world relations.

It is to be hoped that the normal balance of executive and legislative authority may be wholly adequate to meet the unprecedented task before us. But it may be that an unprecedented demand and need for undelayed action may call for temporary departure from that normal balance of public procedure.

I am prepared under my constitutional duty to recommend the measures that a stricken world may require.

These measures, or such other measures as the Congress may build out of its experience and wisdom, I shall seek, within my constitutional authority, to bring to speedy adoption.

But in the event that the Congress shall fail to take one of these two courses, and in the event that the national emergency is still critical, I shall not evade the clear course of duty that will then confront me.

I shall ask the Congress for the one remaining instrument to meet the crisis—broad executive power to wage a war against the emergency as great as the power that would be given me if we were in fact invaded by a foreign foe.

For the trust reposed in me I will return the courage and the devotion that befit the time. I can do no less.

We face the arduous days that lie before us in the warm courage of national unity; with the clear consciousness of seeking old and precious moral values; with the clean satisfaction that comes from the stern performance of duty by old and young alike. We aim at the assurance of a rounded and permanent national life.

We do not distrust the future of essential democracy. The people of the United States have not failed. In their need they have registered a mandate that they want direct, vigorous action.

They have asked for discipline and direction under leadership. They have made me the present instrument of their wishes. In the spirit of the gift I take it.

In this dedication of a nation we humbly ask the blessing of God. May He protect each and every one of us! May He guide me in the days to come!

31

THE DECISION
TO COME TO THE AID OF BRITAIN

F. D. R's "Lend-Lease" Message

June and July of 1940 were somber months for the western democracies. On the fourth of June the British completed their evacuation of Dunkirk. Within a week France fell, and by midsummer the Battle of Britain had been launched by the Luftwaffe. Sentiment in the United States was building up for giving aid in some form to Britain, but how this could be done under the existing neutrality legislation and without involving this country in war was by no means clear. In the spring of 1940 Prime Minister Churchill appealed for military supplies, and as a start the War Department released to Great Britain on June 3 surplus or outdated stocks of arms, munitions, and aircraft. But the British were in desperate need of warships. Of the less than one hundred destroyers they had had available in home waters, almost half had been lost or destroyed. Additional destroyers were needed to help Britain safeguard her trade routes and defend her coasts against the anticipated German invasion.

In July, 1940, an unofficial group of distinguished American citizens calling themselves the Century Group proposed that we offer Britain the destroyers in exchange for "immediate naval and air concessions in British possessions in the Western Hemisphere." The President considered the problem at a Cabinet meeting on August 2, and wheels were set in motion to secure the necessary legislation and to enlist the aid of Wendell Willkie, the Republican nominee for President. To obviate the difficulties of securing Congressional action, the Century Group now suggested that the destroyer deal could be carried out under existing statutes. On that basis President Roosevelt informed Winston Churchill on August 13 that the United States would turn over at least fifty destroyers in return for naval and air bases in British territory in the Western Hemisphere. At Churchill's suggestion these were leased to the United States on long terms. To whip up public opinion F. D. R. arranged to have Ambassador William C. Bullitt deliver a fighting speech before the American Philosophical Society in Philadelphia on August 18, in the course of which he declared that "the destruction of the British Navy would be the turning of our Atlantic Maginot Line."

This was indeed an historic decision, the first step in a more elaborate program of aid embodied under Lend-Lease, and the news of the agreement provoked some attacks. Roosevelt had acted without securing Congressional approval in advance. "Congress is going to raise hell about this," the President told his secretary, Grace Tully, "but even another day's delay may mean the end of civilization. Cries of 'warmonger' and 'dictator' will fill the air, but if Britain is to survive, we must act." The St. Louis *Post-Dispatch* characterized the agreement as "the worst" of all "sucker real estate deals in history," but others regarded it as the best bargain the United States had made since the Louisiana Purchase.

The fifty overage destroyers did not prove sufficient, for as the Battle of Britain waned, the Battle of the Atlantic waxed, and Admiral Raeder's combined sea and air attacks on British shipping were having spectacular results. The danger was mortal. Great Britain needed an increasing flow of supplies, but her dollar assets were approaching the vanishing point. Some new and more grandiose approach was needed. What President Roosevelt had in mind was revealed at a press conference held on December 17. If one's neighbor's house was on fire and one had a hose, one didn't say to him: "Neighbor, my garden hose cost me fifteen dollars; you have to pay me fifteen dollars for it," Roosevelt pointed out. No, instead one connected the hose, helped put out the fire, and got the hose back afterward. This was to be the way with the munitions Britain so desperately needed. For the dollar sign was to be substituted a "gentleman's obligation to repay in kind."

To mobilize public opinion in support of the enabling legislation he was to ask of Congress, F. D. R. delivered a remarkable fireside chat on national security on December 29. "We must be the great arsenal of democracy," he declared. Then, in his great State of the Union Message of January 6, 1941, he requested Lend-Lease legislation and set forth America's objectives. Commenting on the "Four Freedoms" speech, Harry Hopkins, who was soon to direct Lend-Lease, observed to Robert E. Sherwood, the talented playwright who assisted the President in speech-writing, "Don't get the idea that those are any catch phrases. *He* believes them!"

After two months of nationwide debate Congress passed the Lend-Lease Bill, which had been prepared by the Treasury Department's legal advisers. Congress had indicated that it was prepared to support the President's program dedicated to the defeat of aggressors even at the risk of war. Had the Congress gone still further? Had it actually delegated to the President its power to declare war? The Lend-Lease statute authorized the President "to transfer title, to exchange, lease, lend or otherwise dispose of any defense articles," and provided that Lend-Lease could be extended to "any country whose defense the President deems vital to the defense of the United States." This put the decision entirely in the President's hands. Might he not use this authority to render aid to the Soviet Union? some critics asked. That, of course, is precisely what Roosevelt did do when the situation dictated that such action was imperative to the defense of the West. But more immediately the measure saved Britain. "Our blessings from the whole British Empire go out to you and the American nation for this very present help in time of trouble," Churchill wrote to Roosevelt.

Lend-Lease, Secretary of War Stimson admitted in his diary, was "a declaration of economic war." From a different vantage point Winston Churchill described it to Parliament as "the most unsordid act in the history of any nation." Our commitment to the saving of the West was now irrevocable.

ANNUAL MESSAGE [7]

January 6, 1941

Mr. President, Mr. Speaker, Members of the Seventy-seventh Congress:

I address you, the Members of the Seventy-seventh Congress, at a moment unprecedented in the history of the Union. I use the word "unprecedented," because at no previous time has American security been as seriously threatened from without as it is today.

Since the permanent formation of our Government under the Constitution, in 1789, most of the periods of crisis in our history have related to our domestic affairs. Fortunately, only one of these—the four-year War Between the States—ever threatened our national unity. Today, thank God, one hundred and thirty million Americans, in forty-eight States, have forgotten points of the compass in our national unity.

It is true that prior to 1914 the United States often had been disturbed by events in other Continents. We had even engaged in two wars with European nations and in a number of undeclared wars in the West Indies, in the Mediterranean and in the Pacific for the maintenance of American rights and for the principles of peaceful commerce. But in no case had a serious threat been raised against our national safety or our continued independence.

What I seek to convey is the historic truth that the United States as a nation has at all times maintained clear, definite opposition, to any attempt to lock us in behind an ancient Chinese wall while the procession of civilization went past. Today, thinking of our children and of their children, we oppose enforced isolation for ourselves or for any other part of the Americas.

That determination of ours, extending over all these years, was proved, for example, during the quarter century of wars following the French Revolution.

While the Napoleonic struggles did threaten interests of the United States because of the French foothold in the West Indies and in Louisiana, and while we engaged in the War of 1812 to vindicate our right to peaceful trade, it is nevertheless clear that neither France nor Great Britain, nor any other nation was aiming at domination of the whole world.

In like fashion from 1815 to 1914—ninety-nine years—no single war in Europe or in Asia constituted a real threat against our future or against the future of any other American nation.

Except in the Maximilian interlude in Mexico, no foreign power sought to establish itself in this Hemisphere; and the strength of the British fleet in the Atlantic has been a friendly strength. It is still a friendly strength.

Even when the World War broke out in 1914, it seemed to contain only small threat of danger to our own American future. But, as time went on, the American people began to visualize what the downfall of democratic nations might mean to our own democracy.

We need not overemphasize imperfections in the Peace of Versailles. We need not harp on failure of the democracies to deal with problems of world reconstruction. We should remember that the Peace of 1919 was far less unjust than the kind of "pacification" which began even before Munich, and which is being carried on under the new order of tyranny that seeks to spread over every continent today. The American people have unalterably set their faces against that tyranny. Every realist knows that the democratic way of life is at this moment being directly assailed in every part of the world—assailed either by arms, or by secret spreading of poisonous propaganda by those who seek to destroy unity and promote discord in nations that are still at peace.

During sixteen long months this assault has blotted out the whole pattern of democratic life in an appalling number of independent nations, great and small. The assailants are still on the march, threatening other nations, great and small.

Therefore, as your President, performing my constitutional duty to "give to the Congress information of the state of the Union," I find it, unhappily, necessary to report that the future and the safety of our country and of our democracy are overwhelmingly involved in events far beyond our borders.

Armed defense of democratic existence is now being gallantly waged in four continents. If that defense fails, all the population and all the resources of Europe, Asia, Africa and Australasia will be dominated by the conquerors. Let us remember that the total of those populations and their resources in those four continents greatly exceed the sum total of the population and the resources of the whole of the Western Hemisphere—many times over.

In times like these it is immature—and incidentally, untrue—for anybody to brag that an unprepared America, single-handed, and with one hand tied behind its back, can hold off the whole world.

No realistic American can expect from a dictator's peace international generosity, or return of true independence, or world disarmament, or freedom of expression, or freedom of religion—or even good business.

Such a peace would bring no security for us or for our neighbors. "Those, who would give up essential liberty to purchase a little temporary safety, deserve neither liberty nor safety."

As a nation, we may take pride in the fact that we are softhearted; but we cannot afford to be soft-headed.

We must always be wary of those who with sounding brass and a tinkling cymbal preach the "ism" of appeasement.

We must especially beware of that small group of selfish men who would clip the wings of the American eagle in order to feather their own nests.

I have recently pointed out how quickly the tempo of modern warfare could bring into our very midst the physical attack which we must eventually expect if the dictator nations win this war.

There is much loose talk of our immunity from immediate and direct invasion from across the seas. Obviously, as long as the British Navy retains its power, no such danger exists. Even if there were no British Navy, it is not probable that any enemy would be stupid enough to attack us by landing troops in the United States from across thousands of miles of ocean, until it had acquired strategic bases from which to operate.

But we learn much from the lessons of the past years in Europe—particularly the lesson of Norway, whose essential seaports were captured by treachery and surprise built up over a series of years.

The first phase of the invasion of this Hemisphere would not be the landing of regular troops. The necessary strategic points would be occupied by secret agents and their dupes—and great numbers of them are already here, and in Latin America.

As long as the aggressor nations maintain the offensive, they—not we—will choose the time and the place and the method of their attack.

That is why the future of all the American Republics is today in serious danger.

That is why this Annual Message to the Congress is unique in our history.

That is why every member of the Executive Branch of the Government and every member of the Congress faces great responsibility and great accountability.

The need of the moment is that our actions and our policy should be devoted primarily—almost exclusively—to meeting this foreign peril. For all our domestic problems are now a part of the great emergency.

Just as our national policy in internal affairs has been based upon a decent respect for the rights and the dignity of all our fellow men within our gates, so our national policy in foreign affairs has been based on a decent respect for the rights and dignity of all nations, large and small. And the justice of morality must and will win in the end.

Our national policy is this:

First, by an impressive expression of the public will and without regard to partisanship, we are committed to all-inclusive national defense.

Second, by an impressive expression of the public will and without regard to partisanship, we are committed to full support of all those resolute peoples, everywhere, who are resisting aggression and are thereby keeping war away from our Hemisphere. By this support, we express our determination that the democratic cause shall prevail; and we strengthen the defense and the security of our own nation.

Third, by an impressive expression of the public will and without regard to partisanship, we are committed to the proposition that principles of morality and considerations for our own security will never permit us to acquiesce in a peace dictated by aggressors and sponsored by appeasers. We know that enduring peace cannot be bought at the cost of other people's freedom.

In the recent national election there was no substantial difference between the two great parties in respect to that national policy. No issue was fought out on this line before the American electorate. Today it is abundantly evident that American citizens everywhere are demanding and supporting speedy and complete action in recognition of obvious danger.

Therefore, the immediate need is a swift and driving increase in our armament production.

Leaders of industry and labor have responded to our summons. Goals of speed have been set. In some cases these goals are being reached ahead of time; in some cases we are on schedule; in other cases there are slight but not serious delays; and in some cases—and I am sorry to say very important cases—we are all concerned by the slowness of the accomplishment of our plans.

The Army and Navy, however, have made substantial progress during the past year. Actual experience is improving and speeding up our methods of production with every passing day. And today's best is not good enough for tomorrow.

I am not satisfied with the progress thus far made. The men in charge of the program represent the best in training, in ability, and in patriotism. They are not satisfied with the progress thus far made. None of us will be satisfied until the job is done.

No matter whether the original goal was set too high or too low, our objective is quicker and better results.

To give you two illustrations:

We are behind schedule in turning out finished airplanes; we are working day and night to solve the innumerable problems and to catch up.

We are ahead of schedule in building warships but we are working to get even further ahead of that schedule.

To change a whole nation from a basis of peacetime production of implements of peace to a basis of wartime production of implements of war is no small task. And the greatest difficulty comes at the beginning of the program, when new tools, new plant facilities, new assembly lines, and new ship ways must first be constructed before the actual matériel begins to flow steadily and speedily from them.

The Congress, of course, must rightly keep itself informed at all times of the progress of the program. However, there is certain information, as the Congress itself will readily recognize, which, in the interests of our own security and those of the nations that we are supporting, must of needs be kept in confidence.

New circumstances are constantly begetting new needs for our safety. I shall ask this Congress for greatly increased new appropriations and authorizations to carry on what we have begun.

I also ask this Congress for authority and for funds sufficient to manufacture additional munitions and war supplies of many kinds, to be turned over to those nations which are now in actual war with aggressor nations.

Our most useful and immediate role is to act as an arsenal for them as well as for ourselves. They do not need man power, but they do need billions of dollars' worth of the weapons of defense.

The time is near when they will not be able to pay for them all in ready cash. We can not, and we will not, tell them that they must surrender, merely because of present inability to pay for the weapons which we know they must have.

I do not recommend that we make them a loan of dollars with which to pay for these weapons—a loan to be repaid in dollars.

I recommend that we make it possible for those nations to continue to obtain war materials in the United States, fitting their orders into our own program. Nearly all their matériel would, if the time ever came, be useful for our own defense.

Taking counsel of expert military and naval authorities, considering what is best for our own security, we are free to decide how much should be kept here and how much should be sent abroad to our friends who by their determined and heroic resistance are giving us time in which to make ready our own defense.

For what we send abroad, we shall be repaid within a reasonable time following the close of hostilities, in similar materials, or, at our option, in other goods of many kinds, which they can produce and which we need.

Let us say to the democracies: "We Americans are vitally concerned in your defense of freedom. We are putting forth our energies, our resources and our organizing powers to give you the strength to regain and maintain a free world. We shall send you, in ever-increasing numbers, ships, planes, tanks, guns. This is our purpose and our pledge."

In fulfillment of this purpose we will not be intimidated by the threats of dictators that they will regard as a breach of international law or as an act of war our aid to the democracies which dare to resist their aggression. Such aid is not an act of war, even if a dictator should unilaterally proclaim it so to be.

When the dictators, if the dictators, are ready to make war upon us, they will not wait for an act of war on our part. They did not wait for Norway or Belgium or the Netherlands to commit an act of war.

Their only interest is in a new one-way international law, which lacks mutuality in its observance, and, therefore, becomes an instrument of oppression.

The happiness of future generations of Americans may well depend upon how effective and how immediate we can make our aid felt. No one can tell the exact character of the emergency situations that we may be called upon to meet. The Nation's hands must not be tied when the Nation's life is in danger.

We must all prepare to make the sacrifices that the emergency—almost as serious as war itself—demands. Whatever stands in the way of speed and efficiency in defense preparations must give way to the national need.

A free nation has the right to expect full cooperation from all groups. A free nation has the right to look to the leaders of business, of labor, and of agriculture to take the lead in stimulating effort, not among other groups but within their own groups.

The best way of dealing with the few slackers or trouble makers in our midst is, first, to shame them by patriotic example, and, if that fails, to use the sovereignty of Government to save Government.

As men do not live by bread alone, they do not fight by armaments alone. Those who man our defenses, and those behind them who build our defenses, must have the stamina and the courage which come from unshakable belief in the manner of life which they are defending. The mighty action that we are calling for cannot be based on a disregard of all things worth fighting for.

The Nation takes great satisfaction and much strength from the things which have been done to make its people conscious of their individual stake in the preservation of democratic life in America. Those things have toughened the fibre of our people, have renewed their faith and strengthened their devotion to the institutions we make ready to protect.

Certainly this is no time for any of us to stop thinking about the social and economic problems which are the root cause of the social revolution which is today a supreme factor in the world.

For there is nothing mysterious about the foundations of a healthy and strong democracy. The basic things expected by our people of their political and economic systems are simple. They are:

Equality of opportunity for youth and for others.

Jobs for those who can work.

Security for those who need it.

The ending of special privilege for the few.

The preservation of civil liberties for all.

The enjoyment of the fruits of scientific progress in a wider and constantly rising standard of living.

These are the simple, basic things that must never be lost sight of in the turmoil and unbelievable complexity of our modern world. The inner and abiding strength of our economic and political systems is dependent upon the degree to which they fulfill these expectations.

Many subjects connected with our social economy call for immediate improvement.

As examples:

We should widen the opportunities for adequate medical care.

We should plan a better system by which persons deserving or needing gainful employment may obtain it.

I have called for personal sacrifice. I am assured of the willingness of almost all Americans to respond to that call.

A part of the sacrifice means the payment of more money in taxes. In my Budget Message I shall recommend that a greater portion of this great defense program be paid for from taxation than we are paying today. No person should try, or be allowed, to get rich out of this program; and the principle of tax payments in accordance with ability to pay should be constantly before our eyes to guide our legislation.

If the Congress maintains these principles, the voters, putting patriotism ahead of pocketbooks, will give you their applause.

In the future days, which we seek to make secure, we look forward to a world founded upon four essential human freedoms.

The first is freedom of speech and expression—everywhere in the world.

The second is freedom of every person to worship God in his own way—everywhere in the world.

The third is freedom from want—which, translated into world terms, means economic understandings which will secure to every nation a healthy peacetime life for its inhabitants—everywhere in the world.

The fourth is freedom from fear—which, translated into world terms, means a world-wide reduction of armaments to such a point and in such a thorough fashion that no nation will be in a position to commit an act of physical aggression against any neighbor—anywhere in the world.

That is no vision of a distant millennium. It is a definite basis for a kind of world attainable in our own time and generation. That kind of world is the very antithesis of the so-called new order of tyranny which the dictators seek to create with the crash of a bomb.

To that new order we oppose the greater conception—the moral order. A good society is able to face schemes of world domination and foreign revolutions alike without fear.

Since the beginning of our American history, we have been engaged in change—in a perpetual peaceful revolution—a revolution which goes on steadily, quietly adjusting itself to changing conditions—without the concentration camp or the quick-lime in the ditch. The world order which we seek is the cooperation of free countries, working together in a friendly, civilized society.

This nation has placed its destiny in the hands and heads and hearts of its millions of free men and women; and its faith in freedom under the guidance of God. Freedom means the supremacy of human rights everywhere. Our support goes to those who struggle to gain those rights or keep them. Our strength is our unity of purpose.

To that high concept there can be no end save victory.

32

THE DECISION
TO CONTAIN SOVIET EXPANSION

Truman Enunciates a New Doctrine

The late winter of 1947 marked a major turning point in American history. It was now clear that the mutual distrust which had marred the alliance between the Soviet Union and the West during World War II was shaping up into a mighty contest for world domination or liberation, depending on one's point of view. Not only had Soviet foreign policy returned in the first postwar years to active support of revolutionary communism in other countries, but, in addition, Russia had embarked on a program of territorial expansion and penetration reminiscent of Czarist days. The Soviet government had put cruel pressures on Greece, Turkey, and Iran which threatened the independence of those nations.

The prewar Greek monarchy, now re-established on Greek soil, was engaged in a life-and-death struggle with Communist guerrilla forces within Greece, supplied and supported by Greece's Soviet-dominated Communist neighbors, Albania, Yugoslavia, and Bulgaria. Turkey, whose twenty-year nonaggression pact with the Soviet Union had expired in 1945, was being pressured by Russia to yield bases in and near the Bosporus and the Dardanelles, which, if granted, would have made Russia mistress of the Straits. Previously, in an effort to outflank Turkey, the Soviets had kept troops in Iran beyond the period she had agreed upon for withdrawal. As a result of strongly worded American protests Soviet troops were withdrawn.

In Greece the situation remained critical. On February 24, 1947, Secretary of State Marshall brought to President Truman a note from the British Ambassador stating that, owing to the difficulties confronting Britain in fulfilling her overseas commitments, she would have to withdraw all support from Greece by March 30. President Harry

Truman, heir to all the mighty and complex problems of war and peace which he had assumed on Franklin Delano Roosevelt's sudden death at the beginning of his fourth term, had to decide, and within days, whether Russia was to be allowed to take over the eastern Mediterranean or the United States to assume burdens which were becoming increasingly too onerous for a seriously weakened British Commonwealth. Truman was confronted with a hostile Congress, the ill-starred Eightieth, which could be expected to repudiate any decision that was construed as a signal departure from traditional American foreign policy; he was faced with an uphill and seemingly impossible battle for re-election the following year—a campaign which was to be made still more difficult by lowered national morale, high taxes, and inflation; a cautious man might well have procrastinated. But the Man from Independence thrust aside domestic and personal considerations. American diplomatic and military experts had informed him that Greece needed aid, quickly and in substantial amounts. To allow the free peoples of Greece and Turkey to fall before Soviet imperialism would carry ominous implications to Italy, Germany, France, and the whole Middle East. There were serious risks involved, but, as Harry Truman has remarked in his *Memoirs,* "the alternative would be disastrous to our security and to the security of free nations everywhere."

On the morning of February 27 the President told a bipartisan delegation of Senators and Congressmen who called at the White House of his decision to extend aid to Greece and Turkey. No one present dissented. In the days that followed Secretary of the Navy Forrestal, Dean Acheson, and others worked feverishly preparing a plan of action. Truman informed his Cabinet on March 7 that he proposed to ask Congress for the sum of $250,000,000 for Greece and $150,000,000 for Turkey, but that he realized this would be only the beginning.

The President now decided to inform Congress and the nation of the urgency of the situation and the steps that needed to be taken. He realized, as Senator Vandenberg put it, that it was necessary to "scare the hell out of the country." The drafting of the President's message to Congress was first entrusted to the State Department, but Truman was dissatisfied with the version that he was offered. The writers "made the whole thing sound like an investment prospectus," he commented. He returned the draft to Dean Acheson, requesting more emphasis on a declaration of general policy. The rewrite he still felt was a halfhearted statement. The key sentence in the new draft read, "I believe that it should be the policy of the United States. . . ." Truman penciled out "should" and wrote in "must." Elsewhere he struck out hedging phrases. He wanted to make it perfectly clear that his address "was America's answer to the surge of expansion of Communist tyranny. It had to be clear and free of hesitation or double talk."

Nobody had any doubts about what the President intended when he delivered his address to a joint session of Congress on March 12, 1947. The President moved fast. He had the aircraft carrier *Leyte* and nine other naval vessels dispatched to Greece as a token of America's intentions. By impressive and bipartisan majorities both houses of Congress passed the legislation requested. Almost immediately after the President signed the aid-to-Greece bill Secretary of State Marshall, in an historic address at Harvard University (drafted by Charles E. Bohlen, a Russian expert in the State Department), set forth a magnificently conceived program for European economic recovery.

Within the space of a few months the Truman administration had made revolutionary decisions which checked the disintegration of Europe and the westward surge of Soviet imperialism.

ADDRESS [8]

March 12, 1947

Mr. President, Mr. Speaker, Members of the Congress of the United States:

The gravity of the situation which confronts the world today necessitates my appearance before a joint session of the Congress.

The foreign policy and the national security of this country are involved.

One aspect of the present situation, which I wish to present to you at this time for your consideration and decision, concerns Greece and Turkey.

The United States has received from the Greek government an urgent appeal for financial and economic assistance. Preliminary reports from the American economic mission now in Greece and reports from the American Ambassador in Greece corroborate the statement of the Greek government that assistance is imperative if Greece is to survive as a free nation. I do not believe that the American people and the Congress wish to turn a deaf ear to the appeal of the Greek government.

Greece is not a rich country. Lack of sufficient material resources has always forced the Greek people to work hard to make both ends meet. Since 1940, this industrious, peace-loving country has suffered invasion, four years of cruel enemy occupation, and bitter internal strife.

When forces of liberation entered Greece they found that the retreating Germans had destroyed virtually all the railways, roads, port facilities, communications, and merchant marine. More than a thousand villages had been burned. Eighty-five per cent of the children were tubercular. Livestock, poultry, and draft animals had almost disappeared. Inflation had wiped out practically all savings. As a result of these drastic conditions, a militant minority, exploiting human want and misery, was able to create political chaos which, until now, has made economic recovery impossible.

Greece is today without funds to finance the importation of those goods which are essential to bare subsistence. Under these circumstances the people of Greece cannot make progress in solving their problems of reconstruction. Greece is in desperate need of financial and economic assistance to enable it to resume purchases of food, clothing, fuel and seeds. These are indispensable for the subsistence of its people and are obtainable only from abroad. Greece must have help to import the goods necessary to restore internal order and security so essential for economic and political recovery.

The Greek government has also asked for the assistance of experienced American administrators, economists and technicians to insure that the financial and other aid given to Greece shall be used effectively in creating a stable and self-sustaining economy and in improving its public administration.

The very existence of the Greek state is today threatened by the terrorist activities of several thousand armed men, led by Communists, who defy the government's authority at a number of points, particularly along the northern boundaries. A commission appointed by the United Nations Security Council is at present investigating disturbed conditions in northern Greece on the one hand and Albania, Bulgaria and Yugoslavia on the other.

Meanwhile, the Greek government is unable to cope with the situation. The Greek army is small and poorly equipped. It needs supplies and equipment if it is to restore the authority of the government throughout Greek territory.

Greece must have assistance if it is to become a self-supporting and self-respecting democracy.

The United States must supply that assistance. We have already extended to Greece certain types of relief and economic aid but these are inadequate.

There is no other country to which democratic Greece can turn.

No other nation is willing and able to provide the necessary support for a democratic Greek government. The British government, which has been helping Greece, can give no further financial or economic aid after March 31. Great Britain finds itself under the necessity of reducing or liquidating its commitments in several parts of the world, including Greece.

We have considered how the United Nations mights assist in this crisis. But the situation is an urgent one requiring immediate action, and the United Nations and its related organizations are not in a position to extend help of the kind that is required.

It is important to note that the Greek government has asked for our aid in utilizing effectively the financial and other assistance we may give Greece, and in improving its public administration. It is of the utmost importance that we supervise the use of any funds made available to Grece, in such a manner that each dollar spent will count toward making Greece self-supporting, and will help to build an economy in which a healthy democracy can flourish.

No government is perfect. One of the chief virtues of a democracy, however, is that its defects are always visible and under democratic processes can be pointed out and corrected. The government of Greece is not perfect. Nevertheless, it represents 85 per cent of the members of the Greek parliament who were chosen in an election last year. Foreign observers, including 692 Americans, considered this election to be a fair expression of the views of the Greek people.

The Greek government has been operating in an atmosphere of chaos and extremism. It has made mistakes. The extension of aid by this country does not mean that the United States condones everything that the Greek government has done or will do. We have condemned in the past, and we condemn now, extremist measures of the Right or the Left. We have in the past advised tolerance, and we advise tolerance now.

Greece's neighbor, Turkey, also deserves our attention.

The future of Turkey as an independent and economically sound state is clearly no less important to the freedom-loving peoples of the world than the future of Greece. The circumstances in which Turkey finds itself today are considerably different from those of Greece. Turkey has been spared the disasters that have beset Greece. And during the war the United States and Great Britain furnished Turkey with material aid. Nevertheless, Turkey now needs our support.

Since the war, Turkey has sought financial assistance from Great Britain and the United States for the purpose of effecting that modernization necessary for the maintenance of its national integrity.

That integrity is essential to the preservation of order in the Middle East.

The British government has informed us that, owing to its own difficulties, it can no longer extend financial or economic aid to Turkey.

As in the case of Greece, if Turkey is to have the assistance it needs, the United States must supply it. We are the only country able to provide that help.

I am fully aware of the broad implications involved if the United States extends assistance to Greece and Turkey, and I shall discuss these implications with you at this time.

One of the primary objectives of the foreign policy of the United States is the creation of conditions in which we and other nations will be able to work out a way of life free from coercion. This was a fundamental issue in the war with Germany and Japan. Our victory was won over countries which sought to impose their will, and their way of life, upon other nations.

To insure the peaceful development of nations, free from coercion, the United States has taken a leading part in establishing the United Nations. The United Nations is designed to make possible lasting freedom and independence for all its members. We shall not realize our objectives, however, unless we are willing to help free people to maintain their free institutions and their national integrity against aggressive movements that seek to impose upon them totalitarian regimes. This is no more than a frank recognition that totalitarian regimes imposed on free peoples, by direct or indirect aggression, undermine the foundations of international peace and hence the security of the United States.

The peoples of a number of countries of the world have recently had totalitarian regimes forced upon them against their will. The government of the United States has made frequent protests against coercion and intimidation, in violation of the Yalta agreement, in Poland, Rumania and Bulgaria. I must also state that in a number of other countries there have been similar developments.

At the present moment in world history nearly every nation must choose between alternative ways of life. The choice is too often not a free one.

One way of life is based upon the will of the majority, and is distinguished by free institutions, representative government, free elections, guaranties of individual liberty, freedom of speech and religion and freedom from political oppression.

The second way of life is based upon the will of a minority forcibly imposed upon the majority. It relies upon terror and oppression, a controlled press and radio, fixed elections and the suppression of personal freedoms.

I believe that it must be the policy of the United States to support peoples who are resisting attempted subjugation by armed minorities or by outside pressures.

I believe that we must assist free peoples to work out their own destinies in their own way.

I believe that our help should be primarily through economic and financial aid which is essential to economic stability and orderly political processes.

The world is not static, and the status quo is not sacred. But we can not allow changes in the status quo in violation of the charter of the United Nations by such methods as coercion, or by such subterfuges as political infiltration. In helping free and independent nations to maintain their freedom, the United States will be giving effect to the principles of the charter of the United Nations.

It is necessary only to glance at a map to realize that the survival and integrity of the Greek nation are of grave importance in a much wider situation. If Greece should fall under the control of an armed minority, the effect upon its neighbor, Turkey, would be immediate and serious. Confusion and disorder might well spread throughout the entire Middle East.

Moreover, the disappearance of Greece as an independent state would have a profound effect upon those countries in Europe whose peoples are struggling against great difficulties to maintain their freedoms and their independence while they repair the damages of war.

It would be an unspeakable tragedy if these countries, which have struggled so long against overwhelming odds, should lose that victory for which they sacrificed so much. Collapse of free institutions and loss of independence would be disastrous not only for them but for the world. Discouragement and possible failure would quickly be the lot of neighboring peoples striving to maintain their freedom and independence.

Should we fail to aid Greece and Turkey in this fateful hour, the effect will be far reaching to the west as well as to the east. We must take immediate and resolute action.

I therefore ask the Congress to provide authority for assistance to Greece and Turkey in the amount of $400,000,000 for the period ending June 30, 1948. In requesting these funds, I have taken into consideration the maximum amount of relief assistance which would be furnished to Greece out of the $350,000,000 which I recently requested that the Congress authorize for the prevention of starvation and suffering in countries devastated by the war.

In addition to funds, I ask the Congress to authorize the detail of American civilian and military personnel to Greece and Turkey, at the request of those countries, to assist in the tasks of reconstruction, and for the purpose of supervising the use of such financial and material assistance as may be furnished. I recommend that authority also be provided for the instruction and training of selected Greek and Turkish personnel.

Finally, I ask that the Congress provide authority which will permit the speediest and most effective use, in terms of needed commodities, supplies, and equipment, of such funds as may be authorized.

If further funds, or further authority, should be needed for the purposes indicated in this message, I shall not hesitate to bring the situation before the Congress. On this subject the executive and legislative branches of the government must work together.

This is a serious course upon which we embark. I would not recommend it except that the alternative is much more serious.

The United States contributed $341,000,000,000 toward winning World War II. This is an investment in world freedom and world peace.

The assistance that I am recommending for Greece and Turkey amounts to little more than 1 tenth of 1 per cent of the investment. It is only common sense that we should safeguard this investment and make sure that it was not in vain.

The seeds of totalitarian regimes are nurtured by misery and want. They spread and grow in the evil soil of poverty and strife. They reach their full growth when the hope of a people for a better life has died.

We must keep that hope alive.

The free peoples of the world look to us for support in maintaining their freedoms.

If we falter in our leadership, we may endanger the peace of the world—and we shall surely endanger the welfare of our nation.

Great responsibilities have been placed upon us by the swift movement of events.

I am confident that the Congress will face these responsibilities squarely.

33

THE DECISION
TO RESIST THE COMMUNIST INVASION
OF KOREA

*Truman's Announcement that the United States Would
Aid the Korean Republic*

When the year 1950 began it seemed that the Truman policy of containment had been effective. Western Europe and the Near East had been bolstered by economic and military aid. The Soviet Union, thwarted in its efforts at westward penetration by its ineffectual Berlin blockade, but now buttressed by its possession of the atomic bomb, turned its imperialist glances toward the East.

The results of its intrigues came with the staccato suddenness of machine-gun fire. On February 14, 1950, the Soviet and the Chinese Communists signed a treaty of friendship and mutual assistance. This was signal evidence of the collapse of America's uncertain efforts at bolstering the Kuomintang, whose armies had proved no match for the Communist guerrilla fighters, supplied by Russia with captured Japanese equipment. Whether or not this collapse was inevitable or might have been warded off by a more positive policy of aid to Chiang Kai-shek was the subject of a bitter and interminable debate. In a White Paper issued by the State Department in August, 1949, our government had already conceded that "the ominous result of the civil war in China was beyond the control of the government of the United States."

Not only in China, but throughout Asia nationalism and anticolonialism were on the move. The Dutch were forced to grant independence to Indonesia, the British to yield control in Burma, and the French were perilously holding on in Indochina. Where would it end and how far would we go in defending the Far East against communism?

America's intentions were seemingly clarified in an address made by Secretary of State Dean Acheson before the National Press Club in Washington on January 12, 1950. Acheson, spelling out what President Truman had stated a week before, drew a "defense perimeter" beyond which American forces would not venture. The line passed from the Aleutian Islands through Japan, Okinawa, and the Philippines. Beyond this line lay Korea and Formosa, and it was the implication of Acheson's remarks that America accepted no responsibility for their defense. The State Department had impressive support for such a position. General Douglas MacArthur had remarked, "Anyone who commits the American army on the mainland of Asia ought to have his head examined."

In retrospect Dean Acheson's remarks have been considered by many critics as provocative and amounting in fact to an invitation to the Communists to attack Korea. Had the Communists planned such an attack only on the contingency of America's nonintervention, they might have withdrawn once American ground forces were committed and saved face by dismissing the affair as a raiding operation. But they did not. The North Korean Communists and the powers behind them seemed prepared for war regardless of the cost.

Back at Potsdam in 1945 Russia and the United States had agreed to liberate Korea, and soon thereafter had accepted the 38th parallel as a dividing line for the troops of the respective nations. But the liberation and unification of Korea proved an impossible task. Intent on having a regime favorable to themselves in North Korea, the Russians opposed unification, barred the UN commissioners from that territory, and as a result the elections of 1948 only took place south of the 38th parallel. One month after Korea was proclaimed an independent state, with Syngman Rhee as president, the Soviet's Democratic People's Republic of North Korea announced that it too was a sovereign state. In the months that followed pathetically little was done by the United States to build the Korean army into an effective fighting force.

President Truman was visiting in Independence, Missouri, when, on June 24, 1950, he learned from Acheson that North Korean troops had crossed the 38th parallel. At the President's request a special meeting of the Security Council of the UN was convened in emergency session, and by a vote of 9 to 0 approved a resolution declaring that a breach of the peace had been committed by the North Koreans and ordering them to cease their action and withdraw their forces. In his *Memoirs* Truman tells us what he was thinking about as he flew back to Washington. His thoughts went back to Manchuria, to Ethiopia, to Austria, to all those occasions when the democracies had failed to act. He realized that if the Communists were given their way in Korea, no small nation would have the presumption to stand up against a stronger Communist neighbor. The end result would be World War III.

At a Blair House conference that Sunday evening the President's military and civilian advisers were agreed that action had to be taken. Some felt that air and naval aid might suffice; others, that ground forces would be necessary. But all recognized, in Truman's own words, that the situation was "serious in the extreme." When it was evident by the next day that the Korean situation was deteriorating rapidly, Truman gave orders to General MacArthur to use air and naval forces to support the Republic of Korea, but only south of the 38th parallel, and to dispatch the Seventh Fleet to the Formosa Strait. The President speedily lined up Congressional leaders from both parties behind the statement he had prepared, which he gave out to the press at the conclusion of this session. That terse statement, given here, embodied a momentous decision.

"Korea is a small country, thousands of miles away, but what is happening there is important to every American," President Truman declared in a message of July 19, 1950. The western democracies had learned much from the days of Neville Chamberlain and Munich. After seesaw fighting, which brought the Chinese Communists into the war and General MacArthur out of it, a stalemate ensued. In the end the North Koreans were back where they started from. Costly in blood and treasure for the American people, the Korean "police action" had demonstrated that the West had lost neither the will nor the capacity to cope with aggressors.

During the Presidential campaign of 1952 President Truman came under a storm of criticism for having acted first, in the Korean crisis, without Congressional approval. In order to forestall further partisan accusations and to convince Communist China of the basic unity of the

American people President Eisenhower asked Congress in 1958 for a resolution approving in advance such military action as he might order in defense of Formosa.

STATEMENT BY THE PRESIDENT [9]

June 27, 1950

In Korea the Government forces, which were armed to prevent border raids and to preserve internal security, were attacked by invading forces from North Korea. The Security Council of the United Nations called upon the invading troops to cease hostilities and to withdraw to the 38th parallel. This they have not done, but on the contrary have pressed the attack. The Security Council called upon all members of the United Nations to render every assistance to the United Nations in the execution of this resolution. In these circumstances I have ordered United States air and sea forces to give the Korean Government troop cover and support.

The attack upon Korea makes it plain beyond all doubt that Communism has passed beyond the use of subversion to conquer independent nations and will now use armed invasion and war. It has defied the orders of the Security Council of the United Nations issued to preserve international peace and security. In these circumstances the occupation of Formosa by Communist forces would be a direct threat to the security of the Pacific area and to United States forces performing their lawful and necessary functions in that area.

Accordingly I have ordered the Seventh Fleet to prevent any attack upon Formosa. As a corollary to this action I am calling upon the Chinese Government on Formosa to cease all air and sea operations against the mainland. The Seventh Fleet will see that this is done. The determination of the future status of Formosa must await the restoration of security in the Pacific, a peace settlement with Japan, or consideration by the United Nations.

I have also directed that United States Forces in the Philippines be strengthened and that military assistance to the Philippine Government be accelerated.

I have similarly directed acceleration in the furnishing of military assistance to the forces of France and the Associated States in Indo-China and the dispatch of a military mission to provide close working relations with those forces.

I know that all members of the United Nations will consider carefully the consequences of this latest aggression in Korea in defiance of the Charter of the United Nations. A return to the rule of force in international affairs would have far-reaching effects. The United States will continue to uphold the rule of law.

I have instructed Ambassador Austin, as the representative of the United States to the Security Council, to report these steps to the Council.

34

THE DECISION
TO CALL FOR UNIVERSAL DISARMAMENT

Eisenhower's "Open Skies" Proposals at Geneva

Late in 1952 the United States exploded the first hydrogen bomb, and not long afterward the experiment was duplicated by the Russians. Soon England demonstrated her nuclear potential, and in the winter of 1960 France set off an atomic explosion in the Sahara Desert. Four nations, with others certain to follow, possessed the total weapon. Of these, both the Soviet Union and the United States had the demonstrated ability to deliver thermonuclear weapons, as the frightening race for missile supremacy culminating in Russia's spectacular moon shot bore witness.

For years the Soviet Union and the West had been engaged in a cold war. At Berlin in 1948, in Korea two years later, then in the Formosa Strait, and at Suez the world seemed on the brink of catastrophe. At any moment an irresponsible or deranged subordinate might trigger the ultimate weapon and create global devastation. War by miscalculation became an omnipresent possibility. For America the margin of safety was no longer months or even weeks, as it had been in previous wars. It was only minutes away. Everywhere people yearned for a lasting peace, and everywhere the atmosphere was increasingly contaminated by radioactive dust and the fall-out of strontium 90.

Again this was a time for decision. The Eisenhower administration had wavered between a policy of instant retaliation with massive force against aggressors—Secretary of State Dulles' "brinkmanship"—and one of seeking to create a climate of peaceful coexistence between the western democracies and the Communist world. As Dulles' approach met sharp criticism at home and still sharper abroad, the idea of coexistence became increasingly popular in the West as well as behind the Iron Curtain. In December, 1953, President Eisenhower publicly appealed for extraordinary measures to save mankind from the holocaust of a hydrogen war. Within a month *Pravda* and *Izvestia* were publishing articles welcoming a disarmament conference which would "contribute to the freeing of mankind from the terror of atomic bombing." Premier Malenkov reinforced these appeals by a public statement opposing the cold war policy and warning that modern methods of warfare meant the ruin of civilization. Later, under Communist Party pressure, he backtracked and stated that atomic war would lead only to the breakdown of the capitalist system. But it is clear that the peoples of the U.S.S.R. were disturbed as deeply as were the peoples of the West.

President Eisenhower kept the initiative. Late in 1954 he declared:

> Let us recognize that we owe it to ourselves and to the world to explore every possible peaceful means of settling differences before we even think of such a thing as war. And the hard way is to have the courage to be patient, tirelessly to seek out every single avenue open to us in the hope even finally of leading the other side to a little better understanding of the honesty of our intentions.

The Conference at the Summit which the Big Four powers staged at Geneva in July, 1955, marked an interruption in the cold war. The high point of the Conference was President Eisenhower's disarmament proposals, made in the speech given here, which came as a complete surprise to the other participants. The President's object was to test by deeds the Soviet's new profession of its desire to outlaw war. Significantly, no Russian leader directly answered the speech at that time. Principal stumbling block to an East-West disarmament agreement was the issue of German unification, which it was no longer entirely within the power of the Big Four to settle.

Eisenhower's speech triggered a long series of disarmament talks by the major powers. Broken off from time to time, but always resumed on some level, these disarmament talks disclosed increasing evidence that the differences between East and West were narrowing. For example, in 1957 the U.S.S.R. accepted in principle the "open skies" proposal for aerial inspection, first presented by President Eisenhower in his speech at Geneva. Although East and West remained deadlocked over details of inspection, or proposals to continue small underground nuclear tests, progress was made, most notably in the suspending unilaterally of nuclear tests by the U.S.S.R., the United States, and Great Britain, initially proposed for the United States by Adlai Stevenson in his Presidential campaign of 1956. At any moment these tests could be resumed, but President Eisenhower's farsighted proposals at Geneva indicated that it was still possible for the world to look upon the face of catastrophe and draw back before it was too late.

Until a genuine disarmament had been achieved America was not letting down her guard. As President Eisenhower declared in a message to Congress of February 16, 1960, in which he referred to his extraordinarily popular eleven-nation good-will tour to Asia, the Middle East, and Europe:

> My recent travels impressed upon me even more strongly the fact that free men everywhere look to us, not with envy or malice but with hope and confidence that we will in the future, as in the past, be in the vanguard of those who believe in and will defend the rights of the individual to enjoy the fruits of his labor in peace and in freedom.

That America had not let down her guard was dramatically demonstrated to the world on the eve of the ill-fated Summit Conference held in Paris in May, 1960. An American U-2 plane used for photographic reconnaissance was brought down over the Soviet Union. President Eisenhower, perhaps unwisely and certainly in defiance of all traditional ways of handling military intelligence incidents, refused to take the conventional way out and deny that the flight had been ordered in Washington. Instead, he accepted full responsibility for the flight and argued that it was necessary to guard against surprise attack.

Leaving out the question of the wisdom of sending a spy plane over the Soviet Union on the eve of the Summit and abstaining from speculation as to whether the miscalculation merely provided Mr. Khrushchev with a pretext for torpedoing the Conference, the fact is that the failure of the Soviets to accept President Eisenhower's "open skies" proposals made at Geneva in 1955 virtually guaranteed that military intelligence activities of the rival powers would be continued if not intensified, and that mutual distrust would corrode any program of peaceful co-existence.

At Paris President Eisenhower informed Chairman Khrushchev that the U-2 flights had been discontinued, and again proposed the establishment of a system of aerial surveillance to be operated by the UN. In a radio and TV address to the nation on May 26, 1960, the President urged that the Western Allies and the Soviet Union continue the nuclear test and disarmament negotiations. "We are not backing away, on account of recent events, from the efforts or commitments that we have undertaken," Eisenhower pledged. "Nor shall we relax our search for new means of reducing the risk of war by miscalculation, and of achieving verifiable arms control." One of America's major goals, he reminded his listeners, is "a world of open societies."

In short, America wants peace, and while maintaining a posture of strength and vigilance will continue to be patient, resourceful, and conciliatory in pursuing this objective. Peace, the elusive goal of twentieth-century man, holds the only answer to survival. As Lincoln might well have put it, "we shall nobly save, or meanly lose, the last best hope of earth."

PRESIDENT EISENHOWER'S ADDRESS [10]

GENEVA, *July 21, 1955*

Disarmament is one of the most important subjects on our agenda. It is also extremely difficult. In recent years the scientists have discovered methods of making weapons many, many times more destructive of opposing armed forces—but also of homes, and industries, and lives —than ever known or imagined before. These same scientific discoveries have made much more complex the problem of limitation and control and reduction of armament.

After our victory as allies in World War II, my country rapidly disarmed. Within a few years our disarmament was at a very low level. Then events occurred which caused us to realize that we had disarmed too much. For our own security and to safeguard peace, we needed greater strength. Therefore we proceeded to rearm and to associate with others in a partnership for peace and for mutual security.

The American people are determined to maintain and, if necessary, increase this armed strength for as long a period as is necessary to safeguard peace and to maintain our security.

But we know that a mutually dependable system for less armament on the part of all nations would be a better way to safeguard peace and to maintain our security.

It would ease the fears of war in the anxious hearts of people everywhere. It would lighten the burdens upon the backs of the people. It would make it possible for every nation, great and small, developed and less developed, to advance the standards of living of its people, to attain better food, and clothing, and shelter, more of education and larger enjoyment of life.

Therefore the United States Government is prepared to enter into a sound and reliable agreement making possible the reduction of armament. I have directed that an intensive and thorough study of this subject be made within our own Government. From these studies, which are continuing, a very important principle is emerging to which I referred in my opening statement on Monday.

No sound and reliable agreement can be made unless it is completely covered by an inspection and reporting system adequate to support every portion of the agreement.

The lessons of history teach us that disarmament agreements without adequate reciprocal inspection increase the danger of war and do not brighten the prospects of peace.

Thus it is my view that the priority attention of our combined study of disarmament should be upon the subjects of inspection and reporting.

Questions themselves:

How effective an inspection system can be designed which would be mutually and reciprocally acceptable within our countries and the other nations of the world? How would such a system operate? What could it accomplish?

Is certainty against surprise aggression attainable by inspection? Could violations be discovered promptly and effectively counteracted?

We have not as yet been able to discover any scientific or other inspection method which would make certain of the elimination of nuclear weapons. So far as we are aware no other nation has made such a discovery. Our study of this problem is continuing. We have not as yet been able to discover any accounting or other inspection method of being certain of the true budgetary facts of total expenditures for armament. Our study of the problem is continuing. We by no means exclude the possibility of finding useful checks in these fields.

As you can see from these statements, it is our impression that many past proposals of disarmament are more sweeping than can be insured by effective inspection.

Gentlemen, since I have been working on this memorandum to present to this conference, I have been searching my heart and mind for something that I could say here that could convince everyone of the great sincerity of the United States in approaching this problem of disarmament.

I should address myself for a moment principally to the delegates from the Soviet Union, because our two great countries admittedly possess new and terrible weapons in quantities which do give rise in other parts of the world, or reciprocally, to the fear and danger of surprise attack.

I propose, therefore, that we take a practical step, that we begin an arrangement very quickly; as between ourselves—immediately. These steps would include:

To give each other a complete blueprint of our military establishments, from beginning to end, from one end of our countries to the other, lay out the establishments and provide the blueprints to each other.

Next, to provide within our countries facilities for aerial photography to the other country—we to provide you the facilities within our country, ample facilities for aerial reconnaissance, where you can make all the pictures you choose and take them to your own country to study, you to provide exactly the same facilities for us and we to make these examinations, and by this step to convince the world that we are providing as between ourselves against the possibility of great surprise attack, thus lessening danger and relaxing tension.

Likewise we will make more easily attainable a comprehensive and effective system of inspection and disarmament, because what I propose, I assure you, would be but a beginning.

Now from my statements I believe you will anticipate my suggestion. It is that we instruct our representatives in the Subcommittee on Disarmament in discharge of their mandate from the United Nations to give priority effort to the study of inspection and reporting. Such a study could well include a step-by-step testing of inspection and reporting methods.

The United States is ready to proceed in the study and testing of a reliable system of inspection and reporting, and when that system is perfected, then to reduce armaments with all other to the extent that the system will provide assured results.

The successful working out of such a system would do much to develop the mutual confidence which will open wide the avenues of progress for all our peoples.

The quest for peace is the statesman's most exacting duty. Security of the nation entrusted to his care is his greatest responsibility. Practical progress in lasting peace is his fondest hope. Yet in pursuit of his hope he must not betray the trust placed in him as guardian of the people's security. A sound peace—with security, justice, well-being, and freedom for the people of the world—can be achieved, but only by patiently and thoughtfully following a hard and sure and tested road.

35

THE DECISION
TO GO TO THE BRINK
OF THERMONUCLEAR WAR

Kennedy Proclaims a Quarantine on Offensive Weapons to Cuba

At quarter of nine on a Tuesday morning, John F. Kennedy, clad in pajamas and a robe, heard the news which was to bring the Soviet Union and the United States to the brink of thermonuclear war.

The most perilous of the many Cold War crises may be said to have commenced two days earlier. On Sunday, October 14, 1962, the cameras of a U-2 plane, flying over Cuba, furnished incontrovertible evidence that Soviet medium-range missiles were already in place on the island and that sites for intermediate-range missiles were rapidly being constructed.

For several years the increasingly close ties between the Soviet Union and Cuba had been one of the sore points in Soviet-American relations. Those ties dated from January 1, 1959, when the Batista dictatorship had been overthrown. In the months that followed, the bearded, verbose, and impetuous Cuban leader, Fidel Castro, initiated a large-scale social revolution which drove into exile the upper and middle classes and expropriated the property of American citizens and business concerns. Earlier promises of free elections and full political freedoms were quickly forgotten. By the end of 1959, the Communist Party was supreme on the island, and the regime's close economic and political ties with the Soviet Union were patent even to the most gullible. After suspending diplomatic relations with Cuba and clamping down a boycott on her sugar, the United States countenanced an invasion of Cuban territory at the Bay of Pigs by Cuban refugees. This proved a ghastly fiasco. By October, 1962, Castro was actively promoting the overthrow of legitimate governments throughout Latin America. A large segment of United States public opinion demanded direct intervention.

Following the discovery of the Soviet missiles and launching pads, Kennedy mobilized the full might of the United States to secure their removal, making a series of decisions in close consultation with a group of some fifteen key persons.* This "War Council," or "Think Tank," hammered out all the alternatives and finally arrived at a general consensus which met with Presidential approval.

With the "Think Tank" hard at work, with increased air surveillance of Cuba, and with the strictest security precautions in force, the President used the five or six days he felt he could count upon to plan his moves. On Thursday the eighteenth, Soviet Foreign Secretary, Andrei A. Gromyko, unaware that the deception had been discovered, stated in the course of a 2¼-hour conversation with the President and the Secretary of State, that Soviet assistance to Cuba was only for defensive purposes. The President did not reveal his hand.

Pleading an alleged cold in the head, the President returned to Washington unexpectedly on Saturday the twentieth, from a campaign trip to Chicago. That afternoon he affirmed the consensus of the advisory group that a naval "blockade" (a term later changed to "quarantine" by the President) was the most acceptable course of action to take. A strong move, it would still leave the Russians time to back away before lives were lost, whereas an air strike might take on the character of another "Pearl Harbor," escalating rapidly into thermonuclear war. The decision was clinched, subject to a final Presidential word the following day.

Troops moved to Florida, ships steamed to the Caribbean, air defenses went on alert. Letters were drafted to the heads of government of forty-three allies, to West Berlin's Mayor Willy Brandt, to all Latin American nations, and the most vital one of all, to Premier Khrushchev.

On Monday the twenty-second the rapid pace continued. At noon,

---

* This group which varied in number during the crisis usually included Vice-President Lyndon B. Johnson; Secretaries Rusk, McNamara and Dillon; Attorney-General Robert Kennedy; Ambassador to the UN Adlai Stevenson; General Maxwell Taylor, the chairman of the Joint Chiefs of Staff; Former Secretary of State Dean Acheson; Under-Secretary of State George W. Ball; Assistant Secretary of State for Inter-American Affairs Edward M. Marin; McGeorge Bundy, the President's Special Assistant for National Security Affairs; Theodore Sorenson, the President's speech-writer and close advisor; and CIA director John A. McCone.

it was announced that the President would make an urgent speech that evening. In Paris, Dean Acheson called on President de Gaulle of France to inform him of the crisis. In Frankfurt, former High Commissioner of Germany, John J. McCloy, in a private business conference, was called home to see the President. At five in the afternoon, the President and Secretary Rusk briefed twenty leaders of Congress, who had been called back to Washington from the campaign trails. At six, Ambassador Anatoly F. Dobrynin of the Soviet Union was informed of the situation by Rusk. At 6:15, forty-six allied ambassadors were briefed. And at seven, the President went before the nation to deliver a speech that had undergone five different drafts.

The next day brought a hostile reaction from *Pravda,* without a clue as to what the response of the U.S.S.R. would be. Messages of support arrived in Washington from all its European allies. The Organization of American States met and approved by a 19-0 vote a resolution which authorized the use of force to effectuate the blockade.* With the support of the OAS assured, the President issued a Proclamation prohibiting as contraband offensive missiles, their warheads, and electronic equipment and bomber aircraft. It authorized the Navy to stop and search any vessel believed to be carrying contraband to Cuba, to take into custody any vessel which failed to obey directions, and to use force "only to the extent necessary."

Forty-eight hours later, twelve of the twenty-five Soviet ships sailing toward Cuba had turned around. A Soviet oil tanker was intercepted and allowed to proceed without search when it was clear that it was only carrying petroleum. At a session of the Security Council, UN Ambassador Adlai E. Stevenson challenged the Soviet representative to deny that his nation had placed the offensive weapons in Cuba. "I am prepared to wait for my answer until hell freezes over," he declared.

Two replies from the Soviet leader arrived at the White House by Saturday morning, one a rambling, ambiguous letter (still secret) which might have been interpreted as an offer to withdraw the weapons under supervision, if the blockade were lifted and the United States gave assurances that Cuba would not be invaded. The second letter was an

---

* With but a single abstention, Uruguay (which had not received intructions).

offer to trade the Cuban bases for NATO missile bases in Turkey. In his reply, President Kennedy chose to construe Khrushchev's first letter as a bona fide offer, which he promptly accepted, at the same time leaving the door open to possible negotiations at a later date about other outstanding issues, including the Turkish bases.

The next morning Moscow Radio broadcast the Soviet reply. The President's assurance that there would be no invasion of Cuba was regarded with "respect and trust"; furthermore, instructions had been issued to "discontinue the construction of . . . the facilities, to dismantle them, and return them to the Soviet Union." Thus, "there is every condition for eliminating the present conflict." The President welcomed Khrushchev's "statesmanlike decision," and the world breathed a sigh of relief.

In the course of time, the missiles were withdrawn, the bases dismantled or destroyed, and the aerial bombers removed. The United States, however, felt obliged to continue surveillance as ground inspection under United Nations supervision was never effectively agreed upon. The blockade was lifted on the twentieth of November, when Khrushchev promised to withdraw Soviet bombers within thirty days. Dean Rusk summed up the confrontation: "We're eyeball to eyeball, and I think the other fellow just blinked."

REPORT TO THE AMERICAN PEOPLE [11]

WASHINGTON, *October 22, 1962*

Good evening, my fellow citizens:

This Government, as promised, has maintained the closest surveillance of the Soviet military buildup on the island of Cuba. Within the past week, unmistakable evidence has established the fact that a series of offensive missile sites is now in preparation on that imprisoned island. The purpose of these bases can be none other than to provide a nuclear strike capability against the Western Hemisphere.

Upon receiving the first preliminary hard information of this nature last Tuesday morning at 9 A.M., I directed that our surveillance be stepped up. And having now confirmed and completed our evaluation of the evidence and our decision on a course of action, this Government feels obliged to report this new crisis to you in fullest detail.

The characteristics of these new missile sites indicate two distinct types of installations. Several of them include medium-range ballistic missiles, capable of carrying a nuclear warhead for a distance of more than 1,000 nautical miles. Each of these missiles, in short, is capable of striking Washington, D.C., the Panama Canal, Cape Canaveral, Mexico City, or any other city in the southeastern part of the United States, in Central America, or in the Caribbean area.

Additional sites not yet completed appear to be designed for intermediate-range ballistic missiles—capable of traveling more than twice as far—and thus capable of striking most of the major cities in the Western Hemisphere, ranging as far north as Hudson Bay, Canada, and as far south as Lima, Peru. In addition, jet bombers, capable of carrying nuclear weapons, are now being uncrated and assembled in Cuba, while the necessary air bases are being prepared.

This urgent transformation of Cuba into an important strategic base —by the presence of these large, long-range, and clearly offensive weapons of sudden mass destruction—constitutes an explicit threat to the peace and security of all the Americas, in flagrant and deliberate defiance of the Rio Pact of 1947, the traditions of this Nation and hemisphere, the joint resolution of the 87th Congress, the Charter of the United Nations, and my own public warnings to the Soviets on September 4 and 13. This action also contradicts the repeated assurances of Soviet spokesmen, both publicly and privately delivered, that the arms buildup in Cuba would retain its original defensive character, and that the Soviet Union had no need or desire to station strategic missiles on the territory of any other nation.

The size of this undertaking makes clear that it has been planned for some months. Yet only last month, after I had made clear the distinction between any introduction of ground-to-ground missiles and the existence of defensive antiaircraft missiles, the Soviet Government publicly stated on September 11 that, and I quote, "the armaments and military equipment sent to Cuba are designed exclusively for defensive purposes," that, and I quote the Soviet Government, "there is no need for the Soviet Government to shift its weapons . . . for a retaliatory blow to any other country, for instance Cuba," and that, and I quote their government, "the Soviet Union has so powerful rockets to carry these nuclear warheads that there is no need to search for sites for them beyond the boundaries of the Soviet Union." That statement was false.

Only last Thursday, as evidence of this rapid offensive buildup was already in my hand, Soviet Foreign Minister Gromyko told me in my office that he was instructed to make it clear once again, as he said his government had already done, that Soviet assistance to Cuba, and I quote, "pursued solely the purpose of contributing to the defense capabilities of Cuba," that, and I quote him, "training by Soviet specialists of Cuban nationals in handling defensive armaments was by no means offensive, and if it were otherwise," Mr. Gromyko went on, "the Soviet Government would never become involved in rendering such assistance." That statement also was false.

Neither the United States of America nor the world community of nations can tolerate deliberate deception and offensive threats on the part of any nation, large or small. We no longer live in a world where only the actual firing of weapons represents a sufficient challenge to a nation's security to constitute maximum peril. Nuclear weapons are so destructive and ballistic missiles are so swift, that any substantially increased possibility of their use or any sudden change in their deployment may well be regarded as a definite threat to peace.

For many years, both the Soviet Union and the United States, recognizing this fact, have deployed strategic nuclear weapons with great care, never upsetting the precarious status quo which insured that these weapons would not be used in the absence of some vital challenge. Our own strategic missiles have never been transferred to the territory of any other nation under a cloak of secrecy and deception; and our history—unlike that of the Soviets since the end of World War II—demonstrates that we have no desire to dominate or conquer any other nation or impose our system upon its people. Nevertheless, American citizens have become adjusted to living daily on the bull's-eye of Soviet missiles located inside the U.S.S.R. or in submarines.

In that sense, missiles in Cuba add to an already clear and present danger—although it should be noted the nations of Latin America have never previously been subjected to a potential nuclear threat.

But this secret, swift, and extraordinary buildup of Communist missiles—in an area well known to have a special and historical relationship to the United States and the nations of the Western Hemisphere, in violation of Soviet assurances, and in defiance of American and hemispheric policy—this sudden, clandestine decision to station strategic weapons for the first time outside of Soviet soil—is a deliberately provocative and unjustified change in the status quo which cannot be accepted by this country, if our courage and our commitments are ever to be trusted again by either friend or foe.

The 1930's taught us a clear lesson: aggressive conduct, if allowed to go unchecked, ultimately leads to war. This nation is opposed to war. We are also true to our word. Our unswerving objective, therefore, must be to prevent the use of these missiles against this or any other country, and to secure their withdrawal or elimination from the Western Hemisphere.

Our policy has been one of patience and restraint, as befits a peaceful and powerful nation, which leads a worldwide alliance. We have been determined not to be diverted from our central concerns by mere irritants and fanatics. But now further action is required—and it is under way; and these actions may only be the beginning. We will not prematurely or unnecessarily risk the costs of worldwide nuclear war in which even the fruits of victory would be ashes in our mouth—but neither will we shrink from that risk at any time it must be faced.

Acting, therefore, in the defense of our own security and of the entire Western Hemisphere, and under the authority entrusted to me by the Constitution as endorsed by the resolution of the Congress, I have directed that the following *initial* steps be taken immediately:

First: To halt this offensive buildup, a strict quarantine on all offensive military equipment under shipment to Cuba is being initiated. All ships of any kind bound for Cuba from whatever nation or port will, if found to contain cargoes of offensive weapons, be turned back. This quarantine will be extended, if needed, to other types of cargo and carriers. We are not at this time, however, denying the necessities of life as the Soviets attempted to do in their Berlin blockade of 1948.

Second: I have directed the continued and increased close surveillance of Cuba and its military buildup. The foreign ministers of the OAS, in their communiqué of October 6, rejected secrecy on such matters in this hemisphere. Should these offensive military preparations continue, thus increasing the threat to the hemisphere, further action will be justified. I have directed the Armed Forces to prepare for any eventualities; and I trust that in the interest of both the Cuban people and the Soviet technicians at the sites, the hazards to all concerned of continuing this threat will be recognized.

Third: It shall be the policy of this Nation to regard any nuclear missile launched from Cuba against any nation in the Western Hemisphere as an attack by the Soviet Union on the United States, requiring a full retaliatory response upon the Soviet Union.

Fourth: As a necessary military precaution, I have reinforced our base at Guantanamo, evacuated today the dependents of our personnel there, and ordered additional military units to be on a standby alert basis.

Fifth: We are calling tonight for an immediate meeting of the Organ of Consultation under the Organization of American States, to consider this threat to hemispheric security and to invoke articles 6 and 8 of the Rio Treaty in support of all necessary action. The United Nations Charter allows for regional security arrangements—and the nations of this hemisphere decided long ago against the military presence of outside powers. Our other allies around the world have also been alerted.

Sixth: Under the Charter of the United Nations, we are asking tonight that an emergency meeting of the Security Council be convoked without delay to take action against this latest Soviet threat to world peace. Our resolution will call for the prompt dismantling and withdrawal of all offensive weapons in Cuba, under the supervision of UN observers, before the quarantine can be lifted.

Seventh and finally: I call upon Chairman Khrushchev to halt and eliminate this clandestine, reckless, and provocative threat to world peace and to stable relations between our two nations. I call upon him further to abandon this course of world domination, and to join in an historic effort to end the perilous arms race and to transform the history of man. He has an opportunity now to move the world back from the abyss of destruction—by returning to his government's own words that it had no need to station missiles outside its own territory, and withdrawing these weapons from Cuba—by refraining from any action which will widen or deepen the present crisis—and then by participating in a search for peaceful and permanent solutions.

This Nation is prepared to present its case against the Soviet threat to peace, and our own proposals for a peaceful world, at any time and in any forum—in the OAS, in the United Nations, or in any other meeting that could be useful—without limiting our freedom of action. We have in the past made strenuous efforts to limit the spread of nuclear weapons. We have proposed the elimination of all arms and military bases in a fair and effective disarmament treaty. We are prepared to discuss new proposals for the removal of tensions on both sides—including the possibilities of a genuinely independent Cuba, free to determine its own destiny. We have no wish to war with the Soviet Union—for we are a peaceful people who desire to live in peace with all other peoples.

But it is difficult to settle or even discuss these problems in an atmosphere of intimidation. That is why this latest Soviet threat—or any other threat which is made either independently or in response to our actions this week—must and will be met with determination. Any hostile move anywhere in the world against the safety and freedom of peoples to whom we are committed—including in particular the brave people of West Berlin—will be met by whatever action is needed.

Finally, I want to say a few words to the captive people of Cuba, to whom this speech is being directly carried by special radio facilities. I speak to you as a friend, as one who knows of your deep attachment to your fatherland, as one who shares your aspirations for liberty and justice for all. And I have watched and the American people have watched with deep sorrow how your nationalist revolution was betrayed—and how your fatherland fell under foreign domination. Now your leaders are no longer Cuban leaders inspired by Cuban ideals. They are puppets and agents of an international conspiracy which has turned Cuba against your friends and neighbors in the Americas—and turned it into the first Latin American country to become a target for nuclear war—the first Latin American country to have these weapons on its soil.

These new weapons are not in your interest. They contribute nothing to your peace and well-being. They can only undermine it. But this country has no wish to cause you to suffer or to impose any system upon you. We know that your lives and land are being used as pawns by those who deny your freedom.

Many times in the past, the Cuban people have risen to throw out tyrants who destroyed their liberty. And I have no doubt that most Cubans today look forward to the time when they will be truly free—free from foreign domination, free to choose their own leaders, free to select their own system, free to own their own land, free to speak and write and worship without fear or degradation. And then shall Cuba be welcomed back to the society of free nations and to the associations of this hemisphere.

My fellow citizens: let no one doubt that this is a difficult and dangerous effort on which we have set out. No one can foresee precisely what course it will take or what costs or casualties will be incurred. Many months of sacrifice and self-discipline lie ahead—months in which both our patience and our will, will be tested—months in which many threats and denunciations will keep us aware of our dangers. But the greatest danger of all would be to do nothing.

The path we have chosen for the present is full of hazards, as all paths are—but it is the one most consistent with our character and courage as a nation and our commitments around the world. The cost of freedom is always high—but Americans have always paid it. And one path we shall never choose, and that is the path of surrender or submission.

Our goal is not the victory of might, but the vindication of right—not peace at the expense of freedom, but both peace *and* freedom, here in this hemisphere, and, we hope, around the world. God willing, that goal will be achieved.

Thank you and good night.

By the President of the United States of America [12]

A PROCLAMATION

Whereas the peace of the world and the security of the United States and of all American states are endangered by reason of the establishment by the Sino-Soviet powers of an offensive military capability in Cuba, including bases for ballistic missiles with a potential range covering most of North and South America;

Whereas by a joint resolution passed by the Congress of the United States and approved on Oct. 3, 1962, it was declared that the United States is determined to prevent by whatever means may be necessary, including the use of arms, the Marxist-Leninist regime in Cuba from extending, by force or the threat of force, its aggressive or subversive activities to any part of this hemisphere, and to prevent in Cuba the creation or use of an externally supported military capability endangering the security of the United States; and

Whereas the Organ of Consultation of the American Republics meeting in Washington on Oct. 23, 1962, recommended that the member states, in accordance with Articles 6 and 8 of the Inter-American Treaty of Reciprocal Assistance, take all measures, individually and collectively, including the use of armed force, which they may deem necessary to insure that the Government of Cuba cannot continue to receive from the Sino-Soviet powers military material and related supplies which may threaten the peace and security of the continent and to prevent the missiles in Cuba with offensive capability from ever becoming an active threat to the peace and security of the continent:

Now, Therefore, I, John F. Kennedy, President of the United States of America, acting under and by virtue of the authority conferred upon me by the Constitution and statutes of the United States, in accordance with the afore-mentioned resolutions of the United States Congress and of the Organ of Consultation of the American Republics, and to defend the security of the United States, do hereby proclaim that the forces under my command are ordered, beginning at 2:00 P.M. Greenwich time Oct. 24, 1962, to interdict, subject to the instructions herein contained, the delivery of offensive weapons and associated material to Cuba.

For the purposes of this proclamation, the following are declared to be prohibited material:

Surface-to-surface missiles; bomber aircraft; bombs; air-to-surface rockets and guided missiles; warheads for any of the above weapons; mechanical or electronic equipment to support or operate the above

421

items; and any other classes of material hereafter designated by the Secretary of Defense for the purpose of effectuating this proclamation.

To enforce this order, the Secretary of Defense shall take appropriate measures to prevent the delivery of prohibited material to Cuba, employing the land, sea and air forces of the United States in cooperation with any forces that may be made available by other American states.

The Secretary of Defense may make such regulations and issue such directives as he deems necessary to insure the effectiveness of this order, including the designation, within a reasonable distance of Cuba of prohibited or restricted zones and of prescribed routes.

Any vessel or craft which may be proceeding toward Cuba may be intercepted and may be directed to identify itself, its cargo, equipment and stores and its ports of call, to stop, to lie to, to submit to visit and search, or to proceed as directed. Any vessel or craft which fails or refuses to respond to or comply with directions shall be subjected to being taken into custody. Any vessel or craft which is believed en route to Cuba and may be carrying prohibited material or may itself constitute such material shall, wherever possible, be directed to proceed to another destination of its own choice and shall be taken into custody if it fails or refuses to obey such directions. All vessels or craft taken into custody shall be sent into a port of the United States for appropriate disposition.

In carrying out this order, force shall not be used except in case of failure or refusal to comply with directions, or with regulations or directives of the Secretary of Defense issued hereunder, after reasonable efforts have been made to communicate them to the vessel or craft, or in case of self-defense. In any case, force shall be used only to the extent necessary.

IN WITNESS WHEREOF, I have hereunto set my hand and caused the seal of the United States of America to be affixed.

Done in the city of Washington this 23d day of October in the year of Our Lord, 1962, and of the independence of the United States of America the 187th.

JOHN F. KENNEDY

By the President:
  DEAN RUSK
    Secretary of State

THE DECISION TO REACH A *Détente* WITH RUSSIA

Kennedy's Speech at American University

The Cuban confrontation served as a catalyst loosening the alliance structures of both major power blocs and alerting both the United States and the Soviet Union to common interests as well as to areas of conflict.

In the first few months following the crisis, the Chinese Communists edged toward a break with the Soviets, setting off a battery of accusations that Khrushchev was an appeaser of the Capitalist West. On the other hand, hopes that closer Western unity might emerge from the crisis were dampened by French President Charles de Gaulle's decision to veto Britain's application for membership in the European Economic Community.

On January 7, 1963, the United States and the Soviet Union joined together in a letter to U Thant announcing the end of the Cuban missile crisis and expressing the hope that the Cuban settlement would lead to the adjustment of other differences and to the general easing of tensions. On April 5 Moscow agreed to the installation of a direct communications link, the "hot-line" between Washington and Moscow, to reduce the threat of accidental war. On the other hand, negotiations for an agreement on a nuclear test ban had broken off in late January despite mounting world opinion against the perils of testing.

President Kennedy chose the occasion of his address at the commencement exercises of American University in Washington on June 10 to reduce the tensions and perils of the Cold War. His speech followed by two days Khrushchev's decision, then secret from the public, to permit high-level three-power talks regarding a nuclear test ban. Kennedy's speech implemented the conciliatory approach preshadowed both by his Inaugural address and his first address at the United Nations. In announcing to the world that high-level discussions would begin soon thereafter in Moscow and that the United States would suspend nuclear tests in the atmosphere so long as other states would also refrain, he revealed two momentous decisions.

Few speeches by an American President were ever greeted with such worldwide acclaim as President Kennedy's address at American University. *Izvestia* published it in full on the twelfth of June, a treatment reserved for very few official American pronouncements. Weeks later, when Soviet-Chinese negotiations in Moscow broke off, Khrushchev appeared willing, for the first time, to countenance a ban on nuclear tests in the atmosphere, in outer space, and under water, but not covering underground testing.

On July 15 negotiations began in Moscow between W. Averell Harriman, Viscount Hailsham, and Soviet Foreign Secretary Andrei Gromyko. On July 20, a tentative agreement was reached. The one stumbling block which arose—a Soviet proposal to link the test ban to a nonaggression pact between NATO and the Warsaw Pact nations—was hurdled when the United States and Great Britain agreed to consider such proposals *after* the Test Ban Treaty was signed. Kennedy hailed the signing of the Treaty on July 25 as "a shaft of light cut into the darkness." By the time the Treaty was ratified by the United States Senate in September, ninety-nine nations, in addition to the "Big Three" (but not including France and Communist China), had subscribed to it.

It is still too early to evaluate the effect of the Treaty on long-range Soviet-American relations, although some of the more outward manifestations of the Cold War are no longer visible. The Treaty was followed by a new cultural exchange agreement between the two nations and a pact opening consulates. Only time would tell how this decision changed the shape of things to come. As President Kennedy observed in his speech hailing the test ban, "According to the ancient Chinese proverb, 'A journey of a thousand miles must begin with a single step.' My fellow Americans, let us take that first step. Let us, if we can, get back from the shadows of war and seek out the way of peace. And if that journey is one thousand miles, or even more, let history record that we, in this land, at this time, took the first step."

ADDRESS AT AMERICAN UNIVERSITY [18]

WASHINGTON, D.C., *June 10, 1963*

"There are few earthly things more beautiful than a University," wrote John Masefield, in his tribute to the English universities—and his words are equally true here. He did not refer to spires and towers, to campus greens and ivied walls. He admired the splendid beauty of the university, he said, because it was "a place where those who hate ignorance may strive to know, where those who perceive truth may strive to make others see."

I have, therefore, chosen this time and this place to discuss a topic on which ignorance too often abounds and the truth is too rarely perceived—yet it is the most important topic on earth: world peace.

What kind of peace do I mean? What kind of peace do we seek? Not a *Pax Americana* enforced on the world by the American weapons of war. Not the peace of the grave or the security of the slave. I am talking about genuine peace, the kind of peace that makes life on earth worth living, the kind that enables men and nations to grow and to hope and to build a better life for their children—not merely peace for Americans but peace for all men and women, not merely peace in our time but peace for all time.

I speak of peace because of the new face of war. Total war makes no sense in an age when great powers can maintain large and relatively invulnerable nuclear forces and refuse to surrender without resort to those forces. It makes no sense in an age when a single nuclear weapon contains almost ten times the explosive force delivered by all of the Allied air forces in the Second World War. It makes no sense in an age when the deadly poisons produced by a nuclear exchange would be carried by the wind and water and soil and seed to the far corners of the globe and to generations yet unborn.

Today the expenditure of billions of dollars every year on weapons acquired for the purpose of making sure we never need to use them is essential to keeping the peace. But surely the acquisition of such idle stockpiles—which can only destroy and never create—is not the only, much less the most efficient, means of assuring peace.

I speak of peace, therefore, as the necessary rational end of rational men. I realize that the pursuit of peace is not as dramatic as the pursuit of war, and frequently the words of the pursuer fall on deaf ears. But we have no more urgent task.

Some say that it is useless to speak of world peace or world law or world disarmament—and that it will be useless until the leaders of the Soviet Union adopt a more enlightened attitude. I hope they do. I believe we can help them do it. But I also believe that we must re-examine our own attitude, as individuals and as a nation, for our attitude is as essential as theirs. And every graduate of this school, every thoughtful citizen who despairs of war and wishes to bring peace, should begin by looking inward—by examining his own attitude toward the possibilities of peace, toward the Soviet Union, toward the course of the cold war, and toward freedom and peace here at home.

First: Let us examine our attitude toward peace itself. Too many of us think it is impossible. Too many think it unreal. But that is a dangerous, defeatist belief. It leads to the conclusion that war is inevitable, that mankind is doomed, that we are gripped by forces we cannot control.

We need not accept that view. Our problems are man-made; therefore they can be solved by man. And man can be as big as he wants. No problem of human destiny is beyond human beings. Man's reason and spirit have often solved the seemingly unsolvable, and we believe they can do it again.

I am not referring to the absolute, infinite concept of universal peace and good will of which some fantasies and fanatics dream. I do not deny the values of hopes and dreams, but we merely invite discouragement and incredulity by making that our only and immediate goal.

Let us focus instead on a more practical, more attainable peace, based not on a sudden revolution in human nature but on a gradual evolution in human institutions—on a series of concrete actions and effective agreements which are in the interest of all concerned. There is no single, simple key to this peace, no grand or magic formula to be adopted by one or two powers. Genuine peace must be the product of many nations, the sum of many acts. It must be dynamic, not static, changing to meet the challenge of each new generation. For peace is a process, a way of solving problems.

With such a peace there will still be quarrels and conflicting interests, as there are within families and nations. World peace, like community peace, does not require that each man love his neighbor; it requires only that they live together in mutual tolerance, submitting their disputes to a just and peaceful settlement. And history teaches us that enmities between nations, as between individuals, do not last forever. However fixed our likes and dislikes may seem, the tide of time and events will often bring surprising changes in the relations between nations and neighbors.

So let us persevere. Peace need not be impracticable, and war need not be inevitable. By defining our goal more clearly, by making it seem more manageable and less remote, we can help all peoples to see it, to draw hope from it, and to move irresistibly toward it.

Second: Let us re-examine our attitude toward the Soviet Union. It is discouraging to think that their leaders may actually believe what their propagandists write. It is discouraging to read a recent authoritative Soviet text on military strategy and find, on page after page, wholly baseless and incredible claims—such as the allegation that "American imperialist circles are preparing to unleash different types of wars . . . that there is a very real threat of a preventive war being unleashed by American imperialists against the Soviet Union . . . [and that] the political aims of the American imperialists are to enslave economically and politically the European and other capitalist countries . . . [and] to achieve world domination . . . by means of aggressive wars."

Truly as it was written long ago: "The wicked flee when no man pursueth." Yet it is sad to read these Soviet statements—to realize the extent of the gulf between us. But it is also a warning—a warning to the American people not to fall into the same trap as the Soviets, not to see only a distorted and desperate view of the other side, not to see conflict as inevitable, accommodation as impossible, and communication as nothing more than an exchange of threats.

No government or social system is so evil that its people must be considered as lacking in virtue. As Americans we find communism profoundly repugnant as a negation of personal freedom and dignity. But we can still hail the Russian people for their many achievements—in science and space, in economic and industrial growth, in culture and in acts of courage.

Among the many traits the peoples of our two countries have in common, none is stronger than our mutual abhorrence of war. Almost unique among the major world powers, we have never been at war with each other. And no nation in the history of battle ever suffered more than the Soviet Union suffered in the course of the Second World War. At least 20 million lost their lives. Countless millions of homes and farms were burned or sacked. A third of the nation's territory, including nearly two-thirds of its industrial base, was turned into a wasteland—a loss equivalent to the devastation of this country east of Chicago.

Today, should total war ever break out again—no matter how—our two countries would become the primary targets. It is an ironical but accurate fact that the two strongest powers are the two in the most danger of devastation. All we have built, all we have worked for, would be destroyed in the first 24 hours. And even in the cold war, which brings burdens and dangers to so many countries—including this nation's closest allies—our two countries bear the heaviest burdens. For we are both devoting massive sums of money to weapons that could be better devoted to combating ignorance, poverty, and disease. We are both caught up in a vicious and dangerous cycle in which suspicion on one side breeds suspicion on the other and new weapons beget counterweapons.

In short, both the United States and its allies, and the Soviet Union and its allies, have a mutually deep interest in a just and genuine peace and in halting the arms race. Agreements to this end are in the interests of the Soviet Union as well as ours, and even the most hostile nations can be relied upon to accept and keep those treaty obligations, and only those treaty obligations, which are in their own interest.

So let us not be blind to our differences, but let us also direct attention to our common interests and to the means by which those differences can be resolved. And if we cannot end now our differences, at least we can help make the world safe for diversity. For in the final analysis our most basic common link is that we all inhabit this planet. We all breathe the same air. We all cherish our children's future. And we are all mortal.

Third: Let us re-examine our attitude toward the cold war, remembering that we are not engaged in a debate, seeking to pile up debating points. We are not here distributing blame or pointing the finger of judgment. We must deal with the world as it is and not as it might have been had the history of the last 18 years been different.

We must, therefore, persevere in the search for peace in the hope that constructive changes within the Communist bloc might bring within reach solutions which now seem beyond us. We must conduct our affairs in such a way that it becomes in the Communists' interest to agree on a genuine peace. Above all, while defending our own vital interests, nuclear powers must avert those confrontations which bring an adversary to a choice of either a humiliating retreat or a nuclear war. To adopt that kind of course in the nuclear age would be evidence only of the bankruptcy of our policy—or of a collective death wish for the world.

To secure these ends, America's weapons are nonprovocative, carefully controlled, designed to deter, and capable of selective use. Our military forces are committed to peace and disciplined in self-restraint. Our diplomats are instructed to avoid unnecessary irritants and purely rhetorical hostility.

For we can seek a relaxation of tensions without relaxing our guard. And, for our part, we do not need to use threats to prove that we are resolute. We do not need to jam foreign broadcasts out of fear our faith will be eroded. We are unwilling to impose our system on any unwilling people, but we are willing and able to engage in peaceful competition with any people on earth.

Meanwhile we seek to strengthen the United Nations, to help solve its financial problems, to make it a more effective instrument of peace, to develop it into a genuine world security system—a system capable of resolving disputes on the basis of law, of insuring the security of the large and the small, and of creating conditions under which arms can finally be abolished.

At the same time we seek to keep peace inside the non-Communist world, where many nations, all of them our friends, are divided over issues which weaken Western unity, which invite Communist intervention, or which threaten to erupt into war. Our efforts in West New Guinea, in the Congo, in the Middle East, and in the Indian subcontinent have been persistent and patient despite criticism from both sides. We have also tried to set an example for others—by seeking to adjust small but significant differences with our own closest neighbors in Mexico and in Canada.

Speaking of other nations, I wish to make one point clear. We are bound to many nations by alliances. Those alliances exist because our concern and theirs substantially overlap. Our commitment to defend Western Europe and West Berlin, for example, stands undiminished because of the identity of our vital interests. The United States will make no deal with the Soviet Union at the expense of other nations and other peoples, not merely because they are our partners but also because their interests and ours converge.

Our interests converge, however, not only in defending the frontiers of freedom but in pursuing the paths of peace. It is our hope—and the purpose of Allied policies—to convince the Soviet Union that she, too, should let each nation choose its own future, so long as that choice does not interfere with the choices of others. The Communist drive to impose their political and economic system on others is the primary cause of world tension today. For there can be no doubt that, if all nations could refrain from interfering in the self-determination of others, the peace would be much more assured.

This will require a new effort to achieve world law, a new context for world discussions. It will require increased understanding between the Soviets and ourselves. And increased understanding will require increased contact and communication. One step in this direction is the proposed arrangement for a direct line between Moscow and Washington, to avoid on each side the dangerous delays, misunderstandings, and misreadings of the other's actions which might occur at a time of crisis.

We have also been talking in Geneva about other first-step measures of arms control, designed to limit the intensity of the arms race and to reduce the risks of accidental war. Our primary long-range interest in Geneva, however, is general and complete disarmament, designed to take place by stages, permitting parallel political developments to build the new institutions of peace which would take the place of arms. The pursuit of disarmament has been an effort of this Government since the 1920's. It has been urgently sought by the past three administrations. And however dim the prospects may be today, we intend to continue this effort—to continue it in order that all countries, including our own, can better grasp what the problems and possibilities of disarmament are.

The one major area of these negotiations where the end is in sight, yet where a fresh start is badly needed, is in a treaty to outlaw nuclear tests. The conclusion of such a treaty—so near and yet so far—would check the spiraling arms race in one of its most dangerous areas. It would place the nuclear powers in a position to deal more effectively with one of the greatest hazards which man faces in 1963, the further spread of nuclear arms. It would increase our security; it would decrease the prospects of war. Surely this goal is sufficiently important to require our steady pursuit, yielding neither to the temptation to give up the whole effort nor to the temptation to give up our insistence on vital and responsible safeguards.

I am taking this opportunity, therefore, to announce two important decisions in this regard.

First: Chairman Khrushchev, Prime Minister Macmillan, and I have agreed that high-level discussions will shortly begin in Moscow looking toward early agreement on a comprehensive test ban treaty. Our hopes must be tempered with the caution of history, but with our hopes go the hopes of all mankind.

Second: To make clear our good faith and solemn convictions on the matter, I now declare that the United States does not propose to conduct nuclear tests in the atmosphere so long as other states do not do so. We will not be the first to resume. Such a declaration is no substitute for a formal binding treaty, but I hope it will help us achieve one. Nor would such a treaty be a substitute for disarmament, but I hope it will help us achieve it.

Finally, my fellow Americans, let us examine our attitude toward peace and freedom here at home. The quality and spirit of our society must justify and support our efforts abroad. We must show it in the dedication of our own lives, as many of you who are graduating today will have a unique opportunity to do, by serving without pay in the Peace Corps abroad or in the proposed National Service Corps here at home.

But wherever we are, we must all, in our daily lives, live up to the age-old faith that peace and freedom walk together. In too many of our cities today the peace is not secure because freedom is incomplete.

It is the responsibility of the executive branch at all levels of government—local, State, and national—to provide and protect that freedom for all of our citizens by all means within their authority. It is the responsibility of the legislative branch at all levels, wherever that authority is not now adequate, to make it adequate. And it is the responsibility of all citizens in all sections of this country to respect the rights of all others and to respect the law of the land.

All this is not unrelated to world peace. "When a man's ways please the Lord," the Scriptures tell us, "he maketh even his enemies to be at peace with him." And is not peace, in the last analysis, basically a matter of human rights—the right to live out our lives without fear of devastation, the right to breathe air as nature provided it, the right of future generations to a healthy existence?

While we proceed to safeguard our national interests, let us also safeguard human interests. And the elimination of war and arms is clearly in the interest of both. No treaty, however much it may be to the advantage of all, however tightly it may be worded, can provide absolute security against the risks of deception and evasion. But it can, if it is sufficiently effective in its enforcement and if it is sufficiently in the interests of its signers, offer far more security and far fewer risks than an unabated, uncontrolled, unpredictable arms race.

The United States, as the world knows, will never start a war. We do not want a war. We do not now expect a war. This generation of Americans has already had enough—more than enough—of war and hate and oppression. We shall be prepared if others wish it. We shall be alert to try to stop it. But we shall also do our part to build a world of peace where the weak are safe and the strong are just. We are not helpless before that task or hopeless of its success. Confident and unafraid, we labor on—not toward a strategy of annihilation but toward a strategy of peace.

36

THE DECISION TO REACH A DETENTE
WITH RUSSIA

Kennedy's Speech at American University

The Cuban confrontation served as a catalyst loosening the alliance structures of both major power blocs and alerting both the United States and the Soviet Union to common interests as well as to areas of conflict.

In the first few months following the crisis the Chinese Communists edged toward a break with the Soviets, setting off a battery of accusations that Khrushchev was an appeaser of the capitalist West. On the other hand, hopes that closer Western unity might emerge from the crisis were dampened by French President Charles de Gaulle's decision to veto Britain's application for membership in the European Economic Community.

On January 7, 1963, the United States and the Soviet Union joined together in a letter to U Thant announcing the end of the Cuban missile crisis and expressing the hope that the Cuban settlement would lead to the adjustment of other differences and to the general easing of tensions. On April 5 Moscow agreed to the installation of a direct communications link, the "hot-line" between Washington and Moscow, to reduce the threat of accidental war. On the other hand, negotiations for an agreement on a nuclear test ban had broken off in late January despite mounting world opinion against the perils of testing.

President Kennedy chose the occasion of his address at the commencement exercises of American University in Washington on June 10 to reduce the tension and perils of the Cold War. His speech followed by two days Khrushchev's decision, then secret from the public, to permit high-level three-power talks regarding a nuclear test ban. Kennedy's speech implemented the conciliatory approach pre-shadowed both by his Inaugural address and his first address at the United Nations. In announcing to the world that high-level discussions would begin soon thereafter in Moscow and that the United States would suspend nuclear tests in the atmosphere so long as other states would also refrain, he made two momentous decisions.

Few speeches by an American President were ever greeted with such world-wide acclaim as President Kennedy's address at American University. *Izvestia* published it in full on the 12th of June, a treatment reserved for very few official American pronouncements. Weeks later, when Soviet-Chinese negotiations in Moscow broke off, Khrushchev appeared willing, for the first time, to countenance a ban on nuclear tests in the atmosphere, in outerspace, and under water, but not covering underground testing.

On July 15 negotiations began in Moscow between W. Averell Harriman, Viscount Hailsham, and Soviet Foreign Secretary Andrei Gromyko. On July 20, a tentative agreement was reached. The one stumbling-block which arose—a Soviet proposal to link the test ban to a non-aggression pact between NATO and the Warsaw Pact nations—was hurdled when the United States and Great Britain agreed to consider such proposals *after* the Test Ban Treaty was signed. Kennedy hailed the signing of the Treaty on July 25th as "a shaft of light out into the darkness." By the time the Treaty was ratified by the United States Senate in September, ninety-nine nations, in addition to the "Big Three" (but not including France and Communist China), had subscribed to it.

It is still too early to evaluate the effect of the Treaty on long-range Soviet-American relations, although some of the more outward manifestations of the Cold War are no longer visible. The Treaty was followed by a new cultural exchange agreement between the two nations and a pact opening consulates. Only time would tell how this decision changed the shape of things to come. As President Kennedy observed in his speech hailing the test ban, "According to the ancient Chinese proverb, 'A journey of a thousand miles must begin with a single step.' My fellow Americans let us take that first step. Let us, if we can, get back from the shadows of war and seek out the way of peace. And if that journey is one thousand miles, or even more, let history record that we, in this land, at this time, took the first step."

ADDRESS AT AMERICAN UNIVERSITY[13]

WASHINGTON, D.C., *June 10, 1963*

"There are few earthly things more beautiful than a University," wrote John Masefield, in his tribute to the English Universities—and his words are equally true here. He did not refer to spires and towers, to campus greens and ivied walls. He admired the splendid beauty of the university, he said, because it was "a place where those who hate ignorance may strive to know, where those who perceive truth strive to make others see."

I have, therefore, chosen this time and this place to discuss a topic on which ignorance too often abounds and the truth is too rarely perceived—yet it is the most important topic on earth: world peace.

What kind of peace do I mean? What kind of peace do we seek? Not a *Pax Americana* enforced on the world by American weapons of war. Not the peace of the grave or the security of the slave. I am talking about genuine peace, the kind of peace that makes life on earth worth living, the kind that enables men and nations to grow and to hope and to build a better life for their children—not merely peace for Americans but peace for all men and women, not merely peace in our time but peace for all time.

I speak of peace because of the new face of war. Total war makes no sense in an age when great powers can maintain large and relatively invulnerable nuclear forces and refuse to surrender without resort to those forces. It makes no sense in an age when a single nuclear weapon contains almost 10 times the explosive force delivered by all of the Allied air forces in the Second World War. It makes no sense in an age when the deadly poisons produced by a nuclear exchange would be carried by the wind and water and soil and seed to the far corners of the globe and to generations yet unborn.

Today the expenditure of billions of dollars every year on weapons acquired for the purpose of making sure we never need to use them is essential to keeping the peace. But surely the acquisition of such idle stockpiles—which can only destroy and never create—is not the only, much less the most efficient, means of assuring peace.

I speak of peace, therefore, as the necessary rational end of rational men. I realize that the pursuit of peace is not as dramatic as the pursuit of war, and frequently the words of the pursuer fall on deaf ears. But we have no more urgent task.

Some say that it is useless to speak of world peace or world law or world disarmament—and that it will be useless until the leaders of the Soviet Union adopt a more enlightened attitude. I hope they do. I believe we can help them do it. But I also believe that we must reexamine our own attitude, as individuals and as a nation, for our attitude is as essential as theirs. And every graduate of this school, every thoughtful citizen who despairs of war and wishes to bring peace, should begin by looking inward—by examining his own attitude toward the possibilities of peace, toward the Soviet Union, toward the course of the cold war, and toward freedom and peace here at home.

First: Let us examine our attitude toward peace itself. Too many of us think it is impossible. Too many think it unreal. But that is a dangerous, defeatist belief. It leads to the conclusion that war is inevitable, that mankind is doomed, that we are gripped by forces we cannot control.

We need not accept that view. Our problems are manmade; therefore they can be solved by man. And man can be as big as he wants. No problem of human destiny is beyond human beings. Man's reason and spirit have often solved the seemingly unsolvable, and we believe they can do it again.

I am not referring to the absolute, infinite concept of universal peace and good will of which some fantasies and fanatics dream. I do not deny the values of hopes and dreams, but we merely invite discouragment and incredulity by making that our only and immediate goal.

Let us focus instead on a more practical, more attainable peace, based not on a sudden revolution in human nature but on a gradual evolution in human institutions—on a series of concrete actions and effective agreements which are in the interest of all concerned. There is no single, simple key to this peace, no grand or magic formula to be adopted by one or two powers. Genuine peace must be the product of many nations, the sum of many acts. It must be dynamic, not static, changing to meet the challenge of each new generation. For peace is a process, a way of solving problems.

With such a peace there will still be quarrels and conflicting interests, as there are within families and nations. World peace, like community peace, does not require that each man love his neighbor; it requires only that they live together in mutual tolerance, submitting their disputes to a just and peaceful settlement. And history teaches us that enmities between nations, as between individuals, do not last forever. However fixed our likes and dislikes may seem, the tide of time and events will often bring surprising changes in the relations between nations and neighbors.

So let us persevere. Peace need not be impracticable, and war need not be inevitable. By defining our goal more clearly, by making it seem more manageable and less remote, we can help all peoples to see it, to draw hope from it, and to move irresistibly toward it.

Second: Let us reexamine our attitude toward the Soviet Union. It is discouraging to think that their leaders may actually believe what their propagandists write. It is discouraging to read a recent authoritative Soviet text on military strategy and find, on page after page, wholly baseless and incredible claims—such as the allegation that "American imperialist circles are preparing to unleash different types of wars . . . that there is a very real threat of a preventive war being unleashed by American imperialists against the Soviet Union . . . [and that] the political aims of the American imperialists are to enslave economically and politically the European and other capitalist countries . . . [and] to achieve world domination . . . by means of aggressive wars."

Truly as it was written long ago: "The wicked flee when no man pursueth." Yet it is sad to read these Soviet statements—to realize the extent of the gulf between us. But it is also a warning—a warning to the American people not to fall into the same trap as the Soviets, not to see only a distorted and desperate view of the other side, not to see conflict as inevitable, accommodation as impossible, and communication as nothing more than an exchange of threats.

No government or social system is so evil that its people must be considered as lacking in virtue. As Americans we find communism profoundly repugnant as a negation of personal freedom and dignity. But we can still hail the Russian people for their many achievements—in science and space, in economic and industrial growth, in culture and in acts of courage.

Among the many traits the people of our two countries have in common, none is stronger than our mutual abhorrence of war. Almost unique among the major world powers, we have never been at war with each other. And no nation in the history of battle ever suffered more than the Soviet Union suffered in the course of the Second World War. At least 20 million lost their lives. Countless millions of homes and farms were burned or sacked. A third of the nation's territory, including nearly two-thirds of its industrial base, was turned into a wasteland—a loss equivalent to the devastation of this country east of Chicago.

Today, should total war ever break out again—no matter how— our two countries would become the primary targets. It is an ironical but accurate fact that the two strongest powers are the two in the most danger of devastation. All we have built, all we have worked for, would be destroyed in the first 24 hours. And even in the cold war, which brings burdens and dangers to so many countries—including this nation's closest allies—our two countries bear the heaviest burdens. For we are both devoting massive sums of money to weapons that could be better devoted to combating ignorance, poverty, and disease. We are both caught up in a vicious and dangerous cycle in which suspicion on one side breeds suspicion on the other and new weapons beget counterweapons.

In short, both the United States and its allies, and the Soviet Union and its allies, have a mutually deep interest in a just and genuine peace and in halting the arms race. Agreements to this end are in the interests of the Soviet Union as well as ours, and even the most hostile nations can be relied upon to accept and keep those treaty obligations, and only those treaty obligations, which are in their own interest.

So let us not be blind to our differences, but let us also direct attention to our common interests and to the means by which those differences can be resolved. And if we cannot end now our differences, at least we can help make the world safe for diversity. For in the final analysis our most basic common link is that we all inhabit this planet. We all breathe the same air. We all cherish our children's future. And we are all mortal.

Third: Let us reexamine our attitude toward the cold war, remembering that we are not engaged in a debate, seeking to pile up debating points. We are not here distributing blame or pointing the finger of judgment. We must deal with the world as it is and not as it might have been had the history of the last 18 years been different.

We must, therefore, persevere in the search for peace in the hope that constructive changes within the Communist bloc might bring within reach solutions which now seem beyond us. We must conduct our affairs in such a way that it becomes in the Communists' interest to agree on a genuine peace. Above, all, while defending our own vital interests, nuclear powers must avert those confrontations which bring an adversary to a choice of either a humiliating retreat or a nuclear war. To adopt that kind of course in the nuclear age would be evidence only of the bankruptcy of our policy—or of a collective death wish for the world.

To secure these ends, America's weapons are nonprovocative, carefully controlled, designed to deter, and capable of selective use. Our military forces are committed to peace and disciplined in self-restraint. Our diplomats are instructed to avoid unnecessary irritants and purely rhetorical hostility.

For we can seek a relaxation of tensions without relaxing our guard. And, for our part, we do not need to use threats to prove that we are resolute. We do not need to jam foreign broadcasts out of fear our faith will be eroded. We are unwilling to impose our system on any unwilling people, but we are willing and able to engage in peaceful competition with any people on earth.

Meanwhile we seek to strengthen the United Nations, to help solve its financial problems, to make it a more effective instrument of peace, to develop it into a genuine world security system—a system capable of resolving disputes on the basis of law, of insuring the security of the large and the small, and of creating conditions under which arms can finally be abolished.

At the same time we seek to keep peace inside the non-Communist world, where many nations, all of them our friends, are divided over issues which weaken Western unity, which invite Communist intervention, or which threaten to erupt into war. Our efforts in West New Guinea, in the Congo, in the Middle East, and in the Indian subcontinent have been persistent and patient despite criticism from both sides. We have also tried to set an example for others—by seeking to adjust small but significant differences with our own closest neighbors in Mexico and in Canada.

Speaking of other nations, I wish to make one point clear. We are bound to many nations by alliances. Those alliances exist because our concern and theirs substantially overlap. Our commitment to defend Western Europe and West Berlin, for example, stands undiminished because of the identity of our vital interests. The United States will make no deal with the Soviet Union at the expense of other nations and other peoples, not merely because they are our partners but also because their interests and ours converge.

Our interests converge, however, not only in defending the frontiers of freedom but in pursuing the paths of peace. It is our hope—and the purpose of Allied policies—to convince the Soviet Union that she, too, should let each nation choose its own future, so long as that choice does not interfere with the choices of others. The Communist drive to impose their political and economic system on others is the primary cause of world tension today. For there can be no doubt that, if all nations could refrain from interfering in the self-determination of others, the peace would be much more assured.

This will require a new effort to achieve world law, a new context for world discussions. It will require increased understanding between the Soviets and ourselves. And increased understanding will require increased contact and communication. One step in this direction is the proposed arrangement for a direct line between Moscow and Washington, to avoid on each side the dangerous delays, misunderstandings, and misreadings of the other's actions which might occur at a time of crisis.

We have also been talking in Geneva about other first-step measures of arms control, designed to limit the intensity of the arms race and to reduce the risks of accidental war. Our primary long-range interest in Geneva, however, is general and complete disarmament, designed to take place by stages, permitting parallel political developments to build the new institutions of peace which would take the place of arms. The pursuit of disarmament has been an effort of this Government since the 1920's. It has been urgently sought by the past three administrations. And however dim the prospects may be today, we intend to continue this effort—to continue it in order that all countries, including our own, can better grasp what the problems and possibilities of disarmament are.

The one major area of these negotiations where the end is in sight, yet where a fresh start is badly needed, is in a treaty to outlaw nuclear tests. The conclusion of such a treaty—so near and yet so far—would check the spiraling arms race in one of its most dangerous areas. It would place the nuclear powers in a position to deal more effectively with one of the greatest hazards which man faces in 1963, the further spread of nuclear arms. It would increase our security; it would decrease the prospects of war. Surely this goal is sufficiently important to require our steady pursuit, yielding neither to the temptation to give up the whole effort nor the temptation to give up our insistence on vital and responsible safeguards.

I am taking this opportunity, therefore, to announce two important decisions in this regard.

First: Chairman Khrushchev, Prime Minister Macmillan, and I have agreed that high-level discussions will shortly begin in Moscow looking toward early agreement on a comprehensive test ban treaty. Our hopes must be tempered with the caution of history, but with our hopes go the hopes of all mankind.

Second: To make clear our good faith and solemn convictions on the matter, I now declare that the United States does not propose to conduct nuclear test in the atmosphere so long as other states do not do so. We will not be the first to resume. Such a declaration is no substitute for a formal binding treaty, but I hope it will help us achieve one. Nor would such a treaty be a substitute for disarmament, but I hope it will help us achieve it.

Finally, my fellow Americans, let us examine our attitude toward peace and freedom here at home. The quality and spirit of our own society must justify and support our efforts abroad. We must show it in the dedication of our own lives, as many of you who are graduating today will have a unique opportunity to do, by serving without pay in the Peace Corps abroad or in the proposed National Service Corps here at home.

But wherever we are, we must all, in our daily lives, live up to the age-old faith that peace and freedom walk together. In too many of our cities today the peace is not secure because freedom is incomplete.

It is the responsibility of the executive branch at all levels of government—local, state, and national—to provide and protect that freedom for all of our citizens by all means within their authority. It is the responsibility of the legislative branch at all levels, wherever that authority is not now adequate, to make it adequate. And it is the responsibility of all citizens in all sections of this country to respect the rights of all others and to respect the law of the land.

All this is not unrelated to world peace. "When a man's ways please the Lord," the Scriptures tell us, "he maketh even his enemies to be at peace with him." And is not peace, in the last analysis, basically a matter of human rights—the right to live out our lives without fear of devastation, the right to breathe air as nature provided it, the right of future generations to a healthy existence?

While we proceed to safeguard our national interests, let us also safeguard human interests. And the elimination of war and arms is clearly in the interest of both. No treaty, however much it may be to the advantage of all, however tightly it may be worded, can provide absolute security against the risks of deception and evasion. But it can, if it is sufficiently effective in its enforcement and if it is sufficiently in the interests of its signers, offer far more security and far fewer risks than an unabated, uncontrolled, unpredictable arms race.

The United States, as the world knows, will never start a war. We do not want a war. We do not now expect a war. This generation of Americans has already had enough—more than enough—of war and hate and oppression. We shall be prepared if others wish it. We shall be alert to try to stop it. But we shall also do our part to build a world of peace where the weak are safe and the strong are just. We are not helpless before that task or hopeless of its success. Confident and unafraid, we labor on—not toward a strategy of annihilation but toward a strategy of peace.

37

THE DECISION TO COMMIT THE PRESIDENCY TO EQUAL RIGHTS FOR ALL

Kennedy Asks for a Public Accommodations Law

Since the end of the Civil War American Presidents had demonstrated considerable reluctance to assume the political risks attendant upon espousing civil rights for the Negro. Nor did the Supreme Court show any special disposition to take up the cause. To the contrary, the Court declared unconstitutional the Civil Rights Bill of 1875, prohibiting discrimination against Negroes in inns, theaters, and public carriers. One President after another stood silent as Jim Crow came into being and became solidified under the weight of Southern state legislation depriving most Negroes in the Deep South of their franchise and segregating public facilities.

True, there were a few expansive gestures by early twentieth-century Presidents, notably Theodore Roosevelt's invitation to Booker Washington to dine at the White House. While Franklin D. Roosevelt enlisted the enthusiastic support of the impoverished Negro voter of the North and the New Deal performed valiant deeds to rescue the Negro of all sections from the dire poverty of the Depression years, comparatively little attention was paid to the evils of discrimination and to the social problems posed by the Negro, in part the result of the enormous increase in the Negro population in the ghetto cities of the North. On the eve of the Second World War FDR did take a first step. He established a Fair Employment Practices Committee to curb discrimination in war production and government employment. Harry Truman went a step further, by attempting to secure the passage of a permanent Fair Employment Practices Commission and an anti-lynching bill, and the President's Committee on Equality of

Treatment and Opportunity in the Armed Services, set up in his administration, brought about desegregation of the armed forces.

It was the Supreme Court in the fifties, notably with *Brown v. Board of Education* and the ensuing cluster of decisions outlawing segregation in schools and public facilities, which stirred the conscience of the nation. While the *Brown* decision did not bring about a change overnight in traditional patterns of Southern segregation, it enormously heartened civil rights groups, some long established, some new, to take positive action. The drama of massive civil disobedience was ushered in at Montgomery, Alabama, where a boycott of segregated buses took place during the Christmas season of 1956, touching off five years of peaceful civil rights demonstrations.

John F. Kennedy came to the Presidency with a shrewd understanding of the role that Negro voters in urban areas had played in swinging the close election of 1960 in his favor. In addition, he was intellectually committed to channeling the power of the Presidency toward achieving equal rights. Faced with narrow majorities in Congress, however, Kennedy found it expedient to limit himself to a series of executive orders which guaranteed equal employment of Negroes by the Federal government and equal use of Federal facilities, and banned discrimination in the sale of federally financed housing. Even the executive order on housing, redeeming a major campaign promise, was not issued until Kennedy had been in office almost two years. In addition, the President and his brother, Attorney General Robert Kennedy, initiated manifold legal suits guaranteeing the right to vote. These suits were undertaken by the Civil Rights Division of the Department of Justice, under the able direction of Assistant Attorney General Burke Marshall and First Assistant John Doar.

It was not until the last year of his Presidency that Kennedy pressed for effective civil rights legislation. Then, aroused by Negro street demonstrations in Birmingham which had been brutally suppressed by white police, the President decided to request legislation from Congress. Kennedy's decision was doubtless reinforced by the public defiance of the Federal government which Governor George C. Wallace of Alabama had exhibited during the proceedings to integrate the University of Alabama. Just one day after his speech at American

University calling for a reexamination by Americans of the cold war, the President declared that he would "ask the Congress of the United States to act, to make a commitment it has not fully made in this century to the proposition that race has no place in American life or law."

A week later Kennedy in a message to Congress asked for legislation guaranteeing the right of all persons to be served in all public facilities, authorizing the Federal government to participate more fully in lawsuits to end segregation, and giving greater protection of the right to vote.

The passage of the bill was the object of the great assemblage of 250,000 on August 28, 1963, at the Lincoln Memorial. Tied up in Congress at the time of the assassination, the bill became a prime object of President Lyndon Johnson's legislative program. The Kennedy proposal became the Civil Rights Law of 1964 in the summer of that year, and a few months later its constitutionality was upheld by the Supreme Court.

RADIO AND TELEVISION REPORT TO THE AMERICAN PEOPLE ON CIVIL RIGHTS[14]

THE WHITE HOUSE, *June 11, 1963*

Good evening, my fellow citizens:

This afternoon, following a series of threats and defiant statements, the presence of Alabama National Guardsmen was required on the University of Alabama to carry out the final and unequivocal order of the United States District Court of the Northern District of Alabama. That order called for the admission of two clearly qualified young Alabama residents who happened to have been born Negro.

That they were admitted peacefully on the campus is due in good measure to the conduct of the students of the University of Alabama, who met their responsibilities in a constructive way.

I hope that every American, regardless of where he lives, will stop and examine his conscience about this and other related incidents. This Nation was founded by men of many nations and backgrounds. It was founded on the principle that all men are created equal, and that the rights of every man are diminished when the rights of one man are threatened.

Today we are committed to a worldwide struggle to promote and protect the rights of all who wish to be free. And when Americans are sent to Viet Nam or West Berlin, we do not ask for whites only. It ought to be possible, therefore, for American students of any color to attend any public institution they select without having to be backed up by troops.

It ought to be possible for American consumers of any color to receive equal service in places of public accommodation, such as hotels and restaurants and theaters and retail stores, without being forced to resort to demonstrations in the street, and it ought to be possible for American citizens of any color to register and to vote in a free election without interference or fear of reprisal.

It ought to be possible, in short, for every American to enjoy the privileges of being American without regard to his race or his color. In short, every American ought to have the right to be treated as he would wish to be treated, as one would wish his children to be treated. But this is not the case.

The Negro baby born in America today, regardless of the section of the Nation in which he is born, has about one-half as much chance of completing a high school as a white baby born in the same place on the same day, one-third as much chance of completing college, one-third as much chance of becoming a professional man, twice as much chance of becoming unemployed, about one-seventh as much chance of earning $10,000 a year, a life expectancy which is seven years shorter, and the prospects of earning only half as much.

This is not a sectional issue. Difficulties over segregation and discrimination exist in every city, in every state of the Union, producing in many cities a rising tide of discontent that threatens the public safety. Nor is this a partisan issue. In a time of domestic crisis men of good will and generosity should be able to unite regardless of party or politics. This is not even a legal or legislative issue alone. It is better to settle these matters in the courts than on the streets, and new laws are needed at every level, but law alone cannot make men see right.

We are confronted primarily with a moral issue. It is as old as the Scriptures and is as clear as the American Constitution.

The heart of the question is whether all Americans are to be afforded equal rights and equal opportunities, whether we are going to treat our fellow Americans as we want to be treated. If an American, because his skin is dark, cannot eat lunch in a restaurant open to the public, if he cannot send his children to the best public school available, if he cannot vote for the public officials who represent him, if, in short, he cannot enjoy the full and free life which all of us want, then who among us would be content to have the color of his skin changed and stand in his place? Who among us would then be content with the counsels of patience and delay?

One hundred years of delay have passed since President Lincoln freed the slaves, yet their heirs, their grandsons, are not fully free. They are not yet freed from the bonds of injustice. They are not yet freed from social and economic oppression. And this Nation, for all its hopes and all its boasts, will not be fully free until all its citizens are free.

We preach freedom around the world, and we mean it, and we cherish our freedom here at home, but are we to say to the world, and much more importantly, to each other that this is a land of the free except for the Negroes; that we have no second-class citizens except Negroes; that we have no class or caste system, no ghettos, no master race except with respect to Negroes?

Now the time has come for this Nation to fulfill its promise. The events in Birmingham and elsewhere have so increased the cries for equality that no city or State or legislative body can prudently choose to ignore them.

The fires of frustration and discord are burning in every city, North and South, where legal remedies are not at hand. Redress is sought in the streets, in demonstrations, parades, and protests which create tensions and threaten violence and threaten lives.

We face, therefore, a moral crisis as a country and as a people. It cannot be met by repressive police action. It cannot be left to increased demonstrations in the streets. It cannot be quieted by token moves or talk. It is a time to act in the Congress, in your state and local legislative body and, above all, in all of our daily lives.

It is not enough to pin the blame on others, to say this is a problem of one section of the country or another, or deplore the fact that we face. A great change is at hand, and our task, our obligation, is to make that revolution, that change, peaceful and constructive for all.

Those who do nothing are inviting shame as well as violence. Those who act boldly are recognizing right as well as reality.

Next week I shall ask the Congress of the United States to act, to make a commitment it has not fully made in this century to the proposition that race has no place in American life or law. The Federal judiciary has upheld that proposition in a series of forthright cases. The executive branch has adopted that proposition in the conduct of its affairs, including the employment of Federal personnel,

445

the use of Federal facilities, and the sale of federally financed housing.

But there are other necessary measures which only the Congress can provide, and they must be provided at this session. The old code of equity law under which we live commands for every wrong a remedy, but in too many communities, in too many parts of the country, wrongs are inflicted on Negro citizens and there are no remedies at law. Unless the Congress acts, their only remedy is in the streets.

I am, therefore, asking the Congress to enact legislation giving all Americans the right to be served in facilities which are open to the public—hotels, restaurants, theaters, retail stores, and similar establishments.

This seems to me to be an elementary right. Its denial is an arbitrary indignity that no American in 1963 should have to endure, but many do.

I have recently met with scores of business leaders urging them to take voluntary action to end this discrimination and I have been encouraged by their response, and in the last two weeks over 75 cities have seen progress made in desegregating these kinds of facilities. But many are unwilling to act alone, and for this reason, nationwide legislation is needed if we are to move this problem from the streets to the courts.

I am also asking Congress to authorize the Federal government to participate more fully in lawsuits designed to end segregation in public education. We have succeeded in persuading many districts to desegregate voluntarily. Dozens have admitted Negroes without violence. Today a Negro is attending a state-supported institution in every one of our 50 states, but the pace is very slow.

Too many Negro children entering segregated grade schools at the time of the Supreme Court's decision nine years ago will enter segregated high schools this fall, having suffered a loss which can never be restored. The lack of an adequate education denies the Negro a chance to get a decent job.

The orderly implementation of the Supreme Court decision, therefore, cannot be left solely to those who may not have the economic resources to carry the legal action or who may be subject to harassment.

Other features will be also requested, including greater protection for the right to vote. But legislation, I repeat, cannot solve this problem alone. It must be solved in the homes of every American in every community across our country.

In this respect, I want to pay tribute to those citizens North and

South who have been working in their communities to make life better for all. They are acting not out of a sense of legal duty but out of a sense of human decency.

Like our soldiers and sailors in all parts of the world they are meeting freedom's challenge on the firing line, and I salute them for their honor and their courage.

My fellow Americans, this is a problem which faces us all—in every city of the North as well as the South. Today there are Negroes unemployed, two or three times as many compared to whites, inadequate in education, moving into the large cities, unable to find work, young people particularly out of work without hope, denied equal rights, denied the opportunity to eat at a restaurant or lunch counter or go to a movie theater, denied the right to a decent education, denied almost today the right to attend a state university even though qualified. It seems to me that these are matters which concern us all, not merely Presidents or Congressmen or Governors, but every citizen of the United States.

This is one country. It has become one country because all of us and all the people who came here had an equal chance to develop their talents.

We cannot say to 10 per cent of the population that you can't have that right; that your children can't have the chance to develop whatever talents they have; that the only way that they are going to get their rights is to go into the streets and demonstrate. I think we owe them and we owe ourselves a better country than that.

Therefore, I am asking for your help in making it easier for us to move ahead and to provide the kind of equality of treatment which we would want ourselves; to give a chance for every child to be educated to the limit of his talents.

As I have said before, not every child has an equal talent or an equal ability or an equal motivation, but they should have the equal right to develop their talent and their ability and their motivation, to make something of themselves.

We have a right to expect that the Negro community will be responsible, will uphold the law, but they have a right to expect that the law will be fair, that the Constitution will be color blind, as Justice Harlan said at the turn of the century.

This is what we are talking about and this is a matter which concerns this country and what it stands for, and in meeting it I ask the support of all our citizens.

Thank you very much.

38

THE DECISION TO FIGHT A LAND WAR IN ASIA

Johnson Commits American Military Power to Vietnam

The decision to fight a major land war in Southeast Asia was not made in one dramatic moment, as was the case with President Truman's decision to fight in Korea. Rather, the military commitment of the United States resulted from a whole series of small steps taken to plug up a deteriorating situation in South Vietnam.

Saving Vietnam from the Communists never rated a high priority in the military thinking of either the Eisenhower or Kennedy administration. Vietnam in those years represented merely one of a great many fronts where communism was being contained. Although verbal professions of support accompanied by considerable sums of cash were directed toward South Vietnam, only a relative handful of American officers and technicians had been despatched to that area to serve as technical advisors by the end of the Eisenhower administration. In short, in the years dominated by crises at Suez, Lebanon, Berlin, Cuba, and the Congo, Vietnam was never more than of peripheral importance.

Following his meeting in 1961 with Chairman Krushchev in Vienna, President Kennedy showed more concern for so-called "wars of liberation" launched by Communist groups in various parts of the world. The United States stepped up its training for guerrilla war, and by the end of 1961 some 2,000 American military advisors and technicians had arrived in Vietnam. In 1962 the United States contingent in Southeast Asia was augmented, reflecting growing American concern over the civil war in Laos, but the success of the regime of the neutralist Souvanna Phouma temporarily quieted fears.

During the final year of the Kennedy administration, conditions in

South Vietnam deteriorated rapidly. Money and supplies in large amounts contributed by the United States vanished into thin air; desertions among the South Vietnamese troops mounted; dissension in the government and among the people was rife. Following months of demonstrations, in the course of which a number of Buddhist monks set themselves afire in protest against the regime, Premier Ngo Dinh Diem was deposed by a military coup and murdered. The succeeding regimes proved even less stable and competent.

Lyndon B. Johnson inherited these problems when he assumed the Presidency, and during his first months in office he rather cautiously increased the amount of American aid and manpower committed to South Vietnam. American involvement in Southeast Asia underwent a dramatic change during the latter part of 1964 and in the following years. In August of 1964 when United States destroyers were attacked by PT boats in the Gulf of Tonkin, the President authorized Navy commanders to reply and destroy all attackers. The Presidential request that Congress make it clear "that our Government is united in its determination to take all necessary measures in support of freedom and in defense of peace in Southeast Asia" was honored by Congress the next week by the passage of a joint resolution affirming the American commitment. It is this resolution upon which the President based his later decision to escalate the military commitment.

In 1966 the calendar of escalation took on special urgency. On February 7th of that year the President authorized 49 carrier planes to bomb and strafe the barracks and staging areas held by guerrillas in Donghoi as a reprisal for the attack on the helicopter base at Pleiku. A month later, on the 6th of March, 3,500 marines arrived to bolster the security of the Danang Air Base. On the 28th of July, the President announced he had ordered 50,000 more men to Vietnam and that there would be an increase in the draft to cope with the situation. Regardless of the long-range implications of the intervention in South Vietnam, an intervention which raises moral as well as political questions, and regardless of the sharp division of American opinion over the merits of the case for intervention, the United States had by the closing months of 1966 made a major military and fiscal commitment to maintain the stability of Southeast Asia.

STATEMENT BY THE PRESIDENT UPON INSTRUCTING THE NAVY TO TAKE RETALIATORY ACTION IN THE GULF OF TONKIN[15]

August 3, 1964

I have instructed the Navy

(1) to continue the patrols in the Gulf of Tonkin off the coast of North Vietnam.

(2) to double the force by adding an additional destroyer to the one already on patrol,

(3) to provide a combat air patrol over the destroyers, and

(4) to issue orders to the commanders of the combat aircraft and the two destroyers *(a)* to attack any force which attacks them in international waters, and *(b)* to attack with the objective not only of driving off the force but of destroying it.*

RADIO AND TELEVISION REPORT TO THE AMERICAN PEOPLE FOLLOWING RENEWED AGGRESSION IN THE GULF OF TONKIN[16]

August 4, 1964

My fellow Americans:

As President and Commander in Chief, it is my duty to the American people to report that renewed hostile actions against United States ships on the high seas in the Gulf of Tonkin have today required me to order the military forces of the United States to take action in reply.

The initial attack on the destroyer *Maddox,* on August 2, was repeated today by a number of hostile vessels attacking two U.S. destroyers with torpedoes. The destroyers and supporting aircraft acted at once on the orders I gave after the initial act of aggression. We believe at least two of the attacking boats were sunk. There were no U.S. losses.

The performance of commanders and crews in this engagement is in the highest tradition of the United States Navy. But repeated acts of violence against the armed forces of the United States must be met

*The statement was issued following an attack on the U.S. destroyer *Maddox* by Communist PT boats as it patrolled the Gulf of Tonkin.

not only with alert defense, but with positive reply. That reply is being given as I speak to you tonight. Air action is now in execution against gunboats and certain supporting facilities in North Vietnam which have been used in these hostile operations.

In the larger sense this new act of aggression, aimed directly at our own forces, again brings home to all of us in the United States the importance of the struggle for peace and security in Southeast Asia. Aggression by terror against the peaceful villagers of South Vietnam has now been joined by open aggression on the high seas against the United States of America.

The determination of all Americans to carry out our full commitment to the people and to the government of South Vietnam will be redoubled by this outrage. Yet our response, for the present, will be limited and fitting. We Americans know, although others appear to forget, the risks of spreading conflict. We still seek no wider war.

I have instructed the Secretary of State to make this position totally clear to friends and to adversaries and, indeed, to all. I have instructed Ambassador Stevenson to raise this matter immediately and urgently before the Security Council of the United Nations. Finally, I have today met with the leaders of both parties in the Congress of the United States and I have informed them that I shall immediately request the Congress to pass a resolution making it clear that our Government is united in its determination to take all necessary measures in support of freedom and in defense of peace in Southeast Asia.

I have been given encouraging assurance by these leaders of both parties that such a resolution will be promptly introduced, freely and expeditiously debated, and passed with overwhelming support. And just a few minutes ago I was able to reach Senator Goldwater and I am glad to say that he has expressed his support of the statement that I am making to you tonight.

It is a solemn responsibility to have to order even limited military action by forces whose over-all strength is as vast and as awesome as those of the United States of America, but it is my considered conviction, shared throughout your Government, that firmness in the right is indispensable today for peace; that firmness will always be measured. Its mission is peace.

TRANSCRIPT OF THE PRESIDENT'S STATEMENT AT THE WHITE HOUSE NEWS CONFERENCE[17]

July 29, 1965

My fellow Americans. Not along ago, I received a letter from a woman in the Midwest. She wrote:

Dear Mr. President,
In my humble way I am writing to you about the crisis in Vietnam. My husband served in World War II. Our country was at war. But now, this time, it's something that I don't understand. Why?

Well, I've tried to answer that question dozens of times and more in practically every state in this Union. I have discussed it fully in Baltimore in April, in Washington in May, in San Francisco in June. And let me again now discuss it here in the East Room of the White House.

Why must young Americans, born into a land exultant and with hope and with golden promise, toil and suffer and sometimes die in such a remote and distant place?

The answer, like the war itself, is not an easy one. But it echoes clearly from the painful lessons of half a century.

Three times in my lifetime—in two world wars and in Korea—Americans have gone to far lands to fight for freedom. We have learned at a terrible and a brutal cost that retreat does not bring safety, and weakness does not bring peace.

And it is this lesson that has brought us to Vietnam.

This is a different kind of war. There are no marching armies or solemn declarations. Some citizens of South Vietnam, at times with understandable grievances, have joined in the attack on their Government.

But we must not let this mask the central fact that this is really war. It is guided by North Vietnam and it is spurred by Communist China. Its goal is to conquer the south, to defeat American power and to extend the Asiatic dominion of communism.

And there are great stakes in the balance.

Most of the non-Communist nations of Asia cannot, by themselves and alone, resist the growing might and the grasping ambition of Asian communism.

Our power therefore is a very vital shield. If we are driven from the field in Vietnam, then no nation can ever again have the same confidence in American promise or in American protection.

In each land, the forces of independence would be considerably weakened, and an Asia so threatened by Communist domination would certainly imperil the security of the United States itself.

We did not choose to be the guardians at the gate, but there is no one else. Nor would surrender in Vietnam bring peace, because we learned from Hitler at Munich that success only feeds the appetite of aggression. The battle would be renewed in one country, and then another country, bringing with it perhaps even larger and cruder conflict, as we have learned from the lessons of history.

Moreover, we are in Vietnam to fulfill one of the most solemn pledges of the American nation. Three Presidents—President Eisenhower, President Kennedy and your present President—over eleven years have committed themselves and have promised to help defend this small and valiant nation.

Strengthened by that promise, the people of South Vietnam have fought for many long years. Thousands of them have died. Thousands have been crippled and scarred by war. And we just cannot now dishonor our word, or abandon our commitment, or leave those who believed us and who trusted us to the terror and repression and murder that would follow.

This, then, my fellow Americans, is why we are in Vietnam.

What are our goals in that war-stained land?

First, we intend to convince the Communists that we cannot be defeated by force of arms or by superior power. They are not easily convinced. In recent months they have greatly increased their fighting forces and their attacks and the numbers of incidents.

I have asked the commanding general, General Westmoreland, what more he needs to meet this mounting aggression. He has told me. And we will meet his needs.

I have today ordered to Vietnam the Airmobile Division and certain other forces which will raise our fighting strength from 75,000 to 125,000 men almost immediately. Additional forces will be needed later and they will be sent as requested.

This will make it necessary to increase our active fighting forces by raising the monthly draft call from 17,000 over a period of time to 35,000 per month and for us to step up our campaign for voluntary enlistments.

After this past week of deliberations, I have concluded that it is not essential to order Reserve units into service now. If that necessity should later be indicated, I will give the matter most careful consideration and I will give the country due and adequate notice before taking such action, but only after full preparations.

We have also discussed with the Government of South Vietnam

lately the steps that will—we will take to substantially increase their own effort, both on the battlefield and toward reform and progress in the villages. Ambassador Lodge is now formulating a new program to be tested upon his return to that area.

I have directed Secretary Rusk and Secretary McNamara to be available immediately to the Congress to review with these committees—the appropriate Congressional committees—what we plan to do in these areas. I have asked them to be able to answer the questions of any member of Congress.

And Secretary McNamara, in addition, will ask the Senate Appropriations Committee to add a limited amount to present legislation to help meet part of this new cost until a supplemental measure is ready and hearings can be held when the Congress assembles in January. In the meantime, we will use the authority contained in the present defense appropriation bill under consideration to transfer funds in addition to the additional money that we will ask.

These steps, like our actions in the past, are carefully measured to do what must be done to bring an end to aggression and a peaceful settlement.

We do not want an expanding struggle with consequences that no one can foresee, nor will we bluster or bully or flaunt our power. But we will not surrender, and we will not retreat.

For behind our American pledge lies the determination and resources, I believe, of all of the American nation.

Second, once the Communists know, as we know, that a violent solution is impossible, then a peaceful solution is inevitable. We are ready now, as we have always been, to move from the battlefield to the conference table.

I have stated publicly and many times, again and again, America's willingness to begin unconditional discussions with any Government at any place at any time.

Fifteen efforts have been made to start these discussions, with the help of forty nations throughout the world. But there has been no answer. But we are going to continue to persist, if persist we must, until death and desolation have led to the same conference table where others could now join us at a much smaller cost.

I have spoken many times of our objectives in Vietnam. So has the Government of South Vietnam. Hanoi has set forth its own proposals. We are ready to discuss their proposals and our proposals and any proposals of any Government whose people may be affected, for we fear the meeting room no more than we fear the battlefield. And in this pursuit we welcome and we ask for the concern and the assistance of any nation and all nations.

•And if the United Nations and its officials or any one of its 114 members can by deed or word, private initiative or public action, bring us nearer an honorable peace, then they will have the support and gratitude of the United States of America.

I've directed Ambassador Goldberg to go to New York today and to present immediately to Secretary General U Thant a letter from me requesting that all the resources and the energy and the immense prestige of the United Nations be employed to find ways to halt aggression and to bring peace in Vietnam.

I made a similar request at San Francisco a few weeks ago because we do not seek the destruction of any Government nor do we covet a foot of any territory. But we insist and we will always insist that the people of South Vietnam shall have the right of choice, the right to shape their own destiny in free elections in the south or throughout all Vietnam under international supervision, and they shall not have any Government imposed upon them by force and terror so long as we can prevent it.

This was the purpose of the 1954 agreements which the Communists have now cruelly shattered. And if the machinery of those agreements was tragically weak, its purposes still guide our action. And as battle rages we will continue as best we can to help the good people of South Vietnam enrich the condition of their life, to feed the hungry, and to tend the sick, and teach the young, and shelter the homeless and help the farmer to increase his crops and the worker to find a job.

It is an ancient but still terrible irony that while many leaders of men create division in pursuit of grand ambitions, the children of men are really united in the simple, elusive desire for a life of fruitful and rewarding toil.

As I said at Johns Hopkins in Baltimore, I hope that one day we can help all the people of Asia toward that desire—and Eugene Black has made great progress since my appearance in Baltimore in that direction—not as the price of peace, for we are ready always to bear a more painful cost, but rather as a part of our obligations of justice toward our fellow man.

And let me also add now a personal note. I do not find it easy to send the flower of our youth, our finest young men, into battle. I have spoken to you today of the divisions and the forces and the battalions and the units but I know them all, every one. I have seen them in a thousand streets of a hundred towns in every state in this Union— working and laughing and building and filled with hope and life. And I think I know, too, how their mothers weep and how their families sorrow.

And this is the most agonizing and the most painful duty of your President.

And there is something else, too. When I was young, poverty was so common that we didn't know it had a name. An education was something you had to fight for, and water was really life itself. I have now been in public life for thirty-five years, more than three decades, and in each of those thirty-five years I have seen good men and wise leaders struggle to bring the blessings of this land to all of our people.

And now I am the President. It is now my opportunity to help every child get an education, to help every Negro and every American citizen have an equal opportunity, to help every family get a decent home, and to help bring healing to the sick and dignity to the old.

As I have said before, that is what I've lived for, that's what I've wanted all my life since I was a little boy, and I do not want to see all those hopes and all those dreams of so many people for so many years now drowned in the wasteful ravages of cruel wars. And I'm going to do all I can do to see that that never happens.

But I also know, as a realistic public servant, that as long as there are men who hate and destroy we must have the courage to resist or we'll see it all—all that we have built, all that we hope to build, all of our dreams for freedom—all will be swept away on the flood of conquest.

So, too, this shall not happen. We will stand in Vietnam.

39

THE DECISION TO BRING AN END
TO THE VIETNAM WAR

*Reversing Course, Johnson Decides Not to Seek Reelection, Leaving
to His Successor, Richard M. Nixon, the Task of Making Peace in
Southeast Asia*

Time alone can tell what if anything was gained by America's
commitment to a land war in Vietnam. Most protracted in duration,
one of the most inconclusive militarily, the war helped fuel the fires
of domestic discontent and inflation. The war ended the Presidential
career of Lyndon B. Johnson, while winding down the military
intervention proved a major preoccupation of President Richard M.
Nixon's first term and its concluding phases, the initial period of his
second term. Its conduct had worldwide repercussions. It tarnished
America's image as a peace-loving nation, and triggered a great
debate in Congress over the allocation of war powers under the
Constitution.

Never since the Second War with Great Britain in 1812 (the
American Civil War excepted), had the United States been so sharply
divided over the merits of a war. The barrage of criticism against
intervention in Vietnam reached a crescendo by March 1968. The
Têt offensive launched by Vietcong and North Vietnamese forces on
January 30 of that year provided dramatic evidence that, even after
the commitment of 520,000 American troops and three years of
intensive aerial bombardment, a clear-cut victory was impossible of
attainment without major escalation, with all the inherent perils of
triggering World War III.

Within the Johnson administration the Têt offensive spurred a
reappraisal of military strategy and tactics, initiated by the new
Secretary of Defense Clark M. Clifford, formerly a strong supporter

of the involvement. Clifford privately counseled the President to suspend the bombing, resist the army chiefs' request for an additional 200,000 troops, and to negotiate peace. Compounding President Johnson's dilemma was the rising criticism from liberal Senators within his own party. It appeared that Senator Eugene F. McCarthy's seemingly quixotic primary campaign for the Presidency was strengthened by the relatively strong showing he made in the New Hampshire primary on March 12. Four days later Senator Robert F. Kennedy announced that he would also seek the Democratic Presidential nomination. Now the forces opposed to Johnson's renomination had a charismatic leader bearing a prestigious name.

President Johnson kept his own counsel. On March 31, over nationwide TV he announced that he had ordered an end to much of the bombing of North Vietnam, coupling his announcement with a plea for immediate negotiations. At the end of his speech, Johnson dramatically removed himself from the 1968 campaign.

RADIO AND TELEVISION ADDRESS TO THE NATION ON THE VIETNAM WAR

Washington, D. C., *March 31, 1968*

Good evening, my fellow Americans. Tonight I want to speak to you of peace in Vietnam and Southeast Asia. No other question so preoccupies our people. No other dream so absorbs the 250 million human beings who live in that part of the world. No other goal motivates American policy in Southeast Asia.

For years, representatives of our Government and others have traveled the world seeking to find a basis for peace talks.

Since last September they have carried the offer that I made public at San Antonio. And that offer was this:

That the United States would stop its bombardment of North Vietnam when that would lead promptly to productive discussions—and that we would assume that North Vietnam would not take military advantage of our restraint.

Hanoi denounced this offer, both privately and publicly. Even while the search for peace was going on, North Vietnam rushed their preparations for a savage assault on the people, the Government and the allies of South Vietnam.

Their attack—during the Têt holidays—failed to achieve its principal objectives.

It did not collapse the elected Government of South Vietnam or shatter its army—as the Communists had hoped. It did not produce a "general uprising" among the people of the cities, as they had predicted.

The Communists were unable to maintain control of any of the more than 30 cities that they attacked, and they took very heavy casualties.

But they did compel the South Vietnamese and their allies to move certain forces from the countryside into the cities.

They caused widespread disruption and suffering. Their attacks, and the battles that followed, made refugees of half a million human beings.

The Communists may renew their attack any day. They are, it appears, trying to make 1968 the year of decision in South Vietnam— the year that brings, if not final victory or defeat, at least a turning point in the struggle.

This much is clear: If they do mount another round of heavy attacks, they will not succeed in destroying the fighting power of South Vietnam and its allies.

But tragically, this is also clear: Many men—on both sides of the struggle—will be lost. A nation that has already suffered 20 years of warfare will suffer once again. Armies on both sides will take new casualties. And the war will go on.

There is no need for this to be so. There is no need to delay the talks that could bring an end to this long and this bloody war.

Tonight, I renew the offer I made last August: to stop the bambardment of North Vietnam. We ask that talks begin promptly, that they be serious talks on the substance of peace. We assume that during those talks Hanoi will not take advantage of our restraint.

We are prepared to move immediately toward peace through negotiations. So tonight, in the hope that this action will lead to early talks, I am taking the first step to de-escalate the conflict. We are reducing—substantially reducing—the present level of hostilities, and we are doing so unilaterally and at once.

Tonight I have ordered our aircraft and our naval vessels to make no attacks on North Vietnam except in the area north of the demilitarized zone where the continuing enemy build-up directly threatens allied forward positions and where the movement of their troops and supplies are clearly related to that threat.

The area in which we are stopping out attacks includes almost 90 per cent of North Vietnam's population, and most of its territory. Thus there will be no attacks around the principal populated areas, or in the food-producing areas of North Vietnam.

Even this very limited bombing of the North could come to an early end—if our restraint is matched by restraint in Hanoi. But I cannot in good conscience stop all bombing so long as to do so would immediately and directly endanger the lives of our men and our allies. Whether a complete bombing halt becomes possible in the future will be determined by events.

Our purpose in this action is to bring about a reduction in the level of violence that now exists. It is to save the lives of brave men—and to save the lives of innocent women and children. It is to permit the contending forces to move closer to a political settlement.

And tonight I call upon the United Kingdom and I call upon the Soviet Union—as co-chairmen of the Geneva conferences and as permanent members of the United Nations Security Council—to do all they can to move from the unilateral act of de-escalation that I have just announced toward genuine peace in Southeast Asia.

Now, as in the past, the United States is ready to send its representatives to any forum, at any time, to discuss the means of bringing this ugly war to an end.

I am designating one of our most distinguished Americans, Ambassador Averell Harriman, as my personal representative for such talks. In addition, I have asked Ambassador Llewellyn Thompson, who returned from Moscow for consultation, to be available to join Ambassador Harriman at Geneva or any other suitable place—just as soon as Hanoi agrees to a conference.

I call upon President Ho Chi Minh to respond positively, and favorably, to the new step toward peace.

But if peace does not come now through negotiations, it will come when Hanoi understands that our common resolve is unshakable, and our common strength is invincible.

Tonight, we and the other allied nations are contributing 600,000 fighting men to assist 700,000 South Vietnamese troops in defending their little country.

Our presence there has always rested on this basic belief: The main burden of preserving their freedom must be carried out by them—by the South Vietnamese themselves.

We and our allies can only help to provide a shield behind which the people of South Vietnam can survive and can grow and develop. On their efforts—on their determinations and resourcefulness—the outcome will ultimately depend. . . .

Our first priority will be to support their effort.

We shall accelerate the re-equipment of South Vietnam's armed forces in order to meet the enemy's increased firepower. And this will enable them progressively to undertake a large share of combat operations against the Communist invaders.

On many occasions I have told the American people that we would send to Vietnam those forces that are required to accomplish our mission there. So with that as our guide we have previously authorized a force level of approximately 525,000.

Some weeks ago to help meet the enemy's new offensive we sent to Vietnam about 11,000 additional Marine and airborne troops. They were deployed by air in 48 hours on an emergency basis. But the artillery and the tank and the aircraft and medical and other units that were needed to work with and support these infantry troops in combat could not then accompany them by air on that short notice.

In order that these forces may reach maximum combat effectiveness, the Joint Chiefs of Staff have recommended to me that we should prepare to send during the next five months the support troops totaling approximately 13,500 men.

A portion of these men will be made available from our active forces. The balance will come from reserve component units, which will be called up for service.

The actions that we have taken since the beginning of the year to re-equip the South Vietnamese forces; to meet our responsibilities in Korea, as well as our responsibilities in Vietnam; to meet price increases and the cost of activating and deploying these reserve forces; to replace helicopters and provide the other military supplies we need, all of these actions are going to require additional expenditures.

The tentative estimate of those additional expenditures is $2.5 billion in this fiscal year and $2.6 billion in the next fiscal year. . . .

Now let me give you my estimate of the chances for peace—the peace that will one day stop the bloodshed in South Vietnam. That will—all the Vietnamese people will be permitted to rebuild and develop their land. That will permit us to turn more fully to our own tasks here at home.

I cannot promise that the initiative that I have announced tonight will be completely successful in achieving peace any more than the 30 others that we have undertaken and agreed to in recent years.

But it is our fervent hope that North Vietnam, after years of

461

fighting that has left the issue unresolved, will now cease its efforts to achieve a military victory and will join with us in moving toward the peace table.

And there may come a time when South Vietnamese—on both sides—are able to work out a way to settle their own differences by free political choice rather than by war.

As Hanoi considers its course, it should be in no doubt of our intentions. It must not miscalculate the pressures within our democracy in this election year. We have no intention of widening this war. But the United States will never accept a fake solution to this long and arduous struggle and call it peace.

No one can foretell the precise terms of an eventual settlement.

Our objective in South Vietnam has never been the annihilation of the enemy. It has been to bring about a recognition in Hanoi that its objective—taking over the South by force—could not be achieved.

We think that peace can be heard on the Geneva accords of 1954, under political conditions that permit the South Vietnamese—all the South Vietnamese—to chart their course free of any outside domination or interferences, from us or from anyone else.

So tonight I reaffirm the pledge that we made at Manila: that we are prepared to withdraw our forces from South Vietnam as the other side withdraws its forces to the North, stops the infiltration, and the level of violence thus subsides.

Our goal of peace and self-determination in Vietnam is directly related to the future of all of Southeast Asia, where much has happened to inspire confidence during the past 10 years. And we have done all that we knew how to do to contribute and to help build that confidence.

A number of nations have shown what can be accomplished under conditions of security. Since 1966, Indonesia, the fifth largest nation in all the world, with a population of more than 100 million people, has had a Government that's dedicated to peace with its neighbors and improved conditions for its own people.

Political and economic cooperation between nations has grown rapidly.

And I think every American can take a great deal of pride in the role that we have played in bringing this about in Southeast Asia. We can rightly judge—as responsible Southeast Asians themselves do—that the progress of the past three years would have been far less likely, if not completely impossible, if America's sons and others had not made their stand in Vietnam.

At Johns Hopkins University about three years ago, I announced that the United States would take part in the great work of developing Southeast Asia, including the Mekong valley, for all the people of that region. Our determination to help build a better land—a better land for men on both sides of the present conflict—has not diminished in the least. Indeed, the ravages of war, I think, have made it more urgent than ever.

So I repeat on behalf of the United States again tonight what I said at Johns Hopkins—that North Vietnam could take its place in this common effort just as soon as peace comes.

Over time, a wider framework of peace and security in Southeast Asia may become possible. The new cooperation of the nations of the area could be a foundation stone. Certainly friendship with the nations of such a Southeast Asia is what the United States seeks— and that is all that the United States seeks.

One day, my fellow citizens, there will be peace in Southeast Asia. It will come because the people of Southeast Asia want it—those whose armies are at war tonight; those who, though threatened, have thus far been spared.

Peace will come because Asians were willing to work for it and to sacrifice for it—and to die by the thousands for it.

But let it never be forgotten: peace will come also because America sent her sons to help secure it.

It has not been easy—far from it. During the past four and a half years, it has been my fate and my responsibility to be Commander in Chief. I have lived daily and nightly with the cost of this war. I know the pain that it has inflicted. I know perhaps better than anyone the misgivings it has aroused.

And throughout this entire long period I have been sustained by a single principle: that what we are doing now in Vietnam is vital not only to the security of Southeast Asia but it is vital to the security of every American.

Surely, we have treaties which we must respect. Surely, we have commitments that we are going to keep. Resolutions of the Congress testify to the need to resist aggression in the world and in Southeast Asia.

But the heart of our involvement in South Vietnam under three different Presidents, three separate Administrations, has always been America's own security.

And the larger purpose of our involvement has always been to help the nations of Southeast Asia become independent, and stand alone self-sustaining as members of a great world community, at peace with themselves, at peace with all others. And with such a nation our country—and the world—will be far more secure than it is tonight.

I believe that a peaceful Asia is far nearer to reality because of what America has done in Vietnam. I believe that the men who endure the dangers of battle there, fighting there for us tonight, are helping the entire world avoid far greater conflicts, far wider wars, far more destruction, than this one.

The peace that will bring them home someday will come. Tonight, I have offered the first in what I hope will be a series of mutual moves toward peace.

I pray that it will not be rejected by the leaders of North Vietnam. I pray that they will accept it as a means by which the sacrifices of their own people may be ended. And I ask your help and your support, my fellow citizens, for this effort to reach across the battle-field toward an early peace.

Yet, I believe that we must always be mindful of this one thing—whatever the trials and the tests ahead, the ultimate strength of our country and our cause will lie, not in powerful weapons or infinite resources or boundless wealth, but will lie in the unity of our people.

Finally, my fellow Americans, let me say this:

Of those to whom much is given much is asked. I cannot say—and no man could say—that no more will be asked of us. Yet I believe that now, no less than when the decade began, this generation of Americans is willing to pay the price, bear any burden, meet any hardship, support any friend, oppose any foe, to assure the survival, and the success, of liberty.

Since those words were spoken by John F. Kennedy, the people of America have kept that compact with mankind's noblest cause. And we shall continue to keep it.

This I believe very deeply. Throughout my entire public career I have followed the personal philosophy that I am a free man, an American, a public servant and a member of my party—in that order—always and only.

For 37 years in the service of our nation, first as a Congressman, as a Senator and as Vice-President, and now as your President, I have put the unity of the people first. I have put it ahead of any divisive partisanship. And in these times, as in times before, it is true that a house divided against itself by the spirit of faction, of party, of region, of religion, of race, is a house that cannot stand.

There is division in the American house now. There is divisiveness among us all tonight. And holding the trust that is mine, as President of all the people, I cannot disregard the peril of the progress of the American people and the hope and the prospect of peace for all peoples, so I would ask all Americans whatever their personal interest or concern to guard against divisiveness and all of its ugly consequences.

Fifty-two months and ten days ago, in a moment of tragedy and trauma, the duties of this office fell upon me.

I asked then for your help, and God's, that we might continue America on its course binding up our wounds, healing our history, moving forward in new unity to clear the American agenda and to keep the American commitment for all of our people.

United we have kept that commitment. And united we have enlarged that commitment. And through all time to come I think America will be a stronger nation, a more just society, a land of greater opportunity and fulfillment because of what we have all done together in these years of unparalleled achievement.

Our reward will come in the life of freedom and peace and hope that our children will enjoy through ages ahead.

What we won when all of our people united just must not now be lost in suspicion and distrust and selfishness and politics among any of our people. And believing this as I do I have concluded that I should not permit the President to become involved in the partisan divisions that are developing in this political year.

With American sons in the fields far away, with America's future under challenge right here at home, with our hopes and the world's hopes for peace in the balance every day, I do not believe that I should devote an hour or a day of my time to any personal partisan cause or to any duties other than the awesome duties of this office—the Presidency of your country.

Accordingly, I shall not seek, and I will not accept, the nomination of my party for another term as your President. But let men everywhere know, however, that a strong and a confident and a vigilant America stands ready tonight to seek an honorable peace; and stands ready tonight to defend an honored cause, whatever the price, whatever the burden, whatever the sacrifice that duty may require.

Thank you for listening. Good night and God bless all of you.

Elected in 1968 by a narrow edge over Senator Hubert Humphrey, Richard Nixon found no clear mandate from the nation either on foreign or domestic issues. Hence, the new President inched forward cautiously on all foreign fronts, of which Vietnam was merely one of many. Central to the conflict, as Nixon saw it, was the state of Soviet-American relations. Until a dramatic change in those relations, which did not come about for three years, the war continued at huge cost, human and physical.

Within six weeks after President Johnson's speech announcing his withdrawal from the Presidential race, preliminary peace talks began in Paris and were expanded in January 1969 to include the United States, the South Vietnamese, North Vietnam and the National Liberation Front seated around a circular table without name plates or flags, with two rectangular tables on either side. Using a carrot and stick, President Nixon continued the always difficult negotiations. Faced with an offensive in Vietnam that threatened the collapse of the South Vietnamese army and the Saigon regime, Nixon ordered the mining of North Vietnamese harbors and the bombing of Hanoi. Neither Russia nor China reacted in a way that some had fearfully predicted. Likewise during Christmas week of 1972, irked by a stubborn posture on the part of the North Vietnamese and possibly responding to pleas for more time and arms by the Saigon regime, the President authorized a new bombing attack, this time against the major cities of North Vietnam—a decision that Dr. Henry Kissinger, the President's chief negotiator, described in a TV interview in February 1973 as "perhaps the most painful, the most difficult, and certainly the most lonely that the President has had to make since he has been in office."

Finally, in January 1973, after the toughest kind of bargaining sessions, characterized by Kissinger as being filled with "peaks and valleys of extraordinary intensity," an armistice agreement, initiated by Kissinger and signed for the United States by Secretary of State Rogers, was reached. This amounted to a compromise for all sides concerned. It established an International Commission of Control and Supervision, made up of troops from Canada, Indonesia, Hungary, and Poland, to police the uneasy peace. For the United States, which agreed to the withdrawal of its troops from South Vietnam, it guaranteed the return of American prisoners of war held by the North Vietnamese and the Vietcong. It also provided during the first ninety-day period for Saigon and the Provisional Revolutionary Government to set up a National Council of Reconciliation and Concord, which was to plan for elections in South Vietnam.

Not included in the formal agreement, but strongly favored by President Nixon, is United States reconstruction aid for North Vietnam. For the Soviet Union, desirous of pushing on with the SALT II talks and securing liberalized trade agreements and credits from the United States, strong incentives exist for curtailing arms shipments to North Vietnam. As Dr. Kissinger phrased it on January 24, 1973:

* "Peace in Indochina requires the self-restraint of all of the major countries." Only time will tell how well such restraints will be operative, and whether the war-torn peoples of Indochina who have not known peace in our generation can manage to stabilize their internal conflicts and cooperate on a program of mutual reconstruction both sides so desperately need.

40

THE DECISION TO SEEK A DETENTE WITH THE PEOPLE'S REPUBLIC OF CHINA

Richard Nixon's "Ping Pong Diplomacy" Rocks the World

The best-kept secret of this generation proved a tremendous shock, setting off seismic waves in every corner of the globe. The move could have been forecast had not Cold War experts, old China hands, and pundits from the groves of academe kept their eyes on the wrong player. So preoccupied were the experts in watching the dazzling international movements of Dr. Henry Kissinger, Assistant to the President for National Security Affairs, and attempting to deduce from his writings some pattern for future policies, a pattern drawn from theories of balance of power, whether exemplified by a Metternich or a Bismarck, that they all but ignored the quarterback who was directing the plays.

In an article in the prestigious quarterly *Foreign Affairs,* published in October 1967, a year before his election to the Presidency, Richard M. Nixon indicated that he was prepared to depart from his long-time hard line toward Peking. "Any American policy toward Asia," he asserted, "must come urgently to grips with the reality of China." Taking the long view, he insisted that "we simply cannot afford to leave China forever outside the family of nations, there to nurture its fantasies, cherish its hates and threaten its neighbors."

During the early part of his first term, President Nixon made a point of telling the leaders of foreign countries on his trips abroad that he wished to open a dialogue with the Chinese. Particularly helpful to the President as an intermediary was Rumanian President Nicholae Ceausesco. The U. S. Administration was now making it clear that "we were not bound by previous history." If that implied that American-Taiwanese ties were not to be the only strands with the people of China, it also suggested that Nixon was seeking a formula to wind down the war in Vietnam.

China responded in ways characteristically Chinese. Its unusually restrained reaction to the American invasion of Cambodia was a straw in the wind. If no one else got the message, the government at Hanoi did. Then, in the spring of 1971, an American Ping Pong team was invited to Peking. In turn, a Chinese team came to America, while the United States relaxed trade barriers on the shipment of nonstrategic goods to China.

Still, despite these signals, the dramatic events revealed over radio and television by the President on July 15, 1971, caught the entire world by surprise.

PRESIDENT NIXON'S RADIO AND TELEVISION ADDRESS ON CHINA[18]

Los Angeles, July 15, 1971

Good evening:

I have requested this television time tonight to announce a major development in our efforts to build a lasting peace in the world.

As I have pointed out on a number of occasions over the past three years, there can be no stable peace and enduring peace without the participation of the People's Republic of China and its 750 million people. That is why I have undertaken initiatives in several areas to open the door for more normal relations between our two countries.

In pursuance of that goal, I sent Dr. Kissinger, my Assistant for National Security Affairs, to Peking during his recent world tour for the purpose of having talks with Premier Chou En-lai.

The announcement I shall now read is being issued simultaneously in Peking and in the United States.

"Premier Chou En-lai and Dr. Henry Kissinger, President Nixon's Assistant for National Security Affairs, held talks in Peking from July 9 to 11, 1971. Knowing of President Nixon's expressed desire to visit the People's Republic of China, Premier Chou En-lai on behalf of the Government of the People's Republic of China has extended an invitation to President Nixon to visit China at an appropriate date before May, 1972.

"President Nixon has accepted the invitation with pleasure.

"The meeting between the leaders of China and the United States is to seek the normalization of relations between the two countries and also to exchange views on questions of concern to the two sides."

In anticipation of the inevitable speculation which will follow this announcement, I want to put our policy in the clearest possible context. Our action in seeking a new relationship with the People's Republic of China will not be at the expense of our old friends.

It is not directed against any other nation. We seek friendly relations with all nations. Any nation can be our friend without being any other nation's enemy.

I have taken this action because of my profound conviction that all nations will gain from a reduction of tensions and a better relationship between the United States and the People's Republic of China.

It is in this spirit that I will undertake what I deeply hope will become a journey for peace, peace not just for our generation but for future generations on this earth we share together.

Thank you and good night.

The plans to send Dr. Kissinger to Peking were carefully laid and scrupulously guarded. His trip, leaving Washington on July 1 and returning to report to the President at San Clemente on July 13, was announced by a convenient cover story. Kissinger dropped off at Saigon on July 3. Following a two-day stay he visited Bangkok, then New Delhi, arriving at Islamabad, Pakistan, on July 8th. The next day, after dining with Pakistan's then President Mohammed Yah-ya Khan, Kissinger and three aides boarded a plane and flew the 2,500 miles to Peking, while reporters were told that he had a stomach upset and was recuperating in a remote Pakistani mountain resort. Arriving in Peking, Kissinger was whisked off to an official guest house in the suburbs, and, save for a morning tour of the Forbidden City, put in forty-nine hours, every waking hour of which was spent with Premier Chou En-lai. Kissinger returned to Pakistan on July 11th, completely recovered from his stomach upset, and in fact having added another five pounds, a tribute to the hospitality to which he was subjected.

The Presidential radio and TV announcement rocked Taiwan, long allied with the United States and possessing one of the largest non-Communist forces in Asia, as it forecast a gradual reduction in military commitments to that island as well as its diminishing importance in overall American strategy. Not long thereafter the UN voted for the admission of mainland China and expelled Taiwan from the Security Council. It was also an enormous shock to the Japanese, whose Government was briefly told about the Kissinger mission only moments before the President's announcement. Finally, the announcement could not have failed to traumatize the Kremlin, which, despite the United States' intention of according China big-power status, failed to retaliate either by postponing the invitation extended President Nixon for a visit to Moscow in May of '72 or by postponing talks on Soviet-American trade agreements or strategic arms talks—both subjects of common concern to the USSR and the USA. Thus, the President's historic trip to China in February 1972 was followed by a Moscow summit meeting at which numerous joint Soviet-American scientific agreements were entered into, as well as the signing of an agreement mutually limiting each country's nuclear missile forces.

What Red China and the United States agreed upon were, as President Nixon described it, "some basic principles of international conduct which will reduce the risk of confrontation and war in Asia and the Pacific." This meant a mutual acceptance of the policy that the Pacific area not be dominated by any single power, that international disputes be settled without the use of force. The move was generally considered both creative and hopeful, offering a chance to seek genuine solutions instead of violent confrontations.

The President's visit to Peking was followed up by several more on the part of Dr. Kissinger, along with the appointment of David Bruce, a senior member of the United States diplomatic service, as chief of a liaison mission to the People's Republic. Kissinger himself perhaps most aptly summed up the significance of this slow thaw in relations between two giants, so long leaders of bitterly opposed camps, in a White House Press Conference on February 22, 1973.

THE WHITE HOUSE PRESS CONFERENCE OF DR. HENRY A. KISSINGER, ASSISTANT TO THE PRESIDENT FOR NATIONAL SECURITY AFFAIRS

THE BRIEFING ROOM[19]

10:20 A.M. EST

MR. ZIEGLER: You have had a chance to read the communique. As Jerry mentioned to you, it is embargoed for transmission until eleven o'clock, Eastern Standard Time.

Dr. Kissinger left on the 7th of this month, and he has visited Thailand, Laos, the DRV and the PRC and Japan, and returned to the United States on the 20th of this month and is here to talk about his travels and to take some of your questions. He is on the record, of course.

DR. KISSINGER: I noticed that Ron has begun to speak with a German accent. (Laughter)

Ladies and gentlemen, I thought I would begin by making some remarks about my trip to the People's Republic of China, and then take some questions on that, including the communique, and then perhaps make a few additional comments to the briefing that Ron has already given you on the Hanoi communique.

To put this communique into perspective and to elaborate on it for a bit, one should review the evolution of our China policy. When we first began our contacts with the People's Republic of China in 1969 through third parties, and in 1971 directly, the United States had not had any contact with the People's Republic in nearly 20 years; that is, no contact on a really substantial level.

Our early conversations were concerned primarily with building confidence, with explaining each other's position, with establishing channels of communication. Last year our achievements consisted of setting our directions and indicating the roads that might be traveled. After the end of the war in Vietnam, and in these discussions in Peking, we were able to begin to travel some of these roads, and to move from the attempt to eliminate the obstructions and the mistrust to some more concrete and positive achievements.

What happened in these meetings was really a continuation of possibilities that had been outlined during the President's visit and during the conversations between the President and Chairman Mao and Prime Minister Chou En-lai, except that now they took some more concrete form. As the communique points out, we reviewed the progress in Sino-American relations in great detail, and we reviewed the international situations in great detail.

We discussed the principles of the Shanghai Communique, particularly those that dealt with the desirability of normalization of relations, the desirability of reducing the danger of military conflict, the affirmation by both sides that neither would seek hegemony in the Pacific area, and each of them opposed the attempt of anyone else to achieve it, and that the relations between China and the United States would never be directed against any third country.

In that spirit, it was decided to accelerate the normalization of relations, to broaden contacts in all fields, and an initial concrete program for extending these contacts was developed.

Given this new range of contacts, it was decided that the existing channel in Paris was inadequate and that, therefore, each side would establish a liaison office in the capital of the other. This liaison office would handle trade as well as all other matters, except the strictly formal diplomatic aspects of the relationship, but it would cover the whole gamut of relationships. This liaison office will be established in the nearest future. Both sides will make proposals within the next few weeks to the other about their technical requirements, and henceforth it will be possible for the United States and the People's Republic of China to deal with each other in the capital of the other.

Now, in order to give some concrete expression to this desire for the normalization of relationships, it was agreed that a number of steps be taken.

First of all, the Chinese, as a sign of good will, have informed us that they would release, within the same time period as our withdrawal from Vietnam, the two military prisoners that they hold in China, Lt. Commander (Robert J.) Flynn and Major Philip (E.) Smith. They have been held in China since 1967, and 1965, respectively. They will be released within the next few weeks.

Prime Minister Chou En-lai also asked me to inform the President that the Chinese Penal Code provided for the periodic review of the sentences of prisoners and that this provision would be applied in the case of John Downey.

The Chinese Penal Code provides for commutation of sentences on the basis of good behavior. We have been told that the behavior of Mr. Downey has been exemplary and that his case would be reviewed in the second half of this year.

With respect to outstanding issues that have been discussed in other channels, it was agreed that the linked issue of United States private claims against the People's Republic of China and PRC blocked assets in the United States would be negotiated on a global basis in the immediate future. Discussions will begin on this subject between Secretary of State Rogers and the Chinese Foreign Minister next week when both are attending the International Conference on Vietnam in Paris, and we expect these negotiations to be concluded rapidly and in a comprehensive way and we are certain that both sides are approaching them in a constructive spirit and in an attitude consistent with our intention to accelerate the improvement of our relations.

With respect to increased exchanges between the two countries, the Chinese have agreed to invite, during this year, the Philadelphia Symphony by the fall of 1973, a medical group during the spring, scientific groups during the summer, a group of elementary and high school teachers, again during the summer, and increased visits by Congressmen and Senators, as well as athletic teams, an amateur basketball team and swimming and diving teams.

The People's Republic has agreed to send to the United States the archeological exhibit from the Forbidden City, which will probably come in 1974, a group of water conservation experts, insect hormone specialists, high energy physicists, and a gymnastic team.

When the liaison offices are established, possibility will exist for developing further contacts and accelerating this entire process.

The major point we want to make is this: Our contacts with the People's Republic of China have moved from hostility towards normalization. We both believe that it is essential for the peace of the world that the United States and the People's Republic of China act with a sense of responsibility in world affairs; that we are part of an international community in which all nations have a stake in preserving the peace, and that therefore, as the Shanghai communique has already said and as was reaffirmed once again, the normalization of relations between the United States and the People's Republic is not directed against other nations, but is part of a pattern that the President has pursued of building a structure of peace in which all nations can participate and in which all nations have a stake.

It remains for me only to say that we were received with extraordinary courtesy and that the discussions were conducted in what was always described as an unconstrained atmosphere.

Now I will take your questions on China and after that a few comments on North Vietnam.

Q.: Did you come to any agreement with regard to Taiwan and U.S. troops there?

DR. KISSINGER: Inevitably the issue of Taiwan is one in which the People's Republic and we do not have the same perspective. The leaders of the People's Republic stated their view and we expressed our general commitments.

We, of course, continue to maintain diplomatic relations with Taiwan. The level of our troops on Taiwan is not the subject of negotiation, but will be governed by the general considerations of the Nixon doctrine with respect to danger in the area. There exists no immediate plan for any withdrawal, but there will be a periodic review.

Q.: Dr. Kissinger, what will be the rank of the liaison office heads? Will they be Ambassadors?

DR. KISSINGER: Mr. Lisagor has addressed me by my academic title, which is very impressive to me.

The formal title of the head of the liaison office will be Chief of the Liaison Office. And we are not giving any formal diplomatic rank on either side. As soon as the person is selected, which should be within a month, I think his stature will then determine it, but there will be no formal title other than the one I have given.

Q.: To what do you attribute the Chinese decision to send a permanent representative here in view of their previous refusal to have a permanent person any place where Taiwan is recognized?

DR. KISSINGER: The liaison office, of course, is not a formal diplomatic office, but I don't want to speculate on the motive of the Chinese decision.

Our policy had always been clear from our first contact. Certainly from the time that the President visited the People's Republic, he pointed out to Prime Minister Chou En-lai the types of American representation that would be available for establishment in Peking, which ranged from trade missions to various other possibilities, to the idea of a liaison office.

Why the Chinese leaders have decided at this particular moment to accept this and to establish an office of their own in Washington, I would not want to speculate on, except that it is certainly consistent with speeding up the process of normalization.

Q.: Was there any restriction or understanding on the size of the respective delegations?

DR. KISSINGER: No, but we expect it to be of moderate size at the beginning.

Q.: Dr. Kissinger, how about the exchange of journalists and opening of permanent bureaus in both countries?

DR. KISSINGER: This is one of the topics that will be discussed through the existing channel and then through the liaison office. The

Chinese side has indicated that it would be willing to send some journalists over here and it is, of course, clearly understood that we want to increase our journalistic contacts in the People's Republic.

I think there is some understanding in principle with respect to that; the details of which have to be worked out.

Q.: What is the concrete program of expanding trade the communique refers to?

DR. KISSINGER: To begin with, there is already a reasonable amount of trade, much larger than any projection had foreseen two years ago. The initial step in a further expansion has to be the discussion of the two issues I have mentioned, namely the blocked assets and the private claims. When these two issues are resolved, which we expect to be fairly soon, then further steps can be taken.

Up to now, the trade has been essentially in private channels on the United States side and has proceeded more rapidly than anybody projected two or three years ago.

Q.: Dr. Kissinger, do you see the liaison office as something, as far as you can go, in terms of permanent representation, short of diplomatic relations, or do you see something further down the road?

DR. KISSINGER: We have no further steps in mind. This is as far as we can go for the moment.

Q.: Dr. Kissinger, did you have a chance to discuss with the Chinese leaders the possibility of mutual restraints in sending military equipment to Vietnam?

DR. KISSINGER: Our view on the question of military equipment to Indochina is clear and we have made clear to all the countries with which we have talked the importance of tranquility in Indochina to the peace of the world, and Indochina was one of the subjects that was discussed in Peking.

Q.: Dr. Kissinger, could you tell us something of the nature and the details of your discussions with Chairman Mao?

DR. KISSINGER: I am debating whether to spend ten minutes saying "No." or just to say "No." (Laughter)

I will say two general things. One, I obviously cannot go into the details of the discussion. The atmosphere was cordial. Chairman Mao was in apparently good health. and spoke with great animation for about two hours, and extended a personal message to the President, as the Chinese announcement made clear.

Q.: Dr. Kissinger, was there any discussion of a visit here by Chou En-lai or any other senior Chinese representatives in the future?

DR. KISSINGER: There was no discussion of this.

Q.: Were there any secret agreements made in view of the fact you are not discussing the Mao conversations?

DR. KISSINGER: No, the essential nature of what was discussed is contained in the communique and in my explanations. There were no secret agreements.

In an interview with CBS correspondent Marvin Kalb a few weeks before his press conference, Dr. Kissinger presented a realistic analysis of the Administration's changed stance toward the People's Republic of China and the USSR:

> What this Administration has attempted to do is not so much to play a complicated nineteenth-century game of balance of power but to try to eliminate those hostilities that were vestiges of a particular perception at the end of the war and to try to deal with the root fact of the contemporary situation, that we and the Soviet Union and the Chinese are ideological adversaries; that we are bound together by one basic fact: none of us can survive a nuclear war.

41

THE DECISION TO COVER UP THE
WATERGATE BURGLARY

Nixon's Obstruction of Justice

Richard Nixon's decision to cover up the involvement of former
White House aides, former members of his Cabinet, and officials of
his campaign committee in a burglary of offices of the Democratic
National Committee led two years later to his resignation from the
Presidency. During these two years, the press, Congressional committee hearings, and criminal investigations produced revelations of
widespread illegal activities engaged in by members of the Nixon
administration. Throughout, Nixon professed that he had had no
knowledge of any cover-up of the burglary, defended those aides who
were not cooperating with Federal prosecutors—while firing the most
important aide who did, White House counsel John Dean—and
claimed executive privilege to justify refusing to turn over taped
conversations to either Congress or a Special Prosecutor. Finally, after
the Supreme Court rejected Nixon's constitutional contentions, the
release of transcripts of Nixon's conversations provided the "smoking
gun," which brought about universal calls for his resignation, occurring on August 8, 1974.

On June 14, 1972, five men were apprehended while burglarizing
the offices of the Democratic National Committee, located in the
Watergate, an apartment-hotel complex in Washington, D.C. Links
between the accused, the Committee to Reelect the President, and
former White House aides were soon revealed. Still, not until August
5, 1974, would there be direct evidence that as early as six days after
the burglary Nixon had approved a plan to order the FBI to limit its
inquiries and to enlist the CIA in the cover-up effort. Evidence was
destroyed in the office of the President's Chief of Staff, H.R. Halde-

man, and by the Acting Director of the FBI, L. Patrick Gray. Later, the President's personal attorney, Herbert W. Kalmbach, would raise $220,000 which would be paid to the Watergate burglars to insure their silence.

For two years Nixon fired off a series of smoke screens to obscure his involvement. In press conferences, in addresses to the nation, and in written public statements—such as the one reproduced here of May 22, 1973—he asserted his innocence. Forced by Congress to permit his third Attorney General in a year's time, Elliot L. Richardson, to appoint a Special Prosecutor, Harvard Law School Professor Archibald Cox, Nixon claimed executive privilege to avoid providing Cox with tapes of his conversations with his aides. After the U.S. Court of Appeals for the district of Columbia Circuit rejected his contentions, Nixon refused to comply, but instead proposed a compromise by which a hard-of-hearing, elderly Senator, John C. Stennis, would listen to the disputed tapes and verify the accuracy of written summaries, so long as Cox would not in the future seek Presidential documents through the judicial process.

When Cox refused Nixon's proposal, the President, on October 20, 1973, ordered both Attorney General Richardson and Deputy Attorney General William D. Ruckelshaus to dismiss Cox. Both men refused and resigned. As Acting Attorney General, Robert H. Bork then fired Cox, and FBI agents sealed off the offices of Richardson, Ruckelshaus, and Cox. These actions galvanized public opinion and resulted in the introduction of sixteen impeachment resolutions, sponsored by eighty-four members of Congress in the following week.

In July 1974, the House of Representatives Judiciary Committee, chaired by Representative Peter W. Rodino (Democrat, New Jersey), voted three articles of impeachment. By a vote of 27–11 the Committee recommended impeachement on the ground that Nixon "engaged personally and through his subordinates and agents in a course of conduct to delay, impede, and obstruct the investigation" of the Watergate break-in; to "cover up, conceal, and protect those responsible"; and to "conceal the existence and scope of other unlawful activities." The second article, adopted by a vote of 28–10, reflected revelations that were largely the combined result of investigative reporting and the hearings of the Senate Select Committee on Presidential Campaign Activities (chaired by Senator Sam J. Ervin, Jr., Democrat, North Carolina). The evidence exposed campaign "dirty tricks" secretly financed by the Committee to Reelect the President; the misuse of the Internal Revenue Service, the FBI, and the Secret Service to wiretap or harass political opponents on an "Enemies List"; and the operations of a secret investigative unit within the office of the President which engaged in covert and unlawful activities. The President was charged with violating his constitutional oath faithfully to execute the office of President and disregarding his constitutional duty to take care that the laws be faithfully executed by "violating the constitutional rights of citizens, impairing the due and proper administration of justice in the conduct of lawful inquiries, of contravening the law governing agencies of the executive branch and the purposes of these agencies." A third article of impeachment, approved by 21–17, charged the President with disobeying the subpoenas of the House Judiciary Committee, thus impeding the impeachment process.

After release by Nixon of transcripts of three conversations with his aides held on June 23, 1972, his remaining support in the Congress disintegrated. Nixon resigned without admission of guilt, conceding only that he had made "some" wrong judgments, and was taking this action because he no longer had "a strong enough political base in Congress" to carry out his duties. On August 20 the House of Representatives accepted the final report of the impeachment inquiry by a vote of 412–3.

STATEMENTS ABOUT THE WATERGATE INVESTIGATIONS BY PRESIDENT NIXON[20]

May 22, 1973

RECENT news accounts growing out of testimony in the Watergate investigations have given grossly misleading impressions of many of the facts, as they relate both to my own role and to certain unrelated activities involving national security.

Already, on the basis of second- and third-hand hearsay testimony by persons either convicted or themselves under investigation in the case, I have found myself accused of involvement in activities I never heard of until I read about them in news accounts.

These impressions could also lead to a serious misunderstanding of those national security activities which, though totally unrelated to Watergate, have become entangled in the case. They could lead to further compromise of sensitive national security information.

I will not abandon my responsibilities. I will continue to do the job I was elected to do.

In the accompanying statement, I have set forth the facts as I know them as they relate to my own role.

With regard to the specific allegations that have been made, I can and do state categorically:

1. I had no prior knowledge of the Watergate operation.

2. I took no part in, nor was I aware of, any subsequent efforts that may have been made to cover up Watergate.

3. At no time did I authorize any offer of executive clemency for the Watergate defendants, nor did I know of any such offer.

4. I did not know, until the time of my own investigation, of any effort to provide the Watergate defendants with funds.

5. At no time did I attempt, or did I authorize others to attempt, to implicate the CIA in the Watergate matter.

6. It was not until the time of my own investigation that I learned of the break-in at the office of Mr. Ellsberg's psychiatrist, and I specifically authorized the furnishing of this information to Judge Byrne.

7. I neither authorized nor encouraged subordinates to engage in illegal or improper campaign tactics.

In the accompanying statement, I have sought to provide the background that may place recent allegations in perspective. I have specifically stated that executive privilege will not be invoked as to any testimony concerning possible criminal conduct or discussions of possible criminal conduct, in the matters under investigation. I want the public to learn the truth about Watergate and those guilty of any illegal actions brought to justice.

Allegations surrounding the Watergate affair have so escalated that I feel a further statement from the President is required at this time.

A climate of sensationalism has developed in which even second-

or third-hand hearsay charges are headlined as fact and repeated as fact.

Important national security operations which themselves had no connection with Watergate have become entangled in the case.

As a result, some national security information has already been made public through court orders, through the subpoenaing of documents, and through testimony witnesses have given in judicial and Congressional proceedings. Other sensitive documents are now threatened with disclosure. Continued silence about those operations would compromise rather than protect them and would also serve to perpetuate a grossly distorted view—which recent partial disclosures have given—of the nature and purpose of those operations.

—The purpose of this statement is threefold:

—First, to set forth the facts about my own relationship to the Watergate matter;

—Second, to place in some perspective some of the more sensational—and inaccurate—of the charges that have filled the headlines in recent days, and also some of the matters that are currently being discussed in Senate testimony and elsewhere;

—Third, to draw the distinction between national security operations and the Watergate case. To put the other matters in perspective, it will be necessary to describe the national security operations first.

In citing these national security matters, it is not my intention to place a national security "cover" on Watergate, but rather to separate them out from Watergate—and at the same time to explain the context in which certain actions took place that were later misconstrued or misused.

Long before the Watergate break-in, three important national security operations took place which have subsequently become entangled in the Watergate case.

—The first operation, begun in 1969, was a program of wiretaps. All were legal, under the authorities then existing. They were undertaken to find and stop serious national security leaks.

—The second operation was a reassessment, which I ordered in 1970, of the adequacy of internal security measures. This resulted in a plan and a directive to strengthen our intelligence operations. They were protested by Mr. Hoover, and as a result of his protest, they were not put into effect.

—The third operation was the establishment, in 1971, of a Special Investigations Unit in the White House. Its primary mission was to plug leaks of vital security information. I also directed this group to prepare an accurate history of certain crucial national security matters which occurred under prior administrations, on which the Government's records were incomplete.

Here is the background of these three security operations initiated in my Administration.

1969 WIRETAPS

By mid-1969, my Administration had begun a number of highly sensitive foreign policy initiatives. They were aimed at ending the war in Vietnam, achieving a settlement in the Middle East, limiting nuclear arms, and establishing new relationships among the great powers. These involved highly secret diplomacy. They were closely interrelated. Leaks of secret information about any one could endanger all.

Exactly that happened. News accounts appeared in 1969, which were obviously based on leaks—some of them extensive and detailed—by people having access to the most highly classified security materials.

There was no way to carry forward these diplomatic initiatives unless further leaks could be prevented. This required finding the source of the leaks.

In order to do this, a special program of wiretaps was instituted in mid-1969 and terminated in February 1971. Fewer than 20 taps, of varying duration, were involved. They produced important leads that made it possible to tighten the security of highly sensitive materials. I authorized this entire program. Each individual tap was undertaken in accordance with procedures legal at the time and in accord with long-standing precedent.

The persons who were subject to these wiretaps were determined through coordination among the Director of the FBI, my Assistant for National Security Affairs, and the Attorney General. Those wiretapped were selected on the basis of access to the information leaked, material in security files, and evidence that developed as the inquiry proceeded.

Information thus obtained was made available to senior officials responsible for national security matters in order to curtail further leaks.

THE 1970 INTELLIGENCE PLAN

In the spring and summer of 1970, another security problem reached critical proportions. In March a wave of bombings and explosions struck college campuses and cities. There were 400 bomb threats in one 24-hour period in New York City. Rioting and violence on college campuses reached a new peak after the Cambodian operation and the tragedies at Kent State and Jackson State. The 1969–70 school year brought nearly 1,800 campus demonstrations and nearly 250 cases of arson on campus. Many colleges closed. Gun battles between guerrilla-style groups and police were taking place. Some of the disruptive activities were receiving foreign support.

Complicating the task of maintaining security was the fact that, in 1966, certain types of undercover FBI operations that had been conducted for many years had been suspended. This also had substantially impaired our ability to collect foreign intelligence information. At the same time, the relationships between the FBI and other intelligence agencies had been deteriorating. By May 1970, FBI Director Hoover shut off his agency's liaison with the CIA altogether.

On June 5, 1970, I met with the Director of the FBI (Mr. Hoover), the Director of the Central Intelligence Agency (Mr. Richard Helms), the Director of the Defense Intelligence Agency (Gen. Donald V. Bennett), and the Director of the National Security Agency (Adm. Noel Gayler). We discussed the urgent need for better intelligence operations. I appointed Director Hoover as chairman of an interagency committee to prepare recommendations.

On June 25 the committee submitted a report which included specific options for expanded intelligence operations, and on July 23 the agencies were notified by memorandum of the options approved. After reconsideration, however, prompted by the opposition of Director Hoover, the agencies were notified 5 days later, on July 28, that the approval had been rescinded. The options initially approved had included resumption of certain intelligence operations which had been suspended in 1966. These in turn had included authorization for surreptitious entry—breaking and entering, in effect—on specified categories of targets in specified situations related to national security.

Because the approval was withdrawn before it had been implemented, the net result was that the plan for expanded intelligence activities never went into effect.

The documents spelling out this 1970 plan are extremely sensitive. They include—and are based upon—assessments of certain foreign intelligence capabilities and procedures, which of course must remain secret. It was this unused plan and related documents that John Dean removed from the White House and placed in a safe deposit box, giving the keys to Judge Sirica. The same plan, still unused, is being headlined today.

Coordination among our intelligence agencies continued to fall short of our national security needs. In July 1970, having earlier discontinued the FBI's liaison with the CIA, Director Hoover ended the FBI's normal liaison with all other agencies except the White House. To help remedy this, an Intelligence Evaluation Committee was created in December 1970. Its members included representatives of the White House, CIA, FBI, NSA, the Departments of Justice, Treasury, and Defense, and the Secret Service.

The Intelligence Evaluation Commitee and its staff were instructed to improve coordination among the intelligence community and to prepare evaluations and estimates of domestic intelligence. I understand that its activities are now under investigation. I did not authorize nor do I have any knowledge of any illegal activity by this Committee. If it went beyond its charter and did engage in any illegal activities, it was totally without my knowledge or authority.

THE SPECIAL INVESTIGATIONS UNIT

On Sunday, June 13, 1971, *The New York Times* published the first installment of what came to be known as "The Pentagon Papers." Not until a few hours before publication did any responsible Government official know that they had been stolen. Most officials did not know they existed. No senior official of the Government had read them or knew with certainty what they contained.

All the Government knew, at first, was that the papers comprised 47 volumes and some 7,000 pages, which had been taken from the most sensitive files of the Departments of State and Defense and the CIA, covering military and diplomatic moves in a war that was still going on.

Moreover, a majority of the documents published with the first three installments in the *Times* had not been included in the 47-volume study—raising serious questions about what and how much else might have been taken.

There was every reason to believe this was a security leak of unprecedented proportions.

It created a situation in which the ability of the Government to carry on foreign relations even in the best of circumstances could have been severely compromised. Other governments no longer knew whether they could deal with the United States in confidence. Against the background of the delicate negotiations the United States was then involved in on a number of fronts—with regard to Vietnam,

China, the Middle East, nuclear arms limitations, U.S.-Soviet relations, and others—in which the utmost degree of confidentiality was vital, it posed a threat so grave as to require extraordinary actions.

Therefore during the week following the Pentagon Papers publication, I approved the creation of a Special Investigations Unit within the White House—which later came to be known as the "plumbers." This was a small group at the White House whose principal purpose was to stop security leaks and to investigate other sensitive security matters. I looked to John Ehrlichman for the supervision of this group.

Egil Krogh, Mr. Ehrlichman's assistant, was put in charge. David Young was added to this unit, as were E. Howard Hunt and G. Gordon Liddy.

The unit operated under extremely tight security rules. Its existence and functions were known only to a very few persons at the White House. These included Messrs. Haldeman, Ehrlichman, and Dean.

At about the time the unit was created, Daniel Ellsberg was identified as the person who had given the Pentagon Papers to *The New York Times*. I told Mr. Krogh that as a matter of first priority, the unit should find out all it could about Mr. Ellsberg's associates and his motives. Because of the extreme gravity of the situation, and not then knowing what additional national secrets Mr. Ellsberg might disclose, I did impress upon Mr. Krogh the vital importance to the national security of his assignment. I did not authorize and had no knowledge of any illegal means to be used to achieve this goal.

However, because of the emphasis I put on the crucial importance of protecting the national security, I can understand how highly motivated individuals could have felt justified in engaging in specific activities that I would have disapproved had they been brought to my attention.

Consequently, as President, I must and do assume responsibility for such actions despite the fact that I at no time approved or had knowledge of them.

I also assigned the unit a number of other investigatory matters, dealing in part with compiling an accurate record of events related to the Vietnam war, on which the Government's records were inadequate (many previous records having been removed with the change of administrations) and which bore directly on the negotiations then in progress. Additional assignments included tracing down other national security leaks, including one that seriously compromised the U.S. negotiating position in the SALT talks.

The works of the unit tapered off around the end of 1971. The nature of its work was such that it involved matters that, from a national security standpoint, were highly sensitive then and remain so today.

These intelligence activities had no connection with the break-in of the Democratic headquarters, or the aftermath.

I considered it my responsibility to see that the Watergate investigation did not impinge adversely upon the national security area. For example, on April 18, 1973, when I learned that Mr. Hunt, a former member of the Special Investigations Unit at the White House, was to be questioned by the U.S. Attorney, I directed Assistant Attorney General Petersen to pursue every issue involving Watergate but to confine his investigation to Watergate and related matters and to stay out of national security matters. Subsequently, on April 25, 1973, Attorney General Kleindienst informed me that because the Government had clear evidence that Mr. Hunt was involved in the break-in of the office of the psychiatrist who had treated Mr. Ellsberg, he, the Attorney General, believed that despite the fact that no evidence had been obtained from Hunt's acts, a report should nevertheless be made to the court trying the Ellsberg case. I concurred, and directed that the information be transmitted to Judge Byrne immediately.

WATERGATE

The burglary and bugging of the Democratic National Committee headquarters came as a complete surprise to me. I had no inkling that any such illegal activities had been planned by persons associated with my campaign; if I had known, I would not have permitted it. My immediate reaction was that those guilty should be brought to justice, and, with the five burglars themselves already in custody, I assumed that they would be.

Within a few days, however, I was advised that there was a possibility of CIA involvement in some way.

It did seem to me possible that, because of the involvement of former CIA personnel, and because of some of their apparent associations, the investigation could lead to the uncovering of covert CIA operations totally unrelated to the Watergate break-in.

In addition, by this time, the name of Mr. Hunt had surfaced in connection with Watergate, and I was alerted to the fact that he had previously been a member of the Special Investigations Unit in the White House. Therefore, I was also concerned that the Watergate investigation might well lead to an inquiry into the activities of the Special Investigations Unit itself.

In this area, I felt it was important to avoid disclosure of the details of the national security matters with which the group was concerned. I knew that once the existence of the group became known, it would lead inexorably to a discussion of these matters, some of which remain, even today, highly sensitive.

I wanted justice done with regard to Watergate; but in the scale of national priorities with which I had to deal—and not at that time having any idea of the extent of political abuse which Watergate reflected—I also had to be deeply concerned with ensuring that neither the covert operations of the CIA nor the operations of the Special Investigations Unit should be compromised. Therefore, I instructed Mr. Haldeman and Mr. Ehrlichman to ensure that the investigation of the break-in not expose either an unrelated covert operation of the CIA or the activities of the White House investigations unit—and to see that this was personally coordinated between General Walters, the Deputy Director of the CIA, and Mr. Gray of the FBI. It was certainly not my intent, nor my wish, that the investigation of the Watergate break-in or of related acts be impeded in any way.

On July 6, 1972, I telephoned the Acting Director of the FBI, L. Patrick Gray, to congratulate him on his successful handling of the hijacking of a Pacific Southwest Airlines plane the previous day. During the conversation Mr. Gray discussed with me the progress of the Watergate investigation, and I asked him whether he had talked with General Walters. Mr. Gray said that he had, and that General Walters had assured him that the CIA was not involved. In the discussion, Mr. Gray suggested that the matter of Watergate might lead higher. I told him to press ahead with his investigation.

It now seems that later, through whatever complex of individual motives and possible misunderstandings, there were apparently wide-ranging efforts to limit the investigation or to conceal the possible involvement of members of the Administration and the campaign committee.

I was not aware of any such efforts at the time. Neither, until after I began my own investigation, was I aware of any fund-raising for defendants convicted of the break-in at Democratic headquarters, much less authorize any such fundraising. Nor did I authorize any offer of executive clemency for any of the defendants.

In the weeks and months that followed Watergate, I asked for, and received, repeated assurances that Mr. Dean's own investigation (which included reviewing files and sitting in on FBI interviews with White House personnel) had cleared everyone then employed by the White House of involvement.

In summary, then:

(1) I had no prior knowledge of the Watergate bugging operation, or of any illegal surveillance activities for political purposes.

(2) Long prior to the 1972 campaign, I did set in motion certain internal security measures, including legal wiretaps, which I felt were necessary from a national security standpoint and, in the climate then prevailing, also necessary from a domestic security standpoint.

(3) People who had been involved in the national security operations later, without my knowledge or approval, undertook illegal activities in the political campaign of 1972.

(4) Elements of the early post-Watergate reports led me to suspect, incorrectly, that the CIA had been in some way involved. They also led me to surmise, correctly, that since persons originally recruited for covert national security activities had participated in Watergate, an unrestricted investigation of Watergate might lead to and expose those covert national security operations.

(5) I sought to prevent the exposure of these covert national security activities, while encouraging those conducting the investigation to pursue their inquiry into the Watergate itself. I so instructed my staff, the Attorney General, and the Acting Director of the FBI.

(6) I also specifically instructed Mr. Haldeman and Mr. Ehrlichman to ensure that the FBI would not carry its investigation into areas that might compromise these covert national security activities, or those of the CIA.

(7) At no time did I authorize or know about any offer of executive clemency for the Watergate defendants. Neither did I know until the time of my own investigation of any efforts to provide them with funds.

CONCLUSION

With hindsight, it is apparent that I should have given more heed to the warning signals I received along the way about a Watergate cover-up and less to the reassurances.

With hindsight, several other things also become clear:

—With respect to campaign practices, and also with respect to campaign finances, it should now be obvious that no campaign in history has ever been subjected to the kind of intensive and searching inquiry that has been focused on the campaign waged in my behalf in 1972.

It is clear that unethical, as well as illegal, activities took place in the course of that campaign.

None of these took place with my specific approval or knowledge. To the extent that I may in any way have contributed to the climate in which they took place, I did not intend to; to the extent that I failed to prevent them, I should have been more vigilant.

It was to help ensure against any repetition of this in the future that last week I proposed the establishment of a top-level, bipartisan, independent commission to recommend a comprehensive reform of campaign laws and practices. Given the priority I believe it deserves, such reform should be possible before the next Congressional elections in 1974.

—It now appears that there were persons who may have gone beyond my directives, and sought to expand on my efforts to protect the national security operations in order to cover up any involvement they or certain others might have had in Watergate. The extent to which this is true, and who may have participated and to what degree, are questions that it would not be proper to address here. The proper forum for settling these matters is in the courts.

—To the extent that I have been able to determine what probably happened in the tangled course of this affair, on the basis of my own recollections and of the conflicting accounts and evidence that I have seen, it would appear that one factor at work was that at critical points various people, each with his own perspective and his own responsibilities, saw the same situation with different eyes and heard the same words with different ears. What might have seemed insignificant to one seemed significant to another; what one saw in terms of public responsibility, another saw in terms of political opportunity; and mixed through it all, I am sure, was a concern on the part of many that the Watergate scandal should not be allowed to get in the way of what the Administration sought to achieve.

The truth about Watergate should be brought out—in an orderly way, recognizing that the safeguards of judicial procedure are designed to find the truth, not to hide the truth.

With his selection of Archibald Cox—who served both President Kennedy and President Johnson as Solicitor General—as the special supervisory prosecutor for matters related to the case, Attorney General-designate Richardson has demonstrated his own determination to see the truth brought out. In this effort he has my full support.

Considering the number of persons involved in this case whose testimony might be subject to a claim of executive privilege, I recognize that a clear definition of that claim has become central to the effort to arrive at the truth.

Accordingly, executive privilege will not be invoked as to any testimony concerning possible criminal conduct or discussions of possible criminal conduct, in the matters presently under investigation, including the Watergate affair and the alleged coverup.

I want to emphasize that this statement is limited to my own recollections of what I said and did relating to security and to the Watergate. I have specifically avoided any attempt to explain what other parties may have said and done. My own information on those other matters is fragmentary, and to some extent contradictory. Additional information may be forthcoming of which I am unaware. It is also my understanding that the information which has been conveyed to me has also become available to those prosecuting these matters. Under such circumstances, it would be prejudicial and unfair of me to render my opinions on the activities of others; those judgments must be left to the judicial process, our best hope for achieving the just result that we all seek.

As more information is developed, I have no doubt that more questions will be raised. To the extent that I am able, I shall also seek to set forth the facts as known to me with respect to those questions.

LETTER DIRECTING THE ACTING ATTORNEY GENERAL TO DISCHARGE THE DIRECTOR OF THE OFFICE OF WATERGATE SPECIAL PROSECUTION FORCE[21]

October 20, 1973

Dear Mr. Bork:

I have today accepted the resignations of Attorney General Richardson and Deputy Attorney General Ruckelshaus. In accordance with Title 28, Section 508 (b) of the United States Code and of Title 28, Section 0.132(a) of the Code of Federal Regulations, it is now incumbent upon you to perform both the duties as Solicitor General, and duties of and act as Attorney General.

In his press conference today Special Prosecutor Archibald Cox made it apparent that he will not comply with the instruction I issued to him, through Attorney General Richardson, yesterday. Clearly the Government of the United States cannot function if employees of the Executive Branch are free to ignore in this fashion the instructions of the President. Accordingly, in your capacity of Acting Attorney General, I direct you to discharge Mr. Cox immediately and to take all steps necessary to return to the Department of Justice the functions now being performed by the Watergate Special Prosecution Force.

It is my expectation that the Department of Justice will continue with full vigor the investigations and prosecutions that had been entrusted to the Watergate Special Prosecution Force.

Sincerely,

RICHARD NIXON

ADDRESS TO THE NATION ANNOUNCING DECISION TO RESIGN THE OFFICE OF PRESIDENT OF THE UNITED STATES[22]

Good evening:

This is the 37th time I have spoken to you from this office, where so many decisions have been made that shaped the history of this Nation. Each time I have done so to discuss with you some matter that I believe affected the national interest.

In all the decisions I have made in my public life, I have always tried to do what was best for the Nation. Throughout the long and difficult period of Watergate, I have felt it was my duty to persevere, to make every possible effort to complete the term of office to which you elected me.

In the past few days, however, it has become evident to me that I no longer have a strong enough political base in the Congress to justify continuing that effort. As long as there was such a base, I felt strongly that it was necessary to see the constitutional process through to its conclusion, that to do otherwise would be unfaithful to the spirit of that deliberately difficult process and a dangerously destabilizing precedent for the future.

But with the disappearance of that base, I now believe that the constitutional purpose has been served, and there is no longer a need for the process to be prolonged.

I would have preferred to carry through to the finish, whatever the personal agony it would have involved, and my family unanimously urged me to do so. But the interests of the Nation must always come before any personal considerations.

From the discussions I have had with Congressional and other leaders, I have concluded that because of the Watergate matter, I might not have the support of the Congress that I would consider necessary to back the very difficult decisions and carry out the duties of this office in the way the interests of the Nation will require.

I have never been a quitter. To leave office before my term is completed is abhorrent to every instinct in my body. But as President, I must put the interests of America first. America needs a full-time President and a full-time Congress, particularly at this time with problems we face at home and abroad.

To continue to fight through the months ahead for my personal vindication would almost totally absorb the time and attention of both the President and the Congress in a period when our entire focus should be on the great issues of peace abroad and prosperity without inflation at home.

Therefore, I shall resign the Presidency effective at noon tomorrow. Vice President Ford will be sworn in as President at that hour in this office.

As I recall the high hopes for America with which we began this second term, I feel a great sadness that I will not be here in this office working on your behalf to achieve those hopes in the next 2½ years. But in turning over direction of the Government to Vice President Ford, I know, as I told the Nation when I nominated him for that office 10 months ago, that the leadership of America will be in good hands.

In passing this office to the Vice President, I also do so with the profound sense of the weight of responsibility that will fall on his shoulders tomorrow and, therefore, of the understanding, the patience, the cooperation he will need from all Americans.

As he assumes that responsibility, he will deserve the help and the support of all of us. As we look to the future, the first essential is to begin healing the wounds of this Nation, to put the bitterness and divisions of the recent past behind us and to rediscover those shared ideals that lie at the heart of our strength and unity as a great and as a free people.

By taking this action, I hope that I will have hastened the start of that process of healing which is so desperately needed in America.

I regret deeply any injuries that may have been done in the course of the events that led to this decision. I would say only that if some of my judgments were wrong—and some were wrong—they were made in what I believed at the time to be the best interest of the Nation.

To those who have stood with me during these past difficult months—to my family, my friends, to many others who joined in supporting my cause because they believed it was right—I will be eternally grateful for your support.

And to those who have not felt able to give me your support, let me say I leave with no bitterness toward those who have opposed me, because all of us, in the final analysis, have been concerned with the good of the country, however our judgments might differ.

So, let us all now join together in affirming that common commitment and in helping our new President succeed for the benefit of all Americans.

I shall leave this office with regret at not completing my term, but with gratitude for the privilege of serving as your President for the past 5½ years. These years have been a momentous time in the history of our Nation and the world. They have been a time of achievement in which we can all be proud, achievements that represent the shared efforts of the Administration, the Congress, and the people.

But the challenges ahead are equally great, and they, too, will require the support and the efforts of the Congress and the people working in cooperation with the new Administration.

We have ended America's longest war, but in the work of securing a lasting peace in the world, the goals ahead are even more far-reaching and more difficult. We must complete a structure of peace so that it will be said of this generation, our generation of Americans, by the people of all nations, not only that we ended one war but that we prevented future wars.

We have unlocked the doors that for a quarter of a century stood between the United States and the People's Republic of China.

We must now ensure that the one quarter of the world's people who live in the People's Republic of China will be and remain not our enemies, but our friends.

In the Middle East, 100 million people in the Arab countries, many of whom have considered us their enemy for nearly 20 years, now look on us as their friends. We must continue to build on that friendship so that peace can settle at last over the Middle East and so that the cradle of civilization will not become its grave.

Together with the Soviet Union, we have made the crucial breakthroughs that have begun the process of limiting nuclear arms. But we must set as our goal not just limiting but reducing and, finally, destroying these terrible weapons so that they cannot destroy civilization and so that the threat of nuclear war will no longer hang over the world and the people.

We have opened the new relation with the Soviet Union. We must continue to develop and expand that new relationship so that the two strongest nations of the world will live together in cooperation, rather than confrontation.

494

Around the world—in Asia, in Africa, in Latin America, in the Middle East—there are millions of people who live in terrible poverty, even starvation. We must keep as our goal turning away from production for war and expanding production for peace so that people everywhere on this Earth can at last look forward in their children's time, if not in our own time, to having the necessities for a decent life.

Here in America, we are fortunate that most of our people have not only the blessings of liberty but also the means to live full and good and, by the world's standards, even abundant lives. We must press on, however, toward a goal, not only of more and better jobs but of full opportunity for every American and of what we are striving so hard right now to achieve, prosperity without inflation.

For more than a quarter of a century in public life, I have shared in the turbulent history of this era. I have fought for what I believed in. I have tried, to the best of my ability, to discharge those duties and meet those responsibilities that were entrusted to me.

Sometimes I have succeeded and sometimes I have failed, but always I have taken heart from what Theodore Roosevelt once said about the man in the arena, "whose face is marred by dust and sweat and blood, who strives valiantly, who errs and comes short again and again because there is not effort without error and shortcoming, but who does actually strive to do the deed, who knows the great enthusiasms, the great devotions, who spends himself in a worthy cause, who at the best knows in the end the triumphs of high achievements and who at the worst, if he fails, at least fails while daring greatly."

I pledge to you tonight that as long as I have a breath of life in my body, I shall continue in that spirit. I shall continue to work for the great causes to which I have been dedicated throughout my years as a Congessman, a Senator, Vice President, and President, the cause of peace, not just for America but among all nations—prosperity, justice, and opportunity for all of our people.

There is one cause above all to which I have been devoted and to which I shall always be devoted for as long as I live.

When I first took the oath of office as President 5½ years ago, I made this sacred commitment: to "consecrate my office, my energies, and all the wisdom I can summon to the cause of peace among nations."

I have done my very best in all the days since to be true to that pledge. As a result of these efforts, I am confident that the world is a safer place today, not only for the people of America but for the people of all nations, and that all of our children have a better chance than before of living in peace rather than dying in war.

This, more than anything, is what I hoped to achieve when I sought the Presidency. This, more than anything, is what I hope will be my legacy to you, to our country, as I leave the Presidency.

To have served in this office is to have felt a very personal sense of kinship with each and every American. In leaving it, I do so with this prayer: May God's grace be with you in all the days ahead.

LETTER RESIGNING THE OFFICE OF PRESIDENT OF THE UNITED STATES[23]

August 9, 1974

Dear Mr. Secretary:

I hereby resign the Office of President of the United States.

Sincerely,

RICHARD NIXON

[The Honorable Henry A. Kissinger, The Secretary of State, Washington, D.C. 20520]

42

THE DECISION TO PARDON NIXON

Ford Frees His Predecessor of Legal Liability

Nixon's successor was Gerald R. Ford, the first President to attain office through appointment rather than by election. Nixon had appointed Ford Vice President on October 10, 1973, after the incumbent Vice President Spiro T. Agnew pleaded no contest to a single charge of federal income tax evasion and resigned his office, an action coming in the wake of grand jury findings that he had accepted payoffs from construction companies while Governor of Maryland and Vice President.

On September 8, 1974, Ford, now President, granted Nixon a full pardon for all federal crimes he "committed or may have committed or taken part in" during his term in office. No admission of guilt was exacted from Nixon, only that he had made "mistakes." On October 17, Ford, testifying personally before the House Subcommittee on Criminal Justice, stated that "there was no deal, period." Public disapproval of the pardon may have cost Ford the Presidential election in 1976.

REMARKS BY GERALD R. FORD ON SIGNING A PROCLAMATION GRANTING PARDON TO RICHARD M. NIXON[24]

September 8, 1974

Ladies and gentlemen:

I have come to a decision which I felt I should tell you and all of my fellow American citizens, as soon as I was certain in my own mind and in my own conscience that it is the right thing to do.

I have learned already in this office that the difficult decisions always come to this desk. I must admit that many of them do not look at all the same as the hypothetical questions that I have answered freely and perhaps too fast on previous occasions.

My customary policy is to try and get all the facts and to consider the opinions of my countrymen and to take counsel with my most valued friends. But these seldom agree, and in the end, the decision is mine. To procrastinate, to agonize, and to wait for a more favorable turn of events that may never come or more compelling external pressures that may as well be wrong as right, is itself a decision of sorts and a weak and potentially dangerous course for a President to follow.

I have promised to uphold the Constitution, to do what is right as God gives me to see the right, and to do the very best that I can for America.

I have asked your help and your prayers, not only when I became President but many times since. The Constitution is the supreme law of our land and it governs our actions as citizens. Only the laws of God, which govern our consciences, are superior to it.

As we are a nation under God, so I am sworn to uphold our laws with the help of God. And I have sought such guidance and searched my own conscience with special diligence to determine the right thing for me to do with respect to my predecessor in this place, Richard Nixon, and his loyal wife and family.

Theirs is an American tragedy in which we all have played a part. It could go on and on and on, or someone must write the end to it. I have concluded that only I can do that, and if I can, I must.

There are no historic or legal precedents to which I can turn in this matter, none that precisely fit the circumstances of a private citizen who has resigned the Presidency of the United States. But it is common knowledge that serious allegations and accusations hang like a sword over our former President's head, threatening his health as he tries to reshape his life, a great part of which was spent in the service of this country and by the mandate of its people.

After years of bitter controversy and divisive national debate, I have been advised, and I am compelled to conclude that many months and perhaps more years will have to pass before Richard Nixon could obtain a fair trial by jury in any jurisdiction of the United States under governing decisions of the Supreme Court.

I deeply believe in equal justice for all Americans, whatever their station or former station. The law, whether human or divine, is no respecter of persons; but the law is a respecter of reality.

The facts, as I see them, are that a former President of the United States, instead of enjoying equal treatment with any other citizen accused of violating the law, would be cruelly and excessively penalized either in preserving the presumption of his innocence or in obtaining a speedy determination of his guilt in order to repay a legal debt to society.

During this long period of delay and potential litigation, ugly passions would again be aroused. And our people would again be polarized in their opinions. And the credibility of our free institutions of government would again be challenged at home and abroad.

In the end, the courts might well hold that Richard Nixon had been denied due process, and the verdict of history would even more be inconclusive with respect to those charges arising out of the period of his Presidency, of which I am presently aware.

But it is not the ultimate fate of Richard Nixon that most concerns me, though surely it deeply troubles every decent and every compassionate person. My concern is the immediate future of this great country.

In this, I dare not depend upon my personal sympathy as a long-time friend of the former President, nor my professional judgment as a lawyer, and I do not.

As President, my primary concern must always be the greatest good of all the people of the United States whose servant I am. As a man, my first consideration is to be true to my own convictions and my own conscience.

My conscience tells me clearly and certainly that I cannot prolong the bad dreams that continue to reopen a chapter that is closed. My conscience tells me that only I, as President, have the constitutional power to firmly shut and seal this book. My conscience tells me it is my duty, not merely to proclaim domestic tranquillity but to use every means that I have to insure it.

I do believe that the buck stops here, that I cannot rely upon public opinion polls to tell me what is right.

I do believe that right makes might and that if I am wrong, 10 angels swearing I was right would make no difference.

I do believe, with all my heart and mind and spirit, that I, not as President but as a humble servant of God, will receive justice without mercy if I fail to show mercy.

Finally, I feel that Richard Nixon and his loved ones have suffered enough and will continue to suffer, no matter what I do, no matter what we, as a great and good nation, can do together to make his goal of peace come true.

[At this point, the President began reading from the proclamation granting the pardon.]

"Now, therefore, I, Gerald R. Ford, President of the United States, pursuant to the pardon conferred upon me by Article II, Section 2, of the Constitution, have granted and by these presents do grant a full, free, and absolute pardon unto Richard Nixon for all offenses against the United States which he, Richard Nixon, has committed or may have committed or taken part in during the period from July (January) 20, 1969 through August 9, 1974."

[The President signed the proclamation and then resumed reading.]

"In witness whereof, I have hereunto set my hand this eighth day of September, in the year of our Lord nineteen hundred and seventy-four, and of the Independence of the United States of America the one hundred and ninety-ninth."

43

THE DECISION TO YIELD THE PANAMA CANAL

Carter Champions a Treaty with Panama

All too often foreign policymaking is held hostage to the lowest common denominator of jingoistic clamor, with even issues of war and peace heavily influenced by short-term political interest. Only rarely in American history have Presidents willingly risked political disadvantage in order to pursue their conception of the national interest. This is what John Adams did when he sought a diplomatic rather than a military solution with France in 1799. Such was also the case with Jimmy Carter's decision early in his presidency to press forward with negotiations with Panama over the future of the Panama Canal; and, after the treaties had been agreed upon, to invest enormous political capital in seeking their ratification.

The United States won its rights to a Canal Zone ten miles wide across the Isthmus of Panama in 1903 through tacit support for a pocket revolution engineered by promoters of the Canal and dissidents in Colombia's province of Panama. The U.S. helped insure the success of the revolution through the dispatch of warships. American terms for a treaty, which had been rejected by the Colombian Senate, were accepted by Philippe Bunau-Varilla, a French businessman whose authority to negotiate for Panama was doubtful. Unhappy with the terms of the treaty, the Panamanian government caved in under the threat that the United States would withdraw protection of the new republic. The Hay-Bunau-Varilla Treaty granted the U.S. in perpetuity the use and control of the Canal Zone, giving it full sovereignty (including the right of fortification) over the Zone. The U.S. agreed to pay $10 million and an annual fee of $250,000. As President Theodore Roosevelt had commented about his efforts:

If I had followed traditional conservative methods, I would have submitted a dignified state paper of probably 200 pages to Congress and the debates on it would have been going on yet; but I took the Canal Zone and let Congress debate; and while the debate goes on the Canal does too.

The forty-mile Canal, an extraordinary engineering triumph, cost more than $365 million to construct and was opened to traffic on August 15, 1914.

Although by a 1955 treaty the United States agreed to increase annual payments to Panama to $1,930,000 and to guarantee equality of pay and opportunity to non-U.S. citizen employees in the Canal Zone, American control of the Zone was a festering sore. In 1959 mobs attacked the U.S. embassy in Panama City and attempted to invade the Zone. The necessity of reconsidering the arrangement for American control of the Canal Zone was brought to a head by the clashes of January 9–10, 1964 between U.S. troops and Panamanians (provoked when U.S. students attempted to raise the American flag over the Zone), in which twenty-one Panamanians and four American soldiers died.

After a brief break in diplomatic relations, the two nations agreed in April 1964 to renegotiate the Panama Canal treaties. These negotiations, supported by Presidents Johnson, Nixon, Ford and Carter, extended over thirteen years. Preliminary agreements reached in 1967 providing for the termination of exclusive U.S. sovereignty over the Canal Zone were never submitted to the U.S. Senate for ratification and were rejected by Panama. However, on February 7, 1974 the two nations concluded an agreement on *basic principles* to guide the negotiation of a new treaty under which the concept of American control over the Canal in perpetuity was eliminated.

Negotiations with Panama were continued in good faith, but with great political caution, by Presidents Nixon and Ford, in the face of significant opposition in the Senate and on the part of the public. A Senate resolution expressing strong opposition to termination of U.S. sovereignty over the Zone was introduced in 1975, sponsored by thirty-eight Senators, four more than would be necessary to reject the treaty. In the 1976 Republican primaries, President Ford was attacked by candidate Ronald Reagan, who took the position that "When it comes to the Canal, we built it, we paid for it, it's ours and we should tell Torrijos [Brigadier General Omar Torrijos Herrera, head of the Panamanian government] and company that we are going to keep it."

Early in his presidency Jimmy Carter indicated the seriousness with which he desired a resolution of the issue with Panama. Negotiators reached agreement on two treaties, signed by Carter and

Torrijos, on September 7, 1977, in the presence of representatives of twenty-six Western Hemisphere nations. Under the *general treaty* (which will expire at the end of 1999), the Hay-Bunau-Varilla Treaty and other agreements giving the U.S. exclusive rights to the Canal were repealed. For the remainder of the century, the U.S. would continue to be responsible for operation, maintenance, and defense of the Canal, but with Panama assuming increased responsibility until full control would be transferred on December 31,1999. The sixty-five percent of the Zone not vital to the operation of the Canal was to revert to Panama immediately after treaty ratification. During the life of the treaty, Panama would receive thirty cents out of each $1.29 toll per canal ton; a percentage of other revenue from the Canal; and ten million dollars annually from the U.S. for police and fire services; and other payments. The two nations agreed to jointly study the feasibility of a new sea-level canal.

The second treaty, that *Concerning Permanent Neutrality and Operation of the Canal,* provided for the transit of naval and merchant vessels of all nations at all times; in times of peace and war; that, in time of war, U.S. and Panamanian vessels would be entitled to transit expeditiously, while respecting the principle of neutrality which the treaty asserted.

Many, but not all, knowledgeable observers, thought the treaties wise. Carter, like many others, believed it impossible over the long run to defend the Canal without maintaining good relations with Panama. The military foresaw the need for a force of 100,000 to mount a reasonable defense of the Canal. Carter saw the unimpeded use and effective operation of the Canal as more important than its ownership. The moralistic President believed that American behavior toward Panama would be perceived throughout the world as a litmus test of how the U.S. would treat a small and defenseless nation. He viewed the treaties as correcting a seventy-five-year-old injustice.

While President Carter had seldom shown himself to be particularly effective in working with the Congress, a massive lobbying campaign on behalf of the treaties overcame high odds. In July 1977 only thirty-seven Senators were ready to be counted to support the treaties while twenty-five were opposed. The President needed to win over thirty of the thirty-eight remaining Senators at a time when polls indicated that seventy-eight percent of the American people did not want to "give up" the Canal, and only eight percent found the idea acceptable.

In mustering support, Carter personally talked with every member of the Senate, most of them privately and employed his available patronage. He even went so far as to read a textbook on semantics written by California's eccentric conservative Senator (and famous linguist), S.I. Hayakawa. He also had to work to calm the Panamanians, infuriated by the tone of some of the speeches in the Senate. Perhaps central to the ultimate success of ratification was a Statement of Understanding agreed upon by Carter and Torrijos, which interpreted the U.S. right to act against any aggression or threat directed against it, but not including the right to intervene in the internal affairs of Panama. The right of U.S. war vessels to expeditious transit was interpreted as granting them priority of passage. After twenty-two days of debate—the first telecasts of floor proceedings in the Senate—the treaties were both ratified by 68–32, only one vote over the necessary minimum. Three reservations were attached by the Senate to the Treaty of Permanent Neutrality and one to the General Treaty, reflecting the Carter-Torrijos Statement of Understanding.

Ratification did not end the battle. It would take sixteen months for the Congress to pass laws implementing the Treaties. Support in the House of Representatives was razor thin: legislation passed by votes of 200–198 and 204–202. Not until three days before the treaties took effect and U.S. jurisdiction terminated over the Canal Zone (October 1, 1979) was Carter able to sign the implementing legislation.

The struggle left deep political wounds. Six Senators who supported the treaties were defeated for reelection in 1978 and another eleven in 1980, the year that Carter, too, was defeated for reelection.

We can never know what General Torrijos would have done if the treaties had failed in the U.S. After ratification, he said that he would have given orders to the Panamanian National Guard to blow up the Canal. We can, however, entertain the possibility that the U.S. and Panama might have gone to war; that the U.S. would have won the war but the Canal itself would have been closed and damaged. Instead, the U.S. and Panama became allied, committed to partnership in operating the waterway for their common benefit. Torrijos aptly characterized Carter's performance by quoting Abraham Lincoln's remark that the difference between a statesman and a politician is that a "statesman thinks of future generations, but a politician only thinks of the next election."

REMARKS BY PRESIDENT JIMMY CARTER AT THE SIGNING CEREMONY OF THE PANAMA CANAL TREATIES AT THE PAN AMERICAN UNION BUILDING, WASHINGTON, D.C.[25]

September 7, 1977

Mr. Secretary General and distinguished leaders from throughout our own country and from throughout this hemisphere:

First of all, I want to express my deep thanks to the leaders who have come here from 27 nations in our own hemisphere, 20 heads of state, for this historic occasion.

I'm proud to be here as part of the largest group of heads of state ever assembled in the Hall of the Americas, Mr. Secretary General.

We are here to participate in the signing of treaties which will assure a peaceful and prosperous and secure future for an international waterway of great importance to us all.

But the treaties do more than that. They mark the commitment of the United States to the belief that fairness, and not force, should lie at the heart of our dealings with the nations of the world.

If any agreement between two nations is to last, it must serve the best interests of both nations. The new treaties do that. And by guaranteeing the neutrality of the Panama Canal, the treaties also serve the best interests of every nation that uses the canal.

This agreement thus forms a new partnership to insure that this vital waterway, so important to all of us, will continue to be well operated, safe, and open to shipping by all nations, now and in the future.

Under these accords, Panama will play an increasingly important role in the operation and defense of the canal during the next 23 years. And after that, the United States will still be able to counter any threat to the canal's neutrality and openness for use.

The members of the Organization of American States and all the members of the United Nations will have a chance to subscribe to the permanent neutrality of the canal.

The accords also give Panama an important economic stake in the continued, safe, and efficient operation of the canal and make Panama a strong and interested party in the future success of the waterway.

In the spirit of reciprocity suggested by the leaders at the Bogotá summit, the United States and Panama have agreed that any future sea-level canal will be built in Panama and with the cooperation of the United States. In this manner, the best interests of both our nations are linked and preserved into the future.

Many of you seated at this table have made known for years through the Organization of American States and through your own personal expressions of concern to my predecessors in the White House, your own strong feelings about the Panama Canal Treaty of 1903. That treaty, drafted in a world so different from ours today, has become an obstacle to better relations with Latin America.

I thank each of you for the support and help that you and your countries have given during the long process of negotiation, which is now drawing to a close.

This agreement has been negotiated over a period of 14 years under four Presidents of the United States.

I'm proud to see President Ford here with us tonight. And I'm also glad to see Mrs. Lyndon Johnson here with us tonight.

Many Secretaries of State have been involved in the negotiations. Dean Rusk can't be here. He has endorsed the treaty. But Secretary of State William Rogers is here. We are glad to have you, sir. And Secretary of State Henry Kissinger is here too.

This has been a bipartisan effort, and it is extremely important for our country to stay unified in our commitment to the fairness, the symbol of equality, the mutual respect, the preservation of the security and defense of our own Nation, and an exhibition of cooperation which sets a symbol that is important to us all before this assembly tonight and before the American people in the future.

This opens a new chapter in our relations with all nations of this hemisphere, and it testifies to the maturity and the good judgment and the decency of our people. This agreement is a symbol for the world of the mutual respect and cooperation among all our nations.

Thank you very much for your help.

44

THE DECISION TO SEEK PEACE IN THE MIDDLE EAST THROUGH PRESIDENTIAL INITIATIVE

Carter's Camp David Mediation

President Jimmy Carter's successful effort to broker a peace treaty between Egypt and Israel proved to be the most remarkable direct involvement by a President in arbitering a third-party dispute since Theodore Roosevelt's contribution to settling the Russo-Japanese War in 1904. For two weeks in September 1978, Carter focused exclusively on his meetings with Israel's Prime Minister Menachem Begin and Egypt's President Anwar el-Sadat at the Presidential retreat, Camp David, talks held under a complete news blackout. After near failure, the men emerged with significant agreements which, after eleven more days of Presidential shuttle diplomacy in the Middle East in March 1979, ultimately led to the signing of a peace treaty on the lawn of the White House.

The beginning of Carter's term found the Middle East in its perennial state of instability. The Yom Kippur War of October 6, 1973—the fourth in twenty-five years between Israel and its Arab neighbors—had helped Egypt and Syria to regain their national self-respect, but left Israel in control of the Sinai, the Golan Heights, and the West Bank of the Jordan River. By shuttle diplomacy Secretary of State Henry Kissinger had been successful in achieving a cease-fire, a pull-back of forces, and the opening of the Suez Canal to non-military cargoes of Italy. But talks in Geneva under the auspices of the United States and the Soviet Union had not led to further progress.

At the beginning of his presidency, Carter confronted a geopolitical situation in which the Soviet Union appeared to be gaining considerable influence in such marginal Middle East states as South Yemen. Israel, under the leadership of hardliner Begin, was increasingly isolated as a result of the Arab oil diplomacy. On the other hand, Egypt, threatened by Israel, Libya, and possibly Ethiopia, was turning towards the United States under Sadat's leadership. Terrorism, embargoes, boycotts, refugees used as pawns, and strident rhetoric continued to dominate the situation in the Middle East, with still another war looming on the horizon.

The situation was dramatically transformed on November 9, 1977, when Sadat announced that he was willing to go to Jerusalem to seek peace. Invited by the Israeli government, Sadat spent three days in Israel, November 19–21. But the euphoria which resulted from Sadat's visit and cordial reception, was followed by inconclusive negotiations between Begin and Sadat in Ismalia, Egypt, a month later. Sadat found himself attacked by the hardline Arab states, while "moderates" like Jordan's King Hussein hung back from public support of the peace moves. The government of Israel exacerbated the situation by appearing to be promoting settlements on conquered land in the Sinai and on the West Bank.

At the very end of July 1978, Carter decided to go all out for peace—to bring Begin and Sadat together for extensive negotiations. On August 8 the three men announced that they would meet at Camp David. Carter determined upon the isolation of the Presidential retreat, a press blackout while the negotiations were proceeding, and an intensive personal effort. While plans called for a three-day meeting, the negotiations consumed thirteen days.

The three men remained isolated at Camp David (except for a visit to the great battlefield at Gettysburg) accompanied by a few other high officials of their governments—Carter had the assistance, among others, of Vice President Walter Mondale, and Secretary of State Cyrus Vance. Living in little cottages amidst oak, poplar, and hickory trees, the affairs of the rest of the world receded from view. With early discussions between Sadat and Begin proving unconstructive, Carter, virtually abandoning the routine duties of the presidency, met separately with the leaders day in and day out to attempt to find common ground on some fifty distinct issues.

In the end Carter achieved two agreements at Camp David: "A Framework for the Conclusion of a Peace Treaty between Egypt and Israel" and a "Framework for Peace in the Middle East." The first document provided that Egypt and Israel would sign a peace treaty within three months; and thereafter the Sinai would be turned over to Egypt in stages ranging from an initial three-to-nine-month period and to be completed within two to three years. Thereafter, normal diplomatic relations would occur. The second "Framework" provided a five-year transition period on the West Bank and Gaza; the withdrawal of Israel's military government; an intervening local government for Palestinians; negotiation between Egypt, Israel, Jordan, and elected Palestinian representatives on sovereignty. Palestinians were guaranteed the right to elect representatives, determine their own local government, and participate in decisions on their own future. Significantly, the issues of Jerusalem and of Israeli settlements on the West Bank were not dealt with in the two Frameworks.

As the three-month deadline for an Egypt-Israel Agreement passed and both Sadat and Begin refused this time to meet jointly with Carter, the President conducted personal shuttle diplomacy in the Middle East, meeting with Sadat in Cairo, in Jerusalem with Begin— where Carter presided over a meeting of the Israeli cabinet and addressed the Knesset—and then in a stopover in Cairo, where on March 13, 1979, Carter announced achieving a formula for a peace treaty. The Treaty, signed on March 26, 1979, provided for withdrawal of the Israelis from the Sinai; establishment of normal relations; free right of passage through the Suez Canal; and Israel's right to purchase Sinai oil, among other matters. The U.S. pledged $4.5 billion ($3.3 billion in loans for arms purchases) in aid for Egypt and Israel for 1979–81. On the whole, the two nations have observed the peace treaty, although the lack of further progress can in no small part be attributed to the assassination of Sadat in Cairo on October 6, 1981.

CAMP DAVID MEETING ON THE MIDDLE EAST: ADDRESS BEFORE A JOINT SESSION OF THE CONGRESS[26]

September 18, 1978

Vice President Mondale, Speaker O'Neill, distinguished Members of the United States Congress, Justices of the Supreme Court, other leaders of our great Nation, ladies and gentlemen:

It's been more than 2,000 years since there was peace between Egypt and a free Jewish nation. If our present expectations are realized, this year we shall see such peace again.

The first thing I would like to do is to give tribute to the two men who made this impossible dream now become a real possibility, the two great leaders with whom I have met for the last 2 weeks at Camp David: first, President Anwar Sadat of Egypt, and the other, of course, is Prime Minister Menachem Begin of the nation of Israel.

I know that all of you would agree that these are two men of great personal courage, representing nations of peoples who are deeply grateful to them for the achievement which they have realized. And I am personally grateful to them for what they have done.

At Camp David, we sought a peace that is not only of vital importance to their own two nations but to all the people of the Middle East, to all the people of the United States, and, indeed, to all the world as well.

The world prayed for the success of our efforts, and I am glad to announce to you that these prayers have been answered.

I've come to discuss with you tonight what these two leaders have accomplished and what this means to all of us.

The United States has had no choice but to be deeply concerned about the Middle East and to try to use our influence and our efforts to advance the cause of peace. For the last 30 years, through four wars, the people of this troubled region have paid a terrible price in suffering and division and hatred and bloodshed. No two nations have suffered more than Egypt and Israel. But the dangers and the costs of conflicts in this region for our own Nation have been great as well. We have longstanding friendships among the nations there and the peoples of the region, and we have profound moral commitments which are deeply rooted in our values as a people.

The strategic location of these countries and the resources that they possess mean that events in the Middle East directly affect people everywhere. We and our friends could not be indifferent if a hostile power were to establish domination there. In few areas of the world is there a greater risk that a local conflict could spread among other nations adjacent to them and then, perhaps, erupt into a tragic confrontation between us super powers ourselves.

Our people have come to understand that unfamiliar names like Sinai, Aqaba, Sharm el Sheikh, Ras en Naqb, Gaza, the West Bank of Jordan, can have a direct and immediate bearing on our own well-being as a nation and our hope for a peaceful world. That is why we in the United States cannot afford to be idle bystanders and why we have been full partners in the search for peace and why it is so vital to our Nation that these meetings at Camp David have been a success.

Through the long years of conflict, four main issues have divided the parties involved. One is the nature of peace—whether peace will simply mean that the guns are silenced, that the bombs no longer fall, that the tanks cease to roll, or whether it will mean that the nations of the Middle East can deal with each other as neighbors and as equals and as friends, with a full range of diplomatic and cultural and economic and human relations between them. That's been the basic question. The Camp David agreement has defined such relationships, I'm glad to announce to you, between Israel and Egypt.

The second main issue is providing for the security of all parties involved, including, of course, our friends, the Israelis, so that none of them need fear attack or military threats from one another. When implemented, the Camp David agreement, I'm glad to announce to you, will provide for such mutual security.

Third is the question of agreement on secure and recognized boundaries, the end of military occupation, and the granting of self-government or else the return to other nations of territories which have been occupied by Israel since the 1967 conflict. The Camp David agreement, I'm glad to announce to you, provides for the realization of all these goals.

And finally, there is the painful human question of the fate of the Palestinians who live or who have lived in these disputed regions. The Camp David agreement guarantees that the Palestinian people may participate in the resolution of the Palestinian problem in all its aspects, a commitment that Israel has made in writing and which is supported and appreciated, I'm sure, by all the world.

Over the last 18 months, there has been, of course, some progress on these issues. Egypt and Israel came close to agreeing about the first issue, the nature of peace. They then saw that the second and third issues, that is, withdrawal and security, were intimately connected, closely entwined. But fundamental divisions still remained in other areas—about the fate of the Palestinians, the future of the West Bank and Gaza, and the future of Israeli settlements in occupied Arab territories.

We all remember the hopes for peace that were inspired by President Sadat's initiative, that great and historic visit to Jerusalem last November that thrilled the world, and by the warm and genuine personal response of Prime Minister Begin and the Israeli people, and by the mutual promise between them, publicly made, that there would be no more war. These hopes were sustained when Prime Minister Begin reciprocated by visiting Ismailia on Christmas Day. That progress continued, but at a slower and slower pace through the early part of the year. And by early summer, the negotiations had come to a standstill once again.

It was this stalemate and the prospect for an even worse future that prompted me to invite both President Sadat and Prime Minister Begin to join me at Camp David. They accepted, as you know, instantly, without delay, without preconditions, without consultation even between them.

It's impossible to overstate the courage of these two men or the foresight they have shown. Only through high ideals, through compromises of words and not principle, and through a willingness to look deep into the human heart and to understand the problems and hopes and dreams of one another can progress in a difficult situation like this ever be made. That's what these men and their wise and diligent advisers who are here with us tonight have done during the last 13 days.

When this conference began, I said that the prospects for success were remote. Enormous barriers of ancient history and nationalism and suspicion would have to be overcome if we were to meet our objectives. But President Sadat and Prime Minister Begin have overcome these barriers, exceeded our fondest expectations, and have signed two agreements that hold out the possibility of resolving issues that history had taught us could not be resolved.

The first of these documents is entitled, "A Framework for Peace in the Middle East Agreed at Camp David." It deals with a comprehensive settlement, comprehensive agreement, between Israel and all her neighbors, as well as the difficult question of the Palestinian people and the future of the West Bank and the Gaza area.

The agreement provides a basis for the resolution of issues involving the West Bank and Gaza during the next 5 years. It outlines a process of change which is in keeping with Arab hopes, while also carefully respecting Israel's vital security. The Israeli military government over these areas will be withdrawn and will be replaced with a self-government of the Palestinians who live there. And Israel has committed that this government will have full autonomy. Prime Minister Begin said to me several times, not partial autonomy, but full autonomy.

Israeli forces will be withdrawn and redeployed into specified locations to protect Israel's security. The Palestinians will further participate in determining their own future through talks in which their own elected representatives, the inhabitants of the West Bank and Gaza, will negotiate with Egypt and Israel and Jordan to determine the final status of the West Bank and Gaza.

Israel has agreed, has committed themselves, that the legitimate rights of the Palestinian people will be recognized. After the signing of this framework last night, and during the negotiations concerning the establishment of the Palestinian self-government, no new Israeli settlements will be established in this area. The future settlements issue will be decided among the negotiating parties.

The final status of the West Bank and Gaza will be decided before the end of the 5-year transitional period during which the Palestinian Arabs will have their own government, as part of a negotiation which will produce a peace treaty between Israel and Jordan specifying borders, withdrawal, all those very crucial issues.

These negotiations will be based on all the provisions and the principles of Security Council Resolution 242, with which you all are so familiar. The agreement on the final status of these areas will then be submitted to a vote by the representatives of the inhabitants of the West Bank and Gaza, and they will have the right for the first time in their history, the Palestinian people, to decide how they will govern themselves permanently.

We also believe, of course, all of us, that there should be a just settlement of the problems of displaced persons and refugees, which takes into account appropriate United Nations resolutions.

Finally, this document also outlines a variety of security arrangements to reinforce peace between Israel and her neighbors. This is, indeed, a comprehensive and fair framework for peace in the Middle East, and I'm glad to report this to you.

The second agreement is entitled, "A Framework for the Conclusion of a Peace Treaty Between Egypt and Israel." It returns to Egypt its full exercise of sovereignty over the Sinai Peninsula and establishes several security zones, recognizing carefully that sovereignty right for the protection of all parties. It also provides that Egypt will extend full diplomatic recognition to Israel at the time the Israelis complete an interim withdrawal from most of the Sinai, which will take place between 3 months and 9 months after the conclusion of the peace treaty. And the peace treaty is to be fully negotiated and signed no later than 3 months from last night.

I think I should also report that Prime Minister Begin and President Sadat have already challenged each other to conclude the treaty even earlier. And I hope they——[applause]. This final conclusion of a peace treaty will be completed late in December, and it would be a wonderful Christmas present for the world.

Final and complete withdrawal of all Israeli forces will take place between 2 and 3 years following the conclusion of the peace treaty.

While both parties are in total agreement on all the goals that I have just described to you, there is one issue on which agreement has not yet been reached. Egypt states that agreement to remove the Israeli settlements from Egyptian territory is a prerequisite to a peace treaty. Israel says that the issue of the Israeli settlements should be resolved during the peace negotiations themselves.

Now, within 2 weeks, with each member of the Knesset or the Israeli Parliament acting as individuals, not constrained by party loyalty, the Knesset will decide on the issue of the settlements. Our own Government's position, my own personal position is well known on this issue and has been consistent. It is my strong hope, my prayer, that the question of Israeli settlements on Egyptian territory will not be the final obstacle to peace.

None of us should underestimate the historic importance of what has already been done. This is the first time that an Arab and an Israeli leader have signed a comprehensive framework for peace. It contains the seeds of a time when the Middle East, with all its vast potential, may be a land of human richness and fulfillment, rather than a land of bitterness and continued conflict. No region in the world has greater natural and human resources than this one, and nowhere have they been more heavily weighed down by intense hatred and frequent war. These agreements hold out the real possibility that this burden might finally be lifted.

But we must also not forget the magnitude of the obstacles that still remain. The summit exceeded our highest expectations, but we know that it left many difficult issues which are still to be resolved. These issues will require careful negotiation in the months to come. The Egyptian and Israeli people must recognize the tangible benefits that peace will bring and support the decisions their leaders have made, so that a secure and a peaceful future can be achieved for them. The American public, you and I, must also offer our full support to those who have made decisions that are difficult and those who have very difficult decisions still to make.

What lies ahead for all of us is to recognize the statesmanship that President Sadat and Prime Minister Begin have shown and to invite others in that region to follow their example. I have already, last night, invited the other leaders of the Arab world to help sustain progress toward a comprehensive peace.

We must also join in an effort to bring an end to the conflict and the terrible suffering in Lebanon. This is a subject that President Sadat discussed with me many times while I was in Camp David with him. And the first time that the three of us met together, this was a subject of heated discussion. On the way to Washington last night in the helicopter, we mutually committed ourselves to join with other nations, with the Lebanese people themselves, all factions, with President Sarkis, with Syria and Saudi Arabia, perhaps the European countries like France, to try to move toward a solution of the problem in Lebanon, which is so vital to us and to the poor people in Lebanon, who have suffered so much.

We will want to consult on this matter and on these documents and their meaning with all of the leaders, particularly the Arab leaders. And I'm pleased to say to you tonight that just a few minutes ago, King Hussein of Jordan and King Khalid of Saudi Arabia, perhaps other leaders later, but these two have already agreed to receive Secretary Vance, who will be leaving tomorrow to explain to them the terms of the Camp David agreement. And we hope to secure their support for the realization of the new hopes and dreams of the people of the Middle East.

This is an important mission, and this responsibility, I can tell you, based on my last 2 weeks with him, could not possibly rest on the shoulders of a more able and dedicated and competent man than Secretary Cyrus Vance.

Finally, let me say that for many years the Middle East has been a textbook for pessimism, a demonstration that diplomatic ingenuity was no match for intractable human conflicts. Today we are privileged to see the chance for one of the sometimes rare, bright moments in human history—a chance that may offer the way to peace. We have a chance for peace, because these two brave leaders found within themselves the willingness to work together to seek these lasting prospects for peace, which we all want so badly. And for that, I hope that you will share my prayer of thanks and my hope that the promise of this moment shall be fully realized.

The prayers at Camp David were the same as those of the shepherd King David, who prayed in the 8th Psalm, "Wilt thou not revive us again: that thy people may rejoice in thee? ... I will hear what God the Lord will speak: for he will speak peace unto his people, and unto his saints: but let them not return again unto folly."

And I would like to say, as a Christian, to these two friends of mine, the words of Jesus, "Blessed are the peacemakers, for they shall be the children of God."

45

THE DECISION TO TRADE ARMS FOR HOSTAGES WITH IRAN

Reagan Deals with Terrorists

As President, Ronald Reagan's "honeymoon" with the American people lasted almost six years. It ended with revelations that he had approved the covert sale of arms to Iran at a time when official American policy banned aid to governments who were assisting terrorists; that profits from those sales were probably diverted to the Nicaraguan Contras in violation of the spirit, if not the letter of the law; and that members of his National Security Council staff had run amuck in implementing these policies. As a result of this episode, Reagan's management style came under sharp attack. Reagan was portrayed by the review board he appointed—chaired by former Senator John Tower—as remote, confused, and distracted. Months after the news had become public, Reagan clung tenaciously to the widely discredited notion that his Iran policy had not been primarily an attempt to trade arms for American hostages but was prompted by a desire to open up an avenue of communications with alleged "moderates" in the Iran government.

The failure of American policies toward Iran had contributed heavily to the defeat of Jimmy Carter in his bid for reelection in 1980. The long-term intimate relationship between the United States and Iran had ended with the overthrow of the Shah on January 16, 1979, and the emergence of a new regime headed by the Islamic fundamentalist, Ayatollah Khomeini, and overtly hostile to the United States. After the Shah was admitted to the U.S. to receive medical treatment, radical elements stormed the U.S. Embassy in Teheran on November 4, 1979. Fifty-three Americans were taken hostage. Fifty-two would remain in captivity for 444 days. Saturation media coverage and

Carter's obsessive concern for the hostages elevated the matter to a central national concern.

Ronald Reagan came to office vowing that the United States would once again command the respect of both adversaries and allies, and pledged that America would "stand tall." Yet, the Reagan Administration proved no more successful than did Carter in dealing with the terrorism of fanatical groups in the Middle East or in preventing the hijacking of American airplanes and the kidnapping of American citizens. In public statements the Reagan Administration linked the governments of Iran, Syria, and Libya to these terrorist groups and pressured its allies not to deal with them. In practice, however, the United States took military action only against the weakest, Libya, attacking its missile sites in March 1986, and its capital, Tripoli, in April, in what appears to have been an attempt to assassinate Libyan strongman, Colonel Muammar al-Qaddafi.

American approaches to Iran began in August 1985 and appear to have been prompted by a desire to free seven American hostages abducted in Beirut between March 7, 1984, and June 9, 1985, including the CIA station chief in Beirut. Most, if not all, the Americans were held by fundamentalist Shiite terrorist groups with links to the regime of Ayatollah Khomeini.

A second reason for the approaches—the one Reagan insisted was the *only* reason—was to reestablish ties with influential Iranians so that the United States would be able to exert influence during the crisis which presumably would follow the death of the aged Khomeini. In August 1985, although the Secretaries of State and Defense disapproved, members of the National Security Council became involved in facilitating the sale by Israel to Iran of U.S.-origin TOW and HAWK missiles. The Israelis were led to believe that they would then be able to buy replacements from the United States. As part of the deal, the Iranians were to release four or more hostages. Although the President professed that he was unable to remember, the President's Tower Commission concluded that Reagan most likely approved Israel's transfer of arms before it took place, certainly never opposing the notion of such transfers.

One hostage was released as the result of the transfer of 508 TOW missiles to Iran on August 30 and September 14, 1985. During the next few months, members of the National Security Council became increasingly involved in Byzantine intrigues involving the governments and officials of Iran and Israel, and "a shadowy network" of American, Israeli, Iranian, and Saudi Arabian arms dealers and businessmen.

On January 17, 1986, Reagan approved a plan whereby the CIA was to purchase 4,000 TOW missiles from the Department of Defense and, after receiving payment from Iran, transfer them *directly* to Iran. The arrangements were still left to Israel. The Secretaries of State and Defense, rather than informing the President directly of their opposition, seem to have distanced themselves from the transactions.

The 500 TOW missiles were not delivered to Iran until October 29, 1986. Three more Americans were taken hostage in Beirut in September and October. Only one of the original seven hostages and none of the three new ones were released as the result of these new dealings with Iran. The day after the single hostage release, a pro-Syrian Beirut magazine published a story about a secret trip to Teheran made the preceding May by former National Security Advisor Robert C. McFarlane. On November 4 the Speaker of the Iranian Majlis publicly announced the mission. Virtually universal criticism followed in the United States.

As of April 1987, sizable sums of money generated by the arms sales to Iran remained unaccounted for. Some of the funds probably went to support the Nicaraguan Contras. There was, however, no evidence that had come to light to suggest that President Reagan knew of the diversion prior to a briefing by Attorney General Edwin Meese on November 25, 1986. There is no doubt, however, that, because of Congressional restrictions on spending by the Department of Defense and the CIA, the President welcomed private funding of the Contras, and that members of the National Security Council organized channels for the financial contributions to reach the Contras, besides coordinating logistical arrangements to ship privately purchased arms.

The Iranian arms deals shook the nation's confidence in the

President's judgment and management. The Tower Commission, reporting in February 1987, was sharply critical of the manner in which these decisions had been made by the President's administration:

> Established procedures for making national security decisions were ignored. Reviews of the initiatives by all the NSC principals were too infrequent. The initiatives were not adequately vetted below the Cabinet level. Intelligence resources were under-utilized. Applicable legal constraints were not adequately addressed. The whole matter was handled too informally without adequate written records of what had been considered, discussed, and decided.

PRESIDENT REAGAN'S ADDRESS TO THE NATION ON THE IRAN ARMS CONTROVERSY[27]

March 4, 1987

My fellow Americans, I've spoken to you from this historic office on many occasions and about many things. The power of the Presidency is often thought to reside within this Oval Office. Yet it doesn't rest here; it rests in you, the American people, and in your trust.

Your trust is what gives a President his powers of leadership and his personal strength, and it's what I want to talk to you about this evening.

For the past three months, I've been silent on the revelations about Iran. You must have been thinking, "Well, why doesn't he tell us what's happening? Why doesn't he just speak to us as he has in the past when we've faced troubles or tragedies?" Others of you, I guess, were thinking, "What's he doing hiding out in the White House?"

The reason I haven't spoken to you before now is this: You deserved the truth. And, as frustrating as the waiting has been, I felt it was improper to come to you with sketchy reports, or possibly even erroneous statements, which would then have to be corrected, creating even more doubt and confusion. There's been enough of that.

I've paid a price for my silence in terms of your trust and confidence. But I have had to wait, as have you, for the complete story.

That's why I appointed Ambassador David Abshire as my special counselor to help get out the thousands of documents to the various investigations. And I appointed a special review board, the Tower board, which took on the chore of pulling the truth together for me and getting to the bottom of things. It has now issued its findings.

I'm often accused of being an optimist, and it's true I had to hunt pretty hard to find any good news in the board's report. As you know, it's well-stocked with criticisms, which I'll discuss in a moment, but I was very relieved to read this sentence, " . . . The board is convinced that the President does indeed want the full story to be told."

And that will continue to be my pledge to you as the other investigations go forward.

PRAISE FOR PANEL MEMBERS

I want to thank the members of the panel—former Senator John Tower, former Secretary of State Edmund Muskie, and former National Security Adviser Brent Scowcroft. They have done the nation, as well as me personally, a great service by submitting a report of such integrity and depth. They have my genuine and enduring gratitude.

I've studied the board's report. Its findings are honest, convincing and highly critical, and I accept them. Tonight I want to share with you my thoughts on these findings and report to you on the actions I'm taking to implement the board's recommendations.

First, let me say I take full responsibility for my own actions and for those of my Administration. As angry as I may be about activities undertaken without my knowledge, I am still accountable for those activities. As disappointed as I may be in some who served me, I am still the one who must answer to the American people for this behavior. And as personally distasteful as I find secret bank accounts and diverted funds, as the Navy would say, this happened on my watch.

Let's start with the part that is the most controversial. A few months ago I told the American people I did not trade arms for hostages. My heart and my best intentions still tell me that is true, but the facts and the evidence tell me it is not.

As the Tower board reported, what began as a strategic opening to Iran deteriorated in its implementation into trading arms for hostages. This runs counter to my own beliefs, to Administration policy and to the original strategy we had in mind. There are reasons why it happened but no excuses. It was a mistake.

I undertook the original Iran initiative in order to develop relations with those who might assume leadership in a post-Khomeini Government. It's clear from the board's report, however, that I let my personal concern for the hostages spill over into the geopolitical strategy of reaching out to Iran. I asked so many questions about the hostages' welfare that I didn't ask enough about the specifics of the total Iran plan.

Let me say to the hostage families, we have not given up. We never will, and I promise you we'll use every legitimate means to free your loved ones from captivity. But I must also caution that those Americans who freely remain in such dangerous areas must know that they're responsible for their own safety.

Now, another major aspect of the board's findings regards the transfer of funds to the Nicaraguan contras. The Tower board wasn't able to find out what happened to this money, so the facts here will be left to the continuing investigations of the court-appointed independent counsel and the two Congressional investigating committees. I'm confident the truth will come out about this matter as well.

As I told the Tower board, I didn't know about any diversion of funds to the contras. But as President, I cannot escape responsibility.

'MY MANAGEMENT STYLE'

Much has been said about my management style, a style that's worked successfully for me during eight years as governor of California and for most of my presidency. The way I work is to identify the problem, find the right individuals to do the job and then let them go to it. I've found this invariably brings out the best in people. They seem to rise to their full capability, and in the long run you get more done.

When it came to managing the N.S.C. staff, let's face it, my style didn't match its previous track record. I've already begun correcting this. As a start, yesterday I met with the entire professional staff of the National Security Council. I defined for them the values I want to guide the national security policies of this country. I told them that I wanted a policy that was as justifiable and understandable in public as it was in secret. I wanted a policy that reflected the will of the Congress as well as the White House. And I told them that there'll be no more freelancing by individuals when it comes to our national security.

You've heard a lot about the staff of the National Security Council in recent months. I can tell you, they are good and dedicated Government employees, who put in long hours for the nation's benefit. They are eager and anxious to serve their country.

One thing still upsetting me, however, is that no one kept proper records of meetings or decisions. This led to my failure to recollect whether I approved an arms shipment before or after the fact. I did approve it; I just can't say specifically when. Rest assured, there's plenty of record-keeping now going on at 1600 Pennsylvania Avenue.

For nearly a week now, I've been studying the board's report. I want the American people to know that this wrenching ordeal of recent months has not been in vain. I endorse every one of the Tower board's recommendations. In fact, I'm going beyond its recommendations, so as to put the house in even better order.

I'm taking action in three basic areas—personnel, national security policy and the process for making sure that the system works.

First, personnel. I've brought in an accomplished and highly respected new team here at the White House. They bring new blood, new energy, and new credibility and experience.

Former Senator Howard Baker, my new Chief of Staff, possesses a breadth of legislative and foreign affairs skills that's impossible to match. I'm hopeful that his experience as minority and majority leader of the Senate can help us forge a new partnership with the Congress, especially on foreign and national security policies. I'm genuinely honored that he's given up his own Presidential aspirations to serve the country as my Chief of Staff.

'PROPER MANAGEMENT DISCIPLINE'

Frank Carlucci, my new national security adviser, is respected for his experience in government and trusted for his judgment and counsel. Under him, the N.S.C. staff is being rebuilt with proper management discipline. Already, almost half the N.S.C. professional staff is comprised of new people.

Yesterday I nominated William Webster, a man of sterling reputation, to be Director of the Central Intelligence Agency. Mr. Webster has served as Director of the F.B.I. and as a U.S. District Court judge. He understands the meaning of "Rule of Law."

So that his knowledge of national security matters can be available to me on a continuing basis, I will also appoint John Tower to serve as a member of my Foreign Intelligence Advisory Board.

I am considering other changes in personnel, and I will move more furniture as I see fit in the weeks and months ahead.

Second, in the area of national security policy, I have ordered the N.S.C. to begin a comprehensive review of all covert operations.

I have also directed that any covert activity be in support of clear policy objectives and in compliance with American values. I expect a covert policy that if Americans saw it on the front page of their newspaper, they'd say, "That makes sense."

I have had issued a directive prohibiting the N.S.C. staff itself from undertaking covert operations—no if's, and's or but's.

I have asked Vice President Bush to reconvene his task force on terrorism to review our terrorist policy in light of the events that have occurred.

ADOPTING REPORT'S MODEL

Third, in terms of the process of reaching national security decisions, I am adopting in total the Tower report's model of how the N.S.C. process and staff should work. I am directing Mr. Carlucci to take the necessary steps to make that happen. He will report back to me on further reforms that might be needed.

I've created the post of N.S.C. legal adviser to assure a greater sensitivity to matters of law.

I am also determined to make the Congressional oversight process work. Proper procedures for consultation with the Congress will be followed, not only in letter but in spirit.

Before the end of March I will report to the Congress on all the steps I've taken in line with the Tower board's conclusions.

Now what should happen when you make a mistake is this: You take your knocks, you learn your lessons and then you move on. That's the healthiest way to deal with a problem. This in no way diminishes the importance of the other continuing investigations, but the business of our country and our people must proceed. I've gotten this message from Republicans and Democrats in Congress, from allies around the world—and if we're reading the signals right, even from the Soviets. And, of course, I've heard the message from you, the American people.

You know, by the time you reach my age, you've made plenty of mistakes if you've lived your life properly. So you learn. You put things in perspective. You pull your energies together. You change. You go forward.

My fellow Americans, I have a great deal that I want to accomplish with you and for you over the next two years, and, the Lord willing, that's exactly what I intend to do. Goodnight and God bless you.

List of Sources

Unless otherwise indicated, the texts of all Presidential papers are from J. D. Richardson, comp., *Messages and Papers of the Presidents* (New York, 1897, 1911–1914, 1916, 1917)

1 Annals of Congress, 4th Congress, 2nd Sess., p. 2796.
2 Philadelphia *Daily American Advertiser,* September 19, 1796.
3 P. L. Ford, ed., *The Writings of Thomas Jefferson* (New York, 1895), VIII, pp. 143–147.
4 *Narrative of the Expedition of a Squadron to the China Sea and Japan, performed in the years 1852, 1853, and 1854, under the command of Commodore M. C. Perry, United States Navy,* comp. by F. L. Hawks (Washington, 1956), I, 256, 257.
5 U. S. Senate Doc. No. 76 (66th Cong., 1st Sess.).
6 *Congressional Record,* vol. 77, Pt. I, pp. 5–6.
7 *Development of United States Foreign Policy: Addresses and Messages of Franklin D. Roosevelt,* 77th Cong., 2nd Sess., Senate Doc. No. 188, Serial No. 10676 (Washington, 1942), pp. 81–87.
8 *Congressional Record,* vol. 93, Pt. 2, pp. 1980–81.
9 *The New York Times,* June 28, 1950.
10 *The New York Times,* June 22, 1955.
11 *Public Papers of the Presidents of the United States: John F. Kennedy, Jan.* 1–Dec. 31, 1962 (United States Government Printing Office, Washington, 1963), pp. 806–809.
12 *Ibid.,* pp. 809–811.
13 United States Arms Control and Disarmament Agency, *Publication* 17 (June 1963).
14 *Public Papers of the Presidents of the United States: John F. Kennedy,* Jan. 1–Nov. 22, 1963 (United States Government Printing Office, Washington, 1964), pp. 468–471.
15 *Public Papers of the Presidents of the United States: Lyndon B. Johnson 1963–64,* Book II–July 1–Dec. 31, 1964 (United States Government Printing Office, Washington, 1965), pp. 926–927.
16 *Ibid.,* pp. 927–928.
17 *The New York Times,* July 29, 1965.
18 As recorded by *The New York Times,* July 16, 1971.
19 Office of the White House Press Secretary, February 22, 1973.
20 *Public Papers of the Presidents of the United States: Richard M. Nixon, 1973* (United States Government Printing Office, Washington, 1975), pp. 547–555.
21 *Ibid.,* p. 891.
22 *Public Papers of the Presidents of the United States: Richard M. Nixon, 1974* (United States Government Printing Office, Washington, 1975), pp. 626–629.

23 *Ibid.,* p. 633.
24 *Public Papers of the Presidents of the United States: Gerald R. Ford, 1974* (United States Government Printing Office, Washington, 1975), pp. 101–103.
25 *Public Papers of the Presidents of the United States: Jimmy Carter, 1977* (United States Government Printing Office, Washington, 1978), Book II, pp. 1542–1544.
26 *Public Papers of the Presidents of the United States: Jimmy Carter, 1978* (United States Government Printing Office, Washington, 1979), Book II, pp. 1533–1537.
27 *The New York Times,* March 5, 1987, p. A18.